W9-AFJ-406

Euclid Public Library
631 E. 222nd Street
Euclid, Ohio 44123
216-261-5300

THOMAS KENEALLY

AUSTRALIANS

THOMAS KENEALLY

AUSTRALIANS

ORIGINS *to* EUREKA
VOLUME 1

ALLEN&UNWIN

First published in Australia in 2009

Copyright © Thomas Keneally 2009

All rights reserved. No part of this book may be reproduced or transmitted in any form or by any means, electronic or mechanical, including photocopying, recording or by any information storage and retrieval system, without prior permission in writing from the publisher. The Australian *Copyright Act 1968* (the Act) allows a maximum of one chapter or 10 per cent of this book, whichever is the greater, to be photocopied by any educational institution for its educational purposes provided that the educational institution (or body that administers it) has given a remuneration notice to Copyright Agency Limited (CAL) under the Act.

Allen & Unwin
83 Alexander Street
Crows Nest NSW 2065
Australia
Phone: (61 2) 8425 0100
Fax: (61 2) 9906 2218
Email: info@allenandunwin.com
Web: www.allenandunwin.com

Cataloguing-in-Publication entry is available from the National Library of Australia
www.librariesaustralia.nla.gov.au

ISBN 978 1 74175 0690

Typeset in Minion 11.5/15pt by Midland Typesetters, Australia
Printed in Australia by Ligare Book Printer

10 9 8 7 6 5 4 3 2

To four young Australian inheritors of history,
Augustus, Clementine, Alexandra and Rory.

CONTENTS

ACKNOWLEDGMENTS

The idea for this book arose from an editorial meeting, chaired by Patrick Gallagher at Allen & Unwin. So the author owes thanks to all at that table. I must also thank:

Dr Olwen Pryke, gifted researcher on this book, who has now gone on to better things at the State Library of New South Wales;

Judy Keneally, my manuscript- and proof-reading spouse, always a wise reader;

Fiona Inglis, amiable agent, for supporting me through the process and making the contract;

Rebecca Kaiser, a very genial editor-in-chief;

Amanda O'Connell, thorough and percipient copy editor;

Linda Brainwood, tireless picture researcher;

Lisa White, who designed a beautiful book;

And Kathy Mossop, Jo Lyons and Karen Ward who finally herded these pages into one pasture.

Best wishes to them all.

Thomas Keneally

THE WAY THIS BOOK WORKS

In this book I've tried to tell the stories of a number of Australians from the Pleistocene Age to 1860. The people whose tales are told here exemplify the major aspects and dynamisms of the Australian story. For each one I chose to write about, I could have chosen a dozen, a hundred, or in some cases, thousands more. This history therefore sets out to characterise Australia and, above all, individual Australians, in a manner which gives insight into the most significant aspects of the periods I deal with without exhaustively and thus cursorily engaging with every major actor. For example, a number of the explorers are dealt with in salient though not as thorough detail as some others are. The same is true of governors. It is in many cases with the question of how governors impacted upon individuals living on this continent that this book frequently prefers to concern itself. There are some instances where I have used material from my earlier books, *The Great Shame* and *The Commonwealth of Thieves*. I hope that those who are kind enough to read this book find this material altered to give them new perspectives, not too reminiscent of these works. I also hope that through following these histories of particular, though sometimes obscure, individuals, and by examining infrequently reported aspects of the lives of the well-known, I have managed to cast light on at least some of the mysteries of the Australian soul.

CHAPTER 1

DINNER AT CUDDIE SPRINGS

Once there was the All-Sea. Its brew of water and minerals and biology covered the planet. Then the first stones, sediments and bacteria of the great landmass Pangaea broke the surface of the encompassing ocean. They can still be found, these first gestures of ground, the original Mother Earth, in the Pilbara region of Western Australia. The question of whether Australia is old or young jangles in the Australian imagination.

At Taronga Zoo in Sydney there is a globe, at child height, showing Pangaea, the great agglomerated landmass, which remained one huge slab of earth for so long and began to break apart only about 140 million years ago. Pangaea is shown at the zoo in cut sections. A child can move the solid shapes which once made up the enormous single earth-mass on grooves, to create Laurasia in the north and Gondwana, the great southern super-continent. Then, further grooves on the surface enable the child to separate Gondwana into India, Africa, South America, Antarctica and Australia, and slide them to their present locations on the globe. Each of the pieces on this globe is marked with graphics, and as the god-playing child separates Australia from the massive Gondwana, he or she can see pictures of Australian fauna and mega-fauna abandoning the old mother super-continent, choosing Australia as their Mesozoic zoo. The separation of Australia from the rest of Gondwana began 45 million years ago.

It was not all quite as clean as the zoo game indicates. The exotic separating fragment included a version of Australia, New Guinea and Tasmania in the one gigantic landmass, named Sahul by paleontologists. It was all far to the south of where it is now. Over the next fifteen million years, Sahul edged northwards, striving, but not fully managing till three million years ago, to separate itself broadly from the Antarctic and assume a position in the primeval Pacific.

To add to the complicated picture, at various stages Sahul shrank and then expanded again. It was fifteen million years ago, for instance, that Tasmania first became an island, but then, dependent on sea levels, Sahul would regularly take it back into its mass again. The last time Tasmania separated was only 11 000 years ago, when *Homo sapiens* was already occupying the region, at the end of the Great Ice Age.

But Taronga Zoo's idea of exotic animals skipping over water to get on board Sahul/Australia is a potent one. It tells the child that Australia is the continent of exotics and grotesques, and the unique story of the country surely reflects that notion for adults, too.

Modern dating methods show that the arrival of the first Australians occurred at least 60 000 years Before the Present (BP). The people who became the natives of the Australian continent first crossed from the prehistoric south-east Asian district named Wallacea between 60 000 to 18 000 BP, when the Arafura Sea was an extensive plain, when sea levels were 30 metres below where they are now, and there was a solid land bridge some 1600 kilometres wide between Australia and New Guinea, then joined within Sahul. Sahul's north-western coast received only small numbers of individuals from the islands of Wallacea, possibly as few as fifty to one hundred people over a decade.

They may have come by log or canoe; they may even have waded to Sahul at low tide. If experts on human language can be believed, our species had not at that stage achieved speech, but some means of creating human co-operation would have been needed.

Descendants of these first comers still live by the hundreds of thousands in Australia, and the picture of how they lived and what they did with the continent has been revised again and again in recent times. In the early 1960s the proposal that Aboriginal people had lived in Australia for 13 000 years was thought fanciful. But carbon dating showed campfires and tools to be at least 30 000 years old, and these days experts use luminescence dating to claim that campfires and firestick burning date from more than 100 000 years ago. Almost at once as this claim was made, in 1996, at Jinmium in the Northern Territory, Australian scientists dated stone tools as 130 000 years old. If they are right, the original Australians are the oldest race on the planet. Similar remains of human activity, from before the last Ice Age, have been found on the Great Barrier Reef, on an earlier coastal line of cliffs now swamped by ocean.

We must try to imagine the earth as it was then, a country of flamingos and dangerous giant carnivorous kangaroos now known as *Propelopus*, of *Palorchestes*, the bull-sized mammal whose long snout, giraffe-like tongue and massive claws may have inspired Aboriginal tales of a swamp-dwelling, man-eating monster often called the Bunyip. The marsupial lion called *Thylacoleo carnifex* ranged the savannahs, and *Megalania prisca*, a giant lizard, made excellent eating at feasts.

These early Australians believed their ancestral beings had made the visible earth and its resources, and expected the cleaning up and fertilisation done by the firestick. A number of Australian species of tree welcomed fire—the banksia, the melaleuca, the casuarina, eucalyptus—and fire fertilised various food plants: bracken, cycads, daisy yams and grasses. The firestick, in itself and as a hunting device, may have speeded the extinction of the giant marsupial kangaroo, the marsupial lion, the giant sloth, and other species now vanished.

At Cuddie Springs, a lake bed near the north-western New South Wales town of Brewarrina, scientists have found the remains of a meal eaten over 30 000 years ago, when a spring-fed lake brimmed there and was a centre of human and animal existence. Here, in a layer of soil dated between 30 000 and 35 000 years in age, bones of Australian extinct mega-beasts have been found amongst blood-stained stone tools, charcoal and other remains of campfires. The analysis of the tools showed blood similar to that of the giant wombat-like *Diprotodon*. The men who had brought it down and to the cooking fire had not been immune from risk. Also at the site were found wet-milled grass and grindstones or querns, the oldest examples of such implements found anywhere. Aboriginal women thirty millennia past had a milling method which was previously thought to have begun in the Middle East only 5000 years ago.

Thus the triumph of the hunters lies over the bones of this long dead bump-nosed giant, as the triumph of the female millers of seed is evoked by the sandstone grinding basin.

There was a map of Australia in so-called prehistory too, made tribe by tribe across the landmass. The ancestor heroes and heroines had made the spiritual as well as visible earth—the landscape was a ritual, mythic, ceremonial landscape. For tens of millennia before the name Australia was applied to it, there was a clan-by-clan, ceremonial-group by ceremonial-group map of the country. In Central Australia's desert, the Walpiri people used the term *jukurrpa*, Dreaming, to represent the earth as left by the ancestors, and other language groups used similar terms. The Dreaming is seen as something eternal by many white scholars and lay persons, but as one commentator says, it is a fulcrum by which the changing universe can be interpreted—the falling or rise of water levels, flood or drought, glacial steppes or deserts, the ascent or decline of species, the characteristics of animals. Another scholar is particularly worth quoting: The Dreaming 'binds people, flora, fauna and natural phenomena into one enormous inter-functioning world'.

For the individual native, the knowledge, ritual and mystery attached to maintaining the local earth were enlarged at initiation, and further secrets were acquired through life and through dreams. A network of Dreaming tracks existed, criss-crossing the continent, certainly densely criss-crossing the Sydney Basin, connecting one well of water or place of protein or shelter with another. The eastern coastline of New South Wales, built up of Hawkesbury sandstone, standing above the sea in great platforms and easily eroded to make caves, was full of such holy sites. As a visible symbol of that, there exists a huge number of pecked and abraded engravings of humans, ancestors, sharks and kangaroos on open and sheltered rock surfaces around Sydney, as the sandstone proved a good medium for that work.

Natives at particular ceremonial sites re-enacted the journey and acts of creation of a particular hero ancestor, and by doing that they sustained the earth. As in other places the priest became Christ at the climax of the liturgy, during the natives' re-enactment they *became* the hero ancestor. These people would ultimately be called by early European settlers *ab origines*—people who had been here since the beginning of the earth—and though they had not been on Sahul or Australia *ab origine*, they had been in place long enough to make that issue a quibble.

In what is now western New South Wales, near Lake Nitchie, some 6800 years ago, a number of members of the species *Homo sapiens* worked for the better part of a week cutting a pit into hard sediments and making it large enough to take the body of an important man. He was a tall man, some 182 centimetres in height. He had died in his late thirties from a dental abscess. In 1969 the body was found, still seated after millennia, legs bent under his torso, and head and shoulders forced down to fit him into the grave pit and bury him before he putrefied. Daubed with red ochre, a solemn ornamentation, he was interred with scraps of pearl shell which had somehow reached this distant inland location, a lump of fused silica from a meteor and a necklace of 178 Tasmanian devil's teeth. The Tasmanian devil became extinct in mainland Australia nearly seven thousand years ago. This man was a figure of significance and power—his necklace and the care taken to inter him showed that.

Not that the man of Lake Nitchie is the oldest of rediscovered burials in Australia. A female cremation burial from 26 000 years past was found at Lake Mungo in western New South Wales. The light-boned woman's body was not totally consumed by flames when it was cremated on the beach of vast Lake Mungo, and the remaining bones were broken up and placed in a pit. Then half a kilometre distant, but some two thousand years older, a body, almost certainly a woman's, her right shoulder badly afflicted with osteoarthritis, and her skin ornamented with red ochre, was found partly cremated and then buried. Both these people were *Homo sapiens* and it is likely that their cosmology coincided in essentials with that of the Aborigines the first visiting Asians and Europeans would encounter.

Yet what would cause any intrusion on this most ancient of all human cultures? The continent the Aborigines inhabited and nurtured seemed subject to only casual and inexact European interest.

CHAPTER 2

THE MAKASSAR WELCOME

For perhaps a hundred years before the arrival of Captain Cook's *Endeavour* on the east coast of Australia, a fleet of fifty or more Indonesian *prahus*, left the old port city of Makassar (now Ujung Pandang) for the coastline of Australia to seek trepang, a leathery sea cucumber consumed as a health food and aphrodisiac throughout Asia. For the next two hundred years the Yolngu Aboriginals of the tropics knew to expect the Makassar men when they saw the first lightning of the rainy season. The *prahus*, with their tripod masts and lateen sails, made landfall mainly in the land they called Marege, Arnhem Land, or else a long way to the west on the Kimberley coast, known to the Makassans as Kayu Jawa. Each *prahu* carried about thirty crew members, and they dived for the trepang in groups of two to six vessels. Beach encampments of Makassans the Yolngu permitted and welcomed on their coast might have a population of two hundred men at a time. These men gathered trepang by hand or spear but the most common method of collection was diving.

The Yolngu and the Makassans went about their annual time together in a peaceful and ordered way. It was not in the interests of the Makassans to alienate the Aboriginal elders, nor the young Yolngu men they attracted to work with them, nor the young women from whom they sought sexual favours. The Makassans spent most of the day at sea. The trepang was cooked after boiling in a pan of mangrove bark, which added colour and flavour. Next it was dried out and then buried in the sand, to be dug up in time and boiled again. Then it was smoked over a slow fire in a smokehouse assembled from rattan and bamboo carried on the ships. Every few weeks they moved on to a new camp.

These Makassan visits became known to British mariners, who sometimes encountered the *prahus*, and would be one of the reasons the naval officer Matthew Flinders would be encouraged to circumnavigate the continent and thus demonstrate—as one historian says—that the continent was a unified and closed body that could be unilaterally possessed. In 1803 Flinders discovered six *prahus* off the Arnhem Land coast, and greeted their 'Malay commanders' to his ship: 'The six Malay commanders shortly afterwards came on board in a canoe. It happened fortunately that my cook was Malay, and through this means I was able to communicate with them. The chief of the six *prahus* was a short, elderly man named Pobassoo.' Pobassoo told Flinders that there were sixty *prahus* along the coast, and that a man named Salloo was the overall leader. Since they were Muslims, they were repelled by the penned hogs on board Flinders's ship but were happy to take a bottle of port away with them.

That year, as for years before and after, as many as one thousand men, all from the Gulf of Bone in the Celebes (now Sulawesi), were working the Arnhem Land coast. They interbred with the Yolngu people, who traded turtle shells and buffalo horns with the Makassans for steel knives and fabric.

Sometimes Aboriginals sailed on returning *prahus* to Makassar and beyond. A small number of Yolngu settled there, in the Celebes. Those who came back told tales of the city, and the surprise of seeing policemen and soldiers is preserved in dances and song. Young men who visited Makassar came back with enhanced reputations and their knowledge of the Makassar language made them leaders in future dealing between Yolngu and the trepangers.

Coastal communities of the Yolngu traded the foreign goods they acquired with inland groups, so tales of the Makassans spread wider than did the sight of them. Arnhem Land songs of the Makassans and cave wall depictions of them occur throughout the region of Marege, and Marege as a word is still honoured by Yolngu people as a more kindly name than Arnhem Land.

Because of the Makassans the Yolngu people were the earliest Aboriginals exposed to smallpox, yaws and venereal disease, and also to firearms, tobacco and alcohol. Despite these inheritances, the Yolngu to this day will say about Makassans, 'We are one people.'

THE COY COASTS

Known to the trepangers but merely guessed by the Europeans, in 1598 a Dutch geographer, Cornelius Wyfliet, wrote: 'The Australis Terra is the most southern of all lands, and is separated from New Guinea by a narrow strait. Its shores are hitherto but little known, since after one voyage or another that route has been deserted, and seldom is the country visited unless sailors are driven there by storms. The Australis Terra begins at 2 or 3 degrees from the Equator, and is maintained by some to be of so great an extent that if it were thoroughly explored it would be regarded as a fifth part of the world.'

This was a reflection of an ancient belief in the Antipodes—a continent in the southern hemisphere to balance the size of Europe and Asia combined. Hence geographers presumed that the Australis Terra must stretch away far south towards the Antarctic ice.

It has recently been claimed that the Ming Emperor's eunuch admiral, Zheng He, a Muslim, landed in Australia in 1421, in treasure ships of great size and sophistication. As yet, there is no conclusive evidence, but the Ming navy maintained a trading post in Ambon in the Moluccas (now part of Indonesia), so that a Ming vessel coming to the northern Australian coast is not unlikely.

Later, Portuguese entrepreneurs and garrisons were also based in the Moluccas, the Spice Islands west of New Guinea. These were far to the western, Spanish side of the line Pope Alexander IV had drawn to divide the riches of the planet between his two treasured but warring Iberian nations. The Portuguese had got there as a result of their king's marriage with the Spanish king's sister, the bride price being the trading rights to the Moluccas. Had they discovered the great coastline of Australia to the south, they would have kept quiet about it, since the Spaniards would have been able to claim the place, and all its unassessed wealth.

One could say that for purposes of discovery the Australian continent took up a coy position on the globe. It was hidden beneath a screen of islands stretching from the Solomons to Java and Sumatra, wearing New Guinea as its north-eastern cap. It was cunningly lodged west of Cape Horn and east of the Cape of Good Hope, and best approached only by that screaming band of westerly winds, the Roaring Forties, far, far to the south. It was huge but not as huge as the expected mass, and did not lie where that mass was surmised to be.

There were a number of notable Spanish near-misses at encountering Australia. In 1568 a Spanish commander, Alvaro de Mendana, crossing the Pacific from Peru, discovered the Solomon Islands, so naming them—in the spirit of advertising rather than piety—in the hope that Spaniards might assume that these were the isles from which Solomon had got the gold to adorn his temple. Nearly forty years later, a master of one of Mendana's vessels, Pedro de Quiros, petitioned King Philip III to allow him to take three ships to search for the southern continent which de Quiros believed must be south-west of the Solomons. At the island of Espiritu Santo in Vanuatu, de Quiros's flagship seems to have been taken over by its crew. His young second-in-command, Luis de Torres, continued the reconnaissance with his two remaining ships, and searched west, but not far enough to encounter the Barrier Reef and the coast of Australia. Turning north he reached the coast of New Guinea, where he found himself confronted with reefs and islands in a complicated and perilous strait which still carries his name and is a byword for navigational perils.

At least it was proof that New Guinea was not, as de Quiros had thought, part of the Great South Land. De Torres saw the mountains of the mainland of Australia, at Cape York, but believed them to be merely further islands. From the quarterdeck of his vessel, *San Pedrico,* he was only a handful of miles distant.

Nonetheless, de Quiros had already named the continent he was sure existed south of where he was bullied by his crew into returning to Peru and which he would even claim to have discovered. Austrialia del Espiritu Santo was his choice; 'Austrialia' intended as a compliment to Philip III of Spain, who was by blood an Austrian Hapsburg.

In another near-miss, a little Dutch ship named the *Duyfken* had entered Torres Strait from the west in March 1606, a few weeks before de Torres sailed through it. But when nine of the crew were murdered by natives, the Melanesian people who occupied the islands of Torres Strait, the skipper Willem Jansz turned about, and Australia was again left uninterrupted.

Where had Willem Jansz come from? When Philip III achieved hegemony over the Portuguese, he closed Lisbon to the Dutch ships that sailed there to collect spice produce from the Moluccas and elsewhere. Consequently, at the end of the sixteenth century, a group of Amsterdam merchants sent out their own fleet to the Moluccas, the Spice Islands, via the Cape of Good Hope. Suddenly there were many Dutch ships on their way to and from the archipelago which is now named Indonesia. Their preferred route of passage made no sense in an as-the-crow-flies reading of the globe. Initially, once they got around South Africa, the Dutch tried to get to Indonesia by sailing north-east across the Indian Ocean. But they often became becalmed and so much in need of supplies that six out of ten of their crew would die, meaning that the ships stuck on the opaque, unmoving sea were surrounded by the not always successfully weighed-down corpses of their dead crewmates.

The passage that worked best, the Dutch discovered, was to sail round the Cape of Good Hope, but to then reach south to catch the Roaring Forties across the lower quarter of the globe, run east before these gales, and then turn to port and reach north for Indonesia. Given that equation, a number of Dutch ships encountered the Western Australian coast. They named it, without affection, New Holland. Some of them collided with or put in to it.

A master named Dirk Hartog, in the *Eendragt* (Concord), met the deeply indented Shark Bay, one of the westernmost points of the Australian continent, and landing on an island which bears his name, left there a tin plate marked 25 October 1616. Through further such contacts, the west coast of what would prove to be the Australian continent acquired a number of Dutch names, such as Cape Leeuwin, named for a 1623 ship (*Leeuwin*/Lioness) which met with it. Like the south-west coast of Africa, the west coast of New Holland acquired a reputation as a desert of no economic potential.

In a horrifying sideshow to the tide of Dutch voyaging, on 4 June 1629 the *Batavia* of 650 tonnes, a ship more notable in tonnage than most British ships of the day, with more than three hundred on board, became stuck on a reef and sand spit off the Western Australian coast. The captain left the wreck to look for water on the mainland, leaving 268 people behind. Not finding any, he sailed on to Batavia (now Jakarta) for help. Returning to rescue the survivors, he found that a crazed seaman named Cornelisz, with his followers, had beheaded, stabbed and drowned 125 men, women and children.

This news reverberated with the most celebrated of the Dutch captains in the South Seas, a man born near Groningen around 1603. Like the others, he foreshadowed a strong Protestant timbre in the ultimate nation-state of Australia, though it would be the British version that prevailed, not the Dutch. As a young sailor he had enjoyed a rapid promotion within the Dutch East India Company, a sturdily commercial operation not interested in exploration for exploration's sake. But by 1642, Viceroy Van Diemen—his master, the governor at Batavia—gave the captain, Abel Tasman, two ships for exploratory purposes. Tasman's wife and a daughter from his first marriage lived with him in Batavia, the fever port, and he had led a number of well-managed voyages.

At the best, Tasman was to find a route south of New Holland to South America, where the Dutch hoped to erode the Spanish monopoly. 'Slight misdemeanours on the part of such natives [you encounter],' Van Diemen wrote to Tasman before his protégé set sail, 'such as petty thefts and the like, you will pass unnoticed, that by doing so you may draw them unto you, and not inspire them with aversion to our nation.' However, if gold or silver were found, 'appear as if you were not greedy for them, and if gold and silver is offered in any barter, you must feign that you do not value these metals, showing them copper, zinc and lead, as if those metals were of more value to us.'

The men who manned these Dutch ships were tough seamen used to heinous conditions. On a voyage in 1638, looking for a non-existent island in the northern Pacific, Tasman had reached Formosa (now Taiwan) with only fifty of the crew of ninety alive. Things had not massively improved since the previous century and the days of Magellan, one of whose men described the sea biscuit as turned to powder and stinking of rats' urine, the ship's water impure and yellow, and the only fresh meat the aforesaid rats.

Leaving Batavia in August 1642, Tasman's two ships, the *Heemskerk* and the *Zeehaen*, took a zig-zag route through the Indian Ocean to Mauritius and then southwards. Once they had found the westerly gales, for most of their journey they were hurled along at 42 degrees south latitude. At last they came up against the wind-buffeted coast which Tasman called Van Diemen's Land, but which now carries his own name. An attempt to land was made but the weather was too rough. A carpenter swam through the surf with a Dutch flag and took formal possession of the land on 3 December 1642.

A later navigator, the Englishman Matthew Flinders, would name two dominating mountains behind the coast in honour of Tasman's two ships.

Sailing to the south of Van Diemen's Land, after nine turbulent days Tasman encountered the wild west coast of the south island of New Zealand, where three of his Dutchmen were killed and a fourth mortally wounded by Maoris at the site still named Massacre Bay. He returned to Batavia by way of the islands north of New Guinea. Two years later he would explore Australia from North West Cape to Cape York, extending the known map of New Holland.

Back at home in Batavia, he would within two years become a member of the Council of Justice. He and Van Diemen, however, must have been angrily resigned at the letter that came from the Dutch East India Company's managers when they received the news of Tasman's voyage of 1644. 'We do not expect great things of the continuance of such explorations,' wrote the company, 'which more and more burden the company's resources, since they require increase of ships and sailors . . . the gold and silver mines that will best serve the company's turn have already been found, which we deem to be our trade over the whole of India.' By the time Tasman died in Batavia in 1659, New Holland still held no allure for the Dutch.

PIRATING WORDS

Nearly thirty years later, in 1688, a Somerset-born sailor-cum-pirate-cum-journalist named William Dampier—sober, fascinated by nature, and in his late thirties; indeed, the antithesis of the common piratical stereotype—first visited Australia as a member of the crew of the buccaneering ship *Cygnet*, whose Captain Swan had been abandoned, as the result of mutiny, in Mindanao. The *Cygnet* was a captured Spanish prize ship, and after visiting the Celebes accompanied by another prize ship, the crews decided to sail for New Holland, 'to see what that country would afford us'. The *Cygnet* anchored on the mainland near Melville Island, off north-western Australia, and the crew camped ashore for some weeks, eating the local delicacies, dugong, turtle and plentiful estuarine barramundi, with the rice they had brought with them from the Celebes.

These British pirates were amongst the very first Europeans to encounter the Australian indigines. William Dampier found the natives of Melville Island, whose descendants still live there, resistant to the trinkets he and others offered, and made uncomplimentary comments on their appearance and terms of existence. Though the native men threatened the buccaneers with spears, and the women, crying lustily, removed their children from reach, his opinion was that they were 'the miserablest people in the world' and that the Hottentots of southern Africa were 'for wealth gentlemen' by comparison.

The remarks should be judged from the context that Dampier was the closest thing to a monk that a buccaneer could be. He wrote letters home to his wife, he abhorred drunkenness and when on *Cygnet*'s long crossing from Mexico to Guam, when the rest of the crew were howling with hunger on their diet of half a pint of maize a day, Dampier recorded that—given a recent fever—the short rations did him a great deal of good.

Thus, when he wrote of the natives being the most miserable, he was talking from his own less than favoured position of their material culture. The important question of what had held them together as a society for tens of millennia went unenquired into.

The crew careened the ship in King Sound on the north-west coast of the Australian mainland, on a beach with a 10-metre tide, and scrubbed the hull in an attempt to rid it of *teredos* or shipworms. Then they departed west, and though Dampier drew a draft chart of the coast, he lost it with other papers when a longboat he was being rowed ashore in, having insisted on leaving the 'mad crew' of *Cygnet*, capsized off one of the Nicobar Islands.

Back in England, after a time in Hanoi where he was racked by fever, Dampier published an account of his travels: *A New Voyage Around the World*. It attracted attention and made him a celebrity. As a naturalist, he was well on the way to introducing into English more than a thousand new words, including *algatross* (which Coleridge would transliterate as 'albatross' in his famous *Rime of the Ancient Mariner*) *barbecue, cashew, breadfruit, avocado, posse, tortilla* and *chopsticks*. Jeoly, a Mindanao 'painted prince' he had intended to exhibit, was taken away from him by apparent trickery, but his book was his great success. In 1699, he was commissioned as master of the ship *Roebuck* to make a journey into the region of New Holland he had already made famous.

Had he come around the Horn and through the Pacific he might have stolen James Cook's thunder by seventy years, but he did not like the Horn and its icy challenges, and so decided to sail by way of the Cape of Good Hope, thus encountering only those regions which the Dutch had already visited. He landed near present-day Carnarvon at what he called Shark's Bay because his men caught and ate shark there. He would write, 'If it were not for that sort of pleasure which results from the discovery even of the barrenest spot upon the globe, this coast of New Holland would not have charmed me much.' He again described the natives as repellent, the most unpleasing human beings he had ever encountered, 'though I have seen a great variety of savages'.

Dampier spent four months in the west and north-west of Australia, and explored some 1600 kilometres of the unrelentingly dry coast. His men suffered from the hot weather and began to display symptoms of 'the scorbutic', scurvy. The ship was rotting around him, the garbage in the bilges fermenting riotously in the tropic air. *Roebuck* thus became the stinking, worm-impregnated wreck he had to abandon at Ascension Island on the way home.

Later, because the *Roebuck* had been supplied by government, he faced a court martial which declared him unfit to command any of His Majesty's ships. He did command a privateer, however, financed by sundry businessmen, and very unsuccessfully. It was his literary work which would last beyond his death in 1715. The Lilliput of Dean Swift corresponded, in the map Swift printed in *Gulliver's Travels*, with the west coast of Australia, and Gulliver would claim, in the famous book of 1726, that he was a cousin of that adventurous buccaneer, Dampier.

There was evidence of a trading journey to northern Australia, in 1751, conducted by a Chinese merchant. He reached 'the southern coast' where he met indigenous people. The Dutch Resident of Timor wrote, 'Though said Chinese took it for a large island, we do not doubt it will have been the mainland coast of the southland.' This news when it reached Amsterdam sparked great interest in the Dutch East India Company and for a time the idea of trade with northern Australia revived.

But nothing happened.

THE GRAND INTRUSION

In the late 1760s, the Navy Board of Great Britain went looking for 'a proper vessel' that could voyage to Tahiti in the South Seas and observe the transit of the heavenly body Venus across the face of the sun. If experts observed the transit of Venus in a number of locations, calculations could be made which would help yield the accurate distance of Earth to Venus and Earth to the sun. Thus the handmaiden to the European discovery of Australia, or at least its enormous east coast, was the planet Venus. The transit would occur on 3 June 1769, and there would be no reappearance until 1874.

A number of ships were inspected but the one chosen lay at Shadwell Docks: a Whitby (or Yorkshire-built) square stern-backed, single-bottomed vessel named the *Earl of Pembroke*, later to be renamed *Endeavour*. It had been a collier. Its dimensions scarcely do honour to its ultimate and diverse impact—it was only 106 feet (c 32 metres) long overall, only 97 feet 7 inches (c 30 metres) long on her lower deck, where the crew were to live, and a mere 29 feet 3 inches (8.8 metres) broad. She would challenge all her sailors, many of them American colonials, to find space on her decks.

The Navy Board paid £2800 for her. To get her ready to reach Tahiti and beyond and to observe the transit of Venus, they had her towed to Mr Bird's shipway at Deptford, where workmen applied a lining of thick felt on her hull and then fixed further but thinner boards to protect her against the *Teredo navalis*, the ravenous shipworm of the tropics. This was the little tub which in measuring Venus would also find the measure of Australia.

The captain of the *Endeavour*, James Cook, had a background no more startling than that of his little cat. On 25 May 1768 he was appointed first lieutenant, a rank less than notable for a 40-year-old. He had been born in the winter of 1728 in a two-roomed, clay-built thatched cottage in Marton, Yorkshire, a freezing and hilly region. He came from a lowland Scots father and a Yorkshire mother, a combination not unknown to produce a particular form of sturdiness. Cook had sailed on cats like the *Endeavour* since childhood, in the Whitby to Newcastle trade along the east coast of England. Years later, between journeys into North American waters, he had succumbed to Venus in the form of Elizabeth Batts of Barking, whom, on a cold day before Christmas 1762, he had married in her parish church of Little Wakering, Essex. The groom was tall, with a small head and a pronounced nose. James Cook was a man utterly without patrons within or outside the British navy, and a man needed such connections to achieve notable rank. Whereas to find a continent, he needed only his native genius, his apparently indestructible soul and his phlegmatic self-confidence.

Early in 1763, soon after the marriage, Cook was appointed a naval surveyor and was absent on the Newfoundland station for five successive summers, until his appointment to *Endeavour*.

Unlike the later Tahiti-visiting Bligh, he would have no trouble keeping his crew together in Tahiti during the transit of Venus. Cook was a flintier man and not a slave of passion as was Captain Bligh. Cook had the soul of an imaginative functionary, of such talent that if you asked him to survey Newfoundland or find the Antipodes, he would do both with the same straight-faced application, an application, however, of a monumental scale.

Who was this fellow, this apparently two-dimensional naval cipher who greeted the east coast of New South Wales one morning in April 1770? Did he miss a wife, weep for a child? Only Elizabeth Cook, nee Batts, who would live to be ninety-five and die in 1835, who disapproved of his most famous portrait, by Webber, because it made him seem severe, could tell us of the human, sobbing, panting Cook—and did not do so. Other than that, we can surmise he was like the astronauts two centuries later, impermeable to disabling doubt, immutable of faith, unapologetic of skill. He observed all human weakness but was not himself a player in it. In the Webber portrait he has a rugged face turned partly away from us, his Australian children. And when one reads the journals, the face grows no more in human meaning, in the sort of meaning novelists and poets look for. JC Beaglehole's *The Life of Captain James Cook*, a definitive work, addresses this question. Were there terrors, were there stresses? Cook certainly punished, in a manner his masters would have described as exemplary, the desertion—for love's sake—of two of his sailors from Tahiti with their Polynesian mistresses to a remoter island. The elopement led to a mutual hostage-taking by Tahitians and the British, and Cook was concerned not by the stern measures of flogging and clapping in irons to which he sentenced the two men but by the bad relations it generated between natives and the crew.

A moral man who does not seem to have availed himself of any of Tahiti's carnal pleasures before or after the transit, he abhorred the impact of venereal disease, carried by his sailors in an age when the afflictions of Venus were borne by a large proportion of the male and female population of Europe, on the Tahitians. His own rigorous moral standards were apparently all that his beloved Elizabeth at home in Yorkshire could have asked for.

It could seem that Cook's 'coolness and conciseness' dominated, but he could also be carried away by temper—on a later voyage, an irreverent young midshipman named Trevenen, who had been careless about observations, said that Captain Cook did 'a heiva', a Polynesian dance 'of violent motions and stampings', to vent his displeasure.

There is good humour, though, in the way Cook related the anger caused by his rejection of the offer of a native girl in the Tongan islands for use as sexual recreation. An elderly woman 'began first to argue with me and when that failed she abused me . . . sneering in my face and saying, what sort of a man are you thus to refuse the embraces of so fine a young woman, for the girl certainly did not [want] beauty, which I could however withstand, but the abuse of the old woman I could not, and therefore hastened into the boat.'

During his travels, Cook suffered from rheumatism, from a swelling of the groin, and from a condition named *tenesmus*, a chronic paralysis of the bowels. All of these were maritime ailments, caused by a life in dampness and a regime of salt rations which calcified the urinary tract and cut notches in the colon. One can feel a tenderness for this fellow, his nation's forerunner, and a shocking apparition to the Eora people of Botany Bay and the Guugu Yimidhirr far to the north, in today's Queensland, suffering this way, straining above lowered breeches and hose, squatting behind screens of acacia or melaleuca along the coast of which his chart was the first ever made.

THE YOUNG GENTLEMAN

By contrast with aloof Cook, the young gentleman Mr Joseph Banks glimmered with charm. Descended from a family of lawyers who had acquired acreage, Banks was heir to a huge estate at Revesby Park in Lincolnshire, yet was willing for the sake of his mistress, Nature, to confine himself to the narrow, low-ceilinged dimensions of His Majesty's barque *Endeavour* for the best years of his young manhood. He would exchange three years of drawing rooms and country houses and splendid English women to collect exotic plants in far places; clearly his avocation, or botanical hobby, was no small thing to him.

Yet Banks had another reason to escape England. He had an understanding with a young daughter of the gentry named Harriet Blosset, but secretly he hoped it would go nowhere. The *Endeavour*'s extended absence would probably take care of Harriet's irksome expectations of him.

At a dinner at the house of Lady Anne Monson, an enthusiastic plant collector who had done most of her entirely amateur work in Bengal and South Africa, and after whom the great Linnaeus would name a species of geranium, Banks began to talk the accomplished Swedish naturalist Dr Daniel Solander, one of Linnaeus's disciples, into joining the *Endeavour*. First he seems to have induced in Solander a state of excitement, and the next day talked the Admiralty into agreement. Banks chose to take two artists, a secretary, four servants and two dogs on the minute vessel. Tall and personable and exuberant, Banks tended to think that his professional interests should take precedence over the maritime priorities of a narrow Yorkshire salt like James Cook.

Cook's secret orders referred not just to the observation of the transit of Venus. They also required of him that since the discovery of countries hitherto unknown would redound greatly to the honour of the British nation, he was to proceed to the south in order to make discovery of the southern continent, 'until you arrive in the latitude of 40 degrees, unless you sooner fall in with it'. If he did not find any signs of the Great South Land (imagined as far more enormous than the ultimate reality of the Australian continent), he was to proceed to 35 degrees east, very close to what would turn out to be the latitude of a large part of the shelving east coast of Australia. He was to persevere until he fell in with the coast or met New Zealand.

Cook's further orders were, 'with the consent of the natives', to take possession of various places in the southern continent in the name of the King of Great Britain. The official orders also compelled the crew, upon their return to Britain, not to divulge where they had been until they had permission to do so, and the logs and journals of officers and petty officers were to be confiscated.

In sentiments which would frequently be denied in the later history of the continent, Dr Charles Morton, President of the Royal Society and a much admired, fatherly figure who would die before Cook's return, asked him in a document named *Hints* to exercise 'the utmost patience and forbearance with respect to the natives of the several lands where the ship may touch. To have it still in view that shedding one drop of the blood of those people is a crime of the highest nature . . . they are the natural, and in the strictest sense of the word, the legal possessors of the several regions they inhabit . . . they may naturally and justly attempt to repel invaders.'

Lacking a ship's chaplain, Cook was to read prayers on Sundays. Banks, of course, believed in the God of Nature, rather than the God of the Anglican Church. He was a deist, like the French thinkers, and his idea of Providence was of an impersonal Being which, 'careful of the creatures it has created, has benevolently provided against the too extensive multiplication of any species . . .' Like many sailors, Cook seems to have taken the established religion as a given, a bit like Newton's laws, and a godly form for control of sailors.

VENUS

The *Endeavour* crossed the Atlantic and reached Rio de Janeiro, but the viceroy there simply did not believe that this ship, with its scientific gentlemen aboard, was a Royal Naval vessel. Suspecting Cook of either espionage or smuggling, he banned the crew from landing, though some did disembark in disguise. At least, in a nearby bay, Banks and Dr Solander were able to land and collect samples.

Further south, in Tierra del Fuego, Cook managed to find a bay where he anchored and, looking for a watering place, encountered the natives: 'perhaps as miserable a set of people as are this day upon Earth'. Two of Banks's black servants died of exposure on this jaunt from the ship, though Banks's greyhounds, which had been with their master and may have saved him from hypothermia, survived. At sea again, Cook carefully and definitively charted perilous Cape Horn, saying 'that the charts hitherto published had been found incorrect not only in laying down the land but in the Latitude and Longitude of the places they contained'.

As in all Royal Naval vessels, floggings for disobedience and worse were a periodic necessity, and Cook saw such punishment as a regulating device in a ship's population crammed into a tiny space. One young marine stole a piece of sealskin from a comrade, made a tobacco pouch of it, and then hurled himself into the Pacific rather than face Cook and the lash.

Endeavour reached Tahiti more than seven weeks ahead of the transit, and barring some deaths and one suicide at sea, none of the men had scurvy, that tragic-comic disease from maritime melodrama. It is interesting that of all the diseases to which sailors were prone, scurvy frightened them most. It brought on a terrible lassitude, profound depression, acute joint pain, ulcers, tooth loss, appalling breath bespeaking an advancing internal death, and an ultimate closing down of organ function. Dysentery, the bloody flux (a diarrhoea caused by bowel-scarring rations), choleric fevers from bad water, and even yellow fever and typhus were not as universally feared or as statistically lethal as scurvy. On trans-Atlantic, let alone trans-global voyages, scurvy could send men permanently to their bunks and leave ships undermanned or unmanageable. Banks had earlier been worried that he was exhibiting early signs of scurvy and had dosed himself with lemon juice. Cook attributed the defeat of scurvy on *Endeavour* not only to the care and vigilance of his surgeon, but to the serving of sauerkraut ('sourgrout' to the sailors) and portable soup (compacted pea soup), and to dosing anyone who showed symptoms of scurvy with wort or malt.

He had not taken any nonsense about this. Early in the voyage he had ordered men who refused the sauerkraut ration to be flogged. But he had then good-humouredly found more effective methods. 'The sauerkraut the men at first would not eat until I put in practice a method I never once knew to fail with seamen, and this was to have some of it dressed everyday for the cabin table, and permitted all the officers without exception to make use of it and left it to the option of the men either to take as much as they pleased or none at all . . . The moment they see their superiors set a value upon it, it becomes the finest stuff in the world and the inventor a damned honest fellow.'

Ashore, the enthusiastic Banks impressed the Tahitians by bringing down three ducks with one shot, and began to study the Tahitian language. He possessed the Enlightenment thirst to try out, without prejudice, new cultural habits—he had tattoos done on his arm in Tahiti, in part to see how it was to inhabit a decorated skin. (It hurt a great deal, he found.) Meanwhile, 'The women,' wrote Molyneux, the master navigator, 'begin to have a share in our friendship which is by no means Platonic.'

Within a fortnight of *Endeavour*'s arrival in Tahiti, a fort had been finished, redoubts of casks with four-pounder cannon mounted on them and six swivel guns sited. The area was named by Cook Point Venus.

In one end of a large tent erected there, an astronomical clock with a gridiron pendulum was rigged in a double frame of wood, fixed firm and as low in the ground as the door of the clock case would permit, and then enclosed in another frame of wood. 'The pendulum was adjusted to exactly the same length as it had been at Greenwich,' noted Charles Green, the astronomer, a Yorkshireman of biting wit, in his mid thirties. Towards the end of the tent facing the clock and 4 metres from it stood the observatory, consisting of one of the ship's clocks, the astronomical quadrant and the reflecting telescopes set up on a steady cask of wet sand. Throughout Friday 2 June, the entire crew was anxious about weather conditions for the transit the next day, but the dawn of the transit was clear, and the day grew witheringly hot.

'We had every advantage we could desire in observing the whole of the passage of the planet Venus over the Sun's disc,' wrote Banks. Cook was on one telescope, Mr Green on another, and both let Doctor Solander take turns. 'We very distinctly saw an atmosphere or dusky shade around the body of the planet.' All three observers listed a different time for the various stages of the transit, and so did Lieutenants Hicks and Clarke who had set up their own telescopes to the east, and another party to the west. It was a matter of averaging results of the three observation parties, and calculations were collated in the following days.

After the observations, which he would take back to England for comparison with northern hemisphere measurements and to create a firmer set of longitudinal readings, Cook remained to study the Tahitians with the same keen interest that the Tahitians were studying him and Banks. On 13 July 1769, when the *Endeavour* left Matavai Bay, Banks had persuaded Cook to bring along Tupaia, a priest, and Tupaia's servant, a boy named Taiarpa. 'Thank heaven I have a sufficiency,' wrote Banks, 'and I do not know why I may not keep him as a curiosity, as . . . some of [my] neighbours do lions and tigers at a larger expense than he would probably ever put me to.' Banks was also convinced of 'the amusement' of future conversations with Tupaia and 'the benefit he will be of to this ship,' given his navigational capacity and his knowledge of the islands of the South Pacific. Tupaia proved his worth through his encyclopaedic knowledge of the reef depths around the islands Cook chose to visit.

At last they left the archipelago on 9 August, Banks putting it thus: 'Launched out into the Ocean in search of what chance and Tupaia might direct us to.'

Some of Cook's men were showing signs of 'venereal distemper'—probably gonorrhoea—from their own private transits of Venus. Cook's attempt to contain it 'was to little purpose for I may safely say I was not assisted by any one person in the ship'. The natives insisted to Cook that his men had not brought it to the islands; it had come on an earlier ship named the *Dolphin*.

THE TRANSIT OF MERCURY

Sailing south with his lovesick, afflicted crew, by September 1769 Cook had reached the point mentioned in his instructions as the first zone of search for a southern continent: 145 degrees west longitude and more than 40 degrees south latitude. The wind blasts of this region hurled the *Endeavour* about; the men at their mess tables on the crew deck complained all the more because of the lost ease and glories of Tahiti as Cook turned to the north-west. Banks kept working, and in periods of calm weather was rowed about to net jellyfish or shoot seabirds. Banks whimsically described the scene in the cabin: 'Dr Solander sits at the cabin table describing [sketching] myself at my bureau journalising. Between us hangs a large bunch of seaweed, upon the table lays the wood and barnacles . . . notwithstanding our different occupations our lips move very often.'

When the boy at the masthead, Nick Young, shouted 'Land!' he earned himself a pint of rum, and as the east coast of New Zealand's North Island presented itself more clearly, a headland was named in his honour—Young Nick's Head. Not that they were certain where they were. 'All hands seem to agree that this is certainly the continent we are in search of,' wrote Banks, expecting that this might be a northern coast of a huge southern landmass. But Cook himself was more phlegmatic and estimated that this was New Zealand.

Here Cook had his first crisis with native peoples, and it is sad to behold how far his standards had departed from those urged by Lord Morton in his *Hints*. The Maori were Polynesians who had occupied New Zealand, which they called *Aotearoa*, the Land of the Long White Cloud, for about eight hundred years. They lived in fortified villages named *pahs*, identifiable to Europeans as symbols of existing ownership, but there was no *pah* here—the Maori encountered by Cook were probably seasonal visitors.

This landing, Cook in the yawl, probably with Banks and Dr Solander, ended ingloriously in a chase of the soon-to-be famous navigator and the soon-to-be illustrious botanist back to the beach pursued by four aggressive Maori men. These natives, so reminiscent of those of Tahiti, would remain far more truculent than the easygoing Tahitians, and for good cause. The pinnace crew, standing offshore, poured in fire against the four, killing one of them. The next morning, Cook attempted a parley ashore, signalled his intentions were friendly, got the Tahitian priest Tupaia to speak to them—the Maori and Tahitian languages were close—and gave gifts. The Maoris plucked them out of English hands— theirs had been the loss, so their fractiousness was understandable, though Tupaia warned both the crew and the Maori that blood conflict would recur unless everyone behaved well. Almost at once, a Maori, knowing that a steel sword would add a new dimension to his warriorhood, began to run away with Mr Green the astronomer's sword, and someone fired at the man and killed him. The crew of *Endeavour* thus began a pattern of treating natives as potential thieves rather than actual owners.

Later in the day, the *Endeavour* intercepted a canoe full of young men and Tupaia invited them aboard. Instead, the Maori hurled every spear they had at the *Endeavour*. Another volley of musketry killed two or three Maori and another three were taken aboard the ship. 'When we was once alongside of them we must either have stood to be knocked on the head or else retire and let them go off in triumph . . . I am aware that most humane men who have not experienced things of this nature will censure my conduct,' wrote Cook. To give him credit, he acknowledged that 'the people in this boat . . . had given me no just provocation and were totally ignorant of my design'. He was heartsick, but, in an age before anthropology, he was devoted to the idea that his little barque was a travelling tabernacle of European grace and dignity, and that its authority must not be challenged. Europeans, being of a higher culture, should not lose face, even before the most intriguing of savages. These propositions were the armour of his rugged soul, and the uncomfortable question even now is whether he could have endured the long journey without such absolute assumptions. Throughout the entire circumnavigation of both islands, Cook and his crew found the Maori did not understand barter and were likely 'to plunder'. But Cook and his men did not grasp the Maori tradition of gift exchange, and did not understand it when the Maori activated it uni-laterally. Tupaia would in any case assure the crew that the New Zealanders were all liars.

Long after, the Polynesian race would exact its punishment on Cook.

Further north, in a bay in which he hoped to observe the transit of Mercury, his relations with the Maori began better. The telescopes and chronometers were again set up on shore to observe the transit on 9 November, and thereby help determine the longitude of the place. The observations were successful, but soon after a Lieutenant Gore on board became aware a piece of his cloth was missing, and the native who had taken it was back in a canoe, whose rowers brandished their oars in defiance. Gore grabbed a musket and shot the culprit dead. A four-pounder was fired to deter the canoe crew. In later negotiations, the Maori of Mercury Bay received some potato seedlings and were thus the first of their race to make a meal of the earth-apple. A Maori child who experienced the visit would remember later what Cook could not quite appreciate—the bewilderment at the sight of the *tupua*, the goblins or demons; the shock caused by their firearms and implements; and yet the generosity of gifts and the benignity of the chief, Cook, who touched the heads of Maori children as if he wished them nothing but the best.

During the last month of the year 1769, Cook mapped the coast of the North Island of New Zealand. On the west side of the island the coastline was less hospitable and the seas very rugged. He was looking for an inlet in which he could careen the ship, 'she being very foul'.

The careening, the running up of the ship on the shore at high tide so that its hull could be repaired and de-barnacled, was done at Ship Cove in Queen Charlotte Sound in the South Island, where Cook found amongst the local Maori fresh-picked human bone, this and other fairly scattered evidence proving to Cook and Banks that the Maori were cannibals: both claim to have seen the human meat of a forearm. Without doubting the sincerity of Cook or Banks, it was true that evidence of cannibalism was shocking but somehow culturally welcome to the European explorer and his ultimate audience—it showed that barbarous nations must be intruded upon for the savages' own good.

Cook would sail through the passage between the North and the South Islands, proving them separate bodies of land. With two flag-raising ceremonies, he would assume both islands into the mystical body of George III.

Cook had by now fulfilled his orders. He had observed the transit of Venus, hunted for the southern continent where it was presumed to exist—if it existed at all—and would soon complete the charting of New Zealand. He was free in all honour to go home, either by the Cape of Good Hope or by Cape Horn. His instructions declared that in unforeseen emergencies he was to proceed upon the advice of his officers in whichever direction he thought most advantageous to the service. In a great New Zealand fiord surrounded by cloud-concealed walls of near-vertical rock, he called his officers to the cabin for a conference. To honour their uncertainty, he named the place Doubtful Sound. To go home east round the Horn was attractive, not only because that was the fast way, but because he believed it might be a last chance to encounter the Great Southern Continent, the one Dutch New Holland might be part of, but which—should it exist—would soon be encountered to the east and would run far south towards the pole. But he would be in sub-Antarctic ocean, in howling weather and with a leaky ship he would have to career once more to repair it from the damage the Horn might do it. The other relatively safe option was to head north to New Guinea and Batavia. It was decided instead to steer westward until they fell in with the east coast of New Holland, and if they found it, to follow it northwards. It seems that though he consulted the officers, he may have already determined the result. 'I had other and more greater objects in view, viz. the discovery of the whole Eastern coast of New Holland.'

TURAGA LANDFALL

On 31 March 1770, Cook left august New Zealand behind in a bank of its own rain clouds, and turned westwards. The great whale of a south land did not exist, but a prodigious substitute waited out there, across the full-blooded currents of the Tasman.

There was little in it for the sailors. At their mess tables and on deck, or in the captain's cabin if summoned, were the only places they could stand more or less upright. Their sleeping areas fore and aft of their mess were less than 4 feet 6 inches (137 centimetres) in height. Like many British miners, sailors were a race of stoopers. Learning to walk with the ship's motion while so bent over was a skill, but perforce it was second nature, and even Joseph Banks had to stoop somewhat under the low ceiling of the captain's cabin, a space Cook seems to have been generous in letting the scientists make use of. There was a saloon amidships, however, where the gentlemen could stand up and sit relatively comfortably—to work or converse or take meals. But the bunk in Banks's coop, off the main cabin, was so foreshortened that the tall young man had often to stretch out at night on Cook's floor.

The men who were crossing the Tasman Ocean in search of eastern Australia were a race pygmied by the dimensions of their ship. Even so, *Endeavour* was a grail loaded with all the European concepts and gifts. Quite apart from the maritime gifts represented by Cook himself, by Molyneux the navigator and the lieutenants, even by the mischievous American midshipman James Magra, there were the concepts of the Enlightenment and the traditions of humanism carried in particular in the tall frame of young Mr Banks. It is worth reviewing what these concepts were in his case. Above all, he possessed a passion for the new. On the continent towards which they were sailing, in the oldest culture on earth, native people practised what would be called 'maintenance ceremonies', that is, ceremonies to ensure that a particular area, plentiful in water or plant or animal life, would remain as it was, as the hero ancestor had created it, until the next time the people visited. The limitations of food and water sources in New Holland made it so. Whereas Banks and Solander were ready to do away with limits, and to define their world anew. Above all, Banks believed in the supremacy of scientific and philosophic reason over old orthodoxies of thought and belief, and that reason must be followed even if there was a price involved, such as his giving up spacious London for little *Endeavour*, and sleeping on Cook's cabin floor.

A chart Cook owned depicted 'Nouvelle Holland' standing rather in the posture of a huge cat leaning forward on its front paws. Van Diemen's Land was shown on it as those front paws, part of an unmarked straight line running north towards what is known today as Cape York, Australia's northernmost point. The cartographer did not bother even to indent this line with imagined bays. A few broad-stroke waves in it were left to suggest the possibility of a complex coast.

It was not a coast easily found, and the wind and seas did not help. On the night of 19 April, Cook brought the *Endeavour* to in case the land was near, and at five in the morning he set close reeftop sails and merely edged along. And then at six o'clock, the tubercular Lieutenant Zachary Hicks saw the land. It was extending from the north-east to the south westwards, and was 'long'. Cook named the southernmost point he could see Point Hicks, though it is now known as Cape Everard, very close to the present New South Wales–Victoria border. Further south, he could see nothing where Van Diemen's Land should have been. So Cook turned north and began charting the coast or, to quote his famous biographer, Beaglehole, 'brought it out of the shades'.

This was virgin coast for Europeans. The Dutch had not been here, and as far as anyone knew, neither had the Chinese, Makassans, Spanish, Portuguese or anyone else except whatever natives were to be found beyond the string of bold capes and glistening beaches and handsome blue and green hills. Cook would often have to bring the *Endeavour* to at night, because of the vigorous surf off the beaches.

On the afternoon of 27 April, Cook attempted a first footing on the coast by putting off in a yawl with Banks, Solander and Tupaia and the boat crew. But the surf, as so often on this coast, was too strenuous. The next morning, though, a bay presented itself. He entered it around a low headland, and anchored off the south shore of the place that afternoon. He was watched by a few natives, some of them painted with white stripes. From a boat offshore, Tupaia tried to talk to these people, but their language owed nothing to Polynesian. They belonged to the Eora language group, one of at least 250 languages then spoken by people in the continent known as New Holland. To the gifts Cook had ordered thrown from the boat onto the shore the natives showed hostility. Cook said of them: 'All they seem'd to want was for us to be gone.' They knew these visiting spirits on their floating island (*turaga*) were a sign of cosmic disorder, possibly the dangerous dead returned and rampant. Nonetheless, Cook put in for a landing. His wife's young cousin, seventeen-year-old Isaac Smith, soon to become a midshipman and ultimately a rear admiral, a young man who shared Cook's enthusiasm for surveying, was in the boat crew, and as the boat kissed the sandy shore, Cook asked Isaac to jump into the shallows and land first.

From the few empty bark huts that were found, Cook had no inhibitions about removing fizz-gigs, that is, fishing spears. In one shelter they found small children hiding behind a bark shield, and gave them strings of beads. Like many later, these traumatised children of the Gweagal clan thought the wigged and long-haired men to be women spirits fallen from the sky. Dampier had surmised in 1699 that the people he met on the other side of what would prove to be the continent of Australia were relatives of the Negroes. Banks and Cook both took the time in their journals to disagree with this proposition.

Cook could not know what great influence his writings about this place would have in times to come. He said it was 'capacious, safe and commodious'. The land was low and level, unlike so much of the country they had passed on the way up the coast, and its soil was sandy. Much of the inland was lagoon country, where mangrove shrubs and palm trees predominated. Stingrays sheltered in the shallows in front of a land from which rose, when disturbed, pelicans and dazzling parrots and cockatoos.

Here, just south of the present-day city of Sydney, a young seaman from the Orkney Islands, Thorby Sutherland, died of tuberculosis, and death amongst his crew was still rare enough to enable Cook to name the inner south point of the bay in his memory. By now he had carved on a tree, as he had already done at Mercury Bay in New Zealand, his ship's name and date of arrival. The great quantity of stingrays found in the bay led to his first calling it Sting Ray's Harbour. Indeed, the American lieutenant on *Endeavour*, John Gore, went hunting for them in the shallows. Then Banks and Dr Solander came aboard from their excursions ashore, delirious with the range of new plants they had discovered and which, once they affixed samples to drying paper in the normal way, they then had to take ashore again to dry out in the sun. Moved by their exhilaration, Cook decided he had better call the place Botanist Harbour, and the heads at the entrance Point Solander and Cape Banks. Botanist Harbour soon transmuted to Botany Bay. The most famous location of Georgian botany would thus bear the name of Banks's passion and true love, rather than the names of admirals, sailors and bureaucrats (as, for example, Cape Howe and Batemans Bay), or names based on natural appearance (Point Upright, Long Nose, Red Point). Cook also left guidance for future navigators in some of his names: Point Danger, Mount Warning, Point Lookout.

Banks would end up giving his name in particular to a genus of plant which grew up and down this coastline and which would be an iconic plant of the Australian bush, one of those definite markers which said this place is not an imitation of England, nor even of the rest of known creation. The *Banksia serrata*, for example, is gnarled and knobbly, has long leaves with serrated edges, and large, thick flowering fronds, yellow-green and rich in nectar. When the flower dies, the old cone resembles a many-mouthed black villain, and one wonders if it was used as a toy for millennia by Aboriginal children as it would be by the coming generations of white settler children. The *Banksia serrata* would have seventy-six related species all carrying Banks's name.

On the morning of 6 May, helped by a wind change to the south, *Endeavour* left Botany Bay and had a pleasant coastal run. Back on land, the various

Eora-speaking clans who occupied the shore and immediate hinterland considered the departure a deliverance, a successful and happy exorcism of alien spirits. Cook passed the sandstone heads of an apparently shallow bay or harbour which he named Port Jackson, but did not explore. Northwards, he continued his naming tendencies. Port Stephens on the one hand, Smoky Cape on the other, named because he saw smoke inland behind it, fires lit for hunting purposes on the flood plain by the Thunguddi people, whose time of disruption had not yet come.

TO *GANGURRU* REGIONS

Banks and Solander remained industrious, and so did the expeditionary artist Sydney Parkinson, the son of a Quaker brewer from Edinburgh, with so much coastline to sketch and so many novel specimens to draw. Cook's days too must have been extremely busy, as he made his readings on triangulations and added lines to the chart, the very first chart of this coastline. His work was exacting, and he did not fumble his calculations or jump to easy conclusions. Unlike his opinion of Botany Bay, which would later confuse people, his chart of this huge coastline, 2000 kilometres long, was nearly impeccable.

Off Hervey Bay, in what is now Queensland, occurred an incident of grave indiscipline. Richard Orton, the captain's clerk, was so drunk that 'some malicious person or persons in the ship' were able to steal all his clothes and dock part of both his ear lobes. Cook suspected that the culprit was the American midshipman, Mr Magra. Investigations could not prove it, even though Magra had once or twice before 'in their drunken frolics' cut off Orton's clothing, and had said 'that if it was not for the law he would murder him'. Molyneux, the master navigator, also drank a great deal.

Cook considered the cutting of Orton 'the greatest insult [that] could be offered to my authority in this ship, as I have always been ready to hear and redress every complaint that has been made against any person in the ship'. It was interesting that at this great remove from England, Magra and Cook had no doubt that the law prevailed. Some relationships aboard might have been turning rancid, but the travelling was now rendered particularly complicated by the Barrier Reef and the great number of islands all around. One night Cook had to anchor in only 4 metres of water, a mere two and two-thirds fathoms, and a bare half metre more than the ship's draught. The fact that the natives in this region, influenced by the Melanesians to the north, had outrigger canoes—more formidable than the simple craft of the Eora speakers—made him nervous as well. Far north from the point where *Endeavour* had encountered the Australian east coast lay a tropic cape Cook named Tribulation, 'because here began all our troubles'.

The Barrier Reef is not a continuous line of reef but many such lines, and it does not always lie parallel to the coast. To the south it lies further offshore. But by Cape Tribulation the reef cramped Cook in.

It was a splendid night, 12 June, and a man was continuously throwing lead from the bows. The ship now crept on and a little after ten o'clock the man in the bows roared 'Seventeen fathoms!' and before he could swing again, the ship suddenly struck reef. Everything heavy that could be thrown overboard was—the yards and the topmasts were taken down and anchors taken out of the ship with the hope that they could be used for heaving her off. Just a ship's length from the starboard side there was twelve fathoms (21.6 metres) and even more astern.

The ship would not budge, and though letting in very little water the sound of her keel and bottom grinding on the coral was disturbing. The fixed guns and their carriages were thrown overboard, iron and stone ballast, all manner of stores that had rotted and unnecessary casks. But at high water she still would not move. At least there was a flat calm, so that the grinding sound ceased. But as the tide went out again, *Endeavour* heeled to starboard and began to take water. Even the gentlemen took to the pumps. Banks admired the calm of the officers and noticed that the men gave up swearing. Cook hoped that the night tide would be higher. But there was also the horrible chance, given the amount of water that was flooding into the hold, that the ship, its charts and all its news would go straight down. At last, after a day's desperation, the night tide lifted *Endeavour* and she floated and was hauled off by her boats. Banks believed that when hauled off she must surely sink and that the gentlemen and crew would be left in a land where they had no hope for subsistence and with no discourse other than with 'the most unciviliz'd savages perhaps in the world'. But the coral which had holed her had stuck in the hole, and thus plugged *Endeavour*.

The anchors were brought on board and the forward topmast set up, and she edged in towards the land. While she sailed the crew fothered her—that is, passed a bandage of sailcloth entirely round her keel, and tightened it in place. Cook was delighted with Midshipman Monkhouse for undertaking the operation and fulfilling it so well. Though Banks had feared that the men might in panic and desperation run berserk on the ship, the crew had behaved well.

On 16 June, a time of temperate tropic warmth on this coast, Cook was able to run through a narrow channel into a harbour, intending to careen his ship. As the tide receded, the damage could be looked at. A large hole had been torn in the starboard side, but the coral that had come away from the reef had partly plugged the hole and the fother had then sealed it in place. While the ship lay on the sand, propped up by logs, and while the carpenters went to work on its hull, a hospital tent was set up ashore for Tupaia and Mr Green who were both ill. A diet of fresh fish rapidly but temporarily cured Tupaia and improved Mr Green the astronomer, although neither man would live to see the northern hemisphere, and Cook would blame them for neglecting their vegetables.

The high land here was barren and stony, and the banks of a river, inevitably named the Endeavour, and its backwaters were covered with jungle and mangrove swamp. 'A very indifferent prospect,' as Cook said. In Aboriginal mythology the landscape to which Cook was indifferent was the work of a scrub python ancestor named Mungurru. 'Before that old scrub python travelled down to the sea,' said an elder, some years later, 'there was no river there.' The people with whom Cook made tentative contact were the Guugu Yimidhirr. There was early trouble when some of the Aboriginals lit grass as a way of blocking the passage of the English ashore. 'In an Instant, the whole place was in flames,' wrote Cook. There was also argument over ownership of turtles Cook captured. And on 23 June, a previously unsighted animal was seen. It resembled a wild dog but jumped and ran like a hare or deer. The Europeans did not get a good look at one again until 7 July, when on a long walk they saw four of the animals. They outran Banks's greyhounds, who were caught in the dense grass over which the kangaroos leaped. At least that's what the Guugu Yimidhirr people told them they called the beast—*Gangurru*. On 14 July, Lieutenant Gore shot one. 'To compare it to any European animal would be impossible as it has not the least resemblance to any one I have seen,' wrote Banks. 'Its forelegs are extremely short and of no use to it in walking, its hind again are as disproportionately long; with these it hops seven or eight feet at each hop.' Rather like a gerbil, he thought, except this kangaroo weighed 38 pounds (17 kilos) and a gerbil was no bigger than a rat.

A larrikin story remains about this historic naming: that when Cook asked what the beast was called, an Aboriginal, in replying with the word *Gangurru*, in effect said, 'I don't understand the question.' But in fact Cook and Banks and Solander got the name right.

The native people remained wary until at last Cook was able to tow the repaired hulk of *Endeavour* off the beach, rig it and sail north. He found himself in a puzzle of reefs and shoals, afraid that strong seas would cast the *Endeavour* once more on the coral. 'A reef such as is here spoke of is scarcely known in Europe, it is a wall of coral rock rising almost perpendicular out of the unfathomable ocean . . . the large waves of the vast ocean meeting with so sudden a resistance make a most terrible surf breaking mountains high.'

At nightfall the *Endeavour* was only eighty to one hundred metres from the breaking water, 'only a dismal valley' the breadth of one wave away from destruction. In its struggle not to be wrecked, it was pushed out through a hole in the reef with the outgoing tide, but the rising tide again pushed it back into danger. Getting away from the interior of the reef and then escaping the outside of it became a recurrent theme. At a narrow point in the reef through which the *Endeavour* was washed, Cook wrote, 'It is but a few days ago that I rejoiced at having got without the reef, but that joy was nothing when compared to what I now felt at being safe at an anchor within it, such is the vicissitudes attending this kind of service . . .'

It all became much simpler when the reef broadened out into islands around Cape York. Once the northern promontory was rounded, Cook was fairly confident that he could find a passage into 'the Indian seas' and thus home. Cape York was the limit for him—he believed that explorations to the west of it were the business of the Dutch, so just to make the point that he considered his east coast run had turned hinterland British, he once more landed and hoisted the colours and 'took possession of the whole eastern coast . . . by the name of New South Wales, together with all the bays, harbours, rivers and islands situated upon the said coast, after which we fired three volleys of small arms which were answered by the like number from the ship'. For a ship that was barely 30 metres long, the claim its captain made was prodigious.

There were no quibbles about the rights of the sundry tribes of coastal or inland New South Wales, even when their virtues were considered. 'From what I have said of the natives of New Holland, they may appear to some to be the most wretched people upon Earth, but in reality they are far more happy than we Europeans; being wholly unacquainted not only with the superfluous but the necessary conveniences so much sought after in Europe, they are happy in not knowing the use of them. They live in a tranquillity which is not disturbed by the inequality of condition: the earth and sea of their own accord furnishes them with all things necessary for life, they covet not magnificent houses, household stuff, etc.'

Some think that this effusiveness of Cook, and its purely philosophic style, is a departure from the normal, commonsensical or navigational tenor of Cook's journal. Banks had written in like terms: 'From them appear how small are the real wants of human nature, which we Europeans have increased to an excess which would certainly appear incredible to these people could they be told it.'

On 17 August 1770, the *Endeavour* turned towards home. By Batavia everyone seemed ill; Tupaia died before Christmas; and the ship needed long repair. Sydney Parkinson, who had done beautiful paintings of specimens taken by Mr Banks, and Dr Spöring, assistant naturalist, both died, as did a corporal of marines, and then Mr Green the astronomer. Banks, too, caught fever, but recovered. The master Robert Molyneaux died in Cape Town.

When England was reached, it was at first a series of accounts written by crewmen on the delicious nature of their contact with Tahitian women which gripped the popular imagination. 'The women are extremely lascivious,' wrote a crew member. '. . . a virgin is to be purchased here, with the unanimous consent of the parents, for three nails and a knife. I own I was a buyer of such commodities . . .'

It was 29 August 1791 before an officer's letter was published which gave more substantial news. In the meantime, Banks had the immediate problem of avoiding marriage with Miss Blosset, and he and Solander were introduced twice to the King, had dinner with Boswell and Dr Johnson, another with Benjamin Franklin at the house of the President of the Royal Society, and received honorary doctorates from Oxford. Gradually news of the scope of Cook's southern hemisphere visitations penetrated the public imagination. But it came to the European mind as a gradual awakening, not in a thunderclap.

It was Banks in particular who had stepped into glory, the discovery of plants and animals counting for more than the charting of the eastern coast of New Holland and its naming as New South Wales. The pre-eminent Swedish botanist Linnaeus wrote that New South Wales should instead be named Banksia. Cook returned to console Mrs Cook, since their four-year-old girl, Elizabeth, had died three months past. The Admiralty eventually acknowledged that their Lordships extremely well approved of the whole of his proceedings, and the several journals and charts he had presented them with. Cook was introduced to the King at St James on 14 August 1771. He was given command of the *Scorpion*, a sloop, and sent to correct the charts of the English coast. His desire was that he would be sent on another expedition to the South Seas, and that he would command it. He would have his hope.

CHAPTER 3[*]

THE ENGLAND COOK RETURNED TO

A remarkable poem by William Blake, the prophet and artist who lived and worked in Broad Street, London, and knew the truth of the city, seems to summarise the age:

I wander thro' each charter'd street
Near where the charter'd Thames doth flow
And mark in every face I meet
Marks of weakness, marks of woe.
In every cry of every Man
In every infant's cry of fear,
In every voice, in every ban,
The mind-forg'd manacles I hear.
How the Chimney-sweeper's cry
Every black'ning church appalls,
And the hapless Soldier's sigh
Runs in blood down Palace walls.
But most thro' midnight streets I hear
How the young Harlot's curse
Blasts the newborn Infant's tear,
And blights with plague the marriage hearse.

---

[*] Some of the material relating to British society, crime and punishment, and to the administration of Arthur Phillip has also been covered in this author's earlier work *The Commonwealth of Thieves*.

Thus the Britain to which Banks and Cook had brought back news of New South Wales and Botany Bay and the *gangurru* was one suffering from a range of stresses and rages which it tried to treat by imposing severe penalties on acts of discontent, these ranging from sedition to theft.

The British did not possess the great white spaces of a Siberia to serve as a distant outdoor prison for their criminals, but until the late 1770s they had their American colonies, and had habitually used them. As immortalised in popular ballads, foolish young men and minor criminals, perhaps to the number of 120 000, were torn from the breasts of their lovers to be shipped to 'Amerikay'. From about 1650 to the outbreak of hostilities between the Americans and British in 1775 they arrived in Virginia or Maryland or the Carolinas, where American settlers would bid for their labour—generally for seven years—at the auction block. The administrative beauty of this was that the master took over the prisoner, and troubled the authorities only in the case of escape or major unruliness. Sometimes vagrants and the poor—'idle persons lurking in parts of London'—would voluntarily let themselves be transported and sold with the criminals.

London and regional merchants often found this trade in selling the labour of white servants cheaper to engage in than that in African slaves. Based on auction prices in Baltimore between 1767 and 1775, a convict's labour for his total sentence cost between £10 and £25. It was possible for an affluent convict to bid for himself and do his time as, effectively, a free agent. But very few transported convicts could afford to buy their own labour, or return home from Virginia, Maryland or Georgia, even if they survived the 'seasoning period', the first few years of malaria and other diseases which killed two out of five inhabitants of Virginia. The convict engaged in field labour was likely to find an early grave in American soil and never bother the British domestic authorities again.

But in embracing the benefits of transportation for the home nation, the British government sought to solve a domestic issue and barely thought of the impact it had on the colony that received the felons. During the eighteenth century, one North American colonist was left to complain, 'America has been made the very common sewer and dung yard to Britain.' But not once the shots rang out at Concord Bridge, and the Minutemen marched on Boston, signalling the commencement of the American Revolutionary War.

A new Transportation Act of 1780, passed during Britain's very loss of the American colonies, sought to make transportation more obligatory. The reality was that prisoners sentenced to transportation were doing their time not in British colonies but in chaotic, overcrowded prisons while the government waited for the American rebellion to end. The offences for which an individual Briton could be transported under the accumulated Transportation Acts made up an exotic catalogue. Notorious thieves and takers of spoil in the borderlands of Northumberland and Cumberland, commonly called 'moss-troopers' or 'reivers', were subject to penalties of transportation; similarly, persons found guilty of stealing cloth from the rack, or embezzling His Majesty's stores to the value of twenty shillings; persons convicted of wilfully burning ricks of corn, hay, etc or barns etc in the night time (a common crime both in England and Ireland and generally associated with peasant protest against landlords); persons convicted of larceny and other offences; persons imprisoned for smuggling wool to France and the Low Countries and not paying the excise on it (a regular Surrey crime); persons convicted of entering into any park and killing or wounding any deer without the consent of the owner; persons convicted of perjury and forgery; persons convicted of assaulting others with offensive weapons with the design to rob; vagrants or vagabonds escaping from a house of correction or from service in the army or navy; persons convicted of stealing any linen laid to be printed or bleached; ministers of the Episcopal Church of Scotland, suspected of support for Bonnie Prince Charlie, exercising their functions in Scotland without having registered their letter of orders, taken all oaths, and prayed for His Majesty and the Royal Family by name; persons returning from transportation without license; persons convicted of entering mines with intent to steal; persons convicted of assaulting any magistrate or officer engaged in the salvage of ships or goods from wrecks; persons convicted of stealing fish in any water within a park, paddock, orchard or yard. Besides legislation imposing the penalty of transportation, between 1660 and 1819 almost two hundred capital, mandatory death sentence statutes were passed, along similar principles, to add to the nearly fifty already in existence.

One sees in the long list a heavy emphasis on the sanctity of two institutions: property, and the Crown under the Royal House of Hanover. The Irish and certain Scots were resistant to the Crown; and as for property matters, William Blackstone, author of Blackstone's *Commentaries on the Laws of England*, thought with his friends Dr Johnson and Oliver Goldsmith that 'theft should not be punished with death', but Parliament went on churning out statutes which did just that. The lack of a British police force meant that legislators felt they needed to impress the people with the terror of the law.

In theory, frequent public executions should have cut down on crowding in gaols. But even the lawmakers, members of the Commons, might mercifully take up the special cause of this or that prisoner. In a given courtroom, at the bi-yearly Assizes or during the Quarter Sessions, a jury might deliberately undervalue the goods stolen to prevent a prisoner being 'stretched'. Their gratuitous compassion speaks to us still in the court records' description of a prisoner as 'too young' for the full force of the law to operate, or else as 'a poor unfortunate girl' or 'an unfortunate girl of good family'. But if they didn't like a prisoner, juries could just as easily indulge feelings of gratuitous outrage.

King George III also attended to reprieves, sitting in council at St James Palace, and receiving advice and lists of prisoners from judges and recorders. He was severe above all on counterfeiters who presumed to forge his head on coins, otherwise generally accepting the recommendation of mercy from the trial judge, as did the Prince Regent, the future George IV, during his father's illness and lunacy. In the 1770s and 1780s, the royal mercy, flowing across London from St James to Newgate, and out to the county jails of the provinces, helped keep the prisons crammed with transportees who lacked a destination.

As for the individual prisoner, often young, they were aware that when they came in front of the courts, neither judge nor jury would enquire too closely into whether a confession had been beaten out of them. Generally, they appeared without legal counsel. The magistrates they faced at the Quarter Sessions believed one crime unpunished begot another, and questions about the accused's level of want or disadvantage did not delay them for a second. Nor did the idea the accused was innocent till proved guilty influence them. The prisoner had to prove the 'prosecutor'—that is, the victim—had made a mistake in identifying them or was acting from malice. Attorneys were slowly becoming employed both as prosecutors and counsel for the defence, but on magistrates' sufferance.

The trial proceeded more briskly than in modern times—the Georgian version of a day in court was less than a quarter of an hour. Ordinary trials at an Assizes rarely went beyond an adjournment. Major cases all ended with acquittal, transportation or the death penalty—what Londoners called the 'hearty choke with caper sauce', 'nothing more than a wry face and a watered patch of breeches', and 'dancing the Paddington frisk'. Yet capital punishment still took forms other than hanging. Women counterfeiters were subject to death by burning, and the heads of Jacobites (Scottish supporters of Bonnie Prince Charlie) were stuck and exposed on spikes at Temple Bar. About one in eight of those committed for trial was sentenced to death, but (based on figures concentrated between 1761 and 1765), fewer than half of those so sentenced were executed.

For many decades there had been eight hanging days at Tyburn Hill every year, a frightful public but ceremonious spectacle. But from the mid 1780s executions occurred outside Newgate prison itself. There, on a spring day in 1785, James Boswell, the Scottish attorney and writer, watched nineteen criminals, including thieves, a forger, a stamp counterfeiter and others who had illegally returned from transportation, 'depart Newgate to the other world', and then went on to dinner.

CAMPBELL'S HULKS

An Act of Parliament passed in 1783 allowed the removal of convicts from the overcrowded gaols on land to the dismasted hulks of old men-of-war moored in the Thames, and at Portsmouth and Plymouth, where they could serve their time labouring on harbour works pending transportation. The British government was thus temporarily restricted to transporting its fallen souls not across the Atlantic but a few miles ashore by rowboat. The hulks, an eyesore detested by respectable London, condemned by progressives as academies of criminality, and unpopular with convicts, were both a phenomenon and an enterprise. Duncan Campbell, a reputable man and a good Presbyterian Scot, was the hulk-master. He had begun in the convict-transporting business in 1758, carrying felons to Virginia and Maryland. The revolution in America threw the affairs of Campbell and others into disarray. The amounts lost by British creditors in America, when Americans refused to pay British merchants' bills, were of a high order, and Campbell had a dizzying fortune of over £38000 owing to him from gentlemen in Virginia and Maryland. But in modest ways the war in America now compensated him, since he ran the hulks as an enterprise. His initial contract, worth £3560 a year, was for a dismasted hulk (he named it *Justitia*) of at least 240 tons (245 tonnes) to house 120 prisoners, with necessary tools and six lighters for the convicts to work from, as well as medicines and vinegar as a scurvy cure, and means to wash and fumigate the vessel. By 1780 he had accommodation for 510 convicts, and had purchased a French frigate, the *Censor*, and an old 'Indiaman' which he named *Justitia II*. He also set up a receiving hulk and a hospital ship.

On Campbell's receiving ship, the prisoner was stripped of the vermin-infested clothes he had worn in Newgate or elsewhere in the kingdom, bathed, and held for four days quarantine. The high death rate on Campbell's ships and, ultimately, on less well-administered hulks moored in Portsmouth and Plymouth, seems to have been partially the result of diseases prisoners had contracted originally in the common wards of city and county gaols and brought to the hulks with them. 'The ships at Woolwich are as sweet as any parlour in the kingdom,' Campbell argued with some pride, and he had the grace to live near them—at Blackheath just behind Greenwich. But though Campbell had a reputation for decency, the Act of Parliament setting up the hulks called for prisoners to be 'fed and sustained with bread and any coarse and inferior food' as a symbol of their shame, and urged that misbehaviour be punished by 'whipping, or other moderate punishment'.

There was on top of that the hulks' peculiar below-decks dimness, the frock of sewage and waste which adorned the water around them, and the horror of being locked down at night on the cold prison deck and abandoned to the worst instincts of the established criminal cliques. The British thought of the hulks as a temporary expedient, but they would not be able to get rid of their floating prisons in the Thames and elsewhere until 1853—indeed, hulks would make an ominous appearance in Dickens's *Great Expectations*.

Periodically reacting to complaints from their constituents, London's members of parliament and city aldermen kept telling government the prisoners on the hulks should be transported anywhere convenient—to the East or West Indies, Canada or Nova Scotia, Florida or the Falklands. The mayor and corporation of the City of London thought as bad as were the mischiefs so severely felt already, the 'rapid and alarming accumulation of convicts within the kingdom' involved consequences in city prisons and in hulks no human wisdom could foresee.

For by the end of the American war it was obvious British prisons and hulks could not handle the condemned or cause them to disappear. Each prisoner on the hulks cost government £38 a year, and his labour was not worth that. The question was not whether transportation would occur but where.

Yet except for the rebellious North American colonies, no one place seemed the right destination for transportees.

GET RID OF THEM—BUT WHERE?

The question of a destination for the condemned took up a lot of time.

The most significant witness to appear before the Commons Committee on Colonies, in 1779, set up while government was trying to relieve gaol pressure all over Britain, was Sir Joseph Banks, the great naturalist, commentator and society figure.

Even though in the journal of his voyage as a young scientist with Cook, Banks described Botany Bay on the New South Wales coast as barren, he urged the committee to consider that it might be suitable for transportation, and that there was sufficient fertile soil to sustain a European settlement. From there, too, escape would be difficult, he said. The climate was mild, as in the south of France. There were no savage animals or hostile natives. The 'Indians' around Botany Bay he estimated at hardly more than fifty.

Sir Joseph Banks was asked whether he thought land for settlement might be acquired from the Aborigines 'by Cession or Purchase'. Banks said he thought not, that there was nothing you could give the Aborigines in return for their soil. He told the committee that the blacks were blithely nomadic and would 'speedily abandon' whatever land was needed. The concept of New South Wales as *terra nullius*, no man's land, was born.

In the end, the Commons Committee left the question of transportation destinations open, but recommended the building of two penitentiaries, where prisoners would be kept in solitary confinement with hard labour. By 1786, however, no progress had been made on building the penitentiaries and the government had definitely decided to begin transportation again. Crime levels had jumped because of the discharge of members of the army and navy after the war in America. Home Secretary Lord Sydney was left to write, 'The more I consider the matter, the greater difficulty I see in disposing of these people.'

Botany Bay in immensely remote New South Wales, on a coast *Endeavour* had visited in 1770, also had an eloquent proponent in a former midshipman of Cook's, the miscreant James Maria Magra (or Matra) who allegedly had cut Orton's ears one drunken night. But he did not see Botany Bay chiefly as a destination for transportees. At the time he sailed with Cook, he had been financially secure due to his New York colonial family's wealth, but having remained loyal to the Crown in the American war, he had lost all that. He had returned to London from New York in 1781, where he found a great number of fellow American Empire Loyalist refugees living in squalor. Britain was doing little for them, and Magra drafted a 1783 pamphlet addressed to the British government, *A Proposal for Establishing a Settlement in New South Wales to Atone for the Loss of our American Colonies*. American Empire Loyalists should be sent as free settlers to New South Wales, and wives should be supplied to them if necessary from amongst the natives of New Caledonia or Tahiti. 'Settlement could be a centre for trade with East Asia or a wartime base for attack on the Dutch colonies of Malaya . . . And thus two objects of the most desirable and beautiful union will be permanently blended: economy to the public, and humanity to the individual.' Without mentioning convicts, Magra nonetheless brought attention to New South Wales/Botany Bay as a potential destination for awkward people.

Though Sir Joseph Banks promoted Magra's proposal to the government, the incumbent Tories soon fell and the Whigs came to power, and Lord Sydney, a recently ennobled political operator and Kentish squire in his early fifties, inherited the Home Office, including concern for prisons and colonial affairs. Sympathetic to those loyal subjects who had lost their American lands, savings and standing, he was already involved in organising a new home for American loyalists in Nova Scotia, where there would grow a city named in his honour.

On the question of prisons and hulks, though, Sydney remained under pressure from all directions. On 9 December 1784, he wrote to the mayor of Hull, who had asked for the removal of his city's convicts to the hulks, saying that not a person more could be at present admitted to them. Sydney answered similarly to a request from Oxford, and others from a range of counties. Sydney, born Thomas Townshend, already had a solid political career behind him, having been Secretary of War in a previous government and then Home Secretary under both Shelburne and Pitt. He was thought to be a good man who lived an orderly life at his house in Chislehurst, though Oliver Goldsmith, the author and activist, depicted him as the sort of lesser talent with whom great spirits such as Edmund Burke had to deign to negotiate.

At the end of 1785, Prime Minister Pitt and Lord Sydney and his Under-secretary, the former naval purser Evan Nepean, were still looking for a plausible scheme of transportation. They considered Africa, specifically a tract of country on the west coast between 20 and 30 degrees south latitude, near the mouth of the Das Voltas (Orange) River where there were copper deposits. Convicts could be shipped out in slaving vessels which would then proceed up the coast to pick up their more accustomed cargo of African slaves to take to America and the West Indies. The many American families who were still anxious to live under British rule could also be sent to Das Voltas and serve as the discipliners and employers of the convicts. In preparation, the government sloop *Nautilus* was sent to survey the southern Atlantic coast of Africa, but its ultimate report was that the country was barren, waterless, hopeless.

The government also considered a settlement on the Caffre (Kaffir) coast around the Cape. But fears of aggrieving the Dutch in Cape Town made the British pull back.

In March 1786, Londoners and their aldermen yet again petitioned against the unsatisfactory solution represented by the hulks. The aldermen reminded the government that demobilised and unemployed soldiers and sailors could make a mob, and imbued with the fancy American ideas of the rights of man would set convicts free and burn the hulks. The hulks had brought the risk of mayhem and uprising, as well as shipboard epidemics, to within a longboat's reach of shore.

At last, in August 1786, Cabinet plumped for New South Wales, the preposterously distant coast Cook had charted sixteen years past. Londoners rejoiced that a decision had been made to resume transportation. They believed it would mean an end to the river hulks.

A DISCREET OFFICER

The man the government chose to 'take upon him the command of this rabble' of convicts was a 49-year-old Royal Navy post-captain named Arthur Phillip, an old shipmate of the Home Office Undersecretary, Evan Nepean. The fact that Phillip had been a sailor since the age of thirteen and had no experience at all of the British penal system did not worry the Home Office. Lord Sydney wanted any robust and adaptable fellow to mount the flotilla and empty the hulks and prisons for him.

A neighbour of Phillip's in the New Forest, Sir George Rose, Secretary of the Treasury, was involved in the costings of the enterprise, and he supported Phillip's appointment, which Phillip does not seem to have hesitated in accepting. Many officers might have thought it potentially dangerous and unrewarding.

Lord Howe at the Admiralty had written to Lord Sydney of the Home Office on 3 September 1786: 'I cannot say the little knowledge I have of Captain Phillip would have led me to select him for a service of this complicated nature.' But Sydney liked and admired professional officers like Phillip, whom he rightly considered the journeymen of Empire. Yet he was demanding of Phillip a remarkable spectrum of gifts. The man had to undertake a huge navigation and command a number of ships packed with criminals, and on arrival at Botany Bay in New South Wales was required to implement a completely novel enterprise for the Crown, an unprecedented penal and society-making experiment. This blended mission of being commodore not of two or three but eleven ships, as well as captain-general of huge and unvisited territories, and gaoler-in-chief in the netherworld was something for which normal naval service could only dimly prepare anyone. The fact that Sydney thought he could recruit any old reliable officer for it might say more about the pressure he was under than his faith in Phillip. Due to the vulgar urgings of domestic politics, Prime Minister Pitt and Lord Sydney were sending to the ends of the earth a reputable but not glittering fellow, in command of many vessels stocked not with naturalists and artists but with Britain's sinners.

The founding document of this enterprise for Lord Sydney and for Captain Phillip was called, unremarkably, *The Heads of a Plan*, and was devised in Sydney's office by Phillip's friend Evan Nepean. It called for the appointment of 'a discreet officer', and that had been achieved. The term 'discreet' had as rich a series of associations and meanings then as now, but one wonders if it included the idea that Phillip was to keep watch for French incursions into the south-west Pacific, as well as be prison-master. For Phillip, in the past, had been a spy against the French. The *Heads* then concentrated on the business of transportation to New South Wales, rather than on any commercial benefit arising from the new place. New South Wales was a country which, by the temperateness of the climate, 'connected with the remoteness of its situation (from whence it is hardly possible for persons to return without permission)', seemed 'peculiarly adapted' to deal with the increase of felons in the kingdom, and especially in London. The *Heads* covered the process of transportation, the taking on board of two companies of marines to form a military establishment, the provision of rations, and the collection of supplies and livestock on the way at Rio de Janeiro and the Cape of Good Hope.

Towards the end of this *Plan* for settling Botany Bay, Nepean raised the issue of financial and strategic benefits which might arise from the cultivation of the New Zealand flax plant and from the tall trees already growing on Norfolk Island, a place Cook had discovered some 1600 kilometres out in the Pacific from Botany Bay, where a proportion of the felons were to be settled. British manufacturers, wrote Nepean, had claimed that a cable ten inches (25 cm) thick and made of New Zealand flax was superior to an eighteen-inch (46 cm) cable made from European material. Additionally, the *Heads* mentioned the procuring of New Zealand masts and ship timber for the fleets in India.

There has been a great deal of argument about whether this commercial thought was tacked onto the penal plan, or was the real purpose of the whole operation. But the document declares itself at its opening sentence: 'Heads of a plan for effectually disposing of convicts.' And if the proposed penal settlement in the south-west Pacific were to become a trading post, it would violate the chartered monopoly of the immensely powerful East India Company, and upset the Company's trade with Canton and in India. The East India Company's principal, Francis Baring, would quite early complain of 'the serpent we are nursing at Botany Bay'.

It seemed that His Majesty's government desired New South Wales far more as a prison than as a great port, or as an opening for British trade. Phillip was thus, in the strictest penal sense, to be a governor, and not an apostle of British commerce.

THE MYSTERIES OF PHILLIP

To his convicts, Arthur Phillip would later convey the very breath of civil magisterium, even though his early childhood might not have been much more socially elevated than some of theirs. His mother, Elizabeth Breech, had first been married to a sailor named Herbert, who died while still in his twenties of a fever caught during his duty on the Jamaica station. Elizabeth then married Jacob Phillip, a German, a 'native of Frankfurt' and a teacher of languages. Arthur Phillip was born in October 1738, in the family house in Bread Street in the City of London, not necessarily an address of privilege. He was admitted to the charity orphan school at the Royal Hospital for Seamen at Greenwich, apparently as Herbert's son rather than Phillip's, in 1751. The school was for the sons of poor seamen, 'training them up to a seafaring life'. Going thus to Greenwich was a deception which might have added further secretiveness to the boy's aloof nature.

Arthur Phillip's apprenticeship had begun in 1753 in the squalid, grease-laden, profane atmosphere of a whaler built for the Greenland whale fishery. Just after his seventeenth birthday, war—later to be called the Seven Years War—was declared between France and Britain and he entered the Royal Navy as a captain's servant. He experienced the violence of cannonry in an inconclusive battle to save the British-garrisoned island of Minorca. Then, having passed his lieutenant's exam, as a junior officer off Havana in 1761 he survived both Spanish artillery and a wet season in which malaria, yellow fever, cholera, typhus and dysentery killed off seven thousand sailors and soldiers engaged in the campaign.

This prepared Phillip for elevation, even though he lacked the powerful connections so important to young officers. His character in his early twenties combined a dry humour with reserve, efficiency and intellectual hunger. To temper his authoritarian streak he had common sense and was not fast to anger. It is hard to imagine him on a loud stampede through foreign streets, looking for liquor or women.

On 19 July 1763, the Seven Years War having been fought, in St Augustine's, Watling Street, Lieutenant Phillip married Margaret Denison, the widow of a glove and wine merchant, and fifteen to sixteen years older than he was. He does not seem to have been a young man aflame with passion. With the war over he was on half-pay, and the couple lived in Hampton Court for two years, but then went to rusticate at Lyndhurst in the New Forest in Dorset, on Margaret's estate of 22 acres (8.9 hectares), named Vernals. Phillip ran their property as a dairy farm, kept their horses and grew fruit and vegetables. But 'some circumstances occurred' which led to a formal indenture of separation signed by the couple in April 1769. It stated that they had 'lately lived separate and apart'.

Now Phillip applied himself to his alternate vocation. He began to spend time in France as a spy for the Home Office or Admiralty. With a gift for languages and his German coloration he was good at it, but it was an ungrateful business, and Phillip felt he needed to accelerate his naval career. The Portuguese government approached the Admiralty and asked them to second some good officers to help in their fight with Spain over a disputed area, a region known as the Debatable Lands, which ran northward from the estuary of the River Plate on the south-eastern coast of South America. As a token of their claim, the Portuguese had created a colony at the Plate, across the estuary from Buenos Aires, and named it Colonia do Sacramento. The Admiralty recommended Lieutenant Phillip to its Portuguese friends. Collecting his new ship, *Nossa Senhora de Belém*, on the banks of Lisbon's Tagus River, he quickly added Portuguese to the French and German he could already speak.

Phillip got on well with the Portuguese viceroy in Rio de Janeiro, Marquis de Lavradio, who found him a committed combatant against the Spanish coastguard and naval vessels. But in 1776, the Portuguese started to negotiate with the Spanish. Lavradio had already reported to the Portuguese court that Phillip's health was delicate but that he never complained, 'except when he had nothing special to do for the Royal Service'. It was true that many of Phillip's illnesses were associated with a kind of ardent waiting for action to occur, or else with circumstances in which he conducted dangerous work out of the direct gaze of the Admiralty. Ambition was his most restless appetite.

In 1777, the Treaty of San Ildefonso made the Debatable Lands largely Spanish. Phillip resigned his now futile Portuguese commission to seek fresh employment in the Royal Navy and the war against the Americans and their European allies. He had an undistinguished time of it. In the River Elbe, when escorting transports full of Hanoverian recruits for the British army, the onset of river ice forced him ingloriously to run his frigate into the mud at the Hamburg harbourside. During the frustrating months his command *Ariadne* was stuck there, Phillip came to place great reliance in Lieutenant Philip Gidley King, a sturdy young man of undistinguished background like himself, a draper's son.

When in 1782 the Admiralty appointed Phillip captain of the *Europe*, a 64-gun, 600-man battleship, he became at last commander of a ship of the British battle line. He took Lieutenant Philip Gidley King aboard with him, and his clerk, a most eccentric and remarkably placed man named Harry Brewer. Both these men would ultimately accompany him to New South Wales.

The American bosun on *Europe*, a sailor named Edward Spain, would later write an ironic memoir of his time serving with Phillip, and of the relationship between Phillip and Harry Brewer. Brewer was an unmarried seaman of no particular rank—or else he could be counted, at more than fifty years of age, as the oldest midshipman in the Royal Navy. Brewer had for some years skilfully copied Phillip's diaries and journals for him, and had drawn up watch lists and so on. 'Our captain was at that time in slender circumstances . . . and as they both [Phillip and Brewer] rowed in the one boat, no doubt they had their own reasons for wishing to make the voyage together.' Whatever else 'they both rowed in the one boat' might have meant, Spain certainly implied they were short of cash.

At the Cape Verde Islands, said Spain, Phillip 'was perfectly at home for he spoke Portuguese fluent and could shrug his shoulders with the best of them'. Spain would also provide insight into what appears to be a sexual infatuation Phillip suffered. The *Europe* put into the mid-Atlantic island of St Helena, and picked up there four British sailors and their women. 'But don't imagine that it was out of any partiality to any of them, except one . . . and had he given permission to her alone the reason would have been obvious to the officers and the ship's company.' Her name was Deborah Brooks. She and her ship's bosun husband would be on the fleet to Australia, and she would become Phillip's housekeeper.

Phillip's old friend Evan Nepean at the Home Office was now responsible, as well as for prisons, for espionage in France and Spain. It was as one of Nepean's spies in the 1780s that Arthur Phillip, after his return from Madras on *Europe*, became known to Lord Sydney. Though Britain was not at war with France, something like a cold war was maintained between the two nations. Late in 1784 Nepean called on Phillip to journey to Toulon and other French ports 'for the purpose of ascertaining the naval force, and stores in the arsenals'. His leave documents mentioned his desire to see to 'my private affairs', but in November 1784 Nepean gave Phillip £150 for his salary and expenses.

So when the argument about what to do with prisoners condemned to transportation was at its height, Phillip was largely absent from the country.

WHO WERE THE CONVICTS?

The petty crimes of those convicts condemned to transportation frequently contrasted with the cross-planetary transplantation with which they were to be punished. Some characteristic Georgian transportable offences are eloquent in making the point, while those found guilty of committing them reveal much about the upheaval and dislocation suffered by British society following the process known as Enclosure.

For in that era there were changes across Britain which drove many rural poor to the cities and towards crime. Beginning in the 1760s, the revolutionary and disruptive process of Enclosure would transform the landscape of Britain over the next seventy years. Villages had till then been organised under the old system of scattered strips of open land variously owned by peasants and landlord, as well as shared common ground. Under a series of Enclosure Acts, villages were reorganised by Enclosure Commissioners according to new agricultural efficiencies, so that the ground of the chief landlord, of prosperous farmers and various smallholders was consolidated and fenced. In reality, Enclosure drove small farmers and agricultural workers off land their families had worked for centuries. Many smallholders found the expense of fencing their land with barriers of hawthorn and blackthorn beyond them and gave it up. They also discovered that the common land traditionally shared by the community, upon which they and the peasants depended to run their livestock, was fenced off from them too.

Before Enclosure, smallholders and agricultural labourers' families had the right not only to graze livestock on the common land, but to take from it undergrowth, loppings, peat, fish from lakes and streams, sand and gravel, and acorns to feed pigs. Enclosure put an end to those practices, and was occurring in many districts at a time when the great loom factories were coming into being and cloth spun in cottages was less sought after. Traditional village, church and family controls on the way men and women behaved broke down as families sought parish poor relief or became itinerant and set off for cities. For, says an historian of the period, 'Everyone below the plateau of skilled craftsmen was undernourished.'

Over time the new system would cause more than unrest in the countryside. Threatening letters were one of the options for the aggrieved, as in this letter of the Enclosure era: 'Mrs Orpen, I am informed that you and your family whent before last year and glent up what the pore should have had but if you do this year it is our desire as soon as your corn is in the barn we will have a fire ...'

Rather than become scarecrow people of the countryside, many of the rural dispossessed made their way to already crowded cities to become a dangerous under-class who saw crime as a better option than working an 80-hour week as a servant, or toiling for the unregulated and dangerous gods of machine capital.

Esther Abrahams, for example, a young Jewish milliner of about fifteen years who would one day grow old in New South Wales, was indicted for feloniously stealing black silk lace, value 50 shillings, from a London shop while the assistant had her back turned. She was remanded to Newgate, and at her trial in July 1786, her counsel, Mr Garrow, ascertained by questioning that Abrahams stayed in the shop for twenty minutes following the supposed theft. Two doors from the business, however, Esther was said, as if wanting to get rid of the evidence, to have dropped two cards of silk, and also a bit she had stuffed into her purse. Though she called three witnesses who all gave her a very good character, she was found guilty of stealing and sentenced to seven years transportation.

In the public wards of Newgate, she became pregnant and at the end of the following winter gave birth to a daughter, Roseanna. Whether the child came from an alliance of convenience or a prison romance or even a rape, we cannot say, except that all three of these were common in Newgate. A petition for royal mercy had been lodged in February 1787 on Esther's behalf, probably by her parents and local worthies they had interested in her case, but it failed, and soon after the birth mother and infant were sent aboard the *Lady Penrhyn*.

Thomas Barrett was one of a number of First Fleet prisoners who were referred to as 'Mercuries'—in 1782, barely twelve, he was found guilty of stealing one silver watch worth £3 and various other items, when a spinster was showing Barrett and two others the house of a London gentleman available for letting. Barrett made an attempt to escape but was caught and searched by a beadle of Marylebone. At the Old Bailey, Barrett gave an accustomed defence— he said that he had gone with a young servant to rent a house for his master, and the servant picked up a watch during the house inspection and at a cry of 'Stop thief!' the young man offloaded the watch on Tom. If this were the truth, then Tom would endure a short and bitter life for that £3 watch found on his person. He was first sentenced to death in September 1782, then the sentence was commuted. Next he would escape from *Mercury*, a convict vessel bound for Nova Scotia and taken over by the convicts while it was still in British waters. He was recaptured, sentenced to death again, and again received the royal mercy, so finding himself on board the *Charlotte*, where he would prove intractable. In time, while still less than twenty years of age, Thomas Barrett would be the first man to hang in New South Wales.

Margaret Darnell, a woman in her teens, was indicted in April 1787 for stealing a dozen knives and forks, value sixpence, from the shop of an ironmonger and cutler in Holborn near Chancery Lane. Margaret had come into the shop about nine in the evening, wearing a large cloak under which she secreted the goods. The shop assistant pursued her and she threw the goods down just as she left the store. The prisoner's defence was quoted in the Old Bailey papers: 'I was sent for a penny-worth of nails . . . there were two women in the shop when I went in; they went out while I was there; as I was going out I saw the parcel lay; I never touched it.'

Elizabeth, wife of Henry Needham, was indicted for feloniously stealing two pairs of silk stockings, value 30 shillings, from a hosiery shop on a summer night in July 1786, in Sackville Street. She went to trial within two weeks. The prisoner said a particular man had sent her to get a pair of stockings for herself, to make up for a ring of her deceased father's that he had failed to raffle off on her behalf. She told the shopkeeper she was a servant to this man, a perfumer in Bond Street on a particular corner of that thoroughfare. There's no perfumer there, the shopkeeper claimed to have told her. The hosier became convinced she was hiding stolen merchandise and, under challenge, she dropped both pairs of stockings. Nonetheless, the shop assistant was sent to fetch the local

Bow Street runner. At the Old Bailey, near Newgate prison, Elizabeth was found guilty of stealing 'but not privily', and transported for seven years. She would never return to trouble the law officers of London.

And so it went. Isabella Rawson (Rosson) was a laundress, mantua-lace maker and former schoolteacher, tried in January 1787 for stealing three quantities of goods from the gentleman for whom she was laundress. Her loot included a waistcoat and bed curtains taken from her master, Stewart Kydd, a barrister of Gray's Inn. She would go down to the cellar to fetch coals and other things, said Kydd, and stole things from a trunk deposited there. When he returned from the country just before Christmas in 1786, he found that his wife had put Rawson in the custody of a constable. The girl begged he would forgive her; she fell down on her knees and begged for mercy. 'I told her she had no reason to beg for mercy, because she had behaved ungrateful.' Rawson handed over the pawnbroker's tickets she had received when selling the goods.

In court, Mrs Eleanor Kydd's melodramatic evidence was not uncharacteristic of the time. She described going down into the cellar 'and the prisoner seeing me advance up to the trunks to open them, she immediately fell on her knees, and cried out, Madam, I have robbed you; says I, I know very well, Bella, you have robbed me all along . . . She said, Madam, do what you please with me, kill me, I deserve it, if I had twenty lives; says I, You deserve no mercy from me.'

The prisoner made no pretence of innocence and left herself to the mercy of the court. She was found guilty and transported for seven years, giving birth to a prison child aboard the *Lady Penrhyn* which died in infancy.

William Richardson, who would one day be Rawson's husband, had also been a 'Mercury', and was originally tried in December 1783 for an attack with an accomplice on a servant who was walking home to James Street from Chelsea. A handkerchief, a guinea, a crown piece, a silver sixpence and six copper halfpence were taken. Bow Street runners caught the two men in Hyde Park, and the victim would identify them, saying at the trial the night had been moonlit enough for that. Prisoner Richardson threw himself upon the mercy of the court. Both accused were found guilty and sentenced to death, but both were humbly recommended to mercy by the jury.

James Sheers, also Shiers, argued his innocence at length and did not submit as easily as Richardson when charged with a similar crime: feloniously assaulting a man on the King's Highway, in this case the Strand in London, and putting him in fear and danger, taking from him a watch, value 40 shillings, a ring, a seal, a metal key and so on. The offence took place at half past two in the afternoon and the victim-cum-prosecutor said the prisoner jostled him and tore the watch from his pocket. 'I instantly catched him by the collar and with my other hand endeavoured to regain the watch.' Four friends of the victim saw the watch in Sheers's possession.

As, in court, this evidence was given, the prisoner Sheers cried out to ask the victim whether he had been drunk or no at the time of the crime? Witnesses, friends of the prosecutor, said their friend was not drunk. But the prisoner declared that there was a mob all round the prosecutor, they caught hold of Sheers and a woman, stripped them both naked, and unjustly accused them of having the watch. 'I was going to Smithfield market about 5 o'clock and these gentlemen was coming along drunk and had three or four girls with them, and two or three watchmen, and I came up to see what was the matter and they took me. I had not so much as a stick to walk with.'

'Have you any witnesses to call to your character?' asked the court.

The prisoner responded that he did not think he had a friend in the court; it was a very hard case indeed, he said.

The judge, despite Sheers's interesting defence, found him guilty, sentenced him to death but recommended him to the King's mercy. When he went aboard *Scarborough* it was with a sentence of transportation for life.

Yet another intriguing 'Mercury' was Robert Sideway, indicted in September 1782 for stealing a deal luggage box containing various goods including a cloth coat, a linen waistcoat, one pair of silk stockings and one pair of shoes. He had climbed on a coach at the Cross Keys in Wood Street between two and three in the morning and taken the goods. A porter and a watchman intercepted the fleeing man. But the coachman could not definitely identify Robert Sideway as the thief. The prisoner's counsel made much of that and of the fact that the man was dressed in black because it was June 1782 when everyone was in mourning for the King's madness.

Sideway made an accustomed defence—he had heard the watchmen's rattles clacking away to warn of a theft and saw another man in black escape. Later, shipped off on the *Mercury*, he returned to shore and incurred a death sentence, now commuted.

The destination of these people was not to be a home for the chosen, a chosen home, but instead was a place imposed by authority and devised specifically with its remoteness in mind.

THE STATE OF THE PRISONS

The gaols of Britain as experienced by Sideway and the others already condemned to transportation in such numbers in the 1780s had been neglected by government. They were ill-aired, ill-lit and racked with fever epidemics. Crucially, they were run under licence as private enterprises. To be a prison warder was not to be a servant of society but a franchisee, entitled to charge inmates a scale of fees and run a taproom, where liquor could be bought, for profit. John Howard, a prison reformer, discovered in one London prison that the tap, frequented both by prisoners and visitors, was sub-hired out to one of the prisoners. From such sources as the taproom and rooms he could rent out to superior convicts, Richard Ackerman, keeper of Newgate for thirty-eight years and a dining friend of James Boswell and the great Dr Johnson, left a fortune of £20 000 when he died in 1792.

In 1777 the first painstaking survey of conditions in English prisons, Howard's *The State of the Prisons*, was published, and gaol reform became a popular issue. Howard, a Bedfordshire squire, was shocked profoundly by his visits to prisons and became the most famous of prison reformers. In his tract, Howard depicted a cell, 17 feet by 6 (c 5 × 1.8 metres), crowded with more than two dozen inmates and receiving light and air only through a few holes in the door. The 'clink' of a Devon prison was 17 feet by 8 (c 5 × 2 metres), with only 5 feet 6 inches (167 cm) of headroom, and light and air entered by one hole just 7 inches long and 5 broad (17 × 13 cm). In Clerkenwell prison, those who could not pay for beds lay on the floor, and in many other prisons inmates paid even for the privilege of not being chained. Howard claimed that after visits to Newgate the leaves of his notebook were so tainted and browned by the fearful atmosphere that, on his arrival home, he had to spread out the pages before a glowing fire for drying and disinfection.

The most infamous of prisons, old Newgate, was burned down by a mob in 1780. Prisoners were admitted to the rebuilt prison by 1782. New Newgate prison was divided into two halves—the master's side where the inmates could rent lodging and services, and where those who had committed criminal libel, sedition or embezzlement were kept, and then the more impoverished section called the common side. Earlier in the century, the writer Daniel Defoe, who himself had been thrown into Newgate for theft, described it through the eyes of his character Moll Flanders, in terms which seemed to be just as true of the new Newgate: 'I was now fixed indeed; it is impossible to describe the terror of my mind when I was first brought in, and when I looked around upon all the horrors of that dismal place . . . The hellish noise, the roaring, the swearing and clamour, the stench and nastiness, and all the dreadful, afflicting things that I saw there, joined to make the place seem an emblem of hell itself.'

Though prisoners and visitors had access to the taphouse, and there were several communal rooms, a chapel, a separate infirmary for men and women, and exercise yards, only the most basic medicines were dispensed in the two infirmaries. And every day, sightseers came to view the spectacle, as we might now visit a zoo, while prostitutes worked their way around to service visitors and prisoners who had cash, and the turnkeys received a pay-off from this traffic as well. Meanwhile, unless the men and women in the common wards had relatives or friends to bring them food, they lived off a three-halfpenny loaf a week, supplemented by donations and a share of the cook's weekly meat supply. One of the motivations for joining a gang, or criminal 'canting crew', was that if imprisoned, the individual criminal was not left to the bare mercies of the gaol authorities.

In that last winter in England for the many convicts who would soon find themselves on Arthur Phillip's departing fleet, one visitor noted that there were in Newgate many 'miserable objects' almost naked and without shoes and stockings. Women prisoners in the wards were 'of the very lowest and most wretched class of human beings, almost naked, with only a few filthy rags, almost alive and in motion with vermin, their bodies rotting with the bad distemper, and covered with itch, scorbutic and venereal ulcers.'

To what extent did the urgency of the domestic prison problem cause government to be reckless? For was it not reckless to entrust not just one or two but eleven ships to a destination at which, as far as was known, only one other had ever sailed? Could the Home Office and the Admiralty be so sure of Arthur Phillip's competence? In any case they began to see their project delayed specifically for that reason—Phillip's competence. Such was his insistence that the ships be comprehensively equipped, they must have come to wish they had appointed a less fussy fellow. Lord Sydney and Nepean had no desire to create a penal catastrophe and did not want ships sunk or felons wiped out by scurvy, but they had envisaged the fleet would be gone by Christmas 1786. The early sight of convict vessels disappearing down the Thames estuary with sails set was the chief point for the Home Office, not how they fared from the instant of disappearance onwards.

FLASH TALK

While roughly half the convicts of Phillip's flotilla of ships came from regional towns and the countryside, the other half were London convicts from areas north of the Thames River: Stepney, Poplar, Clerkenwell, St Giles and Seven Dials, Soho. (Only a minority came from the South London dockside regions.) In the tenements around St Giles parish, Soho—the famed Rookery of St Giles, also known as Little Ireland for its considerable population of displaced Irish—and in Spitalfields to the east, in squalor unimaginable lived all the classes of criminals. One observer would call the St Giles Rookery 'a honeycomb, perforated by a number of courts and blind alleys, cul-de-sacs, without any outlet other than the entrance'. Another compared it and other criminal slums in London to giant blocks of stone 'eaten by slugs into innumerable small chambers and connecting passages'.

London criminal classes were bonded together by devotion and oaths taken to the criminal deity, the Tawny Prince, duly honoured by theft, chicanery and a brave death on the gallows. And, of course, by the speaking of his language, 'flash' or 'cant', criminal co-operatives or gangs calling themselves 'canting crews'. In flash talk or cant, a *pal* was a pickpocket's assistant who received the *swag* as soon as the pickpocket had lifted it. A *kiddy* was the fast-running child to whom the pal further passed the swag. A *beak* was a magistrate, a *pig* a Bow Street runner. *Tickling the peter* was opening a safe, and a *fence* was a receiver of stolen loot. All these terms mean something to us now through their entry into mainstream English, but at the time they were incomprehensible not only to officers of courts but to the general law-abiding populace.

Cant appeared, amongst other places, in a flash ballad of the time which read:

I have a sweet eye for a plant,
And graceful as I amble,
Fine draw a coat-tail sure I can't,
So kiddy is my famble.
Frisk the cly, and fork the rag,
Draw the foggles plummy,
Speak to the tattler, bag the swag,
And finely hunt the dummy.

A translation would read: I can spot an intended victim, and I have considerable practical skill in the craft of stealth. So I pick a pocket, take the cash, take fine handkerchiefs skilfully, steal a watch and pocket chains, and search for a pocketbook.

'A leading distinction, which marked the convicts from their outset in the colony,' wrote a military officer and friend of Arthur Phillip named Watkin Tench much later, when the convict colony was at last established, 'was the use of what is called the flash or kiddy language . . . This language has many dialects. The sly dexterity of the pickpocket; the brutal ferocity of the footpad; the more elevated career of the highwayman; and the deadly purpose of the midnight ruffian is each strictly appropriate in the terms that distinguish and characterise it. I have ever been of the opinion that an abolition of this unnatural jargon would open the path to reformation.'

In London, the criminal classes availed themselves of many public houses in the City and Spitalfields that were centres for prostitution, the fencing of stolen goods and the division of plunder. 'Hell houses' or 'flash houses' were common names for such places. They were to be found in a number of notorious locations: Chick Lane, Field Lane, Black Boy Alley. Over their half-doors fleeing criminals were free to toss whatever they had plundered and were on the run with. A convict turned novelist would describe a criminal approaching a 'fence' in a house in St Mary Axe: 'There was a box in the wall, so contrived that upon placing any article you wished to dispose of within it and ringing a bell, the box disappeared. After a lapse of a few minutes it again turned, and in lieu of the article left was a sum of money . . . the thieves of London much approved of the principle, as they were never seen by anyone while disposing of their ill-gotten booty.'

Such houses were the former cosmos of many of the men and women who would end in Arthur Phillip's convict fleet.

PHILLIP TAKING PAINS

The Home Office had asked for a discreet officer, and got one. Arthur Phillip could smell disaster in the rushed agenda of his masters and he proved tenacious in his demands for a well-supplied fleet. He wanted the mass of the convicts to arrive at the nominated shore in good health. If he was rushed, they could not. In his little office at the Admiralty, Phillip worked with his clerk, the unkempt Harry Brewer, and as if to focus his mind, wrote a document (on many sheets of paper of unequal size) which represented his philosophy of convict transportation and penal settlement. Not as a visionary, but merely as someone acknowledging the state of British law, he noted: 'The laws of this country will, of course, be introduced in New South Wales, and there is one that I would wish to take place from the moment His Majesty's forces take possession of the country—that there can be no slavery in a free land and consequently no slaves.'

His determination that convicts not be seen as a slave caste would have important results for many of the felons marked down for his convict transports. He had respect for their right to as safe and healthy a journey through the mirror as he could provide. But he did not see their ultimate status as fully equal to that of the free. 'As I would not wish convicts to lay the foundation of an Empire, I think they should ever remain separated from the garrison and other settlers that may come from Europe.'

Through secret caresses between free men and convict women, and other alliances forged on his ships, this would become a proposition already in doubt before the ships even sailed.

The successful tenderer for the overall contract for the fleet was a man named William Richards Jr, a prominent ship-broker of South London. The story goes that contractors dumped their worst produce on Phillip, knowing he could not very conveniently complain. But two reliable young officers of marines, Watkin Tench and David Collins, no strangers to salt rations, would independently agree that the provisions on the First Fleet provided by Richards were 'of a much superior quality to those usually supplied by contract'. Though we have no similar enthusiastic endorsement from any convict, the low death rate during the flotilla's months of voyaging would suggest that Phillip, when visiting the vessels up the Thames at Deptford, and Richards himself, must have been careful at their inspections of barrels of salt beef and pork and flour.

Richards had put a lot of thought into convicts: their quarrels when they had to sleep together four to a berth—he unsuccessfully suggested individual hammocks; their jealousy when some dressed better than others—he thought there should be a standard uniform; the influence which the wicked exercised over the others—he suggested there should be three classes of felons sent on separate ships. Richards would have preferred an intermediate place of transportation at Milford Haven in Wales, with only the worst convicts being sent on to New South Wales.

Indeed Richards was conscientious to the point of crankiness. Under his contract with the Navy Board, he had gone on the river and inspected and chartered five merchant vessels as transports—the *Alexander, Charlotte, Friendship*, the newly built *Lady Penrhyn* and *Scarborough*—and three store ships: *Borrowdale, Fishburn* and *Golden Grove*. The contracts with the shipowners were called charter-parties and were specific about the duties of the shipowners and captains, the number of crew per tonnage, and the form of accommodation, rations, cooking equipment, bedding, fetters, ventilation equipment and so on supplied for the convicts, and the medicines and medical preventives to be taken aboard. Ultimately, as the number of convicts loaded on the ships grew, Richards would need to contract a sixth convict transport, the *Prince of Wales*. The transports were all relatively young vessels, but not purpose-built prison ships, so they required special fitting out by carpenters at the Deptford dockyard in order to be able to receive prisoners on their cargo decks. All were three-masted and over 300 tons (306 tonnes), except the *Friendship*, a 278-ton (284 tonne), two-masted vessel generally described as a brig or a snow.

For Richards and the individual shipowners the cream from this expedition would come after the ships finished off the business of taking the convicts into the void. Some of them looked to receive further charter from the East India Company, authorising them to go to China to load tea. Richards depended on Lord Sydney to apply pressure to the East India Company directors, who exercised monopoly over East Asian trade, and ultimately the company would take up three ships—*Charlotte, Scarborough* and *Lady Penrhyn*—to bring a cargo of tea home from China. That was if they reached Botany Bay in the first place.

Arthur Phillip could not be in Deptford all the time, but the navy had appointed an agent to represent him and it at the dockyards and see that the necessary carpentering was competently done, and all arrangements were properly made for receiving prisoners. The convict prison on each of the ships was fitted out on the lowest cargo deck, where cradles—narrow sleeping bunks in sets of four or six—ran the length of the ship on either side of an aisle. Young Lieutenant Philip Gidley King, Phillip's protégé from *Europe*, was down at Deptford attached to *Sirius*, and described the sort of security being put in place on the transports. He saw that the carpenters were barricading an area on deck with a wooden barrier about 5 feet (1.5 metres) high, and topping it with pointed iron prongs, 'to prevent any connection between the marines and ship's company, with the convicts. Sentinels are placed at the different hatchways and a guard always under arms on the quarterdeck of each transport in order to prevent any improper behaviour of the convicts, as well as to guard against any surprise.' Below, to contain the prison deck, thick bulkheads were positioned, 'fitted with nails and run across from side to side [port to starboard] in the between decks above the mainmast, with loop holes to fire . . . in case of irregularities'. Forward of the prison space was the prison hospital, and the equally dark areas aft of the prison were often reserved for marine privates and noncommissioned officers and their families.

The hatches which gave onto the deck were 'well secured down by cross bars, bolts and locks and are likewise nailed down from deck to deck with oak stanchions'.

The barricaded area on the open deck gave the authorities a place where even the most unruly convicts could be exercised, but many knew that in such close quarters the barriers might in some ways break down, and that there would be contact of various kinds, including sexual contact. For the transports were all very intimate in their dimensions. The largest of them was *Alexander*, 114 feet (34.7 metres) in length and 31 feet (9.5 metres) in breadth, barely more than the width of a decent parlour, and a mere 450 tons (459 tonnes) burthen. On the lower decks no one but a child could stand upright—the prison deck of *Scarborough*, for example, was only 4 feet 5 inches (135 cm) high. The seamen's and soldiers' quarters had similar limitations.

Already, in Whitehall in dismal winter, nameless clerks were attaching the lists of convicts' names to the orders-in-council that authorised transportation. There were no selection criteria for transportees based on health, suitability, trade or sturdiness. A convict of any age, strength and skills could go to Botany Bay. Time already served meant nothing to the bureaucrats either. In some cases the clerks attached the names of convicts who had served five years of a seven-year sentence.

These orders and lists were sent to the keeper of Newgate, to the Clerk of Arraign at the Old Bailey, and the hulk overseer Duncan Campbell. The fitting out of the transports finished, the ships moored at Woolwich, and the first convicts, men and women from the hulks and Newgate, and from some county prisons, were rowed down the wintry river to the *Alexander* and *Lady Penrhyn* on 6 January 1787. Many of them were sick and clothed in rags when received on deck in their prison irons. These were struck off their wrists by a crew member and then the ship's chains were put on, and the transportees descended to the sharp cold and pervasive damp of the prison decks. Down in the chill dimness the convicts were often secured in place by chains which ran through an ankle shackle on each convict. Some masters wanted the prisoners wristlet-ed as well. As yet the convict decks had empty spaces, but the allotted space per felon, when fully loaded, was 18 inches width by 6 feet in length (46 cm × 1.8 metres). The waste arrangements were a series of buckets aft, topped by a plank with holes cut in it.

Even on *Lady Penrhyn*, reserved for women, the master kept the prisoners handcuffed and chained and below decks in those first days, purely out of fear. A poor country girl, Sarah Bellamy from Worcestershire, barely sixteen and sentenced for stealing, would have found the cramped headroom and narrow sleeping space claustrophobic. In the midst of the deck rose the great, groaning mainmast and the trunk of the foremast, like malign, barren trees. Security was uppermost in the masters' minds, and so the ventilation was poor. Add to that the noise of timbers and tide, and the raucousness and bullying of worldly, rebellious Newgate girls, their voices bouncing off the low headroom. For Bellamy, the convict deck must have been a perfect hell, and when Joe Downey, a young sweet-talking sailor soon to be appointed quartermaster, offered his attentions and protection, how grateful she must have been for what he could do to relieve the situation.

Indeed love and lust would penetrate all the clever barricading of the ships, and experienced seafarers knew that and often turned a blind eye to everything except outright disorder. Despite the guarded companionways and gates to the prison decks, and the lack of privacy, prostitution would become a reality on *Lady Penrhyn, Friendship* and *Prince of Wales.*

Perhaps surprisingly, urban working-class women knew better than many country girls how to avoid pregnancy. They would delay weaning if they already had a child; they practised *coitus interruptus*; pleaded illness, including syphilis, and so on. Condoms, made of pigskin and called by Casanova 'English overcoats', and 'armour' by James Boswell, were available in London but were expensive, and therefore essentially a gentleman's device, designed more to avoid venereal disease than to prevent pregnancy.

Meanwhile, Phillip's assigned flagship, the part-victualler, part-frigate *Sirius*, of 540 tons (551 tonnes), named after 'the bright star in the Southern constellation of the Great Dog', and with a crew of one hundred and sixty men, was at the Deptford dockyard, being fitted out with what some called the 'refuse of the yards'. The year had turned and still the fleet had not left. Arthur Phillip typically wrote to Undersecretary Nepean on 4 January 1787. 'I likewise beg leave to observe that the number of scythes (only 6), or razors (only 5 dozen) and the quantity of buck and small shot (only 200 pounds) now ordered is very insufficient.'

Phillip came aboard his ships on 11 January to see the recently loaded men and women, and was appalled by their marginal health and their need of clothing and blankets. Clothing would always be a problem and was not standard in quality or quantity. The navy did not want sailors and transportees to wear heavy wool—wool was worn on the hulks and in Newgate, and infallibly attracted lice and typhus. So the male convicts were given woollen caps, but the jackets issued on board were of blue cloth or the light, compacted woollen cloth called kersey. The male convicts also wore linen shirts, trousers of duck (a tough, close-woven cloth), and stockings made of yarn. In the impoverished landscapes of their childhood, not all of them would be used to stockings.

Again Phillip complained to Evan Nepean, this time that the clothes the women were sent down to the ships in 'stamp the magistrates with infamy'. He ordered that they be supplied with clothing from the naval stores of *Sirius*. He asked the authorities that the ships be moved out of the Thames and down the English coast to Spithead off Portsmouth, where, in the lee of the Isle of Wight, they could anchor on the broad sheet of shoalwater known as the Motherbank. Here, because of distance from shore, the inmates could be unchained and allowed fresh air. Indeed, the fleet would begin assembling there from mid March onwards.

Phillip knew very well that the transports' masters would like the convicts to remain secured and immobilised for as long as possible, to keep the ships safe. But he also knew that for the sake of convict health the felons, male and female, should be unchained once the transports were at sea; that they would need to be unchained if their elected mess orderlies were to come on deck to collect their rations; and that all of them should be freely exercised on deck in good weather.

AT STATION, PLYMOUTH AND PORTSMOUTH

In February 1787, *Charlotte* and *Friendship* headed for Plymouth to collect prisoners from the hulks and gaols there. The two little vessels boarded between them 164 males and 41 females. One of the prisoners loaded from the hulk *Dunkirk* onto *Friendship* was a young, strong, red-headed Norfolk man named Henry Kable. At the time of his sentencing to death in 1783 for burglary, he had been a lad of sixteen, athletically built. Like his father and an accomplice, he was meant to be hanged on a gibbet outside Norwich Castle, but after he climbed the scaffold, he was pardoned on condition of transportation. He saw his father and his accomplice executed.

In Norwich Castle prison after his transmutation of sentence, he had fallen in love with a slightly older woman, Susannah Holmes, guilty of burglary. Their prison child, Henry, had not been allowed to accompany his parents down to the dismal *Dunkirk*, and was being cared for by the Norwich gaoler, John Simpson. Now that Henry was on *Friendship* and Susannah aboard *Charlotte*, the efforts of Simpson to get Lord Sydney to let the baby be reunited with his mother would capture the public's imagination, which extended itself to romantic tales of doomed young felons, but which, unlike the Victorian imagination, did not require that the lovers be virginal or married. Indeed, during their wait at Norwich Castle, Henry and Susannah had requested they be married but had been refused permission. Soon, Simpson came down to Plymouth by coach with the infant, he was presented to Susannah, and she and Henry were both on *Friendship* with their baby, and the family would not be broken up again until late in the voyage.

On 9 March 1787, Lieutenant Ralph Clark, a rather prim, neurotic officer who had volunteered in the hope of promotion, recorded, 'March with the detachment from the barracks to the dockyard and embark on board the *Friendship* transport with Captain Lieutenant Meredith and Second Lieutenant Faddy, two sergeants, three corporals, one drummer, thirty-six privates, nine women and children.'

At the same time the *Sirius*, its tender the *Supply* and the remainder of the ships were anchored on the robust tide of the Motherbank off Portsmouth. Here further convicts and marines were rowed out to the transports. *Scarborough* would receive over two hundred male convicts, and cramped little *Prince of Wales* (318 tons/324 tonnes) some 49 females and one male. A marine garrison of 89 men came from the Portsmouth division.

Though officers of marines were not permitted to bring their families to Botany Bay, some wives of private soldiers, about ten per company, were allowed to travel. A total of 246 marine personnel have been positively identified as having sailed in the First Fleet, with 32 wives and 15 children. Ten further children would be born to the families of marines at sea.

Movement of convicts from London to Portsmouth continued. A report by a gentleman visiting Newgate depicted convicts delighted to be slated for the fleet. One party left Newgate on the morning of 27 February, and a large contingent was moved in bitter weather in six heavily guarded wagons from a Woolwich hulk via Guildford. As this large body of convicts moved through Portsmouth, the windows and doors of houses and shops were closed, and the streets lined with troops.

By the end of the loading process, some fifteen hundred people were spread amongst the eleven vessels. Bouncing around in the lee of the Isle of Wight, the convicts who had never sailed before became accustomed to the noises and motion of a ship and the claustrophobia of their low-beamed, cramped decks.

And even then Phillip was up in London arguing for better supplies, but reactive to the reports of the naval agent and surgeons. The enterprising chief surgeon, John White, a veteran at thirty-one of a decade of surgical practice on naval vessels serving in the Atlantic and Indian oceans, approached Captain Hunter, the Scots skipper of *Sirius*, saying, 'I thought whitewashing with quicklime the parts of the ships where the convicts were confined would be the means of correcting and preventing the unwholesome dampness which usually appeared on the beams and sides of the ships, and was occasioned by the breath of the people.' So, by late March, at least some of the vessels were ordered back into dock at Portsmouth for the prison and soldiers' decks to be fumigated. The convicts were let up on the deck, a mixed blessing in March weather, while the whitewashing of the convict prison was attended to and gunpowder was exploded in small heaps to disperse the vapours associated with disease.

The competent surgeon for the *Lady Penrhyn*, young Arthur Bowes Smyth, came to Portsmouth by mail coach, and gives us a picture of the perils and shocks of being a journeyer in a changeable season. 'A corpse sewed up in a hammock floated alongside our ship. The cabin, lately occupied by the Third Mate Jenkinson, who died of a putrid fever the night before I came on board, and was buried at Ryde, was fresh painted and fumigated for me to sleep in.'

On *Alexander*, eleven convict men, sick on loading, had worsened and died, and as April progressed, morale was low. Some relief was provided by seventy-year-old Elizabeth Beckford, guilty of shoplifting, and 82-year-old pedlar, Dorothy Handlyn, sentenced for perjury, who had become minor celebrities aboard *Lady Penrhyn*, and worth a visit from the gentlemen of the fleet. Beckford would die at sea long before sighting the coast of New South Wales. Handlyn disappeared, perhaps re-landed as absurdly too aged for such a journey.

In April, a Portsmouth newspaper complained that the longer the sailing was delayed the more the port was thronged with thieves and robbers, those who had come down to see their old hulk- and prison-mates and fellow gang members ('rum culls') away. By now the idea of the departing fleet no longer attracted universal applause. One Londoner complained: 'Botany Bay has made the shoplifters and pickpockets more daring than ever. To be rewarded with settlement in so fertile a country cannot fail of inducing every idle person to commit some depredation that may amount to a crime sufficient to send him there at the expense of the public.'

Meanwhile, the Duke of Dorset informed the British government of a journey to the Pacific undertaken by a French nobleman, the Comte de la Pérouse. There were rumours that a race was on to claim the region.

Early in May two late wagonloads of prisoners arrived from Newgate. The prison decks were now filled up and the cargo decks of Phillip's fleet were crowded with water casks and shacks and pens for animals. Phillip would bring his pet greyhounds aboard *Sirius* to add to the noise and clutter. But there was other and more sophisticated freight. At the Board of Longitude's meeting in February 1787, the Astronomer Royal, Dr Maskelyne, had proposed adaptations for three telescopes and the acquisition of a 10-inch Ramsden sextant to serve the marine lieutenant William Dawes, surveyor and astronomer, in making nautical and astronomical observations on the voyage to Botany Bay 'and on shore at that place'. Dawes, on the *Sirius*, was one of the Portsmouth division of marines, a very spiritual young man, who had been wounded in a sea battle with the French in Chesapeake Bay during the war in America, and had volunteered for New South Wales out of scientific rather than military fervour.

On the crew decks, new Brodie stoves, big bricked-in ovens, were kept alight and guarded twenty-four hours a day, producing cooked food for sailors and marines and—if there were time or bad weather—convicts as well. Often the prisoners' breakfast of gruel or pease porridge, and their main midday meal, stews of bread and biscuit, pease and beef, were less satisfactorily cooked in coppers in a shack-galley on the open deck.

When on 7 May Arthur Phillip at last was able to reach Portsmouth from London, with his servants and his clerk, Harry Brewer, he brought with him the Kendall timekeeper which would be used on board *Sirius* to calculate longitude. There too was his old inamorata, Mrs Deborah Brooks. Phillip had a final inspection of his fleet and looked particularly into the availability of caps, porter, women's clothing, and the unloved scurvy-deterrent, sauerkraut.

On board *Sirius*, greeted by the Scots master, John Hunter, Phillip met a marine officer who would become his staunch friend, Captain David Collins, a stalwart fellow of not much more than thirty who was assigned to be Botany Bay's judge-advocate. In an age when boy officers sometimes commanded grown men, Collins had been a fifteen-year-old officer in command of the marines aboard HMS *Southampton* when in 1772 it was sent to rescue Queen Caroline Matilda from Denmark. He had served on land, climbing the slope against defended American positions at the fierce battle at Bunker Hill, at which American sharpshooters caused great casualties amongst British officers. Though married, he was pleased to go back on full wages in December 1786, and willing for the sake of employment to be separated from his wife, who filled his absence by writing romances to enlarge their income.

Collins's military superior, the leader of all the fleet's marines and Arthur Phillip's lieutenant-governor, was Major Robert Ross, a Scot whom some found hard to get on with. John Hunter of the Royal Navy, captain of *Sirius*, was more a companion spirit to Phillip; the sea had ultimate affection over his competing passions for music, the classics and the Church of Scotland. Hunter's first shipwreck had been on a howling Norwegian coast at the age of eight. Just over fifty, he was the sort of officer others might describe as the navy's backbone, though, like Phillip, his career was rendered uncertain by lack of family connections. His fortitude, rigour, energy and tenacity would prove valuable commodities during the voyage of Phillip's improbable fleet, and also once it had reached its staggeringly distant destination.

CHAPTER 4

THE PASSAGE

The First Fleet's prodigious journey began in darkness at 3 a.m. on Sunday 3 May 1787. Phillip's instructions were to punctuate the voyage with calls at the Canary Islands, at Rio de Janeiro, his old home base, and then at Cape Town. The run down the English Channel took three days, with great suffering amongst the women on the convict deck of the *Lady Penrhyn*, the new-built ship whose timbers were still howling and settling and whose master, William Sever, was unfamiliar with her. Uncontrollable seasickness filled the prison's low-roofed deck with its acid, gut-unsettling stench. And, of course, no one could stand up, as the roof hung low, even between the beams. The unrecorded but certain anguish of the adolescent country girl Sarah Bellamy was matched by that of the teenager Mary Brenham, who at the age of fourteen had stolen clothing while babysitting.

Phillip quickly discovered that there was a range of speed and performance between the various ships. Apart from *Lady Penrhyn*, the transports *Charlotte* and *Prince of Wales* were slowed by heavy seas, and their convicts suffered the worst discomfort and seasickness. The handiest sailer was the little snub-nosed tender *Supply*, which could nonetheless safely carry very little sail in really big seas. The *Alexander*, *Scarborough* and *Friendship* were the three fastest convict transports.

By 3 June, the eleven ships reached Tenerife in the Canary Islands, after a journey in which the irons of the convicts, except those under punishment, had been removed, and a routine for allowing the transportees on deck in fine weather had been established. *Alexander*, the unhealthiest ship in the fleet, recorded twenty-one convicts suffering fever, scurvy, pneumonia and the bloody flux in the few weeks since sailing.

South of Tenerife, in the calms, amidst the cram of bodies, the air below decks reached fierce temperatures, and a skirt of stinking waste and garbage surrounded each ship. Wind sails were rigged like great fans, and swung across the deck to blow air below, and while the convicts exercised or slept on deck, gunpowder was again exploded in their prison to disperse evil vapours. The marine officers on *Friendship* found the ship infested with rats, cockroaches and lice, but the women convicts still needed to be battened down on their ill-ventilated deck at night, to prevent 'a promiscuous intercourse taking place with the marines'. Despite the ban on fraternising and prostitution, there were so many alliances between convicts, male and female, and between marines and sailors and sundry women aboard, that one begins to suspect that Phillip and the Home Office were not gravely disturbed that such associations should occur.

Lieutenant Clark on *Friendship* hated the disorderly women and ordered four of them to be put in irons for fighting, which must have been a hard punishment in that climate. 'They are a disgrace to their whole sex, bitches that they are.' Clark was gratified that the corporal ordered to flog one London prostitute and *Mercury* escapee, Elizabeth Dudgeon, later in the voyage 'did not play with her but laid it home'. Liz Barber, another reprobate, abused Surgeon Arndell and invited Captain Meredith 'to come and kiss her cunt for he was nothing but a lousy rascal as were we all'.

When the north-east trades blew, ships were capable of making good time, as on 17 June, when *Friendship* logged a refreshing 174 nautical miles to the *Sirius*'s 163. Phillip was already contemplating splitting the flotilla into fast and slow divisions. Even on a good day for the whole fleet, 26 June, *Friendship* made 29 knots to *Sirius*'s 25.

Phillip knew from the stories of *Mercury* how endemic the dream of mutiny was amongst the convicts, their chief fantasy, and an attractive one in the northern part of the Atlantic from which the newly self-liberated American colonies, champions of men's rights, could most easily be reached. But Phillip seems to have accepted the presence of former escapees and mutineers on his ships with sang froid. One wonders did he ever look at William Blatherhorn of the *Charlotte*, who had escaped from both the *Swift* and *Mercury*, with special attention? Did he look twice at the highwayman Charles Peat of the *Scarborough* who had been sentenced to death for escaping *Mercury*?

'There are so many "*Mercurys*" on board of us,' Clark confided to his wife, on the same day a convict told the commanding marine officer on board the *Scarborough* that two convicts were planning to take the ship over. Both were brought aboard the flagship *Sirius* to have two dozen lashes inflicted by the bosun's mate. The two of them must have hoped that ultimately, when their time was served, their seamanship skills would at least earn them a journey back to Britain, and that in fact would turn out to be the case.

More cheeringly, a group baptism took place on the *Lady Penrhyn*, the Reverend Johnson, the evangelical chaplain, officiating. It was an event of 'great glee' with 'an additional allowance of grog being distributed to the crews of those ships where births took place'. But crossing the equator, the *Lady Penrhyn* and the *Charlotte* came close to colliding with each other, as the *Penrhyn*'s crew was distracted by an officer or bosun dressed as King Neptune apparently rising from the sea to chastise and initiate those who had never crossed the line before.

On 5 July Phillip felt it necessary to reduce the water ration to three pints per person per day, all of it going to consumption, leaving everyone to have recourse to salt water for washing clothes and bathing. Sometimes garments were washed by being dragged on a rope overboard, and one sailor lost a pair of breeches to a shark this way. A convict was washed overboard and lost when he went on deck to bring in the washing during the sudden onset of a storm.

On matters of general health, Chief Surgeon John White and his three assistants were rowed around the fleet when weather permitted to consult with captains and resident surgeons such as Bowes Smyth of the *Penrhyn*, and to inspect health arrangements or undertake care of the convicts.

The run was good to Rio, and on 5 August the fleet stood in the estuary off that city. Private Easty on *Scarborough* had been impressed with the 13-gun salute from the fort. The total deaths since embarkation were 29 male and three female prisoners, which was considered an excellent result. The ships of the convoy had been able to keep in contact with each other, although the journals of the gentlemen indicate that *Lady Penrhyn* was continually lagging.

The Portuguese filled the first boat to return to the *Sirius* with fruit and vegetables 'sent as presents to the Commodore from some of his old friends and acquaintances'. On the second morning, Phillip and his officers were greeted ceremoniously by the viceroy, and that night the town was illuminated in his honour. The English officers could go where they wanted within the city, without escorts.

Collins tells us that while in harbour in Rio, every convict was regularly issued one and a half pounds (680 grams) of fresh meat, a pound (450 grams) of rice, a suitable proportion of vegetables and several oranges. Sailors returning from jaunts even pelted the convicts with oranges. The viceroy set aside an island to allow the expedition to set up tents for the sick and to use as a shore base. Lieutenant Dawes of the marines set up a temporary observatory there. The chief astronomical need was to check the Kendall chronometer of the *Sirius.*

Ashore, young Surgeon White watched religious processions, and was astonished but titillated by many well-dressed women in the crowd, 'quite unattended' and trawling for lovers. He lingered by the balconies of convent novices and students, girls 'very agreeable in person and disposition', and performed a demonstration leg amputation according to the controversial 'Allenson's method' on the patient of a Portuguese military surgeon.

When the fleet departed after a fortnight, the viceroy saluted Phillip with twenty-one guns, and could be forgiven for wondering whether such a varied and implausible expedition would be heard from again.

On *Charlotte*, incorrigible young Tom Barrett was caught trying to pass off counterfeit quarter-dollars made out of pewter and belt buckles. Surgeon White was astonished at how he had been able to create the fakes, given that there were always guards on the hatchway and hardly ten minutes would pass without someone going down to check on the prisoners.

On the long stretch between Rio and Dutch-controlled Cape Town, rancour, ill-temper, cabin fever and paranoia seemed to overtake many of the officers, not least on *Friendship,* and similar rancour and grievances must have filled the convict prison decks. Discomfort, too, was surely felt by all. In late September, on the deck level occupied by marines and women convicts, a sea broke which washed all parties out of their bunks. It must have been harder still for the male convicts on a lower deck. Fortunately, the trip was relatively brisk. On one day *Friendship* logged 188 knots. Cape Town, the Dutch headquarters in Africa, was reached on 11 November.

There, a convict tambour-maker or embroiderer named Eve Langley, sailing on the *Lady Penrhyn* with her small son, Phillip, gave birth to a daughter on a bed of clean straw in one of the shacks on deck. A foremast hand was listed as the father. By now the country girl Sarah Bellamy, and the teenage maid Mary Brenham were showing their pregnancies. There was a common Georgian belief, subscribed to by James Boswell, that sexual abstinence induced gout. The sailors of *Penrhyn* were taking no risk of acquiring the disease.

Surgeon Bowes Smyth of the *Penrhyn* recorded that the women were reduced to 'plundering the sailors . . . of their necessary cloths and cutting them up for some purpose of their own'. The two leaders in this plunder were Anne Colpitts, a Durham woman whose own child, John, died on the voyage, and Sarah Burdo, a young dressmaker guilty of having stolen from a Londoner who rejected her sexual advances. Both convict women would later be midwives in the colony. Because of their 'less exquisite feelings', wrote Bowes Smyth, 'the lower class of women have more easy and favourable births than those who live in affluence'.

Above decks was a babble of complaint from animals. In the fleet, said another surgeon, George Worgan, 'each ship is like another Noah's Ark'. Pet dogs roamed the decks. There were Captain Phillip's greyhounds and horses on *Sirius*, Reverend Johnson's kittens on the store ship *Golden Grove*, as well as on every ship a number of newly purchased sheep, pigs, cattle, goats, turkeys, geese, ducks, chickens, rabbits and pigeons penned in various structures on every deck. Rural convicts and children took comfort from tending animals as they had learned to do from an early age.

After leaving Cape Town, and sniffing the westerlies below Africa, Phillip divided the flotilla into two divisions, the first to be led by the little *Supply*, to which Phillip now transferred. This leading group included the *Alexander*, the *Friendship* and the *Scarborough*, which were now able to crowd on all the sail they had and travel as fast as they liked. On the convict decks it must have been miserable, with the setting in of the sub-Antarctic cold and the heaving seas of the Roaring Forties. Chief Surgeon White, visiting other ships by longboat, found signs of scurvy amongst the women, and ordered them dosed with essence of malt and good wine. Hail and snow came down, and officers like Clark were forced to wear a flannel waistcoat, two pairs of stockings and to keep their greatcoats on continuously. The convicts generally had only their light clothing and their one blanket, and welcomed what crowded warmth they could generate. Ahead, amidst the squalls, lay the south end of the island named Van Diemen's Land, and its perilous coasts.

The first division led by *Supply* sighted Van Diemen's Land's south-western shores on 5 January. It was summer in the southern hemisphere, but it did not feel like it, and on the high ground that could be glimpsed lay patches of snow. Then, less than two days after the first division worked its way around South East Cape, *Sirius*, with the help of its signal guns to attract the attention of other masters, and a large blackboard with the course chalked on it and hung over its stern, led the second division round and headed north. Thus the second division of transports and store ships was much closer behind than Arthur Phillip would have expected. The fleet was now on the last leg towards fabled Botany Bay, using the charts made by Cook as their guarantee of safe arrival.

MEETING EORA

The convicts, soldiers and wives on *Supply*, *Scarborough*, *Friendship* and *Alexander*, the faster vessels, knew they were close to the promised bay of transportation on 16 January in the new year, 1788. All was proceeding normally, yet was tinged with the edginess of near-arrival in a landscape up to then viewed and weighed by a mere handful of Europeans. The many beaches and bays they sailed past were marked by bold headlands and backed by blue mountain ranges with which, as it happened, the infant son of the watching convict, Susannah Holmes, would as an adult become familiar. To what extent did Susannah, holding the baby begotten by her convict paramour Henry Kable, hope for or dread the place? To what extent did Robert Sideway, who had stolen boxes from a coach, a 'Mercury' who might have lived the rest of his life in Nova Scotia, discern this coast as liveable?

Though Prime Minister Pitt and Lord Sydney had authorised Phillip to look at this target coast as a vacancy, the people who had lived here since the last ice age had created their known earth, and whose ancestors had been in the interior regions for millennia longer still, had seen the scatter of ships and were sending reports overland, clan to clan, of the astounding phenomenon.

Eighteen thousand years ago, the coast Phillip was approaching had been a region of cold steppes and sub-alpine woodland. Peaks higher than 1900 metres had glaciers descending them. Now, for the uneasy watchers ashore on this January day of 1788, ice existed only in tribal memory. The coastline had stabilised in its present form about 7000 years Before the Present, when the glaciers melted. Innumerable camping places, stone quarries, burial grounds and sacred sites had been flooded. But in compensation, the coast had began to mature and develop, providing sandstone plateaux, mangrove swamps and lagoons, caves and beaches, all known, all named. Bushland and forest covered most of the hinterland. This, their home, was the south-eastern coast of what would prove to be a southern continent, of which the Aboriginal population, in that last undisrupted week in January, stood at perhaps 750 000 to one million.

The Eora, the language grouping living in the Botany Bay area, were able to track small, stingless native bees to their caches of honey in hollow trees. Apart from nourishing marsupials, lizards, snakes, fish and shellfish were plentiful, but sharks and stingrays, universal clan totems of coastal people, were taboo. 'The Indians, probably from having felt the effects of their voracious fury testified the utmost horror on seeing these terrible fish,' said one officer. But one did not devour one's totem animal, whether bird, mammal, fish or serpent.

As sweet as life might have been on that coast for hunter-gatherers, the conditions for the development of a sedentary life did not exist. Perhaps only one of the grasses which formed the basis for sedentary farming elsewhere grew here, and the only semi-domesticated animal was the native dog or dingo, which hung around the people's campfires and helped them harry kangaroos, wallabies and smaller game in return for meat at the evening camp site.

For the people who now saw the phantasms of the fleet pass by, this coast was the centre of the real world. They would have been astounded that there were, somewhere else, in remote, northern, unholy mists, members of their own species who considered this country a netherworld, a legislated form of hell. Until now, they had not had any reason to think their horizons were about to collapse in upon them.

Captain Cook, who had come this way only once, had made the names he gave to the land's geographic features both bywords for great distance, and also a form of taming: he had reduced the coast to size with European tags. So there were comforting reference points for Phillip and his officers to look for. The officers took professional joy in seeing them come up. King wrote, 'An eminence on the land . . . bore at this time W ½ S 4 leagues which we take for a mountain resembling a hat which Captain Cook takes notice of.' The feature in question was Hatt Hill. Red Point was nine miles (14.5 kilometres) north of this, and then the southern point of Cook's Botany Bay, Cape Solander, named in honour of Sir Joseph Banks's Swedish colleague, came into view.

The *Supply* hauled in for the harbour at a quarter past two in the afternoon of 19 January and anchored in the northern arm of the bay, so that the three closest convict transports following, *Alexander*, *Scarborough* and the little *Friendship*, would be able to see them from the entrance and thus be guided in.

How could the place not fail to disappoint the travellers' long-sustained expectation? No one on the *Supply* made exuberant statements about it. It lay there in its sultry afternoon light, not much elevation to it, despite all the great sandstone cliffs and headlands they had passed further south. It was in part a landscape of shallow hills, eucalypt trees and grass-trees, cabbage-tree palms spread as in a park, with the grass soon to be called kangaroo grass growing between the trees. Otherwise, it was a country of low, indiscriminate earth, open ground in many places, with rank grass: the sort of country that promised there would be lagoons and swamps just behind the shore. Its sand beaches shone with ambiguous welcome in the afternoon sun.

As the *Supply* watched the earth, the inheritors of the earth watched the *Supply*. The Gweagal (Fire clan) of the Eora language group occupied the south shore of the bay and wondered why, after many years, the sky had ruptured again and the phenomenon of a craft as large as an island had returned. The Bediagal on the north side of Botany Bay were galvanised by the same question. Both clans called the newcomers *Beeriwangal*, People of the Clouds. Old men and women began to sing songs of expulsion, and the young repaired spears with animal gut and yellow gum which held the enchanted points of stone or bone in place, and tested throwing sticks for solidity. A young Bediagal *carradhy*, a man of high degree and preternatural physical courage, Pemulwuy, if not actually present, was sent a message that the manifestation was back. Mothers and aunts counselled children to be wary. The last time one of these phantasms had appeared, it had taken a month to expel the dead-white ghosts who had come ashore.

Arthur Phillip knew that Cook had not received an open welcome in Botany Bay eighteen years before. Phillip's task was harder—he did not need merely to be an investigator here. He was meant to make a penal town somewhere in this bay, and continue to live with the 'Indians'. The instructions on this matter had been attached to his commission from the Crown and read: 'You are to endeavour by every means to open an intercourse with the natives, and to conciliate their affections, enjoining all our subjects to live in amity and kindness with them.' Murders, assault and theft committed on and against the natives were to be punished.

At three o'clock the boats were hoisted out from the *Supply* and Arthur Phillip, Lieutenant King, Lieutenant Johnson and the young astronomer William Dawes headed towards the north side of the bay, 'and just looked at the face of the country, which is as Mr Cook remarks very much like the moors in England, except that there's a great deal of very good grass and some small timber trees'. Phillip and his men intended to search the shores of the famous bay for fresh water. A reliable young convict, James Ruse, who had stolen two watches and stood trial on the edge of his native Cornish moors at Bodmin, had been moved to the *Supply* and would always claim he was the first ashore, wading in with Lieutenant Johnston riding, scarlet and glittering, on his back.

For the Eora speakers watching the landing ghosts—red was a colour of peril and war and struggling with spirits.

They noticed, too, as the Europeans drew in towards land that Phillip was missing the very tooth the coastal Aboriginals removed from young men at initiation, an elder sitting on the initiate's shoulder and hammering away with stone pounder and chisel. This compelled their serious attention. Phillip was a dead ancestor improperly returned.

The natives immediately rose to their feet and called to the newcomers 'in a menacing tone and at the same time brandishing their spears or lances'. The usual rituals of arrival took place. Phillip showed them some beads, and ordered one of the seamen to tie them to the stem of a beached canoe. Then Phillip, as a founding act of goodwill, walked towards the natives alone and unarmed. A male native advanced and made signs that he should lay the gifts on the ground. The native, understandably edgy and trembling to be addressing the dead, came forward and took them, and then he and others came near enough to be given looking glasses and other wonders.

Then and in days to come the Eora tried to satisfy these ghosts and cloud-creatures by directing them to water in the hope that, their thirst satisfied, they would leave. Phillip himself was thinking of going. This bay, with its shallow anchorages, unpredictable winds and its doubtful capacity to support an ill-supplied penal settlement, worried him. Because of the fluky winds, the other ships of the first division had still not been able to join *Supply* in Botany Bay.

It was early the next morning that the *Alexander*, *Scarborough* and *Friendship* came round Point Solander, the first bulk of the convicts reaching the place of their sentence according to legislation and orders-in-council. On *Friendship*, the marine lieutenant Ralph Clark noted a great many natives on the point. When the *Friendship* anchored at last, a boat crew from the *Supply* brought aboard some mown grass from the new land, but Clark wrote, 'I cannot say from the appearance of the shore that I will like it.'

We do not know what speculations occurred on the convict deck, but convicts were let up for exercise, and to help catch fish. January is good fishing time in New South Wales, and many specimens were reeled in. A crowd of gentlemen and sailors went into an inlet on the south-west side of the bay and further confused the Eora speakers when they 'ate salt beef and in a glass of porter drank the healths of our friends in England'.

There was a great shift of meaning in operation on those first evenings of British permanency on the east coast of New South Wales. Thereafter, in the wider world, Botany Bay, renowned until then for the exotic, the furthest reach of human investigation and endeavour, famous for both botanic and zoologic conundra, would slowly become a name of scorn. As the English poet Robert Southey would—with mock grandiloquence—write during a pleasant evening with William Wordsworth:

Therefore, old George, by George we pray
Of thee forthwith to extend thy sway
Over the great botanic bay.

For the Gweagal and Bediagal clans of the Eora language group, a similar shift was in progress. The pallid, disturbing ghosts were abounding. One day: one ship, one floating island, one population of ghosts with mysterious outer skins. The next morning: four islands and four populations of strangers. And on the following morning of 20 January, when Captain Hunter on the *Sirius* led the second group of transports around Point Solander, there were eleven of these floating phenomena with their huge and inhuman wings, and infestations of some sort of unquiet returned souls aboard. Some Gweagal and Bediagal, related by marriage, assembled on the southern point of the bay and yelled, '*Werre! Werre!*' across the water. This was their first, undeniable message to the people of the fleet. 'Get out! Begone! Clear away.'

But the officers did not imagine themselves trespassers, and the private marines and, especially, the convicts would have found such a self-description ridiculous.

A more poetic European vision had entered Botany Bay on the just-arrived transport *Charlotte*, in the person of the pleasant young captain of marines,

Watkin Tench. Captain Tench was in his late twenties, the son of a successful and well-connected Chester boarding-school proprietor. During the American war he had been a prisoner in Maryland for three months. Like Collins and other officers, he had volunteered for service on this fleet to get off half-pay. In his striving, often elegant and curious-minded journal, Tench wrote of the arrival of this second division of ships. '"Heavily in clouds came on the day" which ushered in our arrival. To us it was "a great, an important day". Though I hope the foundation, not the fall, of an empire will be dated from it.'

This sanguine and charming young Englishman celebrated the fact that even though the fleet had not been supplied with portable soup, wheat or pickled vegetables, and a small supply of essence of malt had been the only anti-scurvy remedy on board, an extraordinary number of people had survived the voyage of what had been, for the second division of ships, exactly thirty-six weeks since leaving Portsmouth, very nearly to the hour. 'The wind was now fair,' young Watkin wrote, 'the sky serene, though a little hazy, and the temperature of the air delightfully pleasant: joy sparkled in every countenance and congratulations issued from every mouth. Ithaca itself was scarcely more longed for by Ulysses, than Botany Bay.'

John Hunter, too, liked the black mould of some of the earth he saw ashore, and the tall eucalypt trees. Due to the Eora people's fire-stick farming there was less undergrowth crowding the landscape than would later become common.

By contrast, if joy characterised the face of Watkin's commander, the Scot Major Ross, lieutenant-governor of the colony, it would not be evident for very long. Ross's abhorrence for the country set in quickly and profoundly, while on the six ships in which the majority of the convicts were contained, we do not know which emotions were displayed.

Nevertheless, the boisterousness of the convict women and most of the men still kept aboard their vessels, looking out at the land from the deck or through open scuttles, soon echoed around the bay. To some of the felons the country seemed enormous enough to offer room for escape, and those who did not understand the fact that wildernesses were to provide the walls here already planned decamping. Wild elation, dread and depression competed for voice amongst them. Some—despite Tench's sanguine view of their health—were doomed to take cots in the hospital tents Surgeons White and Balmain were erecting ashore.

The wives of marines and their children also looked at the long dun foreshores of the bay with some surmise. They came from the same class as many of the convicts, and shared with them a capacity for stubborn acceptance which would serve them well.

The Europeans, however, were confused. Lieutenant Bradley, Hunter's second-in-command, said that on the one hand boat crews 'amused themselves with dressing the natives with paper and other whimsical things to entertain them'. But the next day, after a landing party began clearing brush from a run of water on the south side of the bay, altering a location where for ritual and ceremonial reasons ferns and grass-trees had been permitted to proliferate, the natives became 'displeased and wanted them to be gone'.

On 22 January, when a seine net was hauled in and the natives saw the quantity of fish the sailors were dragging onshore with it, they 'were much astonished which they expressed by a loud and long shout'. They took some of the fish away, as a matter of right in their eyes, but as a form of primitive pilferage as far as the British were concerned. The next day the natives struck the thieving fishers with spear shafts, took fish 'and ran off with them sensible that what they had done was wrong', wrote Lieutenant Bradley. In fact Lieutenant King had earlier discharged a musket loaded merely with powder, and perhaps they melted away to avoid that thunder. Now and later the material possessions of the Botany Bay people seemed so slight, and their presence so intermittent, that the officers chose to believe that they had not yet left the state of innocence and childlikeness beyond which issues of title to fish, fowl, animals and land became important. Phillip noted that 'What they wanted most was the greatcoats and clothing, but hats was more particularised by them, their admiration of which they expressed in very loud shouts whenever one of us pulled our hat off.'

One day the Eora people indicated by very plain signs that they wanted to know the gender of the men rowing towards them. (No women had yet come ashore.) King wrote, 'I ordered one of the people to undeceive them in this particular when they gave a great shout of admiration.' The Eora had wondered whether beneath their carapaces of cloth the cloud-people were male or female. And as they showed themselves male, they might leave, the Eora surmised, if their desires were sated. 'Pointing to the shore, which was but ten yards from us, we saw a great number of women and girls with infant children on their shoulders make their appearance on the beach, all in *puris naturalibus, pas même la feuille de figeur* [that is, totally naked].' The natives made it clear by their urgings that the men in the longboats could make free with the women onshore. 'I declined this mark of their hospitality,' said King. He urged a particular young woman to put her baby down and wade out to his boat, where she 'suffered me to apply the handkerchief where Eve did the fig leaf'.

Elders and tribesmen would have been confused when the British refused this perfectly good opportunity to exercise their sexual organs, to sate themselves, and then withdraw to sea at last. As for the Aboriginal women, these figures to whom they offered themselves were more virtual than real. Since the great sexual sins of Aboriginal society were to have sex within forbidden blood limits, a dalliance with such phantasms had no moral or tribal meaning.

So the inducements so far offered by the Eora—water, threat, the offer of sex—had not worked, and the ghosts remained in distressing proximity.

BOTANY BAY BLUES

Even Watkin Tench soon shared the general discontent about the fleet's long-anticipated landfall. 'Of the natural meadows which Mr Cook mentions near Botany Bay, we can give no account.' Surgeon White's final judgment would be: 'Botany Bay I own does not, in my opinion, by any means merit the commendations bestowed on it by the much lamented Cook.'

It took Phillip just three days and a few insomniac nights to decide that he would renounce Botany Bay, the most famous inlet in the outer world. He determined to explore the far less famous inlets north along the coast, named in turn by Cook as Port Jackson and Broken Bay. By 22 January, three longboats were prepared with three days provisions for scouting up the coast. Arthur Phillip, Captain Hunter, David Collins, Lieutenant Bradley and a small party of marines were spread throughout the three open boats. Putting out of the bay by dark on Monday morning, they found there was only a gentle swell as light came up on the open, aquamarine Tasman Sea. Sandstone cliffs interspersed with beaches and headlands marked the way north. On the cliffs, several parties of Aboriginals cried out to the three open boats as they proceeded along the coast, 'Werre! Werre! Werre!' That afternoon, Phillip entered the heads of Port Jackson, a dimple on Cook's map of this coastline, named to honour the then Judge-Advocate of the Admiralty. It had not been entered by Cook as he made his way up the coast in 1770. The great sandstone cliffs near the entrance decreased in size to become the weathered south head, whereas the north side displayed perpendicular heights.

Phillip's boats ran around the southern head, up the middle of the tide rushing in from the Pacific. They found themselves in a wide, bright blue bowl of sparkling water. It stretched away on the north and west but particularly on the south side. The foreshores were heights of sandstone thickly covered with dun green forest, interspersed with yellow beaches. Phillip was already enthused, and the general sobriety of his prose would be swept aside when he later told Lord Sydney, 'We got into Port Jackson early in the afternoon, and had the satisfaction of finding the finest harbour in the world, in which a thousand sail of the line may ride in the most perfect security.'

Such absolutes: 'the finest harbour in the world'; 'perfect security'; 'a thousand sail.' The same number of sail Helen had launched in the Trojan Wars. This exuberant sentiment would stand out unapologetically in the midst of Phillip's dutiful official-ese, and it underpinned his decisiveness in declaring this, and not the great Cook's Botany Bay, as the destined place.

The expedition circled to one of the northside bays of this huge, unexpected harbour, which Phillip then or later named Manly Cove, as a tribute to the general style and demeanour of natives who appeared on the beaches that afternoon. Then, in the evening, they headed southwards down the harbour and landed at a place within the southern headland, naming it Camp Cove, since they pitched tents there. They were the very first people from the northern world to take their rest in Port Jackson.

At four o'clock in the morning, that keen taskmaster Arthur Phillip had them on their oars again, with one boat in the lead sounding the way from one bay of Port Jackson to another.

They found that the broad sweep of Port Jackson ran away pleasingly southwards, with much better soundings than Botany Bay. By late afternoon they reached a cove some eleven kilometres inside the harbour of Port Jackson. This place gave excellent soundings close to shore—its good anchorages had been gouged out by a vanished glacier. The party landed on the west side of this inlet, under bushy platforms of rock. They walked around to the head of the cove where the ground was level. Again, there were scattered large eucalypts, cabbage-tree palms and low undergrowth, but more elevation and an utterly less swampy air than at Botany Bay. A good stream densely lined with ferns flowed down the centre of the land and disgorged in the cove. It ran pristinely and plentifully even then, at the height of summer. The ridge on the eastern side struck Phillip and others as a potential site for a public farm. And there were no natives screaming, '*Werre*'. An American, Nagle, a boat-master, a captured former Yankee privateer, remained aboard fishing while the gentlemen made their reconnaissance, and pulled up a good bream. Returning, the governor and his party were in good form; Phillip was very pleased with this cove. He saw the bream and asked who had caught it—it lay silver in the stern like a good sign. He told Nagle to remember that he was the first white man to catch a fish 'in Sydney Cove'.

Perhaps the decision to name the cove to honour the Home Secretary was really as instantaneous as that. Sydney was an English corruption of the French St Denis, but there was no piety in Phillip's choice. A politician was perhaps less likely to forget a place named to honour him, a place whose deterioration might become a reflection on him. Indeed, Phillip had at first intended to name the township he envisaged building in the cove Albion, an ancient name for England, imbued with a certain holiness. But highfaluting Albion would never quite stick, and the convicts and soldiers would quickly come to use the name Sydney Cove, or Sydney Town, or simply Sydney, for their penal municipality.

It already had a long-established Eora name—Warrane. It belonged to a group of Eora speakers named the Cadigal (the Grass-tree clan), and their absence on the day Phillip landed indicated that it was chiefly a place to be visited for ceremonial purposes. Indeed, this whole region of vivid blue skies and water, sandstone headlands and ridges covered in vegetation, sandy bays and ocean beaches backed by marshland, tidal lagoons and mangrove swamps made all the Eora a people united by salt water and a bounty of protein from the sea, from Port Jackson, lying inside its heads, Boree and Burrawara, to Kamay (Botany Bay), and to the hinterland bush.

But their good fortune had passed. For longer than any other population of *Homo sapiens*, and excepting the Makassan contacts in the far north, the ancestors of the Aboriginals had been genetically and culturally cocooned from the rest of the species. Phillip's sailors, soldiers and convicts, already preparing to depart Botany Bay for the more promising Port Jackson, were walking incubators for viruses and bacteria barely before seen on this coast. These micro-organisms too were looking for new landfalls.

WARRANE-BOUND

At first light the next morning, 24 January, when on *Supply* the stock was being watered, and everyone was exhilarated at news of the coming move, the watches on the ships saw two ships just off the coast, trying to work their way into Botany Bay. Amongst the officers visiting each other for breakfast, there were a number of wild surmises. Were they ships from England with a general pardon for all prisoners? Supply ships? A white pennant soon confirmed that they comprised the expedition of the Comte de la Pérouse, who had set out from France nearly three years earlier to explore the Pacific, and who had preposterously turned up just as the British were ending their brief dalliance with Botany Bay.

By the time he appeared off Botany Bay, the comte's two ships, *La Boussole* and *L'Astrolabe*, had doubled Cape Horn, discovered a number of previously uncharted islands, surveyed the coast of Korea, and proved Sakhalin to be an island. Heading south again into the Pacific La Pérouse lost a shore party in Samoa when natives killed his second-in-command and eleven others. A French monk-scientist, Father Receveur, one of two priests on the ships, was fatally ill from wounds received in the Samoan imbroglio, and would ultimately go to his grave on the shores of Botany Bay.

A ferocious north-easter would keep La Pérouse waiting two days to enter the port safely, and tested the seamanship of John Hunter on *Supply* and the other ships' masters as they tacked out from beneath La Pérouse's shadow. Did he too want to make a claim on this enormous coastline? On the convict decks, the hope had already formed that perhaps these two French ships a little way down the coast offered a means of escape.

As La Pérouse finally entered Botany Bay, the *Sirius*, with Phillip once more aboard, was departing. 'The two commanders had barely time to exchange civilities; and it must naturally have created some surprise in M. de la Pérouse to find our fleet abandoning the harbour at the very time he was preparing to anchor in it,' wrote Tench.

Before leaving Botany Bay, a number of marines and reliable convicts had been transferred to the *Supply*, so that as soon as it came to anchor in Sydney Cove, work parties could be sent ashore. Others spent the first night in the ships, but the next day, 26 January, there were scenes of unprecedented activity in bright sunlight in the little inlet. In one place, said Tench, was a party cutting down the woods, while elsewhere a group set up a blacksmith's forge. Soldiers pitched officers' marquees on the west side of the stream, while a detachment of troops paraded, and cooks lit fires on the western side of the cove. Sydney Cove faced north, and the general delineation of the future town was created by its geography. The officers and military were stationed around the banks of the stream. Some ground to the west was to be allotted to officers to grow corn for their animals.

Major Robbie Ross, commander of marines and lieutenant-governor, brought his edginess ashore. He looked on Sydney Cove and its environs with a far more jaundiced eye than other officers. It might have been in part because he had found Phillip so annoyingly secretive about his intentions regarding rations for troops and convicts, the conditions under which rations would be issued, and even on the issue of whether the marines were to be a garrison or prison guards. Ross was feverishly worried about his family in Britain, whom he described as 'very small, tho' numerous'. That was one of the reasons why, upon Captain Shea's death soon after landing, in the corrupt traditions of the army, he made his own son, John Ross, a child just about to turn ten, a volunteer lieutenant, a rank he hoped would be confirmed by the Admiralty with appropriate back-pay benefits.

The other fact was that he hated the place on sight. It looked to him an unyielding place, and he wondered if it were un-redeemed, a place which showed by its heathen strangeness that the Saviour's sacrificial blood, which had certainly rescued his native Scotland, had not washed this far south.

On the very point of the west side of Sydney Cove, Lieutenant William Dawes intended to set up his astronomical instruments for an unprecedented long-term study of the southern sky. He called the place Point Maskelyne (though it now bears his own name), to honour the Astronomer Royal. On that west side too, on level ground beneath the sandstone rock ledges, Surgeon White's marquee-hospital was to be set up, near what Phillip had already assigned as the convict women's camp, the men's camp being closer to the military. The good stream which divided the cove would come to be known before any great passage of time as the Tank Stream, since reservoir tanks would be sunk along its banks to preserve its waters against drought.

THE PASSAGE

On the eastern side of the cove the ground was more open and suited for a public farm and the residences of the governor and his officials. Arthur Phillip's portable canvas house, provided by Messrs Smith of St George's Field, was accordingly erected there, about fifty metres from the water, and a number of tents for trustworthy convicts and those considered not terminally corrupted were put up there too.

In a matter of mere days Sydney Cove would be altered, in Phillip's mind, and to an extent on the ground, from a garden of nomads to a municipality. To celebrate that shift, in the afternoon of 26 January most of the crew of the

Supply assembled at the point where they had first landed in the morning, on the western side of Sydney Cove. The first flagstaff had been fashioned from a sappy pole of eucalyptus and, the British flag being run up, the governor and the officers drank the health of His Majesty and the royal family, then drank success to the new colony while the marines broke the bright sky with several volleys. After this rite, something of greatest significance to the watching Eora happened—many of the white spirits slept ashore, and the night became theirs as well.

If the Gweagal and Bediagal of Botany Bay had been delighted to see the ships depart, they must have been equally confused when they were replaced by the French vessels; and via the well-trodden overland track between Warrane and Botany Bay came news from visiting members of the Cadigal clan to the north that the original ships had merely gone on to infest Warrane, that choice inlet in the great harbour only 11 kilometres to the north.

On that first day, 26 January, the governor found the time to sign a warrant giving his old friend, that ancient midshipman Harry Brewer, a new identity as provost-marshal of the colony. So New South Wales began its long career as a place where men of no description could achieve a label, a post, a self-definition.

CHAPTER 5

ENQUIRIES ASHORE

The disembarkation of the bulk of the troops and some male convicts occurred on 27 January, on feet unsteady after such a long period aboard. After their last breakfast on the ships, all the male convicts, except those who were too sick to walk, gathered up their clothing and bedding and were taken ashore. How strange to leave the convict deck on which most of them, not having landed at Botany Bay, had been for so long, their narrow bed space, their penal womb, and to be reborn ashore. The talkers of cant, and the country fellows ('Johnny Raws') as well, had the urgent business of clearing ground and building themselves shelters, for there were no tenements or even tents for them. Whitehall had decided that it would be good exercise for the men to construct their own habitations. Under instruction from country felons like James Ruse, they began putting together structures of wattle and daub— plaited panels of branches providing the walls, the cracks being filled in with daubed clay, of which there was a plentiful supply on the foreshore of Sydney Cove. Longboats were regularly sent to the north side of Port Jackson in quest of tall straight trunks of cabbage tree (*Livistona australis*) which were used for the corner poles of huts. Roofs were of thatch of cabbage-tree fronds or rushes or bark plastered over with clay, which all made, said Collins, 'a very good hovel'. There were many economic but flimsy structures standing within a few days. Many, however, would be destroyed on 2 February in a characteristically violent Sydney thunderstorm. But for now, wattle and daub was all they had, other than some dockyard canvas sent ashore from *Sirius.*

Those felons sent to cut the tall trees found the timber incorrigible—resistant to adze and plane, knotty and with a mind of its own, a wood indifferent to European purposes. Surgeon White, who had sufficient patients to attend to, would take time to declare of this wood that 'repeated trials have only served to convince me that immediately on immersion it sinks to the bottom like a stone'.

Meanwhile, on the basis of a few days tentative exploration in the bush around Sydney Cove, a cultivated young midshipman, Daniel Southwell, declared that there was nothing deserving of the name of fruit. And with some injustice he declared that the country's quadrupeds were scarcely to be classed above vermin. But he was also resourceful enough to discover that there were many 'salutary shrubs', that balm could be milked from trees, and that a native spinach, parsley and sort of broad bean grew. Many of the productions of the country, he said, were aromatic, and had medicinal properties, and could be used as *fomenta*, poultices on sores. A young surgeon, an Irishman named Denis Considen, a graduate of Trinity College, Dublin, also found various gums and leaves suitable for brewing a form of native tea.

Something else momentous but without ceremony occurred: public stock, largely acquired in Cape Town, was landed on the east side of the cove—including one bull, four cows, one bull-calf, one stallion, three mares and three colts. A range of Western Europe's useful beasts was herded for the first time on this shore, the cattle under the care of a convict named Edward Corbett. As the Eora possessed a Dreaming, so in a sense did the British—a dreaming of harsh-hoofed livestock. For the first time, cattle kicked up the dust of an inadequately super-soiled continent. The Eora had not presented themselves in any numbers at Sydney Cove/Warrane yet, but to those natives looking on, the bestiary of the cloud-people must have seemed puzzling.

On 29 January 1788, when Phillip landed at Spring Cove just inside North Head, twelve natives crowded round the boats, anxious to inspect the newcomers, these owners of fabulous beasts and floating islands. It was the first contact between the races within Port Jackson. The sailors mixed with the native men who were 'quite sociable, dancing, and otherwise amusing them', but the native women were kept well away by their menfolk. The whites could not persuade any of the natives to return with them to the settlement at Sydney Cove. John

Hunter found these Port Jackson inhabitants a 'very lively and inquisitive race', straight, thin, small-limbed and well-made.

ADAM DELVES

In the ideal settlement as envisaged by Phillip, the convict male was to work for the government from seven in the morning until three in the afternoon, with a half-day on Saturdays, and then have time to grow vegetables or pursue some other useful task in his spare time thereafter. By 30 January, the first work party of convicts was put to breaking ground for a government garden and farm on the slope of the east side of the cove and just over the hill, in what became known as Farm Cove. As tools were handed out by the conscientious and always stressed storekeeper, Andrew Miller, the male convicts, directed amongst others by Phillip's manservant, Henry Dodd, showed very little enthusiasm. The first breaking of sod by some anonymous shoveller in the hastily cleared earth of Sydney Cove was unattended by ceremony, or by competition to be the first to sink the shovel, or by any sense of self-congratulation that on this immense shore they few were the first European delvers. The London convicts immediately proved themselves to be the worst workers. Even men as likeable as James Ruse became their enemy once put in a supervisory role. A freed slave, John Cesor or Black Caesar, born in Madagascar, hugely built, was considered one of the few good labourers. Otherwise, the phrase 'Kiss my arse!' was a current and popular one in Sydney Cove—it appears in the early records of the judge-advocate's court in the mouth of a West Country convict named Sam Barsby.

That first slovenly attempt at making a government garden was an early instance in which the realities of the new society were forced upon Phillip. The earth proved rocky, full of lumps of sandstone. Officers, however, and the occasional convict stonemason, thought that the yellowish sandstone was comparable to Portland stone and very suitable for working. But in the bush around no one could find limestone deposits for cement.

The lime trees, the lemons, the oranges, the figs and grapes which had been picked up in the Cape were slowly planted in the government farm, but marsupial rats devoured them eagerly during Phillip's uneasy nights. His sleep beneath the canvas of his temporary residence was restless, since he suffered from renal pain. He also ran into resistance from the officers in a matter amazing for not having been sorted out in England. 'The officers who composed the detachment are not only few in number,' Phillip would write to Lord Sydney, 'but most of them have declined any interference with the convicts, except when they are employed for their own particular service.' So increasingly Phillip was obliged to put some of the more trustworthy convicts in supervisory roles; young, good-looking, well-liked Henry Kable, for example, became a superintendent for the women prisoners who were still to be landed.

In the tents placed for the sick on the west side of the cove, beneath the rocky, bush-embowered sandstone ledges, Surgeon White admitted with some concern that, after the preventive medical success of the fleet, the numbers of sick were increasing. Scurvy, dormant on the ships, suddenly seemed to manifest itself in some of the convicts, and dysentery as well. In that late January heat Surgeon White's sicker patients sat on blankets in the sun and raised their mouths to bite off the air of this place beyond places. White complained that 'not a comfort or convenience could be got' for the sick in those first days.

Lest the Royal Navy sailors on the *Sirius* (who would be returning to Britain soon enough) begin to eat into public stores, Phillip appointed for their use an island not far from the public farm—Garden Island, as it came to be known—on which to grow vegetables for the crew's consumption. Soon Ralph Clark would start using another island in Port Jackson as a vegetable garden, and despite its relative distance down-harbour from Sydney Cove, it would sometimes be plundered by boat crews, and by hungry convicts who could swim long distances.

Phillip gave no priority to building a prison stockade in Sydney Cove. It had always been the plan that the environs would serve as walls to a great outdoor prison. The First Fleet convicts were in the ultimate panopticon, a prison in which all inmates could be readily observed and monitored from a central point, where strangeness hemmed them in, and the sky aimed its huge blank blue eye at them. And yet from the day of landing onwards, a number of prisoners walked the 11 kilometres along a native track down to Botany Bay to bespeak the Frenchmen, and to plead political asylum or offer services as sailors or, when the women were at last landed, sea-wives.

Lieutenant Bradley, a teacher from the naval academy at Portsmouth, had been out surveying the shoreline of Port Jackson, and found on the north side twelve miles (19 kilometres) of snug coves, and—as in Sydney Cove—good depths of water and freshwater streams entering many of the harbour's inlets. At his task, he became aware that the northern shore of Port Jackson, and the southern shore too, carried a considerable population of Eora, 'Indians . . .

painted very whimsically with pipe clay and red ochre'. He came to notice that all the women they met had two joints at the little finger on the left hand missing. 'It was supposed by some to be the pledge of the marriage ceremony, or of their having children.' Most of the men had lost a front incisor tooth and were highly scarred on the chest. Their spears were twelve to sixteen feet (3.7 to 4.9 metres) in length, and they walked very upright.

The term 'Eora', which the Europeans came to use as the name for the Aboriginal people of the area, may have been merely a sample phrase from their language. It may have been the local language's word for 'here' or 'the people about here'. In any event, the language the 'Eora' spoke, like the approximately 250 languages spoken on the continent of Australia in 1788, tended to use the blade of the tongue against teeth and hard palate to create a far greater range of consonants than in English. Australian languages often had six corresponding nasal sounds, where English just has 'm' and 'n'. Transliteration of Aboriginal personal and place names into English would always be chancy and remains so. The sibilants, such as 's' and 'sh', however, were totally absent in Australian languages. Later, Phillip's officers would chuckle at a visiting native's incapacity to say 'candle-snuffer'. Aboriginal words showed case, tense and mood by the addition of meaningful segments, which created very long words, and very long names. Woolawarre Boinda Bundebunda Wogetrowey Bennelong, for example, was the name of the native who would later attract the officers' amusement over the candle-snuffer. Known as Bennelong, he would continue to attract the Europeans' attention, for a variety of reasons.

HONOURING BACCHUS AND GEORGE

Now society in New South Wales really began. The convict women came up from the prison decks to be landed on 6 February. On *Lady Penrhyn*, young Surgeon Bowes Smyth was happy to see them taken off in the ship's longboats, beginning at five o'clock in the morning. Those with goods, portmanteaux or duffel bags full of clothing, decorations and hats which had been carried in the hold were handed their property and toted or wore it ashore, in combination with their aging penal clothes. 'Some few among them,' said Bowes Smyth, 'might be said to be well-dressed.'

How silent the ships must have suddenly seemed to the sailors, as if a soul had gone out of them. The women were landed on the western side of Sydney Cove where bedraggled canvas and huts of wattle and bark delineated their camp. The last of them landed at six o'clock on what would prove to be a typical summer evening, still and hot, but promising a southerly squall. 'The men convicts got to them very soon after they landed,' said Bowes Smyth. And no sooner had the last of the women disembarked than a number of suddenly lonely sailors from the transports also came ashore, bringing grog with them, and the marines were unable or unwilling to keep the women separate from them. The *Lady Penrhyn*'s crew in particular joined in one mass outdoor party, Sydney's first fête of hedonism.

'It is beyond my abilities to give a just description of the scene of debauchery and riot which continued through the night,' wrote Bowes Smyth, whose reliability as a witness is sometimes criticised for his jumping to conclusions about what he claimed to witness from the deck of *Penrhyn*. The evening had turned humid and thunderous, and once the rain began it made an assessment of events ashore a little more dubious still. There was lightning, the sentinel in front of Major Ross's marquee being so intimidated that he abandoned his post. While the night proceeded, one potent stroke of lightning would kill six sheep, two lambs and a pig, all belonging to Major Ross.

The great Sydney bacchanal went on despite the thunderstorm which so unsettled Ross's sentry. Fists were raised to God's lightning, and in the name of the Tawny Prince and in defiance of British justice; the downpour was cursed and challenged, and survival and utter displacement were celebrated in lunges and caresses. 'The scene which presented itself at the time, and during the greater part of the night, beggars every description,' wrote Bowes Smyth.

It is hard to put this idea of wild drinking and orgy together with what we know of at least some of the women. There is little doubt either that some of them were by dark safely with mentors. The forceful young Cockney Jewish convict Esther Abrahams was the passion of 23-year-old Lieutenant George Johnston, a Scot severely wounded by the French as a fifteen-year-old in 1780, but who had now returned to manhood's bloom. The alliance between the Scot and the Jewish girl would ultimately lead to marriage. At the time Lieutenant Johnston became interested in her, when he came aboard the *Lady Penrhyn* in the Thames, she had already given birth to a daughter in Newgate and brought her on board with her. Surely Esther, that night in Sydney, and her daughter, Roseanna, were somehow under Johnston's protection.

Surely, too, Margaret Dawson of the *Lady Penrhyn*, a seventeen-year-old Lancashire girl who had stolen clothing and jewellery to the death-earning value of £22 18 shillings from her master and taken it away with her on the Liverpool–Norfolk coach, joined her lover, Assistant Surgeon Balmain, a 26-year-old Scot whose estate, many years later, she would inherit. But though there were numerous similar cases, the generality of convict women and girls were, willy-nilly, participants in this event which so shocked Arthur Bowes Smyth. Surgeon Bowes Smyth was an evangelical Christian, and so might have been easier to surprise than some, though he had been surgeon on *Penrhyn* for the past ten months and should have been beyond surprising.

There were certainly grounds for a riotous, desperate party of some sort. The women had been on their ships a deranging nine months. They had arrived inextricably in this outlandish and humid summer place; this was the unfamiliar and inscrutable region that would contain their bones. They would be buried in sandstone-strewn earth amongst the angular and tortuous eucalyptus trees. Their frenzy was that of people ejected from the known world and making a rough if brutal bed in the unknown one. Antipodean licentiousness had its beginning here and, almost certainly, Antipodean rape.

'While they were on board ship,' wrote the calmer, though still outraged Watkin Tench, 'the two sexes had been kept most rigorously apart.' (This was not a correct perception.) 'But, when landed, their separation became impracticable and would have been, perhaps, wrong. Licentiousness was the unavoidable consequence and their old habits of depravity were beginning to recur. What was to be attempted? To prevent their intercourse was impossible, and to palliate its evils only remained. Marriage was recommended.'

That was the voice of the Enlightenment, not of the fervent. Social good might arise from a regulated mingling of the sexes, and licentiousness was to be abhorred not so much as an abomination in God's eyes but as a threat to reason and good order.

The orgy prevailed until the dripping, thundery small hours of 7 February, but by noon that same day civic formalities took hold. All the marine officers, their metal gorgets glistening at their throats, took post before their companies, which marched off the allocated, rough-hewn parade ground to adjoining ground cleared for the occasion, 'whereon the convicts were assembled to hear His Majesty's commission read'.

Bowes Smyth and Collins describe a scene which could be seen as Python-esque if one abstracted the symbols and rituals from their potency and from the inherent beliefs of its more significant participants. Phillip, having dressed in full uniform of post-captain and wearing his British and Portuguese awards on his breast, emerged from his palazzo of canvas and proceeded to the ceremonial ground at the head of the cove. Upon arrival, he took off his hat and 'complimented' the marine officers, and the marines lowered their colours to him and paid him respect as governor. The marines then formed a circle around the whole of the convicts, men and women, who were ordered to sit down like so many schoolchildren on the ground. A camp table had been set up with two red leather cases laid on it—the commissions and letters-patent, ready to be unsealed and intoned by Judge-Advocate Captain Collins.

As Phillip stood by, Captain Collins read aloud the documents signed by King George and his Cabinet members which empowered Phillip in New South Wales. Waves of august language rose and perched like birds in the trees: George III by the Grace of God, King of Britain, France and Ireland 'to our trusty and well-beloved Arthur Phillip, Esquire'. Never had a more exceptional claim of territory been uttered than in this commission declaimed amongst the eucalypts and cabbage-tree palms, and heard without comprehension by the no doubt observant Cadigal and Wangal clans of the area. Arthur Phillip was to be Captain-General and Governor-in-Chief over New South Wales, which was an area declared to run from the northern extremity of the coast, Cape York, to the southern extremity of South East Cape; that is, from 10° south to 43° south, or the southern hemisphere equivalent of from the Tagus River in Portugal to Trondheim in Norway. The claim also extended to all the country inland westward as far as 135° east. Whatever was out there, 2400 kilometres or more west of Sydney Cove, a distance greater than London to Moscow, the Crown claimed it. A massive stretch of earth had been mysteriously transformed. It had become, for the first time, estate and realm.

The claim, however, did not run all the way to what would prove to be the west coast of Australia. Phillip knew well enough that the fact it did not go further than 135° east made room for the claims of other nations, especially the Dutch, who had made many landings in what is now called Western Australia. Even though the Dutch despised it as a desert coast and had not yet claimed it, their sensitivities had to be respected. And, to the north, the Portuguese had a long-standing claim on Timor, with which George III and his ministers saw no reason to quarrel, particularly given England's friendly relationships with Portugal. Just the same, it was a massive claim as it stood, close to three-fifths of what would later prove to be a continent of almost 8 million square kilometres, and it was uttered in front of humble, debased and ragtag company, amidst canvas, wattle-and-daub and eucalypts.

The name 'Australia'—Southland—was not mentioned. In 1569 and 1570 respectively, Mercator and Ortellius had used the terms *continens australis* and *australia continens*. Discovering Vanuatu in 1606, Pedro Fernandez de Quiros had posited a southern continent named *Austrialia del Espiritu Santo* and *Austrialia Incognita*. Throughout the sixteenth and seventeenth centuries the terms *Australia* and *Australis* appeared on maps as an ill-defined given. Cook, finding this eastern coast in 1770, thought of it as part of New Holland but did not know if it was a continent or an archipelago stretching away to the west. So he named this east coast New Wales and New South Wales. As a result, in Phillip's commission, the name New South Wales was used, not Australia—the latter name would not then have had international meaning. But the terms New Holland, Botany Bay and New South Wales soon became interchangeable in the mind of the British public.

Arthur Phillip was, by the commissions and letters-patent, to have the power to appoint officials and administer oaths—he would administer one to Collins before that gentleman began his work as judge-advocate. As governor, he had power to pardon and reprieve, punish offenders and to make land grants to civilians. He was empowered also to create a criminal court, a civil court, an admiralty court and so on.

The commission read, the marines fired three volleys to seal this extraordinary advent of authority. The light did not change and the air held its humidity, and somewhere in the huge harbour, native women fished from the insecure platforms of their bark canoes, and a vast, mute electric-blue sky hung sceptically over the giant claims of the British. Wise gods would have laid odds that this exercise could not succeed.

The volleys fired off, Phillip spoke to his charges—Bowes Smyth used the word 'harangued'. There was no exhilaration to what he said. He was not in the mood for eloquence, and perhaps suffered from a certain post-landing depression and the onset of the gritty task. So he offered them no golden promise. He spoke more like a new captain appointed to cut an unruly crew down to size. He told them he had observed them to see how they were disposed. By now, he knew that many among them were incorrigible and he said that he was persuaded that nothing but severity would have any effect on them. If they attempted to get into women's tents of a night, the soldiers had orders to fire upon them. (This would prove an unenforceable threat.) He had observed that they had been very idle—not more than two hundred out of six hundred of them were at work. Phillip told his people that labour in Sydney Cove would not be as severe as that of a husbandman in England who had a wife and family to provide for. They would never be worked beyond their abilities, but every individual should contribute his share 'to render himself and community at large happy and comfortable as soon as the nature of the settlement will admit of'. In England stealing poultry was not punished with death, he said; but here that sort of loss could not be borne and it was of extreme consequence to the settlement that chickens and livestock be preserved for breeding. Stealing the most trifling item of stock or provisions therefore would be punished with death. This severity, he said, was contrary to his humanity and feelings for his fellow creatures, but justice demanded such rigid execution of the laws, and if they stole food, the convicts might implicitly rely on justice taking place. This extraordinary executive decision by Phillip would ultimately scythe down a number of those felons presently sitting and listening to him.

After his plain speech to the convicts, the governor retired to a cold collation in a large tent set to one side.

ISLAND OF INNOCENCE

On 12 February Lieutenant King came to Phillip's tented mansion to take the oath as superintendent and commanding officer of Norfolk Island. The coming settlement on that island was designed for the moment to be a haven for relative innocents—a thirteen to fourteen year old felon named John Hudson was slated for Norfolk Island too, a late attempt to separate him from bad influences. King was 'immediately to proceed with the cultivation of the flax plant, which you will find growing spontaneously on the island'. He was also to secure the island 'and prevent it being occupied by the subjects of any other European power'.

King had gone aboard the *Lady Penrhyn* in the earliest days of February to ask Surgeon Bowes Smyth about suitable women to take to Norfolk Island. Amongst those whose attitude Bowes Smyth praised to King was Ann Innett, a mature Worcestershire woman, a former mantua-maker. In the future she would become King's housekeeper and lover.

Two weeks of storms kept *Supply* off the Norfolk Island coast. But when he landed, King was enthusiastic about what he saw while exploring the central valley and the pine-clad hills with his surgeon, Thomas Jamison. No natives inhabited the lovely island—its later record for drowning and shipwrecks might explain why even the Polynesians had avoided it. King's charges, once ashore, pitched tents on open ground on the south side of the island where there was a gap in the reef in the area he named Sydney Bay and, soon, Kingstown. He settled down to manage the community along the lines determined by Phillip as if it were a large farm and the convicts his farmhands. They split sawed pines to build store-rooms and shelters. They sowed the ground. And it all seemed to go better here. Could this become the penal utopia?

Thomas Jamison, an Englishman who had attended Trinity College Dublin and whom Lieutenant Clark called 'a cunning villain', formed an association with Elizabeth Colley of *Lady Penrhyn*, and produced two illegitimate sons for whom he would provide. But there was also the idyll: one of the young women, Olivia Gascoigne, would soon marry Nathaniel Lucas, a carpenter and cloth thief, by whom she would have thirteen colonial children.

As fresh gales combed the great pines of the island and thunderheads hung low, King was delighted to find turtles on a sandy beach on the eastern side of the island. On 3 March, however, John Jay, one of the *Supply*'s quartermasters, insisted on trying to catch a turtle in the surf 'altho' desired to desist', and drowned. He would not be the last to suffer death in Norfolk Island's turbulent surf.

Later in the month, indeed on St Patrick's Day, King recorded that he had found by experiment, soaking and drying '. . . that the flax plant which Captain Cook takes notice . . . in no manner resembles the flax of Europe'. The finished product was useless.

The lash made its entry into Norfolk Island like the entry of the serpent into Eden. A fourteen-year-old (Charles McClennan) tried to steal rum out of the surgeon's tent and was punished with three dozen lashes. Hail destroyed corn, barley and wheat, and grubs all the potatoes. The sawyers were poisoned by trying out some native beans, and Charles McClennan (also McLellan) was again given lashes for uttering some very seditious and threatening words.

What exchanges occurred between King and his housekeeper, the convict Ann Innett, in his primitive cottage of pine-wood go unrecorded, but it became a connection of some moment, and he would be willing to raise and educate its fruits, which would turn out to be two sons.

THE FOOD QUESTION

On landing, Phillip had implemented his radical plan to provide full rations from the two years of supplies the ships had brought. Convicts were to receive an equal share to men and officers—7 pounds (3.2 kilos) of salt beef or 4 pounds (1.8 kilos) of pork, 3 pints (1.7 litres) of dried peas, 7 pounds of flour, 6 ounces (170 grams) of butter, half a pound (227 grams) of rice or, if it were not available, an extra pound (454 grams) of flour. Females, whether marines' wives or fallen creatures, received two-thirds of the male ration. Phillip had no doubt at all that those rations needed to be protected from bullies and thieves by the sanction of death.

Talkative Major Robbie Ross, and many in the military, thought it appalling to give a lazy or malingering convict the same ration as an industrious one, or as one of His Majesty's marines or, for that matter, as the governor himself. He complained that the convicts were unduly 'sustained by the humanity (I might have said folly)' of the government. His vision was that, within bounds, personal industriousness should be encouraged by imposed hunger, and application rewarded with extra rations.

But Phillip knew that chaos and a wild unofficial market in food would result from an inequity in rations. He was also aware from long naval experience of inspecting opened barrels of rations that the contents were never as copious in reality as they were on paper. The weight of beef and pork was enhanced in many cases by bone and fluid, and the meat, so mummified that sailors and convicts called it 'mahogany', shrank to a much lower weight when the convicts took it to the communal coppers near the women's camp to be cooked. The butter was inevitably rancid and the weight of flour and rice included plentiful weevils. Phillip also knew that rations would soon need to be reduced unless the hinterland and the harbour proved unexpectedly to be bountiful sources of food. Indeed, the first reduction of 12 pounds (5.4 kilos) per every 100 pounds (45.4 kilos) of beef, and 8 pounds (3.6 kilos) in every 100 pounds of pork would be ordered within seven weeks.

Phillip's opening threat about food-stealing was based on a sense that hunger could bring everything undone. A minor ineptitude on the part of Lord Sydney or Evan Nepean or their bureaucrats, or some disaster overtaking a store ship at sea, could lead to a scene of white cadavers amongst the eucalypts, and even of that most feared and unclean phenomenon, cannibalism.

Punishment meted out that February had much to do with food. One Thomas Hill had forcibly taken a quantity of bread from a weaker convict. It must have been a mere morsel for him to have been spared the gallows, but the crime shows that for many in Sydney Cove hunger was already biting, not least because it was almost impossible for Phillip to prevent convicts trading or gambling their rations, and being left voracious for days on end. Hill was sentenced to be kept in irons for one week and fed on bread and water on the little sandstone knob of an island off the eastern end of Sydney Cove. A breeches-maker from Dorset who had as his founding criminal offence stolen a silver watch, Hill became the first man to occupy that rock which would acquire the name Pinchgut.

A West Country fisherman-cum-smuggler named William Bryant was put in charge of fishing in the harbour, and a black market in fish seems to have begun early in Sydney Cove. Of necessity, Phillip blessed him for his skills and his ability to fish the tides. However, the fishing, together with hunting undertaken by Phillip's official convict-huntsman, the Irishman John McEntire, began early to impact upon the food supply of the native people and generate resentment.

In Sydney Cove that February, four young men with robust appetites were caught with stolen butter, pease and pork from the tented storehouse. Thomas Barrett, the young man first condemned to death at thirteen and who had managed to counterfeit coins aboard the *Charlotte* now faced the death penalty for a third time under the terms laid down by Arthur Phillip. Henry Lovell, a London ivory-turner in his mid twenties, and Joseph Hall, another graduate of the ship *Mercury*, also appeared before Judge-Advocate Collins and his bench of officers. The judicial panel condemned them all to hang.

John Ryan, a London silk-weaver, the fourth man involved, also faced the bench. He was sentenced to 300 lashes, being adjudged more a receiver than thief.

Sydney Cove was now to achieve its first executions 'in terrorem, testimony to the Majesty of the Law, a Dreadful and Awful Example to Others'. At five in the afternoon of a late February day, with the summer sun falling down the sky behind them, the marine garrison marched to the place of punishment, probably a Port Jackson fig-tree like the one beneath which the Reverend Johnson had given his first sermons, between the men's and women's camp on the western side of Sydney Cove. All the convict population was compulsorily gathered to see this demonstration. Barrett asked to speak to one of the convicts, a *Mercury* crony, Robert Sideway, who on the *Friendship* had incurred a flogging and chaining. This request was granted and a confidential hugger-mugger passed between them. Then Barrett requested the chance to talk with one of the women but was refused, and mounted his ladder under the tree, as did Lovell and Hall, the nooses hanging level with their necks. But as all three men stood there, Major Ross was approached by a sentry who came running from the governor's tent with a 24-hour stay of execution for Lovell and Hall. They came down their ladders and it was time for the final rites for Barrett. 'The Reverend Mr Johnson prayed very fervently with the culprit before he was turned off, and performed every office appertaining to his function with great decorum.' Barrett, of 'a most vile nature', expressed not the least signs of fear until he mounted the ladder, 'and then he turned very pale and seemed very much shocked'.

He was not the day's only victim. A young convict named James Freeman, sixteen when he was sentenced to death at Hartford and reprieved in 1784, had been given the task of being the penal colony's hangman. Earlier in February 1788 he too had been sentenced to death for stealing flour from another convict, but there was evidence that he stumbled on the flour cached in the woods. Governor Phillip pardoned him on condition he become the public executioner. Freeman hated his work and believed it would make him a pariah, and in the case of Barrett, he delayed fixing the rope and taking Barrett's ladder away for so long that Major Ross threatened to have the marines shoot him. Phillip's old clerk and now the provost-marshal, Harry Brewer, said Surgeon Worgan 'was under the disagreeable necessity of mounting the ladder himself in order to fix the halter'.

Having called on the convicts all to take warning from his fate, Barrett was 'turned off' at last by the convict Freeman. The First Fleet children saw Barrett asphyxiate and piss his pants and were thereby educated in the broad power of authority. What the Cadigal, drawn by the sound of drums and observing from the bush, thought of this strange ritual would be recorded later. They were astonished and appalled. Strangulation was not one of their punishments. They measured retribution in the more calculable currency of blood.

Throughout the century, surgeons and physicians, helped by robust beadles and porters, had stolen the bodies of the hanged from Tyburn Hill and the newer scaffold outside Newgate. But in New South Wales, science had not advanced enough to threaten the eternal rest of Barrett. Overnight a thunderous downpour fell on his grave as convicts darted from camp site to camp site with a petition to the great central presence, Phillip, who would find himself presented the next morning with a written appeal from the mass of the felons begging that the sentences of Lovell and Hall be commuted. The people who signed it knew well enough that the court system was a lottery, that the condemned had probably been worked at by hefty marines and temporary constable convicts before they confessed, guilty as they may well have been.

Phillip let the preparatory rites go ahead. Prim Ralph Clark, leading a guard, collected the two men from Harry Brewer's keeping and marched them to the execution site. Johnson prayed with them as they mounted the ladder and Freeman prepared the nooses. But then the judge-advocate, David Collins, arrived with a commutation of sentence. Lovell was to go to Norfolk Island for life, and Hall to be stuck indefinitely on Pinchgut.

With the beginning of ration reductions, a level of hunger and a great yearning for the lost delicacies of Britain became the lot of all the settlement. Despite the best efforts of William Bryant and John McEntire, fresh meat from marsupials like the kangaroo and wallaby and fresh fish from Port Jackson were in inadequate supply, and much of what was caught went to the hospital. Men and women began to remember with passionate fondness the food pedlars of the English towns, the sellers of watercress, asparagus and chestnuts, cakes, mutton and pork pies and steaming sausages, oysters, fish and fruits in season. How richly they must have talked about the horse-drawn early-breakfast stalls which would set up on some corner or by the approaches of a bridge and sell scalding tea and coffee and hot, fresh bread soaked in butter, all for a halfpenny. The people of Sydney Cove had wronged the cities which had presented them with such delights, and now they were being punished in a shire where the salt of their meat was outweighed only by that of their tears.

A SOLDIER'S TRIAL, AND MARRIAGES

As much as Lieutenant Ralph Clark expected to be bringing down judgment on the heads of the convicts, he was in fact first summoned to a tent near the marines lines to sit on a court martial to hear relatively minor charges against marines. The most interesting case had to do with sexual conflict between a soldier and a convict. Private Bramwell had struck a convict woman, Elizabeth Needham, 'an infamous hussy', according to Lieutenant Clark. She had once tried to shoplift stockings from a West End business and confuse a fashionable hosier, and had already been married when sent to Newgate. Aboard *Lady Penrhyn*, she had become Private Bramwell's lover for part of her time at sea, but when Bramwell asked her to accompany him into the woods behind the camp, she would not go. Since the male convicts had been landed, and she had been free of shipboard coercion, she had met with a convict named William Snailhorn, and she intended to marry him.

'Good God,' wrote Clark, 'what a scene of whoredom is going on there in the women's camp—no sooner has one man gone in with a woman than another goes in with her.' Yet was it all as random and profoundly immoral as he thought? Ashore, there was more future for Elizabeth Needham in Snailhorn than in an authoritarian, woman-beating marine. The marriage between Snailhorn and Needham would endure and produce three native sons.

Bramwell was sentenced to 200 lashes for assaulting Needham. Thus, a marine disappointed in lust was the first non-convict in Sydney Cove to feel the lash on his back. He received 100 strokes on the parade ground at the steel triangle to which he was strapped, and after that was sent to hospital to recover. It was all according to Sydney's and Phillip's plan that convicts and the free be equal before the law.

Impending partnerships were in the air, and so were the ends of partnerships. Virtually as soon as the store ship *Golden Grove* anchored in Botany Bay, the Reverend Johnson had been rowed across to the *Lady Penrhyn* to christen a newborn child named Joshua Bentley. Perhaps, with hindsight, Joshua could be counted the first white Australian. His mother, Mary Moulton, tried at Shrewsbury in March 1785 for burglary with a value of 61 shillings, had been sentenced to transportation for seven years. By the time she left England on the *Lady Penrhyn*, she had already served four years, she was twenty-two, and had become the lover of the sailor Joshua Bentley.

Little Joshua's parents must have known, like Mary Brenham and her sailor, and Sarah Bellamy and hers, that separation was inevitable, since the *Lady Penrhyn* was to return to England via China as soon as it was expeditious for the ship to leave. Some shipboard partners were ready for the separation, but some were bound to each other by desperate love.

On the colony's second Sunday, however, everyone but the sailors was ashore—and indeed, some of them were too, illicitly. The Reverend Johnson held service before the mustered convicts and marines on the east side of the cove 'under a great tree'.

That Sunday is momentous in so far as Reverend Johnson, son of a wealthy Yorkshire farmer, was what came to be called 'Low Church'. He brought Low Church sentiments to Australia, and they remained. He was a member of the Eclectic Society, a movement of evangelical priests and laymen who were influenced by John Wesley, but not to the extent that they abandoned the Established Church and became openly Methodist. Their social program, however, included a desire to reform prisons and to end slavery, and Johnson stood in reaction to a system in which vicars received 'livings', including land, and were often known for the quality of their 'hospitable tables' rather than their hours of prayer.

Before coming to New South Wales, Johnson had gone down to one of the Woolwich hulks run by Duncan Campbell, and found it worse than his imaginings of hell. If there had been any reforming zeal about prisons in Johnson when he was first appointed, meeting the profane convicts ended it. When he first preached from the quarterdeck aboard the fleet in Portsmouth to convicts who had been brought up from below, he tried to interest them in the major theological debates of the day, questions of the nature of free will and grace which lay at the centre of his own consciousness but which made pickpockets laugh. An unsympathetic and agnostic Phillip requested him to begin with and stick to practical moral subjects.

So, in the tale of the First Fleet, Johnson has always held the place of irrelevant and unworldly ninny. But he was respected as a spiritual adviser by the godly Lieutenant Dawes and others. Now, after service read according to the rite of the Anglican Church, children were christened, fruits of the penal experiment and the nine-month voyage. The daughter of Private Bacon and his wife, Jane, was christened alongside the infants of bondage: John Matthew, son of Catherine Prior, West Country highway robber; and Joseph Downey, child of the adolescent felon Sarah Bellamy. Both latter children were sickly from the voyage and suffering in the high summer heat, which might explain their mothers' touching desire to see them baptised. Both would die that month, Sarah's little Joe Downey first, on 29 February—as far as we know the first European child to be received into Sydney's soil.

After the baptisms, five convict couples were edifyingly married by the Reverend Johnson. Ralph Clark said that he was sure some of the people getting married that day had spouses in England. But had Phillip known some of them were married elsewhere, he would probably not have stood in the way of these new alliances. For the betrothed were in a new earth under a new heaven. Their British marriages were of no help in moderating their behaviour here. As Tench had observed, 'Marriage was recommended.'

One of the couples married that day was the young Norwich Castle pair whose destiny had so affected the English public: Henry Kable and Susannah Holmes. This union, between two marginal people in a place forgotten by God, would be an abiding tree, the sort of alliance both Johnson and Phillip required—marriage as a moral rudder. It is in a sense a pity they were not the first order of business that day, for they would have brought great honour to the role of Antipodean Adam and Eve. In another age, those trying to validate the penal experiment would have drawn on the example of Henry and Susannah.

A further couple to bespeak Parson Johnson that day were as exceptional as the Kables. They already had a child between them. Or at least Mary Braund or Broad, a handsome Cornish girl in her early twenties, had given birth to a daughter whom she named Charlotte, the same name as the transport she and her new husband, Will Bryant, had travelled on, and it was presumed Charlotte was Will's child. Mary had been guilty, along with two other girls, of ambushing a Plymouth spinster and robbing her of a silk bonnet and goods to the value of £11 11 shillings. As they stood before the Exeter Assizes on 20 March 1786, all three girls were sentenced to hang. Their sentences were reduced to seven years transportation.

On the dreadful *Dunkirk* hulk, Mary had met Will Bryant, the Cornish fisherman about 27 years of age, convicted exactly two years earlier than Mary at the Launceston Assizes for 'resisting the revenue officers who attempted to seize some smuggled property he had'. He was sentenced to seven years transportation as well, so that he had served over four years in the *Dunkirk* at the time he was put aboard the convict transport *Charlotte*. Smuggling, Will's crime, was considered respectable and valid, particularly in Cornwall. Anyone there who had anything to do with the sea was involved in illegal import. Fishermen down-loaded tax-free wine, brandy and tea from French ships, or from British ones nearing port whose captains wanted to avoid paying tax, and brought the goods ashore, where the distribution networks ran deep inland. Good tables of squires and bishops could not be supplied without men like Bryant. In eastern counties like Sussex, smuggling wool out of England without paying tax on it was a common seafaring activity, and bitterness over the excise men, the customs police, would come close to causing civil rebellion.

Perhaps the excise officers who took Bryant were lucky or numerous or both, for it was not considered a grave sin to kill 'these cruel narks' who wanted to impose their excise on goods from France.

The Bryant who married on 10 February in Sydney Cove was a man in whom a native independence and a dark sense of having been used hard were at work. They created in him a determination to return to the known world, and he was very frank, even with Mary, that he did not see a New South Wales marriage as binding should he escape. Yet, uttering her vows before Johnson on the very edge of things, Mary would come to pay a phenomenal price of loyalty to her spouse.

The sailors felt they were being cut out of the nuptial equation. None of them was permitted to marry his convict maid. They were banned in the women's camp. The male convicts were happy to see the rule enforced against those sailors who had lorded over them at sea and who had been able to attract or buy sea-wives with promises of rations and protection. The very day after the weddings, a carpenter and a boy belonging to the *Prince of Wales* were caught in the women's tents. They were drummed out with a marine fifer and drummer playing the 'Rogue's March' and the boy was mockingly dressed in petticoats. It seemed, though, that the authorities were better at keeping the population of sailors away from the women's camp than keeping the male convicts out.

Yet there was purer, more admirable and tragic love. A sailor named John Fisher, from the *Penrhyn*, gave way to his longing to see his convict woman, Catherine Hart, and their infant son, John. Catherine Hart had been nineteen when tried at the Old Bailey in 1784 for some undistinguished act of theft. The prosecutor/victim addressed the judge in these terms about the goods Hart had stolen: 'My Lord, I value them at 30 shillings in order to save her life, because the wretch's life is of no value to me.' The seaman Fisher swam ashore a number of nights to see his lover and child, and died at Sydney Cove on 25 March 1788 of chest infection and dysentery, Surgeon Bowes Smyth attributing his death to his 'imprudence' in swimming ashore naked. 'He would lie about with her in the woods all night in the dews.'

The women of Sydney Cove would often be as extremely practical about marriage as Phillip would have wanted them to be. For, after John Fisher died, Catherine became the lover of marine Lieutenant Robert Kellow, who would leave her with two of his children when he departed the colony.

AU REVOIR, MONSIEUR LE COMTE

As soon as the British ships left Botany Bay, the French built on its north side a palisade fortification to enable new longboats to be constructed in safety. 'This precaution was necessary,' wrote La Pérouse, 'against the Indians of New Holland, who tho' very weak and few in number, like all savages are extremely mischievous . . . for they even threw darts at us immediately after receiving our presents and our caresses.'

Expecting conflict, La Pérouse was not disappointed. In an ill-defined event on the shores of Kamay—Botany Bay—a number of Cadigal, Bediagal and Gweagal natives were shot and wounded in a confrontation. 'We also have the mortification to learn,' wrote Collins, 'that M. de la Pérouse had been compelled to fire upon the natives at Botany Bay, where they frequently annoyed his people who were employed on shore.' Though this brought a general deterioration in the relationship between the natives and all Europeans, 'we were however firstly convinced that nothing short of the greatest necessity could have induced M. de la Pérouse to take such a step'.

Whatever native mischief la Pérouse experienced, it was notable that the new settlers in Warrane—Sydney Cove—seemed to require no fortification, nor was the judicious Phillip tempted to erect any. Some wisdom told him that a new society could not be created from within a state of siege. Not that the people in Sydney Cove had been pestered by natives, who seemed to stay away from the area in the early weeks.

A French waiter named Peter Parris who had been sentenced in Exeter for burglary would soon become the colony's first successful escapee, after talking French seamen into smuggling him aboard one of La Pérouse's vessels. But after the French left Botany Bay he would be lost in the New Hebrides (Vanuatu) with La Pérouse himself and all the other members of the two French crews.

Before that happened, however, Monsieur de Clonard, the captain of the *Astrolabe*, made a visit to Sydney Cove and told Collins and others that he was frequently visited by convicts. Abbé Monges, a scientific priest, accompanied Clonard on the visit and Clark entertained him by letting him look at the butterflies and other insects he was collecting for his wife.

The courtly hostility between the English and French had never been so remotely played out as here, in Warrane, Sydney Cove.

FINDING AN AMBASSADOR

On the second Saturday of February, two natives came down to the Sydney Cove camp, to within a small distance of the governor's canvas house. They were 'both men pretty much advanced in life' and bore long spears. The governor, determined to be courteous, put on his coat and went out to meet them with a number of officers, and gave one of them a hatchet 'and bound some red bunting about their heads with some yellow tinfoil'. The two visitors sat beneath a tree but refused to go any further into the new town. One of them spent the time sharpening the point of his spear with an oyster shell, perhaps in the hope of showing the force he had to hand and thus moderating the behaviour of the newcomers.

A black African boy from one of the ships came up to look at these elders and they opened his shirt and examined his chest, and by signs begged for a lock of his hair. Surgeon Bowes Smyth cut off a tress. For whatever reason, they put the boy's hair aside in a wreath of grass, and were quite willing to let Bowes Smyth take some of their own. Perhaps they intended to work some ritual of expulsion by using the boy's hair. Perhaps they thought he was one of them, lost.

Whatever their purpose, one could be sure it was unlikely to be idle, and worthy of a better response than bunting and tinfoil. In fact Phillip would soon hear rumours that some of his people had been involved in the rape and plunder of natives, and ultimately in murder, though there was no direct evidence of any of this. Almost certainly the two elders had come, amongst other motives, to observe the people who were so casual in violating the world set up by the hero ancestors, the beings who created the local environment of each clan and language group in the great period of generation known as the Dreaming.

Other contacts made early in that remarkable month of February 1788 seemed to confirm the idea that the natives were very interested in the new people, but were distressed by their unauthorised taking of fish and game. A pernicious trade in native souvenirs had also started between the convicts on land, and even some of the marines, and the sailors of the transports. The sailors knew they would soon be departing and were willing to buy stolen spears, throwing sticks and native nets as mementos. By contrast, Surgeon Bowes Smyth from the *Lady Penrhyn* admired the subtleties of the native artefacts, particularly the lances with the bone of stingray at one end and oyster shell at the other, and acquired one in return for a looking glass, each side being happy with the transaction.

The women's hand fishing lines, if stolen, were particularly difficult for the natives to replace, being arduously spun from the inner bark of the currajong tree. Women would roll long strips of the bark on the inside of their thighs, twisting it together to make the lines. They used the sap of the red bloodwood tree (*Eucalyptus gummifera*) to prevent the line from fraying. They also used bark fibre to make two-ply fishing nets—*carrahjun maugromaa,* a net to catch fish in—and net bags, in which they carried their fishing lines and other possessions, and hung from their necks or foreheads.

Burra, fish hooks, made either of hardwood or of the spiral vortex of shells, were also stolen. The Eora forebears had fished with hooks and handlines and the multi-point spears the Europeans called fizz-gigs—from the Spanish *fisga,* harpoon—for at least two millennia. The men used canoes chiefly to cross from one bay to another, but always fished in the shallows. One European declared that a native had been seen to catch more than twenty fish in an afternoon by standing up in his canoe and striking at fish with his fizz-gig. These were made of the flowering stem of the grass-tree, or of wattle acacia, the four barbs fastened in place by gum. The wooden prongs were sharpened with fire and headed with animal-bone points, sharp fishbones or teeth, or viciously sharp stingray spurs.

Collins says that at convict musters and morning military parades, every person in the colony had been forbidden by Phillip's order from depriving the natives of their spears, adhesive yellow gum, or other articles. But there were obvious violations, and the bad conduct of a particular boat crew led to a landing party in one of the coves in the lower part of the harbour being driven off with spears.

Tit-for-tat, a game the natives played with the same vigour as the Europeans, was now established. A party of Aboriginal men, perhaps sixteen or eighteen, landed on the garden island of the *Sirius* and carried off a shovel, spade and pick-axe. One of the sailors there picked up a musket and got a shot away. A wounded native dropped the pick-axe. Was the attempt to take this item away straight theft, was it the unknowing and accustomed picking up of whatever lay in nature, or was it an attempt at an adjustment of the books? It was, in any case, interpreted on the newcomers' side only as predictable native thievery. Captain Collins lamented, 'To such circumstances as these must be attributed the termination of that good understanding that had hitherto subsisted between us and them, and which Governor Phillip laboured to improve wherever he had the opportunity.' Collins was fair enough to acknowledge that the loss of their fishing lines and other implements must have created 'many inconveniences' for the Eora.

By the end of February 1788, the indigenous people began to shun the settlement. But contact between the two races was a daily occurrence on the water. The natives were scared of the red-coated marines, the two hundred men of the four companies. 'From the first, they carefully avoided a soldier, or any person wearing a red coat,' wrote an observer. The natives called the musket the *gerubber* or *gerebar*; that is, firestick. Obviously they had had demonstrations of its power.

Yet the disintegration of these intrusive white souls might sometimes have seemed almost certain to some native observers, as well as to Phillip and Ross.

As the Antipodean spring came on and the harvest proved bad, Phillip decided that his principal city should be developed some distance inland from Sydney Cove, because of the better farming land away from the coast, and because Rose Hill, as the new settlement would be called, 'was beyond the reach of enemy naval bombardment'. This reference was to a grievance Major Ross had held against him during the previous months in Sydney Cove, and had complained to the Home Secretary about—that the marines had no point, or stronghold, where they could muster and resist civil unrest or enemy attack. Phillip had thus sent part of the garrison, under Ross, and a number of male and female convicts up the Parramatta River to begin a new settlement at Rose Hill (or Parramatta).

Later, the governor accompanied the surveyor-general, Augustus Alt, to Rose Hill to mark out the town. Alt was a soldier with an expertise in surveying, more aged than Phillip, but like him a man raised in a German household. Phillip and Alt were able to converse in German as they worked at this pleasant task of making a British town.

Phillip was also determined to end 'this state of petty warfare and endless uncertainty' between the races. He intended to kidnap one or more natives and retain them as hostages-cum-language teachers-cum-diplomats in Sydney Cove. He explained the reasons for such an abduction to Lord Sydney: 'It was absolutely necessary that we should attain their language, or teach them ours, that the means of redress might be pointed out to them, if they are injured, and to reconcile them by showing the many advantages they would enjoy by mixing with us.'

On 30 December 1788, Phillip sent two boats down the harbour under the command of Lieutenant Ball of the *Supply* and Lieutenant George Johnston of the marines with orders to seize some of the natives. At Manly Cove 'several Indians' were seen standing on the beach, 'who were enticed by courteous behaviour and a few presents to enter into conversation'. Two men who waded out to the boats to talk were seized in the shallows, and the rest fled, but the yells of the two who had been taken quickly brought them back with many others, some of whom were armed with their long spears. One of the captured natives got away. The other captive, a slighter young man, was tumbled into one of the boats.

There was an immediate counter-attack on the boats—the natives 'threw spears, stones, firebrands, and whatever else presented itself, at the boats, nor did they retreat, agreeable to their former custom, until many muskets were fired over them'.

The male native they had fastened by ropes to the thwarts of the boat 'set up the most piercing and lamentable cries of distress'. His arrival at Sydney Cove was a sensation, women and children and off-duty marines milling about him. Most people in the Cove had not seen a native at close quarters for many months. Like everyone else, Tench rushed down from his hut to assess the hostage. He appeared to be about thirty years old, not tall but robustly made, 'and of a countenance which, under happier circumstances, I thought would display manliness and sensibility'. He was very agitated and the crowds who pressed up round him did not help calm him. Every attempt was made to reassure him as he was escorted to the governor's newly a-building brick house, where someone touched the small bell which hung over the vice-regal door and the man started with horror. In a soft, musical voice, the native wondered at all he saw, not least at people hanging out the first-floor window, which he attributed to some men walking on others' shoulders.

That lunchtime, calmer now, intensely observed by Arthur Phillip, he dined at a side table at the governor's, 'and ate heartily of fish and ducks, which he first cooled'. He drank nothing but water, and on being shown that he should not wipe his hands on the chair he sat on, he used a towel 'with great cleanliness and decency'. The gentlemen observed that his front incisor tooth had been removed at initiation. They would note later that, like his fellows, he was able to rest one-legged and motionless, especially during journeys and hunting, with his other leg bent and the foot notched comfortably above the standing knee. Phillip watched him with less flippancy than the crowd who had accompanied him to the governor's house. As part of the potential peace-making between Phillip and the young man, his hair was close cut and combed and his beard shaved. He seemed pleased with his shorn hair, full of vermin as it had been, which he proceeded to eat, and only the 'disgusted abhorrence of the Europeans made him leave off'. He was now immersed in a tub of water and soap and Watkin Tench had the honour to perform part of the scrub.

Despite the young man's accommodating nature, he resisted telling people his name, and the governor first named him Manly, after the cove he came from. To prevent his escape, a handcuff with a rope attached to it was fastened round his left wrist, and at first it seemed to delight him, since he called it *ben-gad-ee* (ornament). In the Government House yard, he cooked his supper of fish himself that night. A convict was selected to sleep in the same hut with him and to be his companion, or as Tench inevitably wrote, 'his keeper', wherever he went.

The next morning, as a cure for his despondency, he was led across the stream and past the parade ground through the men's and women's camps and to the observatory and introduced to Dawes, the young astronomer, who like Collins had a scholarly interest in the natives and would soon start putting together a dictionary of the Eora language. The native could see across the water to the north side of the harbour, where on a sandstone cliff-face a great rock-pecking depiction of a sperm whale had been made by people ritually and tribally connected to him. Spotting also the smoke of a fire lit by his fellows in the northern distance, 'he looked earnestly at it, and sighing deeply two or three times, uttered the word *Gw-eè-un* [fire].' Although depressed and despairing, he consumed eight fish for breakfast, each weighing about a pound.

This young man of subtle and soulful features fascinated Phillip. He ordered that he be taken back to Manly for a visit, so that his people could see he had not been hurt. A longboat carrying armed marines conveyed him close to shore so that he could speak to natives on the beach, or those who edgily waded close. He chatted to his people with a good humour which even survived the return to Sydney. Some of his kinsmen obviously urged him to escape, but he pointed to an iron fetter on his leg. He was taken back to Manly again two days later, but no natives came near the beach this time, so he and his keeper were let ashore to enable him to place a present of three birds into a bark basket left on the beach. He returned to the longboat without having heard a word of either acceptance or rejection. Either his clan considered him vitiated by his contact with the Europeans, or else they were frightened that he was placed on the shore as a bait to attract them, and that they would end up in his position.

He would never be an intimate of his people again, and now he released his real name, or at least one of his names, to his captors. It was Arabanoo. The fleet's children, still impressed by his novelty, would flock around him, and he treated them with great sensitivity—'if he was eating, [he] offered them the choicest morsels,' said Tench. He does not seem to have had a volatile disposition and to have been wistful and sensitive by nature. Since everyone, including Phillip, was enchanted by him, his continued presence at Government House almost became its own point. For he did not learn English quickly, at least not to the point where he could make Phillip any wiser on the grievances of the natives.

And though he was an honoured courtier and ambassador during the day, every night Arabanoo was locked in with his convict.

All Arabanoo's dietary details were recorded by young Watkin Tench, whose account in part patronises Arabanoo, but who was not immune to his fascination. Arabanoo's appetites and actions were therefore of crucial interest. Tench recorded, for example, a small excursion the native had on the *Supply* when it left for Norfolk Island in February 1789. Arabanoo and the governor and other gentlemen were aboard *Supply* simply for the journey down the harbour, but the native was in an agitated state as the vessel was lifted by the great swell of the Pacific through Port Jackson's heads. By now he had been freed from his shackle and was as attached in friendship to Phillip and Tench and others as they were to him, yet he seemed to fear they were taking him out of the known world, and every attempt to reassure him failed. Near North Head, he lunged overboard and struck out for Manly, attempting to dive under the water, 'at which he was known to be very expert'. But his new clothes kept him up and he was unable to get more than his head beneath the surface. Picked up, he struggled, and on board sat aside, melancholy and dispirited. His experience of having clothed himself in alien fabric that took away his power in the water served him as great proof of the inadvisability of his situation. But when the governor and his other friends descended into a boat to return to Sydney Cove and he heard them calling on him to join them, 'his cheerfulness and alacrity of temper immediately returned and lasted during the remainder of the day. The dread of being carried away, on an element of whose boundary he could form no conception, joined to the uncertainty of our intention towards him, unquestionably caused him to act as he did,' wrote Tench.

Arabanoo could not mediate between the natives and the more militant members of the settlement, who turned out to be the convicts and ordinary soldiers. On 6 March 1789, sixteen convicts, feeling vengeful towards the natives, left their work at the brick kilns towards the south-west of the Sydney Cove settlement and, without permission, marched south on the track which snaked along a forested ridge above bushy coastal headlands and beaches on one side, and lagoons to the west, then down to the north side of Botany Bay. They were sick of occasional thefts and depredations, and meant to attack the Botany Bay natives and relieve them of their fishing tackle and spears. So began the first vigilante expedition in New South Wales history. 'A body of Indians, who had probably seen them set out, and had penetrated their intention from experience, suddenly fell upon them. Our heroes were immediately routed ... in their flight one was killed, and seven were wounded, for the most part severely.' Those who ran back to Sydney gave the alarm, and a detachment of marines was ordered to march to the relief of the wounded, but the natives had disappeared and the detachment brought back the body of the man who was killed. At first the convicts claimed they had gone down to Botany Bay to pick sweet tea and had been assaulted without provocation by the natives, 'with whom they had no wish to quarrel'. Gradually, their story developed holes.

Seven of the survivors of this expedition appeared before the criminal court and were sentenced to receive each 150 lashes and wear an iron on the leg for a year, to prevent them from straggling beyond the limits prescribed to them. Tied up in front of the provisions store, they were punished (for example's sake) before the assembled convicts. For this flaying, the governor made a point that Arabanoo should accompany him down to the triangles, and the reason for the punishment was explained to the native, both 'the cause and the necessity of it; but he displayed on the occasion symptoms of disgust and terror only'.

At this time, the ration had been reduced to 4 pounds (1.8 kilos) of flour, 2½ pounds of pork and 1½ pounds of rice. The need for more than that in both quantity and variety was legible in part in the curio-hunting expedition the brick-kiln men had recently engaged in. Phillip had needed, too, to reduce the convicts' working hours: from sunrise to one o'clock now comprised their working day. As in so many other areas, Watkin Tench gives us a frank and telling example of how people lived then. 'The pork and rice were brought with us from England: the pork had been salted between three and four years, and every grain of rice was a moving body, from the inhabitants lodged in it. We soon left off boiling the pork, as it had become so old and dry that it shrank one-half in its dimensions when so dressed. Our usual method of cooking it was to cut off the daily morsel and toast it on a fork before the fire, catching the drops which fell on a slice of bread or in a saucer of rice.'

A shortage of pease, compacted pea porridge, deprived the inhabitants of both Sydney and Rose Hill of their chief source of vitamin B, increasing their vulnerability to infection and showing up in a hollowed-out appearance and leg ulcers. Arabanoo, however, seemed exempted from these rations. In the event he escaped back to his people, Phillip did not want the natives to know that the newcomers' hold on New South Wales was so tenuous, so threatened by hunger.

Phillip had in desperation already sent the *Sirius* to the Cape of Good Hope, stripping the ship of its cannons to allow all the more food to be stowed aboard. But Hunter's vessel was not in the height of repair and there was no guarantee it would be back.

WHO GAVE THE EORA THE SMALLPOX?

The Eora were threatened in a new way too. Sergeant Scott noted on 15 April 1789 that when he went with a party to cut grass-trees for thatching he found three natives lying near a beach, a man and two boys, one of the latter dead from what looked like smallpox, and the other two very ill. It is interesting that the idea of smallpox amongst the natives aroused no great concern for their own safety amongst the Europeans. To a seaman like Arthur Phillip, scurvy was of far greater concern than would be a smallpox outbreak. Though it could be lethal, smallpox was a disease the British were used to. Many Sydney Cove and Rose Hill people of all classes carried the pitted faces of survivors of the illness. The comeliest of the transported women were marked by having suffered the disease earlier in their lives. By the standards of the eighteenth century it was eminently survivable, and on top of that, it seems that from early in the century many Englishmen and women had already been inoculated against it.

The up-to-date Surgeon White had carried with him on Phillip's fleet a flask of 'variolous material', *variola* being the Latin name of smallpox, just in case he needed to inoculate the young against an outbreak in the penal colony. Phillip would soon check with White whether that tissue had somehow escaped its flask at the hospital and thus spread itself to the natives.

Visiting the beach in Port Jackson where the sufferers had been seen, Phillip and his boat party found an old man stretched out on the ground while a boy of nine or ten was pouring water on his head from a shell. The boy had the lesions on his skin too. Near them lay a female child, dead, and, a little further away, her mother. 'The body of the woman showed that famine, super-added to disease, had occasioned her death.' Here was an acknowledgment that Eora were going hungry from the pressure the settlement was putting on their food supplies. Arabanoo worked with his hands digging sand to prepare a grave for the dead girl child. He 'then lined the cavity completely with grass and put the body into it, covering it also with grass, and then filled the hole'. He made no provision for the woman's body.

The man and boy were taken back to Surgeon White's hospital in Sydney Cove and placed in a special quarantine hut.

Boat crews began to see dead natives everywhere, the bodies abandoned by streams and on beaches, or littering caves. The disease disqualified the victim from receiving the normal funeral rituals, it seemed. Either because the natives were too disoriented or too sick themselves, the binding up of a body with various talismanic possessions in a sort of death canoe of paperbark, or the burial in shallow earth, or ceremonial cremation—all of which were previously practised in the Sydney area—no longer occurred.

In Surgeon White's quarantine hut, the older native suffering from the disease kept looking into his son's cot, 'patted him gently on the bosom; and with dying eyes seemed to recommend him to our humanity and protection'. The boy's name was Nanbaree, for his father, shivering, called to him out of a swollen throat. When Nanbaree's father died, the boy is said to have surveyed the corpse without emotion and simply exclaimed, 'Bo-ee [dead]'. It was the gracious Arabanoo who placed the old man's body in its grave. He had been tentative about whether the body should be buried or burned, and Tench read this as his being solicitous about which ceremony would most gratify the governor. His hesitation might rather have come from the fact that he was not of the same blood as the dead man, and so was not entitled to carry out the full funeral rite. In any case, his behaviour that day, his tenderness and generosity towards the ill, persuaded Phillip to release him from his leg bracelet for good.

Nanbaree, the boy, slowly recovered. Despite the Europeans' grasp of the concept of quarantine, the extent of the risk Arabanoo was running in visiting him was poorly understood. Many of the children of the fleet had visited Nanbaree and another native child in hospital, and none of them caught smallpox. A native girl and boy, both about fourteen, had been brought in by the governor's boat. The boy died after three days, but the girl recovered. The names by which she would become commonly known were Abaroo and Boorong.

As smallpox continued to rage among the Aborigines, Arabanoo became Phillip's liaison to the dying. Phillip was anxious that the Eora, who were in utter terror of the plague, should know the frightful disease was not his work, was not some weapon of malice or magic on his part. But the Eora had fled. Arabanoo was taken round the different coves of the harbour to try to make contact with his fellows, but the beaches were deserted. 'There were no footprints on them, and excavations and hollows and caves in the sandstone rocks were clogged with the putrid bodies of dead natives. It seemed as if, flying from the contagion, they had left the dead to bury the dead.' Tench watched Arabanoo lift up his hands and eyes 'in silent agony' and then cry, 'All dead! All dead!', and hang his head in grief. When he spoke, he seemed to have a word for the disease—*galgalla*, he called it, and so did other natives who survived it.

Since it was known that Makassan people regularly visited far northern Australia to collect trepang, Phillip, and ultimately historians, would wonder whether smallpox could have been transmitted from the natives of the north through inter-tribal contact over a huge distance down to the south-east coast of New South Wales.

Phillip asked the question in genuine puzzlement. The port authorities in both Rio de Janeiro and Cape Town had checked for signs of smallpox on board the fleet, and Phillip had been able to say there were none. Nor had there been any sign since. White assured him with some heat that the disease had not arisen from his flask of material, which was unbroken and secure on a shelf. Convicts did not covet it, and Aborigines had not entered White's storehouse and taken the flask. Perhaps there had been a sufferer on the French ships, now gone?

Or had someone amongst the gentlemen, someone who hated the natives and saw them as an unnecessary complication, somehow managed to let the disease loose on them via a blanket or piece of clothing? Experts believe the virus was unlikely to have survived the journey from England in dried crusts or clothing for more than a year. One American sailor on *Supply* had died of it, but he was thought to have caught it from infected Aborigines. Though the disease reached out and struck the Eora fifteen or sixteen months after the arrival of the ships, some two years after they had departed England, the Eora themselves never doubted it to be a deliberate attack.

American experience of epidemics amongst native populations had already taught British surgeons that not all people around the globe had a similar level of immunity or resistance to diseases, and the appalling size and density of the pustules on the bodies of the dead Eora people, as well as the lightning progress of the disease amongst living natives, were noted by White and the other surgeons, indicating the natives had never before been exposed to the contagion.

Arabanoo's nursing of the girl Abaroo and the boy Nanbaree had been the cause of great admiration, and even when he grew ill, Tench and Phillip hoped that the symptoms came from a different cause. 'But at length the disease burst forth with irresistible fury.' Everything possible was done for him, given his centrality in both the affections and plans of Arthur Phillip. He allowed himself to be bled by the surgeons and took everything they had to offer. When he died on 18 May, the governor, 'who particularly regarded him', had him buried in the garden of the brick and stone Government House, and attended the funeral. This would not be the last sign of Phillip's affection for the native people, and his feeling of closeness to Arabanoo must have aroused sneers, comment and rumour amongst some.

Along with Arabanoo, an estimated two thousand Eora perished from the smallpox virus in Port Jackson. A native named Colby would later claim that only three males of his clan, the Grass-Tree clan of Cadi, survived, though he did not mention women or child survivors.

FOOD AND MEN'S MINDS

Among the white community with their resistance to the smallpox infestation, hunger remained the issue. By 1789 the stores were held in two buildings of brick and stone designed and built behind Government House under the supervision of a most promising convict, the bricklayer James Bloodworth, with the help of Harry Brewer, who counted builder's clerk among his former occupations. Of Mr Commissary Andrew Miller, a shadowy and vulnerable figure who managed the supplies, Phillip would say that he fulfilled the task appointed him 'with the strictest honour and no profit'. One morning in March 1789, Miller became aware that a long-running theft of food had taken place amongst the marine sentries, who had made copies of the official keys. One soldier turned King's evidence, and named seven marines from various companies who were in the plot to loot the stores during their rotating sentry duties.

A court martial found them all guilty of plundering the stores. Their execution, carried out on a scaffold erected between the two storehouses, not at the notorious convict hanging tree on the western side of town, was an agony for the corps of marines. Private Easty, who found it sinister that the gallows had been erected before sentence was passed, was in the ranks of marines paraded to witness the hangings. By now his coat, like that of other marines, was faded and worn, and his shoes were falling apart. But the military rituals were still maintained, and he had his Brown Bess musket ready to present arms at the solemn moment. 'There was hardly a marine present but what shed tears, officers and men.' And yet in a strange way the corps accepted the inevitability of this public hanging.

Then, not long before Arabanoo was buried in Phillip's garden, *Sirius* relieved the hysteria over food by reappearing on the broad sweep of Port Jackson. It had had the sort of voyage which makes the question of why any man would be a sailor a conundrum beyond our understanding. During the journey the ship's company was afflicted with scurvy so badly that at one stage there were only thirteen sailors available to man the watch, along with the carpenter's crew. Lieutenant Maxwell went mad off Cape Horn and ordered all sail be put on during a gale. Captain Hunter and the surgeon set to work in Cape Town to address the scurvy amongst the crew. The American seaman Nagle said that the disease was so prevalent that when men bit into an apple, pear or peach, blood from their gums would run down their chins. The best cure, he thought, was fresh mutton and vegetables, 'and the captain allowed us to send for as much wine as we thought fit to make use of, the ship's company recovering daily, till we were well and hearty'.

They had left Cape Town with twelve months supplies for the ship's company, and about four to six months of flour at full ration for the entire settlement, as well as various other stores, including 6 tonnes of barley, sundry private items and stores for officers in Sydney, and medical items ordered by Surgeon White. They had good weather until they got off the South East Cape of Van Diemen's Land. In the darkness of a storm they found the luminescence of surf breaking higher than their mastheads on huge rocks ahead. They found themselves with barely enough steerage room, 'embayed' as the term goes, with a heavy sea rolling in upon them and nothing but high cliffs under their lee and the gale to windward blowing them towards the rocks. Nagle heard Hunter, after giving orders for a combination of sail to be set, cry out above the noise of sea and gale. 'He said she must carry it, or capsize, or carry away the masts, or go on the rocks . . . I don't suppose there was a living soul on board that expected to see daylight.'

On arrival through the heads of Port Jackson and then, to the great joy of all, at Sydney Cove, the *Sirius* looked beaten about, was missing the upper sections of her masts (the fore-topgallant masts), had split the upper part of her stem and lost the figurehead of the Duke of Berwick. Lieutenant Maxwell was brought ashore raving to the hospital, and would never recover his sanity. His family sent him a draft of 70 guineas from England, and in his fits he got hold of a hoe and buried the heavy coins singly all over the hospital garden, declaring he'd have a good crop of guineas the next year. He seemed to represent the madness of exile they all suffered from. If an appropriate ship ever arrived, he would be sent home on it.

How sincerely must Phillip have nonetheless wrung Hunter's hand. There were no newspaper columns or levees to greet Hunter, and yet he had made a remarkable journey without hope of great notice or publicity. What in the northern hemisphere would have gained him renown gained him here an invitation to the governor's dinner table, with the proviso that applied to all officers so honoured, that they bring with them their own bread roll.

CHAPTER 6

THE WEIGHT OF PRISONERS

By August 1787, three months after Phillip's fleet had sailed, the Sheriff of London and Middlesex wrote to Lord Sydney about the problem of overcrowding in Newgate Gaol. Most of the 700 Newgate prisoners were living in crowded wards designed for two-dozen people and crammed with twice as many. The sheriff worried about the coming winter, and the prospect of death from congestive disease and gaol fever (typhus) amongst his charges. Throughout Britain, gaolers wrote to complain that they had been promised that they would be able to move some of their prisoners down to the hulks once the convict fleet had left in May 1787, and this promise had not been kept.

When Lord Sydney was asked about future plans, he told the Treasury he wanted to send at least two hundred women from Newgate and the county gaols to New South Wales, but only when favourable reports of the new colony's progress arrived. Just in case the women could be transported, William Richards (who had fitted out the First Fleet), was given a contract to take up a suitable ship, and in November 1788 officials looked over a 401-ton (409-tonne) ship named *Lady Juliana* at the Royal Navy's Deptford dockyard, and found it to be fit to transport convicts.

Richards appointed George Aitken as *Lady Juliana*'s master. Aitken was conscientious in fitting the ship out, and very willing also to co-operate with the naval agent put aboard, Lieutenant Edgar. Edgar had been Captain James Cook's master, that is, navigator, on HMS *Discovery* during Cook's last voyage in 1776–79. Little Bassey, as his nickname went, was middle-aged, shocked by nothing and determined to look after the women prisoners' physical and nutritional well-being. A younger man, Dr Alley, was surgeon.

By the end of 1788 a new outbreak of gaol fever had been reported from Newgate. At the Old Bailey sessions just finished all windows and doors had been kept open despite the bitter weather, to prevent the spread of the disease. But berths, or cradles, for the convict women selected to board the *Lady Juliana* were not yet ready, and so the prisoners were not immediately moved out of contagious Newgate. The government still hoped to hear reports from New South Wales before they brought the women aboard the ship. If the colony were judged to be in trouble, Captain Aitken might have to transport those aboard *Lady Juliana* to Nova Scotia, despite the hostility of the people of that province to the idea.

It was not until March 1789 that *Prince of Wales* arrived in England with the first news of the colony. Phillip's dispatches, though hopeful, and telling of a struggling yet healthily located place, were counter-balanced by the utterly negative voices of Ross and his ally, Captain Campbell. Undersecretary Nepean put more reliance on Phillip than he did on Ross. There was enough basis to order that *Lady Juliana* could conscientiously be filled up for her journey.

The *Lady Juliana* had been moved from Deptford to Galleon's Reach miles downriver from Newgate. One hundred and sixteen women from the prison were embarked during March and April 1789. There was a woman in the death cells of Newgate who would have loved to be with them. Catherine Heyland, in her mid thirties, had been sentenced to death on 2 April 1788 for counterfeiting, and while male counterfeiting drew only the hanging sentence, female counterfeiting was subject to the traditional punishment of burning at the stake. She had been arrested in a police raid on a front garret in Lincoln's Inn Fields used by counterfeiters. Down Catherine Heyland's bodice, the officials found two bags of counterfeit sixpences. Throughout his own trial, a male counterfeiter frequently reiterated that Heyland had been innocent and he had merely used her as a hiding post. A young Irish girl named Margaret Sullivan had previously been found guilty of a separate act of counterfeiting, and she, like Heyland, was condemned to be publicly immolated by fire. To enable her to complete an appeal for mercy, Heyland's (but not Sullivan's) execution was stayed. The *Times* asked whether mankind must not laugh at long speeches against African slavery when 'we roast a fellow creature alive, for putting a penny-worth of quicksilver into a halfpenny-worth of brass?'.

The Sheriff of the City of London had a similar distaste for burning women, and believed Catherine Heyland did not deserve the death penalty anyhow. What can we make, in our own brutal-by-proxy world, of such public savagery? A Westerner who in this age saw eight friends and acquaintances twitch to death at a rope's end, as did the marine garrison of Sydney, or saw a young woman burned alive, as did any gentleman, woman or child who wanted to be a spectator in Newgate Street, would perforce be offered counselling. Not only did Boswell in the spring of 1785 watch nineteen criminals hanged outside Newgate without its spoiling his appetite, but later the same year he persuaded Sir Joshua Reynolds to attend the execution of five convicts at the same place.

Margaret Sullivan seemed to face her unspeakable death in the spring of 1787 with great courage. She spent her last evening praying with a priest and rejected the offer of a treat of strawberries from the sheriff's wife. As was normal at such times, neighbouring inns the next morning profited from the crush. As two male counterfeiters waited on the scaffold, the chaplain of Newgate preached for three-quarters of an hour. Fifteen minutes after the men died, Margaret Sullivan, dressed in a penitential white shroud, emerged with the priest. And it was all done as ordered. The morning *Chronicle* of 17 March 1787 records that Sullivan was 'burnt, being first strangled by the stool being taken from under her'. City worthies sat on a viewing platform nearby, the horrified sheriff amongst them.

Parliament having risen for the summer of 1788, the sheriff pursued Lord Sydney to the country, was taken to his bedroom, and galloped back to London with a four-day stay of execution, arriving at Newgate two hours before the pyre for Catherine Heyland, whose appeal had been unsuccessful, was due to be set alight.

When, to secure against escapes, *Lady Juliana* moved downriver further to Gravesend, Heyland seemed an unlikely candidate to join it. But out of nowhere, mercy descended on her. George III having recovered from his madness, bells were tolled, cannon were fired, and a restorative deity was praised by choirs in St Paul's. The twenty-three female convicts then under death sentence were brought from their condemned cells the following day to the Old Bailey. These women, all young, in various states of clothing, were told by the recorder that His Majesty had granted pardon to them on condition that they undergo transportation for the terms of their natural lives.

Heyland gratefully accepted, but only sixteen of the women did so. Seven snubbed the King's mercy. One of them told the recorder, 'I will die by the laws of my own country before ever I will go abroad for my life. I am innocent and so is Sarah Storer.' Nellie Kerwin, 29 years old, whom one of her shipmates would call 'a female of daring habits', made a politer refusal of transportation in these words: 'I have two small children; I have no objection to confinement for life; I cannot live long.' She had kept a rakish boarding house for sailors at Gosport near Portsmouth.

The recorder warned them not to try to delay things until after ships such as the *Lady Juliana* sailed. They were given twelve hours to think about it. If they refused this beneficence again, they would be sent down from the bar and, 'You will depend upon it that you will suffer death with the first culprits.' In fact they were kept in solitary confinement and brought back to the dock of the Old Bailey after a month, and seem to have gradually come to terms with their pardons.

In journeying to New South Wales on the *Lady Juliana* and devoting a chapter of his journal to it, the ship's steward, John Nicol, a young Scot, gives us a rare view of the transactions between convict women and seamen. He had a positive nature, believing that aboard one found not 'a great many very bad characters' amongst the women. Most had committed petty crimes, he said. He came to earthy conclusions about why these women were being sent to New South Wales—there was a great proportion who had 'merely been disorderly, that is, streetwalkers, the colony at the time being in great want of women'.

While the ship was still in the Thames, he had seen a young Scottish girl die of a broken heart. 'She was young and beautiful, even in the convict dress, but pale as death, and her eyes red with weeping . . . If I spoke of Scotland she would wring her hands and sob until I thought her heart would burst. I lent her a Bible and she kissed it and laid it on her lap and wept over it.'

It was Nicol's job to go ashore and buy supplies for the ship, but he also shopped for convict women who had brought money with them aboard, particularly for a Mrs Barnsley, 'a noted sharper and shoplifter'. Nicol was a little awed by this potent woman who became *Lady Juliana*'s centre of authority and dispenser of favours amongst the other prisoners. They in return were all pleased to serve her and were rewarded with the groceries Steward Nicol bought for her ashore. To add to her other gifts of personality, she became the ship's midwife, one whom Surgeon Alley very much trusted and thus took advice from. He supported, for example, the women's request for tea and sugar in lieu of part of their meat ration and also suggested that they be supplied with soap. He would eventually ask for 'a supply of child bed linen to be sent on board, for some of the women were pregnant . . . ' Mrs Barnsley had left behind in England a somewhat younger husband, Thomas, a musician by trade, now on the Thames hulk *Ceres*. Elizabeth Barnsley, well settled in on *Juliana*, hoped that she would be joined by him in Sydney.

Nicol had been working aboard *Lady Juliana* for three months when the great love of his life came aboard. Seventeen women from Lincoln Castle, riveted irons around their wrists, had come down to Greenwich, travelling for thirty-six hours roped to the outside seats of a coach. Their condition after such a journey in English late winter weather was pitiable; they were tattered, pale, muddied and chilblained. Nicol, as ship's steward and trained blacksmith, had the not entirely thankless task of striking the riveted county prison irons off the women's wrists on his anvil. (He could present a bill of 2 shillings and sixpence to the keeper of the county gaol for each set of shackles he struck open.) In a smithy shack on the windswept deck women bent low to have the work done, and Nicol fell in love with one of them, despite her bedragglement, in the space of performing his task. 'I had fixed my fancy upon her from the moment I knocked the rivet out of her irons upon my anvil, and as firmly resolved to bring her back to England when her time was out, my lawful wife, as ever I did intend anything in my life.'

Sarah Whitelam, the object of this fervour, was a Lincolnshire country girl, thick-accented to Nicol's ear, and perhaps another victim of Enclosure. Nicol had a broad streak of generosity in his demeanour, which this Lincolnshire girl saw in her extreme situation and latched on to. Not that she struck him as a gross opportunist like some of the London women. 'I courted her for a week and upwards, and would have married her on the spot had there been a clergyman on board.'

During their courtship she told him that she had borrowed a cloak from an acquaintance, who had maliciously prosecuted her for stealing it, and she was transported for seven years for unjust cause. Sarah's true crime, to whose record the love-stricken Nicol had no access, was that at Tealby in Lincolnshire she had stolen an amount of material which included six yards (5.5 metres) of black chintz cotton, a number of gowns, seven yards (6.4 metres) of 'black calamomaco', a pink quilted petticoat and a red Duffin cloak. On the spur of whatever criminality or need, it seemed that she had cleaned out an entire small shop-load.

To allow the sort of courtship which Nicol describes, the *Lady Juliana* must have been a relatively relaxed ship, where for their own good the women were allowed on deck for exercise a considerable amount, and some were permitted access to the sailors' quarters to an extent not openly countenanced on most of the First Fleet. Lieutenant Edgar and Captain Aitken were Georgian pragmatists, not evangelical Christians. In a wooden ship of 400 or so tons, there was not a lot of room for private courting, but the poor of the time were used to cramped quarters, to cohabiting in one-room hutches, to copulating by stealth and with minimal privacy. Space for love was not the issue as Nicol chattered away to Sarah Whitelam; Sarah would be pregnant with Nicol's child by the time the ship left England. Thus, as in the First Fleet, the fallen young of Britain were busy at their associations, generating on whatever terms an enlargement of the convict nation towards which they headed.

A number of friends and family of the women of the *Lady Juliana* made plots to rescue particular women before the transport left the Thames. An attempt at Gravesend on the night before sailing was the only successful one—four women of the convict party below decks went over the stern and into a boat. The escapee whose identity we know was 24-year-old Mary Talbot—one of an army of young shoplifters—who fled the ship with her baby, William. But she was later to be recaptured and would find herself, in the end, without any of her children, wasting on a ship to New South Wales, the *Mary Ann*, and soon enough yielding up her bones to that soil.

In early June, at Spithead off Portsmouth, the ship was joined by ninety women from county gaols and five late arrivals from London who had been rushed down chained to the outside of wagons. The last load of women was brought on in Plymouth, and it was July 1789 when the *Lady Juliana* sailed with a crowded prison deck.

Indeed, John Nicol says there were 245 women aboard *Lady Juliana* as she left Plymouth. 'When we were fairly out to sea, every man on board took a wife from among the convicts, they nothing loath.' As the *Lady Juliana* with Nicol and his pregnant Sarah Whitelam made its solitary way out of English waters, past Ushant and into the Bay of Biscay, it was in a sense a precursor, the first ship of an as yet not fully planned Second Fleet to get away. It carried on board a letter Home Office Undersecretary Evan Nepean had written to his friend Arthur Phillip in Sydney Cove, informing him that 'in the course of the autumn I expect that about 1000 more convicts of both sexes will be embarked from the several Gaols and despatched to Port Jackson'.

EXPIREES

By the time *Lady Juliana* left England, Phillip was faced with the continuing problem of convicts saying their time had expired. Phillip's reply, that he regretted he had no records to verify these matters, was 'truly distressing' to many convicts. Several men told the governor that when the records did arrive, they would want to be paid for their labour as free men. One such man was mangled by his attempts to be heard. John Cullyhorn (probably Callaghan) claimed to have been told by Major Ross that he could now do what he liked, his term having finished by July 1789. He came up over the stream to make a direct appeal to the governor on 29 July 1789 for a full pardon on the grounds that his term was served. In the course of his conversation with Phillip, Cullyhorn asserted that Lieutenant-Governor Ross had told him that there were two years provisions available for any convict who finished their time, and he sought to claim them now. Ross denied having told the convict that, and demanded Cullyhorn be punished as a liar. At Ross's insistence but with Phillip's consent, poor Cullyhorn was charged with calumny and sentenced to receive 600 lashes and to work in irons for the space of six months. That is, the court, its judgment influenced by a need to shut up the turbulent Ross, ordered what a historian would rightly call 'a savage (and illegal) punishment for a free Englishman'. For documents arriving in Sydney later would prove Cullyhorn correct—his time had indeed expired.

Privately, Judge-Advocate Collins was not unsympathetic to such people, who were 'most peculiarly and unpleasantly situated'. But the reality was that Phillip could not afford to advance any person two years of rations. Despite the supplies *Sirius* had brought back from South Africa, in November 1789 the ration was reduced to two-thirds again, since there were only five months of *Sirius's* flour left. Amongst other factors, the storehouse supplies had proved to be appetising to rats and various native marsupials—bush rats, potoroos, possums. Nonetheless, said Collins, 'The governor, whose humanity was at all times conspicuous, directed that no alteration should be made in the ration to be issued to the women.'

Despite abiding hunger, by the end of the Antipodean winter of 1789 the camp of Sydney Cove had taken on the look of a permanent town. Two barracks were finished, two storehouses, and the large brick house the governor occupied. Many male and female convicts had brick huts. But the brick-makers were not always the servants of civilization. Because of ongoing turbulent behaviour at night, and a conviction in the camp that the brickfield convicts, who were camped a little way west of town, came down to the men's and women's area to steal property, a Jewish Cockney convict named John Harris, a *Mercury* returnee, came to Captain Collins and asked him whether a night guard might be established, a patrol of reputable convicts.

This was an early example of the New South Wales conundrum, the overthrow of Phillip's early intention that the positions of the free and the condemned should not become blurred. The convicts began to take on an official importance in the great open air experiment of Sydney that they could not have achieved in Newgate or on the hulks. In a criminal kingdom, a clever and reputable man like Harris ended in a position akin to that of police chief. So, without a free police force to keep order, a night watch of eight convicts was initiated at Harris's suggestion. Collins wrote about this paradox. 'It was to have been wished, that a watch established for the preservation of public and private property had been formed of free people, and that necessity had not compelled us . . . to appoint them from a body of men in whose eyes, it could not be denied, the property of individuals had never before been sacred. But there was not any choice.'

For the purpose of night watch patrols, the settlement was divided into four districts, and three men patrolled each. The night watch was soon guarding the chief settlement not only from the nocturnal evil of convicts, but from marines also. When one of the night watch stopped a marine in the convicts' compound, Ross viewed it as an insult, and Phillip was forced, wearily, to ensure it did not happen again.

John Harris's night guard would ensure, Collins recorded, that by comparison with Sydney Cove, 'many streets in London were not so well guarded'.

A SECOND FLEET

In 1789 aging Viscount Sydney had resigned from the Home Office. His replacement, and Nepean's new superior, was the 29-year-old William Grenville. Grenville, soon to be Lord Grenville, was an enemy of slavery and a campaigner for the emancipation of Catholics from the legal disadvantages which had kept them out of civic life. A future prime minister, he was subject to the same political pressures as Sydney had been, and wrote to the Lords Commissioners of the Treasury in early July 1789, telling them, 'His Majesty has therefore been pleased to signify to me his Royal Commands that 1000 of the said convicts should forthwith be sent to New South Wales.' The dispatch of this thousand was exclusive of the women already on *Lady Juliana*.

The Navy Board immediately called for tenders from merchants to supply ships and stores. William Richards, who had so competently and thoughtfully outfitted the First Fleet and the *Lady Juliana*, bid again, but the successful contractor was this time the largest slave transportation company in Britain—Camden, Calvert and King. It is on the face of it a curious decision for an abolitionist to make. Perhaps Grenville wished to do away with laxities in the Home Office. If as a means of turning a new and more efficient page he gave his ministerial consent to the Navy Board's choice of Camden, Calvert and King, he would come to regret it.

In August the charter-parties for a second fleet of ships were signed by the navy commissioners and the London representative of Camden, Calvert and King. The contractors were to be paid a sum of £17 7 shillings and sixpence for each convict embarked, somewhat less than Richards had quoted. Five pounds would be paid to the contractors once the cabins and bulkheads had been fitted, and £10 when the stores had been loaded and the ships were ready to receive convicts. The remainder was to be paid when a certificate was received in London from the commissary in New South Wales confirming that the stores had been delivered. There was no money held back pending the delivery in good condition in Sydney Cove of the convicts themselves.

The Australian legend that the British dumped convicts in Australia was enhanced and very nearly justified by the horrors which would characterise this core section of the second flotilla—just as the *Lady Juliana* helped generate the concept that women's ships were floating brothels.

The War Ministry had been thinking about New South Wales too and decided that the marines who had travelled on the First Fleet would be gradually replaced. During the summer of 1789, from England, Scotland and Ireland, three hundred men were recruited for a new corps, and the first hundred privates and NCOs, along with two captains, three lieutenants, an ensign and a surgeon's mate would travel on the transports of the Second Fleet. The new unit, the 102nd Regiment of Foot, would be more commonly called the New South Wales Corps, but they were also referred to, whether ironically or otherwise, as the Botany Bay Rangers.

Three transports, *Neptune*, *Scarborough* and *Surprize*, were readied at Deptford for the journey. In the meantime a store ship had been sent from Spithead, bound for Sydney Cove, six weeks after the female convicts in the *Lady Juliana*. The ship in question was a naval frigate of 879 tons (897 tonnes), the HMS *Guardian*, and it left Britain richly burdened with the supplies for which Phillip had asked, and with twenty-five 'artificers', convicts with trades, for whom Phillip had also pleaded. In the crew was fourteen-year-old Thomas Pitt, a cousin of the prime minister. With all it carried, and with its small corps of talented convicts, the *Guardian* represented a secure future for the people of New South Wales. Sadly, it would collide with an iceberg south-east of Africa.

ANTIPODEAN ADAM

Salvation could not indefinitely come from outside New South Wales. One of the iconic figures of redemption from within would be the young Cornish convict, James Ruse. As the clerks who had drawn up the lists for the First Fleet had not hesitated before including people who had already served the greater part of their sentence, Ruse, who had been sentenced to seven years transportation to Africa in 1782 for burglariously entering a house in Launceston, had spent five years on the depressing and brutal hulk *Dunkirk*, moored off Plymouth, before being loaded on the *Scarborough*. Without verification that Ruse's sentence had expired, Phillip nonetheless knew enough about him from his supervisory work at the government farm in Sydney Cove to decide to embark on an experiment with him, and turn him into New South Wales's first yeoman. Ruse had told Tench, who admired him: 'I was bred a husbandman, near Launcester [Launceston] in Cornwall,' and in 1789, when he claimed his sentence had expired (it had), Phillip gave him a conditional grant of thirty acres and convict help to clear it in the promising area known as the Crescent on the riverbank near Parramatta/Rose Hill. Phillip also authorised the issue to Ruse of necessary tools and seed for planting. Full title to the land was withheld until Ruse proved himself the first viable farmer.

Phillip, surrounded by men who regularly told him New South Wales could not serve as a place for settled agriculture, wanted to test whether it was possible for a skilled farmer to live off the land. Above all, he needed to rebut the nihilist voices, such as that of Major Ross, who hated New South Wales with an almost theological passion. 'I do not scruple to pronounce that in the whole world there is not a worse country than what we have seen of this. All that is contiguous to us is so very barren and forbidding that the main truth be said, here nature is reversed.' The perverse behaviour of the convicts confirmed Ross in a sense that he was stuck in an irremediably unregenerate land, a country of contrary, obdurate gods.

Indeed, it seemed to Ross that New South Wales bore the same motto as Lucifer, the fallen angel—*Non Serviam*, I shall not serve. The terms 'will not serve' and 'will not answer' pepper the reflections of many diarists and correspondents, but Ross's above all. Ross, for example, criticised Phillip's choice of Sydney Cove for the settlement, declaring it would 'never answer'.

In the face of Ross's negativity, Ruse would symbolise the resourceful agriculturalist and become a living validation of the idea that the Australian earth was, after all, compliantly fruitful. In truth, not even all Ruse's industry and energy could fully prevail over the recalcitrant, leached-down and grudging earth along the Parramatta River, and he would later move to the more remote floodplain areas along the Hawkesbury north-west of Sydney. At the time he got his land grant, there were others Phillip was willing to free and put to the task of sustaining New South Wales. But that was not to happen until he saw what befell this young Cornishman, and how he set about the task.

A NEW ARABANOO

The other experiment which had been in abeyance was the Aboriginal diplomatic experiment which had ended with Arabanoo's death. Tench says that in making a further capture of natives, Phillip needed, amongst other things, to know 'whether or not the country possessed any resources, by which life might be prolonged'.

Reliable Lieutenant Bradley of the *Sirius* was sent out with two boats to capture natives, a task he found distasteful. Northwards, at Manly Cove, he found a number of natives on the beach, and in the prow of one of the cutters, a seaman held up fish, tempting two robust men, a mature fellow and a young man, into the shallows. 'They eagerly took the fish,' wrote Lieutenant Bradley. 'They were dancing together when the signal was given by me, and the two poor devils were seized and handed into the boat in an instant.' The two captured happened not to be local natives but two formidable visitors from the south side of Port Jackson. Both of them fought ferociously to get away from the melee of soldiers, sailors and convicts, but they were up against numbers, and soon shackles were on them. The other natives rushed from the bush and gathered on both headlands of the cove, shaking their spears and clubs.

Bradley wrote, 'The noise of the men, crying and screaming of the women and children, together with the situation of the two miserable wretches in our possession was really a most distressing scene.' It was a bad day's business, Bradley thought, 'by far the most unpleasant service I was ever ordered to execute'.

At the governor's wharf at Sydney Cove, a crowd gathered to see the natives brought ashore, just as they had gathered to see Arabanoo. The boy Nanbaree, who had survived the smallpox and who now lived at the hospital where White had given him the name of Andrew Snape Hamond Douglas White, to honour White's former naval captain and patron, shouted 'Colby' to the older of the two men and 'Bennelong' to the younger. He had often told Surgeon White about fabled Colby, who was his uncle. Both men still bristled with resistance.

Woolawarre Bennelong (this being just one of many alternative spellings of the name) was judged by Tench to be about twenty-six years old, 'with a bold intrepid countenance, which bespoke defiance and revenge'. He was a man of lively, passionate, sociable, humorous character, and well advanced in ritual knowledge, ritual being the fuel and physics of his world, what kept it in place, what kept it so lovable and abundant. He did not quite have the gravitas and the power of eye to be a full-fledged *carradhy*, a doctor of high degree, a curer and ritual punishment man. He did not seek solitude or penance. But he was well-liked around the harbour, and southwards too, around the shallow shores of Botany Bay, where people lived who were related to him by marriage, language and the great rituals of corroboree dance and other secret, communal ceremonies. Sometimes, it would be discovered, he fornicated with their women and bravely stood up under a rain of ritual punishment spears, took his scars and was proud of them. He had an ambiguous relationship with his least favourite relatives, the Cameraigal of the north shore of Port Jackson, whose women he nonetheless had a passion for and whose country he was at various times permitted to hunt in, fish in, socialise in, and join in corroboree—those dances which were more than dances, which preserved and sustained and continued the earth made by hero ancestors. Bennelong had a range of names in a society where people carried many names, and some of his others were Boinda, Bundebunda, Wogetrowey.

Colby was perhaps thirty, more intractable, somewhat shorter but athletic looking, and 'better fitted for purposes of activity', observed Tench. They had both survived the smallpox—'indeed Colby's face was very thickly imprinted with the marks of it'. Hunter would claim Colby was 'a chief of the Cadigal', and his fuller name was Gringerry Kibba Colby. *Kibba*, or *gibba*, was Eora for 'rock', and would enter the settlers' English before long—the children of the convicts and the free being commonly accused of 'chucking gibbers' at each other. Colby, the rock, behaved like one.

Both natives were taken up to the governor's residence. It was the first time Bennelong and Arthur Phillip saw each other eye to eye, a meeting as fateful and defining as that between Cortez and Montezuma, or Pizarro and Atuahalpa. Bennelong and Phillip in particular were mutually enchanted and attracted, and both Bennelong and Colby could see through the deference other white people offered him that Phillip was the supreme elder—*Be-anna*, Father, as Arabanoo had called him.

A convict was assigned to each of the men until they should become reconciled to their capture. The means used to detain them were in their way severe—they were tied at night to their keepers by both ankle chain and rope, and slept with them in a locked hut. At this treatment, Colby yielded no gesture of reconciliation. Why should he, when he suspected a great infestation that killed his clan had come from these people? He planned escape. Genial Bennelong, 'though haughty', not only got on well with the Europeans but enjoyed the experience of doing so, and was his people's first enthusiastic anthropologist. Beneath his conviviality was a desire to work out what these people meant and, perhaps, how to appease them and even make them go away.

After attempting escape many times, Colby managed it on the night of 12 December 1789, while eating supper with Bennelong and their two minders.

This was bad news for his minder, who received 100 lashes for 'excessive carelessness and want of attention'. But Phillip still considered Bennelong a family member, if a tethered one. Phillip took him with Nanbaree to the look-out post and signal station on the south head of the harbour. Bennelong still wore his leg shackle and despite it was able to put on a display of strength and accuracy by throwing a spear nearly 90 metres against a strong wind 'with great force and exactness'. On the way back the boat stopped near Rose Bay, and Bennelong called to a native woman ashore he was very fond of—one of the Cameraigal, named Barangaroo. Barangaroo and other women waded out and talked, were offered jackets, and told Bennelong that Colby was fishing on the other side of the hill, but had been unable to remove the shackle from his leg.

A captive by night, Bennelong had the freedom of the governor's house by day. At Phillip's table, wrote Watkin Tench, Bennelong was quick to make clear how many of his people had died of the smallpox epidemic the previous year— he claimed that one in two had, 50 per cent. Unlike Arabanoo, Tench observed, Bennelong became immediately fond of 'our viands' and would drink spirits without reluctance, which Colby and Arabanoo had not done. A deadly appetite was imbued in Bennelong. But for the moment, wine and spirits did not seem to have a more perceptible impact on him than on any of the gentlemen who sat around him. He liked turtle, too, which he had never eaten before, but which the *Supply* had brought from Lord Howe Island, an uninhabited isle between Sydney and Norfolk Island. 'He acquired knowledge, both of our manners and language, faster than his predecessor had done.' He would sing and dance and caper, and talked about all the customs of his country in a mixture of rudimentary English and Eora on his side, and rudimentary Eora and English on Tench's and Phillip's. 'Love and war seemed his favourite pursuits,' wrote Tench, 'in both of which he had suffered severely. His head was disfigured by several scars; a spear had passed through his arm and another through his leg; half of one of his thumbs was carried away, and the mark of a wound appeared on the back of his hand.' But they served as a map of his adventures, and as well as telling the stories of his exploits, an exercise he loved greatly, he was also explaining a concept of blood justice, and preparing the European mind for the idea that they too might need graciously to receive similar wounds for crimes. The plunders and even the occupation of earth by the Europeans violated the land. Bennelong hoped they could be taught that fact. It might have been one of the reasons he stayed so long in Sydney Cove, and risked his soul among the cloud-people.

'But the wound on the back of your hand, Baneelon!' Tench asked him. 'How did you get that?' Bennelong laughed and told Tench it was received in carrying off a lady of the Cameraigal on the north shore of Sydney Harbour, across from Sydney Cove. 'I was dragging her away; she cried aloud, and stuck her teeth in me.'

'And what did you do then?'

'I knocked her down and beat her till she was insensible, and covered with blood.'

The story—Tench intending it to be more amusing than it seems to us—is credible despite the presence of that non-Eora word, 'insensible'. Bennelong frequently asked the governor to accompany him with the marines in order to punish and even obliterate the Cameraigal, with whom he had both passionate connection and passionate grievance. As for the governor, Bennelong exchanged his own honorific, Woolawarre, with him, calling him by that name, and thus being entitled to call himself Governor. The exchange of names was meant to do both parties great honour and convey closeness of soul. Woolawarre could have been a very significant name in other ways too, for it seems to derive from the Eora words for 'Milky Way' and 'depart'—Phillip being one who had departed the stars, and really should return there, to those great swirls of light in the night sky.

Phillip told former Home Secretary Lord Sydney in a letter that he hoped Bennelong 'will soon be able to inform us of their customs and manners'. The Europeans certainly got to know of Bennelong's highest order of recreation: *boon-alliey*—kissing women. He spoke much of the Cameraigal women, *Cameraigalleons*, as he called them. They were not so much enemy women, but certainly the women of rivals, and were alluring to Bennelong, especially the woman named Barangaroo, who had him under a spell. This glamour of the foreign and the owned might have led to behaviour appalling in European eyes, but marrying out of their family group was one of the mechanisms by which ancient societies avoided incest.

As part of his British training, Bennelong was required to appear at the governor's table in trousers and a red kersey jacket. On Sundays he wore a suit of buff yellow nankeen from China. Tench observed with patronage but with genuine affection too that he was not the least awkward in eating or in performing actions of bowing, drinking healths and returning thanks. He would raise his glass and drink a toast to 'the King', a term which Bennelong associated ever after with a glass of wine.

There were perhaps two dozen or more clans which participated with Bennelong in the common language of the Sydney area. From the south head of Port Jackson to Sydney Cove, and southwards towards Botany Bay, the people were called Cadi and the tribe were Cadigal, and Colby was an important man amongst that group. (The ending *gal* meant country.) On the south side of the harbour from Sydney Cove westwards, the tribe were the Wangal, of whom Bennelong was a member. On the opposite, northern, shore of the Parramatta River from the Wangal was the tribe called the Wallumettagal. Then, on the broader reaches of northern Port Jackson were the Cameraigal, and at Manly the Gayimai, whom Colby and Bennelong had been visiting when captured. These neat divisions merely scratch the surface of the complexity of clans and families and geography. At particular times they all visited each others' territory, and were connected by favours, gestures, swapped names, marriage, ceremonies and ritual knowledge of how to sustain their shared earth.

By April 1790, the shackle was removed from Bennelong's ankle. Arthur Phillip demonstrated his trust, as he could never do with a convict, by letting Bennelong wear a short sword and belt, Bennelong being 'not a little pleased at this mark of confidence'. Indeed, Phillip seems to have been endlessly indulgent to the fellow. Bennelong's allowance was received each week from the commissary stores by the governor's steward, the Frenchman Bernard de Maliez, 'but the ration of a week was insufficient to have kept him for a day'. The deficiency was made up with fish and Indian corn. For if he were hungry, Bennelong became furious or melancholy.

He was also in love and always had a woman to pursue. On 3 May, he pretended illness, and awakening the servant, the Frenchman Maliez, who lay in the room with him, 'very artfully' begged to be taken downstairs. Bennelong 'no sooner found himself in a back-yard, than he nimbly leaped over a slight paling, and bid us adieu'. Collins was a little affronted that the governor's every indulgence had not prevented Bennelong's decamping. But Bennelong had agendas beyond Collins's imagining, including the necessity of performing ceremonials that were pending, of reporting his experiences of the Europeans, and of moving upon Barangaroo, whom Colby was courting.

John Hunter, hearing of Bennelong's escape, made the joke of the season by saying Bennelong had taken 'French leave' from Maliez. When boat crews, sent around to look for Bennelong, called his name in various coves and bays of Port Jackson, the native women merely laughed and mimicked them.

The British were meanwhile finding there was no comfort for them in the hinterland Bennelong was so anxious to embrace again. Lieutenant Dawes travelled west but was defeated by the great bush-entangled precipices of the Blue Mountains. And a former slave, Black Caesar, who had previously proved himself a competent agricultural labourer, 'a notorious convict and native of Madagascar' delivered himself up to the officer at Rose Hill on the last day of the year. He had managed to stay free only since 22 December, when he escaped in a canoe from Garden Island. He had a musket with him and was able to drive Aborigines away from their campfires and eat what they had been cooking. He had also robbed from gardens in Sydney and Rose Hill. When he lost the musket he found it impossible to subsist and was attacked by the natives and received various wounds. Though he would remain an enthusiastic escapee, he was incarnate proof of the uninhabitable nature of the hinterland.

FAMINE

With a sigh of relief but some concern for his charges, in March 1790 Phillip eventually consigned Ross from Parramatta to the command of Norfolk Island, since Lieutenant King had been pleading a need to return to England, and Phillip thought of him as the most reliable man to send to Whitehall with a true account of the poverty of the penal colony.

For the inhabitants of Sydney Cove, the ration at the time Ross was sent to Norfolk provided daily about 1800 calories (7.54 kilojoules) and 56 grams of protein, a minimum for survival. Tench, passing the provision store, saw a man who emerged with 'a wild haggard countenance having received his daily pittance to carry home . . . I ordered him to be carried to the hospital where, when he arrived, he was found dead . . . On opening the body, the cause of death was pronounced to be inanition.' Both soldiers and convicts found they were not able to fulfil tasks. The clothing store was near empty and some convicts lived in tatters and rags. In their camp the women were resourceful with the needles and yarn Phillip had distributed, but many a guard was mounted in which the majority of soldiers lacked shoes. Intense hunger and depression bred a thousand desperate little thefts.

In this emergency, Phillip 'from a motive that did him immortal honour', released to the general stores the 3 hundredweight (152 kilos) of flour which was his personal store, 'wishing that if a convict complained, he might see that want was not unfelt even at Government House'.

Things were better at Norfolk, and Phillip decided to dispatch around 350 convicts on the *Sirius* and *Supply* to the island with Major Ross and Lieutenant Clark. Amongst those travelling to Norfolk were John Hudson, the chimney-sweep. On the way out of Sydney Harbour, the bulky *Sirius* got itself in an awkward situation near the rocks of North Head, as it had earlier off southern Tasmania, and Hunter again just managed by clever seamanship to avoid disaster and a huge accompanying death toll.

John Hunter and *Sirius* had never been to Norfolk Island before, and at a second attempt to land supplies at treacherous Sydney Bay on the south side of the island, despite Hunter's best efforts, and a complicated series of manoeuvres with sails and helm, *Sirius* was blown stern-first howling and creaking onto the reef, where the surf began to batter her to pieces. Sailors began cutting away the masts and rigging and throwing them over the side in the hope that the loss of weight might refloat her: 'In less than ten minutes the masts were all over the side, the ship an entire wreck,' wrote a midshipman. Provisions were brought up from the hold and stacked on the gun deck. If necessary, some of them could be floated ashore. Sailors were tied to ropes and hauled ashore through the surf.

Male convicts already landed volunteered to swim to the wreck as the sea subsided, and liberate the livestock. Having done so, they also raided the ship's cellar. Ross would issue a proclamation against those who 'in a most scandalous and infamous manner, robbed and plundered' items from the wreck. He declared martial law, fearing the pressure placed on resources not only by the newcomers but also by *Sirius*'s crew, who would be stuck on Norfolk Island for ten months.

Little *Supply* survived and left with Lieutenant King, the outgoing commandant, also carrying to Sydney his convict mistress, Ann Innett, and their two small sons, Norfolk and Sydney, whom King intended to rear as his own, as a gentleman should.

In April 1790, a cheerful phenomenon occurred which Hunter, stuck on the island in a small hut, considered an act of divine intervention. Thousands of birds of a species of ground-nesting petrel arrived on the hills of the island, and continued to land each night for four months. 'A little before sunset the air was thick with them as gnats are on a fine summer's evening in England,' noted Ralph Clark in wonder. They were mutton birds, and nested in particular on Mount Pitt, where they dug their nests like rabbit warrens. Settlers, free and bond, would climb the hill at night with lit pine-knots to search for the birds, who returned at evening to their burrows. Hunter, too, as *Sirius* began to break apart on the rocks, went on such excursions. The parties would arrive soon after dusk, light small fires to attract the attention of the birds, 'and they drop down out of the air as fast as the people can take them up and kill them'. Unfortunately for the species, the mutton bird did not easily rise from flat ground. Its eggs in their burrows were also easily plundered.

Throughout mid 1790, 170 000 birds were slaughtered, and their feathers must have blown hither and thither on the island and coated the surrounding sea.

'They had a strong, fishy taste,' said Hunter. 'But our keen appetites relished them very well; the eggs were excellent.' As on the mainland, people also boiled and ate the head of the cabbage-tree palm. The phenomenon of the birds coincided, however, with a plague of caterpillars and grubs that damaged the crops.

Ross tried a new way to encourage convicts to overcome food shortages, setting up on Norfolk Island his own kind of 'agrarian commonwealth'. He gave allocations of land to groups of convicts, perhaps six at a time, who were jointly responsible for growing what they needed. Thus the convicts would become their own motivators and regulators, and gang up on those who shirked their duties. Ross offered monetary and other prizes to those who put up for sale the most pork, fowls and corn. Felons were thus exposed to the reforming impact of land of their own.

Captain Hunter, who observed the scheme at work, thought that in reality convicts were driven by it to steal from each other's gardens. Under the Ross system, too, the birth of every piglet was to be reported to the deputy commissary and the death of every sow was to be followed by an enquiry. If the cause of the death was found to be an accident or a disease, the government would make up the loss, but if not, the convicts given the care of the pig as a group 'were to be considered responsible and were to be punished as criminals'. Deluded or not, Ross offered his charges the allurements of a far more intense co-operativism than Phillip had in Sydney.

On the mainland, Phillip did not know that the store ship the British government had sent, the *Guardian*, had some months past met icebergs at 42 degrees 15 minutes south, a longitude generally too far north for them. Two boats had been lowered from the *Guardian* to harvest lumps of ice to serve as water for the ship's cargo of livestock. By the time the boats got back to the ship with their iceblocks, visibility had diminished. *Guardian* crept along, its captain looking for a safe passage through, but a semi-submerged ice spur raked open the ship's keel. She tore free, but her rudder was left stuck in the ice. Water flooded into her hull.

Captain Riou fothered his ship; wrapped up the hull in a bandage of two layers of sail. After hours at the pump, some men found the liquor store and drank themselves into a stupor as a means of facing death. The day after the accident, Riou gave those who chose, including the specialist artisan convicts Phillip had asked the government to send, permission to give up the ship and take to the sea in the boats. Most of the seamen left, but the convict artificers stayed aboard the *Guardian*. It would turn out that theirs was the right choice. Only fifteen of those who took to the boats would survive.

Had the *Guardian* been able to continue to Sydney, it would have arrived in March 1790 and saved Phillip from the further reductions to the rations made in April 1790. By that time, weekly, 2½ pounds (1.2 kilos) of flour, 2 pounds (900 grams) of pork and 2 of rice were the limit for each British soul in New South Wales. Because of the energy needed to fish and hunt, an extra measure of rations was set aside for gamekeepers and fishermen. At the cooking fires in the men's and women's camps, prisoners looked covetously at each other's share, and in the marines' huts wives asked their husbands how they were expected to keep children healthy on a few flapjacks a week, insect-infected rice and pork that shrank to half its weight as the brine cooked out. In late April it became apparent that the pork in the storehouse would last only until 26 August at the current low rate of consumption, and the beef similarly.

JULIANA: THE FACE OF SHAME

In the same December *Guardian* hit its iceberg, the leisurely women's convict ship *Lady Juliana* was lying in Rio, and Mrs Barnsley was accompanied ashore by officers to do her shopping. Neither Lieutenant Edgar nor Captain Aitken seemed to have cramped her entrepreneurialism. Nor did they prevent those convict girls who accommodated Spanish gentlemen aboard. The former London madam, Elizabeth Sully, who had run a lodging house at 45 Cable Street, East London, and three of her girls had been sentenced for robbing clients, and now were involved with other former prostitutes in building up funds for their time in New South Wales. After leaving St Jago in the Cape Verde Islands, the *Lady Juliana* was accompanied for some distance by two Yankee slavers making for the Gambia, sailors being rowed over to the *Juliana* for evening recreation.

Naturally, not all convict women were involved in the prostitution—for one thing, Sarah Whitelam, rural beloved of the steward, John Nicol, was by then heavily pregnant. It may have been that Nicol, Surgeon Alley, Captain Aitken and Lieutenant Edgar were in some way facilitators and profiteers of the flesh trade on *Juliana*, and it is hard to see how they could have been opposed to it. But events would soon show that there were more disreputable forms of exploitation than this.

The *Juliana* suffered its own emergency in port. 'While we lay at the Cape,' said Nicol, 'we had a narrow escape from destruction by fire. The carpenter allowed the pitch-pot to boil over upon the deck, and the flames rose in an amazing manner. The shrieks of the women were dreadful, and the confusion they made running about drove everyone stupid.' With the *Guardian* careened and ultimately abandoned on the shore, the women were entitled to feel the vulnerability of their vessel.

Five surviving agricultural work superintendents and some supplies from *Guardian* were put on the *Lady Juliana*. One of the superintendents was a former Hessian officer who had served George III in North America, Philip Schaeffer, who came aboard with his ten-year-old daughter and some vine cuttings which had survived the collision with the iceberg.

All twenty-five of the convict artificers of *Guardian* would need eventually to be delivered to Sydney Cove too. Some of them would be more than willing to join the sexually amiable *Lady Juliana*, but they would need to wait for later British vessels. They were considered by their captain worthy of pardoning, but first their transportation had to be completed.

Back in the Thames, in the squally autumn and cold early winter of 1789, following the departure of the *Lady Juliana* and the *Guardian*, a great crime was in the making. Prisoners from Newgate were being gradually accommodated aboard the newly contracted vessels at Deptford—*Surprize*, *Scarborough* and *Neptune*. *Neptune* was the largest of the three, 809 tons (825 tonnes) with a crew of 83. It was first commanded by Thomas Gilbert who had captained the *Charlotte* in the First Fleet and whose book, *Journal of a Voyage from Port Jackson, New South Wales to Canton in 1788*, was about to be published in London to considerable interest. The *Scarborough*, which had already made the journey once, was half the size of the *Neptune*. The 400-ton (408-tonne) *Surprize* was the smallest of the three and a very poor sailer, and commanded by Donald Trail, a former master to Bligh. Trail had recently commanded one of the Camden, Calvert and King slave ships.

On 15 October 1789 the ships were ordered to move out of the docks to embark soldiers of the New South Wales Corps and convicts in the river. The soldiers were accommodated in the gun rooms, forecastles and steerage areas of the ships, around the convict decks. The rumour was that some of these fellows were less than prime soldiery, ruffians recruited from the Savoy military prison.

Many of this new regiment, particularly some of the young officers, tolerated the inconvenience of being sent so far abroad because they hoped for power, influence and riches from New South Wales. Some, like a scapegrace lieutenant, Anthony Fenn Kemp, who had wasted a fortune of £2 million, were escaping creditors.

Almost all the convicts taken aboard in the river had been confined for some years. Some came directly from Newgate, but the *Neptune* prisoners came as well from the *Justitia* and *Censor* hulks in the Thames. They were a sullen and angry cargo, but well-cowed and already weakened or weakening.

There had been a rough criterion this time for selecting those who went aboard—the idea was to remove the convicts who had been in the hulks the longest time. But that meant they were prisoners who in many cases had served years of their sentences. In committing them to the eighteenth-century equivalent of deep space, the desire to clear out the gaols and hulks seemed to be the primary motive, but it must have occurred to more than a few clerks and officials that it would also ensure that those prisoners serving seven- or fourteen-year sentences were unlikely to return from New South Wales. Thus they must have added names to the lists with the eugenic purpose of locating bad blood permanently in New South Wales without asking too closely what the implications might be for society there. New South Wales was to be the great oubliette, in which convicts could be deposited and forgotten by British society at large.

On *Neptune*, even between Plymouth and Portsmouth, where the men were racked by catarrh and congestive disorders, a number of the convicts had already died, but there was general and unquestioned agreement that it was due to the physical condition in which they had arrived from the hulks and prisons. There were other signs of indifference to convict welfare, however, early on. Either Trail or Shapcote, the naval agent, ordered many of the convicts' chests thrown overboard with their possessions in them. Men and women who had thought to dress better and more warmly while at sea were reduced to the basic ration of convict dress—striped jacket and petticoat, navy shoes, inadequate blankets.

By early December 1789, Undersecretary Evan Nepean had become anxious about reports of the conditions on board the Second Fleet, and told the naval agent that he was to 'examine minutely into the manner of confining the convicts, as it has been represented that they are ironed in such a manner as must ultimately tend to their destruction'. Secretary of State Grenville sent Governor Phillip an ominous dispatch urging him to disembark the prisoners as early as possible when they arrived, 'as from the length of the passage from hence and the nature of their food, there is every reason to expect that many of them will be reduced to so debilitated a state that immediate relief will be found expedient'. It is a letter which reflects some culpability, and indifference to Phillip's problems by the Home Secretary.

Further convicts were collected from the *Lion* and *Fortune* hulks in Portsmouth, as well as from the notorious *Dunkirk* at Plymouth. Male convicts were suddenly told that they could bring their wives on the voyage, if they chose, but only three women and three children had turned up in Portsmouth by 21 December. Three or four other free women embarked in the following days, interesting volunteers, lovers of various convicts willing to take the step, on the eve of Christmas, into the void.

Amongst them was Harriet Hodgetts, wife of a 24-year-old blacksmith-cum-burglar from Staffordshire, Thomas Hodgetts. She had followed her husband down from Staffordshire to London, where she lived with their three small children in acute squalor in Whitechapel. It seems that the churchwardens and overseers of the parish of St Mary's Whitechapel took an interest in the Hodgetts's case and were anxious to get Harriet and her children aboard, since she had no other prospects. Her quarters on *Neptune* were hopelessly cramped—she lived with the convict women. Her revenge was to live till 1850 and give birth to nine colonial children.

NEPTUNE'S MEN

There were two young men aboard the *Neptune* who would have a large place in the story of New South Wales.

One was a young man with a new rank, and a touch bumptious about it. John Macarthur was a little over twenty years of age, and a lieutenant in the 102nd Regiment, the newly created New South Wales Corps, a man of handsome features that must have satisfied the broad streak of narcissism in him. He was a devout duellist, because he was a man of edgy honour—his father was a Scots draper who lived at the back of his business in Plymouth in an era when trade was thought vulgar. His father had been able to 'obtain'—that is, buy—an ensign's commission for John for a regiment intended to be sent to fight the American colonists. In June 1789, when the formation of the New South Wales

Corps was announced, John saw the chance of promotion and his father helped him buy a lieutenancy.

He had married the previous year a robust-spirited and handsome girl named Elizabeth Veal, a Cornish woman who considered her ambitious and volatile husband 'too proud and haughty for our humble fortune'. Indeed it was Macarthur and his fellow officers, not the convicts, who introduced turbulence into Captain Tom Gilbert's *Neptune*.

When the ship anchored in Plymouth in November 1789, Macarthur went up to the quarterdeck and upbraided the captain for his 'ungentleman-like conduct', in crassly rebuffing Macarthur's request for better quarters and called him a 'great scoundrel'. Gilbert responded by saying 'he had settled many a greater man' than Macarthur. The two agreed to meet at four o'clock in the afternoon at the Fountain Tavern on Plymouth Dock, in order to fight a pistol duel. Macarthur faced Gilbert on the stones of the Old Gun Wharf. The two duellists fired, Macarthur's ball sizzling through Gilbert's greatcoat. Then Gilbert's missed altogether. Their seconds came running in and stopped the confrontation, and both men decided that their honour had been satisfied.

But enmity continued. Captain Nepean, commander of the troops on *Neptune*, and Lieutenant Macarthur complained to Evan Nepean, Undersecretary of State and Captain Nepean's brother, that Gilbert would not hand over the keys to the convict deck. Evan Nepean declared, 'I trust that both sides, when out of the smell of land, will find it in their interests to live quietly together.'

As it happened, a decision was reached to remove Thomas Gilbert as master of *Neptune*. Macarthur and Captain Nepean and the New South Wales Corps would eventually bring down bigger fish than Gilbert, but they were pleased with themselves for their first triumph, though it brought to the quarterdeck of *Neptune* the catastrophic Donald Trail.

The other fascinating passenger on board *Neptune* was a young Irishman, D'Arcy Wentworth, aged about 27, a highwayman-cum-surgeon: a voluntary passenger in one sense; a virtual convict in others. He was tall and good-looking and spoke English with an Ulster brogue. He had acquired notoriety in Britain throughout the 1780s as 'a gentleman of the road', whom the public and even magistrates distinguished from 'the lower and more depraved part of the fraternity of thieves'.

Wentworth was the son of an Ulster innkeeper, a relative of the noble Fitzwilliam clan of Portadown. Earl Fitzwilliam, though progressive and wealthy, had no interest in supporting the youngest son of a kinsman, so D'Arcy was left both with a sense of his own worth, confirmed by seven doting sisters, and no wealth to affirm it. In the mid-to-late 1780s he came to London, where the Court of Examiners of the Company of Surgeons certified him an assistant surgeon. He set himself to 'walk the hospitals', but the impoverished Irish medical student did not have the temperament to live quietly and carefully. In criminal society at the Dog and Duck Tavern in St George's Field south of the river, he could pass as a real toff, live fairly cheaply, encounter raffish society, and attract women with his tall frame and his vigorous Irish banter. By November 1787 Wentworth had been arrested for holding up a man on Hounslow Heath. The victim described the perpetrator as a large, lusty man who wore a black silk mask and a drab-coloured greatcoat. The charges were dismissed. But four days later, a gentleman, his wife and a female friend were held up on Hounslow Heath by a solitary highwayman on a chestnut horse with a white blaze. Two Bow Street runners intercepted Wentworth as he returned to the city and brought him before a magistrate. Wentworth stood trial in the Old Bailey in December 1787. Though he inveighed against the press for swinging the jury against him, his victims seemed reluctant to identify him and he was acquitted. By now he was to some a glamorous figure, but one wonders what coercion was used by some of his Dog and Duck associates to prevent a definite identification.

South-east of the Dog and Duck lay the plateau called Blackheath, with Shooters Hill rising from it. In January 1788, Wentworth was the so-called masked gentleman highwayman who rode out of the roadside heath and held up two travellers. In the same month on Shooters Hill, three highwaymen, one of them apparently Wentworth, held up Alderman William Curtis (who owned ships in the First Fleet), and two other gentlemen. These two hold-ups netted goods valued at over £50. One of D'Arcy's accomplices, William Manning, was captured in Lewisham, and an address in his pocketbook led Bow Street runners to Wentworth's London lodgings, where they arrested him again.

Before the magistrates and later in Newgate, Wentworth pleaded his family's good name and said that he had become degraded by the evil influence of the clientele of the Dog and Duck. This time, his trial was moved to Maidstone, where the Lent Assizes met, in the hope of finding a jury who would convict without fear or favour.

That was the month the eleven ships of the First Fleet had gathered on the Motherbank, preparatory for departure, and there was a rumour Wentworth had been sent away on it. Acquitted in Maidstone, again because of uncertainty of identification, Wentworth met Earl Fitzwilliam, his rich young kinsman, in London for a solemn talk. But by the end of November 1788, D'Arcy had been arrested again for holding up a post-chaise carrying two barristers of Lincoln's Inn across Finchley Common north of Hampstead Heath. Stripping the gentlemen of their valuables, one of the highwaymen whispered, 'Good morrow'. One lawyer said to his companion, 'If I was not sure that D'Arcy Wentworth was out of the kingdom, I should be sure it was him.'

The following year, 1789, someone identified as Wentworth asked a surgeon to come and operate on a friend of his, 'Jack Day', suffering from a pistol wound. Wentworth's associate had to be taken to hospital, was grilled by Bow Street officers, and the result was Wentworth's own interrogation and arrest in November.

This time his trial at the Old Bailey was such a *cause célèbre* that it was attended by members of the royal family, including the Duke and Duchess of Cumberland. On 9 December, Wentworth appeared before a lenient judge and his lawyer victims did not prosecute, having known him socially. The jury was pleased to come back with a verdict of Not Guilty, and the prosecuting parties were also pleased to announce that Mr Wentworth 'has taken a passage to go in the fleet to Botany Bay; and has obtained an appointment in it, as Assistant Surgeon, and desires to be discharged immediately'. Earl Fitzwilliam had agreed to fit his kinsman out and pay his fare to New South Wales on the *Neptune*.

In fact, D'Arcy Wentworth had no official position aboard the ship. The quality of Great Britain often got rid of their wild relatives by de facto, above-decks transportation, and Wentworth would be an early well-documented instance of what would become a habitual recourse for embarrassed British families. Now he was alone in a little hutch aboard, bouncing on the swell of the Motherbank, amongst pungent odours and people he did not know, and at 27 was still without a post in life.

NEPTUNE: THE SECOND FACE OF SHAME

Neptune's Captain Trail, a 44-year-old Orkney Island Scot, at one time master to Captain Bligh, took over command of the vessel from the dismissed Captain Gilbert. The *Neptune* now held over five hundred—428 male and 78 female—of the thousand convicts to be shipped. Most of them were housed on the orlop deck, the third deck down, 75 feet by 35 (c 23 × 11 metres), with standing room below the beams of the ceiling only 5 feet 7 inches (1.7 metres). The convicts slept in four rows of sleeping trays, one row on either side of the ship and two down the middle. Lanterns burned on the convict deck till eight o'clock at night, and each ship had to carry the latest ventilating equipment in the hope that air would reach the convicts even in the tropics. In port, and for much of the journey, each convict was chained by the wrist or by the ankles, in many cases on *Neptune* two and two together, and indefinitely so. Trail must have known the impact this would have on individual cleanliness and health.

As usual, each group of six men or women chose their mess steward, and the food these mess orderlies went up to collect morning and evening was cooked in communal coppers above deck. In bad weather the food had to be cooked below deck in the same oven and coppers that were used first for the rations of the crew and soldiers, and the result was that many of the convicts went without cooked food during wild weather; Trail was not concerned.

The sanitary arrangements were very primitive—on the orlop deck large tubs were provided to 'ease nature'. These would be knocked over by accident or carelessness or rough seas. Below decks was thus a damp, under-aired, over-crowded misery.

Among those who came on board the huge *Neptune* from the hulk *Dunkirk* was a lusty young man in his mid twenties, Robert Towers, who had stolen silver tankards and a pint pot from an inn in north Lancashire and then tried to sell them to a silversmith in Preston. His health had gone down a little on the damp lower decks of *Dunkirk*, but on the crowded prison deck of *Neptune*, where he wore slaver shackles around his ankles and wrists, received short-weighted rations and got insufficient air and exercise, he began to feel really poorly. The *Neptune*, at anchor and at sea, would ultimately finish him, though it would take seven months until they brought his corpse up to deck and committed him to a distant ocean. The deck he was thrown from, and all the other decks of *Neptune*, were crowded with the captain's private goods he intended to sell in Sydney Cove.

The three ships now gathered in Portsmouth were joined by a store ship named the *Justinian*, loaded with flour, pork, beef, pease, oatmeal, vinegar, spirits, oil and sugar. There were also 162 bales of clothing and a quantity of coverlets, blankets and cloth, and a portable military hospital, prefabricated for assembly in New South Wales. Four hundred gallons (1820 litres) of vinegar were shipped for use as disinfectant and mouthwash. The three transports also carried supplies.

The wind kept the new convict fleet shuttling between Portsmouth Harbour and the Isle of Wight, but on Sunday morning, 7 January, in the new year of 1790, a westerly allowed them to tack their way down the Channel. The store ship *Justinian* left Falmouth the same day as the other three ships left the Motherbank.

Some of the awesome smells from the convict deck reached the Macarthurs in their little cabin by the women's prison area on a higher deck. Mrs Macarthur found the malodour hard to bear: 'together with the stench arising from the breath of such a number of persons confined in so small a spot, the smell of their provisions and other unwholesome things, made it almost unbearable'. But Elizabeth Macarthur did bear it. In British colonial history she would be recorded as a kindly, loyal and enduring woman, to the extent that she remained clear-eyed even amongst the miasmas of *Neptune*. Her as yet callow husband would be harder to admire so unconditionally.

The seventy-eight female convicts of *Neptune* were housed in a section of the upper deck and were not chained. Unlike the captain of the *Lady Juliana*, Trail denied having made any promise to allow the crew sea-wives, and he punished men who had any unauthorised contact with convict women. Sailors got to women, and vice versa, in any case, through a break in the bulkhead between the carpenters' shop and the women's prison.

As for D'Arcy Wentworth, he seems to have fallen quite passionately in love, passion being his *forte*, with a pretty Irish convict of seventeen years named Catherine Crowley. She had been sentenced in Staffordshire for one of the usual offences, stealing clothing—although in her case it was a considerable amount of clothing. Catherine was sent down from Stafford gaol to London on the outside of a coach with three other girls, and boarded the *Neptune*. With Captain Donald Trail's at least tacit consent, D'Arcy made her his mistress soon after he joined the ship.

So in close quarters on *Neptune* could be found two furiously ambitious young men: one a reclusive, prickly officer, John Macarthur, with his wife, Elizabeth, pregnant; the other the founding social outcast of penal New South Wales, D'Arcy Wentworth, with Catherine Crowley, pregnant. In reality, D'Arcy may have been a more lonely figure aboard *Neptune* than Crowley was. And he remained so, not interfering, not being invited to interfere as a physician in what befell Catherine's convict brethren. Catherine Crowley would have been as surprised as the politer Macarthurs to find out that the child she carried on *Neptune* would one day become Australia's first great constitutional statesman. But all that future was mired in shipboard squalor, stink and dimness, and they sailed towards a place whose survival was unguaranteed in any case.

Twenty-two year old Elizabeth Macarthur kept herself absorbed by writing a stylish journal of the voyage. In the Bay of Biscay the sea 'ran mountains high,' she wrote. Down the coast of West Africa, windsails operated over the deck to keep the lower areas of the ship refreshed, but the terrible heat, particularly in the men's prison deck, could not be dealt with very well. Here was Georgian Hades, the convict deck of an eighteenth-century ship, the Sutton pumps on deck having no air to pump, and men and women locked up with their complex screams and groans and surrenders.

After sailing, the soldiers complained to Lieutenant Macarthur that they were receiving short rations, that they were victims of purloining; that is, short weighting. Captain Nepean did not seem to want to attend to the matter. As Elizabeth sprinkled their little hutch of a cabin with oil of roses, the Macarthurs' rations were also cut by Captain Trail, without resistance by the incapable Lieutenant Shapcote or by Captain Nepean. Nepean dined in Captain Trail's cabin and the two had become cronies, but the Macarthurs 'seldom benefited by their society'.

Captain William Hill, a cultivated and sympathetic young member of the New South Wales Corps, who would make friends of the more intellectual of the officers already in New South Wales, particularly Tench and Dawes, was sailing on *Surprize*, where he did himself great honour by being a critic of the contractors from the start. 'The irons used upon these unhappy wretches were barbarous; the contractors had been in the Guinea trade, and had put on board the same shackles used by them in that trade; which are made with a short bolt, instead of chains that drop between the legs and fasten with a bandage around the waist; like those at the different gaols, these bolts were not more than three-quarters of a foot [c 23 cm] in length, so they [the convicts] could not extend either leg from the other more than an inch or two [c 2.5–5 cm] at most; thus fettered, it was impossible for them to move, but at the risk of both their legs being broken.' Forced inactivity on this scale, Hill feared, was an invitation to scurvy, 'equal to, if not more than salt provisions'.

Even when disease struck, there were no extra comforts offered. 'The slave trade is merciful, compared with what I have seen in this fleet; in that it is the interest of the [slaver] master to preserve the healths and lives of their captives, they having a joint benefit, with the owners. In this [fleet], the more they can withhold from the unhappy wretches, the more provisions they have to dispose of in a foreign market; and the earlier in the voyage they die, the longer they [the masters] can draw the deceased's allowance for themselves . . . it therefore highly concerns government, to lodge in future, a controlling power in each ship over these low-life barbarous masters, to keep them honest.' The beached captain of the *Guardian* had seen the condition of the fleet in Cape Town and bluntly wrote to Evan Nepean: 'If ever the navy make another contract like that of the last three ships, they ought to be shot, and as for their agent Mr Shapcote, he behaved here just as foolishly as a man could well do.'

All four surgeons employed aboard the fleet had already written to Shapcote about the potential seriousness of the convicts' conditions. They urged him to get fresh supplies of beef and vegetables aboard. Surgeon Grey of the *Neptune* wrote that 'without they have fresh provisions and greens every day, numbers of them will fall a sacrifice to that dreadful disease'. Yet at the Cape, Trail made sure his prisoners were securely ironed, which did not contribute to their rehabilitation through whatever fresh fruit and vegetables were acquired ashore.

Surgeon Harris, the military surgeon to the soldiers of the fleet, was concerned about their condition also. William Waters, surgeon of *Surprize*, reported thirty convicts suffering from scurvy. In the *Scarborough* ten soldiers were affected, five of them 'very bad'.

But Shapcote was strangely unconcerned, and may himself have been suffering from the famous lethargy of scurvy or from some other incapacity. He died suddenly in mid May, after dining with Captain Trail and his wife. Between 3 and 4 a.m., a female convict 'who had constantly attended Mr Shapcote' came to the quarterdeck with news of his death.

At Cape Town on 19 February, after an argument with Captain Nepean, Macarthur and his wife, child and servant transferred to the *Scarborough* in protest. Her husband was incapacitated for five weeks by fever, during which time, Elizabeth Macarthur complained, the other New South Wales Corps officers did not make 'the slightest offer of assistance'. He was beginning to walk again as *Scarborough* neared Port Jackson.

In the zone of storms, the empathic soldier Captain Hill felt pity for those 'unhappy wretches, the convicts', who often 'were considerably above their waists in water, and the men of my company, whose berths were not so far forward, were nearly up to the middles'.

The cold, damp, hunger and continued shackling were slowly killing the young convict Robert Towers, and he was aware that when he died, as men were dying every day down on the convict deck of *Neptune*, his messmates would not tell anyone but go on drawing his rations as long as they could, till putrefaction made his condition clear.

CHAPTER 7

CONFIRMATION OF EXISTENCE

In the dispirited colony of New South Wales, June 1790 had opened rainy and hungry, and men and women wondered whether they existed at all any more in the minds of those who had transported or posted them to the ends of the earth. Then, on the evening of 3 June, there was a cry throughout Sydney Cove of 'The flag's up!' It was the flag on the look-out station on the harbour's southern headland, visible from Sydney Cove itself. Tench left a passionate account of what this meant to him and others. 'I was sitting in my hut, musing on our fate, when a confused clamour in the street drew my attention. I opened my door and saw several women with children in their arms running to and fro with distracted looks, congratulating each other, kissing their infants with the most passionate and extravagant marks of fondness.' Tench raced to the hill on which Government House stood and trained his pocket telescope on the look-out station. 'My next door neighbour, a brother-officer, was with me; but we could not speak; we wrung each other by the hand, with eyes and hearts overflowing.'

Watkin begged to join the governor in his boat which was going down-harbour to meet the ship. But a lusty wind, of the kind Sydney folk quickly came to call southerly busters, seemed to be blowing her onto the rocks at the base of the cliffs of North Head. 'The tumultuous state of our minds represented her in danger; and we were in agony.' She survived, however, and the governor sent out a boat to hail her, and when Phillip knew who she was, *Lady Juliana* with a cargo of women in good health, he crossed from the vice-regal boat to a fishing boat to return as fast as he could to Sydney, to prepare for the reception ashore of this new population. Meanwhile the seamen and officers in the governor's cutter 'pushed through wind and rain . . . At last we read the word "London" on her stern. "Pull away, my lads! She is from old England; a few strokes more and we shall be aboard! Hurrah for a belly-full and news from our friends!"—Such were our exhortations to the boat's crew.'

Tench was still overwhelmed as they boarded, so that he saw the women on board this well-founded and well-run ship not so much as the fallen but as 'two hundred and twenty-five of our own countrywomen, whom crime or misfortune had condemned to exile'. Letters were brought up from below, and those addressed to the officers who had boarded were 'torn open in trembling agitation'.

When the *Juliana* came down-harbour and the women finally got ashore on 11 June 1790, they were better dressed than most of barefoot New South Wales, and made their way as strange paragons of health through mud to the huts of the women's camp on the west side of the town. Sarah Whitelam left John Nicol, her sea-husband, aboard. The captain intended a brisk turn-around for the *Juliana*, so Nicol knew a sad parting was imminent.

But the presence of *Juliana*, and ambiguous news of the *Guardian*, was at least a sign that the settlement had not been forgotten by Whitehall. Above all, so was the appearance of the store ship *Justinian*, a few weeks later. 'Our rapture,' wrote Watkin Tench, 'was doubled on finding she was laden entirely with provisions for our use. Full allowance, and general congratulation, immediately took place.' The *Justinian* had taken only five months to make its trans-planetary journey. Profound gratitude and almost personal affection was now directed at *Justinian*'s young captain, Benjamin Maitland, for his ship carried the bulk of the stores Phillip needed, including nearly 500 000 pounds (227 000 kilos) of flour and 50 000 pounds (22 700 kilos) of beef and pork, as well as sugar, oil, oatmeal, pease, spirits and vinegar. Here was the end of famine, and the return to full and varied rations! And from what the *Justinian* told them, the settlement knew to look out for three more convict ships.

The first of the new ships, the *Surprize*, under jury masts from damage in a Southern Ocean storm, was seen from the look-out on South Head on 25 June. By the next day it was anchored in Sydney Cove. The officers from Sydney Cove who boarded it might have expected the degree of health found in the *Lady*

Juliana. In fact, the peculiar disorders of the Camden, Calvert and King ships could be smelled a hundred metres off. Phillip found the ill health of the New South Wales Corps soldiers in stark contrast to the women of *Lady Juliana*, and the contrast with the convicts even more marked, for many of them were dying. Upwards of one hundred were now on the sick list on board, and forty-two had been buried at sea during the journey.

The portable hospital which had arrived by the *Justinian* was assembled to take some of the spillage from White's timber-and-shingle hospital building, for two days later the signal was flying at South Head for the other transports, 'and we were led to expect them in as unhealthy a state as that which had just arrived'.

On *Neptune*, Lieutenant John Macarthur's fever caught at the Cape had spread throughout the ship. In the mad southern seas men and women had expired amongst the jolting, incessant swell, and beneath the scream of canvas and wind. Aboard *Neptune* in particular, according to later witnesses, a black market had broken out for lack of proper supplies. It might cost one shilling and sixpence for an additional pint (about half a litre) of water, a pair of new shoes for a quart (around one litre) of tea or three biscuits, a new shirt for four biscuits, two pairs of trousers for six. Crew members would later sign a statement swearing that they sold food and drink to convicts on board at these elevated prices.

Entering the heads, Trail swung *Neptune* into the northern wing of the harbour, and had his men fetch up the dead from the prison deck and throw them into the water, from which many were later retrieved or observed by convicts and natives. A visit by White and others to *Neptune* showed them that the condition of the people aboard was much worse even than those on *Surprize*. Phillip looked with outraged judgment at masters like Captain Trail but got back the unembarrassed stare of self-justified men with goods for sale. With all Phillip's power, he lacked the capacity to try them before his Admiralty court, so he was reduced to condemning them in dispatches.

No sooner were the convicts unloaded than the masters of the transports, including Trail, opened tent stores on shore and offered goods for sale which 'though at the most extortionate prices, were eagerly bought up'. Since cash was broadly lacking, the goods were in part sold to those amongst the population who had money orders and bills of credit, and even to the commissary for bills drawn on the Admiralty.

Extra tents had to be pitched on the west side of the cove by the hospital to take in the two hundred sick of *Neptune*, carried ashore in their own waste, seriously ill with scurvy, dysentery or infectious fever. Several died in the boats as they were being rowed ashore, or on the wharf as they were lifted out of the boats, 'both the living and the dead exhibiting more horrid spectacles than had ever been witnessed in this country'.

Much of it was attributed, said Collins, to severe confinement, such as had not occurred on the First Fleet. In many cases, convicts had been ironed together for the duration of the voyage. Collins thought, however, that Captain Marshall of the *Scarborough* had done a reasonably good job, even though sixty-eight men had been lost on his ship.

Reverend Johnson, who had entered the below-decks of the first of the three scandalous ships to arrive, the *Surprize*, was galvanised by what he saw. 'A great number of them lying, some half, others nearly quite naked, without either bed nor bedding, unable to turn or help themselves. I spoke to them as I passed along, but the smell was so offensive that I could scarcely bear it . . . Some creeped upon their hands and knees, and some were carried upon the backs of others.'

Later, visiting the hospital, Johnson found many of the ill still unable to move and 'covered over almost with their own nastiness, their heads, bodies, clothes, blankets all full of filth and lice. Scurvy was not the only nor the worst disease that prevailed among them.' Johnson was a little shocked that even in such parlous condition some convicts had not lost sufficient craftiness to beg clothing from him and then sell it almost at once for food, as if their journey had equipped them to act differently.

So many burials took place that people would afterwards remember the dingoes howling and fighting over the bodies in a sandy pit over the hills above the Tank Stream.

Genial Captain Hill, landed from *Surprize*, suffered the normal shock of arrival but was pleased in some respects with his landfall. 'It is now our winter quarters, and had I superior abilities to any man that ever wrote, it would be possible for me to convey to your mind a just idea of this beautiful heavenly clime; suffer your imagination to enter the regions of fiction; and let fancy in her loveliest moment paint an Elysium; it will fall far short of this delightful weather . . . did the gloomy months prevail here as in England, it is more than probable that the next reinforcement on arrival would find a desolated colony.'

But he was not happy with the amenities. 'Here I am, living in a miserable thatched hut, without kitchen, without a garden, with an acrimonious blood by my having been nearly six months at sea, and tho' little better than a leper, obliged to live on a scanty pittance of salt provision, without a vegetable, except when a good-natured neighbour robs his own stomach in compassion to me.' Hill found that people who had lived in huts with their own gardens for some time rarely abused the confidence that was placed in them, and if they did it was to plunder some other convict's garden.

All the healthy male convicts from the Second Fleet were sent to the farming settlement at Rose Hill/Parramatta. Women convicts were put to work making clothes out of the slops, the raw cloth brought out on sundry ships. Allowing for deaths, the population had by now quadrupled to nearly 3000, and so when on 1 August the *Surprize* left for China, Phillip leased it to drop off 157 female and 37 male convicts at Norfolk Island on the way. D'Arcy Wentworth had been working on a voluntary arrangement with Surgeon White, but was now sent to Norfolk Island with his convict paramour, Catherine Crowley, with the provisional post of Assistant Surgeon, based on the help he had given in the grounds of the Sydney hospital. There is no record of how he felt, but perhaps there was angry pride at being on probation and therefore not receiving wages.

When the store ship *Justinian* turned up at Norfolk on 7 August, the ration on the island was down to 2 pounds (c 1 kilo) of flour and 1 pint (c ½ litre) of tea per person weekly, and only fish and cabbage-tree palms and mutton birds and their eggs had saved the population. The *Surprize* joined *Justinian* late that afternoon, but Wentworth and Crowley did not have a high priority for landing, so when the ship had to back off again and go to Cascade Bay on the north side of the island to shelter from a gale, Catherine Crowley gave premature shipboard birth to a son who was to be named William Charles Wentworth. D'Arcy Wentworth helped his son from his mother's womb, cut the cord and washed him, noticed an in-turned eye, but wrapped, warmed and caressed the baby. It took some weeks of tenderness and care to ensure his survival.

Wentworth landed into a turbulent scene, every human's negative passion enhanced by hunger and isolation and the limits of a small island set in consistently dangerous seas. He saw that the officers of *Sirius*, still stranded on the island, snubbed Major Ross and would not pay him the normal respects. There were four other surgeons and assistant surgeons already on the island, and D'Arcy liked most of them: his fellow Irishmen—Thomas Jamison, Dennis Considen and Surgeon Altree—and the former convict John Irving. Irving, sentenced in Lincoln, had served as assistant surgeon on his own ship in the First Fleet, *Lady Penrhyn*. Back in Sydney, he had a grant of 30 acres awaiting him.

Dennis Considen befriended Wentworth at once and began to instruct him in the use of native plants for treating disease, an area of practice in which Considen had been a leader in Sydney. As well as promoting the use of native sarsaparilla and spinach, red gum from angophora trees, yellow from grass-trees, and oil from the peppermint eucalyptus tree, he had found that native myrtle had properties which would serve as a mild and safe astringent in cases of dysentery.

Wentworth was appointed surgeon to the little hamlet of Queensborough, in the interior of the island, to which at first he walked each day. His task was to treat, above all, diarrhoea and dysentery. He also had to attend lashings. Lieutenant Clark seemed to think flogging increasingly appropriate. For some time, Wentworth was a mediator between the lash and convicts. John Howard, a former highway robber, was ordered to receive 500 strokes for selling the slops issued to him by the public store and for telling a lie about it to Major Ross. Wentworth humanely called off the punishment when Howard had received 80 strokes. Wentworth also attended when a man of almost seventy was given 100 lashes for stealing wheat and neglecting his work, and when a young convict boy received thirteen strokes on the buttocks for robbing his master.

When Clark ordered that a young woman receive 50 lashes for abusing Mr Wentworth, she received only sixteen, 'as Mr Wentworth begged that she might be forgiven the other 34'. Clark considered the girl in question—one Sarah Lyons—a 'D/B', his code for 'damned bitch'. Wentworth's tender-heartedness would not save Sarah Lyons from further floggings, but it demonstrated his sentiments.

SELF-SUFFICIENT ADAM

Back on the mainland, something promising was happening. James Ruse, the governor's agricultural Adam, would produce a token 17 bushels of wheat from one and a half acres (0.6 hectares), and by February 1791, Ruse would draw his last ration from the government store, an event of great psychological potency for Phillip, Ruse and all the critics. By then Ruse had met and married a convict woman from the *Lady Juliana* named Elizabeth Perry, convicted of stealing. Elizabeth claimed innocence, and argued that the clothes she was arrested in were her own, and given the shaky nature of the criminal justice system, she might indeed have been right.

The Ruse–Perry marriage rounded out the idyll. Phillip's provisional land grant to Ruse was confirmed in April 1791, the first grant issued in New South Wales. Ruse's place near the Parramatta River would become known appropriately as Experiment Farm. Elizabeth Ruse often heard her husband complain of the unsuitability of this land for farming, and he comforted himself for the smallish returns for his excessive labour and agricultural cleverness by drinking and gambling with other Parramatta convicts, notably Christopher Magee, who had spent part of his adolescence in America and seems to have had republican ideas and to have been a good companion for irreverent conversations.

In late July, another association was about to end. *Lady Juliana* was due to sail for China and home via Norfolk Island, and ship's steward Nicol faced being immediately separated from Sarah Whitelam, his convict woman, and the child they shared. It had been a busy time for John Nicol: 'The days flew on eagles' wings, for we dreaded the hour of separation which at length arrived.' Marines and soldiers were sent around Sydney Cove to bring the love-struck crew of the *Lady Juliana* back on board. 'I offered to lose my wages, but we were short of hands,' said Nicol. 'The captain could not spare a man and requested the aid of the governor. I thus was forced to leave Sarah, but we exchanged faith. She promised to remain true, and I promised to return when her time expired and bring her to England.' He wanted to stow her away, but at times of sailing the convicts were strictly guarded by the marines, and repeated searches were made of departing ships.

Sarah quickly recovered from the disappointment by marrying a First Fleet convict, John Walsh, the day after Nicol's departure, and then being settled on Norfolk Island with him. Nicol remained a seaman, never finding a ship that brought him back to Sydney.

THE WHALE AND THE SPEAR

In July 1790, as *Juliana* made ready to leave, a leviathan came to Port Jackson, a huge sperm whale which entered and became embayed within the harbour. Some boat crews from the various transports went trying to hunt it, and threw harpoons its way without success. Then one morning it rose from the harbour deeps to smash a punt occupied by three marines and a midshipman from the look-out station on South Head. 'In vain they thro' out their hats, the bags of our provisions, and the fish they had caught, in hopes to satisfy him or turn his attention.' Only one marine survived, swimming ashore to Rose Bay.

By late August, however, the whale, still trapped in the harbour, ran itself aground at Manly. The beaching of a whale was a significant event for all Eora people, who gathered together from various clan areas to participate in a great meat and blubber feast.

In the middle of the Eora celebration an expeditionary party from Sydney Cove landed, intending to travel overland to Pittwater. Bennelong, feasting with the other Aboriginals, enquired after Phillip, and expressed a desire to see the governor, with whom, after all, he had exchanged names. The only member of the European party to whom Bennelong expressed repugnance was McEntire, the huntsman, who had an evil reputation amongst the natives.

Surgeon White observed that Bennelong bore two new wounds, one in the arm from a spear and the other a large scar over his left eye. But he insisted on putting into a boat a specially large piece of whale meat as a gift to Phillip. The gift was not ironic—far from it. It was intended to get Phillip to Manly, to the great festival of the whale.

When the message and the blubber arrived back in Sydney, his Excellency was engaged in discussing with Bloodworth, the brick-maker, and Harry Brewer the building of a pillar on South Head to serve as a direction-finder for ships at sea. Now he gathered the weaponry immediately available, and set out in his boat to meet Bennelong. He was accompanied by Captain Collins and Lieutenant Waterhouse of the navy.

Waterhouse was a personable young man, newly promoted to replace the insane Mr Maxwell. He had become infatuated with Elizabeth Barnes, who had come off the *Lady Juliana* three months before, a slightly older woman than he, and probably, as a former prostitute, more worldly. He may have been nervous making this approach to Manly with the governor, given that many thought Phillip somewhat reckless and over-trusting in his dealings with the natives. On landing, Phillip found the Eora people 'still busily employed around the whale'. He advanced alone, with just one unarmed seaman for support, and called for Bennelong, who was mysteriously slow in coming forward. Collins and Waterhouse also landed, and Bennelong now showed himself. So did Colby.

Bennelong seemed delighted to see his old acquaintances 'and asked after every person he'd known in Sydney, among others the French cook and servant from whom he'd escaped, whom he'd constantly made the butt of his ridicule, by mimicking his voice, gait, and other peculiarities, all of which he again went through with his wanted exactness and drollery'. He asked particularly after a lady of the colony, surely Mrs Deborah Brooks, Phillip's housekeeper, from whom he had once ventured to snatch a kiss. When he was told she was well, he kissed the fresh-faced Lieutenant Waterhouse whom he obviously thought had a complexion like that of the lady, and laughed uproariously. But when the governor pointed to Bennelong's new wounds, the native became more sombre. He had received them down in the southern bay, Botany Bay, he announced, and he solemnly pointed out their contours to Phillip.

During this conference, 'the Indians filing off to right and left, so as in some measure to surround them', Phillip remained calm. Bennelong, wearing by this time two jackets, one brought by Phillip and the other by Collins, introduced the governor to a number of people on the beach, including a 'stout, corpulent native', Willemerring. On the ground before Bennelong was a very fine barbed spear 'of uncommon size'. The governor asked if he could have it. But Bennelong picked it up and took it away and dropped it near a place where Willemerring stood rather separate from the rest.

Willemerring was a wise man, a *carradhy*, amongst other things a ritual punishment man invited in from another place, in fact the Broken Bay/Pittwater area. He struck the watching Europeans as a frightened man, and he may have been, but he may have been, rather, a tense and intent man, coiled for his task. This was the time, in Bennelong's mind, for the governor, who had had the grace to present himself, to be punished for all of it: the fish and game stolen; the presumption of the Britons in camping permanently without permission; the stolen weaponry and nets; the stove-in canoes; the random shooting of natives; the curse of smallpox; the mysterious genital infections of women and then of their men—death, in the view of the Eora, particularly unpredictable death, being always attributable to malign magic. There was no malice on anyone's part in this punishment, which explained why Willemerring showed all the nervousness and then unexpected decisiveness of a bridegroom. But the scales needed to be adjusted by august blood, and the most august of all was Phillip's.

Thinking Willemerring nervous, Phillip gamely advanced towards him, as if begging the spear. Captain Collins and Lieutenant Waterhouse followed close by. Phillip removed his own single weapon, a dirk in his belt, and threw it on the ground. Willemerring reacted by lifting the spear upright from the grass with his toes and fitting it in one movement into his throwing stick, and 'in an instant darted it at the governor'. In the last moment before the spear was thrown, Phillip thought it more dangerous to retreat than to advance and cried out to the man, '*Werre, Werre!*'

Given the force with which the spear was projected, Phillip would later describe the shock of the wound to Tench as similar to a violent blow. The barb went into the governor's right shoulder, just above the collar bone, and ran downwards through his body, coming out his back. Willemerring looked at his handiwork long enough to ensure the spear had penetrated, and then he dashed into the woods, with miles to travel to his home ground in Pittwater.

There was instant confusion on both sides. Bennelong and Colby both disappeared, but Phillip's retreat was hindered by the fact that he carried in his body, pointing skyward when he was upright, a lance almost 4 metres long, the butt of it frequently striking the ground as he reeled and further lacerating the wound. 'For God's sake, haul out the spear,' Phillip begged Waterhouse, who struggled but at last managed to break off the spear shaft. Another thrown spear from an enthusiastic native struck Waterhouse in the hand as he worked on the shaft. Now spears were flying thickly, as happened at such exchanges of blood, as the ordinary folk joined in the ritual event.

Phillip was lifted, with the point of the spear protruding from his back, into his boat and brought back across the harbour, bleeding a considerable amount on the way. Since Surgeon White was still away from Sydney on the expedition to Pittwater, the Scots assistant, William Balmain, a quarrelsome man in his mid twenties, took on the task of extracting the spearhead from Phillip. There, at Government House, on a cot, his blue coat sodden with blood, lay the settlement's pole of stability and awesome reasonableness, without whom all might be lost. But the young surgeon earned the joy of Phillip's disciples by declaring the wound non-mortal and by safely extracting the barbed point of the spear. 'The Governor remains in great agonies, but it is thought he will recover, though at the same time His Excellency is highly scorbutic.'

This result would not have surprised the blubber-feasting natives of Manly Cove. They knew it was not intended to be a fatal wound, they knew the barb was meant to be extractable, and they knew Willemerring was an expert at placement. Phillip, though no doubt given laudanum for the pain, had time to order that no natives were to be fired on, unless they first were 'the aggressors, by throwing spears'. White's returning party was fetched back by marines with the news of Governor Phillip's wounding. The boat crew sent to retrieve them told White and the others that Colby and Bennelong had been talking to them and had 'pretended highly to disapprove the conduct of the man who had thrown the spear, vowing to execute vengeance upon him'. Was this a token offered to the wounded Phillip? Were the two natives striking attitudes just to please him?

David Collins was sure that the only reason the spear was thrown was fear on the part of Willemerring that he was about to be seized and taken away. 'The governor has always placed too great a confidence in these people . . . he had now, however, been taught a lesson which it might be presumed he would never forget.'

In general, no one blamed Bennelong for Willemerring's gesture. It was accepted that Willemerring acted out of personal panic, though the people from Sydney Cove found Bennelong's behaviour typically mystifying. But if the accounts of witnesses, including Lieutenant Waterhouse, are looked at, one sees that Bennelong very clearly showed Phillip his own new scars, which his adventures and sins had merited, and that in refusing to give Phillip the spear he asked for, and taking it away and putting it within reach of Willemerring's foot, he had shown it possessed another ordained purpose. The forming-up of warriors in a half-circle creates an impression of a conclave of witnesses to a ritual penalty.

And with considerable perception, in the end Phillip thought that it was a cultural manifestation, that though Bennelong probably was glad his friend and name-exchanger, the governor, had survived, there was no doubt that the natives 'throw their spears, and take a life in their quarrels, which are very frequent, as readily as the lower class of people in England stripped to box'.

The ritual spearing of Phillip seemed to be a new direction in Eora policy, though to put it in those terms is callous to the reality of the bewilderment of the Eora soul. There had been hope for a time that the visitors would vanish, but the ships had increased in number, coming by way of lesions in the cosmos through the gates of the great harbour. Some ships had departed, but now a number had taken their place, and the ghosts multiplied both by new ship-loads and by human generation. And although the many victims of the Second Fleet had been buried in Sydney's earth, this decrease by death did nothing to produce a clear crisis in the camp of the whites, or provide a sign that they would be finally borne away.

Phillip's wound took six weeks to get better, and throughout that time, hoping to use Abaroo and Nanbaree as intermediaries, he had men out looking for Bennelong, hoping there would be reconciliation. Surgeon White was the one to track him down and saw that a momentous change had come about. Bennelong had been joined by his beloved Barangaroo, the spirited woman who had left or been divorced by Colby. Barangaroo already knew that she needed to watch Bennelong very closely, and did so. She did not seem as noticeably pleased as Bennelong to know that the governor was well. Bennelong claimed, through the interpretation of the two children, Abaroo and Nanbaree, to have beaten Willemerring as a punishment. It might have been the truth, another adjustment of universal order.

The party asked Bennelong to help them arrange a husband for Abaroo, someone who could go to and from the settlement without causing trouble. At once, Bennelong suggested Yemmerrawanne, a slender and handsome youth about sixteen years old. He called the lad out of the people milling nearby. Yemmerrawanne offered, said Tench, 'many blandishments which proved that he had assumed the *toga virilis*. But Abaroo disclaimed his advances, repeating the name of another person, who we knew was her favourite.' On a return visit later in the day, though, Yemmerrawanne pressed his suit 'with such warmth and solicitation, as to cause an evident alteration in the sentiments of the lady'.

Now that the wounding of Arthur Phillip had established the principles of responsibility, Bennelong complained to Tench that his countrymen had lately been plundered of fizz-gigs, spears, the gift of a sword, and many other articles by some of the convicts and others, and said he would hand back the dirk the governor had dropped during the attack by Willemerring. The next day, after a search of the settlement, a party of officers, sailors and soldiers went down-harbour again with the collected stolen property.

At the exchange, Tench saw an old man come forward and claim one of the fizz-gigs, 'singling it from the bundle and taking only his own ... and this honesty, within the circle of their society, seemed to characterise them all'. Hunting for Bennelong, they found he was grateful for the return of the materials—they still possessed some unclaimed items, one of which was a net of fishing lines, which Barangaroo now took possession of and flung defiantly around her neck. Bennelong did not return the governor's dirk, however, and pretended not to know much about it. Perhaps it was kept for some chant to be sung into it, something to bring wisdom to Phillip, to end the calamity. Perhaps he had lost it. Watching him imbibe wine they had brought, the officers pressed him to name a day when he would come to Sydney. Bennelong said that the governor must first come and see him, 'which we promised should be done'.

When the governor was well, he travelled by boat down-harbour to visit Bennelong, opening his wound-inhibited arms. His apparent willingness to forgive created not always approving comment among the Europeans. But Bennelong was not ready to visit Sydney Cove yet. It was arranged that the natives would light a fire on the north shore of the harbour as a signal for the Europeans to visit them further.

Again Phillip accepted these terms. Certainly Bennelong was the sort of wilful man who delighted in setting tests, but even so he might have been trying in a way to educate Phillip, who asked to be notified as soon as look-outs saw the signal fire. When it was seen, Phillip and the others set off in their cutters. 'We found assembled, Baneelon [Bennelong], Barangaroo, and another young woman, and six men, all of whom received us with welcome. They had equipment with them—spears, fish gigs and lines, which they were willing to barter.' Bennelong and his party thus attempted to create the principle on which they would make friends with the settlement. Implements and items in general should be bartered, not plundered. 'I had brought with me an old blunted spear, which wanted repair,' wrote Tench. A native took it, carried it to the fire, tore a piece of bone with his teeth from a fizz-gig and attached it to the spear to be repaired with yellow eucalyptus gum, which had been 'rendered flexible by heat'. The meeting was probably considered a success by both parties, but there were major lessons on both sides which remained unlearned.

Another day, Barangaroo, more suspicious than the impetuous, vulnerable Bennelong, did not want her husband to go to Sydney with Tench and White. She snatched up one of Bennelong's fishing spears and broke it against rocks in protest at her lover's gullibility. In the end, the Reverend Johnson, Abaroo and a young convict, Stockdale, remained with Barangaroo as hostages against a safe return of Bennelong and some other men. The boats and the native canoe tied up on the east side of Sydney Cove at the governor's wharf, and then everyone set off for Phillip's residence. There was a reunion at which Bennelong told Phillip that Willemerring was at Broken Bay. Bennelong was delighted to see the governor's orderly sergeant, whom he kissed, and a woman who attended in the kitchen, again probably Mrs Deborah Brooks. But again he snubbed the gamekeeper McEntire. He showed his friends around Government House, explaining what various implements were for. It was now that Bennelong amused Tench by pointing to a candle-snuffer and saying, 'Nuffer for candle', thus avoiding the unpronounceable letter 's'. At last, he departed and was rowed back to Barangaroo, whom they found sitting by a fire with the Reverend Johnson, making fish hooks.

'From this time our intercourse with the natives,' wrote Tench, 'though partially interrupted, was never broken off. We gradually continued, henceforth, to gain knowledge of their customs and policy; the only knowledge that can lead to a just estimate of national character.' But that Bennelong might have been involved in a study of *him* was something not even generous Watkin mentioned.

These gestures of equal trade and of forbearance on the part of Phillip are worth detailing because they would become less and less the spirit of future transactions between the races.

One day in October that year, a sergeant and three soldiers were out beating the bush for an escaped convict when they met up with Bennelong and Colby and a party of other natives. Bennelong asked the sergeant to come south with him and kill a particular man, 'well-known for having lost an eye', the Botany Bay warrior named Pemulwuy. The soldiers joked with him, but he was serious. Down on the shores of Botany Bay he had fought a ritual battle with the father of a desirable girl, and although he claimed to have won the contest, his passions ran high against Pemulwuy, the girl's kinsman. The Bediagal girl, named Karubarabulu, was forthright and not submissive, and Bennelong desired to take her as a second wife.

Bennelong had a temperament which participated passionately in all these inter-clan squabbles, but the difference between himself and Pemulwuy ran deeper than mere scars. Pemulwuy stayed remote from the Europeans. He would never investigate the whites or try to work them out. He wished to exorcise them and restore the normal world. While Bennelong was conciliatory in however puzzling a way, Pemulwuy was a hard-liner. Both would suffer unutterably for the positions they took. Pemulwuy's was the harsher penalty, however. Outlawed by Governor King, he was shot dead by the sailor and explorer Henry Hacking in 1802. On 5 June that year King wrote to Sir Joseph Banks and told him that Pemulwuy's head had been placed in spirits and sent to England via the *Speedy*. Its whereabouts are still unknown.

*

It seemed that a sort of compact now existed between the Eora, in the person of Bennelong, and Phillip's invading culture. Bennelong seemed well aware of his status as chief peacemaker, the one with whom above all Phillip wanted reconciliation, and he was not above asking for material rewards for fulfilling that role. He requested a tin shield—he rightly thought it might save him many a wound—and a brick house in Sydney Cove. The mutual gifts of hatchets and spears, and the intermittent arrival and departure of Eora people in Sydney sealed the deal. Bennelong read the gifts he received from Phillip and others as personal, but also as acknowledgment of Eora rights in this country and in these waters. The officers failed to see them as equivalent exchanges, and remained half-amused by Bennelong's demands for hatchets. They thought they were giving appeasing gifts to troublesome Aborigines, rather than sealing an informal but important treaty.

Yet in Bennelong's opinion, a visible sign of the compact was in the making. As demanded, a brick house was being built for him on Tubowgulle, the eastern point of Sydney Cove. Bennelong had chosen the place himself, according to Tench. 'Rather to please him, a brick house of twelve feet [c 4 metres] square was built for his use, and for that of his countrymen as might choose to reside in it, on a point of land fixed upon by himself.' He had got his shield too—it was double cased with tin and represented an exponential leap for Eora weaponry. Of his new stature with both whites and Eora, Tench observed, 'He had lately become a man of so much dignity and consequence, that it was not always easy to obtain his company.' The point chosen by him for his residence had significance—given its position at the head of the cove (where the Sydney Opera House now stands), it could be seen as a symbol of Eora title to the place. It was almost certainly seen that way by Bennelong, and all Barangaroo's warnings went for nothing.

BENNELONG'S MARRIAGES

The standing of Bennelong, at least in Captain Tench's view, suffered damage from his behaviour towards his second, new and younger wife, Karubarabulu, the young woman from the north side of Botany Bay who, despite the earlier battles over her, had come to live at Tubowgulle, in Bennelong's brick house. One day in November 1790, Bennelong came to the governor's residence and presented himself to Phillip—he seemed to be able to get an interview any time he liked. Holding a hatchet, and trying out the sharpness of it, he told Phillip that he intended to put Karubarabulu to death immediately. Bennelong believed she had committed adultery, and that this gave him the right to bludgeon her to death, and his visit to Government House beforehand was a warning to Phillip not to interfere in laws that were none of his business. Phillip was alarmed enough to set off for Tubowgulle with Bennelong, and to take his secretary, Captain Collins and Sergeant Scott the orderly with him. On the road from Government House down to Tubowgulle, Bennelong spoke wildly and incoherently and 'manifested such extravagant marks of fury and revenge' that his hatchet was taken away from him, and a walking stick was given to him instead. After all, English males were relatively comfortable with the idea of hitting errant women with walking sticks.

Karubarabulu was seated at the communal fire outside the hut with some other natives. Bennelong, snatching a sword from one of the soldiers, ran at her and gave her two severe wounds on the head, and one on the shoulder. The Europeans rushed in and grabbed him, but the other natives remained quiet witnesses, as if they considered Bennelong entitled to his vengeance. Phillip and the officers noticed that the more they restrained Bennelong, the more the other male Aborigines began to arm themselves, as if to support Bennelong's right to what he was doing.

Fortunately the *Supply* was in the intimate cove—on Phillip's orders, it was immediately hailed and a boat with armed sailors was sent ashore, and Karubarabulu was hustled away on this across the cove to the hospital. A young native came up and begged to be taken into the boat also. He claimed to be her lawful husband, which she declared he was, and begged that he might be allowed on board the ship's boat so that he would be away from Bennelong's rage. 'She is now my property,' Tench has Bennelong saying, like a character in an eighteenth-century melodrama. 'I have ravished her by force from her tribe: and I will part with her to no person whatever, until my vengeance shall be glutted.' Bennelong told the governor and others that he would follow Karubarabulu to the hospital and kill her. Phillip told him that if he did, he would be shot at once, but he treated this threat 'with disdain'.

A number of natives visited the girl in hospital and 'they all appeared very desirous that she might return to the house, though they must have known that she would be killed; and, what is not to be accounted for, the girl herself seemed desirous of going'. After an absence of two days, Bennelong—cooling off and perhaps concerned for his relationship with Phillip—came back to Phillip's house and told him he would not beat the girl any further. He himself had a new husbandly shoulder wound from an argument with Barangaroo. His wife and he should go to Surgeon White's hospital and have their wounds dressed, Phillip suggested. But he would not go because he believed Surgeon White would shoot him, and he refused to stay in the settlement in his house because he had come to believe that White, outraged by the damage he had done to Karubarabulu, would assassinate him by night.

The argument was sorted out, however, and soon Bennelong was over in the hospital to have a plaster applied to his shoulder. Once this was done he visited Karubarabulu, and to Barangaroo's outrage took Karubarabulu by the hand and spoke softly to her.

Thus Bennelong's *ménage à trois* remained turbulent. It is remarkable the way Phillip entertained it. Karubarabulu was at last taken to the governor's house so that she could be safe. From the Government House yard, Barangaroo stood hurling curses up at the girl's room, and she grabbed some of Bennelong's spears to launch at the window and had to be disarmed of them by the marine guards at the gate. But in the evening, when Bennelong was leaving to go back to his hut, the girl Karubarabulu, on whom the governor had lavished such care, demanded that she go too, for a messenger had come saying that Barangaroo would not beat her any more and was now 'very good'.

Bennelong continued to confuse the officers with his signals. On the one hand he said a relative had been killed by the Cameraigal, but then was seen on the north shore picking wild fruit with members of that group. And then on 21 November, Bennelong and Barangaroo as a couple pleaded with Phillip to give them protection in his house. The governor did so. Bennelong told Phillip the Cameraigal had killed one of his 'brothers', a friend or relation, and had burned his body. When Phillip said he would send soldiers to punish them, Bennelong was all in favour of such action. The expedition, however, never took place, as it was contrary to Phillip's principles to interfere in tribal tensions.

McENTIRE'S ENCHANTED SPEAR

What brought a new line from Phillip in his dealings with the Aborigines was the murder of his chief huntsman, John McEntire. McEntire, sentenced in Durham, having crossed from Ireland as deck cargo to work on the British harvest, was hated by the Eora but much liked by the gentlemen, including Surgeon White, whom he often accompanied on excursions into the bush to shoot down bird specimens which would ultimately be rendered by a convict artist and appear in White's applauded journal. The long list of infringements of which he was guilty in Eora eyes, including the slaughter of animals the natives considered dedicated by ancestors for their use alone, had not been absolved by Phillip's wounding. On one occasion, when he was hunting, the natives had set one of the indigenous dogs, a dingo, on him, and he had shot it, contrary to the rule of the world that only an initiated male could kill a dingo. McEntire, unlike Phillip, did not have the missing tooth of an initiate.

Preparations were made amongst the Eora for his punishment. Phillip was amazed at this stage to observe that Bennelong entertained at his hut for some nights the man named Pemulwuy, whom he had previously told Phillip and others was his enemy in terms of love. Pemulwuy was a *carradhy*, or as one scholar puts it, a man of high degree, selected in childhood for his piercing, flecked eyes and precocious air of authority. Throughout eastern Australia there were many initiations, processes and tests for the making of a *carradhy*. The candidate was often thrown on a fire while in a state of trance, or hurled into a sacred waterhole. Prayers were recited by the initiate and the elders to the most important clan heroes and sky beings, Gulambre and Daramulan, as the candidate was brought out of the water or fire. The elders woke the candidate from his trance by laying their hands on his shoulders, and he was given quartz crystals to swallow and an individual totem to help him cure people. As in Western rites of preparation for the priesthood, fasting and endurance and time spent alone before the candidate went through initiation were considered important.

A *carradhy* always played a leading part in the rituals of the Dreamtime, for which he was painted with arm blood or red ochre sanctified by chants as it was applied to the skin. All the crises of Aboriginal life were dealt with by magic, by rituals, by spells and by the sacramental paraphernalia owned by the *carradhy*s. The *carradhy*s also interpreted dreams, which were taken very seriously by Aborigines (as by later Europeans). In every generation of Aborigines there seemed to be young men who combined an interest in ritual knowledge with eyes of extraordinary power and a capacity to interpret the dreams of other members of the group.

The powers exercised by *carradhy*s were sometimes symbolised externally by the handling of bones or of crystals of quartz or other rare stones. It was believed *carradhy*s were capable of eroding a human being while he slept by extracting fat from within his body without making a mark. Pemulwuy had a deformed foot which enabled him to make confusing tracks, and the particular characteristics of the eyes, including a strange fleck in his left eye, which went with his office.

It was McEntire's life-blood Pemulwuy would apply himself to. On 9 December 1790, a sergeant of marines took a number of convict huntsmen, including McEntire, down to the north arm of Botany Bay to shoot game. They settled down in a hide of boughs to sleep. At about one o'clock in the afternoon the party was awoken by a noise outside the hide, and saw five natives creeping towards them. The sergeant was alarmed but McEntire said, 'Don't be afraid, I know them.'

Indeed he did but his knowledge seems to have included contempt. He knew Pemulwuy from earlier expeditions. As McEntire advanced, Pemulwuy hurled his spear into McEntire's side. McEntire declared, 'I am a dead man.' One of the party broke off the shaft of the spear and another two took up their guns and futilely chased the natives. Then they carried McEntire back to Sydney Cove and got him to the hospital early the next morning. The governor was at Parramatta at the time, but was shocked by the news on his return.

One of Phillip's characteristics was sometimes to invest affection and unremitting loyalty in people of flawed character who were effective in a limited range of skills; Harry Brewer was one example, and McEntire another. Phillip detailed a sentry to wake the ever loyal Captain Tench. As Tench walked up the hill to Government House in the still, pre-dawn cool of a summer's night, he may have had a sense that for the first time in his Sydney experience, Mars was calling and battle was close.

He met a Phillip who was uncharacteristically enraged. He instructed Watkin to lead a punitive party of armed marines. The governor at first envisaged that Tench's party would track down a group of natives, put two of them instantly to death and bring in ten hostages for execution in town. None of these were to be women or children, and though all weapons that were encountered were to be destroyed, no other property was to be touched. After prisoners had been taken, all communication, even with those natives 'with whom we were in habits of intercourse, was to be avoided'.

Tench was horrified to hear that his party was required to cut off and bring in the heads of the two slain—hatchets and bags would be supplied. In explaining his tough policy, Phillip told Tench that what the natives particularly feared was to lose numbers relative to the other native groups. He had delayed using violent measures because of his belief that 'in every former instance of hostility, they had acted either from having received injury, or from mis-apprehension. "The latter of these causes," added he, "I attribute my own wound; but in this business of McEntire, I am fully persuaded that they were unprovoked, and the barbarity of their conduct admits of no extenuation . . . I am resolved to execute the prisoners who may be brought in in the most public and exemplary manner, in the presence of as many of their countrymen as can be collected." '

The governor at this point asked Watkin for his thoughts, and the young officer suggested the capture of six might do just as well, and out of this number, a group should be set aside for retaliation if any further outrage occurred, and only a portion executed immediately. The governor decided that should Watkin find it possible to take six prisoners, 'I will hang two, and send the rest to Norfolk Island for a certain period, which will cause their countrymen to believe that we have dispatched them secretly.'

McEntire was not dead; indeed he seemed to be recovering at the hospital, but Phillip believed the lesson still had to be taught. On that issue, he met dissent from an officer who greatly respected him.

Lieutenant Dawes was conscience-stricken about the objectives of the expedition and spoke with his friend the Reverend Johnson about its morality. Dawes, though having bravely borne a wound in the American wars, saw himself above all as a student of peoples, a surveyor of surfaces and skies, not as a combat soldier. He had corresponded with William Wilberforce, the renowned leader of the campaign against slavery, and the objectives of Phillip's mission were abhorrent to him. In Sydney Cove he had spent a great deal of time putting together a dictionary of the Eora, a people who liked him greatly, and whom he, in return, admired. Above all, he admired Patyegarang, an Aboriginal girl of about fifteen years named for Pattagorang, the large grey kangaroo, who was one of his sources for his language collection. She became his familiar and stayed in his hut as his chief language teacher, servant and perhaps lover. The language of Patyegarang recorded by Dawes might indicate either that he was a very affectionate mentor or something more. *Nangagolang*, time for rest, Patyegarang said when the tap-to, military lights-out, was beaten from the barracks square near the head of the cove. *Matigarabangun Naigaba*, we shall sleep separate. And *Nyimang candle Mr D*, Put out the candle, Mr Dawes.

It was Patyegarang who interpreted the motives of her people to Dawes. A white man had been wounded some days before in coming from one of the areas down-harbour to Warrane, Sydney Cove, and Dawes asked her why. *Gulara*, said Patyegarang. Angry. *Minyin gulara Eora?* asked Dawes. Why are the black people angry? *Inyan ngalwi.* Because the white people settled here. And further, said Patyegarang, *Gunin*, the guns.

These exchanges must have played a large part in Dawes's refusal to hunt the natives. Phillip told Dawes he was guilty of 'unofficerlike behaviour' and threatened him with a court martial. But Dawes simply refused to submit to one.

Though he ultimately agreed to go, he would later publicly declare he was 'sorry he had been persuaded to comply with the order'. And though this would further outrage Phillip's feelings, Dawes refused to retract his statement.

The expedition was to set out at 4 a.m. on the humid morning of 14 December. Tactful Tench included the New South Wales Corps's urbane Captain Hill in the group. Three sergeants and forty privates made up the rank and file of this first expeditionary force, and some of the low soldiery carried the hatchets and bags for the collection of two heads. The force tramped south on a familiar track between bushy slopes and paperbark lagoons, sighting the Pacific to their left through the contours of the land. They reached the peninsula at the northern arm of Botany Bay at nine o'clock in the morning. They searched in various directions without seeing a single native, so that at four o'clock they halted for their evening camp. At daybreak they marched fruitlessly in an easterly direction, then southwards, and then northwards, often beset by insects in marshy country. Back near the north head of Botany Bay they saw 'five Indians' on the beach, whom Tench attempted to surround, but the five vanished.

After Tench's military expedition set out, the governor had tried to stop Colby going to Botany Bay, offering him a blanket, a hatchet and a jacket to distract him. On top of that, Colby was diverted by food—the officers tried to eat him down. 'It was hoped that he would feed so voraciously as to render him incapable of executing his intention.' He was given a huge meal of 'a light horseman' (a New South Wales fish) and five pounds (2.3 kilos) of beef and bread. But then 'he set out on his journey with such lightness and gaiety as plainly showed him to be a stranger to the horrors of indigestion'. He told the gentlemen he had to go south not to thwart any military expedition, but to see a kinswoman, Doringa, who was about to give birth. But his chief purpose was probably to warn people, especially Pemulwuy and his own *damelian* (his namesake), the Botany Bay native who shared the name Colby.

Meanwhile, the British military force under Tench moved towards 'a little village (if five huts deserved the name)', but no one was there. Some canoes were seen and possibly fired on, because we know that the native known as Botany Bay Colby was wounded. Returning to their baggage, which they had left under the care of a small guard of soldiers, the party saw a native fishing in shallow water about three hundred metres from land. Tench seems to have been relieved that it was not practicable at that distance to shoot him or seize him, so decided to ignore him. But the native himself did not ignore the party. He turned and started calling various of them by name, and 'in spite of our formidable array, drew nearer with unbounded confidence'. It was Colby from Sydney. Tench was under orders to ignore old native friends, but how could he shoot Colby down? Single-handedly, Colby psychologically disarmed the group 'with his wonted familiarity and unconcern'. In theory, his head should have gone into one of their bags. Instead, he recounted how the day before he had been at the hospital for the amputation of a woman's leg by Surgeon White, and he re-enacted for them the agony and cries of the woman.

Overnight he vanished. The British party waded swamps and swore at mosquitoes for the better part of two days before returning to Sydney between one and two o'clock in the afternoon. Private Easty, who had served in the expeditionary ranks, called the return to Sydney 'a most tedious march as ever men went in the time'. Phillip at once ordered a second expedition—his orders for the first had not been a matter of passion but the establishment of principle. He does not seem to have blamed Tench for its failure, since, wrote Watkin, 'the "painful pre-eminence" again devolved on me'. This time the party pretended they were setting off north for Broken Bay to punish Willemerring, but would instead head south once more. Since the moon was full, they would move by night, to avoid the heat of the day. Crossing the broad estuaries of Cooks River and the swamps behind the beaches of Botany Bay, the soldiers carried their firelocks above their heads and their cartouche boxes were tied fast to the top of their hats. Pushing towards the village they had visited the first time, they met a creek which, when they tried to cross it, sucked them down waist-deep into its mud.

There is a perhaps unconscious comedy in Tench's description. 'At length, a sergeant of grenadiers stuck fast, and declared himself incapable of moving either forward or backwards . . . "I find it impossible to move; I am sinking" resounded on every side.' The rope intended to go round the wrists of captured natives had to be used to drag the sergeant of grenadiers free. With their mud-smirched uniforms, the inglorious military pressed round the head of the creek and on to the village. Tench, dividing his party into three so that they could attack from all sides, sent the troops rushing amongst the huts to find them absolutely empty. And now, unless the marines set out for camp at once, the river estuaries they had crossed since the point where they left their supplies and bags would be cut off till nightfall. The struggle back exhausted many soldiers, their physical condition undermined by dietary deficiencies.

Meanwhile, the wounded Irish gamekeeper was still well enough to walk around the hospital. Though many had spoken to McEntire about the appropriateness of openly confessing any injuries he had done the natives, just in case he needed soon to face God, 'he steadily denied . . . having ever fired at them but once, and then only in defence of his own life, which he thought in danger'. He died quite suddenly on 20 January 1791. The surgeons did an autopsy and found pieces of stone and shell inside the lobe of the left lung. Along with the magic which had been sung into them, they had contributed to the lung's collapse.

After missing all the drama of the two expeditions, Bennelong had returned to Sydney with Barangaroo from the Cameraigal ceremonies across the harbour. Phillip saw that Barangaroo's body was exceptionally painted to mark the ritual importance of herself and her husband, red ochre colouring her cheeks, nose, upper lip and small of her back, while dots of white clay spotted the skin under her eyes. Bennelong and Barangaroo proudly wore crowns of rushes and reed bands around their arms. Barangaroo was, after all, a Cameraigal woman, and had returned to her people with her distinguished husband to be made a fuss of. Amongst the initiates was the youth named Yemmerrawanne, he who aspired to marry Abaroo. The initiates had each had a snake-like black streak painted on his chest, and his front tooth knocked out. Yemmerrawanne had lost a piece of his jawbone along with his incisor.

In Collins's journal, the preparations for the knocking out of a tooth are both illustrated and graphically described. The elders danced until one of them fell suddenly to the ground, seemingly in a state of agony. The other elders continued dancing, singing loudly while one or more beat the fallen one on the back until a bone was produced from his mouth and he was free of his pain. This bone chisel would be used on one of the initiates, who believed it to have come from the elder's body. Then one by one the other senior men threw themselves on the ground in this manner, and in each case a bone to be used the following day to remove an initiate's tooth was produced.

For the ceremony, the young initiate, surrounded by spear- and shield-carrying elders, was seated on a kneeling relative's shoulders and the tooth was extracted by a man holding a chisel of bone in his left hand and a striking stone in his right. Collins acquired the name for this tooth-excising ceremony—*erah-ba-diang*, jaw-hurting. Amongst all the names initiated men carried, some too secret to be uttered to the Europeans, there was added after this ceremony the title *kebarrah*, meaning a man whose teeth had been knocked out by a rock.

Bennelong, returned to Sydney, was full of the exhilaration of the recent Cameraigal ceremonies. Corroboree—the Eora word was *carabbara* or *carribere*—was an exultant experience, described by Tench as dances consisting 'of short parts, or acts, accompanied with frequent vociferations, and a kind of hissing or whizzing noise; they commonly end with a loud rapid shout, and after a short respite, are renewed'. Bodies were decorated with white for the dance, and there were waving lines from head to foot, crossbars, spirals or zebra-type stripes. The eyes were often surrounded by large white circles. There were occasional dances of romance as well—Nanbaree and Abaroo performed one for Phillip and the officers.

Bennelong cheerily told Governor Phillip that he had met Willemerring at the Cameraigal festival. In Bennelong's mind this was no more remarkable than it would be to a European to mention that they had met a given judge socially. But to Phillip it seemed another instance to question Bennelong's reliability.

An incident was about to occur which came close to convincing Bennelong to sever his association with Phillip, his name-swapper. After Christmas a raid was made by some natives who dug and stole potatoes—the natives called them *tarra*, teeth—near Lieutenant Dawes's hut. One of the Eora threw his fishing spear at a convict trying to scare the marauders away and wounded him. Led by Phillip, a small party went chasing the potato thieves, and two of them were found sitting with women by a fire. One threw a club, which the marines thought a spear, and three muskets opened fire. Both men fled, and the two women were brought in, slept the night at Government House, and left the following morning.

One of the two natives fired at was wounded. A surgical party led by White and accompanied by some Sydney Cove natives went looking for him and found him lying dead next to a fire. Bark had been placed around his neck, a screen of grass and ferns covered his face, and a tree branch stripped of bark formed an arch over his body. The musket ball had gone through his shoulder and cut the sub-clavian artery. He had bled to death. None of the Eora who went with the surgeon to look for him would go near him, for fear that the *mawm* spirit in him, the spirit of shock or mortal envy, would overtake them.

Bennelong was angry that death had been the punishment for the minor crime of stealing potatoes. At Government House he was plied with food, but refused to touch anything. The fruits of the earth were communally owned by his people, and here were the interlopers making a sop or a bribe out of them. Later, Bennelong appeared at the head of a group of several warriors in a cove where one of the fishing boats was working, and took the fish while threatening the unarmed convicts and soldiers that if they resisted he would spear them. When he next saw Phillip, the governor asked an armed guard into the room during a session in which Bennelong passionately argued the case for taking the fish. Bennelong saw as justice what Phillip saw as robbery. When confronted with two of the soldiers who had seen him from the boats, Bennelong launched into a rambling, insolent protest, 'burst into fury, and demanded who had killed Bangai [the dead Aborigine]'. Then Bennelong walked out on Phillip, and as he passed the wheelwright shop in the yard, he picked up an iron hatchet and disappeared with it.

Amongst the population of Sydney Cove was an anonymous painter who produced a striking watercolour portrait of Bennelong wearing white paint while angry and mourning the news of Bangai's death. Both Phillip and Bennelong had now become exceptionally enraged over their dead. Phillip gave orders that no boat should leave Sydney Cove unless it carried arms, and forbade the natives to go to the western point of the cove, where the crime of potato stealing had occurred. This prevented them from visiting their respected friend, Lieutenant Dawes. But even this breakdown of the relationship could not stop the too-amiable Bennelong from stopping fishing boats to ask how Phillip was, and to find out if the governor intended to shoot him.

Captain Collins had a clear grasp of the policy of 'sanguinary punishments' by the natives, reasoning that, 'While they entertained the idea of our having dispossessed them of their residences, they must always consider us as enemies; and upon this principle, they made a point of attacking the white people whenever opportunity and safety concurred.'

A SUBTLE RESPONSE

When Lieutenant Ball of the *Supply* had been in Batavia in 1790, gathering supplies and sending Lieutenant King on his way to Whitehall on a Dutch ship, on Phillip's orders he had chartered a snow, a small, square-rigged ship to bring further supplies to Sydney. Sailing in *Supply*'s wake, the *Waaksamheyd* (*Wakefulness*) brought with it a cargo of rice and some beef, pork, flour and sugar. By an arrangement not uncommon in emergency food distribution to this day, the British were willing to lose five pounds in 100 of the rice, but after that deduction was made there was nearly a 43 000 pound (79 522 kilo) deficiency in the rice *Waaksamheyd*'s Dutch master, Detmer Smith, landed. Smith had rice and flour aboard which he claimed were his own, and then proceeded to sell to the commissary.

At some stage Phillip would decide that despite Detmer Smith's chicanery, this would be a good ship to contract for taking Captain Hunter, the officers and ship's company of the *Sirius* back to England for the *pro forma* court martial which always followed the loss of a British naval vessel. Phillip also wrote to the Home Secretary, Grenville, by way of the Dutch snow with a new request to match an earlier one he had sent, expressing a desire to return to England on account of 'private affairs' to do with his estranged wife, Margaret, particularly as to what his future might be in the light of any legacy she left him, or bills she expected him to meet after her death. When he had left for New South Wales in 1787, she had been ill and unlikely to live many years, and Phillip saw both potential benefits and horrific legal responsibilities arising out of her death. But in the request he sent Grenville was the added information that for the past two years, 'I have never been a week free from a pain in my side, which undermines and wears me out, and though this colony is not exactly in the state in which I would have wished to have left it, another year may do much, and it is at present so fully established, that I think there cannot any longer be any doubt that it will, if settlers are sent out, answer in every respect the end proposed by government in making the settlement.'

That word 'answer' had arisen again. Yet by the same ship, Collins told his father that 'this colony, under the present system of supplying it, will never answer'. It was as if the place was being asked a question, and gave only a subtle response, which Phillip alone could hear.

Phillip also sent off by *Waaksamheyd* a letter to Sir Joseph Banks which rings strangely to later ears but which grew from the Enlightenment's obsession with skulls as a guide to race and character and as an index to culture. 'The seeds etc. are on board, the flaxseed (a small cask) is marked EN [for Evan Nepean] . . . I am sorry that I cannot send you a head. After the ravages made by the smallpox, numbers were seen in every part, but the natives burned the bodies.' Eventually Phillip was to acquire a skull—we do not know whose it was—and sent it to Banks, who in turn sent it on to Professor Johann Frederich Blumenbach of the University of Göttingen. The male skull had its front tooth missing, as Banks had warned Blumenbach would be the case, 'according to the custom of these savages'. The skull would be used to support Blumenbach's theory that Caucasians were the founding form of the human group, from which other races had degenerated because of climatic variations. Ultimately, the theory would be perverted by Adolf Hitler and the National Socialist Party of Germany to form the core of their racist, pan-Germanic philosophies.

It would take Hunter and other representatives of the *Sirius* till the following year to reach Portsmouth. Their voyage via New Caledonia and Java was marked by Hunter's wisdom and inventiveness. He proved the exact location of the reef-girt Solomon Islands, and discovered a passage between Bougainville and Buka, a passage which would in a much later war in the twentieth century become a graveyard for Australian, American and Japanese sailors. Twenty-two of Hunter's sailors had fever when they left Batavia, and three would die by Cape Town, where at Hunter's insistence the *Waaksamheyd* would wait sixteen weeks, until mid January 1792, to allow recuperation.

In April that year, the snow reached Portsmouth, and Hunter faced his court martial and was exonerated.

CHAPTER 8

INTO THE BLUE

In New South Wales in April 1791, with the *Waaksamheyd* seen off, another exploration of the hinterland was planned. The expedition's aim was to cross the Hawkesbury River near Richmond Hill and then push on to those western mountains whose deep canyons and cliffs had earlier turned Dawes back. Phillip had named them the Carmarthens, but everyone went on calling them the Blue Mountains.

Along with Phillip, Watkin Tench was one of the group and said they intended to find out too whether the Hawkesbury River to the north-west and the Nepean River to the west were one and the same watercourse. Dawes, Collins, White, Colby and a youth named Ballooderry, two marine sergeants, eight soldiers and three convicts who were assessed to be good shots made up the party. Dawes steered north-west by compass, an instrument to which Colby and Ballooderry gave the title *naamora*, to see the way.

The country immediately west of Rose Hill did not much scare Colby, who said that most of the people from there, the Bidjigals, had died of the *galgalla*, smallpox. Further west still was the Hawkesbury River clan called the Booroo Berongal, and encountering one of their encampments, Colby and Ballooderry felt at risk and wanted to burn down the few shelters. When they reached the bushy banks of the Hawkesbury River, the problems the Europeans had walking through the entangled undergrowth and their frequent falls caused amusement to Colby and his young friend. If the person who fell 'shaken nigh to death' got angry with them, even to the governor 'they retorted in a moment, by calling him every opprobrious name which their language affords'. Their general favourite term of insult was *Gonin Patta*, an eater of human excrement.

Again, the Europeans were defeated by the country and were unable to scale the Blue Mountains, which would present themselves to early attempts as either densely wooded, dead-end canyons or else sandstone precipices with no accommodating inclines. Everyone was impressed by the tree-climbing capacity of the Hawkesbury River natives, and a young man gave his coastal brothers Colby and Ballooderry and the gentlemen an exhibition in climbing the smooth and slippery trunks of eucalpyts, looking for possums.

Phillip was excited to tell Sir Joseph Banks later in the year about the journey and to note the difference of the Hawkesbury language from that of the coastal people—indeed, he went so far as to see them as two separate languages. By now Colby and Ballooderry had grown uneasy amongst the inland strangers and were keen to return to known parts. They kept up a chant of 'Where's Rose Hill; where?' On the return journey, the explorers shot ducks which Ballooderry refused to swim for.

It was typical of those early expeditions that bush or water or steep terraces of sandstone would defeat the part-time explorers of Sydney and Parramatta. Yet it still seems odd that the settlers remained confined to the broad dish of the Sydney Basin, and to the coastal regions which opened up to the south of Botany Bay. It is not impossible that Phillip, not expecting much of the interior, was pleased for now to have his charges limited to a finite area.

In fact the most astounding of the journeys of this era of heroic journeying was not one undertaken on land but one plotted and undertaken by the convict couple John and Mary Bryant in the hope of becoming the first to rise from their pit and appear again on the shores of the known world.

For the fisherman–smuggler Will Bryant, the past two years had been hard. In February 1789 he had received a sentence of 100 lashes for dealing in black-market fish. He had been kept on in the fishing service because, as Captain Collins said, 'Notwithstanding his villainy, he was too useful a person to part with and send to a brick cart.' Bryant burned inwardly, however. Like her husband, Mary also resented his punishment.

Expelled with Will from their fisherman's cottage to live in the general camp, not only did she need to listen to the mockery of fellow prisoners and references to her fallen status but was exposed to the full squalor and hardship of the Sydney Cove diet. Into such deprivation was Mary's second child, Emmanuel, born, and baptised by the Reverend Richard Johnson on 4 April 1790. The dilemma of people like William and Mary Bryant was reflected urbanely in a slightly overstated but valid letter Surgeon White wrote in April 1790 to a dealer in hams, tongues and salt salmon in the Strand, London. 'From what we have already seen we may conclude there is not a single article in the whole country that in the nature of things could prove of the smallest use or advantage to the Mother Country or the commercial world. In the name of Heaven, what has the ministry been about? Surely they have quite forgotten or neglected us? . . . This is so much out of the world and tract of commerce that it could never answer.'

When, towards the year's end, the *Waaksamheyd* arrived in the wake of the *Supply*, Captain Detmer Smith and William Bryant made repeated contact with each other. If the English thought little of Smith, Smith was willing to return the favour and at some stage, in secrecy, sold Will Bryant a compass, a quadrant and a chart covering the route via the eastern coast of New South Wales and Torres Strait to Batavia. Then, towards the end of February 1791, Bryant called a meeting with five other convicts in his hut proposing the stealing of the boat in which he was employed. Mary was privy to these arrangements and may even have initiated them. For whatever reason—her persistence, her complete knowledge of the plot, Bryant's affection for her and for his children—she was always considered essential to the escape. A passer-by overheard the discussion, and it was reported to the governor, who ordered that a watch be kept on Bryant.

Because of a recent overturning of the cutter, it had been refitted at government expense with new sails, mast and oars. Bryant's and Mary's accumulated secret cache for their proposed escape included 100 pounds (45 kilos) of flour, 100 pounds of rice, 14 pounds (6.4 kilos) of pork, about 8 gallons (36 litres) of water, a new net, two tents, carpenter's tools, fishing gear, some muskets and the aforesaid navigational aids. Mary Bryant had collected a little pharmaceutical kit too, including amongst it the triple-veined leaves of the native sarsaparilla (*Smilax glycyiphylla*). (Some of her leaves would end up, as souvenirs of her escape, all over the world.)

As seven other convicts accompanied them, they had probably contributed to this serious accumulation of stores as well. They included Samuel Bird, saltpetre thief and a close friend of the Bryants; the Irish stonemason-cum-navigator,

James Martin; the Second Fleet's William Allen, a man in his mid forties who had stolen handkerchiefs from a shop in Norwich; Nathaniel Lilly, who had broken into a house in Sudbury with two other men; Samuel Broome (alias Butcher), a middle-aged Second Fleeter; and James Cox, a colonial cabinet-maker, who had been one of those who had skipped ship as a result of the mutiny on the *Mercury* in 1782. Before he left, Cox wrote a letter to his lover, Sarah Young, in the hut where he pursued his cabinet-making. The letter called on her 'to give over the pursuits of the vices' which, he told her, prevailed in the settlement.

Between nine and midnight on the evening of the day the *Waaksamheyd* departed Sydney, the Bryant party, some of whom were rostered on for fishing that night, stole the government boat and crept down-harbour past the light at the look-out station where Sergeant Scott and his men were obliviously posted. They met with gratitude and exhilaration the pulse of the Pacific racing in through the Heads. The laughter, the curses, the cries of triumph which must have characterised that sturdy cutter as the Bryants and their friends went to meet the moonless night would in coming weeks be imagined and sucked on by those without the skill or endurance to match these escapees. This boatload should have been self-doomed, but it worked with an exemplary degree of co-operation and made its way to Koepang in Timor, part of the Dutch East Indies, achieving the (then) second longest open-boat journey in the world's history.

The Bryants were escaping a colony in which, despite what the *Supply* and the Dutch snow had brought in from Batavia, the ration was, shortly after their departure, reduced again. Though officially at 3 pounds of rice, flour and pork each, it was reduced by a pound in each case to 2 pounds of be-weeviled rice, 2 pounds of reasonable flour and 2 pounds of pork—ill-flavoured, rusty and smoked—the same amount of salt, or else lean beef with bone was measured in as part of the ration. Hunger would again have the effect of driving people to raid gardens, and to make small thefts. In another sense the absent Bryant had a lasting effect on the scrawny, misbegotten society of New South Wales. It was reported to Phillip that Bryant had frequently been heard expressing what was a common sentiment on the subject amongst convicts—that he did not consider his marriage in this country as binding. It was a marriage for the sake of the alternative world in which fortune had placed him, but he asserted to other convicts that it would not bind him should he return to reality, the established and accustomed earth. Phillip, hearing of Bryant's attitudes after his escape, saw how dangerous this concept was to his community, to all the business of inheritance and ordered life of which monogamy was the keystone. Phillip issued an order that no time-served convict could leave behind in the colony any wife and children who could not support themselves.

'This order was designed as a check on the erroneous opinion which was formed of the efficacy of Mr Johnson's nuptial benediction.' Here was another instance of Arthur Phillip declaring that New South Wales was not virtual reality, it was their world, and the contracts made here bound people to the same pieties as contracts made anywhere. Thus, he intended to centre his people's lives in the colony. In so doing, he was making the first families of a non-Aboriginal Australia.

The following year, the by then famous or notorious William Bligh, restored to normal naval command after the mutiny on the *Bounty*, and promoted to post-captain, called again at Koepang and heard the tale of the Bryant party's voyage from the Dutch officials who were still talking about it.

The escape party had explained themselves to the Dutch Governor of Timor, Timotheus Wanjon, as survivors from the wreck of a whaler named *Neptune* in the Torres Strait, and claimed 'that the captain and the rest of the crew probably will follow in another boat'. This was a credible enough scenario. 'The governor,' one of the escapees, Martin, wrote, 'behaved extremely well to us, filled our bellies and clothed double with every[thing] that was wore on the island.'

Koepang proved a delightful place, favoured for recuperation by those who had suffered fevers in Batavia, and a welcome landfall for Mary and the others. Adding a further dimension to the stylishness of their escape, Bryant and his party drew bills on the British government and so were supplied with everything they needed by the administration.

A THIRD FLEET

Already a large third flotilla, the Third Fleet, had been authorised by Whitehall. The contract was made in November 1790, and nine ships would sail on 27 March 1791. For the overall contract, Camden, Calvert and King were to be paid up to £44 658 13 shillings and ninepence, but they had plans beyond that—six of the Third Fleet transports were also chartered to trade in Bombay cotton on the company's account after they had discharged their duty of convict transportation. The other ships of the group would go whaling off New South Wales and in the Southern Ocean. Camden, Calvert and King's ships carried about £30 000 in coin aboard, to lay the foundations of monetary exchange in New South Wales.

The government and its bureaucracies such as the Navy Board, having made such an outrageously inappropriate contract, seemed content or even anxious that the disaster of the Second Fleet should go unreported in London. But via the Second Fleet ships returning, a letter from a literate unnamed female convict from the *Lady Juliana* would make its eloquent way into the *London Chronicle* of 4 August 1791. The woman convict reflected on having seen the victims of Camden, Calvert and King and their officers brought ashore. 'Oh, if you had but seen the shocking sight of the poor creatures that came out of the three ships, it would make your heart bleed. They were almost dead, very few could stand, and they were obliged to fling them as you would goods, and hoist them out of the ships, they were so feeble . . . The governor was very angry and scolded the captains a good deal, and I heard, intended to write to London about it, for I heard him say it was murdering them.' The writer expressed gratitude to the good agent of the *Lady Juliana*—Lieutenant Edgar. For on *Juliana* only three women and one child had died on the voyage.

Sailors who returned to England on the *Neptune* and the other transports eventually swore statements condemning the behaviour of Captain Trail, though it was ultimately for the murder of a seaman that Trail was tried at the Old Bailey Admiralty sessions in 1792, long after the Third Fleet had already been sent.

Neither the Navy Board nor the Home Office welcomed the attention the trial attracted. Why scare off tenderers for the transport of convicts? In the end the charges failed, the judge mysteriously discounting the evidence and directing the jury to bring in a not-guilty verdict.

Subsequently, the Attorney-General produced a report for the King (in July 1792) which attributed the 'unusual mortality' in the Second Fleet to the 'tonnage of the ship being less than was capable of containing for so long so large a number of persons without hazard of their lives'. If this was so, if the tonnage of the *Neptune* had been fraudulently exaggerated as a way of overcharging government, then no one paid for it, the Navy Board simply wanting the whole embarrassment to vanish. Trail, a mass murderer, would return with impunity to the Royal Navy and serve as a master to Lord Nelson. As for Camden, Calvert and King, after putting together the third convict flotilla, the company would thereafter never be used again.

The chief scandal of this Third Fleet would prove to be the short rations for the Irish convicts on the *Queen*. A receipt for these Irish, dated 11 April 1791, was signed by the naval agent and given to the mayor and sheriff of the City of Cork,

Sir Henry Browne Hayes, a United Irishman nationalist who would himself one day be sent to New South Wales for abducting an heiress. The *Queen*'s indent list, however, would be left behind and, echoing earlier oversights, would not reach Sydney until eight years after the convicts had arrived. A future governor of New South Wales, John Hunter of the *Sirius*, complained of the manner of transportation from Ireland as 'so extremely careless and irregular'. For many Irish convicts of *Queen*, their time would expire and they would not be in a position to prove it.

A little before *Queen* left Cork, the nine ships of the Third Fleet proper sailed from England in two divisions: a great number of ships were on the interminable seas making for Sydney Cove. The *Mary Ann* was well ahead with her 150 English female convicts, nine of whom would die at sea. She did not call in anywhere but the Cape Verde Islands for fresh supplies, and that ensured a brisk passage. The converted frigate, HMS *Gorgon*, the store ship which also carried 29 male convicts selected for their trades, would lose only one male.

Separated at sea, *Atlantic*, *Salamander* and the aged *William and Anne* all met up at Rio, and then made the journey to Port Jackson without stopping at the Cape. At least a dozen of the men Surgeon James Thompson had been required to take on the *Atlantic* were so weak at boarding that they were unable to climb the ship's side and needed to be lifted up in a chair. Thompson had taken many pragmatic steps on diet and exercise time on deck to prevent scurvy developing. So that while only nine men had to go from the *Atlantic* to the hospital in Sydney Cove, the smaller *William and Anne* would land a great number of convicts who were very ill on arrival. Its master, Captain Bunker, was ultimately fined for assaulting and beating some of the Irish members of the New South Wales Corps during the passage, so the conditions for the more lowly prisoners must have been harsh indeed. The men who took the job of agent aboard these ships were sometimes older men, cat's paws for the captains. The agent on *Queen*, Lieutenant Blow, would later be reprimanded by the Navy Board for his lack of interest in the convicts' welfare. The second mate, who would later claim he was working on behalf of the captain, Richard Owen, ordered that the leaden weights used to calculate rations be scraped by one of the Irish convicts, who was rewarded with adequate food. The 4-pound (1.8 kilo) weight had 6 ounces (170 grams) scratched out of its base, the 2-pound (900 gram) weight almost 3 ounces (85 grams). The convicts were also cheated by the use of a 4-pound weight in place of a 5-pound weight, and a 3-pound for a 4-pound.

Abel Tasman, the navigator who went further than anyone wanted, with his second wife Joanna, who would outlive him and remarry, and their daughter in 1637. ('Portrait of Abel Tasman, his wife and daughter', 1637, by Jacob Gerritsz Cuyp, oil on canvas. National Library of Australia, nla.pic-an2282370)

Tasman's crew meet and collect the fauna, the black swan, off Rottnest (Rattenest) Island. The 'rats' were in fact marsupials—quokkas. (Detail from 'Swartte Swaane drift op het Eyland Rotternest', 1726 by Johannes van Keulen, engraving. National Library of Australia, nla.pic-an5598203)

New Guinea has a neighbour, one with coastal mountains beyond which Greco-Roman bowmen hunt dragons and lions, and serpents lie. ('Novae Guineae forma & situs', 1593 by Cornelius de Jode. National Library of Australia, map-rm 00389-s5001)

Left: William Dampier, the urbane pirate, poor commander, excellent harvester of new words and literary star, seen here endowed with appropriate sensibility and global reach by an artist of a later generation. ('William Dampier', ca 1850 by William Charles Thomas Dobson, oil on canvas. National Library of Australia, nla.pic-an2272869)

Right: Cook, unreadable as the Sphinx. A junior officer from Yorkshire with no powerful friends except the sextant and chronometer with which he transformed the earth. ('Portrait of Captain James Cook' by John Webber. Museum of New Zealand Te Papa Tongarewa, 1960-0013-1)

The young Banks, rich, sociable and avid, in graphic contrast with the apparently dour Cook. Almost too tall for any below-decks space on the *Endeavour*, he was able to expand the limits of the natural sciences so thoroughly that Linnaeus suggested the new land be named Banksia to honour the botanic bonanza Banks and his associates found on Australia's east coast. ('Sir Joseph Banks', 1773 by Benjamin West. Lincolnshire County Council, Usher Gallery, Lincoln UK/The Bridegeman Art Library/photolibrary.com)

CATCHING AN ELEPHANT.

In a passageway off a courtyard, East End girls prepare to take a lustful client in suit and breeches upstairs and roll him for his possessions. For such co-operative muggings, a number of young women were transported to Australia. ('Catching an Elephant', 1812 by Thomas Rowlandson. Guildhall Library, City of London/The Bridgeman Art Library/photolibrary.com)

A Transfer of Property.

The 'kid' passes the booty to the 'pal', while their associate distracts an innocent, who by his neckerchief and stick and flat hat may be a country visitor, with posters in a printer's window.
('A Transfer of Property', ca 1830. Mary Evans Picture Library/photolibrary.com)

Left: Prisoners about to embark for New South Wales, Van Diemen's Land (or Bermuda, which also took convicts). Though prisoners were often depicted as savage, gross and simian, the convicts in this illustration are wistful and identifiably like normal folk. ('Adieu, Adieu my native land', undated handcoloured lithograph. Allport Library and Museum of Fine Arts, State Library of Tasmania AUTAS001124067836) Right: The young Lieutenant Phillip in 1764, secretive, ambitious, but lacking connections. Yearning for a command, he was at this time married to the considerably older and wealthier Margaret Denison, a union which would not last. She probably paid for this portrait. ('Captain Arthur Phillip RN', 1764 by G. James, oil painting. Dixson Gallery, State Library of New South Wales DG 233)

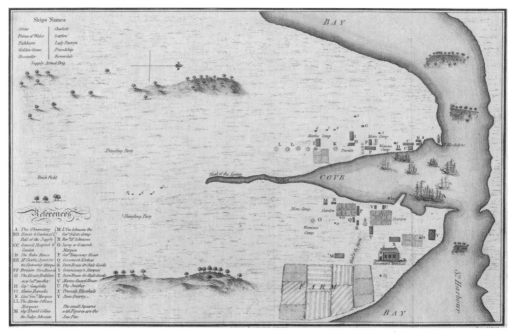

Sydney in April 1788, a map made by an unknown convict. Many of the First Fleet ships and their love-sick sailors still remain to create fist-fights ashore. European-style agriculture is marked here, but uncaptured by this map of an ordered place lies the immensity beyond and the fear within. ('Sketch and description of the settlement at Sydney Cove Port Jackson in the County of Cumberland taken by a transported convict on 16th April 1788, which was not quite 3 months after Commodore Phillips's landing there', 1789 attributed to Francis Fowkes. National Library of Australia, nla.map-nk 276)

Phillip speared in punishment by a Broken Bay Aborigine at Collins Cove, Manly. The whale on which the Eora have been feasting lies partly submerged as the discipline is attended to. This is the work of the convict artist know as the Port Jackson Painter, who may have been Harry Brewer, a middle-aged midshipman, shipmate of Phillip's and provost-marshal. ('The Governor making the best of his way to the boat after being wounded with the spear sticking in his shoulder', ca 1790 by a 'Port Jackson Painter'. The Watling Collection, Drawing 23 © The Natural History Museum, London)

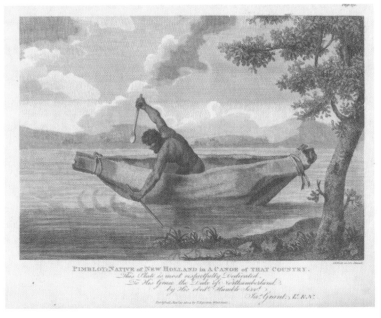

The sole image of Pemulwuy, the Aboriginal leader most resistant of invasion. A *carradhy*, a man of sacred practice and binder and looser of sins and curses, here he is fishing about 1804. His name is rendered 'Pimbloy' by the artist. 'The resemblance is thought to be striking by those who have seen him', wrote James Grant, captain of the naval vessel *Lady Nelson*. ('Pimbloy: Native of New Holland in a canoe of that country', 1804 by Samuel John Neele, engraving from 'The Narrative of a Voyage of Discovery Performed in HM Vessel Lady Nelson, 1803-1804' by James Grant. National Library of Australia)

Bennelong and clansmen on their way to Sydney Cove to enquire into Phillip's health after his spearing.
('Ban nel lang meeting the Governor by appointment after he was wounded by Willemaring in September 1790', ca 1790 by a 'Port Jackson Painter'. The Watling Collection, Drawing 40 © The Natural History Museum, London)

Yoo-long Erah-ba-diang. 7.

An Eora boy is initiated by straddling an elder's shoulders while having a tooth excised with a stone chisel.
('Yoo-long erah-ba-diang', J Neagle, engraving, 1 of a series of 8 plates showing Aboriginal men performing various ceremonies in 'An account of the English colony of New South Wales' by David Collins, 1798. National Library of Australia, nla.pic-an14340273-7)

NOUVELLE - HOLLANDE.

OUI-RÉ-KINE.

Left: Rendered by the invaluable Port Jackson Painter, Bennelong is portrayed in an angry state after Colby's wounding in a ritual battle between Eora clans. Bennelong and Colby would change sides, dependent on who had died or been injured, or who was guilty of abducting women. The ritual lettings of blood resulting from these conflicts were limited by long-established custom. ('Native name Ban-nel-lang, as painted when angry after Botany Bay Colebee was wounded' by a 'Port Jackson Painter', ca 1790. The Watling Collection , Drawing 41 © The Natural History Museum, London) Right: Oui-Ré-Kine (Worogan), a relative of Bennelong's, sketched in 1802 by Nicholas-Martin Petit of Nicolas Baudin's French expedition. The scarrings on her upper arms and breast bespeak unguessed at female ritual. ('Oui-Ré-Kine' by Barthelemy Roger after Nicolas-Martin Petit, engraving from 'Atlas', plate XXI 'Voyage de decouvertes aux terres Australes' by Francois Peron, 1811. National Library of Australia)

Phillip's party on the Hawkesbury in March 1788. Note the apparent dance to the middle right in this coloured drawing by Lieutenant Bradley. Phillip was disappointed by the sandstone escarpments of Pittwater and the lower Hawkesbury. (Detail from 'Broken Bay, New South Wales, March 1788' in 'A Voyage of New South Wales', 1802 by William Bradley, watercolour. Mitchell Library, State Library of New South Wales, ML Safe 1/14 opp. p.90)

John Nicol, an obscure seaman who, like others, begot children on convict women. But unlike them, he kept a journal in which he confesses that as a young purser he had fallen in love with the rural Second Fleet convict Sarah Whitelam as he struck her county-jail chains off. They had a child, but more pragmatic than Nicol, Whitelam married a First Fleet convict named Walsh the day after Nicol's ship, the notorious *Lady Juliana*, left Sydney. ('John Nicol', frontispiece from 'The Life and Adventures of John Nicol, Mariner', 1822. National Library of Australia)

Mary Putland, about 1805. A young widow and Governor Bligh's valiant daughter, in 1808 she defied the officers and men who had come to depose and perhaps execute her father. ('Mary Putland (nee Bligh)', ca 1805 by unknown artist, watercolour. Mitchell Library, State Library of New South Wales MIN 399)

As at the Wexford Vinegar Hill in 1798, the United Irish fought and lost the antipodean Vinegar Hill in 1804. Major Johnston's victory, the first for the eminent Rum Corps, was helped by the fact that he seized the Irish leaders who came to parley. But it does seem that less than three dozen troops defeated over 250 rebels. ('Convict uprising at Castle Hill', 1804, watercolour. National Library of Australia, nla.pic-an-5577479)

Left: Elizabeth Macarthur, a less perturbed figure than her husband the Perturbator. ('Elizabeth Macarthur', ca 1820, by unknown artist. Dixson Gallery, State Library of New South Wales DG223) Right: John Macarthur. The hunger, suspicion, combativeness and restless energy seem evident in this face, and even the 'basilisk [serpent] eyes' of which Governor King accused him. ('John Macarthur', ca 1820, by an unknown artist. Dixson Gallery, State Library of New South Wales DG222)

Esther Abrahams, as the affluent and mature wife of the soldier George Johnston and a woman respected even by Exclusives. An East End Jewish girl sentenced at about fifteen for shoplifting, she had a child in Newgate prison before being sent to New South Wales aboard the First Fleet. Such transformation from felon to matriarch was not uncommon in New South Wales. (Courtesy of Leichhardt Council Local History collection. Reproduced from copy held in their collection)

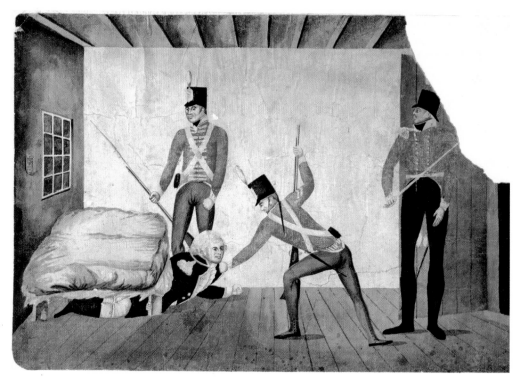

The famous cartoon, unreliable as it is, which has told against Bligh for more than two hundred years. Was he in the room destroying or concealing documents, or was he really, in the full pomp of uniform, under the bed? Commissioned by Sergeant Whittle, this watercolour shows Corporal Michael Marlborough dragging out the governor. The officer on the right is Lieutenant Minchin. All the mutineers have legs like dancers, but Bligh is more grossly rendered. ('The arrest of Governor Bligh', attributed to Sergeant William Minchin. State Library of New South Wales/The Bridgeman Art Library/ photolibrary.com)

The watercolour, 'Costume of the Australasians', is remarkable for the social inclusiveness of colonial society it shows. Two men of substance greet each other on the left, and on the far-right a 'canary', a convict in yellow, carries his burden. Many visitors mention blue dungaree coats or suits which two men in the picture seem to be wearing. ('Costume of the Australasians', ca 1818, by Edward Close, watercolour. Mitchell Library, State Library of New South Wales)

Detail of Port Jackson. The Eora still assert ownership, but that great northern European machine, the flour mill, is evident and permanent in the distance. In the mid-ground are the northern European animals, future wealth on hard hoofs, on whose behalf the Eora and other language groups will lose all. (Detail 'Part of the harbour of Port Jackson, and the country between Sydney and the Blue Mountains, New South Wales' drawn by Major Taylor, 48 Regt., engraved by R Havell & Son, published 1823. National Library of Australia, nla.pic-an5577467

A good-natured London aquatint of 1823 shows a beautiful harbour and a town in good order in which even the convicts working on rocks on the left seem energetic in paying their debt to the law's majesty. This image is at odds with the reports of Commissioner Bigge, then being published, and New South Wales's reputation as a maelstrom of depravity which involved all the figures in this landscape. ('The entrance of Port Jackson and part of the town of Sydney, New South Wales' drawn by Major Taylor, 48 Regt., engraved by R Havell & Son, published 1823. National Library of Australia, nla.pic-an5575513)

Left: George Barrington was such a renowned gentleman pickpocket that his very name became a brand, and after his transportation in 1791, unscrupulous publishers continued to issue tales of his adventures, many of them purporting to be written by him. In fact, he was a haunted soul and chief constable at Parramatta. ('Barrington picking the pocket of J Brown Esqr', 1790, etching. National Library of Australia, nla.pic-an9454411)

Right: The London radical Dr Maurice Margarot, one of the 'Scottish Martyrs' arrested for inflammatory speeches at a British Convention in Scotland. In Sydney with his wife, Citizen Margarot was a plague to an increasingly testy, alcoholic and frightened Governor King. ('Maurice Margarot', 1794, engraving. National Library of Australia, nla.pic-an9727349)

The passionate United Irishman General Joseph Holt, a bugbear for Governor King and under suspicion of planning the slaughter of the administration and its friends. To temper him, King made him attend floggings of more junior United Irish convicts. ('Gen. Holt, the leader of the Irish rebels', 184?-, engraving. National Library of Australia, nla. pic-an9648506)

Three of the seven splendid and ostracised daughters of Wentworth and his wife Sarah, an illegitimate child of convicts. Thus Wentworth passed on his lack of belonging and his repute to a new generation. ('The Three Graces', Hans Julius Gruder, 1868, Vaucluse House Collection, Historic Houses Trust of NSW)

The young radical, Wentworth, scourge of colonial pretension, edgy about his parentage, jealous for the repute of father and his nation, always the outsider, and ultimately to be transformed by increasing wealth into an equally turbulent Tory. ('William Charles Wentworth', ca 1848, copy of lithograph. Mitchell Library, State Library of New South Wales SPF P1/W)

Governor Ralph Darling, who manages to resemble a martinet and man of vengeance in this portrait painted before he left Britain to take New South Wales in hand. ('Portrait of Ralph Darling, Governor of New South Wales, 1825-1831', 1825 by John Linnell, oil on wood panel. National Library of Australia, nla.pic-an3291077)

The young poet from Ulladulla, Henry Kendall, nationalist and friend of republicans and Chartists, who would fight so gallantly to discern an Australian muse and to assert that one could be a man of letters in New South Wales. This face is unmarred by the destitution, alcoholism and lunacy which lie ahead. ('Henry Kendall as a young poet'. Mitchell Library, State Library of New South Wales Pic.Acc.6510)

Left: Young Henry Parkes, the Chartist ivory-turner, poor businessman, but orator so accomplished he could stand atop an omnibus and galvanise a crowd on the subject of ending transportation. ('Sir Henry Parkes', ca 1853. Mitchell Library, State Library of New South Wales PXA 345, 19a) Right: Daniel Deniehy was the brilliant child of Irish convicts, dazzling in spiky oratory and the inventor of the phrase 'bunyip aristocracy' to describe Tory dreams of an Australian House of Lords. The New South Wales constitution would end his republican dream, and alcoholism would mar his life. ('Daniel Deniehy', ca 1860 photograph. Mitchell Library, State Library of New South Wales, SPF P1/D(BM))

Henry Parkes, darling of progressives and sworn to fight the conservatives over the New South Wales constitution, born aloft by admirers after winning a seat in the Legislative Council. ('Henry Parkes, Esq, carried in triumph to the Empire office', Illustrated Sydney News 6 May 1854. Mitchell Library, State Library of New South Wales TN115)

Hobart's first house and its livestock, 1806. It was inhabited by GP Harris, a surveyor set the task by David Collins of surveying and assessing the geographically complex Hobart region. ('GP Harris, cottage, Hobart Town, VD Land, Aug.1806', watercolour. National Library of Australia, nla.pic-an5380489)

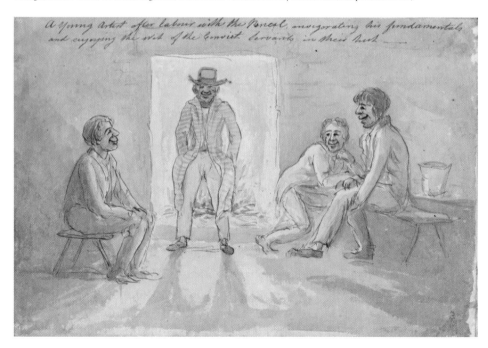

The artist John Richardson Glover emigrated to Van Diemen's Land in his sixties to join his sons. He describes this sketch as being of the artist 'after labour with the pencil, invigorating his fundamentals and enjoying the wit of the convict servants in their hut'. ('A young artist after labour...', 1835 by John Glover, drawing in sketchbook 'Van Diemen's Land'. National Library of Australia, nla.pic-an4623117)

The Irish convict mess orderlies turning up at the cooking shack or coppers on deck found that the cook frequently complained of not being able to work out how to divide the reduced amounts of meat between all the messes. The prisoners appealed to Lieutenant Blow, and he told them to elect one of their own to stand beside the second mate during the weighing. The prisoners also complained to Ensign Cummings of the New South Wales Corps, who in turn asked Lieutenant Blow to intervene, but Blow merely replied, 'My dear fellow, what can I do?'

Magistrates in New South Wales to whom the convicts complained after landing would eventually find that the rations stipulated in the contract with Camden, Calvert and King had not been supplied, that frauds had been committed, and that those who should have seen that the full ration was served had failed to exercise their authority. The magistrates passed the matter on to Phillip, who wrote in his dispatch to the Home Secretary, 'I doubt if I have the power of inflicting a punishment adequate to the crime.'

Little is known about the first Irish convict ship, *Queen*, precisely because it would be so long before their sentencing papers caught up with the prisoners she carried. But if *Queen*'s convicts were like later Irish shiploads, the crimes of the women were at least in part motivated by want when the potatoes gave out in the spring, and shoplifting and theft became an option for those who needed cash or goods to trade for oatmeal. A certain number of the males, about two dozen, were members of an Irish peasant secret society, the Defenders, who had arisen as local groups to protect Catholics against the raids of a similar Protestant organisation named the Peep-of-Day Boys. Many landlords disapproved of the radical, house-burning tendencies of the Peep-of-Day Boys, especially in the Armagh area, where raids and murders of Catholics and burning of cabins and farmhouses occurred throughout the mid 1780s. Some Protestant landlords even advised their Catholic tenants to arm themselves, despite it being illegal for a Catholic to own or carry a firearm. Public sentiment on both sides of the sectarian chasm at first had some sympathy for the men who called themselves Defenders. Feelings deepened, however, when Defenders moved to the offensive against suspected Peep-of-Day-ers, or became vocal, or when they refused to buy any goods from or trade with any business which had Peep-of-Day connections or sympathies.

These people who owned so little were bolstered by enduring myths of the kind which grow amongst the defeated. In their eyes, Christ was their fellow-sufferer and was close to them, and would in the end exalt them, confounding their enemies and destroying the British apparatus of landlord and magistrate. Peasant myths arose which depicted the Irish armed with nothing but cornstalks turning back the armies of England. Such desperately held hopes came to New South Wales with the two dozen or so Defenders and their numerous sympathisers aboard *Queen*.

The forerunner of this Third Fleet, the little *Mary Ann* with her female convicts aboard, appeared off Sydney on the morning of 9 July 1791. She had made the quickest passage yet—four months and sixteen days. But the captain, Mark Munro, not only had no private letters aboard, 'but had not brought a single newspaper'. The officers on the *Mary Ann* could tell Tench, however—that there was 'No war; the fleet's dismantled.'

The women disembarking from *Mary Ann* were all very healthy and spoke highly of the treatment they had received from Munro. Tench thought that Captain Munro should be praised. 'The advocates of humanity are not yet become too numerous: but those who practise its divine precepts, however humble and unnoticed be their station, ought not to sink into obscurity, unrecorded and unpraised, with the vile monsters who deride misery, and fatten on calamity.' The *Mary Ann*, which carried sufficient stores to enable two extra pounds (c 1 kilo) of rice a week to appear on the colony's humble plates also brought the happy news that the store ship *Gorgon* was definitely on the way.

It also brought instructions for the governor confirming British policy that though those convicts who had served their period of transportation were not to be compelled to remain in the colony if they could somehow get home, 'no temptation' should be offered to induce them to quit it. So the mere prison camp was being transmuted into a society, one which operated not only by fear of punishment but by desired and embraced civil pieties. A founding element of New South Wales, and of the embryo nation it would make, was the practical inability of most time-served convicts to leave—the more the population of convicts built up, the more limited the means became of working a passage back home or accompanying a returning gentleman as a time-served servant. This meant that for many of the convicts, in no sense was New South Wales the *chosen* land. It was a netherworld where people got stuck, and having served time became, willy-nilly, citizens of New South Wales.

A later governor (William Bligh) would call the children born in New South Wales 'National Children', but it was an administrative, not a visionary term. Now, with varying degrees of reluctance and acceptance, further time-served convicts moved out during that July of 1791 with their 'national children' to their authorised land grants around Parramatta.

The ships which arrived after *Mary Ann* did not maintain her high standards of care for prisoners. The convicts who were landed sick would have been interested to see the native Bennelong at the hospital, being treated for a form of scabies, which had struck the natives that winter. The surgeons were trying to heal him with applications of sulphur. Bennelong resembled, said Phillip, 'a perfect Lazarus'.

The *Salamander*'s convicts complained loudly that they had not had proper attention paid them. Phillip needed nonetheless to send the ship and her master on to Norfolk Island with convicts, stores and provisions. The majority of the convicts retained on the mainland were sent to Parramatta, employed to open up new ground at a short distance from the settlement.

The slow *Admiral Barrington* and her crew and convicts had suffered a hard time in the Southern Ocean and even off the New South Wales coast, where she was dragged out to sea by a ferocious southerly gale. She had suffered 36 deaths on the passage to Sydney, which she reached on 16 October 1791. The living filled White's hospital.

Mrs Parker, the wife of Captain John Parker of the *Gorgon*, took the trouble when that store ship finally arrived in Sydney to visit the convicts of the Third Fleet then in hospital. She was shocked to find herself 'surrounded by mere skeletons of men—in every bed, and on every side, lay the dying and the dead. Horrid spectacle! It makes me shudder when I reflect that it will not be the last exhibition of this kind of human misery that will take place in this country, whilst the present method of transporting these miserable wretches is pursued.'

In these same grim vessels two convicts arrived in New South Wales who would later become notable entrepreneurs. Simeon Lord was significantly a convicted thief of linen who, once landed, acted as a servant to a captain in the New South Wales Corps. He would later become one of the emancipated convict front men who would retail goods purchased by the officers of the corps. Another entrepreneur in the making, a young felon named James Underwood, would go into the shipping business with Henry Kable. But their glory days were some time off yet.

*

In the midst of all the ill-run, profit-driven ships of the Third Fleet, the store ship *Gorgon* had appeared. 'I will not say that we contemplated its approach with mingled sensations,' wrote Tench, by now a veteran of such arrivals. 'We hailed it with rapture and exultation.' *Gorgon* contained six months' full provisions for about nine hundred people. Lieutenant King, having returned to England to be married, arrived back on the *Gorgon* with the new rank of commander, accompanied by his wife Anna Josepha Coombe, a generous-spirited woman who would look to the welfare of his children by the convict Ann Innett as well as to that of the child she herself was carrying. Obviously King had been frank about his colonial relationship before marrying Anna Josepha between successful conferences with Sir Joseph Banks, Grenville and Nepean. He had returned with assurances about ongoing support for New South Wales, and these he passed on to Arthur Phillip.

Indeed, an extraordinary validating device had arrived on the *Gorgon*, and been delivered to Phillip's office at Government House. It was the Great Seal of New South Wales. On the obverse were the King's arms with the royal titles in the margin; on the reverse, an image of convicts landing at Botany Bay, greeted by the goddess Industry. Surrounded by her symbols, a bale of merchandise, a beehive, a pickaxe and a shovel, she releases them from their fetters and points to oxen ploughing, and to a town rising on the summit of a hill with a fort for its protection. In the bay, the masts of a ship are to be seen. In the margin lie the words *Sigillum. Nov. Camb. Aust.*, Seal of New South Wales; and for a motto, *Sic Fortis Etruria Crevit,* 'In this way Tuscany grew strong'—a reference to Tuscany having once received the criminals of other places.

A BRAND NAME OF CRIME

From the modest brig *Active*, part of the Third Fleet, came Sydney's first genuine celebrity criminal, an Irishman named George Barrington. D'Arcy Wentworth had been a considerable gentleman of the road, but Barrington was a brand name of crime, like Jesse James, Ned Kelly, Dick Turpin or Al Capone. His origins were, as people said then, mysterious, which was almost a synonym for Irish. He was sent to Dublin Grammar School where he stabbed another boy in a fight, was flogged, and in response stole money and ran away. Joining a band of strolling players, he was taught by an expert actor/pickpocket, who took him to London as his protégé. In 1773, his senior partner was transported to North America.

As his own operator, George Barrington achieved the status of prince of pickpockets, living splendidly despite having to spend a year in the hulks. The victims of his confidence tricks and 'lifting' skills included the Russian Prince Orlow, from whose pocket, at Covent Garden Theatre, he managed to steal a snuffbox inlaid with diamonds and said to be worth £30 000. Various peers of the realm were caught out by Barrington, and some of 'the brightest luminaries in the globe of London'. Tried at the Old Bailey in September 1790 for stealing a gold watch and chain at the Enfield racecourse, he was sentenced to transportation for the light term of seven years. The press reported that he had tried to console other rogues in the general wards of Newgate about the fact that they were all to be sent to a country where the natives had no pockets to pick.

After his transportation, his name remained in use in British true crime pamphlets and chapbooks. Having been the generic gentleman pickpocket, he became the generic redeemed thief, and the idea of New South Wales as a place of redemption for deficient Britons gained great currency. In 1793, a small but popular tract named *An Impartial and Circumstantial Narrative of the Present State of Botany Bay*, and in 1802, *The History of New South Wales*, would be published under his name, but may or may not have come from his hand. In the second, more credible book, he is quoted as saying that the appearance of the convicts at the time his ship arrived was truly deplorable, 'the generality of them being emaciated by disease, foul air, etc'.

Phillip, meeting Barrington, found him sober-minded, as if transportation had had an impact on his legendary flamboyance. He was sent to work at Toongabbie, west of Sydney, where he shared a hut with lower-class convicts and an Aboriginal woman. They no doubt found sharing their table with him a great privilege and novelty, and pressed him for stories of his glittering career. But Barrington's seriousness, perhaps partly depression, together with his 'irreproachable conduct' saw him quickly appointed a superintendent of convicts and ultimately a member of the Parramatta night watch. Barrington found there a life not utterly lacking in pleasure: 'having had several young native dogs given to me, from time to time, I take great delight in kangaroo hunting, it is not only an agreeable exercise, but produces a dish for the table, nearly as good as mutton and in the present dearth of livestock is not an unacceptable present'.

He must have been aware of the irony by which publishers in London were profiting in his name. It added to the bitterness of his bread.

GENTLEMAN GO, GENTLEMAN STAY

By the Third Fleet, Governor Phillip received from Secretary of State Grenville a grudging permission to leave the colony: 'I cannot, therefore, refrain from expressing my earnest hope . . . that you may be able, without material inconvenience, to continue in your government for a short time longer.'

It was intended that the bulk of the marine garrison, now relieved by the purpose-recruited New South Wales Corps, should return to England on the *Gorgon*. In deciding what to do in his own case, Judge-Advocate Collins was caught between his dislike of the newly arrived Captain Nepean of the New South Wales Corps and his detestation of the departing Major Ross. Said Collins of Ross: 'With him I would not sail were wealth and honours to attend me when I landed.' And despite his loving correspondence with his wife Maria, he was in an association with Ann Yeates, alias Nancy, a young milliner from *Lady Penrhyn*, who had borne him two sons.

Collins reflected that though the masters of the Third Fleet ships knew they could have brought out a further thousand tons of provisions, instead they had loaded up with copper, iron, steel and cordage for sale at Bombay 'on account of their owners'. Dependent for his survival, like all the other European inhabitants of New South Wales, on this strange balance of beneficence and greed in shipping merchants, he decided that he would seek permission to go home at 'the first opportunity that offers of escaping from a country that is nothing better than a place of banishment for the outcasts of society'.

FINDING CHINA

Speaking their own language, and bound together in many cases by secret oaths and compacts, the Irish who had come into Port Jackson on *Queen* on 26 September 1791 presented particular problems. The officers in New South Wales would have the opportunity to nod as ruefully as any Anglo-Irish magistrate on Irish soil at the Gaelic wrong-headedness of Irish convict refusal to behave like Englishmen, and to speak English. Irish was still the first language of over 80 per cent of Irish hearths, and now it was heard, to the discomfort of the officers and officials, in the fringes of the bushland of New South Wales.

What were they plotting, these strange souls? What was behind their frequent, secret laughter?

One thing about them was the ready—some would say gullible—comfort they took in millennial fantasies. A new century was nearing and there were omens—the French revolution, before that the American—foretelling a successful uprising in their home country. Tom Paine was singing of the rights of the humble and the humble of the *Queen* were aware of it. At the dawn of the new century, the justice of Christ might reverse the order of the world, putting the first last, and the last first. In Sydney and Parramatta there developed amongst the Irish like a fever 'the chimerical idea' of finding China from New South Wales, the idea that it was beyond the mountains and the Hawkesbury to the north-west of Sydney Cove. In terms of the Enlightenment it was a preposterous idea. In terms of their extreme yearning it made perfect sense. Somewhere on earth there *must* exist a veil the Irish could penetrate, beyond which they would reassume old powers and have their remembered spaciousness restored to them. Their ignorance of strict geography was astounding but understandable—the schooling of Irish Catholics was contrary to the penal laws of Britain—so they made up a geography of hope from fragments of information, convinced that New South Wales was part of the same unknown zone as China. They drew their compasses on pieces of paper, with the arrows fixed on north, a practice which would be laughed at by their betters. Yet the Defenders and other secret societies, influenced by Freemasonry, knew there was an inherent importance and a power in the representation of the compass. The north was potent, even if invoked merely on paper, and the Irish convicts, eating bitter rations by the campfires of Sydney and Parramatta, had caught the belief that not too many days walk northwards from the Parramatta River and Port Jackson, a habitable kingdom lay awaiting them.

One sight of the dense bush around Parramatta and Sydney was enough to make many delay their Chinese pilgrimage. The strangeness of the natives, matched by the strangeness of the forests, the tangles of ungodly acacias and melaleucas, the spiteful sharpness of narrow-leaved shrubs determined to survive fire and drought, and the feeling of godlessness and lack of familiar presences in the place had been for three years sufficient to stop most convicts walking away, and promised to be effective well into the future. Yet on 1 November—All Saints Day—twenty male Irish convicts and one pregnant female in Parramatta took a week's provisions, tomahawks and knives, and set out into the bush to find China. A few days later, sailors in a boat belonging to the *Albemarle* transport met the pregnant Irish woman down-harbour. She had been separated from her group for three days. The woman's husband was also later found and gave the same 'absurd account of their design' to officials in Sydney. Thus the proposition of Irish stupidity made its entry onto the Australian stage.

Other men were captured to the north near Broken Bay, and despite their suffering, attempted escape again a few days later. Thirteen of those who first absconded 'were brought in, in a state of deplorable wretchedness, naked, and nearly worn out with hunger'. They had tried to live by sucking the flowering shrubs for their nectar and by eating the wild purple berries which grow on sandstone headlands around Sydney.

Phillip ordered the convicts at Parramatta to be assembled, and told them that if they went missing he would send out parties looking for them with orders to fire on sight, and if they were captured alive he would chain them together with only bread and water during the rest of their term of transportation. The declaration did not staunch the magnitude of Irish hopes. Typically, Watkin Tench visited the convicts who had made the dash for China—it was he who called them 'the Chinese Travellers'. Four of them lay in hospital, variously wounded by the natives. He asked them if they really supposed it possible to reach China, and they informed him that they had been told that at a considerable distance to the north lay a large river, 'which separated this country from the back part of China'. When they crossed this Jordan, they would find themselves among a copper-coloured people who would treat them generously. On the third day of their wanderings towards this hoped-for place, one of their party had died of fatigue, and another was butchered by natives. They had reached Broken Bay and the Hawkesbury River, where the wide entrance and estuary stopped them from going further.

Though a great proportion of the Irish were of farming backgrounds or had agricultural experience, Hunter would later describe them as 'dissatisfied with their situation here', and 'extremely insolent, refractory, and turbulent'. For the Irish combined their dream of China with a keen sense of their small quota of rights. The convicts of *Queen* at Parramatta were the first, for example, to stage an organised public protest. It was held outside the newly built Government House in Parramatta in the humidity of December 1791 and demanded that the issue of rations be changed back from weekly to daily. There was a certain justice in this. A weak or sickly person might be deprived of a week's rations by a bully in one swoop, but if the ration was issued daily, the weak could appeal to the strong to prevent any further, large-scale ration-snatching.

*

There was a pregnant Irish girl named Catherine Devereaux aboard *Queen* who did not seek China but stuck close to camp for the sake of her unborn child, which when born was christened James, taking his father's—the *Queen's* cook's—name: Kelly. James Kelly would reach young manhood under the tutelage of two entrepreneurial former convicts, Henry Kable and James Underwood, and in Van Diemen's Land would become a whaling, sealing and shipping tycoon of some renown.

MERCANTILE DREAMS

Despite a few nods towards mercantilism in the founding of Sydney, it was not a trading post, and Phillip did not want it yet to be one. The Third Fleet transport, *Britannia*, however, going off to whale, returned with seven spermaceti whales in November 1791, having hunted in company with *William and Anne*, which had caught only one whale on its own account. Though the master of the *Mary Ann* had been as far southwards as 45 degrees without seeing a single whale, the *Matilda* stayed off Jervis Bay, south of Sydney, and saw a great many whales, but was unable to chase them because of the weather. The initial performance of the South Seas whale fishery seemed mediocre.

William Richards Jr, who had dispatched the First Fleet, had commercial dreams for the far-off colony he had never seen, and remained in touch with New South Wales through his Botany Bay agent, Zachariah Clarke, who was now the commissary of stores in New South Wales. A visionary eccentric, Richards hoped to reclaim the convict-handling business, and combine it with other forms of trade between the south-west Pacific and Britain. He was willing to receive a land grant and to live permanently in New South Wales as Sydney's shipping magnate. Outraged by stories of the Second Fleet, the devoutly Christian Richards sought the twin beacons of utility: a settled, regular, low-yield market in the conscientious transportation of convicts, and on the other side, high-yield trading with India and China and what he may have been convinced would be an increasing traffic of whalers.

His ideas, an accurate depiction of the future of New South Wales though they were, were not well received. In a year or two he would become bankrupt due to other contracts gone bad, and some of his children would be left to consider New South Wales as an option for free settlement. But far more than anyone else in the penal equation, Richards had desired New South Wales. Not many did.

Even Tench would write, 'If only a receptacle for convicts be intended, this place stands unequalled . . . when viewed in a commercial light, I fear its insignificance will not appear very striking.' He would leave New South Wales, it seemed, with fond remembrance but no desire to return.

In December 1791, as the *Gorgon* lay in Sydney Cove ready to return the marines to Britain, offers were made to the non-commissioned officers and privates to stay in the country as settlers or to enter into the New South Wales Corps. Three corporals, a drummer and 59 privates accepted grants of land on Norfolk Island or at Parramatta, as Rose Hill was by now officially named. The rest wanted to return—indeed, of those who stayed, Tench thought the behaviour of the majority of them could be ascribed to 'infatuated affection to female convicts, whose characters and habits of life, I am sorry to say, promise from a connection neither honour nor tranquillity'. As for tranquillity, only the parties to the relationships could say anything, but it is a matter of record that many of these remaining soldiers and their women were founders of enduring Antipodean stock.

Before packing to leave on *Gorgon*, in the summer of 1791–92, Tench made a reconnaissance around Prospect Hill, south of Parramatta, and the ponds along the Parramatta River. Looking at the settlements with the eyes of a man about to depart forever, Tench gave a report of mixed skill and ineptitude on the part of convict and other farmers, and of New South Wales as something less than a bountiful garden. Its tough and plentiful flora might seem to promise a form of Eden, but in the Sydney Basin it all grew from an ancient, leached and worn-down earth that demanded great skill and determination from those who would profit from it.

For its natural fertility, Tench admired the Parramatta farm of the former sailor and highway robber, John Ramsay. Ramsay had settled there with his wife, Mary Leary, from the Second Fleet. Like Ruse's wife, Elizabeth Perry, Mary Leary might have been unjustly transported, and was a woman with an unresolved and burning grievance against her mistress, the wife of a London attorney. When the lawyer saw some of his wife's clothing on Leary, his wife swore under oath that she had never 'sold her any one thing in my life'. On the farm in New South Wales, Leary probably enlisted her husband's belief in her innocence. No doubt, at their rough-hewn table, she reiterated the extremely credible tale to Captain Tench himself. Tench thought Ramsay 'deserves a good spot, for he is a civil, sober, industrious man. Besides his corn land, he has a well-laid-out little garden, in which I found him and his wife busily at work. He praised her industry to me; and said he did not doubt of succeeding.' By contrast, Tench found Joseph Bishop, former fisherman and convict, had planted a little maize 'in so slovenly a style, as to promise a very poor crop'. To survive as a farmer, thought Tench, a man 'must exert more than ordinary activity. The attorney's clerk, Matthew Everingham, I also thought out of his province, and likely to return, like Bishop, when victualling from the stores ceased, to drag a timber or brick cart for his maintenance . . . I dare believe he finds cultivating his own land not half so heavy a task, as he formerly found that of stringing together volumes of tautology to encumber, or convey away that of his neighbour.'

And so Tench's rural rides went. On 7 December, Tench visited the German settler Philip Schaeffer's farm on the river and approved of his vine plantings. Schaeffer had served as a lieutenant in the Hesse-Hanau Regiment, sponsored by George III, in the American war. Amongst the Americans the Hessians had a reputation for savagery, but Schaeffer and Tench had the bond of having been fellows in arms.

Directly across the river from Schaeffer's 140 acres (57 hectares) lay the more modest but 'very eligible' farm of Christopher Magee, neighbour and crony of the initial farmer, James Ruse. Magee's idyll on the Parramatta River would ultimately prove fragile. Overall, Tench's reconnaissance before departure showed that the Parramatta River area did not speak overly well for the fertility of eastern Australia.

Sydney, where Tench had spent the bulk of his time in New South Wales, was by the turn of 1791–92 the lesser village to Parramatta. In Sydney lived 1259 persons, with 1625 in Parramatta and its farming areas, and 1172 at Norfolk Island. There were just in excess of 4000 European New South Wales people perilously surviving the Sydney experiment.

Robbie Ross was delighted to march the marines aboard the *Gorgon* on 13 December. His now adolescent son, Lieutenant John Ross, was in their ranks. Ross himself had only the week before found reason to fight a duel with Captain Hill of the New South Wales Corps, from which, though both fired two shots, both came away unhurt.

Gorgon dropped down the harbour three days after the marines marched aboard, and vanished back in the direction of the known world the next day. A company of marines remained behind in Sydney Cove, waiting for the arrival of the remainder of the New South Wales Corps.

The *Gorgon* on departure was to an extent not a European but an Australian ark: 'our barque was now crowded with kangaroos, opossums, and every curiosity which that country produced', noted the departing Sergeant Scott, including plants and birds and the other antediluvian mysteries of New South Wales.

By the time the *Gorgon* left Sydney, the twenty-month-old voyager Emmanuel Bryant had died in the Dutch East India Company prison ship moored off Batavia, where Mary Bryant and her two infants were kept prisoner after being picked up by the authoritarian Captain Edwards of the wrecked HMS *Pandora* in Koepang. Captain Edwards, who had been sent to the Pacific to find the mutineers of HMS *Bounty*, had recaptured the escapees in Koepang. He was in the meantime in good lodgings in the elegant Dutch quarter of Batavia, organising passages for himself, his prisoners and the *Pandora*'s company on three Dutch ships to go home by way of the Cape.

Mary Bryant was on her way to becoming the first person tried for return from transportation to New South Wales.

BARANGAROO GIVES BIRTH

Through his gifts of iron hatchets to a number of selected Sydney Aboriginals, including Bennelong, Phillip might have unwittingly created a new elite—the *Mogogal*, the hatchet men. But even ownership of a hatchet did not give Bennelong psychological dominance over his wife Barangaroo Daringah, something of a woman-warrior. She carried two scars from spear wounds received in the give-and-take of inter-clan relations. The spear that caused one of them had passed right through her thigh. She was forceful and good-looking. 'She is very straight and exceedingly well-made,' wrote Phillip. 'Her features are good, and she goes entirely naked, yet there is such an air of innocence about her that clothing scarcely appears necessary.' The septum of her nose had been pierced—an uncommon feature with Port Jackson women.

Tench had described Yuringa, Colby's wife, as 'meek and feminine', but Barangaroo by contrast as 'fierce and unsubmissive'. She seemed slightly older than Bennelong and had two children of a former husband, both of whom were dead, possibly from smallpox. Now she was about to give birth again and Phillip noticed that she, like other Aboriginal mothers, planned to wrap her new baby in the soft bark of the tea-tree.

Before the birth, Barangaroo had visions of being delivered of her baby in Phillip's house, and had already asked him about it. Phillip thought it a mere touching request. But it would give her child a claim on Government House as his place of birth, and seemed to carry with it, apart from genuine affection and reverence, a new strategy—if the ghosts could not be made to disappear, the Eora should try to outclaim and out-title them. Barangaroo thus avoided the hospital, where Phillip wanted to send her, for the obvious reason that it was full of *mawm*, the bad spirits of the dead. In the event, the birth seemed to occur suddenly, and did not take place at Government House. The child was a girl, named Dil-boong.

Then, soon after, at the end of 1791, Barangaroo died. The causes were unknown but might have been the result of either post-childbirth complications or marital contest, the latter seeming for once the less likely. Bennelong and Barangaroo were always fighting, but Tench said, like a good Georgian man, that 'she was a scold, and a vixen, and nobody pitied her . . . the women often artfully studied to irritate and inflame the passions of the men, although sensible that the consequence will alight on themselves'. When Barangaroo was dying, the desperate Bennelong summoned the great *carradhy*, Willemerring, the wounder of Phillip. When he did not arrive in time to save her, Bennelong would seek him out and spear him in the thigh. Indeed, in Barangaroo's honour, or more accurately to adjust the world to her death, many spears were thrown by Bennelong and her Cameraigal relatives, for death was always the result of some sorcery.

In intense grieving, Bennelong asked Phillip, Surgeon White and Lieutenant David Collins to witness his wife's cremation. He cleared the ground where the funeral pyre was to be built by digging out the earth to about 13 centimetres below the surface. Then a mound of sticks, bushes and branches was made about one metre high. Barangaroo's body, wrapped in an old English blanket, was laid on top of this with her head facing north. Bennelong stacked logs on the body and the fire was lit. The English spectators left before the body was totally consumed.

With Watkin Tench gone, David Collins and Lieutenant Dawes and Phillip himself remained as the chief observers of the natives. Collins and others were aware that aside from British–Eora conflict, the old ritual battles of the Eora continued. There had been a confrontation between the Sydney and Botany Bay natives in April 1791 over the uttering of the name of a dead man. The natives knew that the uttered name could summon down havoc from the spiritual realm onto the physical earth. After a death, the deceased became 'a nameless one', said Collins. Mourners often warned Collins and other officers not to use the names of the dead.

An incident occurred in May 1792 which gave the Europeans a further bewildered insight into the rigidity of native law, which matched at least the rigidity of their own—but through a different set of balances. A woman named Noorooing came into town to tell the white settlers of the ritual killing of a south Botany Bay native, Yellaway, who had abducted her. She was clearly not an unwilling abductee, since she threw ashes on herself in sadness and refused all food, and other Aborigines explained that she was *go-lahng*, in a state of ritual mourning and fasting. But soon after, Noorooing herself, travelling in the bush near Sydney Cove, met and attacked a little girl related to the murderer of Yellaway. She beat the little girl so cruelly that the child was brought into town almost dead, with six or seven deep cuts in her throat and one ear cut to the bone. She died a few days later.

The English were not sympathetic to Noorooing, but other Aborigines explained to them 'that she had done no more than what custom obliged her to . . . The little victim of her revenge was, from her quiet, tractable manners, much beloved in the town; and what is a singular trait of the inhumanity of this proceeding, she had every day since Yellaway's death requested that Noorooing should be fed at the officer's hut, where she herself resided.' In some way that the Europeans could not understand, the blood debt had been fully settled by the little girl's death.

Meanwhile, because of white settlement at Parramatta, and the area known as Toongabbie to the north-west of Rose Hill, many of the local Burramattagal clan were pushed west into the country of the Bidjigal. Here the warrior Pemulwuy of the Bediagal from the north shore of Botany Bay began to co-operate with the Bidjigal. If Bennelong had come to some accommodation with the accumulating waves of Europeans or ghosts, Pemulwuy had not. Near Prospect Hill, west of Parramatta, in May 1792, seven native men and two women stole clothing and corn, and a convict worker on the farm fired at a man preparing to throw his spear. The party fled, abandoning nets containing corn, blankets and spears. The natives took a fast revenge. A convict employed on well-digging on a farm near Prospect Hill walked to Parramatta to collect his clothing ration. On the way back he was attacked, his head was cut in several places and his teeth were smashed out. His dead body gaped with wounds from spears.

So here was the contrast. Bennelong was victualled from the store—he took the rations as recompense for damage done to his people. Pemulwuy, who was involved in the murder of the convict, would not deign to receive that sort of compensation. He would not take Phillip's appeasing flour, or any other gift.

AN END TO FLEETS

The age of convict fleets had ended, because transportation by regularly dispatched individual convict transports had begun. Though there would be many more disgraceful ships, the British government had retreated shamefaced from its dalliance with Camden, Calvert and King. It was as an individual transport that a large ship named the *Pitt*, 775 tons (790 tonnes), had sailed on 17 July 1791 carrying nearly four hundred male and female prisoners. The owner of the *Pitt*, George Mackenzie Macaulay, was an alderman of the city of London and one of the Scots merchants of Blackheath—he was what the East India Company called a 'husband'; that is, a contractor who regularly chartered his ships to the East India Company business, and was reputable.

Yet the suffering of the transported remained intense. *Pitt* had originally embarked nearly 450 prisoners, but a complaint about overcrowding was made to the Commissioners of the Navy, and as a result of an inspection it was decided that she could not accommodate more than 410 convicts on the two-level benches which made up the sleeping quarters. On the gun deck, below the quarterdeck, three separate coops in front of the main cabin were set apart for the women's quarters. The fifty-eight women aboard would therefore have better ventilated spaces, though they were equally as crammed as those of the men below.

Smallpox struck the prison deck soon after the *Pitt*'s departure from Yarmouth Roads, and even before the Cape Verde Islands there were fifteen deaths amongst the prisoners. In the doldrums off Africa, the prisoners developed ulcers on their bodies from lack of Vitamin B and showed symptoms of scurvy. A fever struck, killing twenty-seven people—sailors, soldiers and their families—in a fortnight. The crew was left so short-handed that some of the convicts with maritime experience had to be brought up from the prison deck to help sail the vessel.

By the time *Pitt* arrived at Port Jackson in February 1792, a further twenty male and nine female prisoners had died, and one hundred and twenty of the men were landed sick. The hospital was again required to deal with a huge medical emergency. So though Macaulay's ship did not replicate quite the horrors of the Second Fleet, it was still a ship of disgrace. The ship's officers, including the master, Edward Manning, set up a store ashore to sell goods they had brought out at their own expense. Collins wrote, 'The high price at which everything was sold, the avidity with which all descriptions of people grasped at what was purchased was extraordinary.'

The *Pitt* had brought for the commissary store mainly salt beef, enough to extend the provisions of the settlement for forty days, and the ship was employed by Phillip to take a proportion of the supplies on to Norfolk Island.

Also aboard the vessel had travelled Major Francis Grose, on his way to assume command of the New South Wales Corps. He would be Phillip's new lieutenant-governor, and came from a rather more privileged background than Phillip. His father was a renowned antiquary, and his grandfather a jeweller who had enjoyed the privilege of having George II as a client. He had a much more genial nature than Robbie Ross—if anything he would become over time too accommodating to the desires of the officers of his corps for land and wealth. Grose, like the majority of officers, had campaigned as a youth during the American Revolutionary War, fighting in the summer of 1778 at Monmouth Courthouse in New Jersey, a battle site at which the heat may well have killed as many men as were shot, though he was amongst the latter. After nearly six years on half-pay, he was delighted to be appointed lieutenant-governor and chief recruiter of the New South Wales Corps—the sort of task with which he had some familiarity.

Having landed in Sydney with his young family, and inspected his garrison, Major Grose was enthused by what he saw in Phillip's Sydney Cove and Parramatta. 'I find there is neither the scarcity that was represented to me, nor the barren sands I was taught to imagine I should see; the whole place is a garden, on which fruit and vegetables of every description grow in the greatest luxuriance . . . Could we once be supplied with cattle, I do not believe we should have occasion to trouble Old England again. I live in as good a house as I desire; and the farm of my predecessor, which has been given to me, produces a sufficiency of everything for my family. The climate, though very hot, is not unwholesome, we have plenty of fish, and there is good shooting.' There was at last, in Grose's picture, the promise of a settled colony and a habitable place.

Even though Grose saw Sydney Cove in such positive light, it was a hot season, and those male convicts of *Pitt* who had been passed as healthy on landing were put to work cultivating and clearing public ground beyond Parramatta. They found it hard under that hammer of the February sun, in New South Wales's most humid month. Many of them began to join their prison-deck mates in hospital. The advent of full and more justly distributed rations could not save some. The record of burials, chiefly of newcomers, during that late summer is sobering. On 16 February 1792, four convicts were buried, and six the next day, and a further six on 20 February. Five were buried at Parramatta on the next day, a further two the next day, on 23 February a further six, on 25 February a further four. And on 1, 3, 5, 6 and 7 March the burials continued. On 8 March there were five male deaths, and on the following Friday, two more and that of a child, Margaret Tambleton. The regular multiple burials of men continued throughout March.

Yet the vigour of the settlement had affirmed itself for Phillip when in late February he issued fifty-two further land grants to former convicts, chiefly in the Parramatta–Prospect Hill area, all—of course—without reference to any interested Eora or Dharug parties. Nonetheless, the governor wrote to the third Secretary of State he had had to deal with, Henry Dundas, a former Edinburgh lawyer, older than Grenville and a veteran of government that, 'What I feared from the kind of settlers I have been obliged to accept has happened in several instances.' The convict settlers in some cases had grown tired 'of a life so different to that from which they have been brought up' and abandoned their grants or sold their livestock to acquire from ships and from stores like that set up by the master of *Pitt* 'articles from which they do not reap any real benefit'. He regretted, too, that twenty-two time-expired men and nine women intended to go home on the *Pitt*. 'Thus will the best people always be carried away, for those who cannot be received on board the ships as seamen or carpenters pay for their passage.' Even so, it was a minority of convict settlers who had either left without seeking a land grant or had lost or given up their land in this way, and a number of ex-convict farmers by this time had convicts working for them and being supported by them.

SYDNEY'S PARSON

In the Sydney area and along the Parramatta River, the burials continued, but the man who conducted them was thinking of the children of convicts and their education as well. By this time, in early 1792, the Reverend Johnson's house was crowded with often orphaned native children, while Mrs Johnson herself was 'far gone with child', and domestic life was under pressure. Johnson was still engaged with a struggle against Phillip's indifference to religion as anything more than a form of social regulation. The foundations of a church had been laid at Parramatta the previous spring, but before it was finished it was converted into a gaol for secondary punishment, and then into a granary. Phillip had at one stage put aside 400 acres (162 hectares) for church use as a glebe, but did not give Johnson any help to cultivate it. 'What, sir,' Johnson asked one of his London friends, 'are 400 or 4000 acres full of large green trees unless some convicts be allowed to cultivate it?'

He was still holding services at a boat house on the foreshores of Sydney Cove, and in the open, or in any shelter indoors or out he could find in Parramatta or Toongabbie. 'The last time I preached at Sydney was in the open air,' he admitted with reasonable pride, but also some resentment. He was troubled by migraine, and often dreaded the coming of Sunday and the glaring Sabbath sun.

On the day he wrote his plaint he had to bury another six convicts. Death in such numbers must also have been a form of stress on a soul whose resources were limited.

THE DEVIL WITH THE CHILDREN

When the three Dutch vessels Captain Edwards had hired in Batavia reached Table Bay off Cape Town in March 1792, carrying amongst others the *Bounty* mutineers, Mary Bryant and the other Sydney escapees, they found that HMS *Gorgon* with Major Ross and other marines, including Watkin Tench, aboard, was already moored in the roads. Edwards decided to send aboard her the ten remaining *Bounty* mutineers 'and the convict deserters from Port Jackson': Mary, her four-year-old, Charlotte, and four other survivors. Will Bryant had died of fever, and so had their young son. The little girl was in a bad way, and, so too, were some of the marines' children. 'I confess that I had never looked at these people, without pity and astonishment,' declared Watkin of Mary and the other escapees. 'They had miscarried in a heroic struggle for liberty; after having combated every hardship, and conquered every difficulty . . . and I could not but reflect with admiration at the strange combination of circumstances which had again brought us together, to baffle human foresight, and confound human speculation.'

The *Gorgon* left Table Bay for England in early April. None of the children aboard were well, even after spending so much time in a shore camp in Cape Town being nursed and fed healthily for the continuation of their long voyage. Corporal Samuel Bacon and his wife, Jane, had already lost one child on the first evening out from Cape Town: 'It was ill on shore.' A little over two weeks later, the other of the twins of Corporal Bacon died. Clark wrote a few days later, 'This hot weather is playing the Devil with the children—down here it is as hot as Hell—I wish to God we had got twenty degrees the other side of the line [the Equator].'

Edward Divan, son of Sergeant Divan, quartermaster in Captain Campbell's company, born aboard the *Charlotte* on the way out to New South Wales, saw both his younger brothers, Dennis and Mark, committed to the sea from the broiling deck of *Gorgon*. Then Sergeant Andrew Gilbourn's child perished. 'I am very sorry for poor little John—he was a fine child,' wrote Clark. William Mapp, the child of Private James Mapp and the late Susan Creswell, a convict, died a few days later, just as Clark was committing to his journal his hope, if 'this little good breeze continues, that we will be . . . in the same side of the world that my Betsy is in before 12 o'clock at night'.

Mary Bryant heard the weeping and keening of women from the crowded troop quarters, not much preferable to the ones she occupied, where the atmosphere must have been funereal. These lost children had all gone into the making of the great Sydney experiment, and were victims of a most peculiar imperial enterprise.

With so many barely consoled women howling close by, their children worn out by the distance between Sydney and London, Mary must have known Charlotte, who had been through more than any other child aboard, was unlikely to survive. But even though genial Captain Parker allowed Mary and Charlotte regularly on deck, she understood that Charlotte was under the axe of the same dietary exhaustion and fevers as the other children.

'Last night,' wrote Clark on May's first Sabbath, 'the child belonging to Mary Broad [Bryant], the convict woman who went away in the fishing boat from Port Jackson last year, died about four o'clock, [we] committed the body to the deep, latitude 5°25 North.' The ship was surrounded by sharks, which had learned that a regular supply of flesh trailed from this vessel, the child of a marine having died only two days before Charlotte.

The *Gorgon* arrived at Portsmouth on 18 June 1792. Transportation was arranged at once to take Mary and the other escapees to London. A magistrate committed them to Newgate but 'declared he never experienced so disagreeable a task as being obliged to commit them to prison, and assured them that, as far as lay in his power, he would assist them'. As grim as the wards of Newgate were, the escapees all declared that they would sooner suffer death than return to Botany Bay, according to a contemporary broadsheet.

James Boswell, famed companion of Dr Samuel Johnson, generous by nature and with a taste for handsome and robust girls of the lower orders, appealed repeatedly to the Home Secretary, Dundas, a friend of his, and to Undersecretary Evan Nepean for a pardon for Mary and the others. He collected 17 guineas as a subscription for Mary to purchase comforts in prison, and enquired into the nature of her family in the West Country by consulting Reverend William Johnson Temple, his 'old and most intimate friend' down in Devon. The Reverend Temple reported that the Broads were 'eminent for sheep stealing'.

On 2 May 1793, the Home Secretary advised the Sheriff of Middlesex that Mary Bryant had received an unconditional pardon. Released from Newgate, she remained in London, seemingly at Boswell's expense, until the following October. Amongst Boswell's papers is a record headed 'Mary's Money', which lists amounts paid out for her lodgings and for a bonnet, a gown, shoes and a prayer book.

Nearly one hundred and fifty years later, in 1937, amongst Boswell's possessions was found an envelope with the words in his handwriting: 'Leaves from Botany Bay used as tea'. It was the same *Smilax glyciphylla* which Mary had taken on the cutter with her and which comforted the scurvy-ridden and debased citizens of New South Wales.

OH! SHAME, SHAME!

Old Harry Brewer, lucky to have any post at all and still working as provost-marshal and building supervisor without official confirmation from the British government, was conscientiously searching *Pitt* before it left to return to England and found a recently arrived convict woman stowed away, with the connivance of one of the mates, Mr Tate. Tate was brought ashore and tried for the offence and acquitted, so that whether it was to escape New South Wales or for the love of that sailor that the girl was secreted on *Pitt*, we do not know.

Why would she and others not want to flee? For the funerals continued, and the stores were still proving inadequate to sustain healthy lives. 'The convicts dying very fast, merely through want of nourishment,' wrote a newly arrived refugee from bankruptcy, Richard Atkins. 'The Indian corn served out is of little use in point of nourishment, they have no mills to grind it and many are so weak they cannot pound it. At present there is not more than eight weeks ration of flour at two pound [0.9 kilos] per man at the store. Oh! Shame, shame!' Collins expressed the nature of the scurvy in graphic terms—as a very want of sufficient strength in the constitution to digest nourishment.

By now, desperately hungry men and women crept into the maize fields and stole the cobs from the centre of the crops, and being caught were too weak to face punishment. The ration of salt provisions remained as before, but *Gorgon's* flour was giving out. People looked askance at the two pounds of unmilled granite-like maize they were given instead of flour. Imperfectly ground, it could bring on diarrhoea of a near-fatal scale for the malnourished. So it became a byword for useless food, as it did also more than fifty years later during the Irish Famine when the Irish called it, for its dangerous impact on the digestive system, 'Peel's brimstone'.

By May 1792 Collins was grimly relieved so many had perished on and from *Pitt*: 'Had not such numbers died, both in the passage and since the landing of those who survived the voyage, we should not at this moment have had any thing to receive from the public stores; thus strangely did we derive the benefits from the miseries of our fellow creatures!'

A fishery was set up at the South Head look-out station exclusively for the use of the sick. The bulk of game was directed towards the hospitals. The huntsmen were given a reward of two pounds (c 900 g) of flour and the head, one forequarter and 'the pluck' of any animal they brought in. Phillip now found himself issuing maize from the store to supplement shortfalls in other items. Yet the threat of capital and other punishments for food stealing could hardly have entirely prevented the strong stealing from the weak when the chance presented, particularly as the weak, from the time of the Second Fleet onwards, were so numerous. Camden, Calvert and King had a great deal they and their captains would never be called to answer for.

The law of diminishing returns had hit New South Wales. 'Few, however, in comparison with the measure of our necessities,' wrote Collins, 'were the numbers daily brought into the field for the purpose of cultivation; and of those who could handle the hoe or the spade by far the greater part carried hunger in their countenances; independence of Great Britain was merely "a sanguine hope or visionary speculation".'

Indeed, even the First Fleeters' resistance to disease had been depleted by years of poor and reduced rations. Augustus Alt, the British surveyor and former Hessian soldier, was in too bad a condition to attend to surveying farms. A young man named David Burton, whose appointment as Superintendent of Convicts Sir Joseph Banks had recommended and who had come out on the *Gorgon*, took up the task, and Phillip came to like him. Since Phillip was concerned that New South Wales had acquired a bad reputation in the greater world, he asked Burton to prepare a report on the agricultural potential of the Sydney Basin, and Burton spent the summer of 1791–92 doing so. Phillip sent the result to Home Secretary Dundas with the note that Burton 'may be supposed to be a much better judge of the good or bad qualities of the ground than any of those persons who have hitherto given their opinions'. Burton had already remitted sixty tubs of plants and sundry boxes of seeds and specimens to Sir Joseph Banks, his patron, via the *Gorgon*, then by the *Pitt*, and had many tubs ready to send on the *Atlantic*, whenever it should return to Sydney from Bengal.

But sadly the useful Burton was taken away from his grateful governor. He had been out with some soldiers of the New South Wales Corps to kill ducks on the Nepean River. He carried his gun awkwardly, said Collins, and the first time it went off, it 'lodged its contents in the ground within a few inches of the feet of the person who immediately preceded him'. Then, by the river, resting the butt of his piece on the ground, he put his hand over the barrel to pull himself upright. The gun discharged, and the shot entered his wrist, forcing its way up between the two bones of his shattered right arm to the elbow. It took till five o'clock the next day before they got him back to Parramatta, and by then an inflammation had set up in the wound. In the opinion of the surgeons, amputation would have hastened his death, and so he was allowed to die in what could be called peace. Phillip approached young Burton as he lay the evening before his death, and found him very collected. 'If I die, Sir Joseph Banks knows my family, and my intentions towards them—I have brothers, and a father and mother—I wish everything to be sent to Sir Joseph Banks, for my father and mother.' In him, Phillip told Banks, 'I lost one whom I cannot replace and whom I could ill spare.'

Burials of more replaceable people continued into May. On 3 May, three more convicts; the next day, two; on 5 May, three. On the next day, three more. All of them were men from the Irish ship *Queen*, or from *Pitt*. On 8 May, there were another three; on 9 May, four more. 'This dreadful mortality was chiefly confined to the convicts who had arrived in the last year; of 122 male convicts who came out in the *Queen*, transported from Ireland, 50 only were living at the beginning of this month [May, 1792],' noted Collins.

But then, on 20 June, 'to the inexpressible joy of all ranks of people in the settlements', the *Atlantic* store ship arrived, 'with a cargo of rice, *soujee* [a form of semolina] and *dholl* [yellow split pea] from Calcutta'. She also brought two bulls and a cow with her, twenty sheep and twenty goats, which Collins thought of a very diminutive species. But the deliverance from hunger *Atlantic* seemed to offer was illusory. Since it had brought grain and *dholl* only, the ration of salt meat had now to be reduced. Richard Atkins said that in lieu of two pounds (c 900 grams) of pork per week, the stores now gave out one pound (c 450 grams) of Indian corn and one pound of *dholl*. All parties were united in a democracy of want.

Atkins and others were very cheered at the midwinter wheat crop in the Parramatta area, but there was need for more rain. Though the yearly rainfall in the Sydney Basin was approximately 48 inches (c 1220 mm) a year, it was subject to what we now know as the El Niño southern oscillation, which— from the frequent references to drought made in Sydney from 1790 onwards— seems to have had an impact on the first European settlers. The warm water of the eastern Australian currents stops the east–west trade winds across the Pacific, and there is a transfer of warm water to the coast of South and Central America, creating drought in New South Wales. The Eora were used to this phenomenon—it was one of the factors which inhibited their transition to what the Europeans, at least in theory, would have desired them to be: farmers. When it refused to rain in the winter of 1792, one pleasant blue-skied day succeeded another.

To free women for direct or indirect service to the production of crops, the governor suggested to Evan Nepean that ready-made clothing for the settlement should be purchased in Calcutta. The women of New South Wales had been employed until then making clothing out of slops. But there was full enough employment for all the women as hut-keepers, mothers of small children, and at labour in the fields without the further task of making clothing, and in any case there were 'many little abuses in the cutting out and making up of clothing' that could not be wiped out without superintendents. Phillip suggested that frocks, trousers, shirts, shifts, gowns and petticoats be made up in India for the colony, but with a specific thread of a different colour being inserted into the convict provision, so that what was intended for the convicts could not be sold to the soldiers or free settlers.

What sales there were, legal and illegal, still occurred by barter or by bills of various kinds, cheques which were re-endorsed by one payee to a further one. Sometimes there was a list of crossed out payees' names on the back of a bill, with the last legal recipient's uncrossed. People did not always trust this sort of document. Bills could be forged. But the specie of various kinds and nations brought by the Second Fleet did not cover all the necessary transactions even of a modestly commercial place, and so bills had to do. But when the commissary John Palmer, former purser of *Sirius*, sent a subordinate aboard *Atlantic* with a money order for £5 to purchase articles, the purser aboard *Atlantic* devalued it to a mere £1 4 shillings. Thus were all bills discounted, and all New South Wales prices hugely inflated.

Government intervention was essential to moderate prices. Harry Brewer was sent to the master of *Atlantic* with a writ to enquire into the massive, usurious discounting of bills. But the problem remained.

In mid July, as rain came and the last of the stores were being cleared from the *Atlantic*, another signal was made from the South Head look-out station, and the *Britannia* store ship, returned from India, came down the harbour and anchored in the cove. Aboard *Britannia* was twelve months' clothing for the convicts, four months' flour and eight months' beef and pork, so that 'every description of persons in the settlement' could be put back on full issue. Suddenly, Sydney Cove was redolent with the baking of flapjacks and the frying of salt beef. *Britannia* also brought news that Captain Donald Trail of the *Neptune* was being prosecuted, and people were cheered by that and thought that justice and reform were possible.

The new ration situation gave Collins hope for the day when journal-keepers like himself need not 'fill his page with comparisons between what we might have been and what we were; to lament the non-arrival of supplies; not to paint the miseries and wretchedness which ensued; but might adopt a language to which he might truly be said to have been hitherto a stranger, and paint the glowing prospects of a golden harvest, the triumph of a well-filled store, and the increasing and consequent prosperity of the settlements'.

But, as usual, the prospects weren't as bright as they first appeared. Not all the supplies Commissary Palmer received were of high quality. Phillip came along to the storehouses with his dirk and began opening and peeping into a series of ration casks. He was reduced to shaking his head, and instructed Palmer that only such provisions considered 'merchantable' should be paid for. Many of the casks of beef were deficient in weight, and the meat lean, coarse and bony and 'worse than they have ever been issued in His Majesty's service'. Such a claim meant the product was near inedible. Further salt provisions for New South Wales, Phillip counselled, should only be acquired from Europe, since those from other sources, such as India, were appalling. 'A deception of this nature would be more severely felt in this country,' said Collins. 'Every ounce lost here was of importance.' Collins was reduced to considering this cargo from India as an experiment 'to which it was true we were driven by necessity; and it had become the universal and earnest wish that no cause might ever again induce us to try it'.

The deficient food supplies from *Atlantic* and *Britannia* could not prevent some remarkable acts of food theft. In September, all hands were busy bringing in the Indian corn harvest, and even though the seed crop was steeped in tubs of urine to keep it from theft, 'some of the convicts cannot refrain from stealing and eating it'. In a letter to Dundas on 2 October, Phillip wrote of the persistent need for so many articles of food and industry amongst a population which had not eaten amply for four years. They needed iron cooking pots nearly as much as they needed provisions, he said, and then all the cross-cut saws, axes and various tools of husbandry were in short supply or disrepair. And further hunger was inevitable. He went through the sort of weary figures he had been remitting to London since the start: 'There remains at present in this colony, of rice and flour and bread, sufficient for 96 days at two pounds [c 900 g] of flour and five pounds [2.3 kilos] of rice per man for seven days, salt provisions sufficient for 70 days on a full ration, and of peas and *dholl*, sufficient for 156 days at three pounds [c 1.4 kilos] per week for each man.' Even the unpopular maize was now stolen—'Not less than 1500 bushels [c 55 m^3] were stolen from the grounds, notwithstanding every possible precaution.'

Phillip himself remained a victim of the rations and an earth which was only gradually being persuaded to submit to European expectations. The newly arrived son of a merchant friend of Arthur Phillip wrote of the governor at this stage that his health 'now is very bad. He fatigues himself so much he fairly knocks himself up and won't rest till he is not able to walk.'

A GOVERNOR LONGS FOR HOME

By October 1792, Phillip was still waiting to return home. He was anxious now to be relieved, and there had never been any idea that he, the uncondemned, would choose to remain in this temperate, beguiling but harsh garden. He was enlivened when on 7 October the largest ship to enter Port Jackson up to that hour, the 914-ton (932-tonne) *Royal Admiral*, arrived with a large cargo of convicts. The ship also brought one of the last detachments of the New South Wales Corps, as well as an agricultural expert, a master miller and a master carpenter and close to two hundred and fifty convicts. The ship, owned by a London 'husband' who frequently contracted his ships to the East India Company, Thomas Larkins, was the antithesis of some of the appallingly run transports of the past few years. The *Royal Admiral* had embarked fewer convicts than the overcrowded *Pitt* which had arrived earlier in the year and whose men had died in such numbers throughout the New South Wales autumn. The naval agent for *Royal Admiral* was the former surgeon of the notorious but healthy *Lady Juliana*, Richard Alley, and the master and the ship's surgeon collaborated well with him in matters of convict health. There had been a conspiracy of some type on board, but it had been aborted and mildly punished, with one prisoner receiving three dozen lashes and seven others two dozen each. The *Royal Admiral* had made a very fast passage of one hundred and thirty days from Torbay, even though she had spent twenty-one of those days in Simons Bay at the Cape. Then, south of Africa, with the Roaring Forties in her sails, she had made over 4800 kilometres in just sixteen days.

'She brought in with her a fever, which had much abated by the extreme attention paid by Captain Bond and his officers to cleanliness,' Collins recorded. The officers had also supplied the prisoners 'with comforts and necessities beyond what were allowed for their use during the voyage'. The master and officers were speculators nonetheless—they had freighted out over £4000 worth of their own goods to sell ashore.

By this time, the governor judged it necessary to send most arriving convicts straight up the river to Parramatta where work was to be done, since Sydney possessed 'all the evils and allurements of a seaport of some standing'. Phillip felt there would be difficulties in removing prisoners from Sydney once they settled in there. Even within a penal universe, under conditions of hunger, Sydney was already taking on what it would never lose, the allure of a city of pleasures and vices.

The *Royal Admiral* had brought also an important new talent to the colony, a convict who for his special gifts was allowed to stay in Sydney. A Scots artist, Thomas Watling had been amongst the more than four hundred convicts who sailed in the *Pitt*, and had escaped in Cape Town. He had been arrested by the Dutch after the *Pitt*'s departure, put in gaol, and then taken aboard *Royal Admiral* by Captain Bond. Well-educated, and having worked for a time in Glasgow as a coach and chaise painter, he would become the most important artist of early New South Wales. He had been transported in the first place via the temptations of artistry. In Dumfries in November 1788 he had been charged with making forged Bank of Scotland guinea notes. Rather than risk conviction and execution, he pleaded guilty, asked to be transported, and was sentenced to fourteen years.

Upon landing, almost at once he was snatched up by and assigned to Surgeon General John White, who as a naturalist made great use of Watling's artistic skills, especially for drawing rare animals. Watling would find White an exacting master, and would sometimes feel overworked.

Another arrival on *Royal Admiral*, this one significant only in retrospect, was Mary Haydock, aged thirteen when put aboard the transport. She had been convicted of stealing a horse, but her crime seems to have been the Georgian equivalent of joy-riding. She became nursemaid to the family of Major Grose. She had already been courted on *Royal Admiral* by a young agent of the East India Company, an Irishman named Thomas Reibey, who was making his way to India via Port Jackson. He would ultimately return to marry her, and the Reibeys would become wealthy, beginning as civilian associates of the emergent trading force of the New South Wales Corps.

For the newly arrived officers of the New South Wales Corps were quick to sense the advantages of the place and dealt with their state of want by themselves chartering the *Britannia* to travel to Cape Town or Rio for supplies, including boots for the soldiers. Phillip was not easy about it, since it was an interruption to the duty the *Britannia* had in relation to collecting her cargo under East India Company charter. The officers also expected land grants, but Phillip feared that in giving them any, he 'will increase the number of those who do not labour for the public, and lessen those who are to furnish the colony with the necessaries of life'. Collectivist New South Wales was under pressure from these new men, men like the earlier arriving Lieutenant John Macarthur, who was already dreaming of being an importer as a means of becoming a landowner.

Phillip, by contrast, feared too much enterprise would make the penal community of New South Wales hard to control, and that barter would develop in spirits, for which the convicts were crazy. The shops set up in Parramatta and Sydney for the sale of private goods out of the *Royal Admiral* were permitted to sell porter, but they were found to be selling spirits as well, with deplorable results. 'Several of the settlers, breaking out from the restraints to which they had been subject, conducted themselves with the greatest impropriety, beating their wives, destroying their stock, trampling on and injuring their crops in the ground, and destroying each other's property.' In New South Wales, all the rage of exile and want was unleashed by liquor, but the officers of the New South Wales Corps could sniff not a social crisis but an opportunity.

Sir Joseph Banks would later say that 'Governor Phillip . . . was so ill when he left Sydney as to feel little hope of recovery.' In dreaming of his return to England, Phillip must sometimes have imagined death coming from his exhaustion and chronic ailments, but at other, more energetic times envisaged perhaps further military service arising from conflict with republican France. Being in such a remote place as New South Wales at such a crucial time could be itself a torment. Yet he hoped he had done enough not simply to satisfy his masters, but to validate his own honour as an officer, to honour the demands of his culture, and to put its mark on the shore of New South Wales. Indeed, he would leave certain traditions indelibly implanted behind him—an insistence on the supremacy of law, an enlightened authoritarianism rather than republican rights, and a sense of community which the cynics would not have thought possible. Authority and equality were the two trees Phillip planted in Sydney Cove, and perhaps too the tree of grudging co-operative endeavour, into which the convicts were forced by circumstance. He had never invoked happiness, but he had invoked cohesion and its benefits.

So now Phillip had decided. Despite the rationing problems, whose end he saw in sight if the government and private farms were successful, he would sail home on the *Atlantic*, due to leave Sydney in December 1792. For by the time Phillip packed his papers and assembled his samples, he had imposed on this version of the previously unknown earth the European template. There were three and a half thousand acres (1418 hectares) under grant to various time-expired criminals and others. Over one thousand acres (405 hectares) were in cultivation on public land at Sydney Cove and Farm Cove, Parramatta and Toongabbie.

As well, livestock now grazed on land-grant farms, and stock belonging to the public was kept at Parramatta. Though it would later be argued that Australia's ancient, leached, thin soil was not suited to hard-hoofed European animals, such questions did not exist for Phillip. Livestock stood for a European imperative more profound than theology. The new place should be graced by such identifiable, biblical and fruitful beasts.

There were a number of reasons the Sydney enterprise seemed now, and despite all, in a promising condition. One was that the British government was still confronted with an epidemic of crime, and a growth of unrest and rebellious sentiment amongst Methodist radicals and Scottish and Irish seditionists. But Phillip's own stubborn certainties had a lot to do with the experiment's success-cum-survival as well. His insistence on equity in rationing must have been a new experience for many convicts used to the corrupt systems of supply in prison and on board the hulks. His lack of skilled freemen elevated some convicts to civic positions as superintendents, overseers and settlers, and imbued a new sense of opportunity and potential influence. Only in New South Wales did land come to the convict who completed his time, and with it the sense of social order which accompanies ownership. 'A striking proof of what some settlers had themselves declared,' said David Collins, 'on its being hinted to them that they had not always been so diligent when labouring for the whole, "We are now working for ourselves."' Phillip had created a system of punishment and reward which, as repugnant as some of its elements might be to us, reliably provided for the convict and soldier-settler.

In his last days in Sydney, soldiers, convicts and servants carried Phillip's baggage down from his two-storey Government House, past its garden and the edge of public farmland, to the government wharf on the east side of Sydney Cove. When Phillip himself came down on 10 December, finally ready for departure, full of unrecorded impulses and thoughts, unsure of his future but fairly sure of the survival of New South Wales's curious society, the red-coated New South Wales Corps under Major Grose presented arms. They dipped their colours and did him honour.

Phillip must have hoped that, leaving a place so little understood by the world at large, he would have a chance to advance towards greater responsibility and higher glory. But in fact it was with the children of his convict, free and military settlers, whom he was pleased to wave off, that his name would achieve its immortality. Though greater formal honours awaited him, his chief remembrance would be in this cove, in this harbour, and in the continent beyond. And even so his abiding presence in the history of Australia would be more akin to that of a great totem beast than that of breathing flesh. He would not glisten for the children of this and other generations, he would not glow with the amiability or deeds of a Washington, a Jefferson, a Lafayette. He did not seek or achieve civic affection. He would forever be a colourless secular saint, the apostle of the deities Cook and Banks. Yet he would also be lodged not only in our imaginations, but in our calculations of the meaning of the continent and the society.

Thus the New South Wales Corps, which would acquire a questionable reputation, earned or not, correctly saluted Phillip as he passed in his clouds of gravity.

SPIRITING AWAY

One of the most intense fears of the natives was, and would remain, that figures like Phillip would attract men and women out of their accustomed circuits and spirit them away from the Eora world. And it was happening now with Bennelong and the young man Yemmerrawanne, 'two men who were much attached to his [Phillip's] person; and who withstood at the moment of their departure the united distress of their wives, and the dismal lamentations of their friends, to accompany him to England'. They knew no map for where they were going, and only that it was *outer*, and that it was a region of incomprehensible darkness. The risk for Bennelong that he might finish by belonging to neither world was one he bore relatively lightly on this high summer day as he sniffed the aroma of the eucalypts, tinged with smoke from western bushfires, and went aboard the *Atlantic*. It is likely that many of his people thought he was under an enchantment and thus vitiated forever. Some might have thought also that Abaroo's ultimate rejection of Yemmerrawanne as a suitor could have added to that handsome youth's readiness to travel with his kinsman Bennelong.

With Phillip aboard, early on 11 December 1792, the *Atlantic* dropped down-harbour in semi-darkness. It seems Mrs Brooks was travelling on the ship, but not Harry Brewer, who had found in New South Wales as provost-marshal the only post the world was willing to give him. The desert interior of the continent sent a summer south-westerly to send Phillip out of Eora land. Past the Cameraigal headlands of the north shore they sailed, towards a last sight of the beach at Manly where he had taken the chief wound of his incumbency. The principal officers of the settlement, on board to honour Phillip, now bid him goodbye and returned to Sydney Cove.

The marine private and diarist, John Easty, shared Phillip's journey home. He agreed with Phillip that as they left New South Wales, the state of the colony seemed far better than at any time since the settlement was made. Easty mentioned regular ships, good crops of corn and a summer harvest of wheat for cutting. The country was still everywhere covered with wood, and it was with great trouble and fatigue that it could be cleared, he thought. Yet convicts lived in brick huts now because of the good clays of the Sydney Basin. Still, there was 'not a place dedicated to divine worship amidst all the work—a thing much to be lamented by a serious mind'.

The voyage proved uneventful, though Phillip's estranged wife, Margaret, had died by the time he returned to Britain. In her will she had released him from all obligations he had acquired during their relationship. So he devoted himself to defending and explaining his administration to officials in Whitehall, and asked the Secretary of State and the King for permission to resign his governorship permanently on the grounds of ill health. Early the next year, he received a spacious annual pension of £500 to honour his New South Wales service. Phillip now had adequate resources to take a residence in Bath, consult specialists, and take the Bath waters.

His health improved, and he offered himself to the service again. He began to visit, and then married, Isabella Whitehead, the 45-year-old daughter of a wealthy northern cotton- and linen-weaving merchant. He would soon begin to regularly criticise the way things had gone in New South Wales since his departure.

Bennelong and Yemmerrawanne, meanwhile, had stepped ashore with Phillip at Falmouth towards the end of May 1793, to catch the London stagecoach. It was their turn to enter a mystery.

CHAPTER 9

AFTER PHILLIP

Left to govern New South Wales, Francis Grose was not himself a rapacious man, but seems to have been easily influenced by his officers and let them use the colony and its commerce in a manner Phillip would not have approved of. While Phillip had believed in a primitive commonwealth, where soldiers and convicts drew the same rations from the stores, and where convict labour at the government farms would sustain the colony, Grose thought it better to create a private sector consisting of his officers, his men and other colonial officials, in addition to some former convicts and a handful of free settlers. Without authorisation, he granted Other Ranks members of the New South Wales Corps twenty-five acres (c 10 hectares) each, offered land grants in the Sydney Basin to his officers, and awarded the use and rationing of ten convict labourers to each officer. Part of his motivation, he argued, was that he was plagued with ex-convict settlers who wanted to sell their land and livestock and return to England. Though their sheep flocks came from the government flock Phillip had issued to them, if he wanted that flock and its offspring to survive, he had to sell them as well since their wider holdings would ensure the ongoing strength of the sheep population.

When the Rhode Island ship *Hope* appeared in Sydney, Grose was also willing to allow the sale of a quantity of the spirits it carried to civil and military officers. That was a significant decision and one which would in the end beget revolution.

As the barrels of spirit were hoisted from the hold of *Hope*, the liquor business began in New South Wales, with liquor becoming not merely a quencher of spiritual bewilderments in the rag-tag population, but also a standard of exchange and a ticket to power.

Captain Collins recorded that, illegal though it was, the convicts preferred receiving liquor as payment for their labours to any article of provisions or clothing. In changing the convict hours of labour to a morning shift of 5 a.m. until 9 a.m. and then an afternoon shift from 4 p.m. until sunset, it was almost as if Grose were clearing the middle of the day for convicts to do business or tend their gardens. He was certainly creating boozing time. To men and women of small crimes but great, mind-scarring passages to Australia, the numbing power of spirits was much desired, and a string of liquor deaths was soon recorded.

Thomas Daveney, a free man whom Phillip had made overseer of the government farm at Toongabbie and called 'a most useful man', now lived on his own land in Toongabbie, granted to him by Lieutenant-Governor Grose. There he drank himself to death in July 1795 with half a gallon of Cape brandy.

Eleanor McCabe, a First Fleet convict, boarded a boat to Parramatta with her infant and her husband, Charles Williams, alias Christopher Magee, who had land near Rose Hill. With them was a woman named Green. When the boat overturned near Breakfast Point on the river—it was believed because of the drunkenness of all adult parties—both women and the infant were drowned. The eloquent and philosophic Magee, who was a gambling partner of James Ruse and who harboured American republican tendencies, buried his wife and daughter in front of his house, and was seen sitting in his doorway with a bottle of rum in his hand, drinking one glass and pouring another on Eleanor's grave until it was emptied, 'prefacing every libation by declaring how well she'd loved it during her life'.

The colonial love affair with dram drinking had been set going, and it seemed that demons were released into the air. Spirits killed 'a stout healthy young woman', Martha Todd, by inflicting her with fatal gastritis. James Hatfield, a time-expired convict, came from Parramatta to consult the clerks about his coming land grant, drank too deep of the American spirits and died similarly. Another death from intoxication was that of John Richards at the area near Parramatta named the Ponds, a man with a grant of thirty acres, a First Fleeter and former Shropshire burglar. It was as if some were seeking suicide by liquor.

As the officers lawlessy sold and traded liquor around the colony, Grose uttered warnings already unrealistic, counselling the officers that 'it might be relied upon, that if it ever appeared that a convict was possessed of any of the liquor . . . the conduct of those who had thought proper to abuse what was designed as an accommodation to the officers of the garrison would not be passed over unnoticed'.

Convicts found release also in gambling. John Lewis, an elderly convict, had the distinction in early 1794 of being the first man killed in Australia for a gambling debt—having boasted that he carried much money secreted into his clothes, he was found murdered and his body thrown into a ravine, where dingos had mauled it. It was believed that a card player to whom he owed money was guilty, but the suspicion was never proven. Convicts gambled so recklessly that some, after losing their provisions, money and spare clothing on games of cribbage and all-fours, were left 'standing in the middle of their associates as naked, and as indifferent about it, as the unconscious natives of the country'.

More significant than the individual deaths from drinking, and indeed the loss to officers of land former convicts sold them in return for liquor, was the reality that Grose had created a junta, and went so far in legalising it as to begin to substitute his military officers for civil magistrates Phillip had appointed during his later administration.

Because of Grose's casual manners, the rumour got around the convicts that he was not empowered to carry out the death sentence. John Crowe, a sailor aged fourteen when sentenced at the Hertford Assizes for burglary in the summer of 1787, had arrived on the Second Fleet and worked three years on public projects before he was locked up in the Parramatta guardhouse for some offence. He escaped down the river to Sydney, and stole some food from huts before swimming out to the American ship *Fairy*. The American sailors, their notions of freedom already established and given form by Jefferson's Bill of Rights, were always a recourse for the escaping Australian convict. But any ship served as a chance for the desperate. When in 1793 the British *Bellona* was to leave Sydney, two time-expired convicts were allowed to sail on her, but Grose ordered the vessel 'smoked', and so controlled fires were set between decks which brought four other convicts choking and gagging out of their hiding places aboard.

When Crowe was discovered on *Fairy*, he was taken ashore and locked in the black hole of the Sydney guardhouse. Again he escaped, and committed further burglaries in Parramatta. In December 1793, at the age of twenty-one, he was hanged to show that indeed the lieutenant-governor did have that power, and Collins wrote of this cautionary death that 'there did not exist in the colony at this time a fitter object for example than John Crowe'.

Yet even some of Grose's soldiers wanted to get out. In August 1793 a number of them planned to seize a government longboat and sail it to the Dutch East Indies, as the Bryants had. One of them, Roberts, a drummer, was court-martialled and received 225 of his 300-lash punishment, and while 'smarting under the severity' gave up the names of his confederates. Two of the group, a corporal and a private, plundered other soldiers' ammunition pouches and took to the bush. The Parramatta game-killers, convict shooters of kangaroos and wallabies, were sent out to hunt them down, but whenever the two raided a farm they would tell the farmer to let everyone know they would not be taken alive. This mystified good Captain Collins who said that Grose provided his soldiers with comforts, had done away with the equal rations Phillip had so rigorously imposed on everyone, including himself, and 'had indulged them with women'.

The two were captured, and since Grose forbore to have them charged with a capital offence, the corporal was sentenced to 500 lashes, and the private to 800 in an attempt to make them content again with their posting.

Phillip had earlier asked the British government to send to New South Wales free settlers who were intelligent, honest and good at farming. Early in Grose's lieutenant-governorship, a store vessel, the above-mentioned *Bellona*, had arrived from England with so many supplies the storehouses could not contain them all, and provisions and flour were stacked in tiers in front of the store buildings. It also brought, along with seventeen healthy women convicts, the first free settlers to leaven the mass of haphazard convict farming.

Thomas Rose was a middle-aged farmer from Blandford, on board with his wife and four children. They had endured a rough journey in their berths below, for the timbers of *Bellona* seeped with water, and in rough weather admitted it in spurts. Rose was seen by the Sydney authorities as the natural leader of the free-settler group, which included Edward Powell, a farmer from Lancaster, and three other farmers who once had been crew members of the First Fleet's *Sirius*, and so in some sense must have liked the place and now returned to it. They had all been offered assisted passages, a sign of the way future immigration to Australia might work.

This group of perhaps more symbolic than substantial importance was rowed along the Parramatta River to choose land, and settled some eleven kilometres west of Sydney behind a screen of mangroves in an area which was thereafter known as Liberty Plains, near present-day Homebush. Here Rose was awarded 80 acres (32.4 hectares), and later a further 120 (48.6 hectares). The choice is puzzling, since Liberty Plains was a low-lying area of swamps and lagoons, and its tidal sediments held no nutrients. Maybe Rose was over-influenced by Major Grose in the matter. But soon he repented and moved with his family further west to the farmlands around Prospect Hill, and then to the richer alluvial country along the Hawkesbury River at Wilberforce.

Rose and his wife, Jane Topp, were models of sober and inconspicuous industry. Jane, delivered of an Australian son and daughter, lived to see her grandchildren's children, and when she died in 1827 was said to be Australia's first great-grandmother.

BENNELONG RETURNS

In December 1794, Grose returned to England for health reasons, leaving the penal settlement for some months in the hands of the equally amenable and malleable Captain William Paterson, Commandant of the New South Wales Corps. The sixty-year-old bachelor and former captain of the *Sirius*, John Hunter, returned to the colony as governor aboard the *Reliance* on 7 September 1795. He brought with him a few barrels of provisions, a town clock and the parts of a windmill for assembly ashore, and plenty of advice on how to sort out the military officers. Also aboard was the returning Sydney native and familiar of Phillip's, Bennelong. When Bennelong went aboard the *Reliance* at Deptford after two years in England, he had been suffering a bad congestion of the kind that had sent his fellow Sydney native Yemmerrawanne to a grave in Eltham. Hunter wrote that 'disappointment' in England had broken Bennelong's spirit. Whether he meant that in leaving his charges to endure a hard winter in some solitude Phillip had let his spiritual brother Bennelong down, we do not know. But enthusiastic young Surgeon George Bass kept Bennelong warm and alive aboard *Reliance*, and the spring weather off the Azores restored him.

Captain Collins described Bennelong, returned to Sydney, as conducting himself with a polished familiarity towards his sisters and other relations but being distant and quite the man of consequence to his acquaintances. He announced to the Aborigines of Sydney that he would no longer let them fight and cut each other's throats as had happened in the past. He would introduce peace amongst them and make them love each other. He also wanted them to be better mannered when they appeared at Government House. He seemed embarrassed by 'some little indelicacies' in his sister Carrangarang, who had rushed up from Botany Bay to greet him, carrying a little nephew on her back, but having 'left her habiliments behind her'. At table at the white stucco Government House above Sydney Cove, he showed the greatest propriety. But he wanted to track down his former second wife, Karubarabulu, and was upset to hear she was living with a man named Caruey, who had inflicted bitter wounds on a Botany Bay native to establish his permanent title to her. Bennelong sought out the couple and presented Karubarabulu with an elegant rose-coloured petticoat and jacket made of a coarse stuff, accompanied with a gypsy bonnet of the same colour, and for a time she deserted her lover and followed her former husband. But she confused the Europeans when, within a few days, they saw her walking naked about town. Bennelong fought for her and according to one account beat Caruey severely at Rose Bay, using 'his fists instead of the weapons of his country', obviously a medium of combat he had picked up as a temporary Englishman. Whoever won, Bennelong could not restrain Karubarabulu from returning to the younger man. Indeed, Bennelong himself was away from Government House for long periods, leaving his London clothes behind, returning to resume them when he chose and to toast the King with John Hunter.

After his return, perhaps under suspicion that he might have acquired new powers during his absence, Bennelong was commonly accused of causing, by magic, the deaths of Eora people (which appeared, to the Europeans, to be due to natural causes). He was accused, for example, of causing the death of a woman who had reported to others in the camp that she had dreamed that Bennelong had killed her. Sorry ceremonies—minor battles between the clan of the accused and the clan of the deceased—continued. The women who attended them would howl and cry, but then become enraged at the sight of blood, dancing and beating their sides with their arms. Thus the cultural politics of Aboriginal life continued, and despite his speech to his brethren on his return from England, Bennelong became involved.

In December 1797, Colby, the friend of Bennelong, and a young man called Yeranibe faced each other in town and attacked one another with clubs. Yeranibe's shield fell from his grasp, and while he was stooping to pick it up Colby struck him on the head. While he was down, despite the risk of being called *geerun*, or coward, and the likelihood that the friends of the young man would pursue him, Colby hit him again, and then ran away. Yeranibe was looked after by some of the Europeans, but died after six days. Colby spent the time leading up to his young victim's death south of the settlement in the company of friends and relatives. Meanwhile, near town, as a song of lamentation was being sung for the dying Yeranibe by his female relatives, his clansmen suddenly started up and seized their weapons and went off to hunt for Colby. Finding him, they beat him severely, intending to kill him outright when the boy died.

By the side of the road below the military barracks Yeranibe was buried the next day. Every Aboriginal at the funeral seemed determined that Colby must die. In fact a young man related to Colby had to be saved by a soldier from being executed on the spot. Colby realised that he must either submit to 'the trial usual on such occasions' or live in continual fear 'of being taken off by a midnight murder and a single hand.' He decided to face the relatives of Yeranibe, but in town. In that way, he might be able to use his military friends as a brake on the anger of Yeranibe's clan. On the nominated day, Colby presented himself at the rendezvous, near the barracks on the western ridge of Sydney Cove. 'The rage and violence' shown by the friends of Yeranibe overpowered Colby, and when he fell and a group of Yeranibe's kinsmen rushed in to finish him with their spears, several soldiers stepped in, lifted Colby and took him into the barracks.

Bennelong had been present but had not taken any part in proceedings. The impression was that though he could not neglect turning up in some capacity, he had no stomach for the argument. He was armed, however, and when the soldiers stepped in he suddenly became enraged, like a referee who saw a violation of rules, and threw a spear which entered a soldier's back and came out close to the navel. Bennelong was dragged away by the new provost-marshal, an onlooker full of rage at the soldiers who had begun clubbing him with musket butts and inflicted a wound on his head.

The principles of Aboriginal justice would always confuse the British, and the sight of a fellow soldier transfixed with Bennelong's spear (the wound fortunately healed) was not a good way to invite tolerant interest. Bennelong showed little gratitude at being saved from the anger of the military, and next morning he disappeared. He had become, in Collins's eyes, 'a most insolent and troublesome savage'. He was heard to declare that he intended to spear Governor Hunter whenever he saw him, but that proved to be blather.

The normal picture of Bennelong's life promoted by European writers—both Bennelong's contemporaries and of the present day—has him entering a decline, becoming addicted to liquor, and losing his influence with his people.

Indeed, when he died in 1813 on the grounds of the freed convict brewer James Squire at Kissing Point, north-west of Sydney Cove, the *Sydney Gazette* wrote, 'Of this veteran champion of the native tribe little favourable can be said. His voyage and benevolent treatment in Britain produced no change whatever in his manners and inclinations, which were naturally barbarous and ferocious.'

Yet at the time of his death, he was surrounded by at least a hundred kinsmen, which did not indicate a man rejected by his people. As late as 1805, he was now quarrelling with Colby over Karubarabulu, but the fact that his love of that Botany Bay Aboriginal woman was not necessarily requited did not of itself involve a decline. Was the *Sydney Gazette*'s judgment accurate, or did it bespeak attitude more than reality? Was the *Sydney Gazette* aggrieved that, after an early attempt, despite the advantages of having encountered British society, Bennelong had not moved amongst his people as an apostle of European culture? Since he seems to have become a heavy drinker—like many of the Europeans in the Sydney Basin, yet perhaps more tragically given his previous lack of exposure to liquor—he has sometimes been depicted as an archetype of his peoples' tragedy.

Bennelong's son, born of Barangaroo, in some respects followed his father's lead, and shared his curious, sociable nature. He was adopted by the Reverend William Walker, a popular Methodist minister with an interest in the Aboriginals at Blacktown, south-west of Sydney Cove, and elsewhere, and christened Thomas Walker Coke. He would die at the age of about twenty.

In Hunter's time, and then later in Governor King's, Pemulwuy was still at large and leading his relatives and the western natives (the Dharug people) in the wooded regions of the Sydney Basin. He was energetic in razing maize fields, and one party of his warriors came in so close to Sydney that his followers wounded a convict travelling from the brickfield huts on the town's verge to a local farm on business. By 1798 he had decided that because he had been frequently shot at but never severely wounded, he could not be killed by English firearms.

The Hawkesbury Aborigines were similarly at war. An open boat travelling from the Hawkesbury loaded with Indian corn for Port Jackson was overrun while still in the river by Aborigines, a number of whom were killed. It was the second such boat attacked in this way, in what could be considered, in European terms, piracy.

In Sydney, the authorities knew Pemulwuy's resistance was buoyed by what Collins described in 1795 as 'ill and impolitic conduct' on the part of some of the settlers towards the natives. Pemulwuy's warriors had told a young convict they had made friends with that they intended to execute three of the settlers—Michael Doyle, Robert Forrester, a First Fleet thief, and William Nixon—and had attacked two others mistaking them for Doyle and Forrester. The young Englishman, John Wilson, to whom this plan of vengeance was mentioned was remarkably trusted by the various Sydney Aboriginal groups. A former sailor, he had been sentenced to seven years transportation in 1785 for stealing 'nine yards of cotton cloth called velveret of the value of tenpence'. Now he was an emancipist, a free or time-served former convict, but even while he was serving his sentence it was noticed he had a special relationship with the Sydney clans. Achieving his freedom, he began to spend most of his time with them, and such behaviour was repellent enough to his betters for them to consider him 'a wild idle young man'. The authorities had nonetheless used him in excursions to the west, north and south, and he had invented a patois halfway between Eora and English. The Sydney Aboriginals had given him a name—Bun-bo-e. He wore kangaroo skins—not entirely uncommon among the Europeans—and his body was scarred with ritual markings as noticeably as the bodies of tribespeople. Seeing him entering their lives like a man under an enchantment, the Sydney natives must have regretted that it was this young sailor alone whose soul they had caught, who had remembered that in an earlier life he had been one of them. They must have hoped that the others might ultimately find their true natures and follow Wilson, Bun-bo-e, into the real life.

The government was fearful that he might tell the Sydney natives about the vulnerability of Sydney and Parramatta, so in February 1795 they sent him on an expedition to Port Stephens with a young surveyor, Charles Grimes. Here he stepped in on a confrontation with the natives and, talking to them in Eora, saved Grimes from being speared. The Port Stephens natives had already heard good things of Wilson by news passed up the coast via the Hawkesbury Aborigines, and his ritual markings were eloquent to them.

Others did not find living as an Aboriginal so easy. The escaped Parramatta convict John Tarwood and his three mates, who had stolen a boat in 1791 and lived in the Port Stephens hinterland, surrendered in 1795 to a passing ship, despite having survived with the Aborigines and having had wives allotted them. The natives, according to Tarwood, believed that they were the spirits of ancestors fallen in battle and returned from the sea, and one native appeared firmly to believe that his father had come back in the person of one of them and took the man to the spot where his body had been burned. It seemed that the bits of the Eora language they had picked up were not understood by the Port Stephens people, except for one boy, Wurgan, whose mother came from Sydney.

Though Tarwood and his friends returned gratefully, even to embrace European-style punishment, ultimately preferring to do that rather than live amongst natives they said were gentle and courteous to them, over coming years John Wilson continued to straddle two realities and to attract suspicion for seeming to prefer the nomadic life over the settled. He may have been motivated by sexual opportunism, but it was not as if Aboriginal society offered greater chances of gratification than did Sydney itself.

The next time he turned up in Sydney, in 1797, Wilson wore nothing but an apron formed from a kangaroo skin, and told people that the scarifying of his shoulders and breast had been very painful. Interviewed by the governor, he described pastures to the south-west. Hunter decided to use this knowledge, though Collins doubted that Wilson had been, as he claimed, a hundred miles (160 kilometres) in every direction from the settlement. Exploration would prove he was telling the truth.

In January 1798, when a number of newly arrived Irish prisoners seemed ready, like the prisoners of the *Queen* earlier in the decade, to escape and seek what they believed to be a new world of white people, situated this time not north of the Hawkesbury but about two hundred miles (320 kilometres) south-west of Sydney, Governor Hunter, in order to 'save worthless lives', sent off four of these Irish, under an armed guard and with Wilson as guide, to show them that no such deliverance awaited them. The Irishmen soon grew tired of the tangled and spiky bush and returned with the soldiers to Port Jackson, but Wilson and two companions, one of them John Price, a trusted servant of the governor, pushed on into country unknown to Europeans. In the south-west, the Great Dividing Range, which hemmed in the Sydney Basin, retreated westwards, and the three explorers were able to reach the Wingecarribee River, more than 160 kilometres south-west of Parramatta. Wilson's two companions suffered great discomfort and exhaustion in the bush, and were saved by Wilson's bushcraft—his ability to navigate and hunt. The journal of Price, Hunter's servant who accompanied Wilson, was forwarded to Sir Joseph Banks, since it has the first record of the shooting of a lyrebird and the first written reference to the 'cullawine' (koala).

Governor Hunter was impressed enough to send Wilson and two other men back into the same country, and this time the expedition reached Mount Towrang, on the ridge above the site of what would become the town of Goulburn.

Despite the leverage these discoveries gave Wilson in the European community, by 1799 he reverted to 'the wildlife', and the following year was killed by an angry Aboriginal male when he attempted to take a young woman for what Collins referred to as his 'exclusive accommodation'. It was not the first time Wilson had been caught trying to coerce women, some of them extremely young by modern standards. But this not uncommon cause of death amongst Aboriginal males closed out the life of the first European to attempt to live in a way his contemporaries considered savage.

POLITICALS

Though the Irish Defenders would have certainly considered their crimes as political, the authorities chose not to. The first prisoners all parties agreed on as being political and therefore dangerous were a group of five named the Scottish Martyrs—not all of them Scottish, but so named for the place of their arrest and trial. They were representatives of the thousands of men and women who promoted in Britain the ideals of the American and French Revolutions, and Hunter and, later, Governor King found them an administrative annoyance and suspected them of subversion.

In the 1790s, Britain had been swept by radical 'corresponding societies', men and women spreading revolutionary concepts through the mails, with even members of the Royal Navy—turbulent, unpaid, infected by the ideas of the United Irishmen and the French—participating in the passion. It ultimately meant that New South Wales was due to receive a few heroes rather than thieves.

The Scottish Martyrs were sentenced to transportation in 1794. One of them, William Skirving, had been educated at Edinburgh University, a prosperous farmer's son. In the 1790s he became secretary of the recently formed Scottish Association of the Friends of the People, and helped to organise a series of meetings in Edinburgh which were attended by radical members of the association from all over Britain and which government spies also attended. The

Friends of the People had been an almost respectable Whig body founded by Charles Grey, the future prime minister, Lord John Russell and Richard Sheridan, the Irish playwright. But it had in the eyes of government taken on too much French Jacobin (that is, revolutionary) coloration. Its radicalism was directed in large part at the sin of landlordism, the hunger of the masses, general inequality before the law, and republicanism. In December 1793, Skirving was arrested in Scotland with John Gerrald and Dr Maurice Margarot, who had come up from England for the meetings. At his trial for sedition Skirving was accused of distributing political pamphlets and imitating 'the proceedings of the French Convention' by calling other group members 'Citizen'. He was found guilty after the judge directed the jury to consider sedition as 'violating the peace and order of society'. Although sympathetic parliamentarians argued against his sentence of fourteen years in the House of Commons, Skirving was transported.

Dr Maurice Margarot and John Gerrald received similar sentences, as did Thomas Fyshe Palmer, who had written the offending pamphlets. Dr Margarot was something of a star radical, son of a French wine merchant, head of the London Corresponding Society, and though approaching his fifties, sturdy and keen-eyed. He had crossed to Paris in September 1792 to attend the National Convention, to which he extended his congratulations on the execution of Louis XVI. Pamphlets he wrote urged fiscal and electoral reform, shorter parliaments and a broader franchise. Margarot's trial generated mob demonstrations in his favour outside the Edinburgh court. His young fellow delegate to Scotland, John Gerrald, was the son of a West Indies plantation owner. His friends believed he would not survive transportation, because he suffered from consumption.

Thomas Muir, the last of the Martyrs, was a notable and promising young man, the son of a hop merchant from Glasgow and admitted in his youth to Glasgow University. He became a counsel on behalf of the poor and joined the Society of the Friends of the People. In early 1793 he was charged with sedition, but released, upon which he went to France to attempt to persuade the leaders of the revolution not to execute Louis XVI. The day after he returned to Scotland, he was arrested, imprisoned in Edinburgh, tried again and sentenced to fourteen years transportation. Lord Braxfield, who had also tried Skirving, declared in his judgment that 'the British constitution is the best that ever was since the creation of the world, and it is not possible to make it better. Yet Mr Muir has gone among the ignorant country people and told them Parliamentary Reform was absolutely necessary for preserving their liberty.'

Margarot, his wife and the other Scottish Martyrs, except Gerrald, travelled to Port Jackson on the *Surprize*. It had been one of Camden, Calvert and King's overcrowded and stinking death ships in the Second Fleet, but now that England was at war with revolutionary France and many potential criminals were absorbed by the army and navy, there were fewer than a hundred convicts on board, and the Margarots and the others could travel as cabin passengers. But some falling out between Margarot and the others occurred over an alleged plan by them to capture the ship and take it to France. Later, the authorities would dismiss the accusation, but it left some bad blood amongst the Martyrs.

On arrival in Sydney, Margarot and the others were permitted to live in their own cottages exempt from labour, but Dr Margarot urged Lieutenant-Governor Grose to pardon him, claiming he was entitled to 'the restoration of my freedom . . . inasmuch as I conceive my sentence to be fulfilled on my arrival here, that sentence being transportation and not slavery, the latter unknown to our laws, and directly contrary to the British Constitution as it was established in the revolution of 1688'.

Despite failing to gain his desired freedom, Margarot got on well with Grose, and also Governor Hunter. Governor King he disliked. He told King that he intended to report to London on his behaviour, a fact calculated to make King mistrust him. He often entertained the radical Irish who would arrive later in the decade and in the early years of the new century. When King seized the outraged Margarot's papers, he found amongst them evidence of conspiracy with the Irish, denunciations of colonial avarice, and a forecast of Australia succeeding America as the world's chief post-colonial power. Margarot and his wife would ultimately be sent to Norfolk Island with other 'incendiaries'.

After two years in Sydney, having acquired a farm at Hunters Hill, Thomas Muir escaped with the help of the first mate of an American ship, the *Otter* of Boston. He reached Vancouver Island where he boarded a Spanish ship to go into exile in Europe. The Spanish vessel was attacked by a British warship, and a cannonball smashed Muir's left cheekbone and damaged both eyes, and he was recaptured. The French government arranged for Muir's release, and he arrived at Bordeaux in November 1797, went to Paris and campaigned from there with Tom Paine, author of *The Rights of Man*, for parliamentary reform in Britain. But he never recovered from his injuries and died at Chantilly on 26 January 1799.

Skirving had bought a small farm in Sydney, but both he and John Gerrald were in shaky health, and nine days after Gerrald expired of tuberculosis in

1796, nursed by the generous-hearted Thomas Palmer, Skirving fell to dysentery. Palmer would himself perish on the Spanish island of Guam on his way home to Britain after his term of exile expired. But Margarot's seditious house remained at the colony's heart.

UNHINGEING A GOVERNOR

Governor John Hunter, Phillip's friend, suffered as much as anyone from the distance of New South Wales from England and the low priority it inevitably had with a British government struggling with post-revolutionary France. As much as any governor he was subject to sniping reports from various citizens, but none could snipe so efficaciously as John Macarthur.

Macarthur had been appointed by Major Grose, before Hunter's arrival as governor in Sydney, to the post of Inspector of Public Works in New South Wales, and Hunter made friends with him and confided in him until he experienced the fury of Macarthur's unquiet heart when he tried to restrict the trading activities of Rum Corps officers. Captain Paterson, Commandant of the New South Wales Corps, was a youngish man who would become greatly weakened and prematurely aged by a duel he would fight with Macarthur, but despite that, Hunter discovered that he could not rely upon the military, and found it impossible to control its liquor monopoly and trading.

Suffering barely disguised disrespect from the military in town, Hunter found his relief in explorations around Sydney, and in sending back specimens of Australian fauna to Sir Joseph Banks.

In 1799, a dispatch arrived from the Duke of Portland, the Colonial Secretary, recalling him. The sense that he had failed to control the military gentlemen's avarice weighed heavily on him. After returning to England, while serving on half-pay, he wrote a vindication of his administration. In line with the custom of promotion by seniority he became a rear admiral in 1807 and a vice-admiral in 1810. He would die in 1821, but many of his drawings of flora and fauna remain in Australia, at the National Library.

THE HEARTSORE IRISH

As D'Arcy Wentworth served on Norfolk Island with his convict woman and his sickly son, his wealthy cousin, Earl Fitzwilliam, was sent to Ireland as Lord Lieutenant in 1795. He was greeted by progressives with rapture, for it was known he intended to advance the Emancipation of Catholics and make peace with the Irish Whig leader Henry Gratton. Those comfortable with the divided state of the nation fiercely opposed to Emancipation, petitioned London asking for Fitzwilliam's recall. With their powerful connections in Westminster, they were able to achieve it. Hence, the cancellation of Earl Fitzwilliam's warrant and his replacement by a hard-liner, Earl Camden, showed the Irish progressives that justice and independence could be established in Ireland only by force. The Irish people of all classes who formed a crowd all the way to the Dublin Quays, men and women torn between anger at Westminster and respect for Fitzwilliam, and who saw the earl departing on his ship back to England, knew that a cataclysm was coming.

The peasantry, the Gaelic-speaking masses of the countryside, saw rebellion as a chance to adjust the land system in their favour, and, inevitably, to destroy the Protestant Ascendancy. They were the Croppies, the ready foot soldiers of revolution. What was of particular alarm to the British establishment in Ireland was the likelihood that Napoleon might send an army to reinforce any uprising, and that thus Britain would find itself with the enemy not only on the Continent but to its west.

In the countryside remotely placed landlords found their peasantry, many of them future Australian convicts, boldly cutting down their trees to make pikes for the coming adjustment of justice.

> But Ninety-Eight's dark season came,
> And Irish Hearts Were Sore,
> The Pitch-Cap, shears and triangle,
> The patient folk outbore.
> The Blacksmith thought of Erin
> And found he'd work to do.
> 'I'll forge some steel for freedom,'
> Said Pat O'Donoghue.

The early success of the uprising can only be briefly dealt with here, but in Wicklow and Wexford there were pitched battles, and serious action in Ulster. When all seemed lost, after the climactic battle of Vinegar Hill near Enniscorthy in Wexford, a French army landed in County Mayo at Killala, joined up with the United Irishmen, and enjoyed some victories.

When the French ultimately surrendered they were treated well. But the

United Irishmen of Mayo suffered the same excesses of torment as had been employed in the rest of Ireland. In a melee of arrests and beatings, impalings, summary executions and transportations, no one checked too closely into the exact culpability of this or that man. The army butchered anyone wearing a brown Croppy coat found within several miles of any field of action. When the veteran general Lord Cornwallis arrived in Dublin in June 1798 to replace Camden, he was appalled by the excesses of violence his predecessor had tolerated. He wrote to a friend in London of 'the numberless murders that are hourly committed by our people without any process or examination whatever . . . Our friends . . . and their folly in making it a religious war, added to the ferocity of our troops who delight in murder, most powerfully counteract all plans of conciliation.' It was decided by Cornwallis, rather than by London, that clemency must be conceded to men who surrendered. Clemency, however, in many cases would involve imprisonment in typhus-haunted gaols and hulks, and ultimate transportation to New South Wales.

Who were these inflammatory Irish transported to the other side of the world? On the *Minerva* of 1800 and the *Anne* of 1801 were a number of 'prominent leaders' of the 1798 uprising. On the *Anne*, for example, perhaps more than one hundred of one hundred and thirty-seven convicts were guilty of political crimes, at least as they saw it. King called them 'one hundred and thirty-seven of the most desperate and diabolical characters that could be selected throughout that kingdom, together with a Catholic priest of most notorious, seditious, and rebellious principles'. Forty-one were listed as United Irishmen, seven as possessing arms or pikes, four as having been engaged in treasonable, rebellious or seditious practices, three as being involved in unlawful oaths, two as violating the Insurrection Acts, two as being rebel leaders or captains and one of fomenting rebellion. Vaguer offences were also punished, such as those attaching to one Hugh Dolan, 'being from house, a most dangerous man' and to James Delahunty, who was found to be an 'idle and disorderly person and drinking seditious toasts'. Hugh Mohan was found out late at night singing treasonable songs and could give no account for his behaviour.

Thomas Langan from Glin in County Limerick, who arrived in Sydney on the *Anne*, was one of the best-known rebels in the province of Munster, where he went by the nom-de-guerre of Captain Steel. His shipmates on the *Anne* included the United Irish captains Philip Cunningham and Manus Sheehy. Another leader from the Limerick–Kerry border was Patrick Galvin who had arrived on *Friendship* in 1800, along with James Meehan, a young man in his twenties, a surveyor, who would later do great service to the British government in triangulating and surveying the earth of New South Wales.

Philip Gidley King, who became governor of New South Wales in 1800, described the Irish Croppy convicts as 'satanic'. And the Reverend Marsden, Low Church clergyman and high-toned magistrate who arrived in the colony in 1794 to work beside the Reverend Johnson, ultimately wrote a report to the London Missionary Society in 1807, declaring, 'The low Irish convicts are an extraordinary race of beings whose minds are depraved beyond all conception and their whole thoughts employed on mischief.' As for the United Irish leadership, 'leading men in their own country', they were still very dangerous towards a proper government and 'most of them are very wild and eccentric. The advantages of superior education have not been able to correct this part of their national character.' By that stage, the very mercantile, land-owning Reverend Samuel Marsden had personally experienced the rebellious intentions of the United Irish.

Father Dixon of Wexford, the epicentre of the rebellion, was condemned to death by the British army in May 1798, but was saved on the intervention of several leading Protestant loyalists who said he had protected Protestants. His sentence was commuted to transportation. His cousin, a shipmaster named Thomas Dixon, was one of the rebel leaders, and Father Dixon seems to have been guilty by virtue of kinship.

The assumption amongst the authorities was that the priests were dangerous, but in fact the priests were generally against any United Irish uprising in New South Wales, because they believed it would be suicidal. Father Harold, a robust 55-year-old who had written United Irish verse until told to stop by his archbishop had always preached non-violence and restraint but was arrested, his captors ignoring three orders from Dublin Castle, the English headquarters in Ireland, for his release. On the summer evening of his arrival in New South Wales aboard the *Minerva* from Cork, in January 1800, Harold entertained his Protestant clergyman host by singing 'The Exile of Erin', while United Irish prisoners on the beach below cried 'Encore!'

Still opposed to violence, he told Surgeon Balmain in August 1800, in the last weeks of Hunter's governorship, that there were some plans afoot among the Irish of New South Wales to rebel, though he did not reveal the identity of the plotters. William Cox, a lieutenant critical of English excesses in Ireland, who had also sailed on *Minerva*, wrote to Samuel Marsden, the magistrate at Parramatta, reporting his suspicions, and Marsden and Richard Atkins went down to Sydney to tell Governor Hunter who immediately started an enquiry led by the judge-advocate.

The hearing took place in early September and the first witness was Father Harold. Although he said that the planned uprising was well advanced, he believed he could restrain the convicts by moral persuasion and would not name the leader; he declared he would not bring any man by the neck before the authorities unless it were a person who first squandered a thousand lives. He was committed to gaol for withholding the truth. It was assumed he had heard of the plot in the confessional, since under canonical law a priest thus informed may warn of a coming threat, but must not identify the person in whom it resides.

Amongst the names that emerged as potential leaders from witnesses who turned King's evidence were those of Joseph Holt, an eloquent rebel leader from Wicklow, transported on *Minerva*, and Margarot, the Scottish Martyr. It seemed that even during the enquiry the plot was going ahead. One witness said Holt had conferred with two other rebel leaders in a barn at Captain Cox's property at Canterbury, to the south-west of Sydney. Evidence emerged at the enquiry that Holt had waited for a while before committing himself, but it was alleged he then suggested that he lead one party and that a United Irishman named William Alcock, a former British officer, lead another. On the basis of information given by Harold, the authorities were able to track down Bryan Fury, a blacksmith from Longford who also had arrived on the *Minerva* and was said to have made pikes, secretly filing down hinges to make their heads. But none were found in Fury's possession.

Despite the enquiry, the concept for the rebellion remained steady: to gather during Saturday night, 4 March, and on Sunday morning to attack the church in Parramatta during the service, overpowering the soldiers whose arms would be stacked or at their barracks. But one of the proposed leaders, Quinlan, had been found drunk at dawn and was arrested, and Francis King, a deserter from a militia in Cork, took over command. In the uncertainty, not enough turned up to storm the church.

A further ten supposed leaders were arrested—not all of them United Irish-men, or at least not transported for that offence. The authorities persuaded one to turn informer, a young man called John Connell. A new round of floggings was ordered. Father Harold was made to place his hand on the flogging tree when the punishments were carried out at Parramatta, and Joseph Holt was subject to the same order. Amongst those sentenced to punishment varying from 100 to 500 lashes was the young rebel lieutenant Patrick Galvin, and United Irishman Maurice Fitzgerald.

Paddy Galvin said during his flogging, wrote Marsden, that though he was a young man, 'he would have died upon the spot before he would tell a single sentence. He was taken down three times, punished upon his back, and also on his bottom when he could receive no more on his back. Galvin was just in the same mood when taken to the hospital as he was when first tied up, and continued the same this morning.'

Though to Marsden the problem was Galvin's undiminished defiance, the erosion that befell Galvin and Fitzgerald in the physical sense was detailed by Holt with nationalist admiration.

> The place they flogged them their arms pulled round a large tree and their breasts squeezed against the trunk so the men had no power to cringe . . . there was two floggers, Richard Rice and John Johnson, the hangman from Sydney. Rice was [a] left-handed man, and Johnson was right-handed, so they stood at each side and I never saw two threshers in a barn move their strokes more handier than these two man-killers did. I was to the leeward of the floggers . . . the flesh and skin blew in my face as it shook off the cats. Fitzgerald received his three hundred lashes. Dr Mason—I will never forget him—he used to go feel his pulse, and he smiled, and said, 'This man will tire before he will fail—go on.' . . . during this time Fitzgerald was getting his punishment he never gave so much as a word—only one, and that was saying, 'Don't strike me on the neck, flog me fair.' When he was let loose, two of the constables went and took hold of him by the arms to keep him in the cart. I was standing by. He said to them, 'Let me go.' He struck both of them with his elbows in the pit of the stomach and knocked them both down, and then stepped in the cart. I heard Dr Mason say that man was strong enough to bear two hundred more. Next was tied up Paddy Galvin, a young boy about sixteen years of age. He was ordered to get three hundred lashes. He got one hundred on the back, and you could see his backbone between the shoulder blades. Then the doctor ordered him to get another hundred on his bottom. He got it, and then his haunches were in such a jelly that the doctor ordered him to be flogged on

the calves of his legs. He got a hundred there and as much as a whimper he never gave. They asked him if he would tell where the pikes were hid. He said he did not know, and would not tell. 'You may as well hang me now,' he said, 'for you'll never get any music from me so.' They put him in the cart and took him to the hospital.

On 21 October 1800 the *Buffalo* left Sydney Cove for Norfolk Island, to deliver the Irish prisoners, now punished by exile there, and from there for London, with retiring Governor Hunter aboard. Norfolk Island was at that time under the command of Major Foveaux, and there, too, the Irish planned a rising—for Christmas Day. Five soldiers were even recruited—two of them Freemasons in an age when Freemasonry was associated with Irish, French and American republicanism. At a final meeting it was decided that officialdom's women and children could be put to death and a conscience-stricken Irishman presented himself next morning at Foveaux's house 'in much agitation'. Two ringleaders were taken from church parade and summarily hanged within two hours. More than twenty were flogged; the five soldiers amongst them were drummed out of the corps.

After the initial Irish rebelliousness was crushed, the colony was quiet, said King, newly installed as governor, though the arrival of the *Anne* meant the number of rebels in New South Wales who, as King described it, had never dishonoured their oath as United Irishmen was close to six hundred: a regiment of disaffected Irish 'only waiting an opportunity to put their diabolical plans in execution'.

Another ship, the *Atlas*, had left Cork with the former sheriff of that city, Sir Henry Hayes Browne, aboard. Hayes Browne was said by some to be a United Irishman, but was more probably an eccentric, and an opponent of autocracy. Hayes Browne had signed the warrants of the first Irish convicts shipped directly from Cork in 1792, and now had been sentenced himself to transportation as a middle-aged widower with many children for attempting the abduction of a Quaker heiress, Mary Pike, and conducting a spurious marriage with her for the sake of her fortune. The marriage was not consummated, which made wits declare that though he took up his Pike, he was not United. To the disgust of the surgeon John Jamison, Hayes Browne travelled in the cabin section of the ship. On the overcrowded prison deck, which stank terribly from the fermenting bilges, and which was so lacking in oxygen that lights would go out, were the plainer criminals and Croppies, the United Irish rank and file, once more underfed and under-supplied, and chained in their bunks.

The captain, Brooks, was guilty of inventing a mutiny that never occurred so that he could put into the Cape of Good Hope purely for his own trading benefit. His neglect of the convict deck contributed to the deaths of sixty-three male and two women convicts, but he escaped punishment after his ship arrived at Sydney Cove in July 1802. On the *Hercules*, which left Cork in late 1801, there had been a true and horrifically responded-to uprising in which thirteen convicts were shot or bludgeoned to death.

In Sydney, King called a Vice-Admiralty court together to try the captain of *Hercules*, Luckyn Betts, and to perhaps refer charges against him to Great Britain. But the Vice-Admiralty courts, though making exacting and fair enquiries, nonetheless had a record of going softly on ships' masters. In a sense these reprehensible captains were not in the end as great a worry to administrators as were the rebels their ships carried. And for the British authorities the issue was this: if they began sending masters to gaol for crimes against humanity, including manslaughter or murder, they might not be able to find captains and shipowners willing to commit their vessels to transporting convicts.

To the Irish, such an outcome to enquiries on their behalf, as distinct from enquiries into their own activities, merely confirmed their belief that their tormentors would always go unpunished under the Crown.

The words recur in Governor King's dispatches—'diabolical', 'seditious', 'mutinous'. To Governor King the intractable Irish Croppies represented three forms of evil—they spoke their own language; they were by and large Papists, willing in his mind to use the confessional as a mechanism of plotting; and they had been infused with the Jacobinism of their leaders in the failed Irish uprising. And he had to deal with Irish leaders too, gentlemen rebels who had surrendered to the amnesty offered by the authorities and who had travelled in the cabins, men like General Joseph Holt of Wexford, a determined, fiery and resourceful Presbyterian United Irishman.

King reported to the Duke of Portland, Secretary of State for the Colonies, that the mutinous behaviour of the Irish convicts had not ceased even after some of these principal United Irish were sent to Norfolk Island in 1801. And the rebelliousness was ongoing. 'Although everything was ready for general insurrection and massacre yet as no overt act had taken place, I did not conceive myself justifiable in adopting more rigorous measures.'

The hapless and inoffensive priest referred to King on the *Anne*, Father Peter O'Neil, was in reality not diabolical or seditious at all. He had been parish priest of Ballymacoda, a rural area in Cork, an area which provided considerable support amongst the sons of small tenants for the 1798 uprising. Father O'Neil was summarily arrested, and without trial given nearly three hundred lashes with a cat of wire to make him inform on his parishioners. His refusal to do so had guaranteed his imprisonment and transportation. The Lord Lieutenant in Dublin Castle, hearing of O'Neil's rough treatment, signed an order of release, but by the time it reached Cork the *Anne* had sailed.

Perhaps King's low opinion of O'Neil and the other *Anne* convicts was based in part on an uprising amongst the convicts which had occurred in the Atlantic while the prison decks were being fumigated by small, controlled explosions of gunpowder and most of the United Irishmen were on deck. The assumed leader of the revolt, Manus Sheehy, was executed by firing squad on the maindeck.

King dealt with the imagined threat O'Neil was to the good order of New South Wales by shipping him off to Norfolk Island. There he met up with that other priest-prisoner, Father Harold. The Dublin order for release would catch up with Peter O'Neil on Norfolk Island by the end of 1802, and enabled him to go home.

That the United Irish were disaffected was undeniable, but King was aware that half the problem he had inherited came from the improper way they had been tried, imprisoned and transported. 'I beg to submit to your Grace's consideration,' wrote King to the Duke of Portland, 'the situation of several persons who were sent from Ireland during the late rebellion, many of whom without any sentence being sent here against them.' He mentioned men whose behaviour was uniformly good and highly deserving. Father Dixon was one, and also the Reverend Henry Fulton, a middle-aged, progressive Church of Ireland clergyman from Tipperary. An Englishman by birth, Fulton had uttered sentiments considered seditious in the inflamed atmosphere of the time, though his friends claimed that his confession had been extorted 'by fear of a species of torture at that time too common'. This was probably flogging, the pitchcap— pouring hot pitch on the prisoner's head—or repeated half-hangings.

Fulton spent some years on Norfolk Island, where his Christianity showed itself less punitive than that brand pursued by Parramatta's chaplain, Samuel Marsden. He would settle in well, and stay permanently in New South Wales.

To the governor, in the meantime, the Loyal Associations recruited from Sydney to the Hawkesbury to serve as a militia were a comfort—'so many sureties to be of peace and tranquillity'. One of the sergeants of the Loyal Association who kept a musket ready on his farm along the Parramatta River, where he lived with his plentiful offspring and his common-law wife, Sarah Bellamy, was James Bloodworth, founder builder and brick-maker, ready to defend the sovereignty of the King who had transported him.

As for the gentlemen officers, King's garrison, who treated him—as they had Hunter—with increasing contumely as he tried to regulate their trade, still had no fort to which to retire to resist a French regiment of the kind that, appearing from nowhere, perhaps charging in from the Heads, perhaps marching up the old Frenchman's track from Botany Bay, would combine with the Irish and devour the population. Distance and unimportance were the governor's chief protection from the likelihood that United Irish gentry might be in France even then, persuading Napoleon to send a regiment to Sydney to vanquish the not quite martial Rum Corps, as the citizenry had long called the New South Wales Corps.

TRADE AND THE IRISH

In the narrowness of the Sydney flood plain settlement, amongst the population of fallen convicts and quasi-gentlemen, there was sufficient fear and rancour, posturing and paranoia to fill a full-fledged nation, or the court of a Caesar. The tenuousness of the modest society on this charming if less than fertile strand of earth did not diminish the self-seriousness of the gentlemen at all. Indeed such impulses were enhanced here, since all seemed at stake.

The governor was an autocrat according to the writ of his commission, and thus the scope of his power could be offensive to colonial citizens. His first concern, now continuity of supplies seemed assured, was to keep spending in check—no Secretary of State for War and the Colonies ever dismissed a colonial governor for reducing a budget. King was happy to tell the Duke of Portland that he had reduced the number of public ration books by five hundred. The next concern was the trade in liquor, and the third and not unrelated was located in the turbulent breast of one person, John Macarthur, the focus of resistance, of whom Governor Hunter had previously also complained. Macarthur had earlier put up his property for sale to the government and been politely refused by King. It was curious he did so, but the temptation to go home to England was not a stranger to him. Yet he treated any, even the smallest, attack on his property as if it were an assault on his person.

The Scottish Martyr, Dr Margarot, despite being ill, offered his intelligence on the sins of the officers, including Macarthur, to King. The governor, however, did not deign to receive what could have been excellent information.

Not long after, Margarot complained to the Undersecretary in London: 'I was roused in the middle of the night by two serjeants, under false and frivolous pretences. I complained the next day.' Then, at King's muster, Mrs Margarot was compelled to turn up for the count like a common convict woman. 'No man of but even decent education and behaviour could have expected her to attend his levy of female prostitutes and thieves . . . Governor King, however, having laid in a great stock of irascibility towards me, thought proper to vent some of it upon his intended victim, and the next day issued a warrant for apprehending and committing me to gaol as a vagrant.' Hunter, still in the colony, intervened and King's rage was great and difficult to appease.

Maurice Margarot was applying for redress and protection to save not only himself, he said in his letter to London, but the colony. 'The first error of ministry was suffering Major Grose to succeed to that worthy man Gov. Phillip; but the second, and by far the most fatal, is suffering a man like Governor King to succeed Governor Hunter. The first error introduced corruption, but the second will most likely end in ruin.'

CHAPTER 10

A NEW VINEGAR HILL

In the sweltering January of 1804 news arrived in New South Wales of the Irish rebellion led by Robert Emmet in the high summer of 1803 in Dublin. Emmet, wearing a uniform of green and white, had led his followers against Dublin Castle. On the way they had met the carriage of the Chief Justice and his nephew, and piked them to death. The force degenerated thereafter, and Robert Emmet withdrew to the Wicklow Mountains. He, like Irish rebels before him, had been negotiating with the French. The Scottish Martyr, Maurice Margarot, keeping his journal in his little hut in Sydney Cove, already knew about all this from various British radical friends.

When captured, Emmet was hung, drawn and quartered—literally, his body being torn into parts by four horses pulling in different directions. The news spread through the Irish community in the colony. It upset the former sheriff of Cork, Sir Henry Hayes Browne, who had just been released from a six-month sentence in prison for insulting the governor. Mary Turley, the Irish de facto wife of a Parramatta officer, coming down from that town to Sydney Cove in a boat, met an Irishman she knew, Sir Henry Hayes Browne's former servant John Sullivan, who said that if the officer himself had been in the boat he would sooner cut his head off than eat his dinner, and that he hoped the time would shortly come when he would have an opportunity of doing it. Mary Turley charged Sullivan and one of the other boatmen with threatening language. But four witnesses said they had not heard Sullivan make these comments. Turley was charged with perjury but acquitted.

In Parramatta also lived a French prisoner-of-war, François Durinault and his transported United Irish wife, Winifred Dowling. Durinault had given his word of honour that he would not attempt to escape. Joseph Holt called on Winifred and her husband in late January. Durinault told Holt that four men from Castle Hill would call on him later in the day to ask him to lead a planned convict insurrection. Winifred scolded her husband 'that if she saw any more whispering or anything suspicious she would quit the place, for it was by such means the misfortune of her family as well as those of Ireland were occasioned'. Holt warned the Frenchman not to have anything to do with the plotters and promised that he himself would not. He would later claim that he would be a number of times approached to lead the uprising, but always said that with his wife and children in the colony he was not willing to jeopardise them.

Nonetheless, at a junction somewhere between Parramatta and the Hawkes-bury, a number of Irish messengers met each other, carrying intelligence about the uprising. These men were talking about deliverance, redemption, the validation of all they stood for. Yet one of the Irishmen felt very much like Winifred Dowling that rebellion had been the cause of all his misery, and he passed the news that there was an imminent and serious uprising on to the overseer of Captain Abbott. The overseer was a United Irishman from the *Atlas*, who after great thought passed it on to his master. Samuel Marsden, Parramatta's man of Christ, was informed and set off—as in 1800—for Sydney to notify the governor and request more ammunition for Parramatta. In any case, it was a sort of open secret that an uprising was about to take place.

The Munster men, the men from the south and south-west of Ireland, were heavily involved, it was said. Joseph Holt, having rejected leadership of any uprising, stayed at his liberal employer William Cox's house, Brush Farm, and two guards were set, both of them United Irishmen, but loyal to Holt.

At seven o'clock as darkness fell on Saturday 3 March, a convict hut at Castle Hill, to the north-west of Sydney, burst into flames as a signal that the rising had begun. Two hundred convicts at Castle Hill were guarded only by a few convict constables, most of whom joined the rising. The cry of 'Death or Liberty' was heard as they searched for the resident flogger, Robert Doogan, and a number of hated constables. Fortunately for their targets, there were a number of misfires, and no one was killed. Led by the United Irishman Philip Cunningham, the rebels scoured the area for arms, and at one house they found weapons and a keg of spirits.

The plan was that the Castle Hill convicts would march to the Hawkesbury where they would collect other disaffected men and form a force of over one thousand. The combined force would then return to Castle Hill and go on to Parramatta which 'two well-known disaffected persons', unspecified, would assist them to capture. They would plant the Tree of Liberty at Government House there and proceed to Sydney to embark on ships which would be waiting for them. 'Now boys', cried Philip Cunningham, 'liberty or death!'

Cunningham had been the overseer of the government stonemasons at Castle Hill, and had spent twelve months building himself a stone house, as if he foresaw a future in New South Wales. But now he led the Castle Hill convicts to the top of a nearby hill where they divided into parties to raid the surrounding settlements for more arms and volunteers. They raided the convict stations at Pennant Hills and Seven Hills. They took settlers prisoner. One of the settlers escaped and galloped into Parramatta to give the alarm at about 9 p.m. He burst into Samuel Marsden's parlour where the Marsdens and Mrs Macarthur were sitting at supper. (John Macarthur at that time was in exile in England.) 'He told us that the Croppies had risen, that they were at my Seven Hills farm, and that numbers were approaching Parramatta,' Elizabeth Macarthur would later write.

To the Marsdens' and Elizabeth's minds would have come accounts of Croppy atrocities in Wexford. The women would have feared being ravished and piked. For the next hour the drums at the barracks beat to arms and the settlers headed there. They could see the flames at Castle Hill ten kilometres north. A dispatch rider was sent off to alert the governor and the main body of the New South Wales Corps that Parramatta expected an invasion of four hundred United Irishmen. Mr and Mrs Marsden and Elizabeth Macarthur, with the wife and children of Captain Abbott and of the deputy commissary, went down to the river and took boat for Sydney. Even then Elizabeth was full of fear. 'You can have no idea what a dreadful night it was and what we suffered in our minds.'

Parramatta's garrison of soldiers was expecting the rebels to attack and try to capture the arsenal. Instead, on a hill three and a half kilometres from Parramatta, the ex-soldiers and United Irishmen Cunningham and William Johnson drilled their men, looking down towards Parramatta lying in its bowl by the river. From here they could control the road between Parramatta and the Hawkesbury.

In Sydney the beating of drums started a little before midnight, with the firing of cannon. Major Johnston was fetched from his house in Annandale, a few kilometres west of the town of Sydney, and soon after Governor King rode up and told him five hundred to six hundred Croppies had taken up arms and that the call was to march to Parramatta. The governor got to Parramatta quickest, at four o'clock in the morning, and told the anxious men of the garrison that Major Johnston was on his way. A little after five o'clock Johnston arrived with his troops. The soldiers breakfasted on rum and bread. After a twenty-minute rest they marched to Government House, Parramatta.

King's latest information was that the rebels had recently been at the park gate near Parramatta and had retreated to Toongabbie, the work depot nearby. Johnston was to go after them. He sought and got permission to fire at anyone who attempted to run when called on to stop. King also signed off on martial law for a region north and south of the river and westwards.

At Toongabbie Johnston was told the rebels were on the hill above, behind the house of Dr Martin Mason, who had been the officiating surgeon at many a flogging. He had only a small part of the New South Wales Corps with him. But he relied on the fact that his men were at least trained soldiers, some of them having had experience in other British regiments. So he set out to flank the Irish with an advance guard of five soldiers and six to eight local inhabitants, members of the Loyal Association, while he led twenty troops and twelve armed Loyalists up the hill. They found no one there, and marched on through a sweltering summer day. He pursued the rebels for sixteen kilometres and then heard from a mounted trooper that they were only two kilometres further on. The trooper rode ahead, waving a white handkerchief, and caught up to the rebels, calling out to them and telling them that the governor was on his way to talk to them. They did not believe him and took the flints out of his pistol and sent him back. Johnston then sent Father Dixon, whom he had brought with him from Parramatta, to talk to the rebels, but they would not listen.

Johnston and his trooper galloped forward and called to the Irish, most of them wearing shirtsleeves this sweltering day, and asked to speak to their leaders. They invited him to come amongst them. He replied that he was within firing distance of them and that he wanted to avoid bloodshed.

'Death or liberty and a ship to take us home,' was the reply, but in the end two rebels came down the hill. One of them, Cunningham, took off his hat, either as a gesture of obeisance or equality of status. Again Father Dixon cried out for an end to bloodshed. At that moment, as Quartermaster Laycock with the rest of the troops came into view, Johnston pulled a pistol from his sash and put it to the head of one of the leaders, who were innocent enough to think they were operating under a parley and some vestige of British honour in which, despite all, they believed. The trooper did the same with the other leader. Retreating with his two captives, Johnston called on his troops to begin firing, and shooting broke out on both sides. Nine rebels were immediately killed, and many wounded.

Most rebels, however, escaped in the following moonless night and some remained at large well into March. But Philip Cunningham was killed. A United Irish account credibly enough argues that some of the volunteers of the Loyal Association shot Cunningham and his fellow leader, William Johnson, after Major Johnston had left them in the care of Quartermaster Laycock. Johnston himself tellingly reported, 'I never in my life saw men behave better than those under my command, and the only fault I had to find with them was their being too fond of blood. I saved the lives of six miserable wretches that the soldiers would have butchered, if I had not presented my pistol at their heads and swore I would shoot them if they attempted to kill them in cold blood.'

For to make up the numbers of the Loyal Association, many 'volunteers' were convicts serving time, and there was a notable lack of quick pardons for them after the uprising, perhaps as a result of their brutality during it.

Many of the first ten rebels who appeared before court claimed that they had been coerced into taking part in the uprising. Nevertheless, all ten were sentenced to death, to be hung in chains. Marsden noted that four of them were Protestants and two Englishmen. They were executed at the place of their violation, and at Castle Hill, Parramatta and Sydney. Two of the convicts in charge of the bullock carts who were ordered to drive the condemned men to the scaffold went on strike and each received twenty-five lashes.

Other rebels were condemned to flogging or sent to labour in the gaol gang. A number of 'ironed prisoners' in the gaol gang at Parramatta memorialised the governor with their thanks on account of 'your unprecedented clemency' extended to them—'the deluded people distinguished by the name Croppies'.

It is undeniable that a moderating liberal influence operated in King—he was not as remiss or brutal as Earl Camden had been in Ireland. It is hard to this day to say whether that constitutes high or low praise. In the meantime the Irish leadership, dispersed from Coal River (Newcastle) to Norfolk Island, were not in a position to play with the concept of another uprising. The frustrated idea, however, abided amongst humbler convicts.

A STATE OF SLAVES

Governor King would have sent many of the Irish to Norfolk Island except that there were plans now to abandon it and establish a convict settlement at the Coal River, a hundred and twenty kilometres north of Sydney. It would be called Newcastle. A party led by Lieutenant Charles Menzies left from Sydney in late March on two ships with thirty-four prisoners and ten soldiers. The naturalist Frederick Bauer and the ornithologist George Cayley also went, driven by scientific thirst. Amongst the notable United Irishmen sentenced there by the Parramatta bench of magistrates were William Maum and Clarence McCarty, the latter a lawyer. They had suffered a destiny like Joseph Holt, who was sent to Norfolk Island despite its coming (and temporary) disbandment, aboard the *Betsey*, and impressed its captain as a gentleman, 'very finely dressed on landing, in a new blue coat with a black velvet collar, like a gentleman should be—which he was, every inch of him'.

English convicts from the *Coromandel* were mixed in with the Irish at Coal River, but that did not stop Irish disaffection, and six ringleaders of a possible uprising were imprisoned, and two of them sent back to Sydney to face sentences of flogging, after which they were to labour in an iron gang, but with solitary confinement at night. One United Irishman fled to the bush to escape the punishment and died in the hills around the Coal (later, Hunter) River.

The Irish all thought, under the doctrine of Tom Paine and other radicals, that they were slaves. Their masters thought they were miscreants. There could be no meeting of minds.

Many agreed with the Irish convicts. Lieutenant James Tuckey of the *Calcutta*, an Irishman who understood where the rebellions were springing from, wrote a letter to Henry Dundas, now Lord of the Admiralty, suggesting that the regulations which had been both salutary and necessary in the setting up of the colony, 'are now become the most severe grievances'. Tuckey was a friend of Sir Henry Browne Hayes and Maurice Margarot, critics of King's style of autocracy. Copies of the pamphlet of Tuckey's address to Dundas arrived in New South Wales by 1805 or so. William Wilberforce, the anti-slavery campaigner and founder of the London Missionary Society of which Samuel Marsden was the manifestation in New South Wales, could not concur with his protégé's view of things—that close regulation of the convicts was essential—and agreed with Tuckey that the colony was being run on a basis of de facto slavery.

Jospeh Holt, too, wrote of convict labour in the colony in terms that supplied ammunition to the reformers.

> I saw, at the distance of about half a mile, about fifty men at work, and from their appearance, thought they were dressed with nankeen jackets but, to my surprise, I found it to be the colour of their skin . . . they all worked naked, only loose trousers to cover their parts, so I looked at them with the eye of pity. These men were working with large hoes, about nine inches deep and eight inches wide, a small handle about as thick as the handle of a shovel, and they turned up the ground somewhat like it would be dug with spades and left to rot in winter time. Six men to an acre. In the day's work, they can't wear any shoes when at work, nor any clothes on them in the heat of the day.

The treatment of the dead also appalled liberal sentiment. The body of William Johnson, the United Irish leader, hung in chains from a high tree on the road out of Parramatta, subject to putrefaction and attacks by birds. The naval captain William Kent's wife, Elizabeth, sister of John Hunter, pleaded with Governor King to order the burial of Johnson and the other 'martyrs hanged in the sacred cause of liberty'.

If it were accepted literally that they were hung in pursuit of liberty, the concept that they had been slaves was, for many minds, validated. One English convict, John Grant, had been educated along with Coleridge and Charles Lamb at Christ's Hospital. He had been sentenced to death for firing at a solicitor who frustrated his attempts to win the hand of the daughter of Lord Dudley. After a petition from his sister to the daughters of George III, he was reprieved on the eve of his execution and arrived in New South Wales on the *Coromandel* in May 1804. He fell under the influence of Sir Henry Browne Hayes, and frequently wrote of the excesses of Governor King, particularly his brutalities against convicts. The idea he had got from others in conversations around Sydney was that the Irish had rebelled because they had been compelled to work as slaves, 'contrary to the laws of the English Magna Carta . . . and that an English gentleman, peace loving, to whom liberty is dear, finds himself confounded and amazed to see a system of slavery introduced into a colony of his unhappy compatriots'.

'In the name of God, sir,' he asked a loyalist naval lieutenant in 1805, 'what right had this country to seize them and make them work by force? What a horrible slave state that is! There is no justification for it either in justice or politics; on the contrary a wise government should try giving land to them and offering assistance, to make them forget the past, and by such humane and just contact make what were enemies, friends, and [that] would help the Britannic government towards the prosperity of the free settlers in these vast tracts of land.'

He was deported to Norfolk Island in June 1805 and continued to criticise King and, later, Captain Piper, the Norfolk commandant. He was finally banished to the nearby uninhabited Phillip Island as punishment. After four months of living alone and coming close to starvation, he was brought back to Norfolk Island by Piper but was a shell of himself. Returned to Sydney when he received his conditional pardon in 1805 he courageously returned to the theme of slavery: 'This Noble Charter [Magna Carta] is here violated.'

Returned to Sydney in 1808 with his health restored, he later became a chaplain in Newcastle. He had a plough especially made and hired oxen from Sir Henry Browne Hayes to avoid the necessity of accepting assigned convicts or submitting men to the grubbing hoe on his own land. Otherwise, he said, 'I could never have called myself a friend of liberty again.' He would ultimately be absolutely pardoned by Governor Macquarie and in 1811 returned to England.

But he and other friends of liberty in Britain and Australia had released into the air the idea that the convicts were slaves, not in a metaphoric but literal sense. It would become a hard proposition to combat, even though there were obvious differences between slavery and convict transportation which defenders of the system would point out. The offensive concept to many was that as Britain was preparing to legislate the death of one form of slavery, a de facto white slavery seemed to operate in the penal colonies.

CHAPTER 11

THE PERTURBATOR

Lord Hobart, the latest Secretary for War and the Colonies, had already written, in a dispatch to Governor King dated 30 November 1803, that 'the gratification I experienced from the satisfactory view of the situation of the colony is in a great degree alloyed by the unfortunate differences which have so long subsisted between you and the military officers in the colony . . . and which, I am sorry to observe, have latterly extended to the commander of His Majesty's ship, *Glatton*.'

King did not get a chance to acknowledge receipt of this less than glowing letter of appreciation for his efforts until August 1804. So it was not the Irish who brought King down, but the officers. It is not known if he really wanted an ealier vague request to be granted leave to return to England to be so promptly accepted.

Lord Hobart, described as 'amiable and exigent', had done two stints as Lord Lieutenant of Ireland, and it was upon this skilled but relatively colourless fellow that all the great passion of New South Wales was being unloaded by officers, rebels and the governor's besieged supporters. No wonder King had started to drink too much, for his dispatches often display a sense of futility.

His long-running enmity with the officer corps was reaching a climax. King wanted to begin a government store where settlers could buy goods without a scandalous mark-up, putting a stop, he hoped, to what he called 'the late commissioned hucksters'. He came down hard on John Harris, a licensed victualler and retailer of spirituous liquors, who gave spirits to two convicts for their week's ration of salt meat from the public stores. Harris was deprived of his licence and all his liquors were to be 'staved', that is, smashed. But Harris was Macarthur's man, and the staved barrels belonged to him. Macarthur wrote to England to complain to a range of officials, and urged Colonel Paterson to do the same. Consequently, King rapidly developed a detestation of Macarthur which was matched only by his detestation of the Irish politicals. By 5 November 1801 he complained to Downing Street that Macarthur had incited Paterson to write to Sir Joseph Banks complaining that 'my too great economy had occasioned the present scarcity'. He had also bullied the pliant Paterson to write to General Brownrigg at the War Office, King said. Macarthur had led the campaign to rid the officer corps and the colony of Hunter for trying to do away with the bankrupting effects of Rum Corps control of trade. Why shouldn't he achieve the same with King?

Yet the kindly Mrs King and Mrs Elizabeth Paterson, and similarly Macarthur's wife, Elizabeth, were all close and cherished friends, reliant on each other for ladylike society, not least in the new drawing room in Government House, Parramatta, and all of them collaborated in the founding of the Female Orphan School. Perhaps Macarthur thought women operated on a less fraught plain.

Macarthur himself drove the argument with the governor over freedom of trade and sanctity of merchandise and was not above savaging his own side. He became angry at Paterson for keeping up contact and conversation with King and thus standing in the way of Macarthur's attempts to have the governor 'sent to Coventry'. Indeed when the governor invited the garrison officers to dinner, only four failed to turn up, a fact which made Macarthur more implacable and more combative with Colonel Paterson. Gradually, over months, the officers other than Paterson began to shun the governor's table. King felt he could not court-martial Macarthur for his behaviour towards him because most of the men who would sit on the panel 'were so far compromised'.

Manically, or perhaps maniacally enraged when crossed, Macarthur provoked a duel with Paterson, his superior officer, by leaking a letter Mrs Paterson had sent to Mrs Macarthur, and the details of a conversation Mrs Paterson had had with his Elizabeth at the Paterson house. The duel took place in Parramatta and—against the rules of duelling—Macarthur was permitted to load his own pistols. He won the toss to fire first against his commanding officer, did so and severely wounded him in the right shoulder. Paterson could not return fire and by the time his carriage got him back to Sydney he was in a desperate condition from loss of blood.

After some delays, King, who would have liked to challenge 'the perturbator' Macarthur to a duel but felt it inappropriate to his vice-regal status, subjected Captain Macarthur to house arrest on the grounds that the King's Regulations forbade one officer to challenge another under pain of being cashiered. However Macarthur would not give the necessary securities for keeping the peace and insisted on a general court martial, compelling King to 'judge it necessary and indispensable for the tranquillity of the colony and regiment to direct that officer to be sent to England ... Captain Macarthur had quarrelled with Colonel Paterson because he chose to pay me that attention which a friendship of ten years required.'

Indeed, King's allies fulminated against Captain Macarthur in a way not entirely explained by self-interest. Asked to add his voice to King's, the well-connected but alcoholic judge-advocate, Richard Atkins, wrote of Macarthur's 'infamous and diabolical conduct, his rapacity in accumulating a large fortune in so short a time, his extortions on the industrious and laborious settler, which has plunged themselves and families into distress and misery, and considerably impeded the happiness and prosperity of this colony ... unless he is sent Home as a general disturber of the public peace, and as a man who has most essentially injured HM Service, this colony can never enjoy the happiness and prosperity it is HM's wish that all his subjects should be partakers of.'

Surgeon Thompson was similarly asked to comment. 'He came here in 1790, more than £500 in debt, and is now worth at least £20 000 ... His employment during the eleven years he has been here has been that of making a large fortune, helping his brother officers to make small ones, (mostly at the public expense), and sowing discord and strife.' King himself wrote pungently, 'Experience has convinced every man in this colony that there are no resources which art, cunning, impudence, and a pair of basilisk eyes can afford that he does not put in practice to obtain any point he undertakes.'

Macarthur arranged his colonial affairs, concluding by buying a 1700-acre (689-hectare) farm at Toongabbie, and a large flock from Major Foveaux. He left behind, to look after his interest, his wife Elizabeth, the competent, sensible and generous-hearted woman who nonetheless always sided with her husband's frequently excessive stances. Elizabeth had the pain, too, of saying goodbye to her eight-year-old daughter, also Elizabeth, and son John, a year younger still, who were going to England for an education which would separate them from her for years. They were early examples of a notable minority of Australians being sent to Europe for improvement. The 'perturbator' and his youngsters embarked on the *Hunter* for Calcutta. But in the Celebes (Sulawesi) the *Hunter* was dismasted in a typhoon which must have terrified the children, and was obliged to shelter at Ambon, where—in a zone considered Dutch—there was a trading post run by young Robert Farquhar on behalf of the British East India Company. Farquhar was about to be demoted for moving with East India Company troops on a nearby Dutch post, a provocative act, but Macarthur advised him to stand up against his superiors, including the Governor-General of India, Lord Wellesley, and insist his actions were justified. When this strategy bore fruit, and the *Hunter* had been repaired, the young man—who happened to be son to the surgeon and close friend of the Prince of Wales, the future George IV—sent off a letter praising Macarthur to his father, and thus to the prince's circle, as well as to a number of prominent Whigs. With this—and the parcel of fleeces he had already sent to Sir Joseph Banks—Macarthur had a lever he would use to grand colonial advantage.

His next piece of luck was that the chief witness against him, Captain Mackellar, second to Colonel Paterson at the duel, went aboard an American whaler returning to northern waters to present himself as Macarthur's accuser at the general court martial, and the ship was never seen again after leaving Sydney. It could seem to King that Macarthur enjoyed the preternatural luck associated with the being King considered to be Macarthur's uncle—the Devil. These chances would have a powerful impact on the future of the colony and Australia.

Macarthur did not stop fighting the governor in London. Everyone he met, wrote Macarthur to his friend Captain Piper, 'applauds my conduct and execrates Mr King's'. Without a witness for the court martial, the adjutant-general merely reprimanded Macarthur for earlier insisting on a pointless trial in Sydney, but made certain King could not court-martial him on his return.

Wool imports into Britain had been increasingly impeded by the war with the French, and wool manufacturers were keen to inspect the case of wool Macarthur had brought with him. He told them he was the only settler who had separated his merino sheep from his general herds, and that the results were wonderful. He wrote and published a pamphlet, *Statement of the Improvement and Progress of the Breed of Fine Woolled Sheep in New South Wales.* Its thesis was that he, and other likely settlers, could deliver Britain from wool dependency on the Continent. As a document it would have more impact on the manufacturers and government than would any plaint from Governor King. Macarthur submitted the essence of the pamphlet to the Privy Council Committee for Trade and Plantations. Sir Joseph Banks lightly mocked him for his over-enthusiasm—the naturalist refused to believe that millions of sheep could be grazed in New South Wales. Banks spoke of Australian grass as 'tall, coarse and reedy'. But he had never been as far inland as Macarthur.

Macarthur believed that behind Banks's attitude lay King himself, one of Banks's old protégés. However, he was encouraged by the decline of the Tories, and looked for help from the new Whig government which came to power in May 1804 under Pitt, with Lord Camden as Secretary of State for War and the Colonies. Within two months Macarthur was again promoting his cause before the Privy Council. A wool merchant helped him by testifying that Banks's claim about the excessive expense of shipping wool from Australia was false. Then genial old Captain Hunter appeared and urged the council to listen to Macarthur. Thus Hunter, formerly an enemy, was forgiven.

The Privy Council wrote to Earl Camden urging he authorise a conditional grant of pastures to Macarthur. Camden was a man easily influenced—he had been the vacillating and panicky Lord Lieutenant of Ireland who had been presented with the crisis of Irish rebellion against the Crown in 1798. He had been replaced at the peak of the uprising which had resulted in so many convicts being sent to New South Wales. Now, in influencing other Antipodean realities, he was strongly swayed by Macarthur's Whig friends, and signed off on a 10 000-acre (4050-hectare) grant to Macarthur and organised for him to leave the army to devote himself full-time to the wool enterprise.

King, in the meantime, was in increasingly bad odour with the military of New South Wales. He had taken five convicts and mounted them as his own bodyguard. When the Irish convicts from the *Hercules* 'committed some great excesses and left the place they belong to', King sent his private guard to Parramatta to serve under the direction of the officers of the New South Wales Corps, but their services were rebuffed with contempt. On his arrival in New South Wales, King had been enthusiastic in wanting to take over and had been impatient for Hunter to go, but by now he had become a haunted man. The acid of his enemies' machinations and their public contempt had eroded his soul.

A CRISIS IN LAW

King had warned the British government that there would be trouble and perplexity if a professional lawyer were not sent out to New South Wales as Judge-Advocate to 'circumvent the chicane of those miscreants who, from having committed 'the worst of crimes', use their knowledge of those parts of the law which are open to chicane for the most improper purposes'. Two of the three legal officers in the colony were convicts, and could not be officially employed. One of these two was a middle-aged solicitor named George Crossley, who in 1796 had been charged with forging the will of a clergyman, defrauding the heir-at-law. Crossley had allegedly placed a fly in the mouth of the dead testator before tracing the signature with the deceased's hand, so that he would be able to claim that there was life in the body. Crossley survived that trial but was subsequently charged with perjury and convicted. Crossley would become an important source of informal advice for King and, later, the new governor, William Bligh.

Michael Massey Robinson, a literary Englishman, was the other convict lawyer. He had been transported for threatening to publish a verse which accused James Oldham, an ironmonger and alderman of the City of London, of murder. He had journeyed to New South Wales on the same ship as the ailing judge-advocate Richard Dore, and was such entertaining company that Dore made him his secretary. Dore died, but Massey Robinson was still depended on. In 1802, though, he demanded a gallon of rum in payment for the delivery of a bail bond, and perjured himself over it, and though sentenced to Norfolk Island, he had become so essential to Simeon Lord, the emancipated convict, as a general agent and advisor, as well as to other merchants, that a number of the most respected gentry in Sydney petitioned for his pardon. Governor King himself needed Massey Robinson and restored him to his post. Later, his forgery of movement permits was discovered, but glossed over.

It offended the officers that in their legal dealings with government their fate might depend on what convict lawyers told officials. It equally offended settlers that when they went to court, rulings upon which their futures might depend came down from a bench of close-knit officers and a judge-advocate, Richard Atkins, with no legal training.

The nature of the colony's courts and the way they were open 'to chicane' by those Joseph Holt had called 'the huckster officers' would be a trap to bring that eminent explorer William Bligh down. The new governor's determination to bring the trading officers to heel was set, and he applied the same determination to all matters, often treating special pleaders with a quarterdeck irritability and liverishness. So he quickly gave grounds for a log of complaints to be made against him.

BLIGH THE SINNER

The eminent William Bligh, Fellow of the Royal Geographic Society and darling of Sir Joseph Banks, committed his first unpopular act as governor by directing people to quit their houses built within the lines of demarcation of the public domain. 'He has ordered Morant's house and all that row to be pulled down, which has been done, to the total ruin of those poor wretches.' King had granted leases of fourteen years to some of the occupants. 'Some of these people,' wrote one complainant, 'in the erection of their houses, have expended the fruits of many years' industry. These are now forced to quit their dwellings without the least remuneration . . . If one governor can do away the act of a former one, all property of whatever nature must be uncertain.' Later, those who opposed Bligh for meaner reason would embrace the cause of the evicted.

Then, when unpopular William Gore, the provost-marshal, was accused of having 'uttered a false note'—that is, forgery—Bligh directed George Crossley, 'sent here for perjury', to plead for Gore as his counsel.

These complaints were permitted to far outweigh Bligh's reforms—the flogging-as-torture and to extract confession which had marred King's regime was now ended, and promissory notes could only be issued for amounts in sterling, not for quantities of goods. Further, conditions for the arrest of a citizen were made regular. Bligh also looked upon the land as a sacred trust, and was sparing with grants and livestock, and put limitations on the use of convicts—a reform in the eyes of Whitehall but not in those of the officers, free settlers and others.

He quarrelled from the start with Macarthur. By now, Macarthur had been a year or more returned, and was pursuing the sheep business on his grant south-west of Sydney which he had obsequiously named Camden. Macarthur first called on Bligh in 1806 while the new governor was visiting Government House, Parramatta, where King was waiting for a ship home. As they walked in the garden, Macarthur claims Bligh savaged him, and there is a Bligh-like temper to the sentiments Macarthur quoted, even if he was an unreliable witness.

'What have I to do with your sheep sir? What have I to do with your cattle? Are you to have such flocks of sheep and such herds of cattle as no man ever heard of before? No, sir! I have heard of your concerns, sir. You have got 5000 acres of land in the finest situation in this country. But by God, you shan't keep it.'

When Macarthur replied that the grant came from the Privy Council and the Secretary of State, Bligh cried, 'Damn the Privy Council and damn the Secretary of State too! You have made a number of false representations respecting your wool, by which you have obtained this land.'

According to Macarthur, Bligh behaved so irascibly at table that he caused the fragile King to weep, and after breakfast, when Macarthur tried to reiterate Earl Camden's interest in the wool project, Bligh said again, 'Damn the Secretary of State, what do I care for him, he commands in England and I command here.'

Soon Elizabeth Macarthur was telling her best friend, Miss Kingdon, in whose father's manse she had spent the happiest times of her girlhood, that Bligh was violent, rash and tyrannical. It would be easier to dismiss her if she were not such an admirable and genial woman, very loyal to her husband but capable of her own thoughts. Now that he had returned to Australia they lived principally on their property on the Parramatta River, which she thought delightful. She wrote that when they married, 'I was considered indolent and inactive; Mr Macarthur too proud and haughty for his humble fortune or expectations, and yet you see how bountifully Providence has dealt with us. At this time I can truly say no two people on earth can be happier than we are. In Mr Macarthur's society I experience the tenderest affections of a husband, who is instructive and cheerful as a companion. He is an indulgent father, beloved as a master, and universally respected for the integrity of his character.'

There were also complaints from the Macarthurs about King's friend and Bligh's, Mr Robert Campbell, a young man who had come to Sydney from Calcutta in 1800 to open a branch of the family company, Campbell, Clark and Co. He had made such inroads into the officers' trading monopoly that he was by 1804 agent for many of the officers who ironically sometimes complained of his mark-ups. In his position as naval officer of the port as well, he had the opportunity to deal with all vessels that did not come to New South Wales assigned to any particular trading house.

Andrew Thompson, former convict, was also the butt of complaints of those who opposed Bligh. An emancipated Scot with a good practical head, he ran

Governor Bligh's farm, which Bligh's enemies depicted as a demonstration of the governor's rapacity, while his friends lauded it as a useful model farm. Thompson inadvertently gave ammunition to Bligh's opponents when he reported that he had exchanged inferior numbers of the governor's herd of cattle at the Toongabbie yards and obtained good and sufficient ones in their place.

Thompson was rare in being a Scots convict. He had been tried in Jedburgh in 1790 for stealing £10 worth of cloth. He arrived in Sydney in the *Pitt* in February 1792 and served in the men's provisions store for a year, and then at Toongabbie as a member of the police force. In 1796 Governor Hunter appointed him to the Green Hills, that is, Windsor, the main settlement on the Hawkesbury. He stayed there for the rest of his life. He was pardoned in 1798, and built his house overlooking the river on an acre leased from the government. He rose to chief constable and held that office until 1808, during which time he distinguished himself by investigating crimes and capturing runaway convicts, acting as intermediary between Europeans and Aborigines and rescuing settlers from appalling floods.

Bligh was strongly influenced by Thompson's transmissions from the Hawkesbury. For the Hawkesbury folk saw themselves as cut off and victimised by the officers' cartel. They pleaded that the governor might make representations to His Majesty to allow privileges of trade to their up-country vessels and themselves as other colonies had, and that the law might be administered by trial by jury of the people, as in England. They liked the governor for his plans—like King's—to bring down prices with a government store.

Yet two of the first 'respectable' farmers of New South Wales, John and Gregory Blaxland, Kentish men who had been talked by Sir Joseph Banks into emigrating at their own expense, disliked Bligh for his non-compliance with what they saw as their just demands. The Blaxlands had burned their bridges behind them, selling their long-held family farm. They thought Gregory had not been adequately supplied with land, stock and convict labour, and looked at every resource supplied to Bligh's own model farm by Thompson with rancour.

Soon, scrolled-up pipes—anonymous lampooning political doggerel—attacking Bligh began to appear in the streets (as they had during King's governorship), the most noted drawing on the notorious mutiny led by Fletcher Christian on the *Bounty* against Bligh to declare: '*Oh tempora! Oh mores!* Is there no CHRISTIAN in New South Wales to put a stop to the tyranny of the governor?'

THE GRAND IMPASSE

When Bligh was appointed governor, Lieutenant John Putland, married to Bligh's daughter Mary, had accepted a post as his aide-de-camp, even though he was suffering from tuberculosis. Mary was small, vigorous and resembled her mother, who had not accompanied Bligh because she was a very poor sailor. In Mrs Bligh's absence, Mary Putland served as the mistress of Government House, where everyone thought her elegant and amiable.

For a man wary about granting land, on arrival in Sydney Bligh had had Governor King grant him the thousand acres (405 hectares) on the Hawkesbury he used for his model farm, but also 600 acres (243 hectares) at St Marys in Sydney's west for John and Mary Putland. Bligh in return gave a grant to Mrs King which she recklessly named 'Thanks'. This arrangement naturally outraged people like the Blaxlands.

Putland's tuberculosis weakened him. He could not always attend public events with his wife. One Sunday in St Philip's Church, to which she had accompanied her father, Mary fainted when soldiers laughed at the transparency of the new dress her mother had sent from England. She had chosen in the heat not to wear petticoats and the long pantaloons which covered her legs were visible in the light. Bligh verbally flagellated the soldiers responsible, thus making them far from willing servants.

Late in 1807, Mary had written to her mother, 'Pappa is quite well but dreadfully harassed by business and the troublesome people he has to deal with. In general he gives great satisfaction, but there are a few we suspect wish to oppose him ... Mr Macarthur is one of the party and the others are the military officers, but they are all invited to the house and treated with the same politeness as usual.' When John Putland died in early January 1808, to be buried in the grounds of Sydney Cove's Government House, with the remains of Arabanoo and others, Bligh was worried about the effect it would have on his daughter's health. 'She has been a treasure to the few gentlewomen here and the dignity of Government House.'

In late 1807, Bligh and Macarthur had become locked in conflict over two issues. One concerned Judge-Advocate Atkins; the other was to do with the escape of an Irish convict on the schooner *Parramatta*, which made the owners of that vessel, Macarthur and Garnham Blaxcell, a free settler, responsible to pay a bond of £900. Macarthur and Blaxcell refused to pay, and so there was a warrant issued for their arrest. When the warrant was presented on the night of

15 December, Macarthur refused to acknowledge its legality and sent the chief constable away with a note which read, 'I consider it with scorn and contempt, as I do the persons who directed it to be executed.' Macarthur followed the letter into Sydney and was arrested four doors from Government House and committed to appear for trial at the criminal court on 25 January 1808. Now Macarthur brought his Atkins card into play.

Throughout 1807 and into early 1808, Macarthur began to use as a lever and a ploy a near-forgotten debt of £82 9 shillings and sixpence owed him by Judge-Advocate Atkins. In 1801 Atkins had repaid Macarthur with a bill which Macarthur had taken with him to England and which was there dishonoured. On Macarthur's return to the colony, Atkins had promised to pay it, but that had been two years past. Macarthur pointed out that to get justice he would have to 'call upon Mr Atkins to issue a writ to bring himself before himself to answer my complaint'.

Macarthur used this debt of convenience to attack the legitimacy of the court in one of its most vulnerable areas—the position of Judge-Advocate, particularly as held by an untrained drunkard like Atkins. He was also favoured by its other great weakness—its being composed of officers unlikely to bring too harsh a sentence down on one (formerly) of their own.

All through January, as Macarthur awaited his trial, he tried to get Atkins removed, and Bligh said only the British government could do that. There was also an argument over a town lot on Church Hill Macarthur thought was his, but was told by government to give up for 'any situation he may fix on to an equal extent'.

On the night of 24 January 1808, the officers had regimental dinner at the barracks to celebrate the twentieth anniversary of the colony due to occur two days later. The dinner was attended by all nine officers and a number of their friends, including Macarthur's son Edward, and his nephew, Hannibal. The diners could see John Macarthur pacing the parade ground, a hungry presence, while the officers and gentlemen danced with each other to the music of the fife band. On his way home that night to Annandale, Major Johnston injured his arm 'from the over-setting of a gig', so that he was not able to attend the next morning when the court made up of Atkins and the officers sat. The New South Wales Corps had stacked the gallery with soldiers, and even before the indictment could be read Macarthur rose and argued the impropriety of Atkins sitting in his case. When the judge-advocate attempted to put an end to Macarthur's speech and threatened to throw him in gaol at once, Captain Anthony Fenn Kemp threatened the judge-advocate himself with imprisonment. Atkins left the courtroom and went to Government House to report to Bligh. About eleven o'clock that morning the six officers of the bench wrote to Bligh demanding he appoint another judge-advocate.

At 12.30 in the afternoon, the governor wrote back to say he had no power to replace Atkins, and without the judge-advocate, the court could not legally sit. Next Bligh sent a note to the officers demanding a return of the judge-advocate's papers. The officers refused. The papers, according to Johnston's later report, 'led to a discovery that the whole plan of the trial had been arranged, and every question prepared that was to be asked [in] the evidence of the prosecution, by the infamous Crossley'.

While this correspondence was in progress a number of armed constables, most of them convicts, were standing and joking outside the court ready to re-arrest Macarthur and drag him to gaol. The officers instead remanded Macarthur on his previous bail. Late in the afternoon, Bligh's orderly sergeant was sent out to Johnston at Annandale to ask him to come to Government House. Johnston answered that because of his fall he was unable to travel or write.

The following morning at nine o'clock, William Gore, the provost-marshal, arrested John Macarthur at the house of his friend, Captain Abbott. The policeman took Macarthur to gaol, but the officers in the court again wrote to Bligh demanding that he appoint another judge-advocate. The governor spent some hours in consultation with his legal advisers, including the despised George Crossley, the convict lawyer. At last Bligh wrote to Captain Fenn Kemp and the other five officers of the criminal court requiring them to present themselves to face a charge of treasonable practice at Government House at nine o'clock the next morning. A few minutes later a dragoon arrived at Annandale with a letter from the governor, which informed Johnston that six of his officers had been so charged. By his own confession Johnston enjoyed 'temporary forgetfulness of my bruises' and immediately set off in his carriage for the town. In the late afternoon, Johnston turned up not at Government House, but at the military barracks on Sydney's opposing, western, ridge. The instruction went out about the parade ground and neighbouring billets for off-duty soldiers to accoutre themselves for action.

Amongst those who had been at Government House that day was Bligh's United Irish friend the Reverend Henry Fulton, now a magistrate appointed by Bligh, and a very different one from the God-of-Wrath Reverend Marsden of Parramatta. Back home for his dinner, he noted the activity occurring on Church Hill. Fulton rushed to warn Bligh, who was about to sit down to dinner with Robert Campbell and with his daughter in her mourning weeds.

BRINGING A GOVERNOR DOWN

One of the officers intimately involved in the uprising against Governor Bligh was Tipperary-born William Minchin, who seems to have realised that the way to prevent problems was 'to arrest him before he arrests us'. Minchin's attitude to Bligh was partly influenced by Bligh's treatment of Michael Dwyer, a famously respected Irish rebel, suddenly sent to Norfolk Island. Minchin, Dwyer's neighbour in the area to the south-west of Sydney named Cabramatta, had helped support Dwyer's family following his banishment.

Major Johnston, on his arrival at the barracks, immediately released Macarthur who suggested that a letter be prepared and signed by all the civilians present calling on Johnston to arrest Bligh and take over governance of the colony. Macarthur supposedly leaned on the barrel of a cannon to write the letter that declared, 'Sir, the present alarming state of this colony, in which every man's property, liberty and life is endangered, induces us most earnestly to implore you instantly to place Governor Bligh under arrest, and to assume the command of the colony. We pledge ourselves, at a moment of less agitation, to come forward to support the measure with our fortunes and our lives.'

Johnston would later urge a number of pressing reasons for accepting this letter. First, at the barracks he saw 'all the civil and military officers collected, and the most respectable inhabitants in conversation with them. The common people were also to be seen in various groups and every street murmuring and loudly complaining.' It was known that the governor was shut up 'in counsel with the desperate and depraved Crossley, Mr Campbell, a merchant . . . and that Mr Gore [the provost-marshall] and Mr Fulton [the United Irish chaplain] were also at Government House, all ready to sanction whatever Crossley proposed or the Governor ordered'.

So the gentlemen entreated Johnston 'to adopt decisive measures for the safety of the inhabitants and to dispel the great alarm'. It was thought, said Johnston, that the officers making up the court would be thrown into gaol, and it was expected that would be merely the first exercise of excess by the governor.

Johnston accepted the document, compelled, in his account, by the many signatures supporting it. Certainly a number of the disgruntled were at the barracks that day holding a meeting on the situation. Bligh would later say that the military took the petition around after the fact and persuaded over a hundred and fifty to sign it. Whatever the case, Johnston accepted it as his warrant, and the corps, about four hundred available that day from the Sydney garrison, formed up with its band and set off down the hill to Government House on the opposing rise to the refrain of 'The British Grenadier'.

The merchant, Robert Campbell, wrote that he and the governor had just drunk two glasses of wine after dinner when they were told, probably by the Reverend Fulton, that Macarthur had been let loose. The governor went upstairs to put on his uniform and called out to his orderly to ready his horses. Perhaps he meant to face the rebels on horseback, perhaps he intended to flee to his supporters along the Hawkesbury with his daughter. Bligh began working in 'his bureau or trunk' and extracted a number of papers. It was then that he heard Mary Putland raging at the Rum Corps, who had turned up at the gate and forced their way in. As a witness said, 'The fortitude evinced by Mrs Putland on this truly trying occasion merits particular notice . . . Her extreme anxiety to preserve the life of her beloved father prevailed over every consideration and with uncommon intrepidity she opposed a body of soldiers who, with fixed bayonets and loaded firelocks, were proceeding in hostile array to invade the peaceful and defenceless mansion of her parent.' She welcomed the rebels to stab her through the heart but to spare the life of her father.

Campbell and the Reverend Fulton put up a good defence at the front door by refusing to open it, but at last the corps entered via Mrs Putland's bedroom and other doorways, and a search for the governor began. According to Bligh's account he was captured while attending to official papers. 'They soon found me in a back room,' he wrote, 'and a daring set of ruffians under arms (headed by Sergeant Major Whittle), intoxicated by spiritous liquors, which had been given them for the purpose, and threatening to plunge their bayonets into me if I resisted, seized me.'

According to Johnston, writing some months later, 'After a long and careful search he was at last discovered in a situation too disgraceful to be mentioned.' A contemporary cartoon showed him being extracted from under a small bed in full uniform by the searchers, and the image is often accepted as literal truth.

Johnston was in charge of the overthrow, but the revolutionary hero Macarthur was carried by his supporters shoulder-high through the town for a night of jubilation. There was general joy even amongst convicts, and bonfires and illuminations, to celebrate deliverance from Governor Bligh. 'Even the lowest class of the prisoners were influenced by the same sentiments, and for a short time abandoned their habits of plundering. The contemplation of this happy scene more than repaid me for the increase of care, fatigue and responsibility to which I had submitted for the public benefit,' wrote Johnston. Bligh and his daughter would be stuck as detainees in Government House for the next year.

The Sydney rebels, after deposing Bligh, sought an undertaking from him that if he were released from detention he would sail to Britain. But he consistenly refused to give his word on that. In early 1809, however, he agreed to go if he was allowed back on board his ship, the *Porpoise*, and it was only after it sailed from Sydney that he declared the promise had been extorted by force—a credible enough view. He turned for Van Diemen's Land and sailed up the Derwent, looking for hospitality from Lieutenant-Governor David Collins, Phillip's old friend and former secretary, who had founded the settlement of Hobart, after abandoning what he saw as a less desirable site in Port Phillip Bay in present-day Victoria. Collins was in two minds about what had happened in Sydney and was politely remote, giving Bligh accommodation but refusing to become outraged by his situation. During his presence ashore and a-ship in Hobart, Bligh was criticised by Collins for behaviour 'unhandsome in several respects'. Part of this unhandsomeness in Bligh had consisted of compelling local boats to supply the *Porpoise* with produce and paying them with bills he personally issued.

Mary Putland was with him throughout this time. Bligh and Mary left Van Diemen's Land on the *Porpoise* only after he was assured that Governor Lachlan Macquarie had arrived in Sydney. A long period on the *Porpoise* and in Van Diemen's Land, in the company of her aggrieved but irritable father, must have been a time of exceptional stress for Mary, one that she bore with a conviction that her father was transparently in the right. But when the golden-haired Colonel Maurice O'Connell, native of Kerry and a handsome talker, came aboard the *Porpoise* in Sydney Harbour to greet Bligh on his return, Mary determined with her normal strength of mind that she would marry him. The marriage took place at Government House in early May 1810, and a few days later William Bligh returned to England. The O'Connells would leave with the 73rd Regiment to serve in Ceylon (Sri Lanka) in 1815, and in time the colonel became a major general and was knighted, returning to Sydney in December 1838 to command the forces in New South Wales. His and Mary's son, Maurice Charles, was his military secretary, and Mary bore one other son and a daughter, maintaining throughout her life her integrity, and the slightly tempestuous firmness of character she had inherited from her father.

CHAPTER 12

COMES THE AVENGER

On New Year's Day in 1810, the brief and unhappy interregnum of the officers of the New South Wales Corps was put to an end by the landing of a sandy-haired Scottish colonel and his own regiment of infantry, the 73rd. Although he was to be the last autocratic governor, his name was one to be much honoured in the Australian continent—roads, rivers, suburbs and a university would one day have his name attached to them. Yet Lachlan Macquarie, a man lacking patrons, may have been, at 48, the oldest lieutenant-colonel in the army. His father had been a humble tenant farmer from the Hebridean island of Ulva.

That hot day the 73rd marched to the parade-ground on Barrack Hill, the same parade-ground from which the 102nd had moved out two summers before to depose Bligh. The first legally trained deputy judge-advocate, Ellis Bent, who had come to Australia on the same ship, *Dromedary*, as Macquarie and his wife, Elizabeth, shaded himself under an umbrella and read the new governor's commission. In a strong speech, Macquarie promised justice and impartiality, hoped that the upper ranks of society would teach the lower by example, demanded that no one should harm Aborigines, and said that anyone sober and industrious would find a friend and protector in him.

He made quite an impression. No one would have guessed he could be volatile and resent criticism; no one could have guessed how he and Elizabeth still mourned their lost baby daughter; or that when he returned to London after fifteen years service in India he had felt like an 'awkward, rusticated, Jungle-Wallah'. He was august and stable rule incarnate.

D'Arcy Wentworth, former Irish highwayman and now principal surgeon of the colony, appointed after Bligh's overturn, felt uneasy about the man's intentions. Macquarie's secretary had posted a British government proclamation at Barrack Square declaring His Majesty's 'utmost Regret and Displeasure on Account of the late Tumultuous Proceeding in this His Colony, and the Mutinous Conduct of certain persons therein'. All appointments and land grants made under the authority of Bligh's deposers—Paterson, Johnston and Foveaux—were nullified.

It soon proved, however, that Macquarie was not going to enforce the letter of these proclamations. He let the 102nd Regiment—the Rum Corps—stay in quarters at Barrack Square and had his 73rd billeted at Grose Farm, five kilometres out of town, growling and living on bread and potatoes. Elizabeth Macarthur was an old friend of Mrs Macquarie and visited Government House, and so did the former rebel officers, even though Macquarie had been ordered to arrest Johnston and Macarthur, a task he was saved from by the fact they had both left New South Wales. The 102nd was to be returned to England in official disgrace in any case, and perhaps Macquarie's less than punitive actions were a pragmatic attempt to prevent the colony dividing all over again. When Bligh arrived on his ship, *Porpoise*, from Van Diemen's Land, he was no longer governor, but found he would have been ritually re-installed for a day had he been in Sydney earlier. Though Bligh would be entertained by Macquarie until the *Porpoise* left for England in May, to allow Bligh to prosecute the rebels, he developed dark suspicions that Macquarie had opened his mind to them.

But D'Arcy Wentworth found he was still chief surgeon, and thus considered Macquarie a wise ruler.

WENTWORTHS RISING

D'Arcy Wentworth's three sons had a desperate love for their father, and the elder one, William Charles, also loved desperately those who smiled on D'Arcy, and hated with passion those who despised him. For he had spent his early childhood in the little house at Queensborough, Norfolk Island, when D'Arcy seemed prospect-less, and the chief food of the house, other than the occasional mutton bird, fish and turtle, was sea rations. On Norfolk, Wentworth, praised for his competence, impatiently awaited clarification of when his posts might become official.

D'Arcy had gone on residing with the convict Catherine Crowley. In narrow Norfolk, doubts must have been muttered about the little boy, William's, paternity, but D'Arcy remained devoted to the child, and the child would repay him. New authority had not made D'Arcy a martinet. He was liked by gentlemen and convicts both, because of his democratic manner. Without being a philosopher, he had imbibed some of the spirit of democracy driving the American and the French Revolutions, and the coming trans-sectarian rebellion of United Irishmen, many of them of his and higher class, which would break out in Ireland in 1798. He had also had many lessons in the fragility of life, and of the thin filament that lay between respectable and criminal society. Norfolk Island had been his purgatory, and during it, as superintendent at Queensborough, he had developed a gift for supervising agricultural work and for breeding livestock.

D'Arcy had served without pay as an assistant surgeon for some thirty-one months and as a superintendent of convicts for fifteen, when King, then commandant of Norfolk Island, wrote to the Home Office reminding Undersecretary Nepean of Wentworth's good behaviour and calling him 'a real treasure'. Two thousand bushels (73 m³) of maize and five hundred bushels (18 m³) of wheat had been produced under his supervision. King sent a letter to Earl Fitzwilliam too, asking him to use his influence to benefit his exiled kinsman. Fitzwilliam wrote back assuring King that he had spoken to one of the undersecretaries at the Home Office and that D'Arcy would be officially confirmed in the post of assistant surgeon.

Soon D'Arcy was raising swine on his own 60-acre (24-hectare) block given him by King. By May 1792 he received £11 2 shillings for selling six cows to the government, and on 3 May 1794 he sold a supply of pork for £20 7 shillings. Between January and May 1794 he sold grain worth £105 to the public stores. But Major Grose refused to honour the bills which King drew on the Treasury until instructions had been received from Britain. In the economic slump thus caused, Wentworth took advantage by acquiring two additional farms of sixty acres each, running goats on one and pigs on the other.

By the end of 1794 the island's population was made up of settlers and expirees as well as convicts and officials. There was a variety of trades involved in the economy and wheat, maize, potatoes, sugar cane, bananas, guavas, lemons, apples and coffee were all farmed. There were two windmills and a watermill and at Cascade Bay a long wharf.

On 3 October 1795, the *Asia*, an American ship from New York, berthed at Norfolk, and D'Arcy was amongst the settlers who supplied her with meat and vegetables in exchange for tobacco and spirits.

Wentworth, much trusted by Mrs King, treated the bibulous King for gout and 'an almost fixed compression of lungs and breast'. By supporting King, Wentworth gained in status, and King cherished hopes of impressing Earl Fitzwilliam, who could perhaps help him achieve the governorship of New South Wales.

Against D'Arcy's income, Cookney, Earl Fitzwilliam's London agent, began to send shipments of trading goods: cloth, linen, china, combs, paper, pens and general groceries. There were gowns and ribbons of blue, lilac and pink. Wentworth charged moderate prices to maximise goodwill. But for all his growing prominence on the island, he was still seen by some of the establishment as tainted by convictism. By July 1795, he wrote to David Collins about his continued disappointment at the Home Office's failure to commission him as assistant surgeon, and asked to be allowed to return to England. King supported the request. 'How far Mr Wentworth can be spared, I must submit to the Governor; as well as the propriety of his being detained to perform an Office for which he does not receive emolument.'

In January 1796, Wentworth warned Earl Fitzwilliam that since he had not received a single shilling for his service, he would return to Europe. He told Fitzwilliam he had no desire to stay more than an hour in London, nor the smallest objection to re-embarking for New South Wales. Wentworth had sold one of his farms, but kept two others in the hope he could obtain through Fitzwilliam's kindness a situation which would enable him to come back to the island.

This seemed to be a ruse. Only if he failed in Sydney would he think of departing for London. But he hoped that the thought of his notorious relative reappearing in Britain might motivate Earl Fitzwilliam to do something, even though this was a time of great turbulence and distress for Fitzwilliam, recently stood down as Lord Lieutenant Governor of Ireland. Not being aware of any of this, King wrote to Fitzwilliam saying that Wentworth's future conduct in life would be marked by the 'same propriety of behaviour which has procured him the general esteem of everyone here'. He hoped that liberality of soul 'will consign his former wanderings to oblivion'.

That same day D'Arcy and his time-expired wife and son boarded the *Reliance* and sailed for Port Jackson. The five-year-old, rather wizened, William, a clever child who would grow to dominate this locale, saw Port Jackson and Sydney Cove for the first time. The governor, Hunter, though in theory an autocrat still, did not have the power Phillip had enjoyed, because the military oligarchs and their friends ran the colony. Wentworth tried not to make enemies of any side and felt out his way. In 1797 he was plaintiff for recovery of debt in eight cases before the Court of Civil Jurisdiction against prosperous settlers to whom he had supplied trade goods, and sent the proceeds of these cases to cover his debts to Earl Fitzwilliam and to commission Cookney to purchase more goods for him. He received pay for the four years he had acted as assistant surgeon on Norfolk Island, and his belated salary as superintendent of convicts. Cookney sent goods to the combined value of these sums, and D'Arcy was suddenly a well-off New South Wales merchant.

In May 1798, he received two treasury bills for sales to the commissariat, one for £1000 and one for £500, and planned to invest them in the colony rather than remit them to England. He took to wearing a watch, a ring and knee buckles. Governor Hunter did not see him as an enemy, like many of the officers, and invited him to dine at Government House on Christmas Day.

In May 1799 D'Arcy became assistant surgeon at Parramatta. Hunter would grant him 140 acres (57 hectares) there, a couple of kilometres from the Macarthurs at Elizabeth Farm. His acreage was bounded by creeks on either side and by the road to Sydney on the south, and the land lay some six kilometres east of Parramatta township. Here he established his country seat, Home Bush.

As fear increased that the United Irishmen and Defenders would rebel, D'Arcy enlisted in the local loyalist volunteer body with the rank of lieutenant, and his commandant was the Scots emancipist Andrew Thompson, later manager of Bligh's model farm. The floggings that followed the aborted uprising must have appalled D'Arcy, but he kept his counsel on these things. In a sense, he still wanted to keep his head down, and was happy to live in relative seclusion with his convict spouse at Home Bush. Dr Margarot, the Scottish Martyr, wrote of Wentworth: 'A noted highwayman after repeated escapes owing to great protection and interference is at last transported; he ranks as a gentleman, sits at the Governor's table, plunders the colony and amasses a fortune after having twenty times deserved to be hanged.' This was the characterisation which D'Arcy was trying to escape.

Often character attacks were in verse and were left in the street for people to read. And Brigadier General Grose wrote to Major Foveaux on 25 June 1799 noting that some officers of the New South Wales Corps had been so indiscreet as to admit Wentworth to their company. If the Duke of York should learn of any officer disgracing himself by such an association, the officer would be turned out of the service, said Grose. But Wentworth even raised the possibility of buying a commission so that he could associate with officers.

King, returning to New South Wales in April 1800, was advised by Surgeon Balmain to exclude Wentworth from his table, even though Balmain was counted by Wentworth as one of his closest friends.

Catherine Crowley, mother of the boys, had died on 6 January 1800 aged twenty-seven, and her burial at St John's, Parramatta, was conducted by Samuel Marsden. William, then nine, was still small, clumsy and squinting, but he sometimes accompanied his father while D'Arcy transacted business. The attachment remained intense.

D'Arcy had acquired one of the best houses in Sydney and a chaise and horses, and employed two Irish male convicts in 1800, and the next year a female assignee. Governor Hunter had liked him and said that he had behaved 'not only in his official situation but upon all other occasions with the most exact propriety'. But the arrival of King, his champion, actually crimped D'Arcy's activities as the new governor forbade spirits from being landed from any ship without prior approval and written consent. Wentworth did not publicly go against his friend, King. But King summoned him and asked him about the origins of a pipe found in the street which depicted the governor as a tyrant:

> But damn me, while powerful, I'll do what I can,
> According to what I proposed as a plan,
> To make all subservient, humble, and poor,
> Take women and children all off from the store,
> Crush all independence and poverty plant . . .

By 1803, when a cask of Wentworth's madeira was seized on a technicality, Wentworth petitioned the British government and went over at least in part to Macarthur's world view.

THE CONVICT'S CHILD GOES HOME

In 1802 William Charles Wentworth, twelve years old, and his brother D'Arcy, nine, sailed from the world they had always known on the *Atlas*, a ship which traded goods in China and at Calcutta before reaching its destination. In Britain, the conscientious Cookney, Earl Fitzwilliam's agent, acted as their foster father. He sent them to the Reverend Midgley's school in Bletchley, attended also by three of his own sons, and jovial Mrs Cookney welcomed them in the holidays. Letters from William to his father say they were happy at school, and were looking forward to seeing the kindest of parents again. They were eventually joined by their younger brother John, who arrived with the early symptoms of scurvy.

Major Foveaux, one of the rebels against Bligh, was strongly against the Wentworth boys returning to New South Wales, and advised military careers in India, but D'Arcy hoped William would become vendue master, that is, an auctioneer of confiscated goods, or provost-marshal in the colony. But William came home, however, as a young man in 1810 with some accomplishment in Latin and Greek but without any professional training or government appointment. On his arrival, D'Arcy wrote to Earl Fitzwilliam for help in procuring the office of provost-marshal, but Fitzwilliam thought William too young. In 1811 D'Arcy's rapidly increasing influence with Macquarie enabled William to become acting provost-marshal.

Young William, though their future champion, does not seem to have known any emancipists—the time-expired convicts—very well at this stage except for the successful ones: Simeon Lord; William Redfern, the Nore mutineer, who had been accused of participating in the naval mutiny at the Nore in 1797; and James Meehan, United Irishman and Assistant Surveyor. Lord was a fellow magistrate of D'Arcy's, and Redfern was D'Arcy's medical assistant and a family friend. William did not much admire the retired officers who had stayed to make their fortunes in New South Wales. He despised their low origins, their gimcrack manners and postures and their aristocratic ambitions. The most precise expression of this attitude was a pipe on John Macarthur and his family which he probably wrote about 1811, comparing a family like the Wentworths, representatives of true nobility, with the barbarian ancestors of the Scottish 'staymaker' or corset maker. Meanwhile, he rode his father's horse Gig to a well-publicised victory in Sydney's Hyde Park; he was involved in committees to compliment Governor Macquarie; and was a witness at the wedding of Simeon Lord. His closest friend was young George Johnston, son of the Scots officer of the same name and the Jewish convict woman Esther Abrahams. But there does not seem to have been a day when the shadow over his father, the murmurs about D'Arcy's being a convicted highwayman and himself a convict bastard, left him.

William liked the free settler Blaxland brothers too, and was willing to join with Gregory Blaxland and William Lawson, a surveyor, in an attempt to find more land beyond the Blue Mountains. Given D'Arcy's standing with Macquarie, Blaxland hoped that with young Wentworth in his party, Macquarie might soften his disapproval of himself and his brother, both supporters of the rebels against Bligh. In 1812 William Charles Wentworth had received a grant of 1750 acres (709 hectares) on the Nepean River and he probably made a number of exploratory probes into the nearby mountain range with James Meehan.

D'Arcy boasted to Fitzwilliam of William's primacy in the expedition over the mountains, which had found 'a second Promised Land'. In the meantime D'Arcy himself treated Mrs Macarthur's spasms, and certain problems of the governor. Lachlan Macquarie had recurrent urinary problems arising from a bout of syphilis he had suffered in Egypt some years before, as well as dysentery and fever and stress from overwork. By 1810 D'Arcy was principal surgeon, commissioner of police, treasurer of the police fund, magistrate, commissioner for the turnpike and hospital contractor.

IN THE HEART OF EMPIRE

In 1816, D'Arcy Wentworth sent his son William back to Britain in the hope he would achieve a commission in the Guards, but the war against France had ended and made that an unlikely career. Landed at Plymouth, William took the stage to London and arrived in Cookney's warm parlour late in the year, where he sought guidance as to whether he should enter the bar or the church.

He was the sort of young man to whom the sensational romantic poet Lord Byron spoke: gallant, prideful, full of yearning, noble of breeding but carrying a twitchy pride and a mysterious shame. He ultimately resolved to study law, but at the same time thought it politic to reassure his wealthy relative, Earl Fitzwilliam, that it was not his intention to abandon the country that gave him birth. 'I am sensible of the sacred claims which it has upon me—claims which in its present despised state and indigent situation, I should blush ever to be supposed capable of neglecting.'

In February 1817 William enrolled as a pupil at the Middle Temple and declared that he was the son of D'Arcy Wentworth Esquire of New South Wales. He had decided against attending Oxford first, telling his father he was already a better classical scholar than nine out of ten of the graduates. Besides, at Oxford he lacked the means to mix with the nobility and would be treated as one of the vulgars.

He frequently called on the Macarthurs in London, a family he had earlier secretly lampooned. In exile, Macarthur received him kindly as did Macarthur's 22-year-old son, John, who had studied at Cambridge and would soon be admitted to the bar. William had an ambition to marry Macarthur's eldest daughter, Elizabeth, and saw it as a dynastic union. It would be 'the formation of a permanent respectable establishment in the colony,' he told D'Arcy, and 'the accomplishment of those projects for the future respectability and grandeur of our family'. So now the staymaker's daughter was a suitable bride.

Back in Sydney, which Macquarie was improving with the buildings of the contract-forging convict architect Francis Greenway, William's brother John and his friend, young George Johnston, had distributed pipes ridiculing Alexander Riley, the officers of the 46th Regiment, which had landed in the colony in 1814, and George Molle, the lieutenant-governor. All the pipes were motivated by slights against D'Arcy:

> *Of all the mongrels, that to wit lay claim,*
> *The basest bred, that e'er prophan'd the name!*
> *And now farewell thou dirty, grov'ling M'll"*
> *Go with thy namesake burrow in thy hole.*

Molle brought D'Arcy before a bench of magistrates for gross disrespect and contempt in aiding and abetting the publication of the pipes. D'Arcy admitted he knew who wrote them, and that it was not his clerk, Lathrop Murray, a convict bigamist for whose punishment some officers were baying. It was indeed his son William, but D'Arcy was let go as not subject to military jurisdiction. However, the officers of the 46th had their revenge by making a public statement saying the libels came 'from the hand of men so much our inferiors in rank and situation, that we know them not but among the promiscuous class, which (with pride we speak it) have been excluded from intercourse with us'.

*

In Paris in 1817, waiting for the law term in London to commence, William Wentworth began writing his statistical, historical and political description of the colony of New South Wales. There were also some bitter letters exchanged with young John Macarthur over William's borrowings. William typically told his father he would 'pay Macarthur off in his own coin'.

Before he went to France, William had made contact with a reforming member of parliament named Henry Bennet, a rallying point for disgruntled colonials, particularly those who wanted to complain about Macquarie's supposed indulgence towards emancipists. Like Jeremy Bentham, Bennet wanted to prove transportation cost too much, failed to punish, and generated debauchery. Many bureaucrats and Lord Bathurst, the Secretary of State for the Colonies, already believed it.

Bennet had received for presentation to parliament a petition put together by one Reverend Vale and his solicitor Moore, both of Sydney, concerning the punishment of three men who entered the public domain and were sentenced to twenty-five lashes each. Vale and Moore in fact had a grievance towards Governor Macquarie—they had seized the American schooner *Traveler* in Sydney Harbour and claimed her as a prize, and had been punished for it, in Vale's case by a charge of subversion.

From his rooms opposite a riding school in Pimlico, Wentworth had written to warn Bennet that the people who designated themselves settlers in the 'petition from certain inhabitants of New South Wales' were impostors. 'The fact is, the greater part of them are publicans and shop-keepers of the lowest description, who live by preying upon the very vitals of the settlers.' The petition which Mr Bennet had tabled in parliament was full of distinct falsehoods and calumnies, he wrote, and Wentworth had offered to meet Bennet and set him straight. Wentworth had thus been able to tell Bennet that in seven years acquaintance he had never known the New South Wales government to interfere in any of the rights of free people in reference to either persons or properties.

He reported to his father: 'I succeeded in convincing Mr Bennet that so much of the [Vale–Moore] petition as reflected on the Governor's conduct was entitled to no credit, and I am convinced had he seen me before he presented it to the House, that it would never have obtained publicity.'

In 1818 William at last got into chambers at the Temple, which cost his father a great deal to furnish and fit out. He might now become an English jurist, but 'It would require £500 to purchase anything like a tolerable library . . . a soldier might as well be without arms as a lawyer without books.' As soon as his book on New South Wales was published, he told D'Arcy, he would wait upon Earl Fitzwilliam to present him with a copy.

In 1818 D'Arcy turned fifty-six. Maria Ainslie, a 43-year-old convict from Nottingham, had been the woman of the house at Home Bush since the death of Catherine Crowley. All the Wentworth boys loved her for her affectionate nature and lack of pretension. But now D'Arcy, wishing to replace her, had decided to move her from Home Bush to a cottage he owned in Sydney. His son John took offence at the proposal, and refused to talk to the young Mary Anne Lawes, a free servant who had abandoned her husband to become D'Arcy's new mistress. John swore he would not remain under the same roof as Lawes. William regarded the 25-year-old Mary Anne as an opportunist 'who for the single sake of ameliorating her condition ... has abandoned her child, her husband ... burst asunder the ties of nature as of society and stigmatised herself by the violation of every duty'. He described his father as being 'long past the prime of life when he should have expected to inspire love', and hoped that he would have his eyes opened to the folly and disgrace of his conduct. 'In any other person I should reprobate such a miserable infatuation—in him, I can only pity and forgive it.' He saw his father as surrounded by a set of harpies waiting for his last sigh to seize and pillage the fruits of a life of industry and exertion.

Worse surprises were on their way. In 1820, his brother John would die at sea of yellow fever. But it was the previous year that the greater shock came. William was not fully aware till 1819 of his father's four trials for highway robbery. He had heard rumours in Sydney, but probably dismissed them as low-bred jealousy. Now he read in print of the shame of his father's past, exposed in the vivid prose of the House of Commons reformer, Henry G. Bennet.

In his zeal, Bennet was willing to tell anyone about the sins of New South Wales, and in his *Letter to Lord Sidmouth* (the Home Secretary) of February 1819, a notable tract of more than 130 pages, pointed to D'Arcy Wentworth as a prime instance of the New South Wales malaise. Wentworth, said Bennet, was not only a highway robber but had been transported for it, and was now superintendent of police, a magistrate lenient to spirit retailers, and the principal surgeon to boot.

Bennet hoped the ruling Tories would be embarrassed to hear of such a situation. He urged the government to set up a Legislative Council in New South Wales to curb the 'arbitrariness' of the governor.

William was crazed with rage. The furious young colonial presented himself at Bennet's house ready to seek an exoneration of blood, in blood. Already known for his dishevelled hair, in-turned eye, grating voice and clumsy walk, and now engorged with fury, he must have been frightening to behold. He was admitted to Bennet's study, where the gentleman 'changed colour and showed other signs of agitation . . . I commenced by observing that he had permitted himself to give to the world one of the most infamous libels that had ever been published.' Bennet was shocked and agreed that if D'Arcy was not a convict, 'he [Bennet] would make the most ample atonement for what he had written'.

Since he was to bring on in parliament in the next few days his motion respecting the state of the colony of New South Wales, he would then 'take that opportunity of doing you the justice to which you are entitled'. His real target was Macquarie, Bennet admitted, and what he had said was never intended as 'an individual attack' on D'Arcy but was directed against the system pursued by the governor.

Later in the day, William, having consulted Cookney, wrote, 'Sir, since I quitted you this morning, I have found in conference to my father's friend Mr Cookney that your assertion of his having been found guilty on a charge of highway robbery . . . is not founded . . . No one has any right to draw any conclusion but that he was innocent of the crime imputed to him and I can positively take upon myself to say that . . . after his acquittal he protested in the most solemn manner that a jury of his peers had only done him justice. Very shortly after this trial he voluntarily embarked for New South Wales having first obtained the appointment of Superintendent of Convicts.'

This was a misstatement, but a son's misstatement. 'Delicacy like his could not exist in the heart of a felon,' said William. Believing himself descended from a long unsullied line of illustrious progenitors, William felt that the glory of his ancestry was in some degree tarnished by the mere imputation that had been cast on his father's character. 'But twenty-six years of unimpeachable rectitude, during which period he has risen by his single merit to the highest point of distinction and respectability abroad, have not sufficed to silence the venomous tongue of slanderer . . . the suggestion of guilt has been conjured into guilt itself, suspicion into proof, accusation into condemnation.'

The next day, young Wentworth sat in the visitors gallery of the Commons and heard a most thorough withdrawal by Bennet of the accusation in his pamphlet. Bennet withdrew the first edition of his pamphlet too, and corrected the second. But the reality of his father's four charges hurt William and became a spur in his vitals. 'I will not suffer myself to be outstripped by any competitor and I will finally create for myself a reputation which shall reflect a splendour on all those who are related to me.'

Including, of course, the sometimes inattentive Earl Fitzwilliam.

THE COMMISSIONER VISITS

Under pressure from men like Bennet, the Earl of Bathurst, Secretary of State for the Colonies and War, had decided that he was going to send an investigator to New South Wales to look at the question of the cost of transportation and whether it worked as a punishment. Bathurst suggested to John Thomas Bigge, a former judge in Trinidad and his appointed commissioner, that he should investigate all laws, regulations and usages of the settlement with a view to seeing whether transportation should be made 'an object of real terror', and that he should report any weakening of terror by 'ill-considered compassion'.

Macquarie had earlier applied to resign for health and other reasons, and when at the end of September 1819 Bigge came ashore in Sydney, Macquarie was totally taken by surprise and unprepared for him. The liberal-minded Macquarie, who had helped make New South Wales a viable society through his own discretion and labour, found himself subjected to the demands of a royal commissioner who was an aristocrat, a stickler, a man of the law's letter. He was of cramped temperament and lacked a wife to spike his pompousness. Not that Bigge's investigative methods were of the highest order. He accepted attacks on Macquarie and others from witnesses without questioning their bona fides. There was no distinction made between sworn and unsworn testimony. Macquarie himself surmised Bigge's opening question was always, 'Tell me any complaint you have against Governor Macquarie.' In his free time, Bigge found much hospitality at the country house of John Macarthur, who was willing to utter every grievance about Macquarie's preference for emancipists. It was in part through Bigge's ear that Macarthur would have a hand in destroying yet another governor.

Bigge's three reports proved massive when they appeared: one on the state of the colony, published in 1822; one on the judicial establishments of New South Wales and of Van Diemen's Land, published in 1823; and one on the state of agriculture and trade, published the same year. Macquarie knew the reports would be very damaging to him even before they appeared. He had quarrelled bitterly with Bigge over his intention to appoint the former Nore mutineer, Dr Redfern, as a magistrate. Then Redfern accused Bigge of demeaning himself by questioning 'common strumpets in the streets of Sydney' about 'the character of Mr Wentworth and myself'. Macquarie had been calmer in answering before Bigge the sixty-three charges which had been made against him by others.

In the first report, for example, Bigge pointed to the inconsideration of Macquarie in having the Reverend Mr Marsden serve with Mr Simeon Lord, former convict, and the late Mr Andrew Thompson, ditto, as trustees of the public roads. Thus was 'violence done to the feelings of Mr Marsden, which could not be compensated by flattering those of his two . . . associates'. But even more inconsiderate, said Bigge, were the efforts by Governor Macquarie to introduce emancipated convicts to the notice and society of the military bodies. For Governor Macquarie and his deputy, Maurice O'Connell, Mary Bligh's husband, had success in habituating the officers and soldiery of his 73rd Regiment to being polite to convicts.

This was all part of what Bigge would call the 'mismanagement of convicts'. Macquarie sent home for publication his own *A Letter to Viscount Sidmouth*. He left Australia with his family in February 1822, giving place to Governor Brisbane who had orders to enforce some of Bigge's recommendations—the setting up of an appointed Legislative Council, the use of convict gangs to clear land, the sale rather than granting of Crown lands, the accurate registration of prisoners, the creation of Van Diemen's Land as a separate penal administration. Bigge endorsed no legal reforms and did not recommend trial by jury in criminal cases. He left the legal status of emancipists in limbo. But the building program in which Macquarie had engaged was too extravagant, he said, and should be curtailed.

Macquarie and Elizabeth Macquarie were greeted in London by young Wentworth. By the time Macquarie and his wife went north to the Island of Mull to take over a farm his agent had purchased, they were so poor they could not travel by coach but made their way by a small, extremely perilous coasting vessel. Driven back to London by illness, Macquarie died in 1824 of some of the same symptoms of exhaustion and physical damage which D'Arcy had treated in New South Wales.

Having made such a compendium of New South Wales affairs, one which at least the officials in Britain believed, Bigge became a successive investigator into colonies, to the extent that the work itself, which one of his assistants described as 'interminable as the web of Penelope', and the accidents and hardships of travel, certainly shortened his life, as he had shortened Macquarie's.

A HOTHEAD'S PROSE

In 1819, young William Wentworth's book on New South Wales, some of it written in a winter of rheumatic gout brought on by the excesses of life in Paris, appeared in England. It was entitled *A Statistical, Historical and Political Description of the Colony of New South Wales and its Dependent Settlements in Van Diemen's Land*, and William intended it to declare his arrival as his nation's annalist and coming statesman. The book would go through three editions, the second in 1820, the third in 1824, each seemingly dictated by his friends' and father's assessment of the latest situation in New South Wales, or, more accurately, of the forces of exclusivism, that is, the desire to exclude former convicts from public life, which attacked them. First there was a statistical section which contained long extracts from the surveyor and explorer John Oxley's journals. The second section contained historical and political description and, presaging Bigge, argued there should be a Legislative Council since—whether the governor was an acerbic Bligh or a genial Macquarie—the colony suffered from the governor's autocratic powers. At the beginning of the historical section Wentworth placed emphasis on Bligh's administration as an example of unlimited autocracy. He did not mention Bligh by name but described him as 'a wretch whom it would be superfluous to name, as it is needless to hold him to the execration of posterity'. His father had been dismissed as assistant surgeon by Bligh.

The third section had to do with immigration and the advantages of New South Wales over North America for British immigrants. 'I am in great hopes that a large body of Quakers will be induced by my representations to settle in the colony. I have had frequent interviews with them on the subject . . . but the nature of the government is almost considered by them as a decisive obstacle.' But William also spoke of the parlous condition of agriculture, partly due to the lack of a market for grain apart from the domestic needs of the colony. With no market for a surplus, there was no incentive to grow more. Together with frequent losses to drought and unscrupulous creditors, the majority of the settlers were kept in a state of 'poverty, slavery and degradation'. This was 'in some measure imposed on the settlers by their own imprudent extravagance'. But overall, he decided that the chief cause of their trouble was not their 'early habits of irregularity' but 'the actual impolicy and injustice of their rulers'. One of the impolicies, in William's opinion, was the granting of too many tickets-of-leave which undercut the labour supply. He recommended distilleries as a means of using excess grain, and reminded readers that the Select Committee on Transportation in 1812 had recommended it as well, and that it had been recommended by Governor Macquarie but not approved by Earl Bathurst. He argued that distilleries would be good for the moral fibre of the young colonials, because the product was 'depreciated in the estimation of its consumers in exact proportion to its abundance'.

Then Wentworth raised the possibility that the colonists could be goaded into rebellion by British ill-rule, and described how they would be able to ambush the forces of tyranny in the ravines of the Blue Mountains. In this, says historian John Ritchie, he was influenced by Sir Walter Scott's contemporary bestseller, *Rob Roy*, in which Scots used their ravines to good purpose against the redcoats. 'Let the Minister for the colonies then take heed how he acts,' warned the hard-up, gout-suffering young colonial, reaching for eloquence worthy of a Benjamin Franklin or an Edmund Burke. 'His Lordship should know that it is the tendency of colonies to outstrip even legitimate restraints: how then can it be expected that they will long wear the fetters of injustice and oppression?' Wentworth saw New South Wales as an exact or very close replica of Virginia, Georgia or the Carolinas. The result of Britain's refusal to negotiate responsible government, he said, would be 'a spirit which will be handed down from father to son acquiring in its descent fresh force, and settling at length into an hereditary hatred'.

But he argued that although he criticised government, he was not one of those who were sworn enemies of all authority. Nor did he belong to the 'band of ruffian levellers'. He then detailed the commercial disability suffered by New South Wales under the monopoly of the East India Company and recommended that the colony be given parity in trading status with Newfoundland and the West Indies. All these grievances had been included with a petition from the leading emancipists to the Colonial Office in March 1819, which was sent off with Macquarie's endorsement. Since the changes Wentworth recommended were not within the power of New South Wales colonial governments to bring about, it would be up to the British government to effect change.

He was not embarrassed in stating his personal hopes. He had 'the most sanguine expectations of being the instrument of procuring a free constitution for my country'. The idea that finding out that his father was a former highwayman took away his ambition to be the leader of the free immigrants is not borne out by some of his letters, in which he talks a great deal about free immigrants.

Between the 1819 and 1824 editions of his book, Wentworth's attitudes changed according to what was happening to his hopes. The 1820 edition was marked by the still-stinging wound of Bennet's attack on his father. By the 1824 edition, Macarthur, who had prevented William's marriage to his daughter Elizabeth, was described as head of the family which systematically opposed every innovation by which the condition of the community at large was likely to be ameliorated. But Bigge was the *bête noir* of the third edition.

The third edition might also have been influenced by the fact that Wentworth was calling at the time at the Colonial Office, trying to get a pension for his father, and was appalled by the supercilious behaviour of the bureaucrats there, probably because they had read Bennet's revelations. Nonetheless, an annual pension for D'Arcy of £200 was the ultimate outcome.

In 1822, D'Arcy's friend William Redfern and Robert Eager, a Cork lawyer transported for uttering a forged bill, arrived in London to present a petition from the emancipists of New South Wales asking the government to guarantee the legality of their pardons, which had been questioned in the Supreme Court of New South Wales, and to allow them full civil rights, including the right to hold legal office and serve on juries. Wentworth's contacts with Redfern and Eagar would further colour the third edition of his book, especially in its criticisms of Bigge and the flawed way he had collected evidence.

In July 1822 William challenged Bigge to a duel for stating that he was the author of the pipes attacking Molle. And Bigge had reported criticisms of the running of Sydney Hospital under D'Arcy Wentworth, in terms of morality, record-keeping, syphilitic intercourse between patients, nurses throwing warm meat at the patients and so on. D'Arcy Wentworth's defence was that the fact that the female patients were syphilitics inhibited the males from sexual intercourse and the nurses threw the meat to avoid contagion. Bigge would also say that before relinquishing office, Macquarie had granted Wentworth another 3150 acres (1276 hectares) and paid money on behalf of the government for a house he owned in Sydney. Given D'Arcy was a former highwayman, this was seen as part of Macquarie's supposed indulgence towards those directly or indirectly associated with convictism.

Having challenged Bigge to a trial of honour, something Bigge was not designed for, William found police were sent around to his rooms to restrain him, and that added to his fury. Commissioner Bigge was given pause enough to admit he may have drawn an unjust conclusion. The commissioner agreed to delete the offending passage about the Molle pipes before his first report was tabled in the House of Lords, and to insert an apology to D'Arcy in the second report. This did little to soothe the young colonial, since so many men he had grown up with had been maligned.

On 27 February 1823, Wentworth entered Peterhouse, Cambridge's oldest college. At thirty-two, William was much older than most of the undergraduates, but he wanted the éclat of having been to a famous university and he sought through the Chancellor's Prize for poetry to make a mark much larger than that young John Macarthur had. The subject for the prize that year was Australasia. Wentworth's 443-line poem was dedicated to Macquarie.

Wentworth's lines run more sweetly and authentically than those of the poet who won. He did not write of Australia in direct Australian terms, but his preoccupations were identifiably those of the Currency. That the new landscape produced its European interpreters of the first order:

And tho', bright goddess, on the far blue hills,
That pour their thousand swift pellucid wills
Where Warragamba's rage has rent in twain
Opposing mountains, thundering to the plain,
No child of song has yet invoked thy aid
'Neath their primeval solitary shade.
Still, gracious Pow'r, some kindling soul inspire
To wake to life my country's unknown lyre,
That from creation's date has slumbering lain

. . .

Next, the dream that the child might become more glorious than the parent:
And, Oh Britannia! Should'st thou cease to ride
Despotic Empress of old ocean's tide;

. . .

When thou no longer freest of the free,
To some proud victor bend'st the vanquish'd knee—
May all thy glories in another sphere

Relume, and shine more brightly still than here;
May this, thy last born infant, then arise,
To glad thy heart and greet thy parent eyes;
And Australasia float, with flag unfurl'd,
A new Britannia in another world.

In the circumstances, his poem emerges as yet another plaint for recognition, another lever to put beneath the vast stone of the world's indifference and hostility.

By 1823 William Wentworth, a notably unsuccessful lawyer and student, was telling D'Arcy he saw no prospect for himself in England. The New South Wales Act of 1823 had been passed establishing a Legislative Council but failed to introduce trial by jury in criminal cases. The new Legislative Council, said William, was a 'wretched mongrel substitute' for the partially elected one he had recommended. Civil juries were introduced, but based on a property qualification. The Act was to be revised in five years time, and William believed that if he returned to New South Wales he could be in place to influence its revision.

Wentworth's preoccupation with a free constitution was not of great interest to most emancipists. Their main concern, shared by some free immigrants, was trial by jury, which had been a contentious issue for some time. Wentworth knew instinctively he needed to identify his longed-for free constitution with the emancipists' concerns, to put the 'exclusives' in their own barren corner. He was the first Currency child, that is, native-born, who saw a constitutional future of some robustness. But his patriotism, despite his threat about fighting the English in the Blue Mountains, was a British patriotism—he saw New South Wales as 'a new Britannia in another world', as he declared in verse. He now said he would hold no government position in New South Wales as he meant to lead the colony as a private person. He came to an agreement with Robert Wardell jointly to publish a newspaper that would launch his campaign on colonial civil rights. Wardell, a doctor of laws from Cambridge and the same age as Wentworth, was editor of the *Statesman*, a London evening paper. It was an endangered paper, being under the threat of a Tory writ which would very likely finish it. Wardell was happy to escape. He embarked with Wentworth on the *Alfred* for Sydney in February 1824, along with William Redfern and John Mackaness, colonial sheriff designate, all of them tipplers and friends for life.

THE HIGHWAYMAN PASSES

D'Arcy Wentworth had made a heavy loss in being the chief partner in the building of the Rum Hospital in Sydney. The task was undertaken by Wentworth, Garnham Blaxcell and Alexander Riley, a close friend of Wentworth's and, like Blaxcell, a free settler. In return for the construction Macquarie had guaranteed to the partners the right to make a massive importation of rum—205 000 litres— over three years and sell it on whatever terms they chose.

Given the deal on which it was based, a much criticised hospital was built. But as a result of the experience D'Arcy had become less interested in trade within the colony and more heavily involved in the development of the pastoral industry and the export wool trade. Though his sheep were not merinos, the inflated wool market of England at war had returned him a very good price of 69 pence per pound (454 grams). The enforcement of the East India Company's monopoly hampered his interests in whaling and sealing, and Governor Macquarie's port dues threatened to reduce his margin of profit. Then there was a post-war slump in the wool market. But in reality, he flourished.

D'Arcy continued to serve as superintendent of police on a salary of £300 per annum, and, by one of those purely Australian ironies, he and his police had problems with bushrangers on the Parramatta and Liverpool roads. He was also treasurer of the police fund, but, he pointed out to Bathurst, £100 000 had passed through his hands in the eight years he had held the office without his receiving a penny's remuneration. Wentworth and Macquarie both recommended D'Arcy's friend William Redfern to take his place as principal surgeon, but it was not too much of a surprise when Macarthur's friend, the young surgeon James Bowman, instead received the post. Wentworth felt that Bathurst and his ministry had surrendered to all the guff in Britain about convicts being given public office.

Wentworth, however, succeeded Captain Piper as president of the Bank of New South Wales in January 1827, and Mr Cookney wrote from London, recommending his son George and his brother-in-law, Mr James, to Wentworth's protection should they emigrate. The patronage was beginning to run the other way.

D'Arcy did not take much part in the society of the colony despite his popularity with most men and women he met. He had the grief that his son John, a young naval officer, had perished at sea in 1820, but he had also the joy of possessing an extremely dutiful and active son in William, whose book delighted him. And he was proud of D'Arcy junior having marched through his home town, Portadown, as an officer of the 73rd Regiment. He also willingly supported at least seven other children. Annually he gave a dinner to celebrate the anniversary of his arrival in the colony and he was still involved in horse racing. Gradually he resigned his official positions, which had been such a cause of scandal and outrage in Bennet's pamphlet. When he died in 1827 the procession from Home Bush to the graveside was said to be a mile long. Convicts had liked him so well that they competed to be assigned to him, which in a way proved Bigge's thesis that they were not being punished enough.

His name lay on his Antipodean grave as a challenge to his turbulent eldest son. Avenge this man. Avenge yourself.

WHO IS CASTLEREAGH, WHO IS SIDMOUTH, AND WHO IN GOD'S NAME IS BATHURST?

In 1782 the executive business regarding colonies was given to the Home Office, but in 1794, when Britain was imperilled by the French, a Secretary of State for the Colonies was appointed. In 1801 the secretary was designated the Secretary of State for War and the Colonies, and it would not be until 1854 that the two enormous functions were separated.

As for Robert Stewart, Viscount Castlereagh, for whom a New South Wales river of considerable length would be named, he served as a strong servant of repression at home in England, Scotland and Ireland during the Napoleonic era. The viscount was a young and far from unattractive Dublin-born nobleman. When he entered the British Parliament as a twenty-one year old in 1790, Stewart was a Whig who supported electoral reform and Catholic emancipation. By 1795, he crossed the floor to join the Tories, but his position on Irish emancipation and general reform remained the same. His role in quashing the Irish rebellion involved the offer of clemency to commoners who had supported the rebellion, and focusing instead on pursuing rebel leaders. In 1800 he began lobbying in the British and Irish parliament for an official union between the two. His political skills led to the adoption of the Irish Act of Union by both the Irish Parliament and the British, though it instituted two centuries of internecine bloodshed in Ireland.

In 1804 he was made Secretary of State for War and the Colonies and received and replied to dispatches from Hunter, King and Bligh, arguing for the repression of the interests of the officers but at the same time half-believing their complaints. After Pitt's Cabinet of All Talents collapsed, he took up the same job under the Duke of Portland's administration. In this role he became involved in disputes with Foreign Minister George Canning over the failure of the invasion in 1809 of the island of Walcheren. The catastrophe, with thousands dying of camp fever and malaria for no military advantage, certainly distracted Castlereagh from the New South Wales rebellion as Johnston's self-justifications began to arrive in Downing Street, and led to a duel between Canning and Castlereagh, after which they were forced to resign from cabinet.

Three years later, however, Castlereagh returned as Foreign Secretary, and hence he represented the United Kingdom at the Congress of Vienna. He was involved in reaction to the ideas of the French revolution along with the uninspiring Home Secretary, Thomas Addington, Viscount Sidmouth, who was the unapologetic scourge of British demonstrators and protesters. As Home Secretary, Sidmouth brutally crushed radical opposition and suspended *habeas corpus* in 1817, and introduced six vicious acts repressing dissent in 1819 for which Castlereagh was spokesman.

All of these acts suppressing freedom of speech, the press, assembly and association would produce further trials and further transportations. Indeed, Castlereagh was often called on as Leader of the House of Commons to defend Sidmouth's policy, and so attracted the moral disgust of Britons. Shelley wrote, concerning the Peterloo protest and massacre of marchers by British soldiers:

> *I met murder on the way—he had a face like Castlereagh—*
> *Very smooth he looked, yet grim;*
> *Seven bloodhounds followed him,*
> *All were fat, and well they might*
> *Be in admirable plight,*
> *For one by one, and two by two,*
> *He tossed them human hearts to chew*
> *Which from his wide cloak he drew.*

At the end of the summer of 1822 he told King George IV that he was being blackmailed. 'I am accused of the same crime as the Bishop of Clogher,' he confessed, the said bishop having been discovered in the back room of an inn with his trousers down and in carnal congress with a young soldier. The King advised Castlereagh to 'consult a physician'. But Castlereagh (now Londonderry through the death of his father) returned to his fine house at Loring Hall in Kent and committed suicide by cutting his throat with a letter knife.

> *Byron did not mourn him:*
> *Posterity will ne'er survey*
> *A nobler grave than this:*
> *Here lie the bones of Castlereagh:*
> *Stop, traveller, and piss.*

His funeral on 20 August 1822 was greeted with jeering and insults along the entire processional route.

Another home executive who had all these turbulent New South Welsh people on his plate was Henry, Third Earl of Bathurst. He had earlier briefly served under Pitt as Secretary of State and had held other important posts. He was born in 1762 and died in 1834, and so was fifty years of age when he took over at the Colonial Office with the Undersecretary Henry Goulburn and was Secretary of State for the Colonies and War in Lord Liverpool's government from 1812 onwards. These two organised the Colonial Office and made it into a major executive portfolio. They introduced the famous Blue Books, compulsory statistical returns to be filled out by the administration of each colony and returned to England, and set established practice. Bathurst himself, after whom the first transmontane town in Australia was named, was said to be jocular and self-effacing, but was very efficient and indeed had much to deal with in the climactic years of the Napoleonic Wars. As Secretary of State he was involved in Wellington's successful conclusion to the Peninsula Campaign.

He may have been somewhat distracted from Governor Macquarie's New South Wales by the crisis on Napoleon's return from Elba, where it had been the decision of the British government to place him. He would be later left to defend the decision to move him to St Helena in the mid-Atlantic after his defeat at Waterloo.

As well as that, the struggle for the abolition of slavery was in considerable part fought across his desk in the Colonial Office by abolitionists and those in Britain and the plantations of the West Indies who thought slavery had an economic, racial and biblical validity. Other questions such as the removal of 'the disabilities of Roman Catholics', of the laws which made it illegal for them to receive a commission in the army and to hold office, beset him as well, and though he was sympathetic to the Irish he would oppose the Reform Bill. How remote, again, must have seemed the roiling arguments of New South Wales! He did receive submissions from Macarthur, pleading that he be permitted to return to New South Wales, and heard from Undersecretary Goulburn (whose name would also grace an inland town) that the matter would be considered if Macarthur admitted the error of the uprising. Macarthur would not do so, and waited for better terms.

And as a place, short of the noose and available to punish political miscreants, New South Wales remained very much in the minds of government.

CHAPTER 13

RADICAL TRANSPORTEES

Thomas Spence was the apostle of one form of early nineteenth-century radicalism. He was a man driven by Christ's precepts of the equality of man and the evil of unequal possessions. He had arrived in London from Northumberland in December 1792 and over the next twenty-two years organised small groups which met in local public houses where Spence argued the case that 'if all the land in Britain were shared out equally, there would be enough to give every man, woman and child seven acres each'. At night, his supporters walked the streets and chalked slogans such as 'Spence's Plan and Full Bellies' and 'The Land as the People's Farm'. In the early 1800s the authorities believed that Spence and his followers were responsible for bread riots in London. His disciples buried Spence in September 1814 with his dreams unrequited, and created the Society of Spencean Philanthropists. Again, their meetings took place in public houses, including the Carlisle in Shoreditch, the Cock in Soho, the Pineapple in Lambeth, the White Lion in Camden and the Nag's Head in Carnaby Market. The government employed a spy to penetrate the Spenceans and he reported to the Home Office in October 1816 that they were planning to overthrow the British government.

Arthur Thistlewood, the new leader, was convinced a successful revolution was possible, whereas others thought him dangerous and militant. Thistlewood was a former army officer whose improbable design was to take the Tower of London and the Bank of England and thus bring down the government. When nothing came of the plan through lack of support within the society, Thistlewood wrote to 'the Archfiend' Lord Sidmouth—the Home Secretary— demanding payment of £180, the cost of three tickets he had purchased to emigrate to America with his wife and child. When Sidmouth failed to answer, Thistlewood challenged him to a duel. Sidmouth had him arrested for threatening a breach of the peace, he was found guilty and sentenced to twelve months imprisonment at Horsham. Nonetheless, free again, Arthur Thistlewood played an important role in the protest meetings that followed the Peterloo massacre of August 1819, in which a crowd marching in favour of reform and universal suffrage was charged by six hundred Hussars backed by infantry and eighteen marchers were killed. He organised the public reception of Henry Hunt, chief orator of the Peterloo protestors, when he arrived in London after the massacre. The *Times* estimated that 300 000 people turned up to see Hunt and hear speeches. Hunt, however, tried to distance himself from Thistlewood's radicalism.

On 22 February 1820, Thistlewood became aware that several members of the British government were going to dine at Lord Harrowby's house in Grosvenor Square. With a small group of Spenceans he decided to kill the ministers and assembled in a hayloft in Cato Street. But the Spenceans had been set up by a government spy. Thirteen police officers stormed the loft. Several members of the gang refused to surrender their weapons and one police officer was killed by Thistlewood. Thistlewood and four others were found guilty of high treason and sentenced to death. They were executed at Newgate Prison on 1 May 1820 before a huge crowd, deep sighs and groans showing that the mob was not utterly at odds with Thistlewood's plans.

John Harrison, James Wilson, Richard Bradburn, John Strange and Charles Copper were also found guilty, but their original sentence of execution was transmuted to transportation for life, and they disappeared into the New South Wales penal apparatus, creating less paperwork or comment than the United Irish or Scottish Martyrs. But one wonders what attitudes they imbued their Currency sons and daughters with round the hearth-fire.

In some cases, Spenceans who informed against their colleagues were allowed to go to transportation rather than hang. What guilt haunted these men in the fields of Van Diemen's Land and New South Wales? 'It is an ancient custom to resist tyranny,' said one Spencean, William Davidson, in court. '. . . would you not rather govern a country of spirited men, than cowards? I can die but once in this world, and the only regret left is that I have a large family of small children, and when I think of that, it unmans me.'

So did transportation, and the task of finding air within a penal system.

CURRENCY, NOT STERLING

The concern of ex-convicts that they and their issue would remain an underclass emerged very early. In a petition addressed to Governor King in 1801, they complained that in the past (and, they feared, the future) they were considered to be convicts attaint, without personal liberty, property rights, without character or credit, without any one right or privilege belonging to free subjects. They signed it not as emancipated convicts but as 'the emancipated colonists of the territory of New South Wales'.

But King told the Treasury commissioners in a dispatch that he did not like what he saw of the native-born: 'Finding the greater part of the children of this colony so much abandoned to every kind of wretchedness and vice, I perceive the absolute necessity of something being attempted to withdraw them from the vicious examples of their abandoned parents.' Yet this was the generation which by 1820 impressed Commissioner Bigge and others with their probity and calm enterprise. 'That class of inhabitants who have been born in the colony affords a remarkable exception to the moral and physical character of their parents.' They began to be called 'Currency', after the local coinage. If you were British-born, you were 'Sterling', the genuine coin.

In 1810, Macquarie had written to Secretary of State Bathurst describing the colony as 'a convict country'. It was a statement of reality. Nine out of ten of the population were convicts, had been convicts, or were the offspring of convicts. Indeed, the free gentlemen were often determined to hold the line. Lieutenant Archibald Bell, when asked by Commissioner Bigge whether he had any objection to admitting convicts into society, gave the reply: 'I consider them as having once been tainted, unfit to associate with afterwards.' And many Britons at home felt the same way. The Reverend Sydney Smith wrote in the *Edinburgh Review* in 1819, 'New South Wales is a sink of wickedness in which the majority of convicts of both sexes become infinitely more depraved than at the period of their arrival . . . no man who has his choice would select it . . . as his dwelling place.' With a press like this, no wonder British gentlemen with the £250 capital they needed to get a 320-acre (130-hectare) land grant were not yet turning up to take their chances amongst the penal mass.

Even those who had been born free felt stained by association. James Macarthur told Commissioner Bigge that, alas, he had been native-born. The few native-born gentlemen could not hold their heads up, he said, because the native-born were generally a mass of the damned, the children of convicts. The young and gifted bushman Hamilton Hume commented that he hoped to lead an expedition 'altho' an Australian', implying that to be a native told against those who wanted command of things.

Affluent convicts like Henry Kable were in the minority and hoped to consider themselves the middle class of colonial society. It was this group which ultimately had the power to organise and even to send representatives to London to argue their rights. Two of Simeon Lord's native-born sons, Francis and George, worked from a sense of the rights of the respectable Currency over the pretensions of the arrived-free, and became members of the Legislative Council. By 1828 there were around 1167 Currency men to 1601 Currency women. But they were only the first crop of the tainted tree. Many thousands not yet born would have to negotiate the question of whether their origins should be a matter of spiky pride or lifelong regret and denial. And they would also have to interpret what their convict or free parents said about the world, and about Britain. 'Nothing induces me to wish for a change but the difficulty of educating our children,' wrote Elizabeth Macarthur, 'and were it otherwise, it would be unjust towards them to confine them in so narrow a society.' The little creatures all spoke of going home to England 'with rapture'. Like many other native-born, they had 'early imbibed an idea that England is the seat of happiness and delight; that it contains all that can be gratifying to their senses . . . It would be difficult to un-deceive young people bred up in so secluded a situation, if they had not an opportunity given them of convincing themselves.'

As a young man, one of the spikiest, William Charles Wentworth, stood up for the Currency, especially the children of convicts, since he was the son of an Irish gentleman of doubtful legitimacy but also of an Irish convict woman. He accused the wealthier free settlers of wanting 'to convert the ignominy of the great body of the people into a hereditary deformity. They would hand it down from father to son, and raise an eternal barrier of separation between their offspring and the offspring of the unfortunate convicts.'

There were certainly ways in which Currency lads and lasses were pioneering social arrangements unlikely to be seen in other places on earth. Sarah Podmore was the New South Wales born daughter of Richard Podmore, who had been a member of the New South Wales Corps, but he stayed on as a shoemaker, working as the employee of an ex-convict in York Street, Sydney. In 1825 Sarah sought the governor's permission to marry a convict named Joseph Spencer, who had arrived in the colony in 1815, sentenced to transportation for life. In the 1828 census Sarah Spencer *née* Podmore was listed as native-born and her husband, a ticket-of-leave man, that is a convict whose behaviour had been good enough to enable him to be given prior to his sentence expiring permission to work on his own behalf, had been assigned to her as a servant, working as a butcher for her in the town of Liverpool, south-west of Sydney.

Most of the native-born children grew up on modest but adequate farms, and the lack of day-to-day discrimination at that level led to marriage between children of free settlers and the children of convicts. Marriages also took place between sons and daughters of men and women who had been convicted together in Britain, or had arrived on the same ships, or had served in the Royal Marines or New South Wales Corps. Mary Merrick, the daughter of two ex-convicts, married Robert Martin, whose free settler parents had received 100 acres (40.5 hectares) at Mulgrave Place near Penrith as a land grant from Governor King. Mary, her husband and their two children were living with her parents-in-law at Richmond, on the Hawkesbury River, in 1828. Eliza Lydia Griffiths was born in Sydney in March 1794, the daughter of a New South Wales Corps private, Michael Griffiths or Griffin, and his ex-convict wife. Lydia married John Benn, a native-born son of two convict parents and a settler of Pitt Town on the Hawkesbury floodplain.

Farmer Richard Cheers, an ex-convict who received a grant of 30 acres (12 hectares) at Eastern Farms near Ryde in 1792, was leasing half an acre 'on the west side of the cove in the town of Sydney' in 1797, and in 1806 was resident there with his wife, the ex-convict Esther Weaver, and their three native-born children. Originally sentenced for stealing from a man who had refused to sleep with her, Sarah Burdo, one of *Lady Penrhyn*'s midwives, married Private Isaac Archer in 1794, and they later settled at Field of Mars, an area along the Parramatta River put aside for marine land grants. By 1802 they had six children. Sarah farmed with her husband and still acted as a colonial midwife, and by 1828 was living in comfort in Clarence Street, Sydney.

Pierce Colletts, a United Irishman convict who arrived with his free wife in 1801, had 70 acres (28 hectares) in the Nepean district in 1806. The convict father bred his sons James and Joseph 'to the care and management of a farm'. By 1828 he was an innkeeper at Bathurst, and had 200 acres (81 hectares) there, living a contented life being looked after by his 'Colleen Bawn', his beloved native-born daughter.

Matthew Everingham, son of an earl, whose crime had been to steal legal textbooks, had wed Elizabeth Rymes, Spitalfields bed-linen thief from the Second Fleet, and they lived on a farm at Prospect that Watkin Tench had once visited and been not much impressed by. Yet Elizabeth Rymes would give birth and habitation to nine small 'cornstalks' or Currency children.

The native-born children rode their farm horses bareback down dusty tracks, fished and swam in creeks and rivers, and learned bushcraft from each other and local Aboriginal children. A confusing range of opinions would be uttered in Britain and in New South Wales about these national children, just as had been uttered about their parents. It was assumed by many that they must be criminal spawn, abandoned by their 'unnatural parents' or raised amidst scenes of criminal activity and daily debauchery. In fact the colonial experience and later research shows, as the historian Portia Robinson says, that they grew up 'a remarkably honest, sober, industrious and law-abiding group of men and women'. By comparison with British society, the family life of the New South Wales children of ex-convicts and ex-soldiers would be shown, by a government muster taken in 1806, to have been very stable and sturdy. In New South Wales the child labour, hunger and vicious treatment which characterised the factories of Great Britain were missing. Though convict families sometimes lacked funds, they sought to apprentice out their children to equip them with a trade so that they would not be tempted into the youthful follies that had seen their parents transported. Former convicts (including, for example, James Ruse) spoke to other emancipists about apprenticeships for their sons, and many found work in the government dockyards and lumber yards. James Kelly, son of a ship's cook and the convict Catherine Devereaux, serving a sentence of life, was placed with Henry Kable and James Underwood, and by the time he was twenty he knew how to handle a vessel in the wild waters south of Australia and had survived shipwreck at the astoundingly remote sub-Antarctic island named in Macquarie's honour. Other places for apprenticeships were Simeon Lord's enterprises, which trained colonial youths in a number of crafts associated with shipping and chandlery.

Alexander Harris would write that 'The Australians, we must now remark, are growing up a race by themselves; fellowship of country has already begun to distinguish them and bind them together in a very remarkable manner. Whenever they come in contact with each other, even when considerable difference of rank exists, this sympathy operates strongly.'

Nor were they all artisan mechanics, like those trained by Kable, Underwood and Lord. Charles Tompson, transported in 1804, married a native-born girl from the Sydney Orphan School named Elizabeth, and as a literate convict was prized by government. He would come to acquire small businesses in the city and 1500 acres (608 hectares) on the Hawkesbury. Particular about his son and namesake's education, he had young Charles taught in the Windsor government school run by the ex-convict Joseph Harpur, an erstwhile Irish highwayman. Harpur's son also attended, and shared poetic and literary tendencies with Charles Tompson. Young Charles went on to be taught by the Reverend Henry Fulton, the United Irish sympathiser and graduate of Trinity College Dublin. Charles Tompson was the first Currency lad to express the feeling that the world from which his elders came, which they spoke of daily and which he was unlikely ever to see, was a very different one from his extreme southern world. He asked of the Australian spring:

Thou who, unexpected, steal'st serene
Into the bosom of the fertile year
Tell me of climates that I ne'er have seen
And let me feel the fragrance thou dost bear.

As a young man he would complain to Governor Brisbane about the way emigrants were greeted to Australia with land grants. 'Your correspondents, the Australians, are not unreasonable—they are not envious—but the soil is their birthright, their legitimate inheritance!' Lads of industrious habits expected the governor to come good with land, and had done so with some confidence at least since the time of King's administration. The idea of purchasing land was outside their expectations and was seen as a form of imposition.

Before the arrival of Macquarie land grants to the native-born were closely related to the wealth or position of the parent: to those settlers who possessed much, much was further given. The way Macquarie granted land to the native-born, predominantly in lots of 60 acres (24 hectares) made it seem that he judged their claims to be above those of ex-convicts but below those of the free settlers. (Later, as a result of Bigge's recommendations, Darling became the first governor to be ordered not to settle his ex-convicts on small allotments.) Unlike Macquarie, his successor, the godly Brisbane, a keen astronomer, agreed with Bigge and harboured a primary concern not for the ex-convict settlers but for the free sections of the community. 'The bad character of the masses of Inhabitants must in itself be for many an extreme difficulty to settlers from Europe.' He undertook a process of excluding the children of convicts from being granted land, the very policy against which young Tompson complained.

In the meantime, Tompson and Harpur went hunting together, and they would harbour similar nationalist emotions, and Tompson wrote a not consistently gifted song for the anniversary of settlement:

Then live, Australia! Nation young and mild!
Rear still bright Mercy's banner high unfurled
Pardon and peace for Britain's fallen child
Refuge for all the oppressed of all the world.

In 1826 his *Wild Notes from the Lyre of a Native Minstrel* was the first book of verse published by a native son. Charles Tompson dedicated it to the Reverend Fulton. To a boy like Tompson, the experience of a man like Fulton, urbane and generous, would have been a form of liberation.

Like all colonial children, some were creatures of action suited to a raw environment. Others were already concerned to define themselves. The business of worrying over being Australian had begun.

THE POACHING WARS

By the 1790s the authoritarian tendency of British society had cut into all aspects of urban and country life and typified a particularly savage stage of the ancient poaching wars between landed gentry and peasants increasingly squeezed by the Enclosure laws. As enclosure continued throughout the first three decades of the nineteenth century, anti-poaching laws, which already carried the death sentence in some cases, became more strenuous still. In 1828, landlords and gamekeepers were delighted to see a new Night Poaching Act which would increase the sentence for being caught anywhere with the tools of poaching, even in an accused's own premises and quite outside the landlord's grounds, to transportation for fourteen years. The mere intent of poaching could make a man an involuntary Australian. Squires and gentlemen had argued that they were 'entitled to properly regulated . . . amusement and relaxation after the performance of their public duties' and that their residence on their estates had saved the country from anything like the horrors of the French Revolution and contributed instead to the 'virtue and civilisation of the English peasant'.

Not that the poaching class went utterly without sympathy. In the debates leading up to the new Night Poaching Act one of the Whig Lords declared: 'The recipe to make a poacher will be found to contain a very few and simple ingredients which may be met with in every game county in England. Search out a poor man with a large family, or a poor single man having his natural sense of right and wrong, give him little more than natural disinclination to work, let him exist in the midst of lands where the game is preserved, keep him cool in winter, by allowing him insufficient wages to purchase fuel; let him feel hungry upon the small pittance of parish relief; and if he be not a poacher it will only be by the blessing of God.'

Folksongs—from the famed 'The Lincolnshire Poacher' to plaints about and celebrations of poaching—came from Britain, Scotland and Ireland and generally mention transportation as its outcome.

> *Squire Jackson he was unequalled for honour and for reason,*
> *He never turned traitor nor betrayed the rights of man.*
> *But now we are in danger from a vile deceiving stranger*
> *Who has ordered transportation for the boys of Mullaghbawn.*

Indeed amongst the rural poor of Britain, for whom meat had become a scarce commodity since 1750, an enjoyment of the physical challenge of getting some game combined with feelings of defiance against the order of things to produce the crimes of the poacher. Particularly when they operated in parties, poachers might discuss political ideas, darkly asking each other at the local inn whether Genesis did not appoint *man*, not squire, to dominance over the world of animals. One critic of the landlords satirically wondered whether 'there was some sovereign medicinal value in the blood and juices of these animals' which caused the landlords to covet their wildlife so passionately. Peasants intending to hunt for food for their families thus might seek to bind each other to solidarity by taking an oath, and they would thereby become that institution of sedition so dreaded by the authorities: a 'combination'. Such poachers did not consider themselves part of a criminal class, but casualties of tyranny.

A typical poaching incident occurred in 1816 at Berkeley on the River Severn estuary. A poacher trespassing on the estate of Colonel Berkeley was killed by a spring gun set up in the foliage to be tripped off by intruders. This death brought on an outbreak of acts of defiant poaching by outraged young men of the district, and by habitual poachers too. Middling farmers and men with political ideas were willing to participate. A local radical lawyer, 26-year-old William Adams Brodribb, lived with his wife and small children in the village of Moreton, within a long walk of Berkeley Castle, and Colonel Berkeley seemed to Brodribb, a man influenced by Spencean ideas, to be a biblically unjust landlord of the type who would never enter heaven but would make a hell on earth. Brodribb had an ideological sympathy for the poachers, and on the night they gathered at an inn for a punitive poaching expedition against Colonel Berkeley, swore them in, no doubt using a formula common to the forming of secret societies, invoking solidarity, the rights of man and biblical condemnations of wealth. Taking their oath, the poaching party saw themselves as protesters and, almost in the anti-Napoleonic Spanish tradition, guerrillas. They blackened their faces (itself an offence) and intended as instruments of justice to clean out Colonel Berkeley's game. One of their leaders, a young farmer named Allen, specifically forbade the party to fire at gamekeepers, detested because of their setting of man-traps and other instruments of ambush. But as they entered the grounds of the castle, the party of sixteen were fired on by a group of five keepers, and in the overpowering return fire one of the keepers, a man named Ingram, was killed.

The poachers retreated, washed their faces in a stream, and went home. By the first light of day, Colonel Berkeley was gathering a small army of his own to hunt the members of the party down. Eleven of the poachers involved in the affray were caught through Berkeley's strenuous efforts, which included the employment of a Bow Street runner. Amongst those rounded up, though he had taken no part in the poaching expedition, was the attorney-at-law, urbane and godly William Adams Brodribb, father of three. Brodribb was summoned to Berkeley Castle to face a group of magistrates, fellow landowners to Colonel Berkeley, all of whom were known to him and all of whom had some respect for him. He stood accused of administering an illegal oath, and he made his case worse by not denying it and declaring that landlords such as the colonel had brought it all on themselves by setting man-traps.

In Gloucester gaol to the north of their village the captured poachers were able to receive legal advice from their fellow inmate Brodribb. All eleven of them faced the death sentence, and were in the end found guilty of murder or abetting murder by a weeping jury, who thought they were too young and decent to die. Nine of them were recommended to mercy. The tears of the jury were testimony to community ambiguity about the crime the men had committed, evidenced by a ballad of the time:

The law locks up the man or woman
Who steals the goose from off the common,
But leaves the greater villain loose
Who steals the common from the goose.

Lord Eldon, the Lord Chancellor who later introduced a new night poaching law, was like many Englishmen in that he thought poaching a sport and confessed he had tried it himself as a boy. And in the Berkeley court was a local doctor, Edward Jenner, the pioneer of inoculation against smallpox, who wrote, 'My intention is to quit this place, rendered dreary by the tragic scene at this instant about to be enacted on the horrid platform . . . They certainly did not go out to commit murder.'

The next day, the young lawyer Brodribb himself stood trial. He was well-represented and respectably dressed in black, but the jury found him guilty and he was given the statutory sentence of seven years transportation.

All the poachers were reprieved at the end, and were to become Australian transportees. Brodribb was the first to be sent to the old *Justitia* hulk in the Thames that spring, but all of them made it on board the *Sir William Bensley* when it sailed in late summer and entered Port Jackson in March 1817. Brodribb's wife and children would ultimately join him, and he would practise law and acquire land in Van Diemen's Land.

THE SEALERS' LIFE AND GOVERNANCE

It was Surgeon George Bass and Matthew Flinders, two adventurous Lincolnshire men, who first gave news of the abundant islands and seal populations of Bass Strait, which separates the Australian mainland from Tasmania. In 1798, the *Sydney Cove* had been wrecked in the Furneaux Islands of the strait. Two rescue operations to take survivors away from the beaches they had been swept up on were conducted by both Bass and Flinders, and on return to Sydney both men reported specific colonies of seals and their location. That same month, May 1798, an American captain, Charles Bishop of the brig *Nautilus*, arrived in Sydney after an unsuccessful attempt to seal in the Pacific and American waters. He refitted and set out on the first commercial sealing voyage in Australia, at first in company with Flinders and Bass on their handy sloop *Norfolk*. Bass and Flinders were naval officers and not interested themselves in seal harvesting. They wanted to circumnavigate Van Diemen's Land, and show that there was a faster way to Sydney, through Bass Strait (which Flinders had graciously named for his friend), than rounding the dangerous southern capes of Tasmania. 'Mr Bass and myself hailed it [the circumnavigation] with joy and mutual congratulation, as announcing the completion of our long wished-for discovery of a passage into the Southern Indian Ocean,' wrote Flinders.

In the meantime Bishop and his men began the first cropping of the rich harvest of seals in the Furneaux group, Bishop putting a group of fifteen men into Kent Bay on wild and wind-torn Cape Barren Island at the eastern end of the strait. The southern waters had for millennia been the uninterrupted feeding and breeding ground for fur seals, hair seals and elephant seals, and now a new colonial business that involved living far from control in clothing of sealskin and wallaby, on a diet of ship's biscuit and stew made up of anything from wombat to kangaroo to cassowary to mutton bird would begin, and would have its attractions. The bludgeoning of seals, the boiling down of blubber and curing of sealskin for enormously distant markets, if tainted by the stink of putrefaction, was no worse than what men lived with aboard ship or in ill-sewered towns. The gangs scudded from island to island, killing-place to killing-place, in flimsy boats. Their calling was dangerous, but probably less so than whaling. One who certainly liked the life was Samuel Rodman Chase of Rhode Island, an American seaman who would continue his association with Vandemonian sealing for the rest of his life and who married Marianne Letitia, daughter of Van Diemen's Land's Lieutenant-Governor, David Collins. He would inhabit the strait until he drowned in southern waters about 1827.

Leaving the men on Cape Barren Island in place, the *Nautilus* arrived back at Port Jackson on 25 December 1798 with more than five thousand sealskins. As busy as they were with Christmas, the former convicts Henry Kable and James Underwood had time to hear from Bishop.

The next time Bishop visited Kent Bay, in January 1799, he brought back 9000 sealskins to Port Jackson. From 1799 to 1805 there were catches of three, four and five thousand seals. From about 1806, however, the harvest declined, and seals could be found only in places which were dangerous to get a boat to. The methods remained consistent: clubbing was the way of killing the fur seal but the elephant seal was stabbed in the heart so that its blood would drain away and not contaminate the blubber.

Far to the west of the Furneaux Islands, Captain Reid of the *Martha* sighted Kangaroo Island at the end of 1799. Three years later, sealing was firmly established there with gangs living at Point Cowper on the east coast and on the north-west coast as well. Nearly forty years before the Europeans settled the South Australian coastline across from Kangaroo Island, the fires of the sealers were blazing near Kangaroo Head and beneath Billygoat Falls.

Portland Bay on what would be the Victorian coast, not far from the present South Australian border, also served as a base for visiting sealers years before Captain Collins attempted a settlement at Port Phillip in 1804, the one he quickly abandoned to take his convicts and settlers to Van Diemen's Land and the site of Hobart.

In October 1802 Governor King mentioned in a dispatch that he had allocated exclusive rights to seal at Cape Barren Island to the merchants Kable and Underwood. From 1803 the ships of these two redeemed convicts dropped off gangs on islands, and returned later to retrieve sealskins and oil. There were dwelling huts at Kent Bay in 1804 and even a shipyard for constructing a small coastal boat.

François Péron, the young zoologist on the French expedition of Nicolas Baudin, having lost an eye for his country in defence of the revolution, and now travelling on a scientific voyage to chart the Australian coast for French purposes, visited the sealers of Bass Strait and seemed fascinated by them. At the King Island fishery at Sea Elephant Bay he met the sailor Daniel Cooper and ten others who had been landed there from the *Margaret* in June 1802, and described their camp, not yet a permanent year-round settlement. The men, said Péron, lived in four huts or shanties. Daniel Cooper, their leader, occupied one of the hovels with a woman whom he had brought from Maui. A great fireplace fed day and night with tree trunks served to warm the inhabitants and cook their food. A large shed contained a huge quantity of barrels filled with oil, and there were several thousand sealskins dried and ready for shipment to

China. From a butcher's hook hung five or six cassowaries, the same number of kangaroos and two fat wombats. A big copper filled with meat had just been taken off the fire. There was no bread or biscuit when Péron and some of the other French voyagers went to dinner there, but all the sealers seemed vigorous and healthy.

On the lee or eastern side of the New Year Islands, Péron also met twelve Englishmen employed by the Commissary General for New South Wales, Mr Palmer.

Another early report speaks of the Bass Strait sealers as mentally deranged because of long lonely months on gale-swept islands—'their days filled with the stench of rotting carcasses must have had some adverse effect on the minds of men already tainted with viciousness and brutality'. But that picture ignores those to whom it was the only satisfactory way of life left, and to whom a vacuum of authority was a prized environment.

Over on the western end of the Great Australian Bight, in King George Sound, in what is now Western Australia, cropping of the seal population by visiting gangs had also begun. In February 1803, Baudin called there and met Yankee Captain Pendle of the snow *Union*, who was looking for seals but complained there were too few to give him a cargo. Baudin suggested he should try Kangaroo Island, which he did with more success.

After 1804, ships' visits to the sealers became less frequent and between 1805 and 1820 the sealers of Bass Strait became full-time residents of the islands. The Currency lad James Kelly's evidence to the Bigge enquiry in 1820 mentioned these communities. The sealers had houses, gardens and animals, he said, and they collected mutton birds and kangaroo skins as well as sealskins. They used whaleboats to reach the seal colonies.

James Munro, a former Londoner sent to New South Wales for the theft of calico, was changed by a religious epiphany on his way to Australia and became expert at navigating the islands of Bass Strait. From 1820 he lived on Preservation Island, and grew vegetables and bred rabbits for passing whalers and sealers. He also kept their sealskins ready for collection. He would ultimately be made a constable with power to arrest runaway convicts in the strait, and so came to act as liaison between visiting government officials and ships' captains, and the sealers themselves.

Most notable of these visitors was George Augustus Robinson, a pious Englishman and former engineer who sailed to the Furneaux Group in November

1830 to battle the sealers for possession of their islands, which were needed for Aboriginal re-settlement. He also wanted to repatriate the sealers' Aboriginal women stolen from the tribes of north-east Tasmania. He would be defeated on both fronts.

By this time, the population of sealers on Kangaroo Island sold wallaby pelts and salt from the natural lagoons there as well as sealskins. In anticipation of visiting ships, either from America or from Kable and Underwood and others, these goods would be packed on the beach. The merchants came in and took them, and left alcohol, tea and tobacco. The sealers received in kind or money a fraction—perhaps as little as one-hundredth—of what the merchants made. Kable, Underwood, Lord and others, former thieves, had learned from their betters how really to skin a cat.

As noted, the sealers were not alone on the islands. Aboriginal women, especially those from the violently windy Cape Grim country in the north-west of Van Diemen's Land, had been captured as sexual partners and were put to work as well since they knew how to build shelters in that region of constant wind, how to catch fish, dive for shellfish and trap wallabies. They could find birds' eggs, and thread shoes with the sinew taken from the tails of kangaroos. The Tasmanian Aboriginal women also taught the white men how to kill mutton birds, pluck their feathers and squeeze out their oil. By the late 1820s the Bass Strait communities, including the women, were sailing into Launceston to sell mutton bird feathers (for bedspreads), and mutton bird oil for lamps. Their unions were unconsecrated and often based on violence. In 1830, Robinson met seventy-four women living with sealers, and was told of another fourteen living on Kangaroo Island.

Penderoin, a Pennemukeer Aboriginal from Cape Grim, told Robinson that in December 1827 sealers had landed and ambushed a group of his people. One Pennemukeer man, hiding in a tree, threw a spear at the attackers and the sealers shot him, and captured seven women, stealing them away to Kangaroo Island. A few weeks later, in January 1828, another group of sealers opened fire on the Pennemukeer from the caves on the Doughboys Rocks opposite Cape Grim. Landing, they forced the Pennemukeer at gunpoint onto a cliff edge and bound them with cord. Twelve to fourteen women were abducted that day and taken to Kangaroo Island. Since several Pennemukeer died in the raid, Pennemukeer men would later club three sealers to death.

There were even reports of the murder and trading of Aboriginal women. A Bass Strait sealer named Mansell certainly made occasional trades in women. In the Hobart press, the Aboriginal women living with the sealers were presented as animalistic—beaten with the bludgeons used on the seals, and fed after the dogs.

Yet sometimes these transactions were peaceable. As early as 1810 the north-east coastal Aboriginal people met up with sealers arriving in open boats. The sealers were honoured with a corroboree, and sometimes the tribal leaders would negotiate for women to go temporarily with the sealers and come back with meat and other payments in kind—dogs, flour or mutton birds. But such dealings became rarer.

Bushrangers faced with surviving in the seemingly trackless tiers of Van Diemen's Land, however, found exchange with the Aborigines essential. Aboriginal women could be wonderful guides to Europeans on the edges of the viable world. The bushranger James Carrot, for example, was taught by Aboriginal women to make moccasins from untanned kangaroo skin. But he also forced his Aboriginal paramour to walk in front of him wearing round her neck the head of the husband he had murdered. Michael Howe, one of the most famous Vandemonian bushrangers, had an Aboriginal partner and, like many of the early bushrangers, dressed in kangaroo skins and blackened his face, signifying that he had more in common with the natives than with British society.

In south-eastern Van Diemen's Land, a small-boned girl named Trukanini met George Augustus Robinson. The would-be saviour of the Vandemonian natives was appointed by the colonial government to assess their welfare and at the time, in 1829, he was trying to establish a township and haven for the Aborigines on Bruny Island, south of Hobart. Trukanini told him of a family's obliteration: her mother had been murdered by sealers, her sister was abducted by sealers and was believed to be living on Kangaroo Island, 600 kilometres to the west. Her uncle had been shot by soldiers, and her betrothed Paraweena killed by timber-getters. She was willing to help Robinson in return for the protection of her people from the firearms of the interlopers.

Robinson was also becoming aware of a growing and possibly fatal imbalance between male and female in the north-eastern Tasmanian Aboriginals. Some historians claim that the sealers destroyed a number of Aboriginal clans on the north coast of Tasmania through abduction of women and the associated violent conflict which tended to reduce the population of Aboriginal males, as well as, of course, removing women. But it is also ironically true that the sealers let their native wives practise and pass on ceremonial knowledge and beliefs. For all their rough-handedness, the sealers were different from other settlers in that they did not try to convert the Aborigines to Christianity or to suppress their rites.

When the *Astrolabe* under the French explorer Dumont d'Urville called at Kangaroo Island in October 1826 it found a party of sealers who had landed seven months earlier in distress for food. Their mother ship, the *Governor Brisbane*, had been seized by the Dutch government in Batavia, but not before leaving sealing gangs at Westernport and at King George Sound as well as on Kangaroo Island.

Yet when D'Urville offered to take them to Port Jackson, they refused. Three finally agreed to accompany him, one as a seaman, the other two as passengers. One of those who remained was a New Zealand male, and there were Aboriginal women with the party who chose to stay, whether by choice or from fear is impossible to say. The all-important boat steerers, George Thomas and William Bundy, remained. Two other sealing boats from stations along the Kangaroo Island coast turned up while the *Astrolabe* was there, one of the boats including an Aboriginal native from Port Jackson and the other a black American who spoke quite good French. A French expeditioner used two Tasmanian Aboriginal women in the party to draw up a Tasmanian vocabulary which would ultimately be published.

Global politics were reaching out to contain these unofficial settlements of sealers and Aboriginal partners. In 1827, middle-aged Major Edmund Lockyer of the 57th Regiment was sent on an 84-ton (87-tonne) brig, *Amity*, all the way to the present Western Australia to form a settlement on King George Sound before the French could. He landed at Michaelmas Island in King George Sound on Christmas Day. There he found four Aboriginal men marooned, and returned them to the coast when he established his settlement. In the early new year a boat containing men previously dropped by a sealing ship in the Recherche group landed at the settlement. They were accompanied by two native women. They reported they were starving, having been dumped by a ship which never returned. Though Lockyer fed them he removed from their care a seven-year-old half-caste girl named Fanny, whom he sent ultimately to Sydney. As for the men, Lockyer was appalled. 'They are a complete set of pirates going from island to island along the southern coast from Rottnest Island to Bass's Strait in open whaleboats, having their chief resort or den at Kangaroo Island, making occasional descents on the mainland and carrying off by force native women, and when resisted make use of the firearms of which they are provided.' Lockyer recommended that the government should enter the trade each year from November to the end of the following April, but that there should be a severe penalty for killing pups.

Lockyer's settlement was moved in March 1831 to Swan River, but by then the catches for sealers in King George Sound were small in any case.

The sealers, as described by Lockyer, were thus a challenge to action for the Commissioners of the South Australian Company, who in 1836 were about to establish the province of South Australia. It was certainly convenient for them to portray the Kangaroo Island sealers as savages, from whose inroads the natives were now to be saved. A report of the South Australian Company declared, 'The colonisation of South Australia by industrious and virtuous settlers, so far from being an invasion of the rights of the Aborigines, is a necessary preliminary to the displacement of the lawless squatters, the abandoned sailors, the runaway convicts, the pirates, the worse than savages, that now infest the coast of New Holland and perpetrate against the defenceless native crimes at which humanity revolts.'

Yet a letter from South Australian Commissioner John Morphett in the supplement of the same report described the Kangaroo Islanders as 'intelligent, quiet men, having spots of land under cultivation; growing a little wheat, with potatoes, turnips, and other vegetables. They have all expressed pleasure at the opportunity of entering into the relations of civilised life.' Nor was it true that Kangaroo Island was populated by runaway convicts as, unlike the islands of Bass Strait, it did not offer convicts much chance of getting away to Britain, France or America on sailing vessels.

As late as 7 October 1842 the *Perth Gazette* reported that Robert Gamble, originally from Van Diemen's Land, was living on Bald Island, about thirty kilometres to the eastward of King George Sound, with black women and his children by them. By then, the larger island communities had fallen under the influence of government, and of the disciples of Christ.

SOME NOTES ON MATTHEW FLINDERS

After his circumnavigation of Van Diemen's Land with the energetic young surgeon George Bass, Matthew Flinders returned to England in March 1800. He was quickly promoted to the command of HMS *Investigator* and told by the Admiralty to explore 'the unknown coast'—the southern coast of Australia from the Port Phillip area westwards. Before he left for New South Wales, he married a parson's daughter whom he had known since youth, and was passionate enough to try to smuggle her on board. According to one story, the Lords of the Admiralty came to inspect the *Investigator* and found Flinders in the cabin with his wife, Anne, on his knee. Whatever the truth of this tale, even Sir Joseph Banks chastised him and warned him that if he took Anne to New South Wales, he would lose his command.

Flinders reached the unknown coast and began charting, and met the Frenchman Nicolas Baudin and his expedition aboard *Le Géographe*, who were coming westwards, at Encounter Bay in today's South Australia. Having reached Sydney and overhauled there, the young English commander decided to circumnavigate the continent, beginning by going north and making a detailed survey of what is now the Queensland coast and the Gulf of Carpentaria. Because of its un-seaworthiness the *Investigator* had to be careened in Torres Strait, and was found to have rotten timbers. Flinders set his carpenters to work. To his immortal repute, he completed the circumnavigation of the continent in his flawed vessel.

Flinders returned to England as a passenger on *Porpoise* in great desire of seeing Anne, but also to scout out a suitable vessel to complete aspects of the survey which the condition of the *Investigator* had prevented him from doing to his satisfaction and the Admiralty's demands. But the *Porpoise* struck a reef on the Queensland coast and Flinders was left to navigate her cutter more than a thousand kilometres back to Sydney. This time he sailed in a schooner named the *Cumberland*, a small ship of 29 tons/tonnes, which was also in terrible condition. After travelling via Torres Strait, Flinders decided in the Indian Ocean to put in to Mauritius to refit, for he had a French *laissez-passer*, which enabled him to approach French ports. Mauritius was to do great disservice to this honest officer who was in the prime of his life and had much work to do.

The French explorer Nicolas Baudin had written to the governor in Mauritius asking him to treat any English ship forced to moor there with kindness, given that his own ships had been welcomed into Sydney and many of his sick crew treated ashore in Sydney Cove. But the small-minded Governor de Caen imprisoned Flinders as a spy, though later letting him live in the town where he spent time working on his journals. De Caen used the fact that the *Cumberland* was carrying dispatches from Port Jackson as an excuse to detain Flinders even after 1806, when Napoleon gave approval for his release. De Caen justified keeping Flinders in place by suggesting that he was the forerunner of a British intention to absorb Mauritius into the British Empire. Indeed, by 1809 the British were blockading the island and its capture by them became inevitable.

Eventually, from his estate, Revesby Abbey, Sir Joseph Banks wrote to Anne Flinders that he had 'infinite satisfaction in informing you that Captain Flinders has at last obtained his release and is expected in England in a few weeks, and that on his arrival he will be immediately made a Post-Captain'.

At their reunion, Anne was appalled to see her 36-year-old husband grey-headed from his ordeal. But perhaps Flinders's character as a man was seen in his willingness to visit French prisoners-of-war, whose families he had known on Mauritius, and distribute letters and money to them from their relatives. It was the kindness of various French families in Mauritius which had sustained him during his capture and compelled him to this generosity.

At his lodgings in London he suffered from what he called 'either a stone or gravel in the bladder'. He had suffered forms of this complaint almost throughout his entire detention. His diary mentions passing gravel or 'gravelly sand'. Sick as he was, and fevered, with a wife desperately worried for his health, he was delighted to hear that his journals were progressing at the publishers, as was his 'general chart of Terra Australis, or Australia'. He told a friend that he now looked fully seventy years of age. He died the day after his work was published, aged forty.

THE TATTOO AND THE LASH

A considerable number of the convicts transported to Australia carried tattoos on their bodies, and the authorities recorded them as an aid to identification. These marks were acquired not without pain. The tattoos of the day, once cut in the flesh, were made permanent and lifelong by the rubbing in of soot or of black sediment from lamps. Some tattoos recorded the names or initials of the beloved, as with a convict transported in 1828, Laban Stone, a married man with a wife, Sarah, and a son, John, left behind in England. The markings on his arm as recorded in his ship's muster are: 'LS, SS, sun, JS, three, 1831 [probably the year his sentence would end], heart'. Laban Stone thus told the story of his passions and intentions on the length of a limb. A convict Eleanor Swift carried on her arm a tattooed declaration, 'Patrick Flinn I love to the heart'. Sometimes women carried tattoos in less obvious places. Elizabeth Stephens's tattoo, dedicated to 'F. Spooner', could be seen only when she undressed for the surgeon. Simon

Gilbert, a groom found guilty of stealing a bridle, and sent to the hulks to await transportation, had 'Man in irons' tattooed on one arm and an anchor and SG on the other. William Rouse, transported for poaching, recorded his and his wife's birthdays on his arms: 'Wife, R. Rouse, born April 1 1812, of W. Rouse born April 24 1810'. A butcher from Cork, Denis Barrett, carried a Masonic emblem, a harp and the war cry 'Erin Go Bragh!'.

Symbols of enduring affection—sun, oak, anchor or heart—were often set beside a particular set of initials. Other marks included caged birds, a woman resting her hand on a tomb in mourning, boxing matches, cockfights, a man sitting on a cask of rum, Highland warriors, cutters, brigs, schooners and barques. The cross or texts of scriptures often competed for space on the convict's skin with slogans of defiance and phallic jokes or naked women—'obscene marks', as the authorities said. The cross of the crucifixion was most commonly found on Irish convicts.

Some tattoos were acquired in the public houses of working-class London, some from the county jails or Newgate, in which there was ample leisure for self-decoration, and others from the hulks. Some were even acquired on board ship.

The tattoo, wrote one historian, was like a bodily aperture for the imagination—through it the convict could escape exile and loss and return to his pre-transportation days. One convict, Thomas Cavender, would take to his Australian grave the following tattoo on his arm:

May the rose of England never blow,
May the Scotch thistle never grow,
May the harp of Ireland never play,
Till I poor convict greets my liberty. T.C.A. 20 18 30.

The other tattoos, the tattoos imposed by the state, were involuntary. They were scars from the lash, and they marked the bodies of early Australians as distinctly as the exuberantly inked flesh decorations, but these caused lovers to wince, and the bearers to curse and tell dark stories.

There was as well as the lash for women, the practice of humiliating them by shaving their heads—an instinctive way of mocking or denying their sexuality. Though a temporary punishment, it could be enacted painfully and with public derision. Threats to shave female heads en masse, and the exemplary shavings undertaken in the Female Factories, a cross between a female shelter, workshop and prison, caused riots amongst the women, as in Parramatta in 1827, 1831 and 1833, in Hobart in 1827 and 1842, at Moreton Bay in 1836 and Launceston in 1841. Foster Fyans, the Moreton Bay commandant between 1835 and 1837, wrote: 'the loss of hair . . . was held in the greatest dread and abhorrence, often causing disorder and riot, cursing, tumbling and flinging before the constabulary could carry out the sentence, when any other punishment could be carried out without a murmur'.

A convict, O'Connor, mentions a Sunday parade organised by Captain Logan in 1829 at the Moreton Bay settlement (later Brisbane). The female convicts were marched into church that morning in a manner that betrayed Logan's assumption that the church was simply another arena for the control and undermining of the human soul. The women's heads were all shaven, and there were iron collars on their necks with iron chains connecting each woman to the next. Male-size irons were on their legs. The caps they normally wore to church were forbidden to allow troops and convicts to hoot and cat-call at their baldness. Here or there, a lover must have kept his silence or been egged into betraying guffaws.

Physically, it was better than flogging. It is the lash and its scars which both excite and embarrass Australian remembrance. Yet flogging was normal Georgian practice, and not just in penal colonies. It was regularly used in both the British army and navy. Where then to place Joseph Holt's horrifying description of the flogging of Paddy Galvin at Parramatta in 1800, the reduction of the young man's back, buttocks, thighs and calves to jelly? Holt did not think this a normal or justifiable punishment. But then he was in passionate sympathy with the young Irish patriot.

If repeated sentences of flogging were normal, why did the magistrate, the Reverend Marsden, gain repute amongst his contemporaries as a flogging parson? John Skottowe Parker, a liberal-minded superintendent of agriculture at three convict depots during the 1820s—Port Macquarie, Norfolk Island and Moreton Bay—thought the lash a regrettable necessity in environments where officials' lives were threatened by the convicts amongst whom they worked. Parker later wrote, 'I have been an isolated member cut off from society, surrounded by the very worst of my species, compelled to freeze in my breast all those finer feelings of humanity.'

Another notorious flogger, Captain Patrick Logan was a Scottish officer who succeeded to the command of Moreton Bay under a mandate from Commissioner Bigge and Governor Brisbane to be less lenient on convicts.

According to the Sydney *Monitor* in August 1830, there were, under Logan, 'punishment field-days', on which the convict complement was drawn up and 'skulkers' and recalcitrants were selected by the commandant and his overseers from field gangs for ritual punishment—'fifty or a hundred lashes apiece'— in front of their fellow prisoners under the guard of soldiers and constables. The overseers were themselves convicts, yet for the sake of punishment their intentions and selection of victims were considered appropriate by Logan, as if they would not be motivated by spite or bullying, or if they were, that was thought an acceptable part of the system. This scene on the humid banks of the Brisbane River provides *par excellence* a tableau of the petty authoritarianism which would live on in Australian public affairs beyond convict times.

It is sometimes remarkable how calm the voice of the flogged survivor is. Thomas Brookes, a convict at Port Jackson, Newcastle and Moreton Bay, calculated receiving eight separate whippings, totalling 1025 strokes, upon his body. 'They were not comfortable to take,' he commented. 'My back had been cut and chopped, until it was scarcely ever well.' The intense pain of a scourging produced 'a boiling sensation', according to Brookes, 'as if being scorched with a red hot iron . . . we felt we were slaves'. Brookes believed the lash turned men into demons who took their dark rage out on other prisoners.

A convict named Davies at Sarah Island off the west coast of Van Diemen's Land reported, 'The cats and the way they were made and used were the most dreadful things that can be thought of. They had nine tails or rather thongs, each four feet long . . . and each tail had on it seven overhand knots . . . some with wire ends, some with waxed ends . . . [the victim] was immediately sent to work, his back like bullock's liver and most likely his shoes full of blood . . .'

A much-flogged, apparently eccentric convict, Frank MacNamara, known as Frank the Poet, was flogged fourteen times to receive a total of 650 lashes, served three and a half years in iron gangs doing hard labour on roads, docks and in quarries, served thirteen days of solitary confinement and three months on the treadmill near Sydney's Brickfield Hill.

He then spent two years on the hulk *Phoenix* in Sydney Harbour, from which he tried to escape five times, and addressed the superintendent about potential time in solitary:

Captain Murray, if you please
Make it hours and not days.

You know it becomes an Irishman
To drown the shamrock when he can.
[*Drowning the shamrock* is to drink, probably to excess.]

Frank's final punishment was seven years at Port Arthur. There he made a number of attempts at absconding and imagined himself a potential bushranger, bushranging being an assertion of liberty to his mind:

Then hurl me to crime and brand me with shame
But think not to baulk me my spirit to tame,
For I'll fight to the last in old Ireland's name,
Though I be a bushranger,
You still are the stranger and I'm Donahue
[Donahue was a mythic Irish bushranger.]

Despite his numerous punishments, Frank would be permitted to perform for his fellow convicts in New South Wales and Van Diemen's Land during the 1830s and 1840s. On Christmas Day 1842 at the prison settlement at Port Arthur he entertained his fellow prisoners, including the Irish bushranger Martin Cash, with his recitations, announcing himself as he always did at his performances:

My name is Frank MacNamara,
A native of Cashel, County Tipperary,
Sworn to be a tyrant's foe,
And while I live, I'll crow.

Were the more than six hundred lashes given to Frank the Poet of therapeutic value for him or the body of society? They certainly warned other felons not to be too flamboyant. Crowing itself was the triumph for Frank. He never became a bushranger, but he understood the meaning of that gesture of renouncing the settled regions and the orderly progress of a sentence to conclusion.

Moreton Bay remained a harsh place for flogging. In 1836 Captain Foster Fyans was questioned by two Quaker visitors, George Washington Walker and James Backhouse, about flogging, and suggested that the best way to explain it was to have a man flogged so that they could observe the effect, which he himself described to them as follows: 'The first lash, Friend, the skin rises not unlike a white frost . . . the second slash . . . often reminds me of a snowstorm . . . the third slash, Friend, the back lacerated dreadfully . . . the painful feelings then subside . . . for the blood comes freely.'

The Quaker visitors tried out the treadmill too, and found after ten minutes they were exhausted, whereas prisoners would be kept turning the thing for up to fourteen hours at a time.

Although floggings were not officially to be administered publicly after 1820, they were carried out before captive convict audiences—road and chain gangs, groups of assigned servants, and the populations of secondary punishment centres—throughout the 1830s and beyond. There is no doubt that many commandants—for example, James Morisset at Newcastle and later on Norfolk Island—felt their authority enlarged by each stroke of the lash.

Occasionally, convict solidarity surfaced in the face of the lash, and a convict scourger would refuse to do his work, but the system had attended to this possibility by its appointment of overseers and constables, the equivalent of *Kapos* in German concentration camps. These men were often segregated for their own safety from the convict ranks, but if the convict struck out from his humble station amidst the gang, it was often the overseer or constable he targeted, not the officers above. At Moreton Bay, Chief Constable James McIntosh, who was cherished by his commandant for arresting forty runaways, was described by the commandant's convict clerk, William Ross, as one of the most tyrannical men in New South Wales, who seemed 'to delight in human blood'. While at Moreton Bay, three attempts were made on his life—once by a prisoner and twice by Aborigines. The British Parliamentary Select Committee on Transportation in 1838 heard that the most common form of reactive violence in New South Wales was 'the beating of overseers'; that is, of the men responsible for selecting the victims of floggings.

There were many who thought a better way could be found. The liberal governor Richard Bourke expressed fear in an 1832 letter to Morisset, harsh commandant of Norfolk Island, that treatment at the penal stations was 'tending more to harden the heart of the criminal and render him reckless of life' than to produce his reform. 'Something it is said must be wrong in a system which apparently produces greater crime than that which it was framed to punish,' he argued. But when it came to balancing the normal punishment of the lash against ration deprivation, he admitted that flogging was 'the means under providence most likely to effect the reformation of the criminal'.

A colonist, JC Byrne, who travelled from Sydney to Brisbane in the mid 1840s, believed he could unmistakably tell a flogged convict by his face. 'A peculiarity of visage, different from all other men, is recognizable; whilst their countenances are of a dark brown hue, parched and dried up, muscles and all, as if they had been baked in one mass.' What Byrne found most disconcerting was the flogged convicts' hostility to their former masters, and their willingness to sing low ballads full of abuse and the dream of revenge. With the wave of progressive thought that achieved the final abolition of slavery in Britain in 1833, there was a reaction against the universal belief in the lash as essential punishment. The Molesworth committee of enquiry into the New South Wales system appointed a Scots penal visionary named MacConochie to administer Norfolk Island on a merit points system for four years. The experiment rehabilitated many prisoners but any of its failings to modify the behaviour of *all* convicts were taken as proof this system did not work. But MacConochie's replacement, John Giles Price, reintroduced the lash as part of the standard repertory of control, along with the treadmill and suspension by one hand.

But a new penology was emerging in Britain, the so-called 'silent system', which would replace the physical torment of the lash with the mental torment of isolation, involving hours of solitary oakum-picking, and even the removal of strident sounds, such as metal bells, as too stimulating to the criminal senses.

By 1843, the Quaker James Backhouse, visiting Macquarie Harbour convict station on the west coast of Van Diemen's Land, claimed that corporal punishment was not as common as solitary confinement—'with evident advantage'. Later, when he witnessed two floggings in Launceston, he wrote 'this punishment tended to confirm me in its inefficiency compared with solitary confinement'. In his dark and lonely hole, the convict might become, so it was hoped, something like a medieval monk in the stone cells of the Hebrides, or be refined into one of the desert fathers of early Christianity.

GANGS

Lieutenant Jonathon Warner was typical of the young military surveyors posted along the length of the North Road being built from 1826 onwards to connect Sydney to Newcastle and the Hunter Valley. Newly appointed, he found himself stationed at Lower Portland Head on the Hawkesbury River, surrounded by rich floodplains, awesome escarpments, and close to the property of the ex-convict Cockney settler, Solomon Wiseman, who was making a fortune from the road and the ferry he managed. Lieutenant Warner's challenges included not only the doubly convicted men of the work-gang but also the proudly illiterate Solomon himself, who sold produce to feed the gangs. Wiseman was a Thames lighterman who had stolen a consignment of Brazilian wood, but although transported had been able to bring his wife and children aboard his convict ship, and after serving his time had run hotels and a shipping business before founding his own lordly estate on the Hawkesbury. At Lower Portland Head (now known as Wisemans Ferry), he built a large villa, two-storeyed, with wings and extensive outhouses. He called it Cobham Hall after the magnificent place in Kent he must once have seen.

When the travelling judge Roger Therry visited the enterprising Wiseman in 1830, he was half-amused at Wiseman's pride in his lack of education and manners, and his determination that his sons not be subjected to any spoiling from education, and yet, said Therry, Wiseman was earning £3000 to £4000 per year like a genuine aristocrat, just from government rationing contracts. For after the Great North Road had been marked out through his property, Wiseman had applied for a hotel licence, a ferry licence and for supply contracts. The government granted him everything he asked for, since he was so well placed to help. He was difficult to deal with and frequently dishonest, palming off inferior meat and supplies on the gangs.

To a great extent, young Warner was dependent on the co-operation of convict overseers and constables along his section of the road, all of them craftier and more capable of subtle brutalities than he was. He sweated within the uniform of his authority in the furious summer of 1827–28, and had a great problem supplying water to the gangs in the steep terrain through which the road was to be cut. He wrote a disgusted dispatch to the Colonial Secretary, Alexander Macleay, in Sydney in the sizzling days of February 1828, and complained that Wiseman allowed up to one hundred of his pigs at a time to roll in the brackish mud flats of the river and then rush off into a freshwater creek from which he was supposed to supply the gangs with water. He ordered his scourger, Joseph Anderson, to help prevent the stampede of pigs from salt mud to freshwater creek each day. Anderson himself, however, was a problem. Warner wanted him to work on a road gang in between scourging those who committed misdemeanours. Anderson argued that his only duty was to scourge, a task which generally only took him, as Warner complained, a half-hour's labour a week.

The overseers of the gangs along the hills rising out of the point on the Hawkesbury where Wiseman had settled were men whose savage authoritarianism pleased distantly placed officers, but which made them a target for those who had served under them. Henry Martineer, the overseer of Number 9 iron gang, wrote to the authorities asking that, since he now held a ticket-of-leave, he be moved somewhere away from the North Road, 'to any other part of the Department'. Otherwise he would have to resign as an overseer for fear of reprisal. He was not only frightened of convicts, but of crafty old Solomon Wiseman. Wiseman had demanded that Martineer sign off on a greater quantity of fresh meat than the gang required, and had threatened to take Martineer's horse and ride off to a magistrate and have his ticket-of-leave confiscated. Martineer's own superior, Percy Simpson, a free, fully qualified surveyor, had himself several times complained about Wiseman's illicit behaviour, but because the gangs on the North Road were so dependent on the old lag and his sons for supplies, for bringing troops and members of gangs across the Hawkesbury by ferry, and for the use of a number of barracks for soldiers and convicts, there was nothing that could be done.

Under Major Edmund Lockyer, chief surveyor, Percy Simpson was the day-to-day maker of the Great North Road. Simpson was a characteristic man of Empire, looking for a place in the devalued post Napoleonic war labour market for his amalgam of skills. He had been born in Canada, governed the Greek island of Paxos, and now been made superintendent of the road in this most difficult terrain. His gangs' side walls and stone bridges across deep gullies, his culverts and drainage systems, can still be encountered on the back road that was once the colony's chief way north.

Governor Darling had described the convicts in the road gangs as 'the refuse of the whole convict population'. Certainly they were twice convicted, but in unlucky cases the second sentence imposed on them might have derived from a magistrate who knew and dined with the convict's master. It might have also involved what a modern mind would think of as forgivable offences like drunkenness.

Even so, the members of road gangs had a reputation for being plunderers of remote homesteads in their spare time—they would climb up the chimneys of their huts at night to escape or go walking off on Sundays to steal spirits or food or clothing. Sometimes conniving overseers—convicts themselves, or ticket-of-leave men—were accused of being the chief organisers behind the thefts. The convict novelist, James Tucker, depicted overseers who encouraged or forced convicts to run away from the gangs. The overseer would then 'recapture' the convicts as they rested in the bush and receive the reward, which he had undertaken to share with the escapees. The further benefit to an escapee was that he would probably be locked up for a few days without having to work, prior to being flogged, and then may have had further rest while recovering before returning to the road gang. The chance of favouritism for some convicts, and bullying and brutality for others, was an obvious flaw in the system.

Each iron gang contained up to sixty men in irons and was supervised by a principal overseer and three assistants. Road parties, unchained, were made up of fifty men. But Lockyer established also bridge parties made up of twenty-five or more skilled men who in their life before transportation had been carpenters, stone-cutters or masons. These men were given better treatment and allowed more latitude. There were, by 1829, forty gangs spread over hundreds of kilometres working for Lockyer's Roads and Bridges Department; in 1830 ten of the gangs—up to six hundred men—toiled on the Great North Road.

Most of the gangs lived extremely roughly. The members of one gang in the Blue Mountains in the 1830s slept under one blanket each in temperatures that fell below freezing, often in huts too crowded for everyone to lie down. In these cramped quarters, the physical and sexual savageries between young and old, strong and infirm, comprise something over which the imagination might perhaps prefer to cast a veil. When the doors were unlocked in the morning and the men relieved themselves on the iced or frosted ground, they were offered rations which had frequently been fiddled by the overseers in collaboration with the supplier—the arrangement Wiseman was trying to establish with Martineer back on the Hawkesbury. And if Wiseman could frighten a ticket-of-leave overseer like Martineer, one might imagine his power over an ordinary member of the road gang.

Breakfast for the gangs was maize porridge with an ounce (c 28 grams) of sugar. The midday meal was a stew of one pound (454 grams) of fresh or salt meat with one and a half ounces of salt and damper or pudding made with one pound of flour. Part of the latter was to be kept for supper. During the summer months the overseers mustered their convicts at five o'clock in the morning, supervised their breakfast then marched them from their huts to the construction site. They returned to their station at twelve noon for dinner and marched back to work at one o'clock, remaining there until the evening meal at six. At 2 p.m. on Saturdays they were led to a pond or river to bathe and wash their clothing, made distinctive by the use of half yellow and half grey cloth. So marked, the convicts either radiated defiance or kept their heads lowered, knowing they were at least two sentences removed from even conditional freedom.

CONVICT NOVELISTS

Since commerce and the pastoral industry occupied the energies of literate males in early New South Wales and Van Diemen's Land, it fell to convicts to write the first Australian novels, melodramas which despite their exaggerated effects convey the authentic flavour of the time, and the reality of the degradation of the penal system.

The very first novelist was Henry Savery, a well-educated businessman aged thirty-three in April 1825, when he stood trial. Tom Savery, his father, was a Bristol banker. Henry was the sixth son, but considered himself the fifth because one of his brothers had died three days after birth. Hence, the 'Quintus' in the name of his fictional gentleman-convict Quintus Servinton, whose name is also the title of the novel. Savery spent his early manhood in London and married the daughter of a Blackfriars businessman. They moved back to Bristol where from 1817 he was in partnership in a sugar refining, or 'sugar baking', business. In economic difficulties, for a time he edited the *Bristol Observer*, but returned eventually to the sugar refinery. The *Times* reported Savery's arrest in December 1824. He had committed the firm beyond its resources without the knowledge of his partner and had been negotiating money bills for two years with fictitious names and addresses. These fraudulent bills, worth between £30 000 and £40 000, were commonly known as 'kites' and made Savery technically guilty of forgery.

When these irregularities turned up in Bristol, Savery fled to London with his mistress, for he had been panicked by the recent execution of the famous forger Henry Fauntleroy. His wife tracked him down, but he told her to 'Go back! Your route will be traced and my ruin will be effected.' Savery booked passage for the United States on the *Hudson*, soon to leave from Cowes. He seems to have used a variation of the name Servinton for this purpose, and is said to have been arrested only thirty minutes before the sailing hour. When the constables boarded, Savery threw himself into the sea, was rescued, and restrained. He was then put under constant watch because of his suicidal behaviour.

Four months later, in the spring of 1825, he pleaded guilty before Lord Gifford, and was condemned to death by the judge who donned the black cap. One of the prosecutors, seeing Savery struck witless by the sentence, pleaded with the judge for leniency. Savery spent a miserable few days in the death cell, but on the eve of his execution the sentence of death was commuted. He was transferred in July to Campbell's old *Justitia* hulk at Woolwich. From the hulk he joined the convict ship *Medway* which left Woolwich on 20 July 1825 for Shearness, where a young Presbyterian minister, John Dunmore Lang, came aboard. Lang wrote, 'A free passage by a convict ship in those days consisted merely of having an empty space of about six feet [1.8 metres] square in the "tween" decks, with bare walls and without furniture of any kind, together with a soldier's ration.' He found the captain, with whom he had contracted to dine for £70, a 'greedy, unconscionable Scotsman'. Lang, who was to become a political and social activist in New South Wales, probably conversed with Savery who had apparently travelled in separate accommodation from the convicts 'by order of Government'.

Half the convict population of *Medway* had to be sent to hospital on arriving in Hobart for treatment for scurvy. Savery himself was landed in prisoner's dress, his head closely shorn and conducted to the common gaol yard for inspection and assignment. Governor Arthur thought that Savery showed horror and remorse for his crimes. But he seems to have had a rugged ego as well. He worked as a clerk for the Colonial Secretary and then for the Colonial Treasury, receiving £18 per annum plus a ration. His early appointment to such pleasant posts drew attacks from enemies of Arthur, and criticism from the Home Secretary, Lord Goderich. There were also questions about why his forgiving wife was invited to join him, for in 1828 Mrs Savery embarked for Van Diemen's Land. Her original ship was grounded on the English coast near Falmouth, but she bravely tried once more and ultimately arrived in Hobart on the *Henry Wellesley*. But the voyage had provided her a chance for dalliance. On board she met and fell in love with the young Attorney-General of Van Diemen's Land, Algernon Montagu.

In his novel, Savery's (and Quintus Servinton's) admiration of honourable men of business is unstinting, for their standards were what both author and chief character so often aspired to but failed to achieve. Like Savery, Quintus is a sugar refiner. Soon after his marriage to a merchant's daughter from fashionable Bedford Square, Quintus begins to suffer from the fact that he is overstocked, having bought from other merchants just before the market declined. Quintus declares that 'improvident speculations in trade' are like a vice. Recovering, he finds his business burned down. Withdrawing to a rural retreat, Quintus makes the acquaintance of smugglers. 'Mr Carew informed him that one and all in the neighbourhood, rich and poor, gloried in outwitting the revenue officers.' Quintus's ongoing partnership in a troubled business becomes the subject of investigation for 'kites'—forged money bills—'flown' by the partner Mr Kitely. Kitely absconds. Quintus resolves thereafter to build his credit 'upon the shallow and deceitful quicksands of fictitious bills'.

When the date for a payment arrives, 'he provided himself . . . with a fictitious note for £500, the drawers and endorsers of which were creatures of his own brain, having no real existence'. Then Quintus reads in the evening newspaper a report that a particular forger of false bills has been ordered for execution on the following Tuesday. 'You surely do not mean, sir,' asks Quintus, 'it can be forgery to issue paper bearing the names of persons who never existed?' Caught himself, tried and condemned, Quintus Servinton receives many letters of support. Quintus travels to the hulks in a special compartment with a condemned former officer, who is not burdened with chains but is wearing 'a single basil'; that is, a single iron around his ankle. This was the arrangement in the Woolwich hulks, says Quintus, where ordinary soldiers and guards were willing to get people favours for money. Quintus Servinton pays to get an easy job on the shore (where the convicts are landed from the hulks to labour every day) as deputy supervisor of a gang. A doctor ultimately is 'sweetened' into giving him an exemption from labour, and sends him to the hospital ship. His mail is censored, but he is able to pass his letters to his wife, Emily, through the surgeon, a Scot, who appoints Quintus his secretary.

Quintus becomes the target of a faction amongst the convicts who complain to the Home Office about his preferential treatment (as happened with Savery in Hobart). After he is transported and becomes a very useful servant of a member of the colonial gentry, Mr Cressy, he becomes painfully aware that, 'It was a part of the pains and penalties attached to persons in this unfortunate situation, that although in matters of business they might be received, and treated with respect due to former station and conduct, the intercourse between themselves and the free inhabitants went, generally speaking, no further. Anything like familiarity, or approaching to sweet converse, was totally out of the equation.'

In the novel, the interloper in the wife's affection is Mr Alverney Malvers. But Savery depicted him as behaving in a manner admirable, reserved and courteous.

Once reunited with her true husband, the fictitious Emily resolves to return to England and extract a pardon. She succeeds, and it is a matter of poignancy that the novel ends as the tragic author hoped his own life would.

However, when Mrs Savery arrived in Tasmania she found that her husband had exaggerated his circumstances, and there was a great quarrel as a result of which Savery attempted suicide by cutting his throat. He had also been sued by creditors, and Mrs Savery's own possessions, brought out with her, were subject to the suit. Savery was imprisoned for debt in December 1828, and hardly three months after her arrival his exasperated wife left for England with her son on the *Sarah*, and Savery never saw her again. Later, after he received his ticket-of-leave, he would apply for her to be sent out again, but the lady did not reply.

Savery was in debtor's prison for fifteen months. In that time he wrote the non-fiction works *The Hermit of Van Diemen's Land, 30 Sketches of Hobart Life* and *Characters*. Early in 1830, he was released and assigned to Major McIntosh in the New Norfolk district, north-west of Hobart on the Derwent River. It was in the later months of his time with McIntosh that he wrote *Quintus Servinton*. Advertisements appeared in the *Hobart Town Courier* and in the *Tasmanian* in January 1831 to say that the book would soon be published in three volumes. Most copies, it was announced, were to be shipped to England and only a few reserved for sale in the colony. The *Hobart Town Courier* wrote of the book on 19 March 1831: 'though it cannot certainly claim the first rank among the many eminent works of a similar kind of the present day, it is very far from being discreditable to us as a first production of the kind in these remote regions'.

In June 1832, the Colonial Secretary was influenced by a number of petitioners to grant the novelist his ticket-of-leave. By then Henry Savery had become the assistant of Henry Melville at the *Tasmanian* newspaper. But under a general order which forbade convicts to write for newspapers, Savery was deprived of his ticket-of-leave for twelve months. He was suspected of having written a particular article about a police magistrate, but a free citizen journalist who had in fact written it came forward and admitted his authorship. But Savery was caught up in a fight between Governor Arthur and the magistrate. In the coming years he boldly took and was the subject of many litigations. He was not a quiet soul, but on the other hand he had the misfortune of being seen as a proxy for the governor, and thus an easy target. Above all, he could not avoid financial trouble and insolvency proceedings began against him in the late summer of 1838. By that time he had received his conditional pardon and took over a farm at Hestercombe near Hobart. The Board of Assignment disapproved of his leniency towards a convict servant and terminated his right to have one. He began to make up bills with fictitious signatures on the back, a new and complete act of forgery.

There was a story in the *Hobart Town Courier* that Savery had fled to Launceston, hoping to escape to Adelaide. But he was arrested in Hobart and in October 1838 was brought for trial before Algernon Montagu, the man who may have been his wife's lover. Montagu, reviewing Savery's career, declared, 'I will not, however, so far stultify myself as to suppose . . . reformation will be shown by you.' He transported Savery for life to the Tasman Peninsula (or Port Arthur).

Savery died there fifteen months later. His former editor, Henry Melville, declared that he had cut his own throat. A visitor to Port Arthur recorded that on 9 January 1840 he saw Savery in the hospital 'where we had a signal opportunity of drawing a wholesome moral from the sad—the miserable—consequences of crime. There, upon a stretcher, lay Henry Savery, the once celebrated Bristol sugar-baker—a man upon whose birth fortune smiled propitious.' The witness mentioned 'the scarce-healed wound of his attenuated throat . . . Knowing as I once did in Bristol, some of Savery's wealthy, dashing, gay associates, I could not contemplate the miserable felon before me without sentiments of the deepest compassion mingled with horror and awe.'

The other early convict novelist was the author of a manuscript that came out of the Port Macquarie Literary Club, an officially condoned gathering made up largely of educated convicts, from the time when Port Macquarie, north of Port Stephens on the New South Wales coast, served as a station for relatively educated, though fallen, gentlemen. James Tucker was born in Bristol early in the nineteenth century and attended Stonyhurst Jesuit College from 1814. Later he worked on a farm owned by a relative of the same name until a disagreement over the planting of peas led to a split. James Tucker the younger, who had received £5 from his cousin, threatened him with a charge of unnatural crime unless he should pay another £5. His relative put a Bow Street runner on James's track, and he was arrested and brought to the Essex Assizes charged 'with feloniously knowingly and willingly sending a certain letter . . . threatening to accuse James Stanyford Tucker with indecently assaulting him'. Young James Tucker thus received, as improbably as it sounds to the modern ear, a life sentence, and arrived aboard the transport *Midas* in Port Jackson in 1827. In March 1827, Tucker was sent to the Emu Plains agricultural establishment, at the foot of the Blue Mountains, a place which, though dealt with melodramatically in his novel, clearly appalled him with the chicanery and brutality of its convict overseers and constables. In the novel, *Ralph Rashleigh*, he depicts a scene where at the magistrates court awaiting punishment:

> there were a great many men—as usual, from Emu Plains—brought up to answer various charges of insolence to overseers and the majority had already been tried and sentenced to receive various amounts of corporal punishment, from seventy-five to one hundred lashes being the general proportion of the sentences ... One man came out of the presence of the awful conclave of magistrates wearing a countenance radiant with smiles. He declared, 'Oh, I've nobbed it. I've got life to Newcastle.'

Though Newcastle itself was a terrible place, the man delighted in the fact that he was getting away from Emu Plains.

It is very likely that Tucker worked in a road party in 1830–31. There is an intimacy to his knowledge of life on a chain gang in the novel. 'The overseer would next say to him, "Why the devil don't you *bolt* [run away]? I'll give you some grub to get rid of you"; and the poor fellow, willing to earn a few days rest from labour by a sound flogging, would at last agree to abscond.' Three days had to elapse before the reward became available, and then the overseer would meet the absconder in the agreed place and 'bring his prisoner before the magistrates, magnifying his exertions, of course, in making this capture'.

Occasionally, contact with Currency girls, in this case the female children of Irish convicts, refreshed Rashleigh, and perhaps Tucker himself.

> There was no affected squirmishness or reserve among these unsophisticated children of nature ... Their clothing was certainly simple enough, each and all wearing only a kind of pinafore or smock frock reaching from the neck to the ankle and made of very coarse osnaburg, but kept as clean and whole as the nature of their employment allowed. Besides this single garment, each youngster was equipped with a coarse straw hat, but of shoes they had none among them, for probably like nearly all Australian children, they looked on them as useless encumbrances.

They slept on bags filled with corn husks, lacked sheets, and were afflicted, as the Irish said, by 'flaas'. They smoked clay pipes, *dudeens*, as convict women also did. The idea of taking one of these half-wild, possum-hunting, goanna-clubbing girls to wife was not unattractive to Ralph Rashleigh.

By 1833 Tucker had found congenial employment as a government messenger in the Colonial Architect's office in Sydney. In 1837 he was made an overseer himself, in charge of a work gang in the Domain in Sydney. An educated eccentric convict, by being who he was he attracted the attention of meaner men in positions of authority. The severe terms of his ticket-of-leave prohibited drunkenness, but many ticket-of-leavers were habitually guilty of it. However, in September 1839, Tucker lost his ticket temporarily and spent a fortnight at the treadmill at Parramatta for drunkenness. But he received it back again for his part in fighting a fire at the Royal Hotel.

Tucker's ticket-of-leave was—as some but not all were—made out for Maitland in the Hunter Valley. While there he used to creep into Newcastle to meet his friend Alexander Burnett, an educated convict overseer who had taken part in all the Surveyor-General, Major Mitchell's, explorations. From his experience in the Maitland district, Tucker was able to get material for a later play, a comedy entitled *Jemmy Green in Australia*. In 1842, however, he became involved in a not unusual scam, one not utterly removed from fictional creativity. He forged letters purporting to tell two ticket-of-leave holders that their wives in England had died, letters for which he was possibly paid and which would enable the men to remarry.

For his punishment, he was re-sentenced and sent as a class of trusty named a 'special' to Port Macquarie. Port Macquarie, then in its decline as a convict settlement, provided a pleasant interlude in his life. Physically, it was beautiful and temperate, a place of lagoons and floodplains cupped between the Pacific and the mountains of the hinterland. He worked as storekeeper to the superintendent, Police Magistrate Partridge, who encouraged his writing. Old lags at Port Macquarie would later tell what an amusing fellow Jimmy Tucker was. *Jemmy Green in Australia* had its premiere performance there in the barn-theatre named Old Tumbledown. Amongst others of his plays performed there, but now lost, the old lags remembered *Makin' Money*, a satire of the Rum Corps era, and *Who Built That Cosy Cottage?*

When Port Macquarie penal settlement was broken up in 1847, Tucker, by then middle-aged, was granted another ticket-of-leave and stayed on in that port as a clerk and storeman for general merchants. He lodged at the house of

Tom and Sarah Widderson, both ex-convicts and teamsters who used to take stores by bullock wagon from the coast to the New England plateau beyond.

While lodging with them, Tucker wrote two other novels, *Fearless Frederick Fraser* and *The Life of Mary Nayler*, about the lives of male and female convicts at Port Macquarie, neither of which have been found. When he left Port Macquarie surreptitiously in 1849, he left the manuscripts with the Widdersons, in whose care they disappeared or perished. The old lags at Port Macquarie would later say that Tucker cleared out in 1849 to look for gold, but he was found, arrested, convicted and sent to prison at Goulburn, south-west of Sydney. Early in 1850 he again received a ticket-of-leave, but was continuously under supervision by police spies and was ultimately brought to court on a charge of stealing a watch.

The police were unable to prove their point and his ticket was renewed in 1853, this time for Moreton Bay. He was approaching old age, exhausted in his endeavours, and very conscious that the stain of being a convict would never allow him to be left in peace. His adventures in the Brisbane area are not known, but he next appeared as a patient in the Liverpool asylum, near Sydney, where he died from 'decay of nature' in 1866. His novel presciently exhorts us at the end, on behalf of its eponymous hero Ralph Rashleigh: 'Reader, the corpse of the exile slumbers in peace on the banks of the Barwon far from his native land. Let us hope that his sufferings and untimely death, alas, have expiated the errors of his early years.'

CHAPTER 14*

ARRIVING AT THE END OF THINGS

A convict arriving in Sydney or Hobart in the early to mid 1830s encountered prosperous-looking communities where women and men of wealth and property dressed in the best fashion of two British seasons past. The town of Sydney to which the 220 Irish convicts of the *Parmelia* were introduced in March 1834 as they marched from the landing stage to the main depot, ran raffishly inland along gentle hills either side of Sydney Cove. The settlement retained the narrow streets of the original convict camp of the late 1780s. Most houses were cottages with little gardens in front, and such structures clung in random clusters to the sandstone ledges of the Rocks on the western side of the cove. But they took on a more ornate, orderly character in the streets—Pitt, Macquarie—towards the eastern side of town. The landed prisoners heard the cat-calls of old lags as they staggered on unsteady land-legs uptown past St Phillip's Church on its hill, past the Colonial Treasury, the Barrack Square, and saw the town's theatre on the left. The barracks and the offices of government were built of Sydney's honey-coloured sandstone, the most splendid structures of this eccentric seaport.

The town abounded with 'canaries', convicts in government employ, in sallow-coloured jackets and pants, and free dungaree men, poor settlers and occasional tradesmen, who wore cheap blue cotton imported from India. The lean, dishevelled children of convicts, cornstalks or Currency urchins, ran wild,

---

*   Some of the material from this section derives from the author's earlier *The Great Shame*.

grown healthy by the standards of Europe on colonial corn doughboys, salt beef, fresh mutton and vegetables. Convict women on ticket-of-leave stood in gardens or outside public houses smoking Brazil twist in *dudeens*, clay pipes barely two inches long. Laggers, or ticket-of-leave men, wore blue jackets or short woollen blue smocks, and the hats of both convict and free were unorthodox, some of plaited cabbage-tree fronds, some of kangaroo skin. Soldiers and police were much in evidence in front of Customs House, Commissariat Office, Treasury, the post office, and all other government offices. But side by side with this martial formality, male and female sexual services were full-throatedly offered in a manner polite visitors said was more scandalous than in the East End of London. 'A Wapping or St Giles in the beauties of a Richmond,' as one Englishman described Sydney. The abnormal imbalance between male and female gave the flesh trade an added fever, as did dram-drinking—the downing of Bengal rum out of wine glasses.

There was a huge gulf of urbanity and learning between the *Parmelia* men and their fellow Irishman Sir Richard Bourke, whose Government House and stables the line of felons from *Parmelia* passed. Bourke was an improver, though never a radical. He was considered by the Exclusives, the free settlers who wanted to keep the convict class down, to be dangerously soft on serving convicts. He had reduced the power of magistrates in remote areas of the colony to inflict punishment on convict servants. Property owners were always reporting in their paper, the *Sydney Herald*, the organ of the respectable townspeople and the free, as proof of Bourke's 'soothing system for convicts', the impudence and unruliness of their servants and labourers.

Irish convicts were still seen as both very dangerous—most of the mutineers on Norfolk Island recently had been Irish—but also as comically incompetent and unruly. The day after *Parmelia* arrived, the *Sydney Herald* had carried a characteristic tale characteristically told. 'Eliza Burns, a native of Hibernia, favourites whiskey and potatoes, whispered to the bar, that . . . she did on Friday last, in Castlereagh-street, commit an assault with a pair of tongs of some value on the person of Mrs Griffiths. Mrs Griffiths . . . said that the defendant on Friday last, *sans* provocation, threw some water on her, and fetching a pair of tongs from her house, threatened to lay hold of that useful portion of the face, vulgarly termed a proboscis, or smeller.' Mrs Griffith objected that she would 'be deprived of the only pleasure, (except a drop of the cratur occasionally) which rendered life desirable, namely that of the taking of sundry quantities of snuff'.

Just the same, the comfort in all this for the *Parmelia* men marching to the barracks was that they would find plenty of their compatriots, bond and free, ashore, amongst the upwards of thirty thousand prisoners then in Sydney and the bush. Added to this number and still bearing the stigma of former imprisonment were the time-served and pardoned emancipists, who also numbered as many as thirty thousand.

It would be wrong to omit the final buildings *Parmelia*'s felons passed that day. They were the School of Industry and the General Hospital, called familiarly the Rum Hospital. On one edge of the dusty green named Hyde Park lay St James's Church and the courthouse, both splendidly designed by the convict architect from Bristol, Francis Greenway. Across from St James's were the outbuildings and chief barracks of Sydney's convict depot, Hyde Park Barracks.

The superintendent of the Hyde Park Barracks at the time the *Parmelia* prisoners arrived was a young, recently retired military officer of the 40th Regiment, EA Slade. By the time the *Parmelia* men marched into Slade's barracks, the superintendent was an enemy of any program of leniency, and so an enemy of Governor Bourke. Bourke would soon remove him from the magistracy for having abducted a young immigrant woman ashore and for living illicitly with her. Though thought a libertine in his personal life, he was an exacting official with convicts, taking pains to ensure that lashes at the barracks were properly given, and highly motivated to curtail sodomy. He would report three years later, in London before the Select Committee on Transportation, 'When I had the lash inflicted, I never saw a case where I did not break the skin in four lashes.' He was proud to declare that he had standardised the cats used for lashings throughout New South Wales.

The disembarked *Parmelia* men are interesting because they contained amongst their number sixty-two men guilty of so-called Ribbon offences, acts of peasant grievance in a landscape where landlords and middling farmers were under economic pressure and the peasantry burdened by rents and fear of the loss of their small holdings on which their potato crops grew and their existence depended. The 'Terry Alts corps' (a name adopted by some peasant underground groups to honour a County Clare shoemaker falsely arrested for an attack on a landlord), and the Ribbonmen (so-called for an irregular practice of identifying each other by wearing ribbons), were secret societies of cottiers and small farmers, uncentralised but not unorganised, designed to protect, by direct action, small tenants from (amongst other things) unfair rents and the eviction of peasants and small farmers from their land.

The Tory government of Great Britain had in 1829 been persuaded by the Irish Party, led by Daniel O'Connell, 'the Liberator, the King of the Beggars', to pass the Act of Emancipation, thereby granting political and religious rights to Catholics and lifting the oppressive net of acts called the penal laws. Now Catholics could hold office, become majors, magistrates, officers in the army, members of the judiciary and of Parliament. During the Emancipation struggle, which Hugh Larkin well remembered, a peasant could belong to the Catholic Association, the organisational structure behind Emancipation, by contributing one penny a month. Outside Clontuskert parish chapel after Mass on the first Sunday of the month, Hugh's parents, like his wife Esther Tully's, had in the 1820s donated their minimum penny—'the Catholic tax' it was named. After Emancipation, people were persuaded to keep up the payments towards the Liberator's upkeep as a parliamentarian—the 'Repeal tax', aimed at bringing about the repeal of the union between Britain and Ireland by parliamentary means. When that happened, ordinary people believed, unjust rents would be swept away, tenants would have fixity of tenure, Irish spinning and weaving would be protected and encouraged, the narrow franchise would be expanded, the secret ballot would be introduced to prevent landlords terrorising their tenant voters, and Irish landlords would be taxed to support the poor.

These political objectives were ones the Irish, free and bond, would bring to Australia to blend with the Chartism and other British democratic yearnings borne to Australia by a quotient of English political prisoners and progressive settlers. But despite Emancipation, the physical situation for millions of Irish remained appalling, and the voting system disenfranchised them. And regional juries, made up of landowners, abhorred turbulence amongst their peasantry and punished it harshly.

The Galway Free Press reported, as a minor item in the tapestry of conflict between small tenants and large land-holders, that on 9 March 1832 a threatening notice had been pinned on the door of a Mr Simeon Seymour of Somerset House in East Galway, 'stating that unless he complied with the Terry Alt rules and regulations, in raising wages and lowering the rent of lands, that he would meet an untimely fate'.

The 1837 Report on the Poor of Ireland estimated that even with the little rented plots called 'conacre' there were two and a half million persons in Ireland who were in a state of semi-starvation every summer as, the seedlings planted, whole families waited for the new potato crop to appear at the end of the season. Conacre was generally a little plot of an eighth of an acre (0.05 of a hectare), although sometimes as extensive as two acres. It was rented for one season to grow potatoes, or sometimes, oats. Conacre (as well as paid labour, and perhaps an item of livestock such as a pig) was essential for the hungry transit from spring to autumn. These little plots were the only hope of the men who posted the threatening notice at Somerset House. Since they could seek from neither court nor landlord help in adjusting the balance of the world, they turned to secret companies of men of similar mind to themselves.

To administer a Ribbon oath or to take one was an offence meriting seven years transportation; the posting of such a notice as the one quoted above— as with similar notices posted by peasant and political societies in England— could earn you fourteen years transportation. There were two steps left in the Ribbonman's roster of options. The next one was to 'assault habitation'. The last was to shoot the landlord dead.

The young Hugh Larkin was driven—with others—by peasant rage and a fear that he, his wife Esther, and his two sons, if thrown off their quarter-acre (0.1 of a hectare) lot, would become *spalpeens*, 'penny-scythes', that is, summer day-labourers, or else outright beggars. At Mr Simeon Seymour's Somerset House one evening in the spring or early summer of 1833, Larkin was a leading figure of a Ribbon group who, bearing arms stolen or acquired, knocked a door down and uttered threats. This was Assaulting Habitation, and it had a statutory life sentence attached. Tracked down the next day and sent to the Galway Assizes, Larkin had other young Galway Ribbonmen for company in the county jail—one John Hessian, two brothers named Strahane. They were all sentenced at Assizes along with Larkin. The court in Galway was far from his native parish of Clontuskert, East Galway, and so we do not know if his no-doubt distraught young wife had the economic resources even to get to Galway city for the trial, which ended with a life sentence of transportation for Hugh.

Larkin, Hessian and others were fortunate in being men accustomed to management of sheep. So—at the end of *Parmelia*'s voyage from Cork—Irish peasant discontent would be pressed into the service of Australian pastoral ambition. Their penal lives would be spent minding sheep in the great stupor of the Australian bush. Such men were often favoured over thieves when it came to employment in New South Wales.

BEYOND THE LIMITS

The original Nineteen Counties in eastern New South Wales, to which a twentieth north of Port Macquarie had been added, were designed to be the region where government operated and within which land could be alienated, acquired and sold legally. It was considered that this region, three times the size of Wales and containing five million desirable acres, was sufficient for the needs of the colonists. Two hundred and fifty miles (402 km) long at the coast, it ran inland to a depth of one hundred and fifty miles (241 km), where the Lachlan River provided its western boundary. As one commentator said, 'The Nineteen Counties, to all intents and purposes, meant Australia, and the government decreed that they should be viewed as if the sea flowed all around, and not merely to the east.' The borders of this region were named the Limits of Location.

But many of the settlers who employed convict stockmen and shepherds and who owned land within the Limits were very quickly attracted to occupy the great natural pasturage beyond them, and so many of the Ribbonmen of *Parmelia* and many other convicts as well found themselves hundreds of miles out in the hinterland, many days ride away from any magistrate, minding sheep on pasturage which, according to British law, belonged to the Crown and to which they had no right. It was inevitable that men should have settled themselves or their flocks on pasture-lands discovered by explorers beyond the Limits of Location, but they were technically squatters and that was the name given to them. Squatting on land beyond the Limits of Location had begun with absconders, cattle-duffers and sheep-thieves. When the Macarthurs, Wentworths and Bradleys began to invest in the huge unalienated pastures beyond as well as to live the lives of princes within the relative urbanity of the Limits, the power of the squatter became so great that his interests negated the irritation of the British government and began to dominate all other political interests.

The Ribbonman John Hessian was assigned to a landowner/doctor at Broulee near Bathurst, and Larkin was assigned to Goulburn, within the Limits of Location, to a young Currency landowner named William Bradley, the rich and enterprising son of a New South Wales Corps sergeant. Bradley owned land and a brewery and mill at Goulburn, and was also running sheep beyond the Limits to the south-west of Goulburn, in the area known as Monaro. William Bradley took up land in the Monaro in 1834 and though according to the official documents Hugh Larkin was assigned to Goulburn, in fact he would at some stage be sent to work on Bradley's squatted-upon land far to the south-west.

Bradley's own holdings would be greatly increased when other pastoralists had to give up their land in a coming depression in the 1840s. He would also become a member of the Legislative Council of New South Wales when it became part-elected, and worked within it to have the system of squatting legitimised by the home government and by the colonial authority (both of which abominated it but ultimately gave in). His sheep and cattle runs in the Monaro would come to total 270 000 acres (1092 km²). He saw his squatting career as part of the same spirit of progress which moved him to become a promoter and investor in the first Australian railway, Sydney to Parramatta, and to finance the survey for a railway line to Goulburn. Such was the potential wealth derived from the raising of sheep and the export of wool on squatted land, and such was the social respectability of the practice that the daughters of this son of a Rum Corps NCO married into reputable British military and vice-regal families.

As one of fifty men Bradley employed to work under an overseer on his Monaro properties, Larkin exchanged convict clothing for the standard bush uniform supplied by masters—leg-strapped trousers, blue Crimean shirts, and a cabbage-tree hat of plaited leaves. A few kangaroos provided material for a warm coat. Larkin no doubt began as a shepherd, but if he were a good horseman, he would wear Hessian-style boots and spurs for rounding up live-stock on horseback. Mustering stray cattle, riding up escarpments through the great verticals of eucalyptus trees, and armed against attacks from natives, the Ribbonman might have been mistaken for the master.

One of Bradley's protégés in the Monaro area would be a young man the same age as Hugh Larkin, William Adams Brodribb. Brodribb's father had been the young English solicitor mentioned earlier who had administered an oath and acted as counsel to the Berkeley Castle poachers. Brodribb senior had finished out his sentence as a ticket-of-leave attorney in Hobart, and now had become both a farmer and a shareholder in the Bank of Van Diemen's Land.

The younger Brodribb, arriving in Van Diemen's Land as a child in 1818, grew up in respectable Anglo-Scots colonial society, in which the family did its best to forget Brodribb senior's foray into secret oaths. Brodribb the younger arrived purposefully in New South Wales in 1835, when Larkin had been working for Bradley for a year. 'In those days,' Brodribb would remember, 'it was no unusual thing for a squatter to claim 200 or 300 square miles [518 or 777 km²]; land was no object; there was plenty for new squatters'. One stockman tending flocks in a hut in Monaro promised to show Brodribb 'a good cattle station, unoccupied, not far from his master's station, provided I should thereafter feel disposed to settle in that squatting district'. Brodribb's run lay in a deep corner of the Monaro, in a plain made bare perhaps by the firestick hunting methods of the natives who came there in summer. Wooded hills and snow-streaked alps rose above the pastures. Some years later Brodribb stated that in his first year in the Monaro, with a convict shepherd, very probably Larkin, and 'the assistance of a few Aborigines, I washed and sheared my 1200 ewes'. Here the wool press was primitive. Brodribb confessed, '. . . my hut-keeper pressed the wool with a spade, in a rough primitive box made by ourselves on the station'.

He would take cattle and sheep across the Australian Alps to Melbourne and stake out a run near present-day Benalla in Victoria, during which time, by informal arrangement with Bradley, Hugh Larkin worked for him and may have made the huge droving journey under his management. As well as managing his own run Brodribb also managed other squatters' runs, and when the wool price slumped in the early 1840s, he became the manager of Bradley's Monaro operations from 1843 onwards, headquartered—as was Hugh—at Coolrindong Station near present-day Cooma. Ultimately he would move west along the Murrumbidgee and take up land at Deniliquin.

The business of running sheep and cattle on immense and remote pastures obviously fascinated him—he tried to develop a sheep unloading port in Gippsland, Port Albert, and he dealt cheerfully both with remoteness, coarse living under a bark roof, and, until 1844, when he married, celibacy. He too, like Bradley, had no doubts either about the decency or morality of occupying and living on land that at the start of his New South Wales career was considered by two significant parties—the natives and the government—to be an illicit occupation.

After the settlers' runs were given some legitimacy, flamboyantly dressed officials named Commissioners of Crown Lands rode out in green uniforms, hessian boots and braided caps, trailing a few mounted police behind them through the mists or heat hazes, to decide where Bradley's and Brodribb's properties and grazing rights began and ended, and similarly where someone else's began and ended. Boundary lines were drawn with the same informality— natural springs, an Aboriginal tumulus of stone, tree-blazes, ant heaps, and isolated she-oaks all served as markers. Settlers were to pay £10 for every twenty square miles (51.8 km²) of country they occupied, and on top of that a halfpenny for each sheep.

Hugh Larkin, distracted by labour, distance and adequate diet from any clear impulse of rebellion, probably had his journeys too. When the wool had been loaded on its wagon in late spring, that is, October–November, a settler like Brodribb would start out with a reliable man to bring the load overland to Goulburn. From there they would ease it up the Razorback mountain range and down through endless hills to the place called the Black Huts on the Liverpool Road, where Sydney wool buyers posted themselves waiting to buy. In good years, buyers would advance far up the road towards Goulburn on fast ponies. The buyer would cut a slash in an ordinary bale, take out a handful of wool, hoping he had picked a representative sample, and make a bid. These were primitive but significant dealings, for on them colonial prosperity depended. What slave cotton was to the American South, convict wool would be to Australia. The mills of Britain had an illimitable hunger for both.

There were a number of hostelries in the area where the roads from both Sydney and Parramatta met—the Farmer's Home, the Square and Compass, the Woolpack and Old Jack Ireland's—at which the squatters and dealers argued and struck a price, while the Larkins of the system went amongst the wagons looking for someone shipped more recently than them, to hear news of their most distressful country. The wool from the Monaro, bought at the Black Huts, would be taken on to Sydney by the dealer, be shipped to London and turn up at Garraway's Coffee House in Change Alley, Cornhill, where by the light of guttering candles early Australian fibre drew bids based on an unprecedented enthusiasm.

Could Larkin, or men of his ilk, ultimately hope—under ticket-of-leave or conditional pardon—to become graziers and land-holders themselves? Could the Ribbonman be transmuted into an Australian landlord? To establish a station, capital was needed, £5000 for a well-balanced flock, wagon and convict shepherds. But some determined former convicts, starting with small flocks, managed to become the living exemplars for the character Magwitch, the English convict who left his fortune to Pip, in Charles Dickens's novel of 1861, *Great Expectations*.

The Irish convicts cherished the case of Ned Ryan, a Ribbonman who twenty years before had been found guilty of Assaulting Habitation at Ballagh, Tipperary. He had got his conditional pardon in 1830, settled land near the present town of

Boorowa, beyond the Lachlan River north-west of Goulburn, and in time built a house named Galong Castle and was re-united with his wife and three children, one of whom would serve in the Legislative Assembly of New South Wales! The Etonian, classicist squatter might find that his neighbouring pastoralist was a former sheep thief from Ireland or Scotland, or even a former denier of the British system like Ned Ryan. Though rare, the convict who returned home rich, like Orpheus ascending from Hades, would become one of the stock figures of popular literature.

In the winter and early summer of 1837, inadequate snow fell on the Australian Alps above the Monaro to fill the rivers. This was Hugh's first experience of that recurrent but assured Australian phenomenon, drought, the most severe until then experienced by Europeans. There would be five to six such years of blazing suns and poor rainfall. The Murrumbidgee River dried up. Hugh and other convict stockmen had horse races in the dry bed. At night, he would rise in stifling air to see huge walls of flame moving down the wooded slopes, set off by lightning or an Aboriginal hunting fire. Hugh Larkin's Australian education was proceeding apace, and heat and fire annealed him further to this inescapable landscape.

MEETING THE SEASONAL PEOPLE

For the convict shepherd and the night-watchman, as for the stockman riding out from the central station, the day came when the natives appeared out of the screen of forest, old men and warriors ahead, women and children behind, to hold discourse and perhaps to trade. The convict knew these people speared sheep, and if a shepherd objected too strongly, as he was duty-bound to (loss of livestock would show up on his record), they might kill him with spears or a blow to the back of the head with one of the hardwood clubs or stone axes they used to finish off kangaroos.

Convict shepherds and drovers watched them closely, and noticed their womenfolk and their possessions. The young native men of the Monaro in fact carried a variety of purpose-designed hunting spears and two designs of the stunning and felling boomerang. The women carried their dilli bags and finely wrought nets of kurrajong fibre for catching the large, edible bogong moths of the area.

The Ngarigo had occupied for millennia this side of the Australian Alps between the Murrumbidgee and the Snowy rivers. They had ritual and marriage relationships with people named the Walgalu and the Ngunawal to the north, towards present-day Canberra, and with the Bidawal to the south. They encountered in summer the Djila Matang from the western side of the alps, and traded for shells with the coastal Djiringanj to the east. Virtually until the year Hugh arrived in the Monaro, these had been the borders of their feasible world.

They wintered in the milder but still brisk northern Monaro, but came south to the higher Monaro in spring, to feast on the nutty, protein-rich bogong moth, *Agrotis infusa*, 'animated fat-bags' which settle inches deep on trees and in rock crevices to breed. It was in the time of the bogong that Brodribb's and Bradley's men met them. It is possible that Hugh, and certain that other convicts, living on a womanless cusp of earth, made arrangements for the use of an Aboriginal woman. One commentator spoke of 'black women cohabiting with the knowledge and consent of their sable husbands, in all parts of the interior, with white hut-keepers'. But occasional spearings showed that such relationships were not always acceptable to the elders.

The liaison between the Irish convict shepherd and the 'dusky maid' was a fantasy commemorated in a song named 'The Convict and His Loubra':

> *Thy father is a chieftain!*
> *Why that's the very thing!*
> *Within my native country*
> *I too have been a king . . .*
> *You heard, love, of the judges?*
> *They drove me from my throne . . .*
> *The bush is now my empire,*
> *The knife my sceptre keen;*
> *Come with me to the desert wild,*
> *And be my dusky queen . . .*

Aboriginal monogamy was based on blood laws, and was as strict as European morality, and in terms of legal sanction stricter. But the white convict shepherd lay outside the bloodlines and so outside the moral universe of the natives. He was often a contact neither forbidden nor approved; he was a chimera to the Ngarigo as Phillip's men had been to the Eora. Yet, said an observer, 'I am told it is no uncommon thing for these rascals to sleep all night with a lubra . . . and if she poxes him or in any way offends him perhaps shoot her before 12 next day . . .'

In protecting his master's livestock, the shepherd would eventually instigate or witness the collision between European and native, the explosion of the relationship into spear-throwing on one side, the firing of carbines on the other. There were policies designed by anxious governors to protect the natives. After Governor Bourke went home in 1837, the new man Sir George Gipps, an administratively gifted soldier, would appoint Protectors of Aborigines, usually Anglican clergymen, to patrol a remote district and save the native people therein from molestation. These men often came to Australia in answer to an advertisement in the *Church Times*, and believed they would live with their wives and children in a colonial manse amongst other white-robed natives. Instead they were given a dray and dispatched into the interior. Hugh saw one such man moving bewildered through Bradley's and Brodribb's holdings. Like his secular brethren, the Protector found the nomadic quality of Aboriginal life an affront, and tried to keep Aboriginal people near his hut by supplying them with flour, sugar, tea, tobacco.

In 1842 the system of protectors would be abandoned, but the squatters complained that Governor Gipps himself acted as a Supreme Protector who generally blamed problems of violence on settlers and their shepherds, and his efforts in that regard, particularly his prosecution of those stockmen who shot and burned twenty-eight natives at Myall Creek, hundreds of kilometres north-west of Sydney, will be dealt with later in this narrative. Squatters blamed Gipps and not themselves for the seven or eight years of frontier terror and warfare between 1837 and 1845—all without their admitting that the terror cut both ways. The natives would kill whites, one of them complained, 'for no reason at all save their isolation!' Hugh, other Ribbonmen and convicts, saw themselves as possible victims in a sporadic war for which they had not volunteered.

As for Larkin, he survived and having applied unsuccessfully to have his wife and children sent to join him in Australia, after his conditional pardon in 1848 he would marry a young Irish convicted shoplifter from the Parramatta Female Factory, Mary Shields, assigned to Coolringdon as a servant, with whom he would have five children.

CHAPTER 15

THE HEADY BUSINESS OF EXPLORING

Official European exploration in some cases is said to have followed acts of secret penetration and settlement of the interior. But wherever it reported halfway favourable grazing grounds, it was inevitable speculators would avail themselves of these wild pastures.

When the report of the 1813 crossing of the Blue Mountains by Gregory Blaxland, William Wentworth and William Lawson came to Governor Macquarie, he sent his assistant surveyor, George Evans, to follow their tracks and extend them.

Evans did not merely look down upon what Wentworth called 'the boundless champagne', he descended by steep defiles into it, and found grass intermingled with white daisies, 'as in England'. This was a matter of previously unimaginable delight for a man like Evans, to be Adam-in-chief in a new Eden, to enter the untouched Canaan. 'A kangaroo can be procured at any time, also emus. There is game in abundance.' Evans encountered a river running very strongly as he pushed west beyond the present site of Bathurst. He called it the Macquarie, and a lesser stream the Lachlan.

These gestures of fealty to the Scots chieftain back in Sydney did not ensure Evans supremacy. He was passed over, as not quite an educated gentleman, and made second-in-command for the next excursion westwards led by the urbane naval lieutenant John Oxley, who wanted to marry young Elizabeth Macarthur and was considered by her irascible father a far better prospect than Wentworth had been. He established his depot on the Lachlan River to the south of the Macquarie. The large conundrum of Australian exploration had been established. Where did these westward flowing rivers end up? Could it be that they emptied into an inland sea?

The Lachlan became a vast marsh Oxley could not penetrate, even though he believed it to be the edge of the envisaged sea. So he headed north and tried the Macquarie and again was defeated by marshes. Struggling back to the coast, Oxley found rich country which he named the Liverpool Plains, and found a way through the massive cliffs of the Dividing Range to the coast itself. Evans was always at Oxley's side, and in this excursion one sees something that would become a feature of Australian expeditions: the leaders leaving behind horses and men, the latter wondering why they volunteered, malnourished and in a stupor of exhaustion, while a few brave souls tried to find a way out, reach a depot, a waterhole, a remote station or a settlement.

A vigorous though authoritarian surgeon, magistrate and farmer named Charles Throsby, and a Parramatta-born bushman named Hamilton Hume, forcing their way south from Sydney through coastal gorges, came into the Kangaroo Valley, and Macquarie then sent Throsby south-west to find more pasture and open up the plains which had been named after Undersecretary Goulburn. The natives of the Goulburn Plains told Throsby of a great lake and of a river named Murrumbidgee (meaning 'big water'), lying far to the south beyond the lake. Throsby discovered the lake in 1820 and called it George (what else?), and at last found the under-strength Murrumbidgee, reduced by seasonal drought.

A few years later, Allan Cunningham, a botanist who had worked in Brazil on the orders of Sir Joseph Banks, and had now been sent by Banks to investigate the country beyond the mountains in New South Wales and Van Diemen's Land, was ultimately dispatched by Governor Brisbane, first of all to find an easy way into the Liverpool Plains, which he managed to do but not to the governor's satisfaction, and then to look to the far north—to Moreton Bay and the Darling Downs to its west, whose lusciousness as pasture and farming ground pleased all parties.

The young Australian-born bushman, Hamilton Hume, had now squatted at Lake George—to be a squatter one had not only to have some capital but also to be born at a fortuitous time, and to be on site, if not before the official discoverers, then following their fresh wagon tracks. Governor Brisbane soon devised an expedition for him; he decided that one of the ways to find new grazing and a way through the challenging mountain ramparts would be to maroon a gang of convicts on the far northern coast under Hume's supervision and have them work their way south to Sydney. The 27-year-old Hume, who knew well the difficulties of New South Wales terrain and, indeed, of intervening tribes, explained the impossibility of such a project to the governor and refused the job, and fortunately for convict lives the project never went ahead. In any case Hume did not wish to explore northwards. He wanted to go south-west from his Lake George homestead. Brisbane declared that Spencer's Gulf in present-day South Australia should be the target of such a journey. Hume disagreed with him and wanted to end the journey in the Port Phillip area. Hume was supported by William Hovell, an English settler at Narellan, to the south-west of Sydney, who agreed to put in resources and money and to accompany Hume as long as he was acknowledged equal leader. Hovell was a former mariner, and had worked for many years as a master for Simeon Lord. He was a robust and determined man and had navigational skills.

For Hume's part, he sold some of his farming effects to raise his side of the money, and Brisbane at last gave some equipment. Hume and Hovell took with them six convict servants on the promise of freedom, one of them a noted bare-knuckle boxer, Claude Bossawa. Their aim was to reach Westernport on Bass Strait, where in 1804 David Collins had briefly made a settlement for Governor King, before abandoning it and shipping everyone to Van Diemen's Land and the site of Hobart.

To the south of the plains of 'Canberry', they found the Murrumbidgee River in full rage, but Hume and a convict named Thomas Boyd swam it, creating a ferry rope with which they could tow stores, men and animals across. They could see the snow-streaked Australian Alps but steered away south over scrawny hills which gave onto excellent grass, and natural lagoons full of fish and fowl.

Hovell and Hume had soon begun quarrelling, Hume being contemptuous of Hovell's navigational capacities. It was a conflict between British technical skill and raw Currency bush-lore. Bickering away, they encountered all that one would expect: grass fires, carnivorous insects and declining amounts of food. They mounted a hill from which they saw not pasture but jagged terrain heavily covered with forest running away to the west. They called it Mount Disappointment.

Hume and Hovell ended by going on alone, Hume limping from a gash in his thigh, Hovell still highly motivated. He who found pasture became a pet of governors and a darling in his community.

Ultimately, they came to a gap from which they looked down on far-off plains stretching away to the ocean. Coming down to the coast, they believed they were at Westernport but in fact they were at Corio Bay in Port Phillip on the site of the future town of Geelong. Looking to the west, at plains stretching away in that park-like manner which convinced settlers that the Divine Hand had designed them for grazing, would have tempted any man to believe in his own immortality.

Returning to camp they found their men grown mutinous. A promised pardon seemed meaningless out here, in comfortless bush country which seemed to have a lien on their bones. Yet their return journey to Sydney took only five weeks and their news of wonderful new pastoral land around Westernport created a rush by squatters. Negative reports, however, came back from pastoralists who had decamped with livestock to the true Westernport. Hovell's navigational mistake of one degree would go on confusing people for some years yet, but it convinced Governor Brisbane to send a small party of convicts and soldiers to settle Westernport, as King had done twenty years before, for fear that the French would do it first. But what Botany Bay was to Port Jackson, Westernport would be to Port Phillip—less satisfactory water sources, anchorages and hinterlands would typify the two lesser ports.

The quarrels which characterised the journey now continued in the press, for whomsoever had been the true leader of the expedition would be counted a transcendent colonial, and even imperial, figure. The emancipist *Australian* stood up for the virtues of the native-born Mr Hume, declaring, 'Mr Hovell lacks all the qualities befitting a bushman.' But the *Sydney Gazette* lauded Hovell. Without his navigational skills, said the *Gazette*, the party would have been lost. The dispute would continue another thirty years and beyond, English contempt for his colonial-born status souring Hume's old age.

By now another governor, Ralph Darling, after the inadequate rainfall of the winter of 1828, authorised an Indian-born English officer, Charles Sturt, to go back to the Macquarie River and to follow it to its outfall, since the great barrier of reeds and swamp that had stopped others must now be in drought as well. Sturt was old enough to have served under Wellington in the Spanish campaigns against Napoleon and had also seen service on the Canadian border. He had arrived in Sydney in May 1827 in command of the military escort on the convict transport *Mariner*. On that ship he had noticed an interesting phenomenon: when being towed out to sea, many of the women prisoners fell into a state of unconsciousness, with an 'undisturbed countenance and a placid, tranquil pulse'.

A new Surveyor-General, Major Thomas Livingstone Mitchell, was on his way from England to Sydney Cove, and the fact that Darling sent Sturt off without waiting for his arrival caused rancour between the two men. Sturt made his starting point the depot at Wellington Valley on the Macquarie River, which Darling had instituted to protect more urbane convicts from brutalisation, and set out from the station in the heat of the Australian summer on 7 December 1828. He had Hamilton Hume with him, a number of soldiers and seven convicts, and a boat fitted out with sails and carried on a dray drawn by ten oxen. This boat was designed to be the first to break the waters of the inland sea which everyone believed lay beyond the great reed beds of the Macquarie. They were as well provided as a provident officer could make a party in such a situation and still be able to carry everything, the spare shoes and blankets, the horseshoes, rope and tents.

Where Oxley had earlier given up the attempt to penetrate the reed-clogged waters of the supposed inland sea, the reeds still grew three metres high, and beyond them one entered a huge plain with scattered runs of water. Sturt launched his boat in one of the small rivers but got only thirty kilometres before he was stopped by reeds. The local Aborigines cut ahead of them and set fire to the reeds in their path, while leeches and ticks afflicted them intermittently. A crowd of what Sturt called kangaroo flies descended upon the party and bit them crazy in what Sturt later said was the ultimate 'day of torment in my life'. It was indeed a resistant country, as resistant and potentially dark in its effects as Africa. Sturt was left to repeat the sentiment of Oxley—none of this could become the haunt of civilised man.

They were working along a branch of the Macquarie, which would later be called the Bogan, and at last it moved into a noble river, very broad, deep-banked, beguiling and crowded with bird life. Naturally he named it for the governor—Darling. But the water was salty. They would have all perished had not Hume found a pond of fresh water, but in the meantime the saltiness of the Darling convinced Sturt that they were close to the inland sea. However, Hume soon discovered salt springs in the river. They turned back to the drying Macquarie marshes and then found a dried-up river they named for Castlereagh, the Secretary of State. It was meant kindly for a man despised by his many English critics, all of whom would have been amused to find no water in its bed.

The tribespeople in this harsh season brought forward their children and begged for food and Sturt wondered how they could avoid dying out in this withering landscape.

He followed the Castlereagh to its junction with the Darling, and found himself on a plain surrounded by beautiful semi-arid hills. The landscape seemed to call up a vast desert ocean; the distance shimmered like water. But there was no sea. He turned back. His management of the expedition had been impeccable. But he was confused. He had not found a meaningful outfall for the westward flowing rivers.

By the time he got back to Sydney, Major Thomas Mitchell had arrived. He would be the ultimate industrious surveyor, but Darling ignored him and gave Sturt the next westward journey—to trace the Murrumbidgee to its outfall, hoping it would lead into the great inner sea or something else significant. Sturt left Sydney in November 1829. It was his destiny to penetrate the interior distances in their harshest season. Again he took with him soldiers, convicts pursuing a promise, and a dismantled whaleboat carried in drays.

After reaching the site of what is now Gundagai, they followed the Murrumbidgee through sand and desolate country, where, in tune with his reading of the landscape, Sturt found the Aborigines 'sad and loathsome'. At last he took to the river, having his men fashion a mast in the wilderness from a cypress tree. He divided his company in two, taking with him the red-headed George Macleay, son of the Colonial Secretary in Sydney, three soldiers and three convicts. After two days the skiff they were towing, which was loaded with supplies, hit a hidden log and sank. The pork was contaminated and only fit for the dogs. When they camped at night the local natives soundlessly invaded their tents and made off with cutlasses, tomahawks and frying pans. Suddenly the river picked up its pace and tossed them down through narrow banks into a noble watercourse, which Sturt named after the British Colonial Secretary, Sir George Murray. Sturt was not aware that Hume and Hovell had already crossed this river and called it the Hume, but a Colonial Secretary in any case gazumped an Australian-born bushman.

On the banks of the river war-like natives appeared, clashing spears against shields and uttering chants. Fortuitously for the Europeans, young red-headed Macleay was mistaken for an ancestor, possibly because of a missing tooth. An Aboriginal came forward to be the party's protector and strode along the riverbank beside the whaleboat, until it was swept away by increasing current.

They hoisted sail for the first time on 23 January 1830. There was a war party on a spit running out into the river ahead of them, but their accompanying warrior from up the river swam to them and took the leader by the throat and pushed him to the ground. The party made a remarkable sight. Many of them had delineated their ribs with white clay and looked like dancing skeletons. Others were ochre and yellow, highly impressive figures of threat. But now it all turned into a show of hospitality.

They passed the mouth of the Darling and so rowed down into the estuary of the Murray, by now subsisting on damper and tea. They came in February 1830 to a lake which Sturt named Alexandrina, the first name of a princess who would later become Queen Victoria. They could hear the murmur and thud of the surf of the Southern Ocean to the south, into which their river ran. They found it impossible to get to the entrance to the sea, dragging their boat over sandbanks and through shoals, so they turned back in a blistering February. Sturt sent a party under Captain Collett Barker to investigate the various channels of the Murray, and the leader, swimming a narrow inlet towards the eastern sandhills of the river, vanished over the horizon. There he was killed by three tribesmen, a compass strapped to his forehead, which his killers feared was a third eye. The tribesmen dragged the body to the beach in sight of Barker's party, pulled out their spears, mutilated the corpse and sent it swirling out to sea.

It is not to belittle these Australian expeditionary journeys to say they would always become penitential excursions because of the brackishness or absence of water, dwindling supplies supplemented by the occasional protein bonanza from a hunted kangaroo or felled native birds, and disappointments as the party fought its rearguard action back to the safety of Sydney. With Sturt the salt ran out, which they needed so much in the extreme heat. The air was full of glorious birds they could not get close enough to bring down. Handsome native women appeared to entice the men ashore into ambush. And rowing up the Murray, they found their depot deserted.

The men were now dying on their ration of flour. The Irishman Macnamee was raving. Sturt sent two of his soldiers to walk more than two hundred kilometres to the nearest station to find the missing party from the depot upon whom their lives depended. A relief party from Hamilton Plains arrived just as Sturt was pouring out the last of the flour.

The light of the interior had damaged his eyes. He would become blind in the end. It was like a parable. This was what the great suns and spaces of Australia did to the European eye.

DUST AND ENDURANCE

To a people who had brought the dreaming of livestock with them from England, Scotland and Ireland, the man who found new pasture became an Antipodean demi-god. Major Thomas Livingstone Mitchell, a Scots veteran of the Peninsular Wars against Napoleon's armies, was an exemplar of the pasture-seeking kind of explorer, but he did not always succeed in that search. Come to New South Wales as Assistant Surveyor-General, he became Surveyor-General after the death of John Oxley, and his first task was to upgrade the roads of New South Wales, including the one from the Blue Mountains west towards Bathurst. These roads remain in place to this day, though few travellers are aware of Mitchell's part in them. He would ultimately die from pneumonia caught while surveying a breakneck road across the Great Dividing Range from Braidwood, south-east of present-day Canberra to Nelligen near the coast. In his surveys and throughout his more famous explorations, he proved a determined and not always obedient officer, famous for his quarrels with governors from Darling in the late 1820s to Sir William Denison in the mid 1850s.

Mitchell's first endeavour into the interior, after his *bête noire* Governor Darling had gone home, was based on the report of a recaptured convict, George Clark, alias the Barber, who had lived some time with Aboriginal people in the manner of many escaped convicts. To save himself from punishment the Barber announced that there was a river in the north-west named the Kindor, which flowed through wonderful plains to an inland sea.

Mitchell at last came upon the Gwydir and the Barwon rivers but neither of them looked to be mighty streams flowing to a sea. He concluded they flowed into the Darling River, which, of course, had already been discovered by his hated and younger rival, Charles Sturt, with the help of Hamilton Hume. Some of Mitchell's theorising about the interior rivers of Australia had already been disproven by the handsome and personable Sturt.

Soon after Sturt's return to Sydney from his second expedition in 1831, he expressed a desire to settle in Australia, but the damage to his sight forced his repatriation. The rest of his life would not be easy, either in terms of health or prosperity, but Mitchell remained envious of him. He had found new well-watered pastures along the interior waterways while Mitchell had merely been duped by the Barber. Later, having recuperated and regained his sight, Sturt would penetrate the interior of Australia again looking for the non-existent inland sea, trying to breed cattle in country near the Murray but running out of food and needing to be rescued by Edward John Eyre.

Sturt's blindness returned and that, and the sufferings of his men, served once more as warning that the interior was perilous to European bodies and souls. His Australian farm having failed, Sturt was honoured for his sufferings with the post of Colonial Secretary of New South Wales and ultimately retired on a pension of £600, spending his last days in well-watered Cheltenham, a charming English spa town.

In the meantime, Mitchell's second expedition did not earn the gratitude of pastoralists either, but his third, in 1836, to follow the Darling to the sea or discover if it entered into the Murray, was the one which made his name. In fact, he failed to explore the entire length of the Darling River which ran in a great arc through what is now western New South Wales. But south-west of the Murray he turned away and rode into the great pastures of Australia Felix, the western part of modern Victoria. He was lauded by the pastoralists who followed his wagon tracks to the area where previously on the coast the Henty brothers, entrepreneurial Englishmen who farmed at present-day Portland, and their men had been the sole permanent settlers.

Another explorer who, like Sturt, was honoured for his endurance rather than his discoveries was a young Englishman named Edward John Eyre, who was liberal with respect for Aboriginal Australians and their title in the land and whose tough, if sometimes ambiguous, partner in exploration was the Aboriginal Wylie whom Eyre had earlier brought east to South Australia by ship.

Eyre, defeated by the dryness and harshness of the country north of Adelaide, decided to try in 1841 to find a path across the south of the continent to the new colony in King George's Sound, south-east of present-day Perth. The region he would cover was one of the most desolate and apparently featureless on the Australian continent. His journey was in a sense a long romance with the possibility of perishing by thirst, since there was no running water along the way, and frequently it was only the local knowledge of Aboriginals the party encountered that enabled them to drink. To the desert tribes—the Murmirming, the Ngadgunmaia, the Warangu—this flat and desolate country was a precious home to whose resources they were ceremonially bound by ancestry, which they praised and revivified in song, and for which they were grateful. To Eyre, Orpheus in the underworld, it was a great test. Surviving the un-endurable became the entire point of the expedition, in a landcape treacherous not least for its lack of European-style reference points—mountains and rivers and benign springs.

The Aboriginal people of the interior used various way markers, incomprehensible to Europeans, to plot courses in what we would call a 'desert wilderness'—a term meaningless to the Diyari people, for example, who inhabited country between the Simpson Desert and the Sturt Stony Desert, separated from the Strzelecki Desert by Coopers Creek.

The Diyari used *toas*, symbolically painted pieces of wood placed in the ground as important means of communication. The heads of *toas*, often made of gypsum decorated with dots, circles and winding lines, infallibly told one clan where the other was. As with other desert people in the interior of Australia, the Diyaris' movements were dictated by the availability of water. An individual clan would be able to strike out into its traditional country during the winter rains and make use of the standing water which, as warmer weather came, evaporated. They would then retreat to the waterholes along Coopers Creek and the soak holes of the Simpson Desert. Lake Eyre itself would be dry for years on end. In such a country, their indicative markers were life-saving road maps.

The ultimate European endurer was Friedrich Wilhelm Ludwig Leichhardt. Leichhardt was a Prussian, and it is said that part of his motivation for coming to Australia was to avoid Prussian conscription, mainly because it would be an interruption to his passion for the sciences. On arrival in Australia he had hoped to be appointed Director of the Botanical Gardens in Sydney, but did not achieve that post.

His first expedition involved a journey from the Darling Downs, west of Moreton Bay and Toowoomba, to the now phantom settlement of Port Essington on the Coburg Peninsula in the present Northern Territory. He was sponsored by merchants and pastoralists, and on his way across this occasionally arid and then tropic zone, he lost to Aboriginal spears the brilliant and genial young English ornithologist John Gilbert. He arrived in Port Essington—it is said his party staggered in—in December 1845. Returned to Sydney, he too became a licensed hero, having found land of pastoral value, even if it was only gradually taken up, and received subscriptions not only from government but from private citizens. Now his dream was of the ultimate—the crossing of the continent from the Darling Downs to the Swan River in Western Australia. The first attempt was abortive, and it was rumoured that Leichhardt, as competent as he was in the natural sciences and in observing the country through which he passed, was incompetent with men. He was not to be dissuaded, however. He set out again, preferring to skirt the northern edge of the central deserts, and, beyond the last outstation, he disappeared. A number of expeditions were sent to find him but did not succeed, and the Leichhardt legend abounded with rumour and does so to this day. It is not uncommon even now to hear stories of someone who knows, or met an Aboriginal who knows, where Leichhardt finally perished.

By 1860, there were two major parties dealing with the mysteries of central Australia. One was that of John McDouall Stuart, the South Australian government's nominated explorer for crossing the Australian interior from south to north. The second was led by a Victorian, a former goldfields police magistrate and Galway man with all the strengths and weaknesses of his background. Robert O'Hara Burke travelled in co-leadership with an English surgeon, William John Wills. Both of these sets of expeditioners desired to pass through the furnace and stand on Australia's northern coast.

CHAPTER 16

MERRIE ENGLAND

In Britain prior to the Reform Bill in 1832, and even afterwards, people compared their narrow rights in reality to what they might be in a just society. In 1820, a series of protest marches were held in Scotland in favour of a general strike. The protesters were autodidact artisans of a different social class than the more famous Scottish Martyrs of earlier in the century. They were chiefly weavers, who on the eve of the industrialisation of their craft could still work their own hours, acquire literacy and ideas and read the Scottish radical newspaper *Black Dwarf*. There was armed conflict between the protesters and troops at Bonniemuir, while troops who fought their way into Greenock to repress a march had to fight their way out again, killing eight people. Nineteen Scottish social radicals were sentenced to transportation to New South Wales.

It could be said of this second shipment of 'Scottish Martyrs' that, like Dr Margarot before them, they did not abandon their so-called radical views, and did not fail to pass their progressive expectations on to their young, and those they befriended. John Anderson, one of the transportees, would from 1823 until his death in 1858 be the widely respected schoolmaster at the Presbyterian school held in the little church at Ebenezer near Lower Portland on the Hawkesbury River. Another, Thomas McCulloch, became a popular publican and landowner.

Their views were echoed, in 1825, by the journalist William Cobbett who toured southern England reporting on its cultivation and the standard of living of its labourers. The demobilisation of the military in 1815 had put 250 000 soldiers and sailors back in the job market when prices were falling. Farmers cut the wages they paid for labour further as the parish rates they had to pay rose to cover poor relief. 'Judge, then, of the change that has taken place in the condition of the labourers!' lamented Cobbett. 'And, be astonished, if you can, at the pauperism and the crimes that now disgrace this once happy and moral England.' The land produced, on average, he said, what was always produced, but there was a new distribution of the produce. From the grounds of the big manor house, the labourers had retreated to 'hovels, called cottages'. But the threshing machine reduced the need for farm workers in any case. Threshing machines soon became targets for angry peasants, who thus became future transportees.

Crime fell in the good harvest years of 1828 and 1829. But in 1830 riots broke out in the counties across the south and in the midlands, where a great deal of enclosure had occurred, when threshing machines cut down on the need for labour, and workers and their families were forced to apply for poor relief, of which there was not enough to go around. Illegal combinations of labourers, the English equivalent of the Ribbonmen, began to post threatening notices signed 'Captain Swing', their mythic avenger. They also began to wreck machines, burn barns and hayricks, and hough (that is, cut the tendons in the legs of) cattle.

The conservative Australian press, such as the *Herald*, reported the onset of British mayhem, knowing that it would lead to the possibility of fire-spitting radical convicts turning up in New South Wales. A letter from Salisbury published in the *Sydney Herald* of 13 June 1831 shows that as sympathetic as the riots might appear to a liberal mind, they could also be anarchic and savage. A machine foundry was burned down near Salisbury and the mob took a clergyman, and dragged him along the road with a halter around his neck.

There were seven fires in one night. Word was brought that the populace was pulling down Mr White Churcher's farm; the cavalry marched out, and drew up across the London Road; such a scene ensued—the cavalry were attacked and obliged to fly before the crowd, who poured into Greencroft, where they were met by the special constables; the bells of all the churches tolled in alarm, and the staffs went to work, a horrible battle was fought for about an hour, when the constables drove them off. The machinery at White Church Brewery is broken, and sundry barrels of beer were drunk. Milford Mill machinery I saw dashed to pieces, all the neighbouring farmers have had their machinery destroyed, and have been obliged to come down with contributions besides. Blankets and broken machinery are swimming down Salisbury Street. All the shops are shut and the terror is universal.

Some argued that it was the savagery of the authorities that drove events to such an extreme. In any case, for their participation, a total of four hundred and seventy-five rioters were sentenced to be transported, mostly for arson, including the burning of machines. It was not uncommon to have brothers, or fathers and sons amongst the transported rioters. Back in England, between November and January, the hardest time of year, the threshing machine was blamed at many a needy hearth for the hunger of the family.

In September 1831, when the Tory-dominated House of Lords rejected the Reform Bill, there were serious attacks and disturbances throughout England. In London the houses owned by the Duke of Wellington and the bishops who had voted against the bill were attacked. At Nottingham the castle was burned down and there were serious riots in Derby, Worcester and Bath. Dragoons were brought out to attack the crowd in Bristol who burned down one hundred houses, including the bishop's palace, the Customs House and the Mansion House. The mob, like the one which started the French Revolution by liberating the Bastille, set their torches to a number of unpopular citizens' houses and released prisoners from the gaols. 'One body of Dragoons pursued a rabble of colliers into the country, and covered the fields and roads with the bodies of wounded wretches, making a severe example of them.' In London, the government, 'frightened to death at the Bristol affair', gave the military *carte blanche* against 'the malcontents'. Despite the malcontents already transported, the entire United Kingdom was on the edge, and as always the penal colonies of Australia waited to receive the minor or occasional major actors.

A STEERAGE PASSENGER

Henry Parkes, a young journeyman ivory- and brass-turner from Birmingham, was a bounty immigrant; that is, he had his passage paid for, either in large part or in full, under a system operating from 1828 onwards. It used government funds raised through the sale of Crown land to reward shipping companies for landing healthy free immigrants in Australia. The system was at its height between 1837 and 1843, the period in which Henry Parkes and his young wife, Clarinda, travelled to Australia.

The emigrants were recruited by the Emigration Commission, with the system geared towards robust young individuals and families with small children. It was a profitable business if the shipowner and the emigration officials chose wisely. By 1840, for example, an amount of £19 was paid to shipowners for emigrating unmarried female domestics or farm labourers aged fifteen to thirty. Thirty-eight pounds was the bounty paid for man and wife emigrants, £5 per child up to seven years, and £10 for those between seven and fifteen. The control exercised against the danger that the unscrupulous would fill ships with sick and unemployable emigrants was that authorities in Sydney had the right not to accept those selected in bad faith, or to withhold payment of the bounty for them.

The bounty immigrants came not only to the Sydney area, but from 1839 to the Port Phillip District as well. By March 1841, the population of Port Phillip was 16 671, but it grew to over twenty thousand by the end of the same year because of the arrival of bounty immigrants. Sadly, they landed just in time for an Antipodean depression, the first great shake-out of the nascent Australian economy, and so did the young Parkes couple when they at last got to Sydney in 1839.

Parkes was a literate young man of ideas, an autodidact. He had been intermittently educated at Stoneleigh parish school, but while still a child worked in a brickpit and on a rope walk, a long narrow building where laid out hemp was twisted into rope, before being apprenticed successfully to a brass- and ivory-turner. While still an apprentice, like thousands of others he educated himself in the library and lecture hall of the Birmingham Mechanics' Institute. At the age of seventeen he joined the leading Birmingham Chartist Thomas Atwood's Political Union, and publicly and proudly wore its badge. Throughout Parkes's adolescence, Birmingham was the Chartist capital of Britain, and men organised passionately either to petition for their rights or exact them by force. There would soon be revolutionary marches and gestures in the city's streets. The belief Henry and other young Chartists shared was that England held for them no future unless they could wrest from it the objectives of their People's Charter: universal suffrage, vote by ballot, annual parliaments, payment of parliamentarians, abolition of property qualifications for members of parliament and equal electoral districts.

Parkes married Clarinda in 1836, and started his own ivory- and brass-turning business in 1837. The couple regularly attended Carr's Lane Independent Chapel, a Congregational chapel where a remarkable preacher, John Angell James, could be heard. Though aging, Pastor James impressed the young man by delivering two-hour sermons, exquisitely polished, from memory. Those fires not yet lit in Henry by Chartism were ignited by the Reverend James. In these two passions, the chapel and the Charter, he had much in common with many of the respectable young radicals who would be selected for emigration. They must have been aware that they might equally, as a punishment for too much Chartist exuberance, become convicts, as the Welsh Chartist John Frost and his associates Zephaniah Williams and William Jones had. For leading a Chartist riot in Newport, Monmouthshire, they would in 1840 be transported to Van Diemen's Land.

Henry Parkes and Clarinda had married without the full approval of Mr Varney, Clarinda's father, and it seemed to be more Henry's poor prospects and political pretensions than his character which influenced this idea. Just how much Varney's hostility weighed in the scales of young Parkes's going to Australia, we do not know, but it must have had some part, and similar hostility from the potential emigrants' parents must have figured in the emigration of many young couples. So when Henry's ivory-turning shop failed in 1838, he and Clarinda were willing to give London a try, far from Mr Varney's reproach.

The agenda they seemed to have agreed on was that they would give their homeland one more chance in the capital, and if that did not work, they would emigrate. They found lodgings at Haddon Gardens, a furnished room and a good-sized dressing closet where, Henry informed his sister Sarah, they kept bread and cheese and coal.

Throughout that winter they were always short of money. Henry could not put his lathe and other tools to work because he could not afford to collect them from the wagon office. By 6 December, Henry visited the Emigration Commissioners office in Park Street, Westminster because they had made up their minds to emigrate to Australia. He had to be persuasive though—the officials at the office would not at first give him a passage because he was a turner, and therefore self-employed and unlikely to be employed by any settler. He complained, 'There are crowds of applicants every day at the Immigration Office for them to choose out of . . . They will not take anyone who has a young and helpless family, except such mechanics as carpenters, masons, smiths, shoemakers, etc. etc.'

But he and Clarinda were accepted in the end. In the meantime there were many certificates to be acquired—a certificate of good behaviour and references from four respectable citizens of Birmingham. They had been counselled that they would be at sea for four months, and 'as there is no washing allowed on board, we must have at least fifteen changes of clothes etc. each, be they ever such poor ones.' Henry's sister and mother were pressed into labour to make them. His well-used books, including the works of Shakespeare and the novel *Caleb Williams*, were exchanged for shirts and pants.

William Godwin's 1790s classic, *Caleb Williams*, was a book which spoke to the young Parkes's condition. It concerned a young worker who felt himself a victim of 'unrecorded tyranny'. Like Parkes, he was literate and political, and 'my improvement was greater than my condition in life afforded room to expect'. Now Caleb's tale would help clothe Henry for emigration. Like many emigrants, Parkes gathered seeds to take with him, half a pint of marrow-fat peas, half a pint of scarlet runners, and fine carrot seeds.

The young couple could not wait to go. The Australian colonial propaganda Henry had read at the shipping offices and elsewhere led him to believe, as he told his sister at home in Birmingham, that in Australia mechanics could earn a whopping 40 or 50 shillings a week. Sugar cost a mere 2 shillings a pound, tea 2 shillings, beef tuppence a pound, wine sixpence a bottle, and rent was only 4 shillings. 'My hopes are not extravagant, though I make sure of getting rich and coming home soon to fetch all of you. I had forgotten to say the climate is the healthiest in the world.'

But fast escape was impossible. The ship that was leaving before Christmas, and could have delivered them from the discomfort of the rest of the winter on land, was fully occupied, and the next ship would not leave until the end of March. Clarinda and Henry had to endure a cold, final English Christmas. In the months they had been in London, they had been able to afford only one piece of bacon, and it had tasted like a mix of soap and fish. Their water came from the Thames, into which all the city's sewage and putrefaction—bodies human and animal, and the offal of Smithfield—drained. The cold fogs choked Henry and at night the noise of gin-soaked Cockneys and howling of cats frayed the couple's nerves.

Henry had time to compose his farewell verses, *The Emigrant's Farewell to His Country*. Many such farewells would be written by yearning young men and women awed by the decision they had made, but his has survived.

I go, my native land, far O'er
The solitary sea, to regions, where the very stars
Of Heaven will strangers be,
To some untrodden wilderness
Of Australasia's land—a home, which man has here denied,
I seek at God's own hand.

As for his father and mother, he bequeaths them nothing save his tears.

I leave them in a busy town,
Where pale mechanics toil
In irksome manufactories,
Shut from the sun and soil.

Having tramped about London all Christmas Eve trying to sell some of his ivory work, but not succeeding in doing so, Henry was sad to report that his and Clarinda's only Yule fare, after two or three days without anything to eat, was their landlady's daughter's plum pudding and wine. But now he faced a challenge that most prospective emigrants, having set their mind on departing, must have feared most. His parents and sister read in the popular magazine *Bell's Life* an account, which proclaimed itself to be an official report, of the harshness of life in New South Wales. Parkes consoled himself that certain people in his boarding house knew more about Australia than did someone in Birmingham. He wrote defensively to his concerned relatives, 'A girl that was apprenticed to Miss Irvine [their landlady] went out to New South Wales some years ago. She returned to England about four years ago, the wife of a celebrated missionary. She made Miss Irvine's her home during her stay in London. After laying out several hundreds of pounds in expensive articles of furniture she went back again to New South Wales, more glad again to leave than she was when she arrived in her native land. So you see, we can obtain some news about Australia without going far a-field.'

The family wanted him to have likenesses painted of himself and Clarinda, and sent him money for the purpose, but he had to use it to pay for expenses. Over the winter Clarinda had become pregnant, but the young couple received little support—a mere shilling in fact—from Clarinda's father. By comparison with Mr Varney, Parkes's father sent a pound on the eve of their departure.

Henry had time before going to the ship to be idolised as a poet by the old ladies in his lodging house, for the *Charter* published his verse. One old lodger made him a present of an ivory tablet, a set of reading books, a shoe-lift and a paper knife. They would have been wiser to give him cash, for by the time he and Clarinda boarded the emigrant ship *Strathfieldsay*, he had only the seven shillings that his sister had sent to have the images made. 'Just enough to take us to Gravesend', he lamented, but consoled himself that another poem of his would appear next month in the *Village Magazine*.

To enter the steerage of even a well-run emigrant ship daunted Clarinda and Henry, as it did other emigrants. 'The hole allotted to steerage passengers had a most miserable appearance at first . . . The large hold of the ship, where the goods generally are stored, is divided in about the middle by a deal partition. The apartment towards the forecastle, or front of the ship, is allotted to the male steerage passengers; the other, towards the cabins in the poop, or the back part of the ship, to the females. There are two rows of berths, one above the other round each compartment. The berths are three feet by six feet [0.9 by 1.8 metres] just affording room to two persons to lie down. They are separated from each other by a slight low deal board about 10 inches [25 cm] high, so that when we are all in bed, our bodies rising higher than those boards which separate, it seems as if we are arranged side by side in one immense bed all round the place.' The Parkes couple slept—like others—on straw mattresses, with a double blanket and a rug. They had to share their deck and the hold with a cow and a calf, twenty-four pigs, thirty sheep and numerous geese and fowls.

The emigrants were divided into messes, eight persons to a mess, each taking a turn at being mess captain for a week. This task involved getting the provisions for the mess from the ship's steward, to see to their being cooked, and to wash the dishes. Meals were nothing but beef and soup and biscuit, though there was plenty of it.

On board, Parkes recorded, were many farm labourers from Sussex. 'A rude set,' Parkes found his fellow steerage-dwellers, the average urbanity further diminished by a crowd of 'Irish-real emeralds' who came aboard at Plymouth. Some passengers fled the ship before it left Plymouth Sound. 'Came last night, a young Jew from London forfeited his passage money and left the ship the other day heartily tired of it. A man who was going out free also ran away last Sunday morning, as soon as we got here, and left all his clothes behind him.'

But the young Parkes couple had no option other than to stay the course.

THE ALMA MATER OF IMMIGRANTS

Though he was a sturdy young man, Henry Parkes would have found it difficult to read on the *Strathfieldsay*, since rude immigrants subjected working-class readers to ridicule. The rowdiness of the young men was inescapable, and was often compounded by marital quarrels or the cries of sick children, all in the terrible, dim, cheek-by-jowlness of steerage. And in storms, as one observer of an emigrant ship recorded, there would be 'boxes . . . all adrift, flying about from one side to the other, with nearly fifty whining sick squalling children to complete the misery'.

Light was also the enemy of the intellect in steerage. In better kept ships a lantern was meant to be in reach of each berth, and oil lamps and candles might have been supplied by purser or passengers. Sometimes lights were made out of animal fat rendered down into a tin cup and supplied with a cotton-wool wick. These kinds of lights were often a good recourse also for the Australian bush, where the mutton-fat lamp was the only assured lighting.

Though steerage was irksome for Parkes, for some it was a tragedy. Sarah Davenport's husband had been a soldier, and he and his wife had heard from friends in New South Wales and Port Phillip that there were good opportunities in both those places. They paid their debts and were told by the immigration authorities in Manchester that they would have to find £2 for each of their four children. Unlike the delays which beset Henry Parkes and his wife, the Davenports got to Liverpool on 4 October 1841 and resided in the dormitories of the emigrant depot, passed the board of commissioners the next day, and went on board their immigrant ship the day following—it sailed that evening. But the vessel went aground on a sandbank as 'roughs were bawling nex my galley', and as Sarah was nursing her violently ill children. Nonetheless, 'I did not wish to begin life again in old England—I wanted to make a fresh start in a new country.'

After some weeks ashore they went on board the *Champion of Glasgow*. Ten days out from England a girl was coming down the hatchway with some gruel for her mother and was pitched by the sea off the ladder. Sarah was sitting at her berth with her infant son, Albert, on her knee. The boiling gruel splashed his head and he died four days later. 'I could not cry one tear—I was stund— the young woman's name was Ema Patmore and a good young woman she was aged about 15 . . . she could not cry but in one short month she died and was buried in the sea.' The shock of Albert's death brought on premature labour in Sarah Davenport, 'and that babe was thrown in the sea—I was almost dumb with grief—I thought my trials was heavy but I cried unto God to help me for my children's sake'. Her husband was in some sort of shock too. His kindness seemed to have vanished and he wandered the deck querulously. Some of the other women were very kind to Sarah, however, and she rallied herself with the idea that she must make herself useful. She helped a woman who was confined on New Year's Day and went on deck to get her something hot from the galley as a wave struck which washed part of the galley away and sent Sarah sprawling under a longboat. Sarah went below, assessed her cuts and bruises, put on dry clothes, tried a return trip to the galley, and succeeded.

Just as they landed in Port Jackson in February 1842, Mrs Patmore's own infant also died. There were ten deaths on the *Champion of Glasgow* but ashore lay the kindnesses and ready dispensing hand of the former convict Dr Bland, who issued prescriptions and pills as he rode about Sydney. Sarah Davenport, like many a steerage immigrant, praised the surgeons aboard her ship. Most immigrants had better luck than her, though few could exceed her in ruggedness of soul. Sarah and her husband and children would ultimately settle on the Murray at Albury.

A Scots woman, Sarah Brunskill, travelling to South Australia in 1838, had similar bad fortune. It was common that young children suffered dehydration and convulsions from the combination of seasickness and harsh salt rations. If there was a cow aboard, it was possible to address the problem in most cases. But, 'At ten minutes after seven in the morning our dear boy breathed his last on my lap. Oh! How can I proceed! My heart is almost ready to burst. Soon after four his body was confined to the deep about ninety miles from Oporto.' The same day Sarah Brunskill lost her boy, her daughter was also taken by measles. 'About half past twelve her dear spirit flew to that mansion from which no traveller returns, so you see in less than twenty-four hours our darlings were both in the bosom of God.'

Sarah Brunskill would settle with her husband on land near Adelaide, rejoiced in the speed with which the sun dried her clothes and, although she had intended to return to Britain after prospering, died an Australian matriarch at the age of eighty-seven.

Emigration was hard in a number of ways for young mothers, especially in cramped steerage, since they did not always realise that for the sake of preventing the spread of infection they had to consign babies' napkins to the sea. An immigration manual instructed that, 'These cannot be used again on board ship, and must, the moment they are removed, go through the porthole.'

Even without nappies, the water closets in steerage often malfunctioned or overflowed, but the early Victorians were used to living with the smell of sewage. To cut the fetid air below deck, surgeons added fumigants to charcoal burners and burned tar in swinging stoves. Chloride of lime mixed with vinegar gave off an unpleasant creosote odour, but probably saved lives.

There was a bad typhus epidemic on the emigrant ship *Manlius*, which put into Port Phillip Bay in 1842 from Greenock in Scotland. Forty-four immigrants had been buried at sea, a great number for what was, by the standards of the age, an apparently well-run ship. Typhus was a fever transmitted by the body louse, and was also known as spotted fever, gaol fever, ship fever, colonial fever, camp fever and, in Ireland where it would soon kill hundreds of thousands, famine fever. Children were underrepresented among the typhus dead because it did not usually attack those under about fifteen. Thus one Scottish couple died on *Manlius* and left behind five orphan children aged between two and twelve. The captain was savaged by the colonial press, and the reports were inevitably picked up by British journals. In some ways this impeded immigration, but it certainly helped to make shipowners scrupulous.

The ship was quarantined at Gellibrand's Point near Williamstown, where a further seventeen passengers died. The government refused at first to reimburse the shipowner with the bounties for the arrivals but, after an enquiry, decided that neither the owner nor the surgeon was to blame for the outbreak of the disease. Like those who enquired into the behaviour of convict transport masters, the colonial and British authorities were anxious not to be too harsh in judgment, lest shipowners be discouraged from bringing immigrants.

Generally the journals of immigrants were full of praise for their ships, captains and surgeons. But perhaps the most remarkable tribute to a captain is that of Ellen Moger, who would land at Holdfast Bay, in the new colony of South Australia, in 1837, to walk with her husband and daughter across gibbers and through a thirsty landscape to the site of Adelaide. Ellen wrote, 'Our captain took great notice of our children when he saw them gradually wasting away and would send for them into his cabin and give them port-wine, almost daily. In fact, wine and water was the only nourishment they took for weeks and that was given to them too late.' So Emily, the daughter who trudged cross-country to

Adelaide, was the only one of four Moger children to have survived—indeed, at sea, the Mogers had lost three in the space of twelve days. 'They could eat none of the ship's provisions and our vessel was not like many of the vessels that were sent out, provided with one or more cows for the accommodation of the sick.'

It was to such sturdy-souled steerage passengers of the immigrant ships that Charles Harpur, son of a convict schoolteacher, addressed his *The Immigrant's Vision*:

> *Their Truth an abode on the forest-clad hills*
> *Shall establish, a dweller forever,*
> *And Plenty rejoice by the gold-pebbled rills,*
> *Well-mated to honest endeavour,*
> *Till the future a numberless people shall see,*
> *Eager, and noble, and equal, and free,*
> *And the God they adore their sole monarch shall be—*
> *Then come, build thy home in Australia.*

THE SCOTTISH WAVE

Despite the high profile of the Scottish Martyrs, Scots had not been much represented amongst the convicts, but semi-compulsory emigration to Australia remained an established British style and had its impact on the Highlanders and Islanders.

Until the early 1800s lairds—landowners—had hung on to their crofters, or peasants, and resented those who had emigrated to North America. To absorb some of the human overflow on their estates they had founded Highland regiments, but with the Napoleonic wars long over, the men of the regiments were back home, prices had fallen, and the lairds were, compared to their ancestors, hard up. Like those of many Irish landlords, their estates were encumbered with debt. Improvement of the estates, by replacing tenants with revenue-producing livestock, was a way out for the burdened gentry of both Ireland and Scotland. How fortuitous and providential it was—for the landlord, if not for the individual crofter, his wife and their hungry and squalling children—that just as the landlords of the Highlands and Islands came to bemoan their region's density of population, the new world, and notably the Australian colonies with their willingness to underwrite migrant ships, cried out for more people.

Many lairds, even—and especially—those most sentimentally attached to the traditions of Scottish culture, became remorseless evictors of their tenants. The methods of clearing off the crofters from their notoriously squalid huts were often the same as those used in Ireland—military and constables at the ready, then the roof crushed in, even the house set afire. Betsy McKay, who lived in Skye in the valley of Strathnaver, remembered years later that her family's farm had been attacked by a burning party which fired the house at both ends. Another witness remembered pulling one old lady out of the house after it had been set on fire. *Oh, Dhia, Oh Dhia, Teine, teine*, she cried in Erse, the Gaelic of the Scots. 'Oh God, oh God, fire, fire.'

One commentator described a clearance or eviction of an entire village: 'For some days after the people were turned out one could scarcely hear a word with the lowing of the cattle and the screams of the children marching off in all directions.' Many of those screaming children would come to Australia as bounty emigrants. On the Isle of Skye, more than 40 000 people received writs of removal, and in some places one family was left where there had been a hundred. The owners and the gentlemen co-operated with the immigration agents to send off many ships of poor tenants between 1837 and 1839. As the novelist Sir Walter Scott wrote, the day would soon come when 'the *pibroch* [a bagpipe call to assemble] may sound through the deserted region, but the summons will remain unanswered'.

Those evicted would become, in many cases, bounty emigrants, lured by speakers such as the New South Wales Presbyterian minister John Dunmore Lang, who was honoured at a public breakfast at the port of Greenock, his native city. He had come back to Scotland to attract Highlanders and Islanders to Australia. He predicted that whatever befell Britain itself, there would always be a Britain while such people as the Scots emigrants, descended from the ancient state, speaking the ancient language, pursued their fortunes and their Presbyterianism in a far place. Lang believed the Scots would make 'the hills and vales of Australia resound with the wild note of the *pibroch* and the language of the ancient Gael'. Scotland would not lose the emigrants; Scotland would be enlarged by their translation to Australian places. On a Sydney pier, a Presbyterian minister addressed the arrivals on the *Midlothian* in 1837 in similar terms, and told them in Gaelic that they would raise 'the altar of God' in the areas they occupied—in their case the charming valleys of the Manning and the Clarence rivers in northern New South Wales. The Thunguddi of the region did not yet know what blessings were on their way.

Australia was a popular choice for Scots immigrants because it looked for common labourers and 'artisans of very ordinary quality'. Or, more accurately, the Colonial Office did. As in England, a bounty was offered to immigrants to Australia—£10 was paid to the shipowner for every immigrant Scot safely landed in Australia.

Previously, landlords had placed tenants close to the shoreline where they could gather and process kelp for them. Their crofters held very small plots of land as well and paid rent generally in the form of labour and services. The chief work they did was picking kelp along the coast and processing it. Crofters called the kelp 'tangle', in fact, and used the name kelp itself to represent the ashes produced from burning the tangle. Its ultimate use was in glass and soap manufacture. But in the 1820s, the taxes on foreign imports of flax and kelp were abolished, and the lairds, having organised their estates around flax and kelping, could not compete with the foreign imports, and were left short of a source of income. And so too were the kelpers robbed of their usefulness.

Throughout the 1820s and 1830s Australia slowly became one of the chief destinations of displaced Scottish Islanders and Highlanders, even though the journalist William Cobbett declared that it was the worst of all possible destinations. The number of official executions, he said, was challenged by the number of murders of landowners by their servants and murdering natives. 'If any man, not actually tired of his life, can prefer immigrating to a country like this to immigrating to the United States he is wholly unworthy of my attention.' But he assumed the crofters had no informed choice in the matter. They were largely in the hands of the evicting landlords, despite their fears the natives of Australia spirited people away from their houses and that they were never seen again.

REINVENTING SCOTLAND

Alistair MacDonnell, sixteenth laird of Glengarry, a Skye landowner and still a man in his prime, was receiving £60 000 income a year from an estate which cost him £80 000 to run. His father had been the prototype for the heroic laird Fergus McIvor in Sir Walter Scott's literary sensation of 1810, *Waverley*. The Glengarrys were the clan that had given their name to the Scottish cap worn (to this day) by Highland regiments. Now the glory was hollow, and Alistair MacDonnell decided all this talk about recreating Caledonia in Australia was the answer. A visitor to Glengarry about the time MacDonnell was to leave for Australia saw tenants beside 'the great man's gate' in mud hovels he believed Eskimos would be appalled to reside in.

MacDonnell set sail in 1842 with his family, his servants, some prefabricated timber houses and his piper, all with the intention of making Caledonia anew in Australia. He was bound for Gippsland, a grazing region east of Port Phillip, for whose discovery the Polish adventurer Paul Strzelecki took credit, attaching the name of the governor to it, but which in fact had earlier been reconnoitred by a young Skye emigrant named Angus McMillan. It seemed from 1840 on to be a Scots preserve, where squatting leases were taken by Skye men who generally employed other Skye men as drovers.

By the regulations then in force in New South Wales (of which the lands encompassed by present-day Victoria were then part), MacDonnell was entitled for a fee of £10 per annum to hold an area of 20 square miles (51.8 km²), on which he might place five hundred head of cattle or four thousand sheep. He chose a site for his head station and residence on the banks of a Gippsland river, the Tarra. Now, if he succeeded, old Scotland, communal and cohesive Scotland, could be reborn in Gippsland in Australia.

His clansmen built a house for him, huts for themselves, and stockyards, and he bought five hundred dairy cattle for £10 each, and the business of dairy farming commenced in the land of the Kurnai, the Aboriginal tribe of the region. Young Scots bailed up the cows each morning and put on the leg ropes, and sat on the stockyard fence as the milkmaids moved in to draw the milk. But all the milk and butter was consumed on the station, and only a little inferior cheese could be made. The MacDonnell farm, however, was popular with young Scottish drovers, and one visitor was the youth Donald Macalister, who came to make arrangements for the shipping of some cattle and sheep. He, his drovers and shepherds had a pleasant time at MacDonnell's with songs and whisky and a piper playing, and the men and milkmaids dancing. But there was much in Australia which mocked the conventional idyll. On the road to MacDonnell's one day, Donald Macalister was distracted by one native while another rushed him from behind and threw a spear through his neck. His riderless horse arrived at MacDonnell's, and his body was found stripped of everything but trousers and boots. His upper body had been mutilated. It was a payback killing.

Lachlan Macalister, his uncle, was a former army captain and officer in the Border Police and was not going to let this murder go strenuously unchastised.

As an ironic Gippsland court clerk, George Dunderdale, wrote, 'It was, of course, impossible to identify any black fellow concerned in the outrage, and therefore atonement must be made by the tribe.' The Kurnai were found encamped near a waterhole at Gammon Creek. 'Those who were shot were thrown into it, to the number, it was said, of about 60, men, women, and children; but this was probably exaggeration ... the gun used by old Macalister was a double-barrelled Purdy, a beautiful and reliable weapon, which in its time had done great execution.'

It seems that Macalister's posse of Gippsland Scots was unabashed about the casualty rate. But even the gunning down of indigenes could not guarantee Scotland-in-Australia.

For the dairy business at MacDonnell's farm ran at a continual loss. In the end, he could not keep the recreated tribal situation afloat. He sold his cows cheaply to dealers from Sydney, and intended to return to Scotland. On the eve of his departure for Sydney by schooner, a farewell dinner was given by the Highlanders at the Old Port near Port Albert on the lagoon system of the Gippsland coast. All wished the young chief well, and his going depressed them. It showed there was something about the pastoral realities of Gippsland that fought against their desire for clanship. 'The family tree of Clanranald the Dauntless had refused to take root in a strange land,' observed Dunderdale.

CHARLES DARWIN'S NEW SOUTH WALES

Towards the end of his service as naturalist on HMS *Beagle*, young Charles Darwin, whose research would rock the foundations of the world, decided from his visit to Sydney that there were many serious drawbacks to domestic life in the colony, 'the chief of which, perhaps, is being surrounded by convict servants. How thoroughly odious to every feeling, to be waited on by a man who the day before, perhaps, was flogged, from your representation, for some trifling misdemeanour.' The female servants were the worst, he thought, for they taught the children of the house the vilest expressions if not the vilest ideas.

There was sometimes a strong bond, as much as Darwin disapproved of it, between the child and the convict servant, since the servants tended not to 'peach' on children to their parents. One thinks of the bond between the Wentworth children and D'Arcy's housekeeper–lover, Maria Ainslie. But Darwin was right that there was an extra layer of class difficulty between servants and masters in New South Wales—the inferiors being in this case not just members of the lower classes but convicted criminals. Similarly, he could not but be worried that settlers' sons in the age group sixteen to twenty would often be sent off to take charge of distant farming stations, and that these young men were doomed to associate entirely with convict stockmen.

He also noticed the tension between the edgy and often clever children of the rich emancipists and the free settlers, and indeed the colonial snobbery of up-jumped Currency folk towards honest immigrants. It was the rich emancipists, not the immigrants, who believed they were the measure of society, though the 'Ultras' like the Macarthurs, who saw themselves as inhabiting the mountain-top of society, gave them a run for that title. The surgeon Peter Cunningham wrote, 'The pride and dignified hauteur of some of our ultra aristocracy far eclipse those of the nobility in England.'

In walking about the town, Darwin was impressed by the contrast with his experiences of South America. 'Here, in a less promising country, scores of years have done many times more than an equal number of centuries have effected in South America.' His impulse was to congratulate himself for being an Englishman. But there was a misgiving: he was not sure how profound the reformation of the former convicts was. Darwin thought that as a genuine system of reform, New South Wales had failed. 'But as a means of making men outwardly honest—of converting vagabonds most useless in one hemisphere into active citizens of another, and thus giving birth to a new and splendid country—a grand centre of civilisation—it has succeeded to a degree, perhaps unparalleled in history.'

Travelling to Bathurst he liked the state of the macadamised roads, but was shocked by the dimension of savagery apparent in the iron gangs under the charge of sentries with loaded arms. This oddity was matched by that of the flora: 'The trees nearly all belonged to one family, and mostly had their leaves placed in the vertical, instead of as in Europe, in the nearly horizontal position: the foliage is scanty, and of a peculiar pale green tint, without any gloss.'

Altogether, he decided, nothing but the sharpest necessity would cause him to emigrate. Meeting a party of natives, the touring party from the *Beagle* was able to give the leading Aboriginal a shilling if his men would perform spear-throwing for the amusement of the travellers. A cap was placed thirty metres away and the throwers transfixed it with spears launched from throwing sticks at great speed and force. Even so, Darwin felt that this was a race in decline, a people of value reduced now to sideshow performers. He acknowledged that wherever Europeans trod, death struck the indigenes. 'The varieties of man seem to act on each other in the same way as different species of animals—the stronger always extirpating the weaker.' He did not, however, make this observation as men convinced of European supremacy would, though he has often been accused of just such a supposition. He was speaking not of racial superiority but of infection and the gun. However, long after he had died, his ideas would influence the relationship between black and white in Australia.

CHAPTER 17

'ALL FREEDOM AND SENTIMENT'

The press in New South Wales began as *the* press, a single unit, a wooden and iron press Phillip had brought with him and which sat for more than a decade in a shed behind Government House. Here a convict occasionally ran off a government notice or edict. But the man who would turn it to the function of a newspaper did not arrive in the colony until towards the end of 1800. George Howe, transported for robbing a mercer's shop, had been born in St Kitts in the West Indies and had then worked in printing in London. Soon after he arrived in Sydney, Howe became the government printer and in 1802 printed *New South Wales General Standing Orders*, claimed to be the first book produced in Australia. Howe was not without a journalist's skill and persuasiveness, and Governor King authorised the founding of the *Sydney Gazette* as a weekly newspaper, printed in the same shed as the decrees had been, in 1803. The paper was carried on at the risk of Howe who, though he had been pardoned in 1806, did not receive a salary as government printer till 1811. Even then it was only £60, and when subscribers to the *Gazette* fell behind in their payments, he frequently became desperate. He had five young children to feed, the offspring of his alliance with a convict woman, Elizabeth Easton. He was driven to try to keep a school, and to trade in sandalwood from New Zealand, and by 1817 he was one of the original subscribers when the Bank of New South Wales was founded by emancipists and some exclusives. He died in 1821.

It was his eldest son, Robert, who maintained the *Gazette*, started *The Australian Magazine* and published the currency lad Charles Tompson's book of verse.

Robert Howe's paper was suspected of being a tool of government, yet was often liberal and certainly not timid. Howe was horsewhipped by D'Arcy Wentworth's great friend William Redfern in the street one day, and another disgruntled reader assaulted him with a bayonet and wounded him. Yet his newspaper was not emancipist enough nor national enough for the young returned-home William Wentworth.

On 14 October 1824 Wentworth and his fellow lawyer and drinking companion Robert Wardell launched a weekly newspaper, the *Australian*. They were influenced in part by the fact that the first Legislative Assembly of New South Wales, to which John Macarthur and his nephew Hannibal Macarthur had been appointed, did not contain a single spokesman for the nativist or emancipist side, a role which Wentworth himself had hoped to fulfil. Wentworth and Wardell were also appalled that when on 24 October 1824 lists of those deemed eligible to serve as jurors were fixed to the doors of Sydney's churches, no one who had come to the colony as a prisoner was on them. Wentworth used the courthouse and his paper to challenge this decision. Full of combativeness, when he was elected a director of the Bank of New South Wales, ill feeling between the exclusives and emancipists on the board grew intense, and so the exclusives resigned to found their own institution, the Bank of Australia, in 1826.

Wardell looked after the day-to-day running of the newspaper and wrote most of the copy. Wentworth wrote some editorials and paid more than £4000 in 1824–25 as his share of the capital and running costs. Wardell and Wentworth's editorial brio made Governor Brisbane give up any attempts to censor the milder *Gazette*. Barron Field, the colony's new Supreme Court judge, said of the *Australian* that it was the equivalent of producing a radical newspaper in Newgate.

On 26 January 1825 occurred a great dinner hosted by Wardell and Wentworth at which the thirty-seventh anniversary of the colony was toasted. They drank to a House of Assembly, freedom of the press, trial by jury and to the Currency lasses. The ex-convict poet Michael Massey Robinson called on them to drink to, 'The land, boys, we live in'. About the same time copies of the third edition of Wentworth's book reached New South Wales and the emancipists hailed its author as their spokesman.

William Wentworth's interest in Currency and emancipists must have been redoubled by his association with a young plaintiff named Sarah Cox, a twenty-year-old daughter of two convicts, in a breach of promise suit in the Supreme Court against a sea captain who traded between Sydney and Van Diemen's Land. By the time the jury awarded her £100 damages plus costs, she was two months pregnant with Wentworth's child. He had repeated the pattern of his father in finding his partner amongst the despised. Miss Cox had grown up in a modest home at Sydney Cove next door to her father's ship and anchor smithing workshop.

In 1825 at an estate Wentworth rented near Petersham, his and Sarah's daughter, Thomasine (or Timmy), was born out of wedlock. Wentworth would buy Petersham from Captain Piper and stay with Sarah on weekends and spend the rest of the week in Sydney. Sarah was a serene, practical woman, black-haired, with a high forehead and searching eyes. Though her father's business was successful in Sydney, he had left a destitute wife, Margaret, and their three sons and infant daughter in Shropshire surviving on poor relief. Sarah's mother was Frances Morton, transported for life on a charge of stealing.

Governor Brisbane was summoned home in 1825 after trying to leave the day-to-day running of the penal and colonial engine to his New South Wales Colonial Secretary, Frederick Goulburn, whose brother had been undersecretary in the Colonial Office from 1812–21, and the results were seen as not effective. Brisbane had given six days and nights of the week to his astronomical observations at Parramatta, and to writing papers on astronomical matters, in order to gain what he most desired—a doctorate from the University of Edinburgh.

The new governor, Ralph Darling, decided to take on the scurrilous press. He wanted to enact a statute that would allow him to bring editors to court on charges of seditious libel. And he wanted to drive the papers out of business by imposing a fourpence stamp duty on each copy sold. Even Robert Howe of the *Gazette*, a man with such a debt to government, wrote material that mocked his intentions. Darling had recruited the sort of bodyguards who escorted judges and conveyed prisoners to Assizes in Britain. 'The new javelin men,' wrote Howe, 'intended for the purpose of conducting prisoners to and from the Criminal Court and to do duty generally over the gaol, are now equipped, and make a most formidable appearance. The uniform is a blue coat, with a yellow binding on the edges, and grey trousers: with a terrific long spear . . . Really we shall begin to think ourselves in old England yet.'

Darling's efforts to control the press were also opposed in New South Wales by Chief Justice Forbes and in London by James Stephen, the legal counsel to the Colonial Office.

One of the deciding issues for both the press and the governor was the case of two privates of the 57th Regiment, Joseph Sudds and Patrick Thompson, who deliberately committed theft in a Sydney shop so that they could change their condition to that of convicts. Darling changed the sentence of seven years transportation to one of the outer penal stations to seven years hard labour, and put them in prison laden with irons and with spiked iron circlets around their necks which made it impossible for them to recline. Though he did then anxiously seek the advice of his judges on the propriety of his changing the sentence, Sudds died. Here, said Wentworth, was tyranny red-handed. The day Sudds died, the *Australian* and a newer paper, the *Monitor*, savaged Darling.

In a joint opinion Sir Francis Forbes, a liberal-minded man who had previously been Chief Justice of Newfoundland, and his friend Justice Steven ruled against the governor, saying that Darling had in effect set aside the court's sentence and imposed a new, illegal, sentence by executive fiat. The governor, like all other citizens, was subject to the rule of law, it was decided. His sentence should be overturned, declared the court.

The *Monitor*, the newest paper in the colony, had been founded in 1826 by a former lay preacher and social worker named Edward Smith Hall. Hall's editorial position was based on sincerely held ideological conviction, and there was thus a sense in which he was more dangerous than Wentworth. Colonel Henry Dumaresq, clerk of the Legislative Council, aide to Darling and also the governor's brother-in-law, complained in a report to the Colonial Office that assigned servants went up to five miles (8 kilometres) to read the *Monitor* in the evenings, and soldiers as well as convicts were constantly seen reading the paper. Thus, argued Dumaresq, a dangerous sense of unity amongst the prisoners and soldiers was building and disaffection to the Crown was being created. The security of the colony depended on stopping such a thing.

Dumaresq also felt under threat from other organs of the press. When Robert Wardell wrote an article in the *Australian* critical of him, Dumaresq challenged him to a duel. They met in a field at Homebush, and each fired three shots at the other, all of which missed. Wardell's second was William Wentworth, who persuaded him to apologise. Honour had been satisfied, and the parties all rode fraternally back to Sydney for breakfast. But the duel was in itself an attempt to control the press. Now that the terror of a bullet had failed, Darling proposed legislation which would establish a licence system for newspapers, provide for its forfeiture upon conviction for any blasphemous or seditious libel, and confer on the governor an unconfined discretion to revoke the licence. A second proposed bill would impose a stamp duty on newspaper sales.

Under the New South Wales Act all legislation required a certificate from the Chief Justice to the effect that the legislation proposed was not repugnant to and was consistent with the laws of England. Darling, with the assent of his Legislative Council, enacted the new provisions concerning stamp duty and criminal sedition even though Chief Justice Forbes had warned him he might not be able to provide the requisite certificate.

Colonel Arthur, the lieutenant-governor in Van Diemen's Land, had just passed strict laws against the press and his right to do so had been approved by a certificate issued by Chief Justice Pedder of that territory's Supreme Court. These laws included a licensing fee for all newspapers.

In Sydney, Chief Justice Forbes was a well-liked and respected man. He refused to permit the adoption of the practice, then still current in England, by which judges kept court filing fees for themselves. As a result Australian judgeships would never develop into commercial posts or 'valuable rights of property'. Forbes also liked to run proceedings with a minimum of formality. It was after his departure for England that the bar had his successor insist that the full paraphernalia of technical pleading based on the English model be used in New South Wales courts. Forbes had even been against the wearing of wigs. 'On many occasions I've been compelled to take off even the little band from my neck—you have never sat in a crowded court with the thermometer at 100 [38°C].' There was an outcry at this, of course. 'I have given the best possible refutation to one part of the charge against me, by putting on a wig—and it will be a great consolation, when I find my brains boiling under it in summer, to know that I'm performing my duty and silencing a great scandal.'

In the end Forbes refused to certify the stamp duty of fourpence Darling wanted to impose on each newspaper in New South Wales. 'By the laws of England,' Forbes decided, 'the right of printing and publishing belongs of common right to all His Majesty's subjects, and may be freely exercised like any other lawful trade and occupation . . . To subject the press to the restrictive power of a licenser, as was formerly done, both before and since the Revolution [of 1688], is to subject all freedom of sentiment to the prejudices of one man.'

Darling's Stamp Act had already been enforced by the government awaiting Forbes's certification. The day the provisions were first enforced, the *Monitor* was printed with a black border. Edward Smith Hall planned to evade the tax by turning his newspaper into the *Monitor Magazine*, a stitched book adorned with a border of mitres 'out of unfeigned regard for our venerable Archdeacon, one of the *Septem viri* [seven men]', that is, for Archdeacon Scott, one of the Legislative Council. Robert Howe published a 'humble remonstrance' against the proposed laws. He estimated that the duty would cut his weekly circulation from 2000 to 600 and cost him £1200 a year.

Only Wardell refused to pay the stamp duty. Darling suspected that was because Wardell was a friend of Judges Stephen and Forbes. Certainly, Forbes would visit the home of Stephen, and their table talk would come to the ears of the judge's son Francis, an associate of Wentworth, Wardell, Mackaness and others whom Darling detested.

When Forbes ruled against the duty, Hall was delighted to greet at his door one of the colonial bureaucrats who had come to return his stamp money. But Darling now set himself to curb the press by prosecutions for criminal libel. He had especial rancour for the 'republican' outpourings of an agitator such as Hall, whom he called 'Thersites', after the rancorous soldier in the *Iliad*, or 'the Australian Cobbett', after the English journalist who recorded the plight of the British underclass. Hall would receive a jail term and fine for libel in 1829. So too did EA Hayes, the journalist Wentworth and Wardell sold the *Australian* to.

For Hall was the one who most firmly believed that it was up to the press to protect citizens from tyranny: 'We are the Wilberforces of Australia who advocate the cause of the Negroes [convicts] . . . Packed juries, and magisterial juries on magisterial questions, and taxation without representation, cannot long exist in the burning radiance of a free and virtuous press.'

Darling, meanwhile, had worked out yet another tactic to defeat 'the republicans'. In August 1827 a convict printer not formally assigned to Hall was suddenly withdrawn from the *Monitor* office, and when Hall tried to retain him he was fined by the Police Court. Then, early in March 1829, the assignment to Hall of two convict printers and one convict journalist was revoked by the governor. When one, Tyler, came to work anyhow instead of reporting to the barracks, he was gazetted as a prisoner illegally at large, arrested and sent to Wellington Valley in the west of New South Wales. Hall not only failed to obtain his release by *habeas corpus*, but was fined for harbouring a runaway convict.

All these judgments came from lower court magistrates despite the fact that the Supreme Court had recently ruled the governor could cancel an assignment of a convict only if he intended to remit the rest of his sentence. So both sentences were quashed in the Supreme Court in June 1829. Tyler was returned to his master who, however, was himself in Parramatta gaol. Darling was outraged by the Supreme Court decision and it was not until July 1830 that the Crown law officers in London upheld the right of the governor to revoke assignments as he saw fit. When that decision came through to Sydney, Darling again arrested Tyler, but was later rebuked by the Colonial Secretary in Whitehall for acting from political motives in doing so.

To silence Hall, still writing 'libels' in prison, Darling talked the Legislative Council into passing unanimously a new law based on one of Britain's repressive Six Acts of 1819, which were enacted after the savage suppression of dissent in regional British towns, and in particular after the army's massacre of rioters in Peterloo. This made it mandatory for the court to impose banishment to a place of secondary punishment on any person convicted of seditious libel for a second time, and was designed to stop the gaol in Parramatta becoming an editorial base for attacks on His Excellency's administration. The governor must have enjoyed fantasies of Hall being 'sorted out', at the best, in the intellectuals' work camp at Wellington Valley. The *Australian* bitterly condemned the Act and gave up publishing editorials. Where the editorial would have appeared, there appeared instead a picture of a printing press chained up by a military officer, the printer hanged on his own press, and all taking place within the confines of a large 'D'. Hall, too, left a blank place where his leader should have gone. He put in its place the figure of a coffin with a black epitaph.

As for Hayes, editor of the *Australian*, he was liberated from prison in January 1831 when two young Sydney radicals, Francis Stephen, the son of the judge, and CD Moore, brother of the Crown's solicitor, paid his £100 fine. Stephen, a barrister, was suspected of having being the true author of the seditious libel for which Hayes had suffered.

Hall resumed his editorials and wrote one savaging the baroque cruelty of Captain Logan's settlement at Moreton Bay. And news of Darling's new Act reached London in July 1830 at the time parliament was in the process of repealing the sections of the English statute of 1819 that related to banishment. The colonial Act thereby became inconsistent with English law and in January 1831, Earl Goderich, the Whig Secretary of State for the Colonies, disallowed it.

Darling was discouraged from bringing any further prosecution against Hall. Hall continued to publish the *Monitor* even though he did not pay sureties or licence fees, for he said he could find no one to stand pledge for him.

On 29 January 1829 Robert Howe of the *Gazette* was killed in a boating accident in Sydney Harbour, leaving his estate in the hands of trustees. The Reverend Ralph Mansfield, a Wesleyan missionary who had joined the staff of the *Gazette* as joint editor, was appointed editor at £300 a year and with a one-quarter share of the profits. Ann Howe, Robert's widow, colonial-born, had not been the easiest of wives, but seems to have been a woman of considerable acumen. She resented the arrangement and organised Mansfield's dismissal in June 1832. The *Gazette* under Mansfield had faithfully reported Darling's reply to an address from leading exclusives in July 1831, when the governor had denounced the claim to freedom of the press as a specious pretence of newspaper editors, describing them as 'the infatuated incendiaries who have attempted to assail my character as they have the character of many others, and to disturb the colony'. Darling also attacked Wentworth's criticism of him as a 'gross and absurd compound of base and incredible calumnies'.

With the institution of civilian juries in 1830 the time was right for a counter-attack. Hall, represented by Wentworth, brought three civil actions for libel against Mansfield of the *Gazette* and won two of them, getting £52 in damages. Wentworth also laid a criminal information against the Reverend Mansfield for criminal libel against himself in the reporting of Darling's words, the governor himself being immune from prosecution, and Mr Mansfield was fined £10. Wentworth did not mind the contradiction of principle involved in using the law to curb Mansfield's liberty of the press.

In March 1831, Goderich notified Darling that he was to be relieved. Darling felt he had been treated shabbily by the Colonial Office. But there were noisy celebrations of the governor's departure in October that year.

The office of the *Australian* was illuminated with a transparency—a series of lights—depicting the triumph of the press over the tyrant. 'Rejoice Australia! Darling's reign has passed!' it told its readers. 'And Hope, once more, reanimates our Land.' The *Monitor* gave two hogsheads of liquor to the crowd who had turned up to look at its coloured transparencies which declaimed, 'Liberty to the press unfettered by the Darling Necklace' and 'He's off!' They set off fireworks and made toasts.

But it was on the lawns of Williams Charles Wentworth's newly acquired house at Vaucluse, and in the hearts of his fellow campaigners that the most frenzied joy was found. From the deck of the governor's departing ship, *Hooghly*, the lights of Vaucluse and the celebrations there were visible. By invitation, Hall gave a speech, and the band cheerfully played 'Over the Hills and Far Away' while four thousand ordinary people, refreshed by copious potations of Wright's strong beer and 'elated by the fumes of Cooper's gin, did justice to their kind host's tables loaded with beef and mutton'.

The new governor, the Irish liberal Sir Richard Bourke, who arrived in Sydney on 3 December 1831, favoured trial by jury, representative government and full civil rights for emancipists. And he told the gangling young Undersecretary at the Colonial Office, Lord Howick, the future Earl Grey, that 'without free institutions where the press is wholly unrestricted no government can go on'.

In this new era, Robert Wardell, Wentworth's friend, still in his prime, was riding around his Petersham farm when he saw a suspect and makeshift camp. It belonged to three absconded convicts with whom he exchanged angry words. One of the three, Jenkins, shot him through the heart, not knowing that he was killing a champion of the convict class.

THE PRESS OF THE 1830s

In June 1833, the *Sydney Gazette*'s editorship was given to a charming, poetic but alcoholic emancipist named Edward O'Shaughnessy, transported from Ireland in 1824 for the crime of collecting taxes under false pretences. O'Shaughnessy initiated theatre criticism in Australia, by covering the productions of Barnett Levey's Theatre Royal. In 1834 he published an explosive pamphlet, *Part Politics Exposed*, on the misuse and brutalisation of convict servants, which would appear under the pen-name 'Humanitas'. It was the work of William Watt, a sub-editor and educated convict, in love with the proprietress, Ann Howe.

This was an important shot in the argument over convict transportation, one which would no doubt be heard by the liberals in Britain who equated the assignment of convicts with slavery, and would get plenty of evidence of that from Watt's pamphlet. It was mainly directed at a master named Major Mudie of Castle Forbes, Patrick's Plains in the Hunter Valley, of whom one observer said, 'Mudie spoke of the men he employed in terms of an executioner: "Nothing could wash away their guilt or obliterate its brand." Mudie had been appointed a magistrate by Governor Darling, and he and his magistrate neighbours would meet for dinner and beforehand, in the parlour, condemn each other's assigned convicts to floggings.

When five of his men absconded, stole weapons and fired at Mudie's superintendent, they were brought to trial on a capital offence under the Bushranger Act. A private donor hired the Irish lawyer Roger Therry to defend them. In his pamphlet, Watt recorded that Hitchcock, the most intelligent of the five men, said he had no ground to offer in his defence, but he implored the government to enquire into their past floggings; the frivolous excuses resorted to for the purpose of depriving them of their liberty after they had served a period that entitled them to its partial enjoyment by being granted tickets-of-leave; the merciless infliction of the lash; the bad and insufficient food they had received, and so on. Hitchcock asserted that an old cow had died alongside a creek on a Sunday and had been cut up on Monday and served to the men. 'I have seen the overseer take out his meat full of maggots,' testified one of the men, 'and wash the meat, and throw salt on it for the men's use.' The flour was tailings mixed with smut and rye. It should not be so on a large and well-regulated estate, argued 'Humanitas'. It was generally presumed that on the ill-managed and small farms, oppression could be worse still.

Hitchcock requested permission that he and his fellow prisoners might exhibit their lacerated backs to the public gaze, but this request was not granted; indeed it would have been considered highly irregular in terms of the jurisprudence of the day. The Solicitor-General, John Hubert Plunkett, 'humanely forbore', said Therry, to insist on execution in the twenty-four hours after the sentence and agreed to their having a reasonable time to prepare for death. Three were hanged in Sydney, and two of them at Castle Forbes. They were aged between twenty and thirty-two.

The bodies of his absconders hanging in the wind, Mudie turned his attention to William Watt of the *Gazette*. Watt was charged with having passed a printed piece of paper from the *Sydney Herald*, founded in 1831 and a conservative voice which derided the *Gazette* under O'Shaughnessy as 'the prisoners' paper. The piece of paper, Mudie believed, libelled a third party, but Watt was acquitted. Mudie then attempted to have Watt deprived of his ticket-of-leave on the grounds of an immoral relationship with a convict woman. This intimacy, said Therry, had ended many months before. In hearing the case ten magistrates, all of whom hated the liberal Governor Bourke and suspected Watt was his creature, attended the court.

In fact Bourke had already decided that Watt had assumed a position in society 'inconsistent with his condition'. He sent him to Port Macquarie, then the station for educated felons. It was a compromise. The exclusives wanted Watt punished for lending ammunition to the reformers, colonial and imperial, by being put into a work gang.

Watt travelled to Port Macquarie in style as a cabin passenger attended by his foursome of servants. In February 1836 a Supreme Court injunction transferred control of the *Gazette* from Mrs Howe to Richard Jones, a Tory merchant notorious for his diehard opposition to Bourke's liberal reforms. Mrs Howe had by then herself shifted to Port Macquarie, where she married and lived with William Watt. She threatened to withdraw her assigned servants, the nine pressmen and compositors who produced the *Gazette*, but Jones bought her off with a weekly allowance of £5. Watt exercised his charm to win the friendship of the local police magistrate, Major Sullivan, but alienated the harbourmaster, Captain Geary, who caused his ticket-of-leave to be cancelled. Watt seems to have absconded then, but after a month was arrested and given fifty lashes by his former friend Sullivan. After a period on a road gang, he was assigned to his wife as her servant, but drowned while crossing a tidal creek at Port Macquarie in January 1837. In the same year, Mudie lost his magistracy, claimed that 'through his secret connection with functionaries of the government, Watt actually ruled the colony', and withdrew to England in dudgeon.

The *Gazette*, under Jones, turned into a Tory mouthpiece that harped on convict insubordination, and reviled WC Wentworth as a demagogue and Governor Bourke as the champion of the unwashed. Its editor, George Cavanagh, left in 1838 to found the *Port Phillip Herald* in Melbourne, and in the new decade, the *Sydney Herald*, which had become the *Sydney Morning Herald* and published daily, would drive it out of business.

Left: Methinna. This Tasmanian Aboriginal girl, seen on Flinders Island in 1845, was adopted and then abandoned by Lady Jane Franklin. ('Methinna VDL' 1845 by JS Prout, drawing © The Trustees of the British Museum AN76222001) Right: The young Trugernanner or Truganini, once said to have been the last Tasmanian Aboriginal. She knew that many of her Aboriginal sisters had been carried off by sealers. ('Trugernanner (aka Truggernana or Truganini)', 1837-1847 by Thomas Bock, drawing © The Trustees of the British Museum AN00094643_001_l)

Behind the regimented line of the chain gang lies a world of chicanery and suffering, and at the centre of it, the convict supervisor. ('The chain gang mustered after a days work...', 1853? by Frederick Mackie, lithograph. National Library of Australia, nla.pic-an4767719)

Left: 'Emigration of Females to Sydney under Sanction of Government', reads the poster on the wall. In 1833, this young, sweet-faced woman was on her way to be someone's servant. But her main objective was appropriately marital, and she would be helped by gender imbalance of the colonies. ('Emigration in search of a husband', 1833 J Kendrick, etching. National Library of Australia, nla.pic-an6589596) Right: Steerage on bounty vessels to Australia was as cramped, interminable and hard on the health as it was on ships to the Americas, as the woman on the lower bunk at the right of the picture could tell us. (Steerage bunks of European emigrants sailing to America, 1870. Courtesy of photolibrary.com)

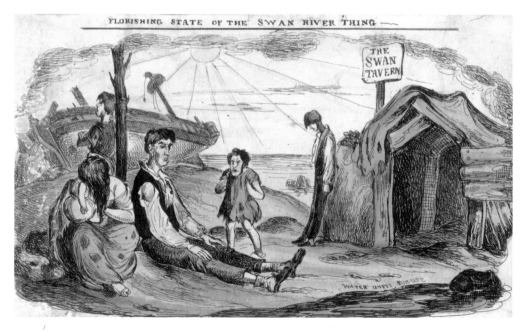

An English cartoon of about 1830 portraying the flourishing state of the Swan River colony. Some of those who, while in Britain, had read the prospectus too enthusiastically and signed up, would have looked wryly at this artist's work. ('Florishing State of the Swan River thing', 1830 by William Heath. Mary Evans Picture Library/ photolibrary.com)

This 1828 plate, 'Plucking or Peeling', depicts Thomas Peel of the Swan River emigration scheme snatching the feathers from a white swan, a symbol of the scheme. He reflects that 'Cousin Bob's letter did the job, etc.', his cousin being Robert Peel, Home Secretary and future prime minister of Great Britain. The signpost points to 'the best part of the Swan River settlement, only to be got at through the hands of Mr Thos Peel'. Tom Peel himself would be plucked. ('Cousin Thomas, or, the Swan River job', 1829 by Robert Seymour, etching. National Library of Australia, nla.pic-an6016587)

Londoners arrive to buy tickets to see Augustus Earle's panorama of Sydney, which opened in 1829. The ticket seller offers Hell as an alternative, and the daughter of the family calls the panorama she is about to see a picture of 'the Naughty Place'. In the meantime, a pickpocket attempts to guarantee his own transportation. Like most jokes, this one demonstrated entrenched attitudes. ('New panorama, a startling interrogation', published by T McLean, 1829 April 1, etching. National Library of Australia, nla.pic-an6589613)

PORTRAIT OF YAGAH,
CHIEF OF THE SWAN RIVER.

The head of Yagan, an elder of the Swan River region. There was a fashion for the study of 'native' or 'savage' heads in nineteenth century Europe, so that Aboriginal remains were often sent off for supposed scientific study on matters of race and the gradations of Homo sapiens. ('Portrait of Yagan, chief of the Swan River', Geo. Cruickshank delt., R. Havell sculpt, print, pub 1834. National Library of Australia, nla.pic-an7404365)

Left: The young Quaker, Louisa Clifton, who lived under canvas in the failed settlement of Australind, yet who kept a journal whose delicacy and wit is worthy of a drawing room in London. (Watercolour of Louisa Clifton, ca 1839. Courtesy State Library of Western Australia, The Battye Library BA 1073) Right: Practical Major Mitchell who found Australia Felix and was loved for it. ('Sir Thomas Livingstone Mitchell', ca 1850s by William Hetzer, calotype. Mitchell Library, State Library of New South Wales a143002)

The Thunguddi of the Macleay in about 1842, as seen by the young surveyor Clement Hodgkinson before the major impact of grazing and cedar-cutting. The robustness of the men is a testimony to the traditional life Hodgkinson is unwittingly bringing to an end with his plumb line and theodolite. ('Dance of defiance of the Yarra-bandini tribe', 1842? By Clement Hodgkinson, drawing. National Library of Australia, nla.pic-an6617620)

53. Paradise on the Bellinger River? Hodgkinson seems to imply as much in this drawing of about 1843.
('Natives spearing fish in the Bellengen River', 1843? By Clement Hodgkinson, drawing. National Library of Australia, nla.pic-an6617600)

The penal system bred out stations, some for punishment of secondary crimes (crimes committed after transportation). Tragic James Tucker, convict novelist and playwright, was sent to Port Macquarie when his ticket-of-leave was cancelled for being drunk in Parramatta. ('Port Macquarie', ca 1840 by Joseph Backler, oil painting. Mitchell Library, State Library of New South Wales ML 356)

While images of flogging have become Australian clichés, it is true that the remote convict settlement at Moreton Bay was renowned for routine flagellation, even under the genial Foster Fyans. ('Flogging a convict at Moreton Bay', unknown artist, etching from 'From the Fell Tyrant or the Suffering Convict' by William Ross, 1836. Mitchell Library, State Library of New South Wales ML365/R)

MURDER OF CAPT FRASER.

of the Stirling Castle.

Captain Fraser of the wrecked *Stirling Castle* is impaled by natives on Great Sandy Island in 1836. The idea that Eliza Fraser, his young wife, here naked, was now at the mercy of 'savages' titillated the popular imagination and made the ultimately rescued Eliza a British celebrity. ('Murder of Captain Fraser' from 'Shipwreck of the Stirling Castle…' by James Curtis, 1838. National Library of Australia)

The drover (possibly an assigned convict) meets the natives somewhere in Australia around 1840. (Detail from 'Cattlemen and natives by gum trees', ca 184- by ST Gill, watercolour. National Library of Australia, nla.pic-an2376895)

EDWARD GIBBON WAKEFIELD.
Founder of New Zealand.

(FROM A RARE PRINT IN THE POSSESSION OF THE AUTHOR.)

Twice an abductor of young women, Edward Gibbon Wakefield devised, in prison and after release, a scheme for the systematic colonisation of 'waste land' in Australia, a continent he would never trouble with a visit. ('Edward Gibbon Wakefield Esqr.' by Benjamin Holl, engraving, published 1826. National Library of Australia, nla.pic-an9928451)

Well-ordered Adelaide 'animated and bustling', gracefully surveyed and designed by Colonel Light, as Wakefield would have been gratified to behold it. Yet few of its inhabitants did not carry in their heart some disappointment—or at least the acute memory of trial and disappointment —from encountering the limitations of Wakefield's theories. ('Adelaide, Hindley Street from the corner of King William Street, looking west', ca 1846. Courtesy of the State Library of South Australia, SLSA:B15276/41)

Under his new land provisions, Governor Gipps squeezes the squatters in a wool press in this cartoon of 1845. No one else in Australia or the Empire though squatters were being harshly treated; indeed, many people considered they had got away with a great acquisition or near-theft of land. ('Ways and Means for 1845, or taking it out of the Squatters', 1845, Raphael Clint & Edward Barlow publishers, lithograph. Dixson Library, State Library of New South Wales DL PXX 66/8)

The contrary view—Gipps's squeezing of this 'Monarch of more than all he surveys' seems to have had little influence on his survival. ('Squatter of NS Wales Monarch of more than all he surveys', 1863 by ST Gill & Dr JT Doyle, drawings. Mitchell Library, State Library of New South Wales PXA 1983, f. 41)

Tutor, mountaineer, composer, and friend of Washington Irving's on the American frontier, as Superintendant and then Lieutenant Governor of Port Phillip, the cultivated La Trobe was faced with challenges from querulous squatters and the restiveness of gold-seekers. ('Charles Joseph La Trobe', 1855 by Sir Francis Grant, oil on canvas. Pictures Collection, State Library of Victoria mp003623)

Collins Street, 1839, a target for overland drovers from New South Wales and a centre for the Scots arriving from land-cramped Van Diemen's Land. As is common in such vistas, the natives, in this case the Yarra group, watch from the edges. ('Collins Street, town of Melbourne, New South Wales', 1839 by William Knight, watercolour. National Library of Australia, nla. pic-an5695310)

COLLINS STREET
TOWN OF MELBOURNE
NEW SOUTH WALES 1839.

John Buckley had lived with the Port Phillip natives since 1804. Such men, generally convicts, were not as rare as earlier commentators declared. Here Buckley is greeted by the first Melbournians. ('The first settlers discover Buckley', 1861 by Frederick William Woodhouse, oil on canvas. Pictures Collection, State Library of Victoria mp010578)

The Yarra tribe in European clothing, posed for a journey inland. ('The Yarra Tribe starting for the Acheron', 1862 by Carl Walter, photograph. Pictures Collection, State Library of Victoria b19553)

The design on one side of a handkerchief manufactured in quantity for distribution around Gippsland in the hope that one of them would be discovered by the mythical missing white woman of the region. The design showed a young woman telling a man of the missing person. The reverse was printed with advice in English and Scottish Gaelic, advising her that there were fourteen armed men searching for her and urging her to 'rush to them when you see them near you. Be particularly on the look out every dawn of morning'. La Trobe and others ultimately concluded the lost white woman did not exist. ('White woman of Gippsland' handkerchief. Pictures Collection, State Library of Victoria is000684 and is000683, digital enhancement courtesy of the Public Record Office of Victoria)

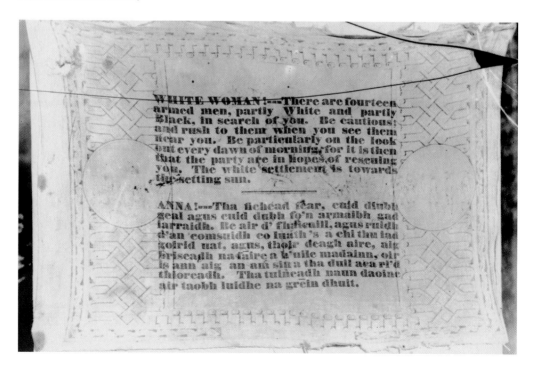

Black mounted troopers escort a prisoner from Ballarat to Melbourne in 1851. Up to 1854, there was considerable use of Aboriginal police on the goldfields under their commander Henry Dana. ('Black troopers escorting prisoner from Ballarat to Melbourne', 1851 by William Strutt, pencil and watercolour in 'Victoria the Golden; scenes, sketches and jottings from nature, 1850-1862'. Reproduced with permission of Parliamentary Library, Parliament of Victoria)

Miners thronged to the Chinaman John Alloo's (Chin Thum Lok's) restaurant in Ballarat. ('John Alloo's Chinese Restaurant, main road Ballarat', 1855 by ST Gill, lithograph. National Library of Australia, nla-pic.an6016195)

A highly staged photograph of miners taken about 1858. It is delightful for the glimpse of genuine diggers it gives us. ('Group of diggers', ca 1858 by Richard Daintree and Antoine Fauchery, photograph. Pictures Collection, State Library of Victoria b22463)

The rush of gold-seeking newcomers created a canvas town south of Melbourne and the Yarra River, depicted here as extraordinarily orderly and well laid-out. ('Canvas Town, between Princess Bridge and South Melbourne in 1850s' by De Cruchy & Leigh, lithograph. Pictures Collection, State Library of Victoria b28555)

From drawing-rooms to the very doors of the court, the acquittal of the Ballarat rebels was greeted with great civic enthusiasm. ('Acquittal of the Ballarat Rioters in 1855', *The Illustrated Australasian News*, June 25 1887. Newspapers Collection, State Library of Victoria mp005883)

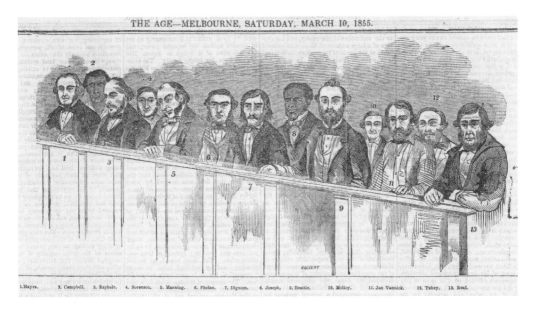

The accused standing trial for their part in the Eureka uprising. Timothy Hayes is on the extreme left, Raffaelo Carboni third from the left, and his friend the African American John Joseph sixth from the right. ('Rebels in the Dock', *The Age*, March 10 1855, p. 6. Newspapers Collection, State Library of Victoria)

Anastasia Hayes, schoolteacher, one of the seamstresses of the Eureka flag, spirited Irishwoman. After the uprising, she helped Dr Doyle during the amputation of Lalor's arm. Her husband abandoned her after his acquittal, and went to South America. (Public Record Office of Victoria, PROV 12970/P0001, Hayes Family Photographs, Unit 1: Anastasia Hayes)

This painting is entitled 'Eureka Slaughter'. The attack on the stockade occurred on a Sunday when fewer men were manning the palisades. The soldiers were from the 40th and 12th Regiments and were fortunate not to be fighting the Russians in the Crimea. ('Eureka Slaughter', 1854 by Charles A Doudiet, watercolour, pen and ink on paper, 16.3x23.9cm. Collection: Art Gallery of Ballarat, purchased by the Ballarat Fine Art Gallery with the assistance of many donors, 1996)

CHAPTER 18

NEW HOLLAND

The western side of what Flinders's navigation in 1802–03 had proved to be a continent was still known as New Holland. It was more than two and a half million square kilometres of arid and semi-arid earth, some of the oldest on the planet. Its spacious and well-wooded south-west was considered promising by the few who had seen it. Yet for more than twenty years after Flinders's great circumnavigation it had not generated in any British cabinet or in any colonial governor an urgency to occupy and consecrate it to the Crown.

In 1822 as a result of lobbying by the London representatives of Macarthur and other pastoralists, the British government reduced the import duty on Australian wool, and it was then that the Australian Agricultural Company, set up by royal charter in London, was granted 405 000 hectares of land north of Newcastle on the continent's east coast to raise sheep and sow crops.

This phenomenon impressed a naval officer named James Stirling. Stirling had begun his naval life at the age of twelve, but unlike Arthur Phillip he had a powerful patron, his uncle, Rear Admiral Charles Stirling. By the age of twenty-one, he was commanding naval sloops attacking American shipping and forts on the Mississippi delta, and he was able to avoid going back on half-pay until 1818. He was resolute and rancour had not yet marked his nature.

He was prodigiously fortunate in 1823 to marry, on her sixteenth birthday, a jovial young woman, Ellen Mangles, whose father was a director of the British

East India Company and head of the family's own shipping line. In the 1820s there was a great deal of French naval activity in the Pacific, and Governor Darling was ordered to create a number of outposts on the Australian continent. Captain Stirling was given the command of HMS *Success* and was to sail to Sydney with a cargo of money and then voyage to the far tropic north to collect convicts and garrison from Melville Island, where a settlement had recently been established. Darling had already sent a garrison to King George Sound in present-day Western Australia. On his arrival in Sydney, Stirling argued that the monsoons would prevent him getting to Melville Island for some months, and that he would be better employed for the moment looking at the west coast of Australia, particularly at a river in the south-west discovered by one of the Dutch captains and named the Swan.

Darling liked the idea, but the Colonial Office did not. In Stirling's words, it sniffed out his interest in the site as a settlement, and 'trembled at the thought of the expenditure involved'. Nonetheless he made a reconnaissance to the Swan with a botanist from Sydney named Charles Frazer and they were both very impressed with the country. Stirling then took off for the Melville Island garrison, and thence returned to his duty on the East Indies station. It was when he was sent home sick with a stomach ailment that he was able to talk to his father-in-law about the fine country around the Swan. Helped by the Mangles family he assembled a syndicate, and relentlessly harried the officials at the Colonial Office to give the group government approval and grants of land. Stirling had no one idea on how settlement should proceed—he had many. He thought of founding an association such as had been used to settle Georgia and Pennsylvania, but influenced by events in eastern Australia, also wondered about floating a syndicate like the Australian Agricultural Company.

Stirling had further luck in that in May 1828 Sir George Murray, an aging Scottish general and friend of the Stirling family, became Colonial Secretary. Stirling had by then placed articles on the proposed colony in English newspapers and popular magazines. One of Stirling's advocates, the merchant HC Sempill, compiled on the basis of the captain's description a most attractive description of a country he had never seen. The Swan River, according to Sempill, had one of the finest climates in the universe and was suited for the production of cotton, silk, tallow, provisions, linseed, hemp, flax, corn and vines. The county was of an open and undulating character with excellent soil; it was beautifully, but not too much, wooded, well adapted for wool growing and the raising of stock, and the coast and river teemed with fish.

Sempill also pointed out the proximity of the Swan River to the Cape of Good Hope, Mauritius, the Indian sub-continent, Batavia and New South Wales. He foretold low prices for provisions. A commissioner would sail in the first immigrant ship, escorting the immigrants to their destination with the sole purpose of assisting their settlement. 'Engagements with young, stout and healthy labourers and mechanics of good character are in the course of arrangements.' The immigrant, Sempill promised, would not have to wage hopeless and ruinous war with interminable forests and impenetrable jungle, 'as he will find extensive plains ready for the plough share'. He would not be 'obliged to mingle with, and employ those bearing the brand of crime and punishment; and as no convict of any description of prisoner will be admitted into the colony, those who established property and families will feel that their names and fortunes cannot be mixed hereafter with any dubious ideas as to their origin. Land so situated, without tithes, taxes or rent, under the special care and protection of His Majesty's Government, and where the British laws will be rigidly and uprightly administered, cannot fail being worth the attention of every industrious and discerning Briton.'

Sempill circumvented the decision by government not to pay the wages of labourers by promising to put interested and worthy labourers into contact with settlers of capital who would require their services. Another whom Stirling enlisted to his cause was Thomas Peel, a young gentleman of independent fortune related to the Home Secretary. Peel had thought of settling in New South Wales and investing his money there, but in 1828 was attracted by the more savoury reports of Swan River. The syndicate of financiers he joined offered to take ten thousand settlers with appropriate stock and stores to the new colony within four years and place them each on 200 acres (81 hectares) of land, in return for which the syndicate wished to receive four million acres (1 620 000 hectares) of land itself.

The Colonial Office was under pressure from Captain Stirling and the syndicate either to grant them the right to develop the place under a proprietary charter or to proclaim it a new Crown colony of which Stirling would be governor. The appointment of Sir George Murray, old general, famed lover and friend of the Stirling family in the Colonial Office in May 1828 and of another Stirling friend, Horace Twiss, as Undersecretary, meant that the Colonial Office was sympathetic, yet did not wish either to grant a charter or to incur expenses.

Stirling somehow persuaded Murray that the colony could be founded and flourish without government expense. But the Colonial Office beat the reward the syndicate of investors was seeking down from four million to one million acres. Members of the syndicate dropped out, except for Thomas Peel. While he hesitated, a former convict from New South Wales, Solomon Levey, offered to enter with him into a ten-year partnership in the Western Australian endeavour. Levey was to finance the exploitation of the proposed one million acres; Peel was to be its resident salaried manager.

Levey was one of the emancipist merchants who had risen in the time of Macquarie. He had been transported for seven years as an accessory to the theft of 90 pounds (41 kilos) of tea and a wooden chest. He began his business career in Sydney soon after arriving, and was dealing in real estate and supplying the government store with various goods while still under sentence. On 8 February 1819 he received an absolute pardon. He became pervasively successful in business in the Pacific. His ships visited the islands of Bass Strait and the Southern Ocean for sealskins. In the 1820s he had a base in Tahiti from which he imported island products; he owned a rope factory; he had grazing properties and land grants within the Twenty Counties. He became a proprietor of the Bank of New South Wales, advocating low interest rates and associations between the bank and English banking firms. In 1824 he added his name to the petition that Redfern and Eager took to London asking that the emancipists be allowed to do jury duty.

He went into partnership with another entrepreneurial emancipist named Daniel Cooper in 1825, and they formed an enterprise which involved import and export, the buying of wool, shipping, whaling and sealing. He was back living in London when he met Peel.

Their venture would not be a happy one. To begin, Peel concealed his partnership with an emancipist from the Colonial Office. And when he ultimately received his land grant south of Perth, he faced angry charges that he had been favoured by his cousin, the Home Secretary Robert Peel. By his agreement with the Colonial Office Peel had been granted priority to 250 000 acres (101 250 hectares), which he chose off the map on the southern banks of the Swan and Canning rivers, with a further 250 000 acres to be allotted once he had landed four hundred settlers. After twenty-one years, if improvements had been made on this first half-million acres, the remaining half-million would be allotted. The other problem for Peel was that the press, which did not understand the vastness of Western Australia, declared that after a 250 000-acre grant, there would be nothing left for settlers.

The government announced in January 1829 that the first shipload of immigrants was to be landed before 1 November 1829 if priority of choice of land was to be retained. The Peel settlement failed, in part because of native resistance, and Peel, dressing in hunting garb, was left to haunt the landscape in old age. The *Gilmore*, the Peel–Levey partnership's first ship bearing 179 recruited immigrants, put to sea, but would arrive in New Holland six weeks late and by then his best land had been chosen by others.

TALKING TO THE SULKY ONE

Much earlier than Peel's arrival, on 2 May 1829, Captain Fremantle of HMS *Challenger* took possession on behalf of Stirling of a large stretch of land at the mouth of the Swan River. Stirling arrived on 18 June with his wife, civil officials and a small detachment from the 63rd Regiment on the store ship *Parmelia*, and proclaimed the colony on a bright afternoon beneath Mount Eliza. Rarely had a settlement been made on the basis of so little knowledge of the nature of the hinterland. It was decided that there would be a port at the river mouth, later named Fremantle, and a main site upriver, just beyond the point where the river named the Canning entered the Swan. This settlement would be named Perth, to honour the seat Sir George Murray held in the House of Commons. It was already the meeting place of a tall and sinewy people who called themselves Bibbulmun, though they would later be more commonly named the Nyoongar, the word in their language for 'man'. In the cosmos of the Bibbulmun the most significant creature was the Rainbow Serpent who had to be persuaded, flattered and appeased ceremonially into continuing to provide the elements of life. The Bibbulmun often called the Rainbow Serpent 'the Sulky One', because they knew from millennia of experience that their beloved country required exertions, priestly and physical, from them, and that the Sulky One must be conciliated into making plenty possible.

Now the arrivals, knocking down a tree, raising a rag, singing a song, unleashing thunderous smoke into the air, were also placing themselves in the power of the Sulky One. And many of them were ambiguous about it, and many others appalled.

On the *Warrior*, for example, everyone was dissatisfied with the rations provided for the voyage by Mr Sempill, the charterer. One passenger wrote,

'The rascality of Sempill has at length arrived at a crisis altogether intolerable.' But more crucial was the quality of the water. It was difficult even for a cabin passenger to get sufficient to keep flesh clean. Aboard the *Warrior* were a number of young men of the Bussell family, the orphan children of a Church of England minister. John Bussell had met up with a Captain Molloy, who was already intending to emigrate, at a ball in Southampton, and decided that his three younger brothers needed somewhere spacious. The four brothers travelled steerage to save money but had dogs and some poultry with them, a corn mill, an *Encyclopaedia Britannica*, compasses and a thermometer.

The town of Fremantle, said one *Warrior* passenger, 'was composed of a good number of miserable-looking tents, most of which were grog shops'. And George Bussell at first saw the sand surrounding the settlement as snowdrifts, 'a delusion, however, most forcibly contradicted by the intense heat of the sun and the glare it occasions'.

Fremantle could be seen as graceless with its one hotel. In unloading his cattle, Captain Molloy, a middle-aged and retired captain of infantry, saw them dash away into the scrub, since there were no stockyards to hold them. Goods were simply unladen anywhere on the beach. 'I was obliged to keep watch night and day,' said one passenger, for though there were no convicts there were still thieves and desperate people. The places where a settler's goods and furniture were landed were widely scattered, dependent on the tide and which beach was chosen by a particular lighter. Women wept for broken china and broken and sea-ruined furniture.

Vernon Bussell described his Fremantle tent thus: 'The pole was surrounded with guns, three double barrels, two single and three rifles. Over them were hung four braces of pistols and two cutlasses, the table a slab of wood supported by three desks and our seats consisting of a saucepan and a bucket turned upside-down and the door crowded with dogs, who were not allowed to come in.' One had to be very young like Vernon, or a particular kind of human, not to be a little chastened by the conditions.

Newly arrived colonists were to enrol their names in the register, receive permission to reside, and call on the governor. A charter boat would take people up the Swan River to the settlement of Perth. The river, its wide reaches, black swans and verdant foreshores were enchanting to many, and consoled them in the extreme choice they had made. But the settlers who came by *Warrior* were told that the best land, along the Swan and the Canning, was already taken. The officers of HMS *Sulphur* and HMS *Challenger*, who had arrived in 1829, had taken up most of the river frontages. 'It was the opinion of not a few that the Governor had acted very improvidently in giving . . . an extent of river frontage to one individual. It would perhaps have been better, to have made a square mile [2.3 km²] the maximum of any grant on a river.'

One visitor to Perth noticed idle servants infesting the main street—'hulking lazy fellows and exceedingly insolent; but what else could be expected, from their previous character, having been, I believe, mostly taken from the workhouse?' Those who had expected that the earth and their servants would be tractable were disappointed on both scores.

On a large eucalyptus tree the written newspaper of the place was attached, in the form of public and other notices. A visitor, EW Landor, saw the governor's written permission for one individual to practise as a notary, another as a surgeon, and a third as an auctioneer. 'There did not appear to be an opposition tree, and so much the better; as although a free press may do good to a community arrived at a certain state of perfection, yet I think it may be doubted how far it can be serviceable in an incipient colony.'

Three hotels had been licensed by January 1830. If tent life got too much for a family, they might stay, perhaps, in the one named the Happy Immigrant.

The governor's house was on the banks of the river, 'a commodious wooden building'. Captain Stirling's young wife, twenty-three years old, despite her wealthy background endured the fierce summers with grace, and with what everyone agreed was a lack of pretension which might have been welcome in her husband. A young gentleman visiting for tea said that she was 'a pleasant contrast to the bridling and haughtiness of some half-bred persons whom I remember at home'.

Before he left London, Captain Stirling had been offered a grant of 100 000 acres (40 500 hectares) with priority of choice. He (and his brother) hoped to select land in Geographe Bay, south of Perth. Settlers would later claim that Stirling continually changed his mind about where to choose land, 'and on the discovery of any new or fertile district he has immediately appropriated the best part of it to himself, thus severely checking enterprise and the spirit of exploration amongst the settlers, who cannot afford either the time or the money to explore land for the Governor'.

Indeed in Western Australia were available acreages that would make a European's head spin, and it was a proud feeling to write home and boast of the extent of grants, but the size of the enterprises required a labour force which generally did not exist.

EW Landor describes his and his brother's experience. Having been condemned to death by three eminent physicians, and being unable, like the wealthy, to go to Italy, his brother had had the climate of Swan River recommended to him. 'My younger brother . . . was a youth not eighteen, originally designed for the Church, and intended to cut a figure at Oxford; but modestly conceding that the figure he was likely to cut would not tend to the advancement of his worldly interests, and moreover, having no admiration for Virgil beyond the Bucolics, he fitted himself out with a Lowland Plaid and a set of Pandaean pipes, and solemnly dedicated himself to the duties of a shepherd.' Landor and his brother left England in April 1841, taking with them a couple of servants, four rams, a bloodhound, a mastiff bitch and a handsome cocker spaniel. They also shipped a vast assortment of useless lumber. 'Nine-tenths of those who emigrate do so in perfect ignorance of the country they are about to visit and the life they are destined to lead. The fact is, Englishmen as a body know nothing and care nothing about colonies. My own was merely the national ignorance.' The Englishman's idea of a colony, said Landor, was of a miserable place, a black hole, where exiled spirits sighed for a glimpse of the white cliffs and a taste of 'the old familiar green-and-yellow fog of the capital of the world'.

As for the Bibbulmun, 'When we first encountered on the road a party of coffee-coloured savages, with spears in their hands, and loose kangaroo-skin cloaks (their only garments) on their shoulders, accompanied by their women similarly clad, and each carrying in a bag at her back her black-haired offspring, with a face as filthy as its mother's—we by no means felt inclined to step forward and embrace them as brethren.'

Landor quickly pressed his legal qualifications with Stirling and was appointed commissioner of the Court of Requests while his previously sickly young brother ran the family farm. Such honest settlers were further discontented when those who had been granted good land near the settlements did not remain there or develop it. Early on, the common talk when settlers got together was about their having been misled by the reports of Captain Stirling and Mr Sempill. As a later-comer, Landor described the country thus: 'The first impression which the visitor to this settlement receives is not favourable. The whole country between Fremantle and Perth, a distance of ten miles [16 kilometres], is composed of granitic sand, with which is mixed a small proportion of vegetable mould. This unfavourable description of soil is covered with a coarse scrub, and an immense forest of banksia trees, redgums, and several varieties of eucalyptus. He also notices the xanthoreas or grass tree.' However, 'the traveller at his night bivouac is always sure of a glorious fire from the resinous stem of the grass tree, and a comfortable bed from its leaves'.

Perth looked attractive to the Landor brothers, with its luxuriant gardens of grapes and figs, melons and peaches, bananas and plantains. 'The town has a never failing supply of fresh water from a chain of swamps at the back, and the well is fed by them and never dry . . . No park in England could be more beautiful than the grounds around some of the dwellings.'

Yet the fate of many a Western Australian settler was a hard one. At first, said Landor, the settler was satisfied with finding that he could sell enough produce to pay his way, as long as he lived economically and showed a reasonable degree of good management. But unexpected expense, such as an illness or legal fees, could throw his economies awry. 'He forgets, however, the principles on which he came out to settle; he begins to complain that he is not making money. It is true he leads an easier life than he did in England; he is not striving and struggling for existence as he was there, but he is making no money. His wife asks him daily, in the pleasantest connubial key, why he brought them all from England, to bury them there, and see nobody from morn to night? What, she urges, is to become of their children? Will Jonadab, their firstborn, be a gentleman like his maternal ancestors? But how, indeed should he, with the pursuits of a cow-boy and the hands of a scavenger? . . . Is she to endure this forever, and see her daughters married to men who wear long beards and blucher boots?'

But Stirling never grew sick of it. He stuck on, and administered the Swan River settlement from June 1829 until August 1832, when he left on an extended visit to England during which he was knighted, and he was then back as governor from August 1834 until December 1838. He was succeeded by a young bureaucrat named John Hutt, a bachelor whom colonial maidens considered with interest but who earned a certain unpopularity for following Whitehall's orders too exactly.

One of the issues facing Hutt was whether the natives were British subjects or not. The Nyoongar were unwittingly in something of a cleft stick—if not subjects, they could be shot; if subjects, they frequently came foul of the law. 'By declaring the savages to be in every respect British subjects,' wrote Landor, 'it becomes illegal to treat them otherwise than such.' Thus, 'the poor native, who would rather have been flayed alive than sent into confinement for two months previous to trial, whilst his wives are left to their own resources, is heavily ironed, lest he should escape, and marched down some sixty or seventy miles to Fremantle Gaol, where the denizen of the forest has to endure those horrors of confinement which only the untamed and hitherto unfettered savage can possibly know'.

OH MR WAKEFIELD

Handsome Mr Hutt, the new governor at Swan River, was a disciple of a visionary Briton named Edward Gibbon Wakefield, a flawed yet passionate seer. Wakefield's father had been a friend of the utilitarian philosopher Jeremy Bentham, and his grandmother, Priscilla Wakefield, was one of the founders of the Savings Bank in England. Edward Gibbon, historian, was a relative, and Elizabeth Fry, the famed Quaker prison reformer, his cousin.

As a young man Wakefield, on leave in 1816 from service as secretary to the British envoy at Turin, eloped with Eliza Ann Frances Pattle, a ward in Chancery. Through the influence of the Lord Chancellor the marriage was approved by parliament and Wakefield went back with Eliza to the Turin legation. The couple had a daughter, and then a son, ten days after delivery of whom, in July 1820, Eliza died.

Wakefield had a substantial income from this marriage. And yet in 1826 he abducted a fifteen-year-old heiress, Ellen Turner, from her school, married her in Gretna Green, then fled to Calais. Ellen was persuaded to return to her parents and Wakefield came back to England to stand trial. He and his brother William, the latter as accomplice, were convicted of statutory misdemeanour, and on 14 May 1827 were each sentenced to three years imprisonment. Had he received a seven-year sentence, as was not uncommon with abductors, he would have been transported. This time parliament annulled the marriage.

Wakefield was an enquirer and while he was in Newgate he examined his fellow prisoners and tried to assess how effective their punishments were, and as a result of his study produced a tract, *Facts Relating to the Punishment of Death in the Metropolis* and also *Swing Unmasked, or the Causes of Rural Incendiarism*. Two years later, he produced a further two pamphlets on punishment and populist politics.

While still imprisoned, he devised a plan for colonising 'Australasia', published in June 1829 under the misleading title *A Letter From Sydney, The Principal Town Of Australasia*. It would create a stir in Sydney when it arrived the following

December. In Australia it was reviewed as having been written by 'a penny a liner from Grub Street'. That did not negate its influence.

Though he had never visited the southern continent, Wakefield claimed in the pamphlet that the Australian colonies were suffering from chaotic granting of free land, shortage of labour and consequent dependence on convicts. He argued for a more systematic exploitation of 'the wasteland' of the Crown as a means of providing money for the emigration of labourers. If the price for Crown land were made sufficient, high enough to discourage labourers from immediately acquiring land they could not use, such tribulations as those of Thomas Peel of the Swan River settlement would be avoided. Settlement should expand in contiguous blocks and the volume and pace of immigration should be related to available land. Deficiency of labour and a congenial society would attract capital, encourage immigration, assure prosperity and justify the rights of the colony to elect representatives to its own legislature. British society, in its most advanced form, would thus be transplanted to everyone's benefit.

The social structure Wakefield envisaged was hierarchical but mobile, allowed for free institutions, and would consult settlers on such matters as the appointment of officials and land sales. The pursuit of self-interest (as defined by Adam Smith, whose work he had edited), would lead to ineffable social harmony, Wakefield claimed.

Wakefield was an awkward speaker but had a great deal of personal magnetism. And though there's something inherently comic in a man dreaming up colonial schemes for Britons to apply their dreams, capital, bodies, families and breath to while in Newgate, it cannot be denied that Wakefield's theories had serious results. The *Spectator* wrote: 'The imprisonment of Mr Edward Gibbon Wakefield in Newgate will probably prove the source of the most essential benefit to the country.'

Indeed, Wakefield's ideas made up what one historian calls 'a seductive package'. Like the Greek colonies of old, the new colonies Wakefield proposed were to have balanced populations based on all classes of society; they would be extensions—not denials—of civilisation. Through such colonies 'Britain would become the centre of the most extensive, the most civilized and, above all, the happiest empire in the world'. Wakefield's claim that his theories were scientific, though perhaps shaky, gave them an attraction to the enlightened. In the penal colony autocratic and temporarily appointed officials had little common feeling with the pulse of colonial life. A Wakefield colony, in contrast, would be a true society. Having harboured colonies of the fallen, the enemies of God, society and reason, Australia was now to become the continent of model and reasonable and Christian settlements. In particular, the area now known as South Australia would be home to these idyllic societies.

Unlike Western Australia, however, with all its problems, South Australia was to be subjected, beneficially, said Wakefield, to divided authority. The Colonial Office would appoint a governor who was to be responsible for affairs of state other than land sales and immigration. Land sales and immigration were to be under the control of a board of commissioners, set up in 1835 with Robert Torrens as chairman and Roland Hill, the later inventor of the penny post, as secretary. The board was to preside over the sale of all land alienated from the Crown at a price of at least 12 shillings an acre, much less than Wakefield's ideal 'sufficient price'. The money from sales was to be used to foster immigration by poor labourers. The allotted area for sale comprised 802 511 square kilometres. All this huge area was designated, without thought for the Aboriginal inhabitants, as 'wasteland of the Crown'.

The colony had to be self-supporting. The commissioners were authorised to raise £200 000 to finance the first settlement and the foundation of government, and £50 000 against the sale of land to begin the immigration program. At this stage land was selling for 5 shillings an acre in New South Wales. The board advertised its prospectus and attracted attention in the press. Settlers bought into the enterprise sight unseen; sight merely described in most flattering language.

After demand dried up they dropped the price of all land to 12 shillings an acre. Finally Angas saved the speculation from total collapse by forming the South Australian (Land) Company as a philanthropic and business venture to buy out the balance of the land, and by December 1835 sufficient land had been sold to initiate the colony and a £20 000 guarantee was lodged by the board with the Treasury.

Behind this lucre lay the hope of a new society free from political patronage and the evils of a privileged church. So it was a perfect place for Robert Gouger, one of Wakefield's collaborators, a former inmate of debtor's prison, a dissenter in religion and a radical in politics. Gouger had submitted plans for the disposition of land and provision of worthy labourers to the Colonial Office and became secretary of the South Australian (Land) Company. The company dissolved itself in 1833 and Gouger dominated a new South Australian Association with the classicist parliamentarian George Grote.

John Hindmarsh, a naval captain, was appointed governor—as in most cases the Colonial Office could think of nothing better than to subject the Australians to military officers, which in some cases, Bourke and Gipps of New South Wales for example, had worked remarkably well. A reputable 25-year-old solicitor named James Hurtle Fisher would give up his London legal office to become the resident commissioner. The colony would achieve self-government when its population reached 50 000. Meanwhile, a nominee council would assist the governor.

All was set for a colony whose society would be not only superior to New South Wales's but superior to Britain's itself.

RE-ESTABLISHING PORT PHILLIP

Port Phillip in the south-east of the Australian mainland first gained its settlers from Van Diemen's Land, that lovely and august island whose mountains, east and west, hemmed settlement to its central valley running from Hobart to the coast north of Launceston. For several years before the occupation of Port Phillip, most Van Diemen's Land settlers who had any capital at all were interested in the coast to their north across Bass Strait. Whalers and sealers had already built huts at Port Fairy and Portland, in today's western Victoria. The Hentys, an English family, had pioneered more permanent settlement there. Their leader was Thomas, a gentleman sheep farmer from Sussex who sold up his property at the age of fifty-four to set sail for Australia, bringing with him his flocks and seven of his well-educated sons. (Another son would ultimately deliver Henty's wife and his sturdy daughter, Jane, to Launceston.) The Hentys were amongst the unlucky immigrants who arrived in Van Diemen's Land on their chartered ship just after free grants of land had ceased in 1831. One son, James Henty, tried Western Australia, but considered the land granted to the family there too poor to be worth working. In their own vessel, the Hentys began investigating the coast of the mainland. After three reconnaissances, in November 1834 another son, Edward, was 'much pleased' with Portland Bay, far to the west of Port Phillip, with its 'extraordinary vegetation and good climate'. Inland he found plenty of good grass. The Hentys began farming there in earnest; they had no other options, and they hoped the land they had occupied would in time be confirmed as theirs. Whalers stole their beef, but then they got involved in whaling as well. They were a family-based, uncondoned version of the South Australian (Land) Company. Their area would later be visited by the surveyor and explorer Major Thomas Mitchell, who would be astounded to find them there and who would name the region Australia Felix. Later it would be more commonly named the Western Districts and the Hentys would become mythic for their impertinent land grab. But when their father died in Launceston in 1839, the tenure of the Hentys was still insecure.

Meanwhile the Port Phillip Association had been formed to settle the desirable bay of that name. In 1827 the lawyer Joseph Gellibrand and the bushman John Batman, a Sydney-born Currency lad and son of a saltpetre thief, applied for a land grant there but were thwarted. There was further collaboration with Charles Swanston, manager of the Derwent Bank in Hobart, a very energetic person in all this, JH Wedge, the Van Diemen's Land government surveyor; James Simpson, Commissioner of the Caveat Board; two Scottish brothers, William and Duncan Robertson, who backed Batman financially; and a George Mercer of Edinburgh. Accompanied by an Irishman, three English servants and seven Sydney Aboriginals to act as intermediaries for the Port Phillip tribe, Batman was to find a place suitable for settlement. It was on this visit to Port Phillip that he made a treaty by which the Doutta Galla tribe 'sold' about a million acres (405 000 hectares) of land to the Association in exchange for small quantities of trade goods.

Batman now sold his land in Van Diemen's Land and suddenly had £10 000 to invest on the mainland. He was impatient, as if he knew his time was short. He had lived what many called 'an abandoned life' and was probably already suffering from the nasal form of syphilis which would cause his wife, Eliza Callaghan, to spurn him, and which would kill him in four years time. He was in a mood to make final arrangements. Both Batman for the Port Phillip Association and the Hentys pushed ahead in blithe hope that their requests for land grants would be recognised. They were both in direct negotiation with the Colonial Office when the initial settlements were made, doing their best to force it into assuming responsibility for them and extending legitimacy of possession and protection to them.

In Sydney, Governor Bourke was worried because he knew 'much evil' must follow without proper controls in the new southern settlement. Unlike some at the Colonial Office in Whitehall, he thought it would be best to impose reasonable conditions on Mr Batman and his associates, to consider the total capital expended by them, and to recognise the occupation of Port Phillip. Meanwhile Governor Arthur of Van Diemen's Land, worked on by the bank manager and Association member, Swanston, gave them as much discreet support as he could. Arthur hoped that the Port Phillip settlement might come under his purview, but in a proclamation of August 1835 Bourke made it apparent that it came under his, and he warned off all trespassers and declared any treaty made with the natives illegal.

Without legal force to their settlement, the Association played on Arthur's humanitarianism by stressing their desire to Christianise and civilise the Aboriginals. 'This is all Stuff,' wrote Arthur frankly to Bourke, 'and it is better for all parties to be sincere, and plainly state that the occupation of a good run for sheep has been the primary consideration—if not the only one.'

James Henty, Thomas Henty's able eldest son, back in London, besieged the Colonial Office for acknowledgment of the Portland Bay settlement. In the meantime the Port Phillip scheme had created a great frenzy of enthusiasm amongst the young and the discontented in Van Diemen's Land. In May 1836 Governor Bourke ordered a representative to proceed from the Goulburn district to report on the new settlement. The man declared 'the Port Phillip residents appear to be treating the blacks with great kindness and are endeavouring to instil habits of industry into them,' foreshadowing that the land would need to be fought for. Yet there had been spearings, he admitted.

The convict population of Van Diemen's Land had been a mere 568 in 1817, but by the early 1830s the numbers were in the thousands, and it was these men and women, assigned to Vandemonian masters who moved to the Port Phillip area, who created the labour for the expansion of the pastoral industry into the Western Districts, Australia Felix. The life for both squatter and servant was barbarous: often torpid, occasionally interspersed with brutality. Yet the pastoralists were not like the bounty settlers—they had capital and they meant to go home and live in comfort when they had earned their fortunes. Many of them got caught, nonetheless, by the scale of their hunger for wealth or by other attachments.

So many personable young men now departed Van Diemen's Land that it caused one young lady of Hobart, Jane Williams, to call the new country 'that dreadful Port Phillip'. The young Vandemonians were responsible for more than 300 000 sheep grazing in Port Phillip in 1837. By 1839 intending settlers from Van Diemen's Land formed more than half of total arrivals, even though emigrant ships had begun to arrive directly from Britain.

Under pressure of the spearing to death of the squatter Charles Franks, and one of his partner's convict shepherds, Governor Bourke appointed Captain William Lonsdale to Port Phillip as police magistrate. A Customs Officer and tide waiter were also appointed, given the constant intercourse with Launceston. To further formalise matters, the Port Phillip Association's representatives were summoned to Sydney 'to arrange the terms on which the Association will be permitted to retain some small part of the land they have taken possession of'. The expenses of the new establishment were to be 'defrayed from the revenues of the Crown lands'. While the members of the Association were not given land, they were to be allowed a remission of £7000 on any land they bought at auction.

From their lush corner of the greater Port Phillip region, the Hentys, too, continued to wage a paper war with the Colonial Office and the Sydney government until they won title to their land in 1849. Major Mitchell's account of Australia Felix had already attracted a great number prepared to invest and settle in the district. The flow from Van Diemen's Land to Australia Felix—as well as to Port Phillip itself—was on.

Meanwhile, one early arrival in the Association's settlement found a town of three or four wattle and daub huts, a few turf huts and about twelve or fifteen tents, some of these being only tarpaulins put across a pitch-pole, supported at each end by a forked stick stuck in the ground. This is how Magistrate Lonsdale found the settlement too, when he arrived to be its magistrate. Yet by then the population of the whole district 'exceeded 5000 souls . . . and more than 100 000 sheep'. Bourke named the village Melbourne to honour the prime minister of Great Britain and directed that a town be properly laid out. Land was to be put up for sale at both Melbourne and its port, named Williamstown. He travelled to Geelong and visited the stations of Thomas Manifold and Philip Russell, youngish, vigorous men from Van Diemen's Land, and could not entirely dislike them for taking their chances.

The settlers at Geelong, a new port servicing Australia Felix, asked for protection and from Sydney Bourke dispatched Captain Foster Fyans as a police magistrate. He also saw that it was necessary that appointed or elected members from Port Phillip attend the legislature at Sydney, even though the natural commercial partnership would be with Launceston or Van Diemen's Land in general. A judge of the Supreme Court of New South Wales would hold Assizes twice a year at Port Phillip. Then there was the matter of land tenure to consider.

Bourke had ordered one hundred town allotments be surveyed for Melbourne, and similarly a few at Williamstown. Otherwise the unsurveyed reaches of the new pastoral region spread away without apparent limit, and those who took it were to pay the usual not very onerous licence fees.

The Crown Lands Commissioners should exercise their wit to prevent crises between blacks and whites, Bourke decided. There were hopes that the natives could be persuaded to settle in villages and make themselves useful under the generous aegis of the chief protector, George Augustus Robinson, who had struggled to protect the Van Diemen's Land Aboriginals. In that vast country, Bourke could not prevent the occupation and exploitation of land by squatters. He sought, however, to ameliorate the effect upon the native inhabitants.

The first Sydney-side overlanders (that is, from the Sydney side of the Murray River and the Australian Alps, were Joseph Hawdon from near Batemans Bay, and his assistant, John Gardiner, an Irishman who had lost his tenancy in County Meath and was hungry for success in Australia. With convict and ticket-of-leave stockmen, they drove cattle from the Murrumbidgee to Melbourne in December 1836 and sold them at £10 per beast. Other journeyers from the Sydney side could follow the deep ruts which had been left by Major Mitchell's boat-carriage. By June and July 1837 there were numerous overlanders following this same route and by 1840 it was said that there were 20 000 cattle between Yass and Melbourne, moving slowly southwards. Some of these parties went through to South Australia, the hospitable Hentys providing them with accommodation at Portland, whereas others sent their stock to Adelaide by ship. Meanwhile, Joseph Hawdon, from the Cowpastures near Sydney, took two months from the Murrumbidgee to Melbourne but others were not so fortunate—some found their assigned men unmanageable as soon as they were beyond the reach of a magistrate's court; others had to treat their flocks as best they could when scab and catarrh broke out in them. One typical overlanding party composed of thirty men, an overseer and two natives. There were 5000 sheep, 600 horned cattle, twenty horses, two pigs and forty working bullocks besides a variety of dogs. 'Our provisions and baggage are carried by four bullock drays and two horse carts. The sheep are enclosed every night in strong nets which are fastened at top and bottom to stakes driven into the ground and are watched all night by one of the men. The cattle are watched all night by two men who walk around them until they lie down, and come to them again just before dawn of day, when they rise to feed.'

At night horses and working bullocks were hobbled and three tents were put up—one for the overlander and his overseer, another for the shepherds and a third for the six men who drove and watched the cattle. The rest of the men slept under the drays. The provisions were flour, beef, tea, sugar and tobacco.

Governor Gipps, who succeeded Richard Bourke, would remark on the quality of the overlanders: 'Young men of good families and connections in England, officers of the Army and Navy, graduates of Oxford and Cambridge, are . . . in no small number amongst them.' All of them were convinced of their future fortunes. After the overlanders came the first fresh arrivals from overseas, eager young men who had read the treatises on sheep and cattle in *The Library of Useful Knowledge*, in Major Mitchell's *Travels in Australia* and in Mr Waugh's *Three Years' Experience*. Many of them were from the lowlands and border area of Scotland, because the fares to Australia for a gentleman were cheaper than those from London by a differential as great as £50 for cabin passage and £20 for steerage.

Neil Black, a partner of Neil Black and Company of Liverpool, was the son of a Scots farmer from Argyllshire and had a little capital of his own. Taking his chances in Australia, he much preferred Melbourne to Sydney, finding it to be more of 'a Scots settlement', though its streets were hazed with dust, and an open sewer crossed the main thoroughfare. He would buy a run named Strathdowney. The names of locations in Skye, the Hebrides and the Highlands would compete with local Aboriginal names to be given to pastoral runs throughout the Western District.

Between 1839 and 1840 the population of the entire Port Phillip region nearly doubled to 10 291 because of arrivals from overseas, including assisted immigrants. Squatters such as Neil Black were able to sponsor immigrants under bounty schemes. By the middle 1840s when Port Phillip was divided into five regions, there was scattered settlement in each of them. But there were only forty-four runs in Gippsland compared with seven times that number in the rich Western District.

The men from overseas by now outnumbered the Vandemonians in the total population, but immigration from Van Diemen's Land continued. Those with capital always brought with them ex-convicts to swell the numbers of the labouring population. By 1841 newcomers had to *buy* stations, and it was already hard to find suitable new runs. The government had been defied in the initial making of the settlement and it remained, as Sir James Stephen, British Undersecretary for the Colonies, said a 'systematic violation of the law' which was 'countenanced and supported by the society to which they [the squatters] belong'. Stephen was aware of the fact that the founding minor crimes of Australian penal society were nothing compared with the audacity of the squatters. When it came to varieties of crime, the squatters' was the most spacious. Though these men violated the law on a huge scale, they did not see it in those terms, and operated from the mandates—biblical, ideological and personal—which had most validity for them.

Melbourne, Geelong and Portland had become depots and meeting places for squatters from up country and whalers from the sea. Here was society created by white men almost exclusive of women, and concerned almost wholly with work. Portland remained a whaling town and throughout the winter every inhabitant was alert for a whale blow, and when the alarm was given there was a scramble to take to the boats. At night the whalers roystered and fought in the streets and scandalised the inhabitants. In the small white-walled encampment of Port Fairy, the whalers and squatters caroused in the Merrijig Inn.

Sophie de Montollin, the wife of the superintendent of Port Phillip and governor-to-be of the ultimate colony of Victoria, had grown up in an environment of privilege as the daughter of a Swiss Councillor of State. She had met earnest young La Trobe when he arrived in Switzerland after travelling across the prairies with his famous American friend, the writer Washington Irving. His own book, *The Rambler in North America*, had just been published. Though an Englishman, Charles La Trobe had spent a great deal of time in Switzerland, and was probably educated there before becoming a mountaineer and a tutor to 'good' families. He was brave, intelligent and pious—a devout Moravian Methodist whose family had campaigned passionately against slavery. In 1835, though not wealthy, he must have seemed a good, reliable fellow to Sophie.

He was offered the superintendency of the Port Phillip area because he had acted successfully as a rapporteur for the British government in determining how West Indian slaves could best be equipped for freedom. He was to have the overall management of the aggressive gentlemen who wished to occupy Port Phillip by mutual arrangement and without administrative claptrap. Sophie de Montollin settled with a will into the La Trobe hut in Port Phillip. Her husband was more tentative in his decisions—especially since he had to answer to a new governor, Gipps, in Sydney, and to the Colonial Office, and to deal with determined graziers. He was lord of a process he could not control.

THE COLONY OF THE SAINTS

The dominant spirits of South Australia were ambitious middle-class townsmen, often radical both in politics and religion. South Australia was their great gamble both in terms of real estate and Utopian hope. Hindmarsh, the first governor, as a fifteen-year-old had been the only officer to survive on the quarterdeck of the renowned *Bellerophen* at the Battle of the Nile in 1798. Some South Australian Company commissioners would come to wish it were otherwise. He had been promoted by Nelson himself on the victory and had lost an eye like his hero. Hindmarsh subsequently had a dogged rather than a dazzling naval career, and now he was still dogged, and not necessarily a complete captive of the capitalist mysticism of the leading settlers. With the best will in the world, however, it would be hard for a governor to know where his administrative power ended and the economic and commercial powers of the commissioners began. Before leaving London, Hindmarsh met and was charmed by Edward Wakefield, and thus, man to man, approved of his system. But an immigration agent, after meeting Hindmarsh, declared that South Australia would have 'a little quarterdeck government', narrow and hidebound. Hindmarsh was probably not the right person to deal with the hoped-for forthright, upright, Protestant settlers of South Australia. And to him, the place was a posting, not the thorough destiny it represented for the settlers. He knew its relative imperial value. 'Pray, where is South Australia?' one of the younger princes asked during the House of Lords debate on the South Australian bill. 'Somewhere near Botany Bay,' replied the Lord Chancellor.

Hindmarsh arrived on the *Buffalo*, disgruntled, and concerned for his family of three daughters, a wife and a son. One observer wrote, 'They have no place where they can walk or breathe unpolluted air. The bulwarks of the *Buffalo* are six foot [1.8 metres] high. On both sides of the main deck are rows of filthy hogs, kept in pens, generally in a horrid state of dirt and uncleanliness.' In landing, Mrs Hindmarsh's piano fell into the sea: culture was drowned.

By the time he arrived in South Australia Hindmarsh had already come into conflict with the commissioners of the South Australian colonisation scheme. He quarrelled with Surveyor-General Colonel Light over the site of the capital of the colony. He also argued with Resident Commissioner Fisher. He suspended

Robert Gouger and other public officers, and the commissioners complained of him to the Secretary of State for the Colonies.

Despite the squabbling, on 28 December 1836 the province of South Australia was proclaimed in the earlier manner of Western Australia, by a huge gum tree on a grassy plain studded with peppermint gums and melaleucas, near the sand dunes of Holdfast Bay and at the mouth of Patawalonga Creek (near today's Glenelg). The governor's private secretary read the proclamation, a flag was hoisted, a party of marines fired a *feu de joie*, and a cold collation followed in the open air. The governor went about shaking hands with the colonists and congratulating them on having such a fine country. Then he mounted a chair and offered a toast to the King. The Adelaide hills sat behind the gathering of new settlers, the yellow kangaroo grass ran amidst trees all the way to their peaks. The natives of this rich coastal area looked on openly.

The settlers, whether at Holdfast Bay or at Kangaroo Island where some others had landed, were meeting the full-blown summer reality of the place—the heat and the insects. 'I can recollect perfectly well,' one South Australian entrepreneur remembered, 'the disconcerted and dismal look with which most of the first party regarded, from the deck of the ship, the dried and scorched appearance of the plains, which, to their English ideas, betokened little short of barrenness.'

The local tribe, the Kaurna, seemed friendly. One of them, Panartatja, was taken out to a ship and dressed up in European clothes and would be dubbed Jimmy Rodney. Because of its dryness, South Australia might have had fewer than thirty thousand indigenes, but the number is merely an informed guess. They interested Hindmarsh, who wrote of them, 'Instead of being the ugly, stupid race the New Hollanders are generally supposed to be, these are intelligent, handsome and active people, being far better looking than the majority of Africans. The women exhibited a considerable degree of modesty.'

Now the first-comers were camped, like eastern convicts long before them, under canvas amidst scorched summer grasses, awaiting the delineation of their capital by the surveyor, Colonel William Light.

Light was the son of a Portuguese Eurasian mother and an East India Company adventurer father, and had lived the early part of his childhood in Penang. He had fought in forty engagements in the Peninsular War without being wounded, and had reconnoitred the French lines by pretending to ride forward in the manner of a man severely injured. In the 1820s, he fought with the Spanish liberals against King Ferdinand and was badly wounded, and in the same period he and his mother were swindled out of their Penang property and wealth. At the time of his appointment he was suffering from tuberculosis. His relationship with his beautiful English wife had soured and they had separated. In South Australia he cohabited with a woman named Maria Gandy, an arrangement which meant that the founding settlers avoided him socially.

The work load laid down for Light by the governor and commissioners would have killed him, had tuberculosis not claimed him in any case. He was to find, first, a commodious harbour, safe and accessible at all seasons of the year. Second, a considerable tract of fertile land immediately adjoining. Third, an abundant supply of fresh water. And so on, ending with tenth, a site for a gaol. One thing in which Hindmarsh and the commissioners were enlightened was in the instruction that Light would 'make the streets [of the colony's capital] of ample width, and arrange them with reference to the convenience of the inhabitants and the beauty and salubrity of the city; and you will make the necessary reserves for squares, public walks, and quays'.

So Light was required, within a few months, to examine all the good harbours on 2400 kilometres of coast, found the first town and as many secondary ones as he had leisure for, and complete a complicated survey of about 40 500 hectares of country sections. All this in unexplored country, in the midst of a heatwave, amongst natives already alienated by the riffraff of whaling and sealing gangs, who had stolen their women away to Kangaroo Island.

Hindmarsh was angry that the location of the capital had been left to Colonel Light. He wanted it to be either right across Spencer's Gulf (near present-day Port Lincoln) or at Encounter Bay, near the mouth of the river which would become known as the Murray. By the time Light found the little river called the Port Adelaide River and the harbour upstream and the attractive Adelaide Plains, the first settlers were already there, pitching their tents. Heat and flies and mosquitoes were their lot. A 13-centimetre centipede scared the new colonial secretary, Robert Gouger in his tent. Mrs Gouger was six months pregnant and found the huge temperature range—between 41 and 10 degrees Centigrade—hard to deal with. Just the same, George Stevenson, the first editor of the *South Australian Gazette and Colonial Register*, noted in the diary he kept with his wife: 'We are all delighted with the aspect of the country and the rich soil of the Holdfast Plains. Mount Lofty and the hills before us are wooded to the very summits . . . on the plain there are numerous splendid trees of the eucalyptus species. The *banksia rosa marinafolia* was in great beauty. I have seen the Pickaway Plains of Ohio and traversed the prairie of Illinois and Indiana, but the best of them are not to be compared with the richness of the Holdfast Plains.'

Now Light's surveying equipment was applied to a landscape that had been subject to other and different readings over four millennia. In fierce and characteristic heat, with the breath of the Australian interior blowing on him, the city was laid out, a metropolis of imagination and fire whose limits were 'the enchanted hills', the Mount Lofty Ranges. In this landscape there were no geologic complications to distract Colonel Light. Many of the streets had a 30-metre width. A minimum width was 20 metres. But the terraces were broader still.

THE MAIDEN OF AUSTRALIND

Plans for a second Wakefieldian settlement followed the proclamation of South Australia. Under the aegis of the Western Australian Company, settlers were to take up land south of Perth, previously part of Thomas Peel's allotment. The new settlement, subject to the authority of the governor of Western Australia, was to be named Australind, to honour the hope that its produce would become the basis for trade with India.

Louisa Clifton was a young gentlewoman of devout Quaker family who had been chiefly familiar with her parents' house at Wandsworth, just outside London. Her highly respected father, Marshall Clifton, seemed to seek no life beyond that of the capital, where he had served as secretary of the Admiralty Victualling Board. But he came home as early as 1839 engorged with a new enthusiasm. He was to be Chief Resident Commissioner of the Western Australian Company. Louisa read the company prospectus on Australind. 'It is hardly possible to conceive a finer situation for a Town.' It was a region of plentiful fish and exotic native birds, said the prospectus, including the famous black swan. It told the intending emigrant that land had been set aside for a college, pleasure gardens, hospital and observatory—which all implied that the town would quickly become a version of the world he was leaving.

The Clifton family was related to Quaker reformers such as Elizabeth Fry, and to Edward Gibbon Wakefield, the systematic colonisation man, himself. If the move to Western Australia frightened Mrs Clifton as much as it inspired her husband, it also, with good reason, alarmed the wide-browed, lustrous-eyed, handsome girl Louisa. Though pursued by a suitor in England, Louisa wrote, 'I chose Australia; dearest Mamma's bitter tears have decided my wishes.' Her suitor seemed shamefully relieved to see her off and gave her a packet of seeds.

A week before the Cliftons' ship left London, however, Lieutenant Grey arrived from Western Australia to say that the land intended for the settlement had been resumed by government. Grey also declared that the area was a veritable Sahara in any case. In early 1840 the emigrants set sail into this vacancy of promise, and after an average passage on a ship named *Parkfield*, landed and made contact with Western Australian surveyors at Port Leschenault, 165 kilometres south of Perth, who quickly came to the conclusion, by talking to the newcomers, that the whole effort was amateurish and unrealistic.

In the first place, 'Papa's' agent, sent ahead, had gone mad. But even so Louisa's vigour of soul let her be cheered by the pretty aspect of the inlet and the shoreline. From here Mr Clifton set off with others to survey the new site of Australind, about 12 kilometres to the north of present-day Bunbury, and Louisa fulfilled the Christian duty of visiting the man who had become deranged. 'He was lying nearly naked, dirty beyond anything, on a mattress in the corner of his tent.' The poor man told Louisa that he wouldn't like his wife, who had already landed, to stay in this country. At last the *Parkfield* carried them down from Port Leschenault to their encampment site. Mrs Clifton and Louisa were both charmed to see the neatly pitched tents and the beautifully wooded riverbanks.

Still the women did not land, though within a few days the young men were off ashore on a kangaroo hunt with Governor Stirling. At last, the women came ashore into the camp and *Parkfield* sailed away, and Louisa and her mother and sister became tent-dwellers. Louisa was revived by camp life. 'An immense fire of branches was soon lighted on the level ground a little distance below our tent, water boiled, and tea made, and having fortunately got up our plate chest containing knives and forks, teacups etc., we sat down to a welcome repast, and with more comfort than we could have imagined possible. I wish you could have seen the interior of our new abode, some sitting on the ground, others sitting on our mattresses rolled up; I making tea on a gun case seated on a hassock in the midst. By degrees all the young men collected to this centre of comfort and sociability.' Memories of the solid comfort of a fully equipped London house were not permitted to cheapen the edge or resolve of life here and now. Louisa had brought with her a chest of clean linen and patterns and books and found that they had been all dampened, and she was compelled to turn the lot out onto Western Australia's harsh ground to be dried in the sun.

When a party of male settlers visited the camp, she was not impressed by what Australia had done to them. 'Colonial Society! How little captivating or refined it is!' One of the visitors was 'vulgar and unprepossessing, young, rough, and of course in dress, to English eyes anything but a gentleman. The want of gentlemanly dress is an additional friction to "taste". A very stupid dinner. I felt low spirited and requiring to be drawn out rather than to exert myself in conversation.' It must have been bewildering and disappointing for a woman sustaining a ladylike life under canvas to discover the limitations of potential colonial husbands. Verbal sniping between men and women was common in the camp, but Louisa was determined not to let her standards slip and sink to the level of waspishness. Her brother, Gervase, had been very offended by a Miss Spencer's unkind treatment and 'unladylike conduct'. Had they been Englishmen or Englishwomen on a grand tour of Europe, Louisa could not have set her fellow settlers higher standards.

Her father began to clear woods, or, more accurately, 'set some Indians to clear'. At last, at the end of May 1841, the first public building, the storehouse, was finished and on a day of streaming rain, forty settlers were entertained in it, with the head carpenter and the thatcher prominent amongst them. Kangaroo soup, kangaroo pies and steaks, pork, beef, pease pudding and suet puddings were served. Soon thereafter, a year after the founding of the colony, the Cliftons received a party of visitors who included a Mr Eliot, Louisa's future husband as it turned out, in their new habitation. 'As the whole roof had not been thatched, the rain dripped through the canvas thrown over the aperture and the table and plates wetted and it obliged all the ladies to sit high up the table, so that poor Robert was left at the bottom with the children, Miss S., and our stupid young men.'

Yet in this scatter of tents and half-finished huts, 'I was in hopes that I had obtained the first contribution to our Australind museum in the form of some skins of beautiful birds that he [Mr Eliot] begged me to accept . . . He is a very droll person and I cannot quite understand him; truly and thoroughly amiable in the best and highest sense, and gentlemanly in every feeling.'

Sheets of water came through their roof still, and Louisa and her sister, Ellen, slept habitually in wet beds. 'But I found it acceptable nevertheless, being dead tired . . . No future settlers can suffer what we do; for when others come they will find things made for them and our experience available . . . Friends in England should be made acquainted with this Australian coast in this season . . . I feel horrified to think of people blindly coming out at any time of year, to be exposed to such awful weather as this.'

Louisa was speaking of the Western Australian winter, when a desert-like cold prevailed at night and all the year's rain fell in fiercely concentrated bouts. At last, the Cliftons' house of thin planks, with a rush thatching and a floor composed of a layer of bricks packed close and tight upon the sand, was finished. The news that her English suitor did not intend to follow Louisa to the colony made her declare that she was finished with men for good. The situation of two Aborigines brought before her father for theft evoked her best, but unavailing, feelings of Quaker compassion. 'Some of them will be sent, I fear, to Rottnest [gaol] . . . but being deprived of liberty and independence so dear to wild man, they soon die of broken hearts . . . When will justice appear upon earth? Not I fear while white man who professes Christianity falls so far short of acting up to its first principles.' In 1843 the Western Australian Company ceased to operate and its Australind holdings: land and any company equipment. Most emigrants had to go elsewhere—the labourers to look for work. Marshall Clifton lived on in the area on an Admiralty pension.

Louisa also stayed, having married George Eliot in June 1842, and began an honourable career in the hinterland as a settler's wife, the mother of young colonials, and an exponent of kangaroo cuisine.

CHAPTER 19

MYALL CREEK . . . AND BEYOND

In the 1820s outposts like Bathurst, to the west of the Blue Mountains in New South Wales, had barely more than a hundred settlers, and the dream of the surrounding Wiradjuri was that they might be driven off forever. The leader of Aboriginal resistance in the area was a man named Windradyne (also dubbed by the white settlers 'Saturday'). The Wiradjuri had been affronted by the destruction of native game, and did not understand why shepherds and pastoral foremen were so aggrieved when, in compensation, the tribespeople slaughtered livestock.

Windradyne's idea was like Pemulwuy's before him—of consolidating scattered clan groups into a larger and more militant group. The Bathurst commandant was a man of tyrannous nature named James Morisset—he later became commandant on Norfolk Island—and his 1824 imprisonment of Windradyne in leg irons seems to have accelerated rather than stopped Aboriginal attacks. Aboriginal people were shot at on sight, or treated to flour laced with the arsenic dip used to cure scab in sheep. Windradyne survived a massacre over the taking of potatoes in which he saw members of his family group shot down, and became more militant still. Some Wiradjuri under his leadership attacked a hut and stockyard which had been built on a ceremonial site about which they had earlier made a protest. Three station hands were killed in the attack. The next day they killed four further hut-keepers and shepherds. These were shocking killings—every settler was haunted by the possibility of being a corpse studded with spears.

Meanwhile, the *Sydney Gazette* had been appalled to hear of the killing of Aboriginal innocents, who were, after all, British subjects. The *Gazette* declared, 'The adoption of the most determined measures must be speedily resorted to, to effect the suppression of such wanton and horrid murder.'

'Philanthropus', writing to the same paper on 5 August 1824, agreed: 'I suppose the New Hollanders to be *human creatures* and that their maker has taught them more than the beasts of the earth. I think they have with myself, and all other men, one common ancestor . . . Hence I have been led to estimate even the least one of these, my despised and injured brethren, at more value than all the sheep and cattle on Bathurst Plains; than all the flocks and herds in the territory of New South Wales; than all the animals in the whole world!' Another letter-writer sympathetic to the Aboriginals and appalled at the idea that they should be hunted down for the sake of sheep, nontheless argued a fine point in the same journal during the same debate, 'They are the *inhabitants*, but not the *proprietors* of the land.'

It was a rare settler who could disapprove of acres of land 'reclaimed by our industry', as a Methodist minister later put it. Even if malice did not operate, the two dreamings—Aboriginal and European—of what should be done to the earth were in conflict with each other, and there was a sense in which that was a trigger for all the tragedies.

Morisset did send an overseer and four of his men to Sydney to stand trial for killings on the O'Connell Plains, south-east of Bathurst. They were all acquitted, and the lesson became apparent—one was unlikely to be found guilty of the murder of natives, particularly if there was provocation and no record was made. A settler named William Cox told a public meeting in Bathurst, 'The best thing that can be done is to shoot all the blacks and manure the ground with their carcasses. That is all the good they are fit for! It is also recommended that all the women and children be shot. That is the most certain way of getting rid of the pestilent race.'

Certainly somewhere near twenty shepherds and hut-keepers were killed, but the losses on the Wiradjuri side were probably five times that number, and increased after the governor, Sir Thomas Brisbane, in August 1824 proclaimed martial law west of the mountains and sent a detachment of the 40th Regiment to Bathurst. The soldiers in Bathurst now numbered seventy-five and there were an equal number of enraged settlers willing to join them on any expedition. A group of Wiradjuri camping on the banks of the Macquarie to the north-west of Bathurst was attracted to a party of soldiers who laid out some food as bait and then shot down thirty of them. Another detachment of soldiers forced a party of Wiradjuri over the cliffs at Bells Falls. Many of these people had had no involvement with any of the attacks on the huts.

After two months Wiradjuri society had been torn apart, and survivors had to hide in the remotest gorges of the country. Leading his family and some survivors over the Blue Mountains and down to Parramatta to surrender, Windradyne gave himself up. Some whites wrote 'Peace' on a sheet of cardboard, attached it to a straw hat and made Windradyne wear it. His life spared, he would be a reduced man until his death as a result of a tribal fight in 1829.

When the Liverpool Plains, in the area surrounding present-day Gunnedah, were settled in the 1830s, the memory of how things had been done in the Bathurst area was still fresh. This time the tribe in question was the Kamilaroi. A number of young male settlers had moved into the area from other parts of New South Wales and lived the harsh slab-timber and bark-roof life of squatting with their assigned convicts. There were some four thousand Kamilaroi in the area in 1836, and the normal skirmishes took place. One posse of pastoralists, drovers and mounted police rode through the area for two weeks and executed eighty Kamilaroi people. Then, when the Kamilaroi came down the valley of the Gwydir from their winter quarters in the spring of 1837, they were horrified to see the damage done to their land by grazing animals. There were immediate retaliatory killings of livestock and conflict arose over the misuse of Aboriginal women by settlers.

The tragedy for the Kamilaroi was that Lieutenant Colonel Kenneth Snodgrass was for two months, over New Year 1838–39, the Administrator of New South Wales, awaiting the arrival of Governor Gipps. Snodgrass was a man of pastoral bent and, in answer to complaints of pastoralists about the activities of the natives, sent the commander of the New South Wales mounted police, Major James Nunn, to the Liverpool Plains with the instructions: 'Use your utmost exertion to suppress these outrages. There are a thousand blacks there, and if they are not stopped, we may have them presently within the boundaries.'

Major Nunn and his party of twenty-three mounted police arrived near the settlement of Manilla in early 1838 and joined up with a posse of local stockmen. At first light on a January morning, they surrounded an Aboriginal camp on the northern bank of the Namoi River. In desperation, one group of surrounded

Aboriginals accused another group of being the raiders of cattle and Nunn accepted their word, taking the 'wild' group prisoner. One of them was shot, and the others let go. At Waterloo Creek, on the Namoi River, the captives were massacred—up to fifty Kamilaroi were shot. A similar encounter had earlier taken place at Ardgowan Plains Station. When Nunn and his party arrived at Gravesend Station, they were in triumphant mood, and grateful pastoralists put out the welcome mat for the major all the way back to Sydney. At Tamworth the hands who worked for the Australian Agricultural Company cheered him, but when he saw the new governor, George Gipps, there were no congratulations. Gipps was appalled at the licence Nunn had taken and so was the Attorney-General of New South Wales, the Irishman John Hubert Plunkett.

Plunkett had been good friends of both Daniel O'Connell, the famed Liberator of Ireland, and of the liberal governor Richard Bourke. He and Bourke had framed legislation for Irish-style national schools in New South Wales; they had stood against any attempt to establish an official church; they believed that colonial self-rule should not be delayed. Now Plunkett and his new governor, Gipps, decided it was time, despite the difficulties, to prosecute those who took the lives of Aborigines. It was apparent to Nunn that this was the view of the Secretary for the Colonies, Lord Glenelg, as well. Though he was a hero on the frontier, he was not considered one in Whitehall. But because he had operated on Snodgrass's orders, it was decided nothing could be done about him. Nor was Snodgrass indicted.

Henry Dangar was a long-established pastoralist of Cornish background who lived in the Upper Hunter Valley, but also had a station on Myall Creek which ran from the Gwydir River on the northern Liverpool Plains, near present-day Inverell. The people on Myall Creek were relatives of the Kamilaroi named the Kwiambal, and the Kwiambal group and the stockmen on Dangar's property got on well together. The station was run by a man named William Hobbs with the help, amongst others, of two assigned convicts transported for life—George Anderson and Charles Kilmeister. George Anderson had a relationship with a young Kwiambal woman named Impeta, and was sympathetic to the natives, and so it appeared was Kilmeister. The stockmen would often join the Aboriginal people after work for socialising on the banks of the creek.

When some of Dangar's station hands went off to bring cattle in closer to the station, Hobbs followed them to guard against stragglers in the herd. The men with the main herd met a posse, led by a man named John Russell, an emancipist, and including five assigned convicts, all armed, and travelling—with their overseers' sanction—to 'deal' with the natives. One of the men was a black Liverpudlian, John Johnston, and another an Irishman named Ned Foley, who had been transported for the same crime as Hugh Larkin—assaulting habitation. Russell asked the drovers if there were any Aboriginals living on the Myall Creek station. They replied that there were about twelve women, twelve children and sixteen men. They were anxious to protect the Aboriginal people by saying that they had been there for many weeks, and that therefore they could not be the blacks who had caused trouble further down the river.

Back at Myall Creek a superintendent from a neighbouring station had arrived and commissioned ten Kwiambal men to go downstream and cut bark. So the men were absent when Russell's posse, grown considerably in number, turned up at the station, galloping up to the homestead with every display of their intentions.

The Aboriginal women and children ran from the creek to Anderson's hut, believing that their white friends would protect them, while Kilmeister went out to meet the posse. He was relaxed with them, since he knew most of them. With the Kwiambal huddling around him, Anderson asked Russell what his plans were. He was going to tie them all together, he said, and take them 'over the back of the range' to frighten them. Russell and others forced their way past Anderson. The Aboriginals called out to Kilmeister and Anderson to save them. Kilmeister did not resist, but Anderson protested. A woman who claimed to be the spouse of Yintayintin, one of the Aboriginals who worked round the station, was left behind, and another woman was also excused in an attempt to win Anderson over. Anderson also managed to hide a child in his hut. The prisoners were led away and later two shots were heard but no more.

Two kilometres out in the bush near a new stockyard lay a heap of twenty-eight butchered Kwiambal bodies, including Charlie, the three-year-old station favourite. Most of the children had been decapitated by swords and the adults had been hacked to death.

The next day the killers seemed in excellent spirits as they breakfasted at Myall Creek, discussed the best features of their horses and made occasional reference to the killings. Anderson was particularly appalled to hear them speak of the pack rape of one of the younger women. When they saw Anderson's disgust, Russell, the leader of the party, asked Ned Foley to stay with Anderson and make sure he did not do anything 'unwise'. That day they burned the bodies, with Kilmeister accepting orders to tend the pyre.

The Kwiambal bark-cutters had arrived meanwhile at a nearby station where the overseer, Eaton, knew that they would be in danger from the posse. He sent them and all the people from his station into the hills. A small number of them were pursued, caught by the posse and shot.

At Myall Creek, the manager, William Hobbs, arrived back the next day. He began quizzing Anderson and Yintayintin. Kilmeister had gone off with the posse on their latest excursions, and now returned. Later that afternoon Yintayintin took Hobbs to the stockyard massacre site, which he would later describe as 'horrible beyond description'. Hobbs did not know what to do, but at last decided he must write letters outlining what he knew of the massacre to the police magistrate at Muswellbrook and to Henry Dangar. Public opinion in pastoral areas disagreed with Hobbs's intentions and with what he had set in motion, and Dangar would soon dismiss him, perhaps under pressure from other pastoralists.

The Attorney-General decided that Kilmeister, John Russell, John Johnston, Ned Foley and seven others were to be charged. The men brought down to Sydney were tried in the Supreme Court for the murder of Daddy, an old man whose body had been most identifiable at the site. The senior prosecutor was Plunkett himself, and his junior was another Irishman, dapper little Roger Therry. Chief Justice Dowling gave strong instructions in favour of conviction, but it took the jury a mere fifteen minutes to acquit the men. When the verdict came in the court broke into loud applause. The Attorney-General now cut back on the number of accused and charged seven of the men with the murder of four victims including the three-year-old boy, Charlie. Many newspapers called for the release of the prisoners and the *Herald* attacked Gipps as a zealot.

Henry Dangar, as he had at the first trial, paid for the defendants' counsel. But Anderson and Hobbs were potent witnesses. The seven were found guilty of the murder of a child unknown, and Governor Gipps confirmed their sentence. The seven waiting in the condemned cell were the subject of kindnesses from various men with pastoral interests, who probably gave them the false comfort of assuring them they would not hang. And although they were willing to confess to their crime, they felt grievously unlucky, since, as they said, killing Aboriginals was a common activity on the frontier. They must have wondered why Major Nunn could kill so many, and they had to swing for a lesser number.

Justice Burton, in sentencing them, had indeed mentioned his sympathy over their transportation and their remote placement on stations far from the improving influence of churches and the institutions of civilisation. Pastoral associations all over New South Wales angrily demanded a reprieve. The *Herald* pleaded, 'Where, we ask, is the man endowed with even a modicum of reasoning powers, who will assert that this great continent was ever intended by the creator to remain an unproductive wilderness? . . . The British people found a portion of the globe in a state of waste—they took possession of it. And they had a perfect right to do so, under the Divine authority, by which man was commanded to go forth and people, and till the land.'

The *Herald* also declared that there was a chance that this judgment would encourage more vengefulness against the natives, and sadly, vengefulness and secrecy now became the established mode. Plunkett's hope had been to protect the Aborigines from molestation and intrusion upon their rights to the same extent that the emancipists were protected. Things would not turn out as well as that.

CONTESTING THE LAND

The idea that Australia consisted of waste lands waiting to be seized by enterprising Europeans was both in law and at the popular level a common belief in the nineteenth century. Indeed in 1819, the law officers of the British government had declared Australia to be *terra nullius*, land belonging to no one prior to British occupation. But there was barely a season in which the concept of *terra nullius* was not challenged—by Aboriginals and sympathetic Europeans. Debate over the legitimacy of the settlers' seizure of land would emerge very early. Captain David Collins had written in the 1790s, 'But, strange as it may appear, they [the Aboriginals] have also their real estates. Bennelong, both before he went to England, and since his return, often assured me that the island of Me-mel (called by us Goat Island), close by Sydney Cove, was his own property; that it was his father's, and that he should give it to Bygone, his particular friend and companion. To this little spot he appeared much attached; and we have often seen him and his wife Barangaroo, feasting and enjoying themselves on it. He told us of other people who possessed this kind of hereditary property, which they retained undisturbed.'

The debate over waste land versus native title raged over the years in the colonial press, especially following incidents such as the surrender of Windradyne and the massacre at Myall Creek. It was just as heated in the huts of the hinterland

and around the fires of stockmen. In 1844, a young man named Henry Mort living on the frontiers of settlement in Queensland described to his mother and sister in England the conversation he had had with his fellow educated stockmen: 'Had a very animated discussion on the "moral right of a nation to take forcible possession of a country inhabited by savages". John and David McConnell argued it was morally right for a Christian nation to extirpate savages from their native soil in order that it may be peopled with a more intelligent and civilised race of human beings, etc., etc.' Certainly even Henry Mort had no doubt that the ministers of the Church of England should carry the sacred torch of civilisation and religion so that the 'darkest and most remote recesses of heathen barbarism may be illuminated thereby'.

A normal justification for settlers in moving onto Aboriginal lands was a reference to the Bible, and in particular to God's Old Testament instruction to go forth and multiply and subdue the earth, as quoted by the *Herald* in the wake of the Myall Creek trials. The Aborigines had failed to subdue the earth and thus left it open to those who were willing to. Christopher Hodgson, a parson's son who had farmed the Darling Downs west of Brisbane, wrote of his years in Australia, 'Thus far the creator of the universe is just, in that He allows the superiority of civilisation over barbarism, of intellect over instinct or brutish reason . . . the world was made for man's enjoyment and created not as a beautiful spectacle, or spotless design, but as a field to be improved upon.'

The political radical Presbyterian JD Lang was inevitably attracted to this basic issue. He was sympathetic to the natives, but he had a not uncharacteristic take on the subject for a man of his period. In a speech to the meeting of the Moreton Bay Friends of the Aborigines, he was reported as saying that the settlers 'were certainly debtors to the original Australian Aborigines, for they had seized upon their land and confiscated their territory. In doing that he did not think they had done anything wrong . . . The white man had indeed only carried out the intentions of the Creator in coming and settling down in the territory of the natives.' Later, though, from his questioning of Aboriginals, he decided that 'particular districts are not merely the property of particular tribes; particular sections or portions of these districts are universally recognised by the natives as the property of individual members of these tribes'. If an owner decided to burn off grass on his land, 'which is done for the double purpose of enabling the natives to take the older animals more easily, and to provide a new crop of sweeter grass for the growing generation of the forest', then tribes from all about would be invited in, the landowner giving his permission for all to come to the land and hunt its wild animals. 'I have often heard natives myself tell me, in answer to my own questions on the subject, who were the Aboriginal owners of particular tracts of land now held by Europeans; and indeed this idea of property in the soil for hunting purposes is universal amongst the Aboriginals.'

At a meeting of the Aboriginal Protection Society in Sydney in 1838, Richard Windeyer, a young barrister who had been scandalised by the Myall Creek massacre, and who was campaigning to have Aborigines permitted to give evidence in court, nonetheless spoke on similar lines as Lang in Moreton Bay. As quoted in the *Colonist*, 27 October 1838, 'He disagreed with the sentiments that the natives had been usurped by *fraud and violence by the Europeans* He could not look upon the natives as the *exclusive* proprietors of the soil. Nor could he entertain the ridiculous notion that we had no right to be here. He viewed colonisation on the basis of a broad principle laid down by the first and great Legislator, in the command He issued to man to multiply and replenish the earth the land belonged to him who should first cultivate it.'

Captain Sturt, said Windeyer, had stated in his journals that he had travelled three hundred miles (480 kilometres) and only met one family. Now, he wished to know, 'whether these three hundred miles belonged to this one family? No. He only had a title to lands, who first bestows labour upon it.'

And yet there was an abiding uneasiness. 'If we have no right to be here,' said Windeyer, 'we have nothing to do but to take ship and go home.'

Occasionally a less ambiguous statement would appear, such as that in the *Launceston Advertiser* of 26 September 1831. 'Are these unhappy people, the subjects of our King, in a state of rebellion, or are they an injured people, whom we have invaded and with whom we are at war? . . . They have never been subdued, therefore they are not rebellious subjects, but an injured nation, defending in their own way their rightful possessions, which have been torn from them by force.'

Such opinions did not wash so well, said EW Landor, the Western Australian lawyer settler, once you had to live amongst the nomads. 'The most prominent idea in the imagination of a settler on his first arrival at an Australian colony is on the subject of the natives. Whilst in England he was, like the rest of his generous minded countrymen, sensibly alive to the wrongs of these unhappy beings . . . Full of these noble and ennobling sentiments, the immigrant approaches the scene of British colonial cruelty, but no sooner does he land, than a considerable change takes place in his feelings. He begins to think that he is about to place his valuable person and property in the very midst of a nation of savages, who are entirely unrestrained by any moral or human laws or any religious scruples, from taking the most disagreeable liberties with these precious things . . . We have acted exactly as Julius Caesar did when he took possession of Britain . . . We have a right to our Australian possessions; but it is the right of conquest, and we hold them with the grasp of power.'

Such would often be the language of the frontier—'You don't know them as we know them.' That was the rhetoric in Moreton Bay, as the settlement at Brisbane was transforming itself from penal colony into a commercial port serving a rich hinterland. 'If we hold this country by the right of conquest,' the *Moreton Bay Courier* of 9 December 1848 wrote, 'and if that right gives us a just claim to its continual possession, we must be empowered to enforce our claim by the strong arm, when necessary. One law *must* apply to our conquered nations.'

Edward Curr, a former Van Diemen's Land pastoralist who had become an early Port Phillip settler and conservative, and had seen the process of encounter between the nomads and the pastoralists frequently, could understand the Aboriginal side. He believed as a rule of thumb that whenever there was encounter between Aboriginal tribes and white pioneers, a war began which lasted from six months to ten years according to the nature of the country. If the Aboriginals had many fastnesses to retreat to, the war was longer. 'Hence the meeting of the white and black races in Australia, considered generally, results in war. Nor is it to be wondered at. The White Man looks on the possession of the lands by the Blacks as no proper occupation, and practically and avowedly declines to allow them the common rights of human beings. On the other hand, the tribe which has held its land from time immemorial and always maintained, according to native policy, the unauthorised digging up of one root on its soil to be a *casus belli* [reason for war], suddenly finds not only that strangers of another race have located themselves permanently in their lands, but that they have brought with them a multitude of animals, which devour wholesale the roots and vegetables which constitute their principal food, and drive off the game they formerly hunted. They are also warned that they are not to hunt the livestock that is present on the land which they consider theirs. The tribe, being threatened with war by the white stranger, if it attempts to get food in its own country, and with the same consequences if it intrudes on the lands of a neighbouring tribe, finds itself reduced to make choice of certain death from starvation and probable death from the rifle, and naturally chooses the latter.'

Curr's reflections show that pioneers did indeed often understand the dilemma they presented to the natives, as well as the dilemma the natives presented to them. White men took women from amongst the natives, but no extra enlightenment came thereby. It is not to excuse anything to recognise that killing might become the way out not only for commercial frustration (the decimation of flocks), not only for cultural frustration (the apparent refusal of Aborigines to give up their claim to land and sites of importance), but even from moral frustration for a problem which seemed to test a wisdom greater than normal men possessed.

Edward John Eyre, the South Australian explorer, declared in his *Journals of Expeditions of Discovery*, 'that our presence and settlement, in any particular locality, do, in point of fact, actually dispossess the Aboriginal inhabitants'. The localities most cherished for grazing and cultivation were also the places where Aboriginal food was most easily procurable. In South Australia in 1840, however, Governor George Gawler and his Land Commissioner, Charles Sturt, had to explain to a group of leading, disgruntled settlers why the Aboriginals would be given the right to select land as reserves before the British did. For South Australia, both at the level of its charter and by government instructions was meant to recognise native rights. Charles Sturt wrote to the settlers on 1 August 1841: 'I am desired by His Excellency to say, in reply, that it is to him a matter of deep surprise that persons of intelligence, like yourselves . . . should consider any rights that any European possesses to the province as preliminary to those of the Aboriginal inhabitants. Those natural indefeasible rights which, as His Excellency conceives, are vested in them as their birthright, have been confirmed to them by the royal instructions to the Governor, and by the Commissioners' instructions to the resident Commissioner.'

Elsewhere, though, native attacks put any idea of 'natural indefeasible rights' out of settlers' minds. In 1840, the Port Phillip pastoralist David Waugh went to Melbourne on business and when he returned to his station, having taken out his squatter's licence and procured supplies, he found that the local Aborigines had killed the two men left in charge of the sheep and plundered the head station, putting its stockman to flight. The losses were considerable—638 sheep were destroyed or died from wounds.

There had been similar depredations by Aboriginals in Van Diemen's Land. One account tells us, 'Mr Bell's house and servants attacked on Great Jordan Lagoon; the natives kept at bay from the house, but one man received a spear through the thigh. Mr Hopley murdered about a mile from Mr Betts', James Macarthy desperately wounded. February 12 1830, Mr Howells' dwelling burned, Mrs Howells and her children narrowly escaping the flames.' And so on.

A quarter of a century later, in the Wide Bay area around Maryborough, north of Moreton Bay, many stores and houses were robbed and two settlers were killed, and again stock losses were considerable.

A young Irish lawyer, GF Moore, who had landed in Western Australia in October 1830, within a month found himself on the first punitive expedition in that colony against natives, a fracas which became the murderous battle of Pinjarra, south of the Swan River settlement, provoked by a number of raids by the Nyoongar people. Moore came from the robust Protestant tradition of County Tyrone. As soon-to-be Secretary of the Agricultural and Horticultural Society, Moore was an apostle of agriculture, an upholder of colonisation. Yet he was not closed to the value of the indigenes and had a sympathetic concern for them, ultimately learning their language and recording some of their stories, though 'he wished sadly that they would not steal his pigs'. He published a descriptive vocabulary of *The Language In Common Use Among The Aboriginals of Western Australia.*

The Nyoongars were a remarkably tall and robust group of Aboriginal people. Their tribe, said Moore, 'had long been indulging in almost unchecked commission of numerous outrages and atrocious murders'. Amongst the killings was that of Private Nesbitt of the 21st Regiment and the spearing of a civilian.

The punitive expedition was led by Captain Stirling, the governor, and came at last upon undulating hill country with nutritious food for cattle where the voices of many natives were heard. 'The moment was considered propitiously favourable for punishing the perpetrators . . . should this prove to be the offending tribe. His Excellency rode forward two hundred or three hundred yards with Mr Peel and Mr Norcott, who knew the natives and their language, and commenced calling out and talking to them for the purpose of bringing on an interview. No answer was returned because the noise of the natives seemed so clamorous.' The instant they saw a party of advancing police, the natives, about seventy in number, 'started to their feet, the men seized their spears and showed a formidable front before retreating, gradually quickening their pace until the word "forward" from the leader of the gallant little party brought the horsemen in about half a minute dashing into the midst of them, the same moment having discovered the well-known features of some of the most atrocious offenders of the obnoxious tribe'. Norcott recognised one 'celebrated for his audacity and courage' and announced that 'these are the fellas we want, for here's that old rascal Noonar'. The native turned around and cried, "Yes, yes, Noonar, me," and was in the act of hurling his spear at Norcott in token of requital for the recognition, when the latter shot him dead. The identity of the tribe being now clearly established, and the natives turning to assail their pursuers, the firing continued, and was returned by the former with spears as they entered the river.'

It is not just to say that a godly, civilised, companionable and curious man like Moore would colour the truth, but everything seems to go conveniently for the attackers—Noonar is identified, then identifies himself, then threatens Norcott's life before being shot in self-defence. The identity of the tribe is absolutely established and the natives turn to assail their pursuers—that being the reason the firing continued. When the governor's rearguard came up, the Nyoongars were subject to crossfire and took to the river, hiding amongst the roots and branches and holes in the banks or lying in the water with their faces only uncovered. But they were still treacherous, in Moore's account, 'ready with a spear under water, to take advantage of anyone who approached within reach'. Those who exposed themselves 'were gradually picked out of their concealment by the cross-fire from both banks, until between 25 and 30 were left dead on the field and in the river'. On being assured of personal safety, eight women and some children emerged from their hiding places and were detained as prisoners until the end of the battle.

Having, no doubt with sincerity, established the guilt of the victims, Moore was not abashed by the potential numbers of dead. 'It is . . . very probable that more men were killed in the river, and floated down with the stream. Notwithstanding the care which was taken not to injure the women during the skirmish, it cannot appear surprising that one woman and several children were killed, and one woman among the prisoners had received a ball through the thigh.' During the height of the fire, a number of men cried out that they were females and should be spared, 'but evidence to the contrary was too strong to admit the plea'. Perhaps half of the male population of the tribe was wiped out, including 'fifteen very old and desperate offenders', and so the bugle sounded the ceasefire. Captain Ellis had been badly wounded in the right temple by a spear and a constable had received a wound above the right shoulder. After a consultation over the prisoners it was resolved to set them free, 'for the purpose of fully explaining to the remnant of the tribe the cause of the chastisement which had been inflicted'.

There is intense sorrow in these events—the sorrow of the suddenly and cruelly stripped-down DNA of the tribe, and the sorrow in the fact that the views of the time and the tenuousness of European settlement in Western Australia made such a scene philosophically, scientifically and theologically inevitable. For a man to say round the campfire that night, after the women and children had been let go, and as the supplies on the packhorses were unloaded to make damper and to cook beef, that the Nyoongar had died for their country would have been a proposition laughed to scorn, even though sophisticated minds, from Stirling's to Moore's, were gathered round the crackling wood.

It was a further misfortune for indigenes that the great passion of late eighteenth- and early nineteenth-century science, on whose behalf people from Phillip onwards sent back Aboriginal skulls for study in Europe, was phrenology. This so-called science dismissed the Aboriginal skull and brain as substandard. In the *Colonial Literary Journal* of August–September 1845, a correspondent wrote under the name 'Aneas': 'The Aboriginal cranium appears to be large, although in reality the brain is not so ... The great preponderancy of the brain in the New Hollander, as in all savage nations, lies in the posterior parts of the head—the seat of the passions, and inferior sentiments; the moral and intellectual portions, with few exceptions, are very deficient.'

With eminent men assuring the settler of the primitive nature of the Aboriginal brain, there was less reticence about putting a bullet in it. An allied myth which condemned the Aboriginal was that native ownership had been bloodlessly yielded up due to the cultural inferiority of the Aboriginal. As one phrenologist said in November 1851, 'The Cape Caffre and the New Zealanders, possessing superior phrenological development to our Aborigines, have each cost the British nation much blood and treasure to subjugate, while the dim twilight intellect of a New Hollander yields his country a bloodless conquest.'

In 1838, the missionary Lancelot Threlkeld, who had tried to train the Hunter Valley natives in agriculture, attacked the pseudo-science of phrenology as 'this miserable attempt' to deduce that Aborigines 'have an innate deficiency of intellect rendering them incapable of instruction', a belief that led men to the idea that they were merely 'part and parcel of the brute creation'.

This made it all the more valid to exploit their labour. One commentator wrote of early Queensland: 'Gladstone [the town] would suffer much from want of labour, if the despised black were not to be found, for a small piece of tobacco or a handful of flour . . . ever willing to render any service required of them. Many a time that I noticed a native groaning under a heavy load of bark, that he was carrying on his naked back to some white that would perhaps swear at him, not give him the promised tobacco or flour, and if he hung about his dwelling, bring out a pistol [and] threaten to shoot if he did not move off.'

Ultimately it was the unwillingness of the natives to accept the eminently better—in white eyes—European order of things which most bemused settlers. W Ridley, a member of the Select Committee on the Native Mounted Police, Queensland, in 1861 wrote, 'Bungaree, who after taking prizes in Sydney College, speaking good Latin, and behaving as a gentleman in elegant society, returned to the bush, and then entered the black police, once said, in a melancholy tone to Lieutenant Fulford, "I wish I had never been taken out of the bush, and educated as I have been, for I cannot be a white man, they will never look on me as one of themselves; and I cannot be a black fellow, I am disgusted with their way of living."'

The identical tension was reported by Sir George Grey in his *Journals of Two Expeditions in North-West and Western Australia*: 'The officers of the *Beagle* took away with them a native of the name of Miago, who remained absent with them for several months. I saw him on the northwest coast, on board the *Beagle*, apparently perfectly civilised; he waited at the gun-room mess, was temperate (never tasting spirits), attentive, cheerful, and remarkably clean in his person. The next time I saw him was at Swan River, where he had been left on the return of the *Beagle*. He was then again a savage, almost naked, painted all over, and had been concerned in several murders.'

Yet Grey was sympathetic to Miago. When he landed, he said, none among the white people would be truly friends of his—they would give him scraps from their tables, but the very outcasts of white society would not have treated him as an equal. He could not have married a white woman, he had no certain means of subsistence open to him. Grey thought he himself faced with the same dilemma would have made the choice Miago did, and gone back into the bush.

Often, on the frontier, reflections on the native enigma were not as subtle.

George Dunderdale, a clerk of the court in Gippsland who had travelled widely both in the United States and Australia, knew the rawness and directness of the treatment of natives in the region. Charles James Tyers, the Crown Lands Commissioner for Gippsland, was questioned by Dunderdale about his *modus operandi*. 'He was informed that some cattle had been speared and he rode away with his horse to investigate the complaint . . . Traces of natives were soon discovered, and their probable hiding place in the scrub was pointed out to Mr Tyers. He therefore dismounted, and directing two of his black troopers armed with carbines to accompany him, he held a pistol in each hand, and walked cautiously into the scrub. The two black troopers discharged their carbines. The Commissioner had seen nothing to shoot at, but his blacks soon showed him two of the natives a few yards in front, both mortally wounded. Mr Tyers sent a report of the affair to the Government, and that was the end of it. This manner of dealing with the native difficulty was adopted in the early days, and is still used under the name of "punitive expeditions". That judge who prayed to heaven in his wig and robes of office said that the Aborigines were subjects of the Queen, and that it was a mercy to them to be under Her protection. The mercy accorded to them was less than Jedburgh [a border town in Northumberland where stock thieves were said to be summarily strung up] justice: they were shot first, and not even tried afterwards.'

CHAPTER 20

LOST WOMEN, LOST TRIBES

European fears about the peril white women faced from Aboriginals on the frontiers expressed themselves in two extraordinary incidents. The *Sydney Herald* of 28 December 1840 carried a letter from the usually phlegmatic Angus McMillan, discoverer and resident of Gippsland. On the coast near Corner Inlet, McMillan had found at an abandoned Aboriginal camp a cache of European clothing, male and female, including a new brown Macintosh cloak stained with blood. There were various items of cash, decorations, British blankets, a thermometer tube and a musket, and a number of London, Glasgow and Aberdeen papers of 1837 and 1838. There were two children's copy books, one Bible printed in Edinburgh and one set of the National Loan Fund regulations respecting policies of life insurance. Enclosed in three kangaroo-skin bags was the dead body of a male child about two years old. The local physician, Doctor Arbuckle, examined the body and found the child to be European.

McMillan's party had caught a glimpse of Aboriginal males driving women in front of them. One of them 'we noticed constantly looking behind her, at us . . . on examining the marks and figures about the largest of the native huts we were immediately impressed with the belief that the unfortunate female is a European—a captive of these ruthless savages'.

This sighting established the existence of the lost woman for many people on the frontier and in Melbourne. The story, as if drawing on people's nightmares, revived periodically. As one poet in the Melbourne *Argus* wrote,

Unhappiest of the fairer kind;
Who knows the misery of thy mind,
Exposed to insults worse than death
Compell'd to breathe the pois'nous breath
Of a rank scented black;
To yield to his abhorr'd embrace,
To kiss his staring, ugly face,
And listen to his clack.

The power of the concept of the tender white woman subjected to heathenish embraces of savages was not peculiar to Gippsland or to Australia in general. But it provided a further reason to pursue and harry the blacks, especially the Kurnai, who, as well as allegedly keeping a white woman against her wishes, were doing a certain amount of concrete harm to stock and shepherds.

Some Kurnai were also dying in revenge killings between clans, produced by deaths from imported infections. No death was un-caused in the eyes of Aboriginal society, and punishment for increased deaths that we would consider 'natural' was compounded by the Aboriginal need to readjust the balance of the world by often deadly retaliation. George Augustus Robinson reported in 1844 that the Westernport tribes had been all but wiped out on this basis by the Brataualung of the Port Albert area. Then Melbourne Blacks led by Lal-lal and Billy Lonsdale killed at least thirty Brataualung in 1847. Thus death compounded itself amongst the indigenes.

In 1846 there were further reports of the sighting of a white woman; again the Aboriginals were said to be driving her before them. That year John McDonald, proprietor of the Scottish Chiefs Hotel in Melbourne, wrote to the *Argus* to say that he believed a woman named Anna MacPherson was the captive of the blacks of Gippsland. She had been a passenger on the *Britannia* which had sunk on the Gippsland coast in 1838. A Sydney source claimed that she was the Irish wife of a brewer, a Mrs T Capel. Others said her name was Lord. A public meeting was held in Melbourne and a subscription was gathered to send an expedition to Gippsland. Led by a former trooper named de Villiers and by the businessman James Warman, the party took off for Corner Inlet, carrying with them a number of handkerchiefs on which was printed in English and Gaelic: 'White Woman!—there are 14 armed men, partly White and partly Black, in search of you. Be cautious; and rush to them when you see them near you. Be particularly on the lookout every dawn of morning, for it is then that the party are in hopes of rescuing you. The white settlement is toward the setting sun.'

What the expedition found was not a white woman but the skulls of dead Kurnai—the banks of streams and rivers were sown with them. A native seemed to intimate, however, that the white woman was living with a man called Bunjeleene in the Snowy Mountains. Another native mentioned that the white woman liked to sing Psalm 100, 'Make a joyful noise unto the Lord, all ye lands'.

While de Villiers and Warman were searching for the woman, Captain Henry Dana, a squatter and head of the border police, was moving with his posse from Cape Otway to the west of Melbourne, where he had been massacring natives, to Gippsland in the east. He had found that armed and uniformed natives were willing to kill distant tribespeople to whom they were not related by blood or mysteries. Warman's expedition and Dana's, independently of each other, tracked the mysterious white woman into the Snowy region.

Warman found plenty of signs of Dana's work—Snowy River Aboriginals lying dead of gunshot wounds. The native police, said a shocked Warman, were 'harpies of Hell misnamed police' and there were Europeans who were not far behind them in savagery. Dana's expedition claimed to have come close to finding the woman—they had found a native cloak allegedly belonging to her. One party claimed to have seen her footprints, but according to the *Argus* back in Melbourne, Bunjeleene concealed her whereabouts by putting possum skins on her feet.

There were some who dared surmise the white woman did not really exist and was a figurehead washed ashore from a wrecked ship. But another expedition was sent out under Sergeant Walshe of the border police and contact was made with Bunjeleene, who presented the party with a female native from Port Phillip, and said he had no other alien women. In the end Bunjeleene and his two wives and two sons were held at native police headquarters at Narre Warren. One of his wives died there and then, in late 1848, so did Bunjeleene.

Now men began to report seeing the remains of a white woman and child put to death. Doctor Arbuckle examined bodies at Eagle Point and said that there was no doubt of one of them being a white female 'which was easily evident from her head'. She had supposedly been murdered by Bunjeleene's brother to stop another man enjoying her.

The Gippsland Land Commissioner, Charles Tyers, would conclude 'my firm opinion is, and it is the opinion of Mr La Trobe, that there never was a white woman amongst the blacks'. He believed that no less than fifty Kurnai had been killed in the hunt for the woman. But even after the fruitless searches, the myth survived, enlivened by the tremors and twitches of European frontier males, men who would have disdained to show any superficial fear, men who could be described as doughty, but who could not deny the profound and unsolicited manias of the inner soul. There was even a story that the woman had survived and returned to Scotland to her husband in Lorn. Indeed, Campbell Macleod, a direct descendant of the Campbells of Lorn, was at Buchan in Gippsland when he heard that one of the native police had found part of a Bible in the bush and went out looking for the woman. Instead he found nice grazing country on the Snowy and took possession of it.

Relative to this tragic chimera of the white woman of Gippsland are the remarks of the droll George Dunderdale, the Lancashire man who was clerk of the courts in Gippsland. He wrote of the Kurnai, 'When a race of men is exterminated somebody ought to bear the blame, and the easiest way is to lay the fault at the door of the dead.'

In the other great tale of a captured white woman, the woman at least existed. She was Scottish, as some claimed the phantom of Gippsland to be. Her name was Eliza Fraser, the wife of James Fraser, Scots captain of the *Stirling Castle*, a 500-ton (510-tonne) brig, and a man in his fifties ailing from an unspecified disease. At the point where the Great Barrier Reef extends three hundred kilometres out into the Pacific, the *Stirling Castle* jagged itself irretrievably on an outcrop of the Great Swain Reefs, now Eliza Reef. When the ship struck and foundered, the survivors took to the lifeboats. Amongst them were the sickly Captain Fraser and his pregnant wife, Eliza, a woman in her mid-thirties. A few days after leaving the wreck, rowing southwards towards the settlement at Moreton Bay, Eliza gave birth in the well of a longboat to a baby who died soon after.

The story of Eliza then intersected with the equally remarkable one of her ultimate convict rescuer, whose exceptional experience of remote New South Wales formed a fitting prelude to Eliza's rescue.

MOGWI

An Irishman from County Louth, John Graham was transported in 1824 for concealing lengths of hemp in his apron and removing them from the premises of his master. He travelled to Australia from Cork on the same transport as brought notorious Captain Patrick Logan of the 57th Regiment. Logan's name would become associated with Moreton Bay and the energetic exercise of the lash and treadmill. The ship's guard and convicts disembarked at Sydney in 1825.

Graham was first assigned to work on the Darling mills, a steam-powered flour mill outside Parramatta. On a night in September 1826, however, he stole objects valued at 37 shillings. He was sentenced to secondary transportation for seven years, and was shipped just before Christmas 1826 to the relatively new Moreton Bay penal settlement, a place designed to fulfil the hope that transportation would become an object of fear. Governor Brisbane, for whom it would be named, had decreed that it be a harsh place. Between 1826 and 1842 under the command of Logan and others, it became a place of howls and degradation. During a six-month period in 1827, more than one-third of the convict population received punishment.

A valley on the river on which the penal settlement stood was a communally held treasure of the native people of an extensive area. Seasonal plenty in one form of food or another always allowed Aboriginals to gather for overarching ceremonial duties. On the Murray River it was wild fowl and freshwater crayfish in springtime, whereas in the Australian Alps it was the bogong moth. A stranded whale presented an occasional bonanza for all coastal peoples. To the north-west of the Moreton Bay settlement, great numbers of natives, a thousand or more, are estimated to have gathered every third year for the feast of the bunya-pine nut. The bunya pines showed fruit every year in January and February, but produced a lavish supply of edible seeds or nuts only every three years. The seeds were roasted and eaten or could be ground into flour. To partake of the festival people came up the coast to the Bunya Mountains and Blackall Range from the Richmond River (in present-day northern New South Wales), and across from the (Queensland) coast running north to Fraser Island.

The first commandant, Bishop, and his successors tried to get on with the native people of the region and induced them to return runaways or bushrangers. The Aboriginals did not particularly want to receive the *mogwi*—the white ghosts—and thus returned many prisoners, the Aboriginal women in the bush often screaming so loudly at the apparition of an escaped convict that soldiers were guided to the escapee.

The initial act of running or absconding was relatively easy. During January 1826 twenty men ran. In the twelve months from February 1828, 123 men out of a total convict population of 415 tried it, and most returned soon to camp to face a flogging of from 100 to 300 lashes. That same year thirty-two convicts were given 300 lashes for absconding and 171 men each received 100 lashes. Nor did this stop under later commandants such as the sociable Irish veteran soldier Foster Fyans, who had been reprimanded on Norfolk Island for going soft on the former naval captain turned thief John Knatchbull, and was not willing to take that risk again.

John Graham first ran from the penal settlement in mid July 1827. Though a small man, he was lithe, and had good luck in the hinterland and did not return to give himself up until he had calculated his seven-year sentence of transportation had expired, in 1833. Graham was one of those absconders who were recognised by the Aborigines as a recently dead loved one returned to the earth. The local Aboriginal practice of removing the skin from a corpse made the white skin of the convict convincing, though it created uneasiness—as would any resurrection. Yet it was on this basis that a number of convicts managed to live in the bush in various directions from Moreton Bay.

Graham later claimed that when he first encountered Aboriginals they called him Moilow after a recently deceased elder. His clan territory was identified to him. Moilow's widow, Mamba, accepted him as her returned husband and he acquired two grown sons. He learned to nourish himself on game, fish and the flour made from pounded coastal bracken.

On a search northwards in partnership with an escaped Leicestershire convict, George Mitchell, Graham pushed up the coast intending to reach the Gulf of Carpentaria and the Makassan *prahus*, and the two of them were probably the first Europeans to cross the Tropic of Capricorn by land. On the way they spent three months amongst the tribe on what would be ultimately named Fraser Island. North of Hervey Bay, however, they were turned back by the absence of succouring Aborigines, a shortage of food and difficult terrain. The explorer Allan Cunningham would later interview Graham and had no doubt that he had reached the vicinity of Broad Sound and Shoalwater Bay north of present-day Rockhampton, before returning to the tribe who had taken him in, the people of the Noosa area.

Another escapee, James Davis, who returned to Moreton Bay after years amongst the natives, had cicatrices on his chest, wore necklaces and armlets and went by the Aboriginal name Duramboi. When John Graham, believing his sentence expired, turned himself in, he was similarly marked and was similarly very secretive about major Aboriginal ceremonies. The Presbyterian preacher John Dunmore Lang met James Davis in 1845 and was fascinated by the phenomenon of the escapee turned Aboriginal Lazarus. 'I was much pleased with the good feeling exhibited by the man [towards Aborigines], who appeared sincerely to regret this loss of [Aboriginal] life as well as property.' Davis assured Lang that if he, 'or any other person at all acquainted with the habits and feelings of the natives', were employed as a liaison, then peace and harmony could be maintained between the squatters and the Aboriginals.

In south-eastern Queensland there were three mutually unintelligible Aboriginal language groups—Panjalangic to the south of Brisbane, Durrbulic in the Brisbane area and Waka-kabic in the area to the north where Graham, Davis and most other absconders lived with the natives. The Waka-kabic speakers were the prime keepers of the bunya-pine ceremonies which occurred near present-day Dalby. For ceremonial reasons the absconding convicts would be passed from tribe to tribe, as John Dunmore Lang said, like a blind man being passed around soliciting charity in Scotland. Some of them were so long with the Aborigines that they forgot English. Of Davis, son of a Glasgow blacksmith, Lang noted, 'he could not speak "his mither's" tongue'. Another escapee, David Bracefield or Wandi, 'the great talker', could not remember English for some time after his return, and often combined Waka-kabic and English into a sort of dialect.

Bracefield had spent some time with Graham in the Maroochydore–Noosa area in 1829, but gave himself up after two months. When he next absconded in 1831 he moved to the north of Graham's area. There he was adopted as the reincarnated son of Eumundy or Huon Mundy, a powerful man of the Noosa hinterland, who protected him for the next six years before he again gave himself up. Bracefield would then abscond once more in 1839, and stayed in the bush until the abandonment of Moreton Bay as a penal settlement.

After John Graham's return to confinement in 1833, he found that time endured while absent from Moreton Bay did not count towards time done, and so he was still stuck in the settlement. The natives would turn up in groups of six or seven to visit him, most particularly male relatives. When they left, 'it was distressing to witness their grief, yelling and tearing their skin,' Captain Foster Fyans recalled.

Because of Graham's usefulness as a negotiator with the surrounding Aboriginal people, he was treated as a trusty and achieved the status of a constable or convict overseer. His knowledge of the coast north of Brisbane was also valued by Foster Fyans, and led to his inclusion in the party sent to rescue the *Stirling Castle* survivors.

RESCUING ELIZA

News of the wreck of the *Stirling Castle* came to Moreton Bay through two of the crew being found on Bribie Island, but also by way of Aboriginal visitors to John Graham at the convict settlement. An expedition commanded by Lieutenant Otter and including Graham set out at once by ship for the Noosa River—in those days named Huon Mundy's River after the well-known Aboriginal elder of the hinterland. Landed, Graham reverted to nakedness and greased himself with charcoal and animal fat, taking with him some bread and a potato, since his tribe loved carbohydrates. First he learned of the presence of two 'young ghosts' near Lake Cooroibah and, finding them, bought them back from the natives, saying that they were his two sons. The next morning, after the ship had moved to Double Island Point, Graham went into the bush again, carrying bread once more. He came upon two women who told him that Eliza Fraser had been taken to the ceremonial area of Worwa near Lake Cootharaba. He learned also that Baxter, the ship's second mate, was nearby at the southern end of what would ever after be named Fraser Island where the longboat originally put in and where Captain Fraser had died, or been killed.

First Graham repaired an old bark canoe and paddled across to Fraser Island or Tomé, where he met natives he knew and talked them into fishing so that he and the weakened Baxter could eat. He also told them that there was good fishing along the coast of the mainland and that he had heard of a whale coming up on a beach to the south. Thus he got back to the mainland and moved south to where Lieutenant Otter and his party waited. On the afternoon of the day he returned to Double Island Point with Baxter, Graham started off for Worwa, forty kilometres away. He let Otter's party of convicts, soldiers and sailors follow him but they were to halt and wait at a spot he would mark with an arrow. They were to avoid hostage-taking.

By nightfall Graham was two-thirds of the way to Worwa and dined on a two-metre snake he had killed. On the track the next morning he met some people who told him that Eliza Fraser had been claimed by a man named Mothervane, who had identified her as the spirit of his wife's sister. When Graham arrived at the site he was greeted by his kin and saw that Eliza was in a bark shelter guarded by his kinsman, Dapen. He began to talk, claiming that Eliza was his dead wife, Mamba. An argument developed about the validity of this claim but Mamba's father supported Graham, especially after he began to tell stories of the journeys he had made with Mamba's spirit. 'All the coast blacks here stood on my side,' wrote Graham later, 'and said I always told the truth.' Dapen then said, 'Come uncle, I was watching my aunt; that the mountain blacks should not come near while you were talking.'

He urged Graham to depart with Eliza immediately before the opposing inland Aboriginals could make trouble, especially since Mothervane was present and gave up his claim to Eliza with a bad grace. Much later it was surmised that Mothervane may have been the escaped convict Bracefield, who lived amongst the tribe to the north of the Noosa people. When she emerged from the shelter, Eliza's appearance seemed strange to Graham: 'On her head was a sou'wester, the smell of the paint kept the blacks from taking it. Around her loins were part of the legs and waistband of a pair of trousers, which covered part of her thighs, wound round with vines twenty fold as well for delicacy as the preservation of her marriage and earrings which she concealed under the vines.'

Taking Dapen's advice, Graham recounted, 'I rose, reached out my hand, saying come with me. God has made me your deliverer. Fortitude was what I now called upon from Heaven to assist me in seeing a woman survive.'

They left Worwa accompanied by four of his kinsmen, and took Eliza across the lake by canoe, where Otter had reached the arrow Graham had marked in the sand. Fourteen hours later they got to the ship. At Moreton Bay Graham was an instant hero. He was praised for having exhibited 'noble conduct'. Foster Fyans wrote to Governor Bourke from Moreton Bay in 1836: 'From the intelligence and firmness displayed by this man, I am certain should His Excellency at any future period think a survey of the North Coast advisable, Graham would be a most useful man in the undertaking.'

From the time Eliza arrived in Moreton Bay, or certainly from the time she arrived in Sydney, her story began to change in a way that was prejudicial to the natives she had been amongst. There was no questioning she had had a horrifying experience, tormented by loss of a child and a husband, perhaps tormented too by jealous Aboriginal women. But soon she was accusing the Waka-kabic speakers of being cannibals, and perhaps she felt that thrilling word was necessary to insert into her story when later in Britain she became the central actor in her own tale in theatres and at fairs. In Sydney, she depicted Graham as having rescued her from a totally malign mass of natives rather than from his not unsympathetic kinsmen. By the summer of 1837, when Eliza was in Liverpool, Graham had become one who himself had been captive amongst the savages, and had arrived just as she was about to be ravished by an aged native. Her story appeared in America and throughout the British Isles in chapbooks in which Graham was helped by Huon Mundy who lifted her round the middle 'with his gigantic arms' and ran to the beach where Graham was waiting with a canoe. And on it went.

Some form of pardon did come to Graham and thereafter he vanished from the record, into the anonymous mass of old lags. Over time, too, Bracefield's name became unreliably but indelibly associated with the rescue.

The idea of white women lost to heathens and their lusts, and then rescued, was such a fertile seed in the Victorian imagination that few could resist enhancing the reality, even Eliza herself.

CHAPTER 21

MOLESWORTH'S COMMITTEE

Everyone—Major Mudie, James Macarthur, the Reverend Lang, every pastoralist who employed convict labour as well as every commentator who thought such employment immoral—wanted to bring their evidence to the Select Committee of Parliament on Transportation which met during the spring and summer of 1837 in a drafty committee room of St Stephen's Hall, Westminster, where the British Parliament then still sat. And whoever it was, whether Mudie or Lang, apologist or opponent of the system, each wanted to give the committee his thoughts not just on the convict assignment system, but on the effect the system had on the whole society of New South Wales and Van Diemen's Land.

The committee chairman, Sir William Molesworth, was a wealthy and noble-hearted young man, twenty-seven years of age, who dressed superbly but was also a radical. He had in fact founded the *London Review* as a radical organ, and then acquired and edited the *Westminster Review* with the philospher of radicalism, John Stuart Mill. Though he disapproved of the state of debauchery to which the system of transportation and assignment had reduced New South Wales, he was not beyond debauchery himself. Yet as a radical he was mindful always of the poor and the slave. He had been disfigured in childhood by scrofula and this had resulted in teasing about his looks while he was at boarding school, an experience which gave him sympathy for other marked men and women.

Another member of Molesworth's committee, Lord Howick, was the young

George Grey who entered parliament in 1829 and had a remarkable future as Earl Grey. Lord Howick disapproved of assignment but did not want to see the committee recommend the total abandonment of transportation which Molesworth himself obviously desired.

The Presbyterian minister JD Lang was available and anxious to give evidence since he was already in Britain recruiting Scots emigrants. In line with his capacity to damn both sides of a question, he disliked emancipists for their presumptions and exclusives for their sins. He told the gentlemen of the committee that transportation could work as a punishment, 'but it has not been hitherto subjected to a fair trial in the colonies of New South Wales and Van Diemen's Land for lack of free population'. Society's tone was created by the convicts, 'instead of by a virtuous population'. As for assignment, he pleased the committee by declaring it 'is unequal in its operation, and consequently unjust to the convict'. It depended for its severity on the character of the master. 'If the master is of a mild disposition, the convict is treated with much indulgence; on the other hand, if he is of an austere and severe disposition, the convict experiences that severity.' There was nothing that could be done to prevent this unevenness, in Lang's opinion.

Lang thought the number of assigned convict servants in Sydney and their ready access to 'ardent spirits' was the cause of dissipation and licentiousness which would lead inevitably to more crime. There were fewer temptations for convicts assigned as field labourers in the interior. Even so, all assignments should be discontinued, he argued. Would there not be a great want of labour? he was asked. Not if proper exertions were made to bring in free immigrants, said Lang.

As for the convict road parties, 'They have opportunities of escape, and they avail themselves of these very often to prey upon the settlers.' Lang thought road parties should therefore be discontinued too, except maybe outside the Twenty Counties, the located districts. Within the settled districts there was a deficiency of superintendents, and, of course, too much ease in getting those 'ardent spirits'. As for the chained gangs, they were under more vigilant superintendents, and found it harder to flit away. A great number were also employed on the streets of Sydney, repairing the roads. As for the government's employment of convict mechanics, he did not like the special preferences they had been receiving, though there were fewer of them now than previously. Before 1830, almost all the mechanics in the colony either were convicts or had been convicts. They had been permitted to work 'over-hours' on their own account. Sir Richard Bourke had received a petition from the free mechanics of Sydney either in 1832 or 1833 requesting the government distribute the convict mechanics all over the territory, or not to employ them at the public works, as it interfered with the profits of the free mechanics' labour. He had complied. This had been the sensible way to proceed, in Lang's view.

By the questions it asked, the committee, so certain that convict transportation was morally indefensible, obviously knew very little about the details of the system. When a convict woman is married either to a ticket-of-leave man, or to a free man, she becomes free? they asked. Lang told them that she was free as long as she conducted herself with propriety. But if she got drunk—as was frequently the case—she was liable to be sent to the Female Factory or to have her ticket-of-leave cancelled.

Then came the significant question: 'You said that the assignment of women tended to demoralise them; is not the sending them out there to become the wives of the emancipists and ticket-of-leave men tantamount to rearing up a criminal population for that colony?'

Lang said he did not think so. Marriage had a reformatory impact on many. But then the question was, 'Do you think that is good as a punishment; is it a good description of punishment, merely to send a woman out to be married?' Certainly not, said Lang. But the disproportion that existed between the sexes was a great source of crime and depravity, and should be addressed.

'There is an action and reaction in the colony perpetually going on between the classes of society originally depraved and those which have, ostensibly at least, a better character,' he continued. The impact of the assignment of educated convicts, for example, to become editors of newspapers was 'the very worst possible . . . The only paper in the colony that was published three times a week was under the management of individuals of that class [O'Shaughnessy and Watt] so lately as the year 1835. The influence of these individuals on the press was virtually directed to the abolition of the moral distinctions that the law of God has established in society, to persuade the community that the free immigrant portion of the population was really no better in point of character than the class from which they had emanated, the convicts . . . they were perpetually endeavouring to persuade the community that their situation was the result of misfortune and not of misconduct.' They also sought 'to impress on the community that the mere fulfilment of the man's term of transportation restored him, to all intents and purposes, to the same condition in society as the man who never had been a convict.'

A committee member, Mr Bulwer, rather aggressively asked Lang did he consider the people who attended meetings in support of the legal rights of former convicts, men such as Sir John Jamison, WC Wentworth, Henry O'Brien, Doctor William Bland, Thomas Wills, Edward Cox, Henry Cox, George Druitt and others to be suspect characters. Lang moderated his tone a little, going so far as to say that though they were respectable they were too heavily influenced by wealthy emancipists who made their money by running public houses, and money lending. Lang was also not impressed that many schoolteachers and tutors in private families were convicts or ex-convicts. 'There is at this moment the son of an English clergyman in New South Wales who was educated by a person of this class, and who is now a convict [himself] under sentence of transportation for life in Van Diemen's Land.' John Dunmore Lang certainly believed that the amount of immorality amongst the Australian mass, free and convict, was higher than in England. The number of couples living in 'concubinage' particularly concerned him.

In truth, the Reverend Lang was in favour of the abolition of transportation as it then operated in New South Wales. A border should be drawn near Port Macquarie and the whole land north of that should be used for a new experimentation in transportation. The Highlanders of Scotland should be the settlers introduced into a new system, under which convict labour would prepare the settlements for immigrants. The funds derived from the sale of Crown land should be employed exclusively for that purpose. Free immigration was the only means 'by which we can get rid of the evils which that system [convict transportation] has entailed upon the colony hitherto'. Bringing in a numerous population of Scots free settlers 'would give a high value to land, and then, that population would be enabled to pay for the land such a price as would repay all the advances of government'.

Such were the dreams of a Scots visionary expressed in a wintry room in Westminster to a committee determined to end transportation to eastern Australia.

Another witness before the committee, the English Benedictine William Ullathorne, who had heard the confessions of brutalised Norfolk Island prisoners about to be hanged for rebellion, agreed with Lang that transportation had not produced reform amongst convicts. The committee probably had in hand in any case his pamphlet, *The Horrors of Transportation briefly unfolded to the People,* published that year in Ireland and England. Major Mudie had also written a book, *The Felonry of New South Wales,* in which he condemned the malice of convicts and the discipline-softening measures introduced by Governor Bourke limiting what local magistrates could do to punish disobedient or insolent assigned servants. Even EA Slade, a former superintendent of the convict barracks and inventor of a special no-nonsense whip for use on the premises, wanted to give evidence along the same lines as Mudie. However, Ben Boyd, a squatter of the regions far south of Sydney, argued, 'I believe there is no employer of labour in the colony who would not prefer a ticket-of-leave man to a bounty immigrant; for my own part, although I came out here at first with all my English prejudices against the prisoner class, I now from experience prefer them so decidedly, that I have at this moment but few immigrants in my employment.'

The committee's final report was an attack on the penal system of New South Wales. It brought an end to convict assignment in 1838, and ultimately an end to transportation.

CHAPTER 22*

THE GIRL FROM THE FEMALE FACTORY

Like many Australians trying to deal with the past, the author became interested for family reasons in one unexceptional young convict woman who seemed in background, crime and penal experience to represent a multitude of her kind. At the Limerick City Court of Sessions in the autumn of 1837, thirteen Irish labourers and servants were unremarkably sentenced to seven years transportation each. One of these was an auburn-haired, small-boned, handsome young woman of twenty-two years named Mary Shields.

Other women sentenced at the same court session were Catherine Mongavan, who had stolen £5 13 shillings, a third of the average yearly wages in Ireland; Martha Walker, who had stolen a sheet; and Rosanna Daly, who had shoplifted ribbon. Mary Shields had been found guilty of stealing clothes from a Timothy Reardon. Since her occupation was given as that of servant, she may have been Mr Reardon's servant. It was recorded also that she was a native of Tipperary, so she and her parents very likely belonged to the mass of landless or evicted peasantry who wandered into cities and took what work they could find.

This young woman, only five feet one-and-a-quarter inches (155 cm), bore the indications of want. She was already the mother of a small son and infant daughter. She had been married at eighteen in May 1834 to a man named

---

* Some readers will have encountered events narrated here in the author's *The Great Shame*, although emphasis will differ from that earlier account.

John O'Flynn in St John's Church, Limerick. Their first child was baptised at St Michael's Church, Limerick, in October 1835, and was named Michael. A daughter, Bridget, was baptised in December 1837.

Not all people sentenced to transportation were in fact transported, and for the first phase of her sentence Mary, in Limerick City gaol, was still in contact with her husband and children. In fact, children often accompanied their parents to prison. Mary's son, Michael, was of an age, about two years old, to want to be with his mother, and since he would be shipped with his mother, must have been at least part of the time in the wards of the gaol with her.

We know something of Irish criminal offences, and the date of Mary Shields's crime, in the summer of 1838, has some significance. The potato did not last after early summer, and the new crop was not harvested until September. Shields was at least a city woman, receiving a cash salary. But unlike peasants she had no fattened pig to sell to buy summer oatmeal and as the price of food rose as the season advanced, it was not uncommon for rural and city women to steal goods to convert stolen clothing into cash, or to steal food directly.

Like most of the women who were to accompany her to Australia, Mary had no previous conviction. More Irish female convicts—as compared with convicts from the rest of Britain—were married women; more of them were mothers of young families; more came from the country. Apart from Dubliners, few were described as 'of the Cyprian tribe', that is, prostitutes. Fewer, too, had been found guilty of crimes of violence such as assault or highway robbery.

The bill for an Irish Poor Law had passed the British Parliament on 31 July 1838, three months before Shields's crime. The Limerick workhouse would not be ready to receive its poor until May 1841. Yet the probable truth is that had the workhouse existed as a safety net in her day, Shields would still have committed her crime. To many people, even after the workhouses were in place, a minor crime committed to deal with a needful emergency would prove preferable. Smith O'Brien, the famed Irish member of parliament who would himself one day be a convict in Van Diemen's Land, had warned in the Commons that the workhouse would prove alien to the Irish. They not only feared the indignity of make-work stone-breaking, or the endless pushing of the spoke of a mill-wheel; they feared, above all, the separation of women from men and children from parents.

When a number of prisoners including Mary were moved to Dublin to board their transport, she took her son Michael with her. What became of her infant,

Bridget, is not known. She would not be the first child left behind with relatives, nor Michael the first child to accompany his mother aboard.

Though chained at wrist, or even at waist or ankle, and guarded by soldiers detailed from the Limerick garrison, the group of felons and children could hardly have seemed much of a threat to the social fabric. The housemaid Catherine Bourke, cloak-stealer, as well as being sixty years of age, was only five feet (152 cm) tall. Rosanna Daly, a nineteen-year-old cook, was four feet ten inches (147 cm). Bridget Lonrigan, a 25-year-old single kitchenmaid and clothes thief, also reached less than five feet.

It was a harsh business getting to the ship. Shields and the other Limerick women imprisoned with her would be conveyed in bitter air not to Cork, 80 kilometres away, but far across-country to Dublin. From Tullamore in County Offaly, they would have been put on the decks of a barge, and subjected to the mockery and occasional kindnesses of bargees as they traversed the locks along the Grand Canal to Dublin, to august Kilmainham gaol by the Liffey on the edge of the city.

There must have been gossip about ships and destinations. She would have heard of the notorious *Neva*, which left Cork in early 1835 with one hundred and fifty Irish women convicts and over fifty of their children. Four months after departure, in July, on the far side of the earth in Bass Strait, *Neva* struck on an unmarked rock which ripped her rudder out. All but twenty of the female convicts and all their fifty-nine children were drowned.

Mary's ship was to be the bark *Whitby* of 431 tons. Throughout January and February 1839, one hundred and thirty prisoners and twenty-nine of their children were rowed out through the misty estuary of Dublin Bay and arrived in piercing cold on the damp prison deck. In the struggles for space, rations and warmth, Michael was both burden and protection. Not that the other women were hardened criminals. Only three of them had done serious prison time. Whatever their slyness, sullenness, loudness, they were normal, powerless women, most of them in grief.

On 16 February 1839, Captain Thomas Wellbank signed the Lord Lieutenant's Warrant, acknowledging the 'several bodies' he had received on board, and their prison shifts, jackets, petticoats, etc. The surgeon superintendent on *Whitby* was the naval man John Kidd, who found Mary to have brown hair, brown or chestnut eyes, ruddy complexion, and 'marks of scrofula under the chin or right jaw'. Called the King's Evil because it was believed that the touch of a monarch could cure it, scrofula was something she caught by her parents' hearth, while drinking the normal staple of buttermilk from a cow infected with bovine tuberculosis.

Surgeon Kidd would note that like Larkin before her, she had reading but not writing. Thus, as a small girl, she must have attended a hedge school, an unofficial school run in the open or in a barn by Irish itinerant scholars—the only source of learning for her class.

Many of the children aboard were young and delicate, said Kidd, and 'several of the women old and infirm'. He kept the women busy with sewing and exercise on deck, and as in most well-run ships, the noise of some crewman's fiddle and the distant thump of jigs was heard through the mists by occasional winter promenaders ashore. The time of anguish and noise came on 18 February. *Whitby* left Ireland, as so many transports did, in the midst of the season of storms.

A veteran surgeon, Peter Cunningham, who made six journeys to Australia, frankly recommended cohabitation between convict women and sailors and guards. He proposed that these sexual alliances were to the benefit of all parties. They provided the women, he said, with extra comforts—tea and occasional spirits—and provided the sailor with washing, sewing and cleaning. It was axiomatic in the case of the Irish that Dublin women were more susceptible to these arrangements than women from the outer counties, and more evangelical surgeons did not approve of the procedure anyhow. Cunningham tells us that the sound of the Rosary recited in Irish was heard each evening from the convict deck of Irish ships—an indication of a muscular morality. But as ever, except in the much earlier and notorious case of the *Lady Juliana*, the little island of a women's ship left in the record more questions than answers, carrying within it its own net of accommodating secrets. Kidd's journal gives not the slightest direct information on what arrangements were permitted or suppressed aboard *Whitby*.

Progressive bureaucrats in Whitehall, however, who hoped that these women might become the mothers and improvers of Australia, would have been gratified to hear that only Mary Hegarty, a Londonderry child's maid, eighteen years of age, had been treated for syphilis, the one case of that nature Kidd found aboard. Hegarty would survive the disease to receive her conditional pardon in 1846.

It was surprising how many of the prisoners were going to a reunion. Amongst others, Eliza White of Dublin travelled in hope to her convict husband, Christopher Reilly. Jane Ramsey, a Protestant kitchen maid, was also on her way to her husband, and Mary Carroll, a 39-year-old dairymaid wanted to show her convict husband her two and a half year old son whom he had never seen. A sixty year old, Ann Murray, also had a relative on his way to New South Wales: her son, aboard the *Waverley*, a ship for males which left from Dublin a week after the *Whitby*.

Sir George Gipps, a studious army engineer with a taste for research who had taken over from Governor Bourke the previous year, had written to Whitehall about the inferior quality of rations on ships coming from Ireland. Early in his New South Wales career, he had ordered a more modest study made of the rationing of two Irish ships. 'A simple perusal of this report will, I hope,' he wrote to Colonial Secretary Glenelg, 'induce Your Lordship to cause an inquiry to be made into the mode of victualling these ships . . .' But plain tastes and the fact that hunger was no stranger to them, equipped most of the *Whitby* women to survive be-weevil-ed flour and the rancid barrels of bony and unsavoury beef and pork.

In late June 1839, *Whitby* at last sailed through the sandstone headlands of Sydney Harbour. The drag of sea slackened. Mary heard raucous Australian birds call from the bushy heights above Watson's Bay.

The skills of the *Whitby* women, advertised by government, brought relatively light demand, and none for women with children. So, with perhaps this or that sailor dwelling on a woman's face and fearing her loss, on 1 July the women and their infants were rowed down-harbour and landed on the western side of Sydney Cove. Lined up unchained, they were lectured by a number of colonial wives, members of the Ladies' Committee, who gave them sisterly, evangelical advice on the perils and possible rewards ahead of them.

Five Irish nuns of the Charity order had come from Cork the previous December to look after and protect their convict sisters. There were two or three of them at the women's section of the Hyde Park barracks in Macquarie Street. The others Mary Shield would encounter at Parramatta, acting as visitors at the Female Factory, which was to be her home. Detention in Sydney was brief. The *Whitby* women and children were brought back down to the water, put into whaleboats by constables, and rowed up the Parramatta River, a broad waterway with islands, inlets and fine juts of sandstone, and, further up, mangrove swamps.

It could be a pleasant journey in Sydney's mild winter. In the intimacy of a whaleboat, something like normal male society was now temporarily restored to Mary. The constables and oarsmen were all former or serving convicts, some honourable men, some rascals. The journey was only 23 kilometres as the crow flies, somewhat more by the bends of the river, and many fine picnic places lay along the way. Until the 1830s the trip to Parramatta had sometimes taken constables and women three days. Liquor travelled with the parties, and in camps set up early—so it was surmised by the Colonial Secretary of New South Wales—evening bush orgies had been the pattern. By the *Whitby* women's time, the journey was meant to take only one long day, or in exceptional circumstances two, and the presence of children would have helped mute wilder behaviour. Boats still generally stopped for refreshments at Squire's Public House, a large slab-hut inn at Kissing Point, above a beach surrounded by sandstone ledges and bush. Here was a sandbar which boats kissed against, but it had a repute, too, for convict sexual recreation. Squire's Inn provided Mary with her first Australian drink and social occasion, and she was partial to both.

The Female Factory for which the women were bound was built in 1821 at Parramatta on 1.6 hectares on the riverbank, and was judged necessary because of the perceived fallen nature of the women, but also because of the degraded nature of society. The disproportion of males to females in convict society—one hundred male convicts to every seventeen women, had called the place into being, to save females from prostitution. At first the factories produced cloth known as 'Parramatta' or 'Georgetown', after the respective Female Factories. But by the time the women of the *Whitby* arrived, there was no consistent work done at the Parramatta site. Its reputation was questionable but not as bad as that of the Cascades Female Factory, which was seen as a de facto brothel for the town of Hobart. The Cascades Factory was certainly the scene of scandalously high mortality amongst infants and young children who inhabited the place with their mothers and, like the Parramatta Factory, it was now continuously overcrowded. The Parramatta and Cascades Factories were not the only ones in the colony—there were at this stage or later similar Factories at Newcastle, Port Macquarie, Moreton Bay, and at Launceston and Ross and elsewhere in Van Diemen's Land. But the Factories would always have an ambiguity of intent— were they a haven or a gaol, a workshop, hospital, marriage bureau?

The Parramatta Factory had been designed for all possible purposes by the talented convict Francis Greenway, the Bristol architect transported for forging a contract. Behind its 2.7 metre walls, it was three storeys high, and was meant to house three hundred women. Within a year of Mary Shields's arrival there, it held 887 women and 405 children. Since free immigration for deserving poor spinsters from the British Isles was taking jobs once given to convict women, women accumulated in the Factory. In some ways the Factory was an extended, land-based version of the convict deck. 'Major' Mudie, the severe Hunter Valley magistrate, disapproved of the Parramatta Factory on the grounds, as he would ultimately tell the Molesworth parliamentary committee, that 'So agreeable a retreat, indeed, is the Factory, that it is quite a common thing for female assigned servants to demand of their masters and mistresses to send them there and flatly, and with fearful oaths, to disobey orders for the purpose of securing the accomplishment of their wish.' By contrast, reformers said that many convict women arrived with 'good resolutions' at the Factory, making their imprisonment unnecessary and degrading. 'The assigned servant of Mr Keith was charged by her master with refusing to obey her mistress' orders. The woman would deck herself out with lace on Sundays and when desired to remove so many furbelows refused to do so. For this disobedience, she was sentenced to three months in the Third Class [the penal wing] of the Female Factory.'

A master's complacency over an assigned convict's sexual behaviour could also lead to the cancellation of the right of assignment and the woman's at least temporary transfer to the Factory. This occurred with Mary Ann Waters, for example, who was encouraged by her master and mistress to accommodate other lodgers sexually to help support the master's family.

In the dormitories, women competed for space through sly stratagems and by maintaining a phalanx with those from the same ship and county. *Whitby* women stuck together against women from earlier arriving ships such as *Lady Rowena*, *Diamond*, *Sir Charles Forbes*, *Surrey* and *Planter*. The English women from these last two ships had their own encampment in the Factory's long dormitories, but the Irish had a larger one, and many of the arguments over space and food were conducted with that Irish raucousness which would become an Australian characteristic, but which polite people mistook for lowness of soul. The Sisters of Charity did their best to mediate, and may have understood better than male officials that the Factory made a woman edgy and assertive. Those who lost the fight would wither under melancholia, die, or be sent to join the mad at Tarban Creek.

A few months before Shields's arrival at Parramatta, Governor Gipps had as part of his new initiative dismissed a tipsy matron and a strait-laced and incompetent superintendent. All Gipps could fall back on was a pragmatic but venal couple who had earlier been sacked from the post—the Bells, George and Sarah. During Shields's time at the Factory, the Bells were its day-to-day managers. They had in their care three categories of women. Category 1 consisted of women like Mary who were eligible for assignment, had the right to go to church on Sundays, receive friends at the Factory, and earn wages if there was something for them to do. Category 2 were returned assignees, and Category 3 those undergoing punishment. The Category 1 single women were sometimes 'drawn up in a line for the inspection of the amorous and adventurous votary, who, fixing his eye on a vestal of his taste, with his finger beckons her to step forward from the rank'. There was a colonial song about this extraordinary process.

> The Currency Lads may fill their glasses,
> And drink to the health of the Currency Lasses,
> But the lass I adore, the lass for me,
> Is a lass in the Female Factory . . .

It was often with no previous acquaintance with the man at all that a young woman would choose an unpredictable marriage over life in the Female Factory.

The Factory's Sunday clothes were designed perhaps to attract the attention of a newly pardoned drover or shepherd in church: a white cap, straw bonnet, long dress with a muslin frill, a red calico jacket, blue petticoat, grey stockings, shoes, and a clothes bag to store all these in between Sundays. For weekday wear the women had plainer garments: calico caps, serge petticoat and jacket, and an apron.

The continued existence of the Factories as part women's refuge and part-prison was never resolved into the one reality under any administration.

Gipps had been horrified to find that the women of the Factory were completely idle, apart from cooking and washing for themselves. The year before Mary Shields's arrival, the Governor decided that he would introduce a supply of New Zealand flax which could be picked by the women and turned into mesh for fishing nets and screens for fruit trees. From 18 October in the year of Mary's arrival, the public was informed too 'that needlework of all sorts is performed at the Female Factory in the best possible manner and at very moderate charges'. The Colonial Secretary set a scale of prices—slips 1 shilling and sixpence; shirts from 1 shilling and 10 pence; baby's gowns upwards of sixpence. None of the Factory's operations was particularly profitable for the government, but Gipps favoured them for their rehabilitative aspects.

Lady Elizabeth Gipps, daughter of a British major-general and a woman of progressive mind, had the best behaved thirty or so of the Factory women visit Government House, Parramatta, to receive lessons in needlework. Mary Shields walked up the driveway of the vice-regal residence to attend these sessions, and breathed the urbane air of a civilised household. In the parlour, the women awed to reticence for once by this elegantly genial British lady in her thirties who sat down amongst them along with her housekeeper, the classes proceeded, though they were interrupted in the early 1840s by Lady Gipps's bad health.

With whatever skills she possessed, Mary was motivated to maternal vigour to ensure her son's rations. When he reached the age of five, some time in 1840, Michael was taken from her and sent to one of the orphan schools in Parramatta, probably the one founded by the Sisters of Charity. Contact between Mary and Michael was permitted, especially on Sundays. The boy was growing up amongst the children of other convicts, yet the orphanages of Parramatta did not seem to be schools for criminality. Michael would not come to manhood lawless.

Mary spent a largely unrecorded four years in the Factory's rowdy sorority. Though no notable misdemeanour or illness raised Shields to public notice, she suffered from the way the prison-cum-refuge was run. Embezzlement of funds, over-ordering and short-rationing were the *modus operandi* of steward and matron, Mr and Mrs Bell. News of Factory dissatisfaction eventually reached Governor Gipps, and he agreed to meet a delegation of convict women. 'They represented that they'd been sentenced to be transported, but not to be imprisoned after transportation ...' They contrasted, 'I must say, with great force and truth', their treatment with that of women in prison in Britain and Ireland.

About the time of the appeal to Gipps, two women detained in a small cell started a fire, and their screams were heard throughout the Factory. One hundred women packed into one of the dormitories broke their door down to get to their threatened sisters. But the constables and the Bells got there first and freed the two women. Abuse and recriminations were exchanged between the two sets of rescuers. Bell used colourful insults, and the women began breaking doors and windows. A detachment of military arrived at the double, but the insurgent women subjected them to a volley of stones and pieces of broken furniture. Eighty of the rioters were arrested and confined at the Factory or Parramatta gaol. Since Mary Shields was soon to be included in a list of the 'best conducted', she was obviously not one of those imprisoned after the riot.

By now the commissary officials of the colony were investigating Bell, and found that for the past two years, 'Mr Bell's expenditure appeared to be inconsistent with any means he was known to possess.' The Bells and Mrs Corcoran, the sub-matron, had also been depositing money in the Savings Bank beyond their means. Mrs Corcoran, however, was now willing to give evidence that Bell had been withdrawing rations for one hundred more children than the Factory contained and selling the excess to Parramatta innkeepers, and that Mrs Bell had needlework done on her own account, and often kept money paid for needlework. Corcoran claimed the prisoners were never issued meal, and the supply of bread to the children was intermittent. She said Mr Bell liked the women's company too, and took a number of the prisoners to town on drinking sessions, and so on. The matter of the Bells, reported now to the Home Secretary Lord Stanley, drew a passionate response. But the Bells survived in the job because, after a trial with other managers, it was found that they were the only ones willing to endure the running of the place.

Even though convict assignment had ceased in 1838 Governor Gipps, upon the Molesworth Committee's recommendation, in March 1843 approved a scheme to place some of 'the best conducted women' with reputable employers. Mary Shields was due for her ticket-of-leave that year, after four years of her sentence, so it is a little mystifying that her release was cast in official papers as part of this plan of reward. In any case, by April 1843, twenty-two women were selected for the scheme, and then in June a further eleven were added, amongst them a number of the *Whitby* women, including Mary. Applications from potential employers were to be accompanied by references from clergymen or magistrates, and the Colonial Secretary took the trouble to draft a special set of rules for the employment of these women. They were to be paid between £8 and £10 per year—Gipps said he wanted this group to have purchasing power from the day they left the Factory. Money the women earned was to be sacrosanct and not taken by the police.

Middle-aged Cecily Naughton and her children were to go to Campbelltown, no more than a day or two's ride away. Mary Carroll, who had a convict husband, was to remain as close as Penrith, barely 25 kilometres from the Factory. But another *Whitby* woman, Anne Morrow was to be sent by ship to distant, beautiful Port Macquarie, four hundred kilometres up the coast, and Mary

Smith and Mary Gallon to Yass, a remote town in the interior at the limits of the old Nineteen Counties.

Three women were to travel initially to the inland town of Goulburn—Mary Shields; Bridget Conelly, who had arrived on the *Diamond* from Cork in March 1838; and Margaret Carthy whose transport, *Sir Charles Forbes*, had put into Sydney on Christmas Day 1837. Shields had been applied for by William Bradley of Lansdown Park, Goulburn.

Each of the three women carried on her person her ticket-of-leave, indicating that she was permitted to stay in the district of Goulburn. The women were to present their papers on demand to magistrates and police along the way, in the knowledge that any dallying or diversion from their approved route would be reported. This was their first extended and open experience of a society which was said to be the most debased on earth, and of a landscape in which any European woman was a rare sight likely to release male frenzy. How they negotiated it, how they evoked protection and respect from some men to balance the savage intentions of others can only be surmised. Ticket-of-leave men driving wagons or droving sheep watched them pass, and there were also men to ignore or fraternise with amongst the crowds of English and Irish convicts in road and timber-cutting gangs. Unhappy and angry felons, some in chains, brushed their eyes over the travellers in sullen desire. That these three came from the Female Factory was evident in their well-kept clothing, and women from the Factory possessed a certain éclat. Whether it was swamped by the male brutality of their surroundings we do not know.

By day, the three women travelled on their own recognisance on the outside of coaches—the fares consuming part of their 10-shilling advance—or took rides on wagons, walking up the steeper grades. They took pains to look like nobody's fools, not that they could have seemed an impressive company. Margaret Carthy was a squat worldling, a Dubliner, 155 centimetres, with light blue eyes. Brown-eyed Bridget Conelly, the marks of smallpox on her face, the tallest of the three at 160 centimetres, was from Galway and therefore an Irish-speaker. The offences of all three women were identical: stealing clothes.

The authorities did not want to see women molested or prostituting themselves around the night encampments, so police magistrates would have assigned the three travellers shelter in empty cells or unused police shacks. To the Factory women, a roof was welcome, for the Australian winter nights were growing frosty, and in the mornings a skin of ice needed to be broken on the washing pails.

The browned, dusty country Shields, Carthy and Conelly journeyed through was beginning to revive after some hopeful winter rains and to show an occasional burst of green now that the biblically long drought was ending. In this countryside, drought and land speculation had obliterated a great number of William Bradley's fellow entrepreneurs and squatters. William Brodribb, Hugh Larkin's employer, had had to abandon his pastoral lease in the Monaro and was pleased to be given well-paid work managing Bradley's ever-increasing squatting leases beyond the Limits of Location. The Bank of Australia also failed that year of Mary's release, and some of the oldest free settler families were swept away by this disaster. The emancipists' bank, the Bank of New South Wales, survived, underpinned by the massive trading deposits of the late Samuel Terry, 'the Botany Bay Rothschild', a convict who had been transported for stealing four hundred pairs of stockings in Salford, Lancashire, and who made his fortune speculating in property in Sydney and rural areas.

One of the chief signs of the recent economic crisis which the three women bound for Goulburn noticed from the start of their journey was the stench of boiling-down works in the bush, and on the outskirts of every settlement. Earlier that year an Irish settler from Mayo named Henry O'Brien had decided that the few pence value bankruptcy sheriffs put on sheep could not be a correct assessment. He conducted an experiment in his premises in Fort Street, Sydney, boiling down sheep for the tallow used in the manufacture of candles and soap. O'Brien reasoned that a sheep could produce twelve to fifteen pounds (5.4–6.8 kilos) weight of tallow even if starved. Eight hundred tolerably fat sheep would cost £109 to boil down and deliver to London, where the tallow would sell for £350. O'Brien thus calculated that, boiled down, a sheep was worth 6 shillings. There was a bottom value to livestock. It could be said therefore that a Mayo man had saved European New South Wales from economic devastation—but at an environmental price. As flocks of sheep were driven to tallow houses and boiling-down vats, the foulness of the process pervaded the country, increasing the suspicions of the native people that these white intruders were an accursed and poisonous race.

Having crossed the Razorback Range and then sloped down Towrang Hill, the women approached the Goulburn police magistrate, who arranged for them to be delivered to their employers. Mary, at the end of her institutional existence, said goodbye to the last of her Factory comrades. She went in the first instance to Lansdown Park, Bradley's home near Goulburn, a fair imitation of a British country estate, which employed dozens of convicts and former convicts. Recently elected to the new Legislative Council of New South Wales, representing the County of Argyle, Bradley had left management of his business within the Limits to a young Englishman, John Phillips, to whom Mary would have presented herself. She was not to stay long, however, in the defined regions, but was slated to work as housekeeper or servant in the Monaro bush with the manager of the huge Bradley sheep runs further south, Mr Brodribb.

When Mary and her son, Michael, went off on a wagon to the far south, they still had to travel about the same distance as already covered, and in wilder and less administered country. The wagon advanced over the Limestone Plains and gradually upwards into the broad, grand, windy, stone-strewn, mountain-rimmed reaches of the Monaro, where European women became a rare phenomenon, and where men might feel liberated by suffering and distance from restraints they might have chafed under in the church-ed and saint-ed world. Young Michael served as something of a protection as mother and son took their rest in rough company, in overseers' and shepherds' huts along the way.

The homestead at which Mary and Michael arrived at last, their Factory neatness jaded by distance, lay beyond Cooma Creek at a place named Coolringdon. The main house was certainly nothing like Lansdown Park. Brodribb planned to marry, though, and to introduce refinements. Inside the slab timber and bark walls, on the packed earth floor, Mary found an occasional excellent item of furniture, and good linen and silverware, and bound editions of the Latin and Greek classics as well as volumes of sermons, histories, and even novels.

The bark kitchen where Mary fulfilled some of her duties was separate from the house. The huts of the workers on the station stood nearby, of no more elevated construction than that of the master. In one of them resided her future lover, Hugh Larkin, whose Irishness and humour were, she clearly felt, close to her own.

CHAPTER 23

THE POOR EMIGRANT ASHORE

The ship bearing young Henry and Clarinda Parkes anchored in Sydney Harbour on 25 July 1839, after Clarinda had given birth at sea to a baby girl just after they cleared Bass Strait. The couple possessed two or three shillings when the anchor was let go, and 'the first news that came on board was that the four-pound loaf was selling at half a crown [two shillings and sixpence]!'.

On landing, they could not afford a carriage and Clarinda had to walk a mile across town, her infant in her arms, to 'a little low, dirty, unfurnished room, without a fireplace'. It would cost them 5 shillings per week rent. 'When she sat down within these wretched walls overwhelmed with fatigue, on a box which I had brought with us from the ship, I had but threepence in the world, and no employment.' At length, 'completely starved out', Henry took a job inland from Sydney as a common labourer with Sir John Jamison, whose model property, Regentville, lay near the Nepean River some 58 kilometres from Sydney. Though Sir John agreed to a yearly wage of £25 for Henry to work in his 6-hectare vineyard, Henry Parkes's status as a labourer would have put him in contact with the common assigned criminals who tended Sir John's vines and good horses, Sir John being the enthusiastic chairman of the Turf Club.

At work in the vineyard, Henry met a convict transported two years before from his own home town, Birmingham. The convict, 'who evidently knew the circumstances, brought me a share of his rations'. And when for some reason

Parkes had to travel through the bush in the middle of the night, an old lag touched him by insisting on carrying luggage for him 'out of pure respect'. But he and Clarinda ate the same rations as the convicts. Thus Parkes, a free Englishman, had the chance to comment on the complaints made by many convicts about what masters gave them to eat. He told his sister that they each received weekly 10½ pounds (4.8 kilos) of beef sometimes unfit to eat; 10½ pounds of rice—of the worst imaginable quality; 6¾ pounds (3 kilos) of flour, half of it ground rice; 2 pounds (900 grams) of sugar; a quarter pound (114 grams) of inferior tea; a quarter pound of soap ('not enough to wash our hands'); and two figs of tobacco ('useless to me'). And this from a master considered to be a reputable one. Parkes had no time to make a vegetable garden since 'the slave masters of Sydney require their servants to work for them from sunrise till sunset'.

The Parkes's marriage bed consisted for the first four months of their habitation at Regentville of a disused door laid on cross-pieces of timber, lined with a sheet of bark off a box tree and covered with articles of clothing for warmth. The hut's walls and roof admitted sunshine, rain, moonlight and wind. Their boxes, coming up from Sydney on Sir John's dray, had been broken open along the way, and almost everything worth carrying away was stolen. 'I made this first a very grave complaint, but only got laughed at for my pains, and told that was nothing.'

Towards the New Year Henry and Clarinda and the baby returned to Sydney, where he found employment with Russell Brothers, Engineers and Brass Founders, in George Street, getting 5 shillings per day finishing brass work. He did not like the work much and thought he might need to return to the country after all. The town of Sydney was an execrable place. 'I have been disappointed in all my expectations of Australia, except as to its wickedness; for it is far more wicked than I had conceived it possible for any place to be, or than it is possible for me to describe to you in England. For the encouragement of any at home who think of immigrating, I ought to add that I have not seen one single individual who came with me in the *Strathfieldsay* but most heartily wishes himself back at home.'

But slowly Parkes began to meet kindred souls—not least a bookseller named McGee of Pitt Street, of whom he was a client. And by September 1840 he had got work as a Customs House officer, and things were better. 'I spend most of my time on board ships, where I have a great deal of leisure to write poetry.' Some of it was published. And Robert Lowe, a member of the Legislative

Council, a descendant from one of the most illustrious families in England, had not thought him undeserving of his kindness, Henry said. 'I lately sat down to table with some of the most respectable merchants in Sydney.' He had 'a more comfortable home than it was ever my lot to possess in England', and was accumulating books again, though regretting that poor Clarinda spent a solitary life apart from the company of their daughter, 'our dear little blue-eyed ocean child', Clarinda Sarah.

Like many, however, whose future would prove entirely Australian, he did not think he would finally settle there. From ships' officers he collected books and newspapers but also heard stories of commercial chances in Java, Manila and Calcutta.

Parkes saw the onset of the colonial depression. 'The merchants of Sydney are all in a state of bankruptcy.' (And the four-pound loaf, he remarked, was now only 8 pence.) He believed too many immigrants were arriving for everyone's good. 'A week ago there were eight vessels lying at anchor in the harbour, all crowded with emigrants! And though many of them have now been engaged to go into the interior, I am afraid great numbers will not be able to obtain employment.' The cry for increased immigration came from those who wanted to keep labour prices low and keep Britons in the role of coolies, said Parkes.

He had fellow feeling for the uncertain futures facing the immigrants. They were permitted to remain on board their vessels for up to ten days after their arrival in Port Jackson, but then had to come ashore and find their way into society. One young woman, who left one of the immigrant ships when the ten days were up, was found by a policeman sitting on the Queen's Wharf and was taken to the watch-house. The next morning she was brought before the magistrate charged with being drunk, and though she stated it was faintness, she was sentenced on the oath of a policeman to sit one hour in the stocks. 'What encouragement for persons to come to Australia!'

Parkes confessed that when he went home in the evenings, his daughter would run to him with the plea, 'Father, take us in a big ship to see Grandfather and aunties in England, do, Father!' But distance from England had its benefits. It made him willing to offer peace to his father-in-law. 'Tell Mr R Varney that his daughter is comfortable, and as happy as a virtuous woman in her situation can be. Tell him it is time any enmity he may feel towards me should cease, though in some measure he may have had cause for it. The fact of our being separated to the opposite extreme of the earth, should, I think, help to make us friends.'

Pleased to report that the greatest poetical personage of Birmingham was now living in Australia—the Chartist-leaning, independently minded Miss Louisa Twamley, now married to the Vandemonian pastoralist Charles Meredith— Parkes himself was preparing for press a volume of verses, *Stolen Moments*, for which he had subscribers for one hundred copies. By now he knew Charles Harpur, the Australian-born poet. 'I am now more happily situated,' he wrote, 'but there is much bitterness at best in the lot of an exile.' His poetry would emphasise the banished British spirit and potential Australian democratic glory. Seeing convicts working to level Pinchgut Island in Sydney Harbour, Parkes's eye caught one of them. Perhaps he was the subject of some bitter urban or rustic arrest, Parkes mused.

> *He perchance is one*
> *Who yonder lifts the pickaxe in the sun*
> *To level Pinchgut Island! If e'er joy*
> *Gladdened your heart on England's shores, oh Never*
> *Forget that Englishmen are banished here forever.*

PASTORAL MIGHT

While convicts struggled with poor rations and hoped for tickets-of-leave and free emigrants battled to survive the economic downturn, patriots, patriarchs and pastoralists were at work in the politics of the colony. In 1842 an Imperial Act granted New South Wales, which still included Victoria, the right to elect twenty-four members to a legislature. A £20 rent or licence fee franchise was the basis of the Electoral Act, and there were democrats, from Charles Harpur the poet to Henry Parkes the customs officer who considered it far too high. It was not corruption of society by convicts which worried these men, it was the concentration of political power, whether in New South Wales or Whitehall, in the hands of the pastoralists, the men who, living under bark, had grown the Golden Fleece in the great distances and ennui of the bush.

The gentry were already hostile to the extension of the Land Commissioners' powers by Governor Gipps in 1839. In 1842, for example, William Lee had his squatting licence cancelled when his servants, moving herds westward beyond Bathurst into unauthorised areas, fought with Aboriginals. There was a fierce, denunciatory public meeting at Bathurst. The meeting asked the government to grant licences on the advice of three local magistrates, but Gipps believed this would give regional settlers the power to administer for their own benefit the vastness beyond the Twenty Counties and even the Crown lands still within. Gipps had earlier written, 'As well might it be attempted to consign the Arabs of the desert within a circle, traced upon the sand, as it would be to confine the graziers or woolgrowers of New South Wales within any bounds that could possibly be assigned to them.'

A great political crisis emerged in April–May 1844 when Gipps stated new terms under which settlers and squatters could occupy land. He and the British government were appalled that squatters could occupy unlimited acres for a mere £10 licence fee. He now proposed that squatters pay a licence fee for each run of twenty square miles ($52 \, km^2$), that the squatter could buy his land over a long period at not less than £1 per acre, and that to achieve security over his land, the squatter should purchase a 320-acre ($1.29 \, km^2$) homestead area which would secure his title to the run for eight years, and that he pay £320 every eight years to renew his rights. Gipps wanted this revenue to finance more immigration. Though he did not know it, the potato blight which would bring famine to Ireland and Scotland and which would produce great waves of immigration was but a few years away.

The pastoralists reacted to these modest ideas with fury. To fight Gipps the Pastoral Association in New South Wales and its Port Phillip counterpart, the Mutual Protection Society, began lobbying in Britain and locally, predicting the ruin of their industry if licence fees on squatting land and the collection of quit rents within the boundaries went ahead. The Committee on Land Grievances came into being, as gentry like Ben Boyd, WC Wentworth, Henry Dangar and others refused to accept the right of the imperial government to control land policy, a stand, as Gipps said, 'in opposition to all Constitutional Law and the positive enactment of Parliament'. At a meeting in Sydney, to the delight of genuine republicans, Wentworth—no longer young, now a pastoralist operating beyond the Limits, and well on his way to becoming a Tory—played the republican card by arguing that the Crown had been acting as 'but the trustee for the public'. All land taxes not sanctioned by the Legislative Council of New South Wales were illegitimate, he said. Ben Boyd, with land holdings on the south coast of New South Wales and over the mountains to the interior, argued that the payment of a £10 licence fee should vest the occupier with freehold over an area twenty miles square ($52 \, km^2$). One squatter suggested, 'The best thing they could do with Sir George [Gipps] now would be to Bligh him.' Another thought that twenty good stockmen would defy 'any regiment in Her Majesty's Service'; a third, that the soldiery would switch loyalties in return for twenty acres (8 hectares) and a few cattle apiece. The revolutionary spirit amongst squatters was strong.

The attempt of the squatters to take up Australian nationalism for their own ends impressed some. One who was initially attracted to their cause was Robert Lowe, the patron of Henry Parkes, an albino lawyer who had come to New South Wales with his wife for his health. After taking some months rest, he had sought a place in the Legislative Council and was appointed by Gipps. Lowe declared, 'If the representative of Middlesex claims a right to control the destinies of New South Wales, the representative of New South Wales should have a corresponding influence on the destinies of Middlesex.' But the urban liberals ultimately saw through the pastoralists' rhetoric, and Lowe withdrew his support from the squatters. 'I would give them every encouragement,' he said, 'but to give them a permanency of occupation of those lands—those lands to which they had no better right than that of any other colonist . . . I can never consent to.' He decided that having thought they fought for liberty, 'he found they fought only to defend their breeches pocket'.

But Wentworth, in particular, fought on with the same intensity and gift for vituperation which had characterised every aspect of his life. Of Gipps's plan he declared to cheering supporters that it was 'an imposition such as a lord puts upon a serf—fit for Tunis and Tripoli—worthy of the Dey of Algiers—it is intolerable, it is a nuisance which should not be endured'.

Throughout the 1840s the argument about whether Australia was to be 'a sheep walk forever' (to borrow a later phrase from Robert Lowe) would continue, along with struggles between and within sects and amid a bewildering and coruscating display of political passion.

CHAPTER 24

FETCHING SPOUSES

Hugh Larkin had by the time of Mary Shields's arrival at Coolringdon served ten years of his life sentence. Eighteen months earlier, on 21 December 1841, he had filled out a form he got from the police magistrate in the new village of Cooma, forty or so kilometres away. It was an application to have his wife, Esther, and their children, Patrick, then ten and Hugh, eight, sent to Australia at the British government's expense. 'The Petitioner is desirous of being reunited to the family from which he was separated at the time of his transportation.' William Brodribb certified that 'the Petitioner above named has been in my service since the month of March 1834, during which period his conduct has been such, that I respectfully recommend his Petition to the favourable consideration of His Excellency . . .' Hugh's application was signed too by a police magistrate and a clergyman.

In his arduous broad-stroke handwriting, Hugh gave Esther's address as Lismany, Galway, of the parish of 'Cluntowescirt nr Laurencetown'. As referees he nominated Walter Lawrence Esquire of Belview, Laurencetown, County Galway and the Right Reverend Thomas Cowan, Bishop of Loughrea, County Galway. Hugh could have found out these men were alive and willing to be referees only from Esther. In her late twenties in 1840, she would have hiked by road to Loughrea to bespeak the bishop, or lobbied him while he was in Clontuskert parish on a pastoral visit. Similarly, she took a short walk south through country in which she knew every cabin, fence, nuance of stone and mound and field, and up the long avenue to Belview House, to ask Mr Lawrence for the use of his name so that she might be removed from the familiar to an Australian future.

More than a year earlier, Esther had made her own appeal to Dublin Castle asking the Lord Lieutenant to look upon her situation with the eyes of pity and send her and her boys by free passage to New South Wales. Perhaps Hugh had received a letter from Esther and was operating on the basis of Esther's stated willingness to cross the mighty ocean. Their combined applications would surely be Esther's ticket out of a connection which, at the large house, in the cabin, in the field, poisoned the spirit.

Having filled in the form, Larkin must have enjoyed the heartiest Christmas yet of his Australian exile. From assignments all over the Australian bush, other men also applied for reunion. James Doolan, a shipmate aboard *Parmelia*, wanted his wife, Margaret Egan, and two children to join him. Stephen Doyle of the *Lady McNaughton*, serving seven years for a Ribbon crime, had applied for his wife, Jane McCone of Banbridge. But he had been flogged in January 1839, for losing sheep on Patrick's Plains. A year later he was flogged again. His application would be marked, 'Not Recommended on account of punishment.'

Hugh's petition needed to make its way by bullock wagon and mail coach to Sydney, where two months later a Colonial Secretary's clerk checked Larkin's record and wrote, 'Nothing recorded.' On that basis, Governor Gipps himself inscribed the petition, 'Allowed.' In May 1842, the Colonial Secretary in Sydney told the Superintendent of Convicts to apprise the successful applicants.

Dependent on shipping availability, the approving document would have reached Ireland in the summer of 1842. There was no problem with the way Hugh had addressed the petition. Laurencetown was a well-known market centre, Lismany a few kilometres north of it. Since Esther was still in the parish of Clontuskert, in Laurencetown or Lismany, under the eyes of relatives and the clergy, it was not likely that a lover delayed her. In early 1840 she had been more than willing to voyage to Australia, in fact desperate to. If she did ever receive the invitation to travel, it may have been an elderly and ailing parent who halted her departure—it may even have been Hugh's mother. Or perhaps Esther found she did not have the financial means to travel with her sons to the port of embarkation, or acquire the food and range of clothing required for the journey. Or maybe she never received the approval: sometimes, for reasons of inefficiency on the part of the Irish constabulary, laziness, malice or loss of documents, the papers were not delivered.

The most likely, and most pathetic, explanation for Esther's failure to reach Australia was the success of the anti-transportation movement. Convict transportation to New South Wales was ended by a Royal Order-in-Council in August 1840, implementing the recommendation of the Molesworth Committee. But the wives of convicts could receive free passage only on convict vessels. Even when Esther Larkin made her petition in February 1840, it was already nearly too late to link up with the last women's ship, the *Margaret* from Dublin.

The renewal of transportation seemed Esther's best hope. Then, about 1848, arrangements were made for convicts' wives to travel on emigrant ships. But all these adjustments would be too late for Hugh and Esther. There were still transports travelling to Hobart. But it was probably assumed by a bureaucrat within Dublin Castle that Esther, landed in Hobart without connecting transport, might be reduced to prostitution. So, probably for lack of a ship, Esther remained in Galway, and all enquiries and demands she made at barrack gates in Ballinasloe and at constabulary posts in the countryside were futile.

The Colonial Secretary in Sydney had signed Hugh's ticket-of-leave on 1 June 1843. He was lucky to be far from towns where the malicious or the righteous might report him for some peccadillo. But near-freedom brought no hope of an Australian hearth. The dream of showing Esther the bush, of introducing his sons to its particular grandeurs and squalors, of eating meat and damper with them in quantities to make them cry out in wonder, could no longer be entertained without pain.

By the time Mary Shields and her son ascended the slight slope where the homestead of Coolringdon stood, Hugh was entitled to go out and seek employment where he chose; to set up in business in his own right if he wished. Like many convicts who rubbed along well enough with a master, he chose to remain in this isolation, in the rawness and splendid space of that rising plain. He might never get his conditional pardon if he went off to some district more administratively fussy, or fell foul of new masters. The arrival of Mary may also have been a cause of his sticking with Brodribb.

Vivacious Mary must have been a wonderful relief to the weight of languor which afflicted the bush. William Forster, a future premier of New South Wales, described his life as a stockman on the Molonglo Plains to the south of

Coolringdon as being that of 'a miserable sort of outlaw . . . exerting the whole of my faculties in taking care of sheep and cattle'.

Even the squatters were reluctant to bring their families into the remoter country. Squatting was a form of exile from the defined world aimed at setting a man up for life. When the squatters finally won security of tenure in 1846–47 many of them began to settle, enlarge and refine their habitations, bring in furniture, raise families and cherish books and a piano in the parlour. That had not yet happened at Coolringdon, however, on the rawest edge of the Upper Monaro.

A BIRTH IN THE BUSH

Mary Shields quickly became inured to her work in William Brodribb's slab timber and bark homestead. Apart from the bush flies, ants, large—but not particularly vicious—spiders, and the occasional hut-intruding brown or red-bellied black snake (a particular terror to the natives of snake-free Ireland), the homestead must have seemed freer and more pleasant than the Female Factory. As the Australian spring came on, in the rush of activity around shearing when excitement, talk and the flow of liquor was at its peak in the Monaro, she and Hugh Larkin took each other as partners. The following July, screaming at a bark ceiling, she gave birth on a bed of sapling and leather strapping to a boy. Though an observing Anglican, Brodribb seemed philosophic about these liaisons between felons, even if both were married to others, as in this instance; such flexibility, shocking to visitors from Britain, was not considered extraordinary in New South Wales.

Brodribb himself was to be married that year, 1844, and would bring his wife, Eliza Matilda Kennedy, to Coolringdon. She was a cultivated young woman who had grown up on her father's pastoral stations. In the bush's natural democracy, her own children in years to come would play around the woolshed with convict children such as the Shields–Larkin son, perhaps under the care of Michael O'Flynn, Mary's Irish son, who was nearing ten years of age when his half-brother was born.

Mary Shields's new child was baptised Thomas by Father Walsh at the end of August 1844. The priest gave the couple the usual talking-to for begetting an Australian bastard. If wise, Hugh took this in silence. After all, Mary's sentence would be fully served by October the following year. She would then be free to live and marry as she chose, on the basis that she knew that her first husband had died, or that she was willing, as many were, to tell the authorities he had. Besides, like other convicts, Hugh must have thought that if authority could make his marriage to Esther a dead letter, he was, in return, entitled to be indifferent to the letter of authority, even to the canon law.

Now that ceaseless tragedy was the daily order of famine-struck Ireland, those transported earlier lived lives almost of banal well-being in their distant quarter of New South Wales. Hugh Larkin and Mary Shields did not escape the average, bitter nineteenth-century bereavements, though. In December 1847, a second child, Mary, was born and lived only eleven days. Hugh performed his own baptism of her, pouring the waters over her head, having been trained from childhood in the importance and potency of the rite. With the mother still ailing, he took the small coffin and his dead child by cart to burial somewhere in that immense country. Mary had now lost both daughters she had given birth to: O'Flynn's Bridget and Larkin's Mary, and that must have weighed appropriately on her.

It was apparent to her that they must marry for the sake of young Tom Larkin, now three years old. On the one hand, there was no doubt that Hugh and Mary, being now dead to the Old World, could still not permit themselves to marrying outside the church. But the priests were not as easily convinced. In their eyes the fact wives or husbands in the northern hemisphere were unreachable did not justify new unions at the earth's extreme south. An Attorney-General of New South Wales, the Irishman Roger Therry, who lived thirty years in the colony, was well aware of the marriage stratagems of some of his convict brethren. He told of how a man transported from Cork had left his wife and two children behind in Ireland. On becoming free, he wished to marry within the colony. He was able to produce a letter, complete with a Cork postmark forged in Sydney in red ink on the corner of the envelope. The letter, purporting to be from his brother in Ireland, indicated that the man's dear wife had died in the bosom of the Holy Catholic and Apostolic Church, a touch which worked well, said Therry, with the clergy.

In the end, Hugh and Mary managed to marry just before Hugh's conditional pardon was granted, when in theory he still needed permission from the Convict Department. This wedding prior to Hugh's freedom could have occurred only because both Esther Larkin and John O'Flynn had died in Ireland or else through the use of subterfuge of the kind mentioned by Therry. In any case, the ceremony took place on 16 March 1848, the eve of St Patrick, at Sts Peter and Paul's Catholic Church at Goulburn.

The marriage came at the end of an Australian summer and of another fatal Irish winter. News of the immutable Famine was in every paper they flinchingly read to each other, or had read to them. The Famine fell over their plentiful bush table, and made its claim upon them at dead of night, when they were released from distracting labour and lay together, as spouses in this hemisphere, wondering at what was happening in the parallel universe.

There was now a new governor in New South Wales. Well-meaning George Gipps had left in 1846 in a state of failing health and with the general disapproval both of the progressives, who saw him as too much a servant of the Crown, and of the squatters who believed him to be too lenient towards Aboriginals and indifferent to their problems of tenure. The new governor, Sir Charles Augustus FitzRoy, had fought at the age of sixteen at Waterloo, and had experience of colonial government in both St Edward's Island in Canada and in the Leeward Islands of the West Indies.

It was FitzRoy who, on 1 June 1848, signed the conditional pardon of Hugh Larkin. In this ornate document, towards the bottom of its page of print and penmanship, lay the clause: 'Provided always . . . that if the said Hugh Larkin, shall at any time during the continuance of the term of his said Sentence, go to, or be in, any part of the United Kingdom of Great Britain and Ireland, then this Pardon shall thenceforth be and become wholly void . . .' He could not take his dark, knowing benevolence even temporarily back to Galway to encounter his sons.

Hugh had an intention now to give up the remote stations. He and Mary left that boulder-dotted high plain, going away as their own people, possessed of freedom of movement and the rights of ambition. In late October 1848, Hugh bought for £25 a town allotment in Cowper Street, Goulburn, and set to work to build a house upon it and opened a small store. An infant, Anne, born of Mary Shields/Larkin on 30 November 1848, was healthy, and like her elder brother Tom, now five years old, would live on into another century. These colonial children, speaking in a potent, crow-harsh Australian accent, confirmed for their parents their distance from the Irish disaster, but also evoked other children who spoke more liquidly in Limerick or Galway.

The future seemed promising for the Larkin children, but utterly limitless for the children of their parents' former employer, the two young Brodribb daughters and a small son. When, en famille, the Brodribbs had visited the parsonage at Cooma one weekend, the elder daughter had come out from her mother's bedroom, with her hair nicely dressed. Brodribb wrote, 'My friend, Alex H-, who was present, remarked to me, "She will be a handsome woman." I thought I never saw a finer looking child.'

But in the middle of 1849, when Hugh and Mary were establishing themselves in Goulburn, Brodribb's wife, Matilda, fell ill, and almost at once his daughters too. It was diphtheria. The doctor from Cooma 'had their hair cut off, and cold applications applied to their heads'. At the end of July 1849, in the same room where her mother and sister lay, Brodribb's eldest daughter died. Brodribb rode by phaeton forty kilometres to Cooma for a coffin. Eight days later the second daughter died in great suffering. Mrs Matilda Brodribb recovered, but the 'loss of our daughters weighed heavily on her mind'.

William Bradley, Brodribb's employer in turn, also suffered more immediate grief than his former employees and convicts. During his journey to Europe, he lost his sickly wife, Emily, whom Italy was meant to cure.

But for the moment, Hugh Larkin's Australian wife and children bloomed. Soon they would share the pews of Sts Peter and Paul with Irish farm labourers and maids, desperate bounty emigrants from the Shannon estuary, part of the huge exodus of souls from Famine-ravaged Ireland.

Though the greatest mass of starving refugees would go to England, America and Canada, some thousands of Irish men, women and children reached Australia as a result of the Famine, including 4000 workhouse orphan girls. Two of the Irish emigrants who came from the peak of the Famine to Australia were Peter Lalor and his brother, while three other brothers went to America, where the discovery of gold had added an extra layer of attraction to the emigrant proposition. The Lalors came from a highly political family, and Peter's would soon be a resonating name in the goldfields of Australia.

MARY AND THE THUNGUDDI

One Irish girl who succeeded in joining her (soon-to-be) husband in the Antipodean wilderness was Mary McMaugh, who arrived in Sydney with her mother aboard the *Montmorency* in mid 1849. In this case her betrothed was not a convict but a free emigrant, an Irishman two or three years older than Mary, named Jack Vaughan, and it had probably been decided some time before in Ireland that Jack would come out first, establish a homestead and then send for her—this would be one of the patterns of emigration from the British Isles and Ireland.

Both Mary and her husband seem to have been the children of better-off Catholic farmers who survived the Famine, and Mary and her mother also successfully negotiated the risks of an emigrant ship—another matter of endurance. Yet Mary was shocked to see her fellow countrymen in the chain gangs of Sydney, a sight the locals were inured to.

From Sydney, Mary left alone by ship for Port Macquarie, the outlying penal station northwards along the New South Wales coast. Here again she observed chained men quarrying, occasionally lifting their morose eyes to take in the traveller. In the small port her fiancé was waiting for her—a fine, strong man, as she described him, though 'the hard bush life had roughened him'. She seemed, however, more stimulated than afraid when he described the life he led in the upper Macleay, and his narrow escapes from natives. Their marriage took place in the fort at Port Macquarie, and on horseback with a half-caste guide named Billy, they left for the town of Kempsey on the Macleay River, with its two pubs and a salesyard out the back of one of them. Stockmen and 'overlanders' here were booted and spurred, with bright Crimean shirts and colourful handkerchiefs around their necks. Jack said such men, flush from cattle sales, would ride their horses into the bar and call for drinks for all hands.

From Kempsey Billy the guide accompanied them towards 'my mountain home', upriver, at Myall Station, Myall being a common term in New South Wales for 'wild native'. They passed through groves of bush full of game, and the gorgeous, unaccustomed birds seemed to excite rather than alienate Mary. Her husband told her the names of trees, bushes and animals of this new world. She heard the cat-bird cry like a human baby.

At a farm where they stopped near Toorookoo Crossing (now Toorooka) she listened to a forthright farmer and his wife tell the story of their recent deliverance from Thunguddi attack. The Thunguddi had occupied the headwaters and the valleys of the Macleay, Hastings and Manning rivers for millennia, they were sturdy people, and from conversations with such neighbours as these she began to discern the difference between corroboree, ceremonial dance, and the initiation ceremony *capeharra*.

Now Mary and her husband rode on towards 'pinnacle after pinnacle, towards blue-green mountains'. When they reached the ridge above Myall Station, station hands, dressed in Crimean shirts, moleskins, boots and cabbage-tree hats, presented themselves. Dogs came out to greet them. As for the house: 'I was surprised to find it very neat and tidy, and when I learnt that this poor, ignorant black woman was the housekeeper, my astonishment knew no bounds.'

The Thunguddi people were not, of course, all so benign. A party attacked the overland mailman at Big Flat, hacked him to pieces and beheaded him. To the Vaughans, this was an attack on civil existence itself, on the networks which connected them to the outer world. Soon after, the milking cows began coming home with spears in them. For fear of attack on Myall Station, Mary's husband formed an outstation further down the river, closer to the mounted police barracks at Belmore River, and they lived there, now with two infants to whom she had given birth with the help of the Thunguddi housekeeper. When Jack was away, Mary dreaded the natives appearing and spent the night hours sleeplessly waiting for an attack. 'Some of the blacks had been employed by white people, but had drifted back to their tribes again. These were the worst class—most daring, treacherous and cunning.'

The fact was that these former servants had received an education in how genuinely the white settlers believed themselves to be here to stay, and they also knew what treasures a homestead might hold. Vaughan decided on the policy of making the Thunguddi scared of him, and this certainly seemed to his wife the right procedure. Vaughan 'became such a terror to them that they feared him exceedingly and I think (under Providence) preserved me and my children'.

For he was often away with his men, and Mary's only protection was an old Aboriginal man at the front door with a spear, and another at the back. She believed they, too, would spear her if she turned her back, but one night when a party of Thunguddi made what could be called a demonstration outside the house, she found one of the old men hiding under a bed. Soon after, in a form of defiance, she returned to the head station with her two boys.

Here she found a horse, impaled by a spear, standing dead against the stockyard fence. Though the stockmen slept with pistols, the Thunguddi raided the gardens, and carried off maize in their bags of kurrajong fibre. After Vaughan's stockmen had met up with some Aboriginals roasting stolen bullocks, a small squad of native police and two white police were posted to the station to protect against further raids. But some kilometres away, cedar cutters had an unprotected camp, where—supposedly safe in numbers—they felled the then-plentiful and tall wild cedar and floated it downriver on the next 'fresh'. They had employed a native named Smoker who showed the cutters the best clumps of cedar, and caught fish for them, and took honey from the hives of stingless native bees. It appeared Smoker secretly advised his clan on how to attack the loggers' camp. If that is true then his kinsmen would pay a high price ultimately, but in the short term their raid left the dead cutters heaped up in front of their huts. One wounded cutter, Sparks, survived.

At the end of a pursuit by the border police and stockmen far upriver, so many Thunguddi were killed that the place of the slaughter—like the creek on the Liverpool Plains and other such places in Australia—was named Waterloo, thereafter and to this day.

To Jack Vaughan and his wife Mary, drought was an enemy too. Wild apple and oak trees had to be cut down to stop the cattle starving, and Vaughan took stock for sale hundreds of kilometres across rivers and mountain ranges to the market in Maitland, near Newcastle. While he was gone the kitchen and storehouse took fire from burning embers scattered by a cruel wind blowing through a bushfire. Though Mary's boys struggled bravely, the fire obliterated the house as well.

Then, when the drought ended, the river came down like a torrent, and cattle were drowned, their carcasses stuck fifteen or more metres up trees. Young Mrs Vaughan accepted it with a deep-set equanimity. It was the nature of Australian seasons, and Australia was not a country for soft souls.

Myall Station was remote country, but remoter still were the ravines beneath the New England escarpment where the last major population of the Thunguddi was now situated. These groups were led by a man named Blue Shirt, but one day, riding far up the river, Vaughan captured Blue Shirt single-handedly and brought him back to the border police. It was reported that Blue Shirt was 'kicked to death' by a police horse, and no further enquiry was made of his fate.

Not all depredation was the work of the natives. A pleasant young Scot named Ellis had arranged with Vaughan to live at Myall Station to learn bushcraft. Mary enjoyed his company greatly. He was summoned home by a family loss, said his farewells to the station hands, and on the way to Kempsey, drowned above Dan's Falls. There were signs that a theft had taken place from his satchel, which was sent on to his mother in Scotland, still containing his letters and journal. Some disreputable figures who had ridden down from New England were suspected of the murder, but in that immensity, as with Blue Shirt, nothing could be proved.

The Thunguddi were still not utterly reconciled to the loss of their long, paradisal valleys. A new stockman who rode out to visit Dan's Falls was found there beheaded, wounded eight times with spears and his horse wounded as well. He was buried, as bushmen were, in a sheet, and wrapped in a sheath of bark.

How welcome to Mary Vaughan was the racing season when once a year the family went into the growing port town of Kempsey for the races there. It was a vivid scene—good gigs, fine dresses, conviviality. Racing clubs were one of the ways Australians built sociability across massive distances. But ultimately Mary and Jack returned to the testing loneliness of the upper Macleay Valley, and there one day, when gold had been discovered in New South Wales and Victoria, and when Sydney and Melbourne had been transformed to more than mere outposts, Jack Vaughan's horse rolled on him and crushed him in that hilly country he had wrested from the Thunguddi. The man who had captured Blue Shirt was put on a bier at the homestead, and his and Mary's boys helped bury him beneath the august blue hills of the Kookaburra Range. Mary would continue to occupy Myall, her sons married and stayed in the area, and her descendants are still found in the upper Macleay Valley.

CHAPTER 25

CANADA BAY

An uprising which would send Canadian and American rebels to Australia began in Lower Canada—the present-day Quebec—in 1837. It grew from the refusal by the government—run by a British governor and an appointed legislative council—to address the political hopes and land aspirations of an increasingly poor and, above all, democratically thwarted group named the *Patriotes*, a French-speaking party, led by merchants and intellectuals.

But it was not only French-speakers who were involved in the unrest of 1837–8. A reform movement was also operating in Upper Canada—today's Ontario. Radical reformers there wanted to build an economy based on that of the United States, with the same degree of democratic control over revenues and expenses, and a check on the granting of land grants to people of influence. The leader of the radicals, William Lyon Mackenzie, instigated an armed insurrection after the lieutenant-governor intruded in the elections of 1836 to make sure that he had a conservative legislature.

This rebellion was brutally crushed by British troops, but American activists, border supporters of the rebels, moved into Canada in 1838 to continue the fight. They ran into a well-organised military resistance co-ordinated by the new lieutenant-governor of Upper Canada, Sir George Arthur, who had previously ruled Van Diemen's Land.

The trials of the French-speaking, Anglo and American rebels read shamefully and involved tainted 'evidence' manufactured under the broad aegis of martial law. The various charges thus proved on which the rebels were transported included high treason, misprision of treason [attempted treason] and lawless aggression. A number of them were condemned to death. Some travelled to the hulks in Britain before being transported to Van Diemen's Land.

Most of them, however were loaded aboard the *Buffalo*, which reached Hobart in February 1840. The Yankees were landed there, while the Canadians were sent on to Sydney.

The approach of the *Patriote* rebels in the *Buffalo* alarmed the residents of Sydney. The Protestant mainstream was horrified sufficiently by the proliferation of Irish papists sunk in superstition, and now their equally rebellious French counterparts were to join in the New South Wales equation. The *Herald* reminded Sydneysiders: 'The only instance of any united attempt to overturn the government here was after the arrival of the Croppies in 1804, and it was many years before the seeds of disorder and riot were crushed.'

There was a public insistence that the *Patriotes* be sent to Norfolk Island, and the first Catholic bishop of Sydney, John Bede Polding, who came aboard *Buffalo* to hear their confessions, indeed exhorted them to accept that hard fate. Yet nine days passed, and the indications grew that the *Patriotes* would remain in Sydney. Governor Gipps decided that they would stay together as a group in the Longbottom prison camp along the Parramatta River. The 'beautiful little village' of Concord steeled itself for the arrival of the rebels at the camp on the western shore of Hen and Chicken Bay.

A platoon of soldiers met the *Patriotes* on the beach and escorted them to the main barracks about a kilometre away. The superintendent there received them ungraciously. They slept on the floor of their huts with only one blanket to protect them and were forbidden to speak. Their clothes were branded with 'LB'—Longbottom Barracks. Yet the Canadians abashed the guards by being good workers. They were put to work loading stones from barges onto bullock carts, taking them a little way inland and pounding them down to make road gravel. The superintendent considered appointing one of their number, Maurice Lepailleur, as work overseer, because he noticed Lepailleur was generally respected by the prisoners—a departure from normal practice. Removed, he was given the job of gatekeeper. A rather forthright *Patriote* named Louis Bourdon finally got the job instead—not such a popular choice. Meanwhile, Lepailleur noticed that even their luxuries, their ounce of brown sugar a week, was best described as 'left over filth, full of little bits of wood and rice'. The rations normal to the convict condition appalled them. The cooks among them did their best to create pâtés, tourtières, soups and other French-Canadian dishes, but they could not perform miracles with rotten meat. By August 1840, some of the men showed the effects of malnutrition. A 190-centimetre innkeeper from St Martine named Shèvrefils was desperate for food and a number of his friends gave him their bread rations.

Apart from unloading stone, some of the French Canadians burned charcoal, and others made bricks. Lepailleur was appalled to be made gate sentry, but it gave him time to keep a journal, and even to keep one for an illiterate prisoner named Basile Roy. He watched traffic go by on Parramatta River, and was surprised to find that the Sydney area was not as fertile as the Château Guay Basin in Lower Canada. Down the road in Sydney, Father Brady, secretary to Bishop Polding, waged a writing campaign on the *Patriotes*' behalf, to get them better treatment and if possible some form of pardon.

After three months the authorities felt secure in withdrawing the military guard assigned to the Canadians, and the Sydney papers began to comment favourably on their industry. Lepailleur in his gatekeeper's hut nonetheless still chafed, as many of them did, at being 'the slave of everyone, not only one person, but all those in authority'. Back in Château Guay, he had been bailiff, postal courier, farmer, father of two sons and a man of substance. Here, apart from the general ignominy of his lot, Bourdon the overseer began to act like a martinet towards him and everyone else. 'Strangers have not despised us as much as our convict officers have,' complained Basile Roy. They were chagrined to be marched to church in ranks like common criminals and brought back in the same manner.

Louis Dumouchelle, transported with his brother Joseph, took ill, and extraordinary pressure was required to get him moved to the hospital in Sydney's Macquarie Street. There he found that being nursed by convicts was a hard cure. The sick were often brutalised, and Lepailleur saw a man die after the convict nurses had shaken and beaten him in an effort to make him stand. The man died while tied to the end of his bed as punishment for letting his sheet slip to the floor.

Louis Dumouchelle eventually died in Sydney Hospital hallucinating that he was reunited with his wife. His brother saw the limits placed on convict dignity when his body was placed naked in his coffin. Fearful that they might follow

Louis into the Australian earth, the other *Patriotes* became devout, joining the lay brotherhood of Our Lady Help of Christians. The air over the Longbottom station was nonetheless rent not by the singing of hymns to the Virgin Mary but by *Patriote* drinking songs.

Contrary to official policy the *Patriotes* received newspapers, both local and the occasional overseas edition—a boy delivered them to Lepailleur the gatekeeper on Parramatta Road every morning. Newspaper opinion had come totally round to them. JD Lang's *The Colonist*, for example, which had once feared them as a papist threat, now called them 'unfortunate men'. 'No mention or complaints are heard from them, and they pay implicit obedience to any orders they receive. Every evening they congregate near their . . . house for the purposes of prayer. After they are locked up each division may be heard for a short time, imploring the Supreme Being and then all is hushed till the morning, when they return to their severe probation.' The exception was the *Herald* which felt that if they were treated kindly it would be unfair 'to the well-behaved Protestant prisoners'.

The men were able to get drink too, from the Bath Arms across Parramatta Road from their camp, owned by an accommodating German named Emmanuel Neich, who also supplied more reading material, including books in French. The *Patriotes* were confused, however, to find that there were no names in the English dictionary for Australian fauna or flora. There was no 'cockatoo' or 'goanna'; no names for the fish many caught to supplement their lean diet.

In 1841, in an exception to the general restrictions on convict assignment, Governor Gipps let it be known that the Canadians could be assigned. The deputy-surveyor, Samuel Perry, and Captain McLean were the first to apply. McLean was the principal superintendent of convicts, and had installed a system of good wages and conditions for assigned men—wages were to be paid into the Savings Bank of New South Wales in the men's names.

There was a depression beginning in New South Wales, and that fact delayed assignment for many, but as the numbers dwindled inside the Longbottom stockade, so did the morale of those left. There were fretful rumours that their wives and children would be shipped out. Lepailleur's longing for his wife was such that when a woman on Parramatta Road stopped in front of the gate and looked into the settlement, it was all he could do to refrain from running out and greeting her as his spouse.

The *Patriotes* were all excited to hear from Father Brady that Bishop Polding had mentioned their case to government while he was in England, and that they might receive their tickets-of-leave as early as February 1842. In the meantime Emmanuel Neich, the innkeeper, had decided to take a *Patriote* himself and applied for Maurice Lepailleur. In fact, Lepailleur was assigned to Hamilton C Sempill, a Darlinghurst magistrate close to Governor Gipps, and was happy to escape the barracks; it was one step closer to his wife, 'dear Domitile'. He began working as a painter and labourer.

News of the Canadians' impending tickets-of-leave indeed came through in February, and by the month's end every *Patriote* had left Longbottom. There was a celebratory dinner at the Jew's Harp Inn on Brickfield Hill, which belonged to a French immigrant, Jean Meillon. Here a number of the *Patriotes* lived after receiving their tickets-of-leave and while looking for work. Lepailleur scrubbed floors and acted as a handyman there. In March, John Ireland, who owned the Plough Inn on Parramatta Road, gave him employment. Lepailleur painted coaches and houses and lettered post office carts on behalf of his master, since the Plough Inn was a changing place for coaches. He worked also for Alexander MacDonald who had supplied the Canadians, while they were at Longbottom, with peaches and watermelons to supplement their diet, and helped to build a house and family tombs for him in St Anne's cemetery at Kissing Point across the Parramatta River. He also worked for his old friend Emmanuel Neich at the Bath Arms. He even worked for a time for William Charles Wentworth at Vaucluse.

The stonemasons amongst the *Patriotes* worked on the foundations of the new Paddington Army Barracks. Bourdon, the former overseer, found his work manufacturing lathes from tree branches exhausting. Another *Patriote*, Rochon, bought two blocks in Kent Street, borrowing money from the small Canadian community, and brought in *Patriote* tradesmen, including Lepailleur, to work on them. Whatever their grievances, the Canadians tended to support each other. Dr Newcombe for example, a 77-year-old *Patriote*, lived with another Canadian in the Longbottom area.

The freed Canadians were impressed as other visitors were, by the amount of drinking in the colony, particularly Lepailleur. Mrs Stone, the wife of one of his employers, was a pretty woman but she drank as much as a man, and was rapidly becoming deranged and dishevelled. Hippolite Lactôt found 'Intemperance was *de rigueur*; sobriety the exception, amongst women as it was for men.' Once a woman convict, intoxicated and just released from the Female Factory, stood in the middle of Parramatta Road screaming drunken curses outside the house of another ex-convict woman. When a *Patriote* sent a police guard to protect her, she turned her back, 'lifted up her clothes and showed . . . her bum, saying that she had a "black hole" and slapping her belly like the wretch she was'. The Canadians were utterly unaccustomed to such drunkenness and displays of crudeness in women.

The community's sexual mores also fascinated the *Patriotes*, shaken by the experience of prisoner celibacy as they were. Jean-Baptiste Trudel and Désiré Bourbonnais went to help a woman who was being beaten by her Portuguese husband, and Bourbonnais was reported to the police for doing so. The Portuguese man paid the police off to prevent prosecution. And Lepailleur wrote once of a woman and her husband, the wood warden of Concord: 'She was drunk and he punched her and beat her with a whip. It was her New Year's present . . . we hear more women crying in the night here than birds singing in the woods during the day. I think every husband beats his wife.' When working at Ireland's hotel, Lepailleur was shocked to hear men boast of having committed gang rapes. And yet he, the alien ingrate rebel, was supposedly the lowest of the low in this society.

When Bishop Polding returned from England, the Canadians were told that they should present themselves the following Sunday at St Mary's. They did so in their best suits, expecting expansive news. Polding told them only that British Colonial Secretary Lord Stanley was favourably disposed towards them and that they should have patience. The bishop had not invited them into the presbytery, and said a few words to them on the church steps. They went away complaining, in the spirit of the Irish, that though a priest he was, after all, an Englishman.

The Canadians were increasingly tempted by local women—Joseph Dumouchelle ran away with Mrs Charles Nicholls, a woman from Concord. Tracked down, he was found to have some minor possessions of Nicholls's in his keeping. He was arrested and sent to the Hyde Park Barracks, to serve a six-month sentence for theft, even though Mrs Nicholls praised his ardour by comparison to her husband's. At the barracks, despite his brother's death at the hospital, he worked his way into it, pretending illness.

While walking in the Domain, Louis Bourdon, the officious overseer, was offered escape by officers of a French whaling ship which was in port. The officers downplayed the danger, even though the captain or owner of the ship was subject to its being impounded if an escaped convict were found aboard.

Bourdon realised that escape would still mean exile from Lower Canada, and capture would mean his being sent to Norfolk Island. Just the same, he determined to try. He went on board, leaving sundry debts behind, and made his way to New York and ultimately, after pardons came through, to his home village.

In Canada, *L'Association de la Déliverance* had been working for some years to promote a pardon for the *Patriotes* and to support 'their families, their property, their honour, their liberty, their life'. A fund was raised to restart them in life, once pardoned or released. All the *Patriotes* were indeed pardoned by the British government by March 1844, and were repatriated by January 1845. Lepailleur was reunited with his 'chère Domitile'. One *Patriote*, Joseph Marceau, stayed on in New South Wales and farmed in the Dapto region, south of Sydney, having married a nineteen-year-old Englishwoman.

In the meantime, Sir John Franklin in Hobart had told the North Americans transported there that their circumstances were without precedent, and that they must not hold conversation with the other prisoners, as 'they were a desperate and hardened class'.

The Americans and non-Québécois Canadians were put to work on the roads and quickly noticed that the overseers and clerks took the choicest mutton and left the scrag ends to the convicts. There was no sugar, tea, coffee or tobacco. Macadamising the roads meant 'levelling down hills and levelling up valleys, breaking stones and drawing them in hand carts to where they were wanted'. It was desperately tough physical labour. Four *Patriotes* bolted after months on the gang, but were recaptured and sent to Port Arthur for the remainder of their time. One party was sent to work on a new gaol in Hobart. They would frequently go out at night by climbing through the chimney of their hut, though its door was locked, and jumping to the earth and going away to steal potatoes, which they would bring back and drop down the chimney to their associates. Those discovered in these outings were flogged and given three months hard labour in irons or were sent to the coal mines on the Tasman Peninsula. Ultimately, in February 1842, the Americans were allowed to take their tickets and settle in one of six specified districts.

The rebel, Snow, worked on the property of a member of the Legislative Council, taking in the harvest. In October 1842 he got the news that he had received a pardon along with twenty-eight others. They returned home on an

American vessel, the *Steiglitz*, a whaler from Sag Harbor, New York. None of them were tempted to stay. 'We had thought of the moral influence exerted upon the minds of children of the free population by being associated with and surrounded by so many of the most vicious human beings the world ever saw; we had in countless instances seen total depravity personified', he later declared of the island colony.

THE RELIGIOUS DIVIDE

As shown by the suspicion attending the arrival of the *Patriotes* in Sydney, Protestant–Catholic tension was evident even in the early years of Australia. But the Catholics were also fighting their own internal battles. The fledgling Catholic Church in the colony was divided roughly along an English–Irish axis, even though in Sydney the English Benedictine bishop and lover of cricket, John Bede Polding, got on well with the apostle to the Irish convicts, the affable reformed alcoholic Father John McEncroe. But McEncroe was too much a political radical for the tastes of most of the English Benedictines, even though his politics reflected those of his congregation, bond and free. And in Hobart, the Irish Father John Joseph Therry fought the English-born Bishop Willson over control of church property for fourteen years. In August 1849, a letter signed 'An Irishman' appeared in the Hobart press sneering at 'Bishop Willson and his anti-Irish clergy'. It claimed that birds of passage like them did not deserve a cathedral built with Irish money. The *Irish Exile*, a flamboyant journal run by a charming and tragic alcoholic revolutionary named Patrick O'Donohoe, supported Therry, depicting Willson as 'upholding British supremacy under the veil of Catholicity'. Indeed, near the end of his career, Willson would argue that an Irishman should succeed him, chiefly because an Englishman could not hope to control the Hobart diocese.

The English Benedictines (Willson was not one) tended towards conservatism, but in Van Diemen's Land, as in New South Wales, Catholics of Irish background associated with the local 'Australian' faction whose objectives included resistance to transportation, a free market for free labour, self-government and the vote. Father Therry, for example, made clear that his opposition to transportation was as great as his opposition to stigmatising former convicts, so plentiful in his congregation, with criminality.

Under Irish pressure, the Catholic Church supported the multi-establishment of churches, tolerance and social harmony, whereas the Anglican Bishop

Broughton protested against the Catholic Bede Polding's recognition as a prelate at an 1839 Government House levee. Bishop Nixon, the Anglican bishop of Van Diemen's Land, similarly objected to Robert Willson adopting the title of 'Catholic Bishop' in 1842. The leading liberal Catholics of the day admired separation of church and state, not only because of progressive opinion but also because it was the best condition under which they—essentially a non-Establishment church—could operate. The Scots Catholic intellectual and journalist William Duncan suggested to Dr Lang, the Presbyterian leader, that the Catholics and Presbyterians unite to support this principle, which was reflected in Governor Bourke's New South Wales Church Act. But Lang did not like the Church Act for its capacity to spread papism. By contrast, Catholics like Caroline Chisholm, a familiar sight in the 1840s riding her grey horse, Captain, and leading columns of young female immigrants into the bush, where in distant towns she had set out employment offices for them, made sure it was a committee composed of clergy and laity of all denominations that supervised her emigrants' home in Britain and her depot and outlying offices in Australia.

The Vatican, however, was suspicious of the new nationalisms and secular democratic pieties, and there was always a sensitivity in the Catholic Church about new ideas. With this anti-intellectual streak came mainstream Catholic suspicion of the secular schools Governor Bourke had legislated for. So a priest like McEncroe, much loved in the houses of the native Irish and by the members of work gangs, grew to be the enemy of a multi-denominationalist like William Duncan. Yet McEncroe was a social liberal too, an enemy of the concept that something as precious as the human soul should be left at the mercy of *laissez faire* economics of the kind that were keeping the Irish at home poor and would visit the huge calamity of the Famine upon them. He wanted the New South Wales government to establish a state bank to issue credit and discount small bills, and relieve the poor with loans. McEncroe was also a supporter of the anti-transportation movement, and he was anti-squatter in Australia as he had been anti-landlord in Ireland, and belittled the Pastoral Association and its pretensions. In men like McEncroe his friends could meet an increasingly common Irish Catholic phenomenon—the man who was strict on dogma and unyielding on religious observance, but radical in political thought. Indeed, the Presbyterian JD Lang later described him as Australia's first republican.

Another problem, both within the Catholic Church and between religions, was the tendency to use Irish nationalist emblems at Church events. The Attorney-General, John Plunkett and the lawyer Roger Therry—both Irish— shared Duncan's view that this simply created anti-Catholic bile and bigotry, most vehemently expressed by local members of the Orange Lodge, the Irish loyalist society founded in the 1790s to protect the state against the inroads of papism. The local Orange newspaper, the *Sentinel*, railed frequently against the 'papal democratic mob', and found support in the Melbourne *Argus*. Their major charge against Catholics was that they planned domination of the judicial system from the Supreme Court down to the constabulary. Even the Presbyterian Lang gave the Orangemen ammunition by saying of Caroline Chisholm's female migration schemes that they were 'extending the Romanism of the colony through the vile, Jesuitical, diabolical system of "mixed marriages"'. Ribbonism was active in Sydney, declared the *Sentinel*, and you could see it demonstrated on St Patrick's Day and on Boyne Day, the day decent Protestants marched to celebrate their deliverance from the priest-ridden horrors of papism.

The week around Boyne Day 1846, Melbourne suffered the tensions of civil war. In the midst of potential mayhem, the *Sentinel* declared that it opposed general cemeteries where Catholic bones presumed to seek burial with those of the children of God. Fortunately, sectarian activity confined itself to mutual insult and fist-fights, but the antagonisms had been set in place and would last for more than a hundred years.

Meanwhile, the brilliant William Duncan's Scottish blend of urbanity, learning and liberalism, disseminated in his paper, the *Weekly Register*, was not what Irish Catholics wanted to read. They took to a more tribal paper, *The Freeman's Journal*. When Duncan's paper went out of publication, he took a job as a customs officer in Brisbane, where he would work the rest of his career.

The Irish enmity to the English Benedictines came to its head in the reaction to Father Gregory, a shy Benedictine monk who became vicar-general of the Sydney diocese. As is a common Irish reaction, his English austerity was mistaken for contempt. It was believed that he too quickly showed alarm or, some would say, dislike for the raggedness and ignorance of much of his Irish congregation. To them, his liking for the company of the higher officials and councillors of the colony seemed a betrayal, and being born in Cheltenham, unlike many of his flock he did not want to see Catholicism captured by Irish nationalists or turned into an instrument of cultural vengeance against Protestants. In the period in which he ran the diocese—1846–48—the Christian Brothers found him so authoritarian, supercilious and negligent of their feelings and needs that they returned to Ireland. A section of the Irish Sisters of Charity went to Van Diemen's Land rather than submit to his intrusion in the running of their affairs, including their fund-raising for Catholic schools and a hospital. As discontented colonials used to complain to Whitehall of governors, discontented Irish denounced Gregory to Rome. Nonetheless, his report to Rome on the new Constitution for New South Wales which was being proposed in the early 1850s shows that he saw common cause with the Irish. 'The Bill recently granted by the Imperial Parliament for a new arrangement of the Legislature in the Colony, will also, it is probable, be serviceable to the cause of Catholicism, inasmuch as by the extension of the voting franchise, the influence of the labouring and trading classes will be rendered more able to cope with that of the wealthy landowners and capitalists who are almost exclusively Protestants.' Ultimately, an Act of 1851 removed all religious discrimination in New South Wales. Anglicans, Catholics, Presbyterians, Jews, Methodists and Wesleyans were legally equal before the state and the law. In practice, there were still battles to be fought.

CHAPTER 26

DEMOCRACY

By 1848, Henry Parkes, former labourer, brass-finisher and customs officer had earned enough to turn shopkeeper, selling a miscellany of items from his premises in Hunter Street, and had founded and led an Artisans' Committee which secured the election of the lawyer Robert Lowe, the first populist candidate, to the New South Wales Legislative Council. One of Lowe's policies was to reduce the reserve price of land to 5 shillings an acre, leaving squatters in possession until bona fide settlers purchased the land. It was a form of unlocking the land which would ultimately become popular many years later.

There was inevitable conflict between the old gentry who had bought or been granted their land and the squattocracy who had acquired it cheaply. 'Between the counties and the districts,' wrote Benjamin Boyd, himself a squatter, 'there always has been, and will be, bitterness of feeling and dissension. The old settlers cannot forgive the squatters their long leases; the squatters cannot forgive the old settlers their free grants of land.' But of the gentry who did not become squatters, only a few survived the economic rigours of the 1840s.

Squatting nonetheless was contrary to the idea of a 'merrie Australia', an Australia of villages. Indeed free men did not like to work on remote stations. Ex-convict overseers allegedly found pleasure in tormenting them for their enviable condition. Fear of Aboriginal spearing acted as a disincentive too. The work was monotonous. Payment was by orders drawn in Sydney that the workers had to go and collect. They might find on arrival that their employer's credit was not worth anything. The free working class therefore failed to meet the woolgrowers' need for labour.

So the squatters were the chief voice favouring renewal of transportation, and it was one of the motives behind the establishment of the Moreton Bay Separation Movement, pushing for an independent colony in what is now Southern Queensland. But by common consent the ideal immigrant was a young married Briton; he, his wife and his children promised the best hope of a community sound in moral health and amenable to high ideals. The clash between men who wanted a continuing supply of cheap convict labour and those who wished for reputable artisans was very deep.

As the Currency poet Charles Harpur vividly declared in 1845,

Hark Australians! Hark, the trumpet
Calls you to a holy fight!
Round the Evergreen, your standard,
Gather, and as one unite!
Shall the Monarchists condemn us
Into slavery and shame?
Or shall Truth endiadem us
With the stars that write her name?
Shall yon bright blue heaven, in roofing
This green golden land, afford
But a wide and splendid dwelling
For the villain and his lord!
And not a great dome of merit—
Not an open region be
For the outward marching spirit
Of immortal liberty.
Down with Wentworth! Down with Martin!
Murray, Marsh and all their clan!
Sticklers for the rights of cattle—
Sneerers at the rights of man!
We were slaves—nay, we were viler!
Soulless shapes of sordid clay,

Did we hound not from our Councils
Wolves and foxes such as they . . .
By the equalising glory,
Of the cause with which we start!
By the blood of honour thrilling,
Through each patriotic heart!
By the majesty of manhood
Righteously and nobly free,
We will pause not till Australia
All our own—our own shall be.

In the atmosphere in which he wrote this, Harpur knew that in New South Wales a little over one thousand people occupied 44 million acres (almost 18 million hectares), and a similar disproportion in land ownership existed in the Port Phillip region.

THE TOYSHOP MOB

By 1848 Henry Parkes, former bounty immigrant, was a political force. The room behind his shop in Hunter Street, which sold everything from ivory by the tusk and pound to musical instruments, stationery, desks, whales' teeth, boxing gloves, pomade pots and Malacca canes, was a meeting place for the literary and political radicals of Sydney. Some called this grouping 'the toyshop mob'.

In February 1849, Earl Grey announced the resumption of transportation to New South Wales. He had yielded to the desires of the pastoralists, and was sending to the colony a number of trusty convicts known as 'exiles' on a ship named *Hashemy*. Parkes's parlour was one of the epicentres of outrage at Earl Grey. Even though Parkes's short-lived paper was named the *Empire*, the air was full of republican rhetoric, particularly from the Reverend Lang and a little dandy of a Currency man, Daniel Deniehy. Respectable liberal leaders of some means would fight for control of this newest cause, since they were frightened that the toyshop radicals would use the betrayal by Earl Grey to take New South Wales in some drastic revolutionary direction. After all, only the previous year, the French had overthrown a king and installed a poet, Lamartine, as president of France. As for the Irish working classes and former convicts, their brothers and sisters at home, in that most distressful country, were dropping into ditches, fodder in their hunger for opportunistic diseases. The Legislative Council would condemn Earl Grey's decision, to make possible revolutionaries feel they had friends at the top.

Shops closed the Monday after the *Hashemy* arrived in Sydney in June 1849, and thousands of people made their way to Circular Quay. Parkes had hired a horse-drawn two-decker omnibus which carried a banner declaring, 'Defiance'.

Rain began to fall, but the crowd did not move. Parkes's friend Robert Lowe was there, though no longer popular with the lower classes who had helped elect him to the Legislative Council. Even so he got a laugh when he said he no longer wanted to be identified as a 'toy' of Parkes's Constitutional Association, so-called to assure the enemies of the 'toyshop' that all they wanted was reform within the British Constitution, a claim which would prove itself utterly true in Parkes's case. But when he spoke at length, Lowe was aflame. 'I can see from this meeting the time is not too far distant when we assert our freedom not by words alone. As in America, oppression is the parent of independence, so will it be in this colony ... And as sure as the seed will grow into the plant, and the plant into the tree, in all times, and in all nations, so will injustice and tyranny ripen into rebellion, and rebellion into independence.'

This statement, said the *Herald*, was met with 'Immense Cheering'. But the truth was that most people there that day were looking for redress within the British Constitution; they did not want, or even contemplate, independence. Even Lowe might have been merely raising the American Revolution as a spectre to frighten the British government into constitutional action.

But when a delegation, including Lowe and Parkes, took the motions and petitions from the meeting to Government House, they found the garrison out and guarding the fences of the Government Domain. Let in, they met the new governor, Sir Charles FitzRoy, the aristocrat who combined earthy tastes with superciliousness towards political activists, particularly lower-class activists like Parkes. The governor said he had assured the people of Port Phillip that the prison ship *Hashemy* would not land its cargo there, and so it would have to dock in Sydney. The delegation left in the cold of a June dusk, outraged at FitzRoy.

The exiles aboard *Hashemy* must have looked at the shore and longed for a landing, and wondered why, when in the past far worse lags had been landed, they could not be brought ashore without creating a vast public riot. But travellers on two bounty emigrant ships also in the harbour looked at *Hashemy* with a jaundiced eye too. They had been promised an Australia where in the main they would not have to compete for their bread against convicts. Scots who had escaped the potato blight of the Highlands but not yet landed, glowered at the *Hashemy* trustys.

The governor's ill-grace was a great rallying call for another mass meeting a week later. A few years before, the loss of his young wife, whose skull had been crushed in a coaching accident at Government House, Parramatta, when FitzRoy had been demonstrating his talents as a 'whip', had brought from the colonists an extraordinary outflow of public grief. Since then, however, FitzRoy and his sons had scandalised many with their sexual appetites.

From the top of his bus, Parkes said that now the heavens smiled on their endeavours whereas the week before they had wept for the gross injustice represented by the convict ship. Lowe spoke to a motion upbraiding the governor for his rudeness. Parkes then spoke to a motion moved by the lawyer Alexander Michie—'That it is indispensable to the well-being of the colony and to the satisfactory conduct of its affairs, that its government should no longer be administered by the remote, ill-informed, and irresponsible Colonial Office, but by Ministers chosen from and responsible to the colonists themselves, in accordance with the principles of the British Constitution.'

The convicts were nonetheless landed from *Hashemy*, and some were applied for as assigned servants now that that was again temporarily possible, and the rest were sent up to Moreton Bay. But it was apparent to FitzRoy and Earl Grey that no more convict transports could come to Sydney.

CHAPTER 27

EAST INDIAMEN

The abolition of slavery in Britain in 1833 had helped create a system of indentured labour by which large numbers of Indians were shipped to Britain's African and West Indian colonies as a cheap labour force. Some entrepreneurs and pastoralists in Australia, faced with the end of transportation, now thought of Asian labourers as an answer, particularly in light of the harsh economic conditions of the late 1830s. Though there was already a great deal of commercial and general contact between Calcutta and Sydney, Australian progressives were opposed to the concept of indentured labour, and Australian craftsmen and workers did not want to compete against 'coolies', whose labour was so much cheaper than their own.

Nonetheless, in 1836, John Mackay, who had arrived from India where he had lived for twenty-eight years, began to test the interest on the part of New South Wales pastoralists in importing coolies, and in conversation with an uneasy Governor Bourke told him that their clothing was simple and scanty, their dwellings small, yet they produced work fully equal to Europeans in any agricultural job 'excepting the plough'.

Those, like Mackay, interested in employing coolies were quick to point out that when the indentured labourers returned to India, they would take with them 'not only improved manners, customs, arts, agriculture and laws, but also the blessings of Christianity'. And so, the opponents of slavery were told, this was not slavery; this was the spreading of the light.

The edgy governor therefore received 'the Hill Coolie Proposal', a letter from 'certain flock owners' begging him to consider 'the urgent necessity that exists of sending to Bengal for shepherds, cow herds, labourers and household servants'. The government was expected to pay the expenses of recruitment, passage and provisions during the labourers' voyage to Australia.

Through June and July 1837 a Legislative Council committee of landowners considered the matter. Hannibal Macarthur and John Blaxland were members, and the chairman was Colonel Kenneth Snodgrass, the Scot who had earlier authorised Major Nunn's murderous expedition against the Kamilaroi. John Mackay argued before the committee that Hindus should be recruited, because in his opinion Muslims were more addicted to opium, wine and spirits. William Charles Wentworth, stepping down to make his own submission, disapproved on the grounds that Indians would destroy racial purity. William Lawson mildly objected to the scheme as it would not provide a 'permanent increase in the labouring population'. The Indians, if recruited, were to be eunuch agricultural labourers.

Some of those giving evidence were on the edge of bankruptcy, given the slump in the price of wool and the long-running drought, and their attitudes towards labour costs were thus influenced. All of them were about to take heavy losses, including Hannibal Macarthur. Among these witnesses was John Edie Manning, registrar of the Supreme Court of New South Wales, a young man with a wife and five children whom he had brought to the colony. As Colonial Director of Intestate Estates, he had hoped to be able to derive income through their custody and administration, but due to reforms he lost that perk. He also had land grants at Rushcutters Bay, but when these were sequestered in 1841 his debts amounted to £30 000. In the end he was not saved from bankruptcy by Indian labour, and there is doubt that he would ever have been.

The committee's report came down in favour of more migrants from Britain, but noted briefly that Indians were a hardy, industrious race likely to give 'immediate and temporary relief' to the labour shortage. There were problems with the paganism, habits and colour of the Indians, the report said, and yet, out of necessity, the committee concurred in the expediency of granting a bounty of £6 sterling for every male Dhangar, or hill labourer, of Bengal, who would be embarked before the end of 1837. The governor, Sir Richard Bourke, forwarded the committee's rather apologetic recommendations to the Colonial Secretary, Lord Glenelg.

The coolies left Calcutta on the *Peter Proctor* with a native surgeon in 1837 and reached Sydney in late 1837. In February 1838 fifteen coolies absconded from two properties in the Sydney basin, Mr Abercrombie's of Glenmore Distillery and Mr Haslingden's property. The chief constable of Parramatta apprehended them hiking west near the modern township of Wentworth Falls, with the ambition of walking home to India. Appearing before a bench of magistrates seven days later, one of them, Madhoo, complained of insufficient food and clothing as well as the non-payment of wages for the two months they had been working. The rags they had on, the *Monitor* reported, seemed to be the tattered remains of the clothing in which they had left India. They were also not getting enough *dholl* and rice to keep them well-nourished.

Mackay was prepared to drop charges if the labourers would return to employment. Madhoo agreed on condition that they received sufficient food and pay, and clothes were issued monthly. Here was something convicts had been unable to apply in any coherent way without being destroyed by it—industrial action. It was not the first such case in Australia, but an early one.

Edward Smith Hall of the *Monitor* wrote about these 'unhappy maltreated Heathen British subjects'. The coolies of Mr John Lord were working well, however, on the remote Williams River in what would become Queensland, and Mackay complained that the Indian coolies who went west had been 'seduced to abscond' by local progressives. Though the *Herald* said 'More and more labour from India should be the cry of the colonists of New South Wales', there were attacks from the *Australian* against the 'Eastern slave trade'. It reported that of ten unfortunate coolie passengers on the *Emerald Isle* in 1838 from Calcutta to Sydney, two ran away at Mauritius, one of them died in a miserable condition on the beach at Adelaide in South Australia, and another perished in a state of idiocy brought on by cold, hunger, ill-usage and neglect.

In July 1838 the New South Wales Legislative Council passed new resolutions in favour of continuation of convict transportation, because in some ways it was beginning to seem more acceptable than immigration from India. Sir William Molesworth in the House of Commons that year denounced the importing of Indian labourers into New South Wales as 'a new species of slave trade'. The *Australian* asked more potently, 'Shall this, our country—shall Austral-Britain—become the Emporium of the Eastern slave trade? Shall our future generations be a mixed race? Shall the inveterate prejudices of colour and caste—shall Hinduism and Mahomedanism—be transplanted and take deep root in this

Christian, British soil!' In terms of humanity towards the coolies themselves, some argued that the Indians were so poorly informed on where they were going to work that they thought Mauritius was a company village in India, and were appalled when they found themselves at sea.

In 1838, the British Cabinet initiated a bill for the protection of the coolies, and there was an order-in-council that the human traffic should stop until regulations could be worked out to protect the recruited labourers. Legal opinion was clear that this applied to Australia also. In January 1839 a petition was drawn up by pastoralists and addressed to the Queen and both Houses asking for the continuation of convict transportation and assignment. The petitioners agreed that one cheap alternative to transportation would indeed be to supply themselves with coolie labour from India, but that would 'inflict on this colony injury and degradation only inferior to what has occurred in the slave states of the union in America'.

Major Lockyer of Ermington outside Sydney, who had spent sixteen years in India, was one who criticised convict thieving and claimed that convicts cost twice as much as Indians. People of like mind to him had not abandoned the coolie option. Indeed in June 1841 a petition for coolie labour was signed by 202 colonists.

Governor Gipps, however, like Bourke before him, commented negatively on the evils which would result from coolie labour. And once the governor opposed indentured labour, James Macarthur declared he had strong views against it too, and withdrew his petition. Many landowners were angry with Gipps, and the *Herald* accused Macarthur of 'mawkish sensibility and courtly simpering'.

That same year James Stephen at the Colonial Office in Whitehall enunciated the principle that Australia should be a land 'where the English race shall be spread from sea to sea unmixed with any lower caste. As we now regret the folly of our ancestors in colonising North America from Africa, so should our posterity have to censure us if we should colonise Australia from India.'

The issue rolled on through the 1840s, especially after the formation of a Coolie Association by Australian landowners. They drew up a memorial in favour of more coolie importation but the governor, receiving it for transmission to England, asked them, 'Gentlemen, are you sure that the great body of the colonists is with you?' Indeed, in the electoral campaign for city representatives to the Legislative Council in 1843, there was a 'No Coolie' ticket.

WC Wentworth and Captain Maurice O'Connell, both committee members of the Coolie Association, tried to depict themselves as 'the working men's friend'. For if the colony collapsed economically, they said, it was the workers who would suffer. On the other side, Henry Parkes's friend, the literary Scot William Duncan, was removed from his position as editor of the *Chronicle* by the Catholic vicar-general for being too anti-coolie, and thus too political.

With the income-based franchise for voting for the Legislative Council set high, Wentworth was able to beat the anti-coolie ticket massively. Soon after the elections, however, a broadside announced, 'Operatives of Sydney arise! Your interests are at stake!!! Attend at the Race Course on Monday next, January 16th [1843], to defeat the objects of the Coolie men.' William Hustler and Robert Cooper, emancipist merchant, the chief anti-coolie organisers and candidates for the Legislative Council, argued that if workers were needed there were 'hundreds and thousands of their starving brethren in England' who were to be preferred to 'black slave labour'. Henry Macdermott, an advocate for white labour, opposed coolie labour because of the 'vices peculiar to the natives of India', which went unspecified but were wildly guessed at.

An anti-coolie petition signed by 1421 artisans and small businessmen was forwarded, with Governor Gipps's opinion in its support, to Queen Victoria. The British Colonial Secretary Lord Stanley told Gipps that he should acquaint the labouring classes of New South Wales that the Queen had read their petition, and that Her Majesty's government had no plans to permit the immigration of coolies into New South Wales. The British government did not wish to create a new colonial underclass in New South Wales, and neither did what were generally condemned as 'the democratic classes' in the colony. The only exception allowed to the ban was the employment of Indian sailors and menial servants, and in October 1844 a number of such 'servants' arrived to work under the aegis of a man named Friell on his property at Tent Hill, north of Glen Innes. A year later they walked away, complaining to the magistrates of Glen Innes about their clothing, rations and wages.

Still the coolie faction fought on. Robert Campbell, grandson of Sydney's early merchant of the same name; Robert Towns, the Geordie sea captain and merchant; and WC Wentworth (also Towns's brother-in-law) commissioned a Calcutta firm to obtain one hundred 'menial servants' in 1845. But even the *Herald* disapproved of this display of back-doorism.

Robert Towns would always be interested in cheap labour from Asia and the Pacific islands. He had arrived in Sydney in 1827 as captain of his own ship, and six years later married Sophia Wentworth, William's seventeen-year-old half-sister who had arrived back from England that year in Towns's ship *The Brothers*. Towns's relationship with his Indian coolies was not smooth. He was a famously tough employer, who took his virtues from Quakerism and the Old Testament. All the coolies working at his depot at Miller's Point went on strike, and spent two days at the police office in Sydney complaining to the magistrates. The complaints were—as usual—to do with irregularity of pay and inappropriate food; meat and flour were being handed out instead of the rice and *dholl* their contracts had specified. The coolies declared that they were Brahmins, and meat would make them ritually unclean. They won their case in the end, but for several days beforehand were left begging in the streets.

The meat problem resurfaced in April 1849, when six of Wentworth's coolie servants were charged with absconding. The verdict imposed by the magistrates was that though the agreement remained, the coolies had to spend a week in prison, court costs were to be deducted from their wages, and, presumably, if they wanted to avoid hunger, they had to eat meat.

The *Australian* pointed its finger at all these problems. The coolie was more expensive than the Irish, it said, being a 'poor slender half-built man, made out of rice and *dholl*'. Between the Indians' failure to be 'meek and mild Hindus', and the lack of enthusiastic support from government, things were not flourishing for the coolie faction. Friell said that his coolies at Tent Hill were indolent and that they had cynically accepted their passage to Australia, never intending to give good service.

Soon there was discussion about Chinese labourers, with employers speculating whether they would prove to be less unruly.

TRADING IN TEA

Singapore, once it was established as a British free trade port in 1819, had begun to attract a lot of trade from Makassar, and inspired the creation of a similar northern Australian port that could attract Makassan ships and become the basis of trade with the Celebes (now Sulawesi), the Moluccas and China. Three attempts were made to create such an outpost on the far northern coast of the continent: Fort Dundas on Melville Island, for five fraught years from 1824 to 1829; Fort Wellington at Raffles Bay on the Coburg Peninsula, east of present-day Darwin from 1827 to 1829; and tragic Victoria at Port Essington, also on the Coburg Peninsula, from 1838 to 1849, where the remains of British soldiers, their wives and children lie amongst the termite mounds and spinifex to mark an unwise effulgence of British planning. For all these places were unsuccessful in attracting the Makassan fleets for trade, and all of them were fever and malaria ports.

Port Essington, and its township Victoria, east of present-day Darwin, seemed particularly accursed, and unsuited for its hopes of being the new Singapore. Even in the year of its founding, 1839, twelve people were killed by a cyclone. There was not commercial gain at any time. No ships came for trade and supplies. No settlers came to join the garrison, convicts and the Italian priest Father Angelo Confalonieri, stranded there by shipwreck, and its chief annalist. Traces of the graves of soldiers' wives, children, and other victims of malaria and unspecified fever can still be found there amongst the Coburg Peninsula's termite hills and scrub. The hated town and its always termite-infested buildings, when abandoned in 1849, were destroyed by the navy's cannon-fire.

Even so, all the early traders of Sydney, emancipist and free, had contact with the British trading houses in Asia. The young Scot Robert Campbell, son of the laird of Ashfield near Greenock, Scotland, and trading from warehouses at Dawes Point, Sydney Cove, had his brother in Calcutta, and John and Gregory Blaxland were related by marriage to Hogue, Davidson and Company of Calcutta. Walter Davidson was a young man who had drawn on John Macarthur's advice when the shipwrecked Macarthur and his children fetched up in the Celebes on their way to England, and had done him services which had led to Macarthur's being rewarded with British impunity and Australian land. He came to Sydney with John Macarthur in 1805 and, on instructions to Governor King from the British government, had been granted 2000 acres (810 hectares) next door to the Macarthur estate in Camden. He formed a trading partnership with Macarthur and took a ship to Macau with a mixed cargo, mostly sandalwood from Fiji, for the Chinese market. This was in defiance of the East India Company's trade monopoly, which as early as 1806 Governor King had tried to break, pleading that the new colony ought to have access to the China trade, to export sealskins, trepang, sandalwood and other colonial produce. The British East India Company had resisted the idea, and King was forced to forbid the locals to trade with China. Yet monopoly rights were steadily eroded. Whaling and sealing companies made special arrangements with the East India Company to enable them to operate in the South Seas from

1798. By 1813, the Company had lost practically the whole of its monopoly rights except for the China trade and trade in tea.

China tea, sweetened by sugar, had become an early solace of exiles, received from a master by a convict as a reward, or as inducement to good work, something which could be withheld for bad behaviour. Seated at a fire, a man or woman could let the warm fragrance caress their faces and dream of a world unmarred or a homeland restored. The colonial appetite for tea was even more intense than that of Britons.

The tea would not be drunk with milk, as later became the Australian habit. It was green tea, and drunk with sugar derived first from the Philippines, and later from Mauritius, when it came under British rule. This thirst for tea and sugar in New South Wales had been an engine in the development of Australia's earliest international trade, because the trade in tea made the Australian merchant houses look for something other than cash with which to pay for it—goods such as sandalwood, trepang, sealskin and tortoise shell. Many of these early houses were run by emancipists—Henry Kable of the First Fleet; Simeon Lord; James Underwood, Kable's partner; that entrepreneurial powerhouse Solomon Levey; and later, the Kable and Underwood apprentice James Kelly.

Cargoes of sandalwood and trepang would be landed in Sydney from the islands in ships owned by wealthy emancipists such as Kable, Underwood, Lord and Levey for re-shipping—in a complicated system using neutral vessels to circumvent the East India Company's monopoly—to China. By 1834, even the China monopoly was abolished.

Meanwhile, Walter Davidson had stayed on in Macau, setting up a base there. He was soon the man to go to in the Portuguese colony so close to China, and much of the tea with which the colonists were comforted and Aborigines bribed with came through him.

He had been in Sydney enough to be involved with Macarthur in the imbroglio over Governor Bligh, but left Australia permanently after the rebellion and, despite the Portuguese trying to evict him, remained in Macau until 1822, trading all that time with Australia. The problems of doing business over these enormous areas were softened by reliance on family ties, school friendships, Freemasonry and relationships like that between Macarthur and Davidson.

With the ending of the East India Company monopoly in 1834, trading with China opened up a little, but a crisis developed between the British and the

Chinese over opium imports as payment for tea, and Guangdong, the centre of the tea trade, was blockaded by the British. The bold Geordie Robert Towns, now New South Wales magistrate, merchant and landowner, considered himself a free agent and tried to break the blockade, sailing his ship, the *Royal Saxon*, past the point of demarcation known as the Bogue. He was unsuccessful, and much chastised by the British for his attempt.

Ultimately, as China was humiliated in the Opium Wars and forced to make further trading concessions, Walter Davidson moved his base to Hong Kong and put tea warehouses in various Chinese ports. The ships to collect the tea would arrive in the Pearl River after the north-east monsoon in October and leave for Australia before the south-west monsoon began in March. They would time their return to Australia to avoid cyclones in the Coral Sea and would arrive off Sydney about May. But gradually Australia's trade with China in tea transferred itself to India—it was in British interests that it should do so, and there was a shift from green to black teas, associated with the growth of dairying and the availability of fresh milk. The end of convict transportation in the 1840s also brought an end to the masters' demands for cheap teas for their convicts to drink.

Australia's exports to China continued, but now suited the tastes of the large European enclaves in Chinese ports where there were foreign concessions and thus large European populations. Australian merchants shipped butter and cheese, racehorses for the Shanghai and Hong Kong jockey clubs and, increasingly, coal supplies for European steamships. Chinese imports included opium which was often smuggled into Australia because, though not illegal, it was heavily taxed. But as in the earliest penal times, there remained a triangle of trade involving China, Australia and Britain.

WHAT ABOUT CHINESE?

In the early years of the colony there had been a scattered arrival of a number of skilled Chinese tradespeople—carpenters, furniture-makers and cooks, some brought in by wealthy landowners. In 1829 the Macarthurs at Elizabeth Farm employed a Chinese cook and a Chinese gardener, but even earlier in the decade the newly arrived young Presbyterian minister John Dunmore Lang employed two Chinese men, Guong and Tchiou, primarily to make household furniture, but also so that he could explore whether there was a relationship between the spoken languages of China—in their case probably a Cantonese dialect—and those of Polynesia. Guong and Tchiou probably arrived in Sydney on the *Calder* in 1822 and were allowed to land by the Colonial Secretary, who had already that year allowed ten Chinese labourers to be brought in on the *Westmoreland*. Chinese carpenters ordered from brokers in southern Chinese ports arrived in Melbourne in 1836 and in 1842 at Port Adelaide, and the great enthusiast Lang proposed that a Chinese tea plantation be started at Port Macquarie.

In the 1840s the Peacock Inn in North Parramatta was owned by a Cantonese man known as John Shying, who had been born Mak Sai Ying in Guangdong in 1796 and had come to New South Wales as a free settler in 1818. He married an Australian woman, Sarah Thompson, and after Sarah's death, another Australian, Bridget Gillorley. A complaint made about girls of Irish background—as Bridget was—was that they were likely to marry Chinamen, the supposed lowness of one calling to the lowness of the other. Shying returned to China in 1832 where he stayed for five years pursuing business and family matters, but came back to Sydney in 1837.

Low Kong Men, a British subject born in Penang, the son of a Cantonese merchant, came to Melbourne in 1843 in his own vessel. He spoke English and French as well as Cantonese. Within a year he had established in Bourke Street the Kong Men Company, importers of tea and other delicacies. He owned a fleet of six ships, some of which were engaged in collecting trepang from Torres Strait. By 1850 he was so well established in Melbourne that he organised Chinese clubs, settled disputes between Chinamen and tried to mediate in their relations with the Crown.

During the First Opium War (1840–42), when the Chinese resisted British attempts to use Indian opium to pay for increasing imports of China tea, Australian pastoralists, disenchanted with the Indian coolie experiment, discussed the desirability of importing Chinese coolies as cheap labourers, but they were unable to do so until the war was over. Then, in 1847, amendments to the Colonial Master and Servants Act made it attractive to import Chinese labourers into Australia. The first shipload of indentured labourers arrived in Sydney in October 1848 from Amoy (Xiamin), organised through the agency of J Tait, a British merchant house in that port. There, in a depot on the agency grounds, the labourer, recruited by Chinese middlemen, signed a Chinese-language contract concerning pay and rations, and undertook a five-year exile to some as yet unknown station in the remote Australian bush. On arrival in Sydney, the labourer would sign an English-language contract not always identical to the one he had signed in the Amoy depot.

The arrival of Chinese coolie labour was immediately unpopular among Australian workers, the same people who had been involved in the abolition of convict transportation. Australia would receive between 1847 and 1853 approximately 3500 Chinese indentured labourers. They represented in their very persons a challenge to the home government and to the European settlers' concerns over wages and race. These latter sentiments would ultimately win; the importation of Chinese labour would represent the peak of the large pastoralists' economic and political power.

Benjamin Boyd, an exceptional entrepreneur who had been involved in the founding of the Royal Bank of Australia in London, used its finances to move a number of his ships and himself to New South Wales. By 1844, after only two years in the colony, he and the bank controlled 2.5 million acres (just over 1 million hectares) on the coast, in the Monaro and the Riverina. He added a new twist to the indentured labour issue by bringing in Pacific Islanders, generally Melanesians, to work in his whaleboat crews and on his sheep stations. In 1847, for example, ships of his brought to Australia 185 men and seven women from small Melanesian islands such as Ouvéa and Lifou in the Loyalty group, from Tana and Aneityum in the New Hebrides (now Vanuatu) and even from a Polynesian island beyond Vanuatu. The men were to work as shepherds, labourers or seamen for five years at £1 6 shillings a year with food, clothing and bedding supplied. White shepherds at this time were earning £25 a year, so Boyd seemed to do very well out of his Islanders.

Scrupulous people accused Boyd of virtually kidnapping the natives to bring them to Australia, but an enquiry by the Attorney-General of New South Wales dismissed the accusations. The Legislative Council's Committee on Immigration of 1847 reported unfavourably that the 'boundless regions of the Australian continent capable of containing millions of our fellow subjects may thus be occupied by a semi-barbarous or even savage race'.

Some of Boyd's Islanders who were assigned to his mountainous stations in the Monaro suffered severely from the winter cold, and others could not get accustomed to the great stretches of plateau and Riverina plains, and returned to Twofold Bay—Boyd's base on the New South Wales south coast—begging him to transport them home. By the end of 1847, only sixty of his original Islanders remained with him.

In 1851 that other thrusting entrepreneur Robert Towns owned thirteen ships that were involved in the Pacific trade. He imported eight shiploads of Chinese labourers in the early years of the 1850s. When his *Arabia* arrived from Amoy on 22 December 1851, it was found that ten out of 189 Chinese coolies had died aboard. The captain, Chilcott, had been in the habit of tying quarrelsome Chinese to the rigging and flogging them, and had even resorted to throwing hot tea over them. Towns noted, 'You have the services of these men for five years at a rate not exceeding one-quarter you are obliged to pay for your own countryman.'

For a ship named the *General Palmer* another broker signed up 332 labourers on five-year contracts. This journey was a disaster—by the time the ship dropped anchor in Sydney, 63 Chinese and one crew member were dead of dysentery. The enquiry showed that although *General Palmer* was a good ship there had been no place to separate the sick from the healthy. The men had no changes of clothing, nor any blankets, and the only water closets provided were chains flung over the stern on which the sick men had to balance themselves. Some of the men, weakened by dysentery, had simply fallen off the chains and drowned.

In the infamous case of *St Paul*, a French ship bound from Hong Kong to Australia in 1858 with 327 Chinese labourers aboard, only one man, Ah Fung, made it to Sydney. The ship had been wrecked on Russell Island off New Guinea. According to Ah Fung, reliably so or not, some of the European crew escaped by small boat to the north coast of Australia while the Chinese left on the island were progressively killed and eaten by the local natives.

The squatters in the northern sections of New South Wales, that is, in future Queensland, were the biggest users of indentured labourers from China. Many Chinese indentured labourers were employed also to clear land around the farms and townships of Narrandera, Hay and Deniliquin in south-west New South Wales. They were a mobile workforce who, hired out, would set up their own camp, work and move on. Time off was usually spent in the Chinese quarter of the nearest big town.

There were at this time similarities between the pressures on the individual Chinese male and those on the Irish and the Scottish Highlanders. They were likely to have joined local gangs and secret societies to create a network of support for themselves in a landscape where their hold on land was shaky. They may have come from a background of clan warfare, common in Guangdong, where mercenaries were often hired by both sides. Some of those who ultimately came to Australia may have served as mercenaries or members of militias, or rebels during the Taiping uprising of the 1850s. If a man wanted to escape Guangdong for any reason, the estuary of the Pearl River was crowded—since the Treaty of Nanking—with the masts of foreign vessels.

Ching Dynasty law allowed more than one marriage, and the chief purpose of marriage was not the fulfilment of the married couple but the production of male heirs for the perpetuation of the ancestors' line, and the recruitment of an extra woman to help in the house and farm. If a man was married before he migrated, it was accepted he would not take his wife with him. He would come back to his home village once he had made his pile. While he was away, if he did well he was permitted to take a second wife and maintain two households. If he was single when he migrated, he would return home, after saving enough money, to marry, stay for a few months, and then return to the place of migration without his wife. Thereafter, he would visit his home village as often as he could afford.

One upsetting problem for the indentured Chinese labourers, as for the Indians, was that they had signed contracts stipulating rations of rice, and in many cases flour or even readily available meat rather than the more expensive rice was supplied. By not providing rice, employers were effectively breaking the Chinese contract, though the English-language contract may well have been different. Another problem stemmed from the lack of reference to clothing in the contracts, which meant that labourers had to purchase new clothing from station stores where prices were infamously high. As well as that, pastoralists were willing to take a sizeable portion of the exchange rate between Amoy dollars and sterling, downgrading what the Chinese men received.

The indenture system came to be called the 'truck system'. It was essentially a system of thraldom, making the Chinese labourers a captive labour force—in getting employees to chalk up purchases from the station store against unearned wages, employers were forcing their coolies into a situation of debt peonage, which could be enforced by recourse to the law. The coolies were unable to accumulate money to buy their way off the station they were indentured to.

This was the case of Kang who signed with TML Prior of Logan River near Brisbane in November 1851 to work for 12 shillings per month. Kang cleared out on the rough track to Brisbane when his master told him that he had a debt of £2 18 shillings and tuppence. Labourers often absconded or turned themselves in to the magistrate—the same thing, since both involved leaving their work—when they found that through technicalities or the hard bookkeeping of the master they owed money. Kang, when confronted with the bill, told Prior he would shoot him. Absconding brought Kang a sentence of three months work on the Newcastle breakwater. He was also sentenced to keep the peace for twelve months and enter sureties totalling £80 or undergo twelve months imprisonment for the threat to Prior. The Attorney-General overturned this last sentence, which had been imposed by a magistrate sympathetic to Mr Prior.

Two men named Pekie and Chiok Kaon absconded from their station similarly owing amounts of more than £3. The magistrates always returned the workers to their masters after they had served their hard labour, and the masters retained the men's contracts. Fortunately for the Pekies of the back blocks, the masters did not usually bring charges for absconding because they knew they would lose three months hard labour from the coolie they had invested in. But they tried to use locking them up in the cells at regional police stations as a chastening tool, after which the owner would not turn up to court. The lock-ups were harsh. The Tenterfield one was described as 'a wooden box for prisoners in the centre of a common hut', and was capable of causing 'all but the most recalcitrant labourers' second thoughts.

Sometimes, Chinese labourers would set out on their way to the magistrate to press charges against their master for being ill-used or having wages withheld, but would be charged with a countersuit of absconding for this brief absence. Such was the case of Huey Bow, who was charged with absconding after requesting that he be discharged by his master given that his five-year term had been completed the previous month. He had not been willing to re-hire himself for a further twelve months. When he claimed his wages, he was told that he owed the station £29 8 shillings for lost sheep. His employer obtained a warrant for Huey Bow's arrest for absconding, on which charge the labourer was found guilty and fined £4 pounds 4 shillings with costs of £1 pound 4 shillings. In this case Huey Bow was charged only with absconding and not with losing sheep or destruction of property, a prosecution that would have meant a longer gaol term. He had no choice than to drag himself back to labour for his master to pay off his debts.

Barteong, who had been employed by Dr Barton of Brisbane and left requesting his wages, was arrested not for absconding but for vagrancy. Though the magistrates did not order Barton to pay the wages he had withheld, they believed that Barteong had been justified in leaving Barton's employment, since Barton was paying wages on a yearly basis which the contract did not permit.

One coolie named Sang was charged with assault and battery on his master Robert Fleming, for which he was found not guilty. Sang stated that he was still owed £10 for the past year's work.

When facing the benches and courts of the colony, Chinese labourers generally suffered from a lack of legal representation. A number of Chinese labourers acted as interpreters, notably Zuan Zing in Goulburn and Tinko, Isim and Gan Som in Brisbane. But Gan Som, or Ganson, was deterred from continuing because of threats from his countrymen. In a few cases, employers acted as interpreters, particularly in a case of assault brought by one coolie against another.

The greatest abuse of Chinese labourers within the court system involved a master, PJ Bertelson of Boonerah near Shellharbour and two labourers named Tong Chou and Ke Tiam, who had been charged with assault of their master. They were eventually pardoned on the basis that they had not understood the charges laid against them, nor were they able to offer any defence due to the lack of an interpreter. Bertelson had himself offered to act as interpreter for the accused, an untenable situation.

The affinity between 'the merino magistrates' and the employers of indentured Chinese reached a peak with the bulk signing of warrants by magistrates for employers, who then needed only to fill out the necessary information whenever a warrant was required. This saved the pastoralists going to the magistrate every time they wanted to charge a coolie, and quickened up the time within which the recalcitrant employee was admitted to the lock-up.

Overall, despite many misunderstandings and deliberate abuses on the part of employers, the Chinese were considered 'good shepherds, yet they are difficult to manage'. A lot of problems ceased as understanding of the English language and laws grew amongst the labourers. As their contracts expired, they often found they were able to demand wages closer to what white labourers earned.

CHAPTER 28

GOLDEN EPIPHANY

One sultry night early in 1851, on a trans-mountain farm near Orange, New South Wales, a devout Methodist farmer's son William Tom, Cornish-born, was working in a shed by lamplight, hammering together a wooden box shaped like a child's cradle, but with compartments inside it and an upright handle attached to it. Once it was completed, a party of men placed the cradle on the bank of the creek below the Tom homestead, under the command of a hulking, black-moustached 34-year-old Englishman, Edward H Hargraves. They shovelled in gravel and rocked the cradle so that heavy grains of gold would remain in its tray. When they did not have much luck, they put the cradle on a horse and moved it some 16 kilometres to Lewis Ponds. Here, where Hargraves and the local publican's sons had already found grains of gold by panning, they ended with sixteen grains of gold in their cradle.

Hargraves, a proud Orangeman, took to his horse and headed east for Sydney to announce the find. He believed from American experience that there was more reward in announcing the discovery of gold in workable forms than in digging it. While in San Francisco the previous year, he had written to a Sydney merchant: 'I am very forcibly impressed that I have been in a gold region in New South Wales, within three hundred miles of Sydney.'

To go to California, he had left his wife and five children behind in the coastal New South Wales town of Gosford, but he had not relished the drudgery of fossicking, especially not in the blizzards of winter or the slush of the Californian spring. Until he could get home again he knew he was in danger of being beaten to what he thought would be a world-altering and life-transforming discovery of Australian gold. In the first month of the Californian rush, February 1849, a young man called Chapman had brought 38 ounces (1.08 kilos) of gold from Glen Mona station near Amherst, 160 kilometres north-west of Melbourne, into Brentani's jewellery shop in the city. The superintendent of Port Phillip District, Charles La Trobe, had to send black troopers to disperse the men who quickly gathered with pick-axes and shovels at Chapman's find. Later, realising the effects of the California rush more fully, La Trobe regretted having acceded so easily to the station owner's demand that force be used to stop miners trespassing.

In January 1851 Hargraves returned to Australia and told people in Sydney he would find a goldfield in the interior. He had heard from the Colonial Secretary, Edward Deas Thomson, that gold had been found in quartz in Carcoar, near Orange, but when Hargraves, on the way there, stopped at the settlement of Guyong, west of Bathurst, he saw in the local inn specimens of copper, pyrites and quartz, of the kind he had seen in Californian goldfields, from a nearby copper mine. Hargraves borrowed a tin dish, a hand pick and a trowel and headed north-west with the publican's son, John Hardman Australia Lister. It was a warm day in the bush, a day when the ancient landscape seemed set in its ways and resistant to sudden revelations. In the valley of the Lewis Ponds Creek, a creek which did not run in dry weather, they found a waterhole and made the usual pannikin of tea, and then Hargraves announced he would attempt to pan for gold. He saw the gleam of a gold grain at the bottom of his pan. He washed, in total, six dishes for six grains. Others might consider it a nugatory amount—certainly the drinkers at Guyong's Wellington Inn ignorantly did that evening. But having been in California, Hargraves knew what it meant. These grains of gold were mere scrapings from the lode. By the waterhole in the bush that morning, he had made a famous speech, with only young Lister to listen. 'This is a memorable day in the history of New South Wales. I shall be a baron, you will be knighted, and my old horse will be stuffed, put into a glass case and sent to the British Museum.'

Britain's minor criminals often had lusted for gold, and the flashy pickpocket George Barrington had extracted it from the pockets of gentlemen and nobles. Yet in outcrops all around the huts of convict shepherds and in the alluvium of creek beds lay undetected grains and lumps. By the very nature of geology, the Spanish reefs of solid gold were an impossibility. Nonetheless many Europeans were ready to indulge dreams of El Dorado.

The Toms and Lister were anxious not to draw in a rush of diggers. To reassure them, Hargraves, before leaving for Sydney, devised on a sheet of paper under the presumptuous words 'On His Majesty's Service' a deed allowing them to mine the richest point of the creek. Hargraves named the area Ophir in honour of the biblical goldmine, and gave Lister and the Toms the exclusive right to the gold, though he probably guessed the paper was worthless. But to the young Australians, it meant they were possessors of their own Ophir, their own King Solomon's mine, their own biblical vein. If others came to claim it, they had Hargrave's document to establish their prior ownership.

In fact, Hargraves knew that by a set of ancient statutes all gold belonged to the Crown. That was why he had gone to Sydney—to seek a reward. The government had been worried about the number of young men who had left the colonies for California. This discovery would reverse things. In his red overcoat he waited three hours for another interview with Deas Thomson. Thomson was not at first impressed. Hargraves expediently forgot about the baronetcy and asked him merely for £500 as compensation for the expense of his expedition. Meanwhile, Lister and William Tom found nuggets of fine gold at Yorkey's Corner near Bathurst. Lister picked up a 2-ounce (57-gram) nugget on the ground. Back at the Tom homestead they balanced gold on the scales with sixteen new sovereigns borrowed from the widow Lister. They had found 4 ounces (113 grams) of gold.

Secretly, despite his undertaking to Lister and the Toms, Hargraves wanted to attract crowds of men to Ophir, since the richer the goldfield the greater his reward from the government. After making his claim to Deas Thomson, who, like many an official, seemed a little bemused as to its significance, Hargraves returned to Bathurst, where he lectured on his discovery, displayed pieces of gold and told his audience where they could find it. As a result, the local Commissioner for Crown Land rode fast out to Ophir to find eight or nine men digging there. They showed him the deed Hargraves had written out. Hargraves himself left Bathurst with a group of mounted horsemen to whom he pointed out good places to dig and wash.

The fifty kilometres of track to Ophir were soon marked by dray wheels and horses hooves. When Hargraves escorted the government's mineralogical surveyor Samuel Stutchbury, an English mineralogist and biologist, to Ophir in May 1851, the diggers, in the throes of gold fever, barely noticed their arrival. They felt they were a long way from authority. Ophir was, after all, 275 kilometres from Sydney and the contact was via mail coach over a slippery and boggy mountainous road, its last stretch only a horse trail.

Back in Sydney Deas Thomson showed Hargraves's specimens to a man newly arrived from California. The man laughed and said that the gold obviously was found in California and had been planted at Ophir. The official reaction to Ophir was thus confused and delayed. Gold was not mentioned when the Executive Council met in Sydney on 13 May. Yet hundreds were coming up the bush track from Bathurst to Ophir, inflamed by headlines which declared Ophir 'a second California'. By the time the government reacted, it was too late to ban the digging of gold, since hundreds were at it and could not be stopped. The local Crown Lands Commissioner, a loyal servant who knew his law, served the diggers at Ophir with notices to desist, but they ignored him.

When this disobedience was reported to Sydney it became clear there were not enough policemen and soldiers to suppress it. There was also the perceived risk that policemen and soldiers would themselves join in the frenzy. James Macarthur suggested martial law, but Deas Thomson thought that too extreme.

On 22 May, Sir Charles FitzRoy, the governor, wrote his first dispatch to England concerning the new discoveries and suggested that Hargraves was exaggerating. But before this dispatch was put on board a ship, a pencilled report arrived from Stutchbury saying that many men were panning an ounce of gold or even two every day with only a tin dish. Stutchbury apologised for using pencil: 'There is no ink yet in the City of Ophir.'

FitzRoy now proclaimed the Crown's right to all gold found in New South Wales, declaring no man could dig it up without buying a licence. The charge would be 30 shillings a month. Naturally the miners resisted the first attempts to impose licences, and soon the inspector of Sydney police was preparing to take reinforcements to the goldfields. A detachment of troops was also readied in Sydney. No one could decide if beyond this initial crisis lay an enlarged world or the decay of everything they knew. Fever struck all, in the sense that no one had a calm opinion of what was happening.

JD Lang, in his prison cell in Parramatta, where he was serving a criminal libel sentence under the Darling laws, believed the immigrants attracted to New South Wales, along with the independence and wealth associated with digging, would ensure the colony's political vigour. He wrote: 'The announcement of this wonderful discovery in our land is tantamount to an authoritative proclamation ... that Australia henceforth shall be free ... through the resist-less influence of her coming democracy.'

An experienced but hard-up magistrate, John R Hardy, former Cambridge blue in cricket and a man to reckon with, was appointed the new Commissioner of Crown Lands for the gold district. He had an escort of ten deputies armed and mounted, and between them they were to issue licences, administer the diggings, arbitrate between diggers and, in Hardy's case, sit as a justice in the Court of Petty Sessions. By the time he reached Ophir in early June 1851 there were a thousand men camped along the creek. Hardy behaved sensibly, allowing diggers to work for several days until they had enough gold dust to pay for a licence. All went peaceably, and Hardy thought Ophir as quiet as an English town.

Deas Thomson, however, now insisted that all men buy a licence before they lifted their first spadeful of gravel. Hardy protested, but went along. He thought it unfair, but the system was meant to be unfair, in the hope of forcing the agricultural labourer or the farmer back to his normal work. Policemen were instructed to smash the cradles and tools of unlicensed men. The licences were still fairly readily paid, however, Hardy estimating that at least half the now 1500 men at Ophir found on average £1 worth of gold each day. Jewish merchants moved from tent to tent buying gold. Everyone was doing well, and there was little disorder.

Within three months the number of diggers at Ophir had begun to ride home. Governor FitzRoy, who had grown fond of the licence revenue, was suddenly anxious that a new field be found. He appointed Hargraves a Commissioner of Crown Lands and sent him to find new Ophirs in south-western New South Wales. His journey was not productive. Next FitzRoy asked the help of the Reverend WB Clarke, a formally trained geologist. Clarke had not been surprised by Hargraves's discovery—he already knew some of the geology of New South Wales was gold-bearing. He did not want to leave his parish of St Thomas's in North Sydney, but in the end he undertook the trip into the bush, being able to preach to miners and pastoralists on Sundays, since one of the conditions of the gold licence was that the Sabbath be observed. His journeyings were exhaustive, and he found sites from Omeo, south of the Alps in the Port Phillip area, all the way up into the Darling Downs. God had put the gold there, he knew, but its results tested his faith, since the goldfields seemed to generate drunkenness, were driven by a worship of Mammon, and the chance of violence hung over them.

On top of Hargraves and Clarke's explorations, the miners themselves were searching northwards from Ophir to the Turon River. Gold was sprinkled thirty kilometres along the Turon—'as regular as wheat in a sown field', reported Hardy, who despite his own wages being sequestrated to pay his debts, was not tempted to leave his post and harvest those ears of precious metal. On the Turon, he recorded meeting a group of sixty unlicensed diggers who had all found at least £3 worth of gold for the day. 'I was beset by a crowd all thrusting their pound notes into my face, and begging me to mark the boundaries.' The Turon would have a population of 67 000 during 1852, centred on the instant town of Sofala, whose hotels and lodging houses had calico walls not even decorated to imitate brick, as was the case with the canvas hotel walls of San Francisco. In Sofala, most men wore the long, curved throwing knife which enabled them to prise gold from cracks and wedges in the bedrock, and they carried arms to protect their gold. Yet the murder rate was low.

At a sheep station 80 kilometres north of Bathurst, an Aboriginal minding the sheep of Dr Kerr, his master, cracked an outcrop of white stone with his axe and saw a reef of gold. He told his master and overseer. Some gold-studded quartz was packed into a trunk and taken to Bathurst by wagon. Dr Kerr kept the gold taken from the site, since Aborigines were not eligible to apply for a licence.

William Charles Wentworth was worried that his workers would desert his estate at Camden, and even some of the Chinese coolies were leaving their masters and clearing out to the Turon. Governor FitzRoy expressed his amazement to Deas Thomson after the Government House porter took the road to the diggings, carrying a government-owned shovel with him. Thomson, the husband of Anne Bourke, the former Governor Bourke's daughter, was something of a calming influence. He had discussions with the American consul in Sydney who told him that the rush could bring good results for the colony if a licence system was maintained and if there was adequate policing. By planting some good press in Europe and the United States, said the consul, the authorities could expect a boom in immigration and the spread of wealth amongst ordinary folk.

The authorities remained locked between dread and hope. The population of the diggings dropped off that cold winter of 1851, and then in the springtime, to the relief of Thomson, many diggers left their claims to shear and take in the harvest. Meanwhile many residents of the Port Phillip area—since November 1850 the newly created colony of Victoria—were clearing out to the New South Wales goldfields. It was the turn of the new Lieutenant-Governor of Victoria, Charles La Trobe, and his thirty-member Legislative Council (twenty of whom were elected) to worry about an exodus of working men. As representative government began in the new colony of some 18 000 population, the place was aflame with gold fever as well as unmanageable and devastating bushfires.

GOLDEN VICTORIA

In granite hills at Ballarat, 110 kilometres north-west of Melbourne, an elderly man named John Dunlop found gold, and so in early August 1851 did the blacksmith Thomas Hiscock at the village of Buninyong under the mountain of that name, just south of Ballarat. The squatters in the area included a former sea captain named John Hepburn, an early promoter of the Port Phillip District. They were all men who had come to the area in the late 1830s and the 1840s, and lived in slab timber with their ticket-of-leave stockmen, often Vandemonians. They had survived the burning seasons of drought and the biblical floods, and the downturn of 1842. They had in their way dealt with the Kulin people, whom they considered a further force of nature, driving flocks away and needing to be pursued by Captain Henry Dana and his native border police recruited from the tribes of Gippsland. In an attack on a shepherd in May 1844, the Kulin natives were able to drive off 780 sheep. Dana's black police and some police regulars were quickly on site, and chased them northwards, shooting dead their leader Lillgona. La Trobe warned the regular police to proceed with moderation, but the pastoralists did not like such pussyfooting forbearance, and the extent of both good and bad which occurred in the land of the Kulin before gold manifested itself remains unknown.

Despite the cold winter of frosts and snowfalls on the hills, diggers came up the road from Geelong, 60 kilometres to the south on the western edge of Port Phillip Bay, walking and pushing barrows loaded with cradles and pans, food and tents, or riding on carriages or with hired bullock teams, with all their gear wrapped in canvas and a California-style cradle on top, all making for Ballarat and the Yarrowee Creek which cut its valley. At the new-found field the Gold

Commissioner, Doveton, and his Aboriginal troopers recruited from throughout the region, and even from beyond the Murray River in New South Wales, found eight hundred to a thousand men digging in the area.

A journalist from Geelong witnessed a meeting the diggers, summoned at eight o'clock one night by gunshot, held to decide on the miners' attitude to licence fees. A group of as 'picturesque-looking individuals who ever ornamented canvas assembled around a large watch-fire kindled beneath the gloomy stringy-bark trees'. There opinions were uttered which would come to bedevil the Crown in future years. One man described himself as free and hard-working, willing to pay a fair share to government—but not 30 shillings a month. Another asked, 'How can I be expected to pay a shilling a day to the Commissioner? It's a burning shame.' Perhaps more significantly, another said, 'It's more than the squatter pays for twenty square miles.' Another: 'I spent all the money I have fitting myself out for the diggings, and now I am to be taxed before I have been here a week.' Another: 'This is Port Phillip, d'ye see? Here is a specimen of independent government. I should like to know what right the government has to tax us £18 a year.' Another: 'I'll ding my cradle first.' Then: 'That would only be serving yourself out. I propose we get up a memorial to Mr La Trobe and that we all sign it.'

So Ballarat goldfield politics began. The memorial told the government that the 30-shilling monthly fee was 'impolitic and illiberal', that the gold in the Buninyong field could not support such an impost, that the new Executive Council (of four members, appointed by La Trobe) should in any case give diggers a period of grace to work their claims, and that if these sane propositions were not acceded to, the miners would move to Bathurst in New South Wales.

A few men came to the commissioner's tent to buy their licences and when leaving 'were struck and pelted by the mob'. But under the protection of the black troopers others paid, and by afternoon the commissioner ran out of licence forms. In the Legislative Council in Melbourne, Dr Francis Murphy, a member of the Irish and colonial bar, condemned the licence fee as 'unproductive, unequal and vexatious'. He asked that it be replaced by a duty on gold. Murphy was a conservative lawyer trained at Trinity College, Dublin, yet for his motion to succeed he needed the diggers to resist paying the fee, but in the end they did not, because the field was rich enough to make the 30-shilling monthly charge seem a minor expenditure. Once men found how much gold there was beneath the pastures they began to pay up. But their opinions remained as expressed in that first meeting—especially the complaint that in lean times they were being billed more than squatters.

For each had a mere 2.4 metre square to dig in, unless they formed a team and combined the leases. Once alluvial gold had all been panned or was considered an inadequate return, the miner had to dig down through soft earth and gravel, using local timber to line and support the shaft. Next he met layers of clay, red and yellow, sticky and heavy to dig. Then harder clay still, studded with gravel, then a seam of blue clay rarely more than 13 centimetres thick in which the gold lay. Sometimes this blue clay was 3 metres down, sometimes 9 metres, sometimes not there at all. That kind of hole had a name—a shicer.

The impact of all this displacement of earth and felling of trees on Ballarat's bosky valley was prodigious. The forest disappeared, the landscape became a maze of clayey holes. The miners did their best to wash the clay and mud off at the end of each day, but it penetrated their skin.

La Trobe was aware that the Colonial Office in Whitehall wanted him to deal with the new state of affairs without spending imperial funds. How to cope with the expense of new emigrants and new townships? 'The gold revenue must be charged with it,' he jotted in pencil on a letter from his Auditor-General.

La Trobe made a significant visit to the Ballarat field after it had been open a month. He talked to the diggers, stood on heaps of clay above the shafts, and glanced down into the pits into which Mammon would draw them, even at the risk of cave-ins, six days a week. He got the impression that a great deal of lucky wealth was emerging from the shafts, and was aware of the pressure these fortunate fellows were imposing on government. For example, he talked to a team of five men who had dug 136 ounces (3.8 kilos) of gold one day and 120 ounces (3.4 kilos) the next. He heard of one digger washing eight pounds weight (3.6 kilos) of gold from two dairy-maid dishes of clay, and of a partnership of diggers finding 31 pounds (14 kilos) of gold in one day. His impression was that the diggers could very easily pay for the government's new expenses.

There were very soon 5000 diggers at Ballarat, though the number dropped off towards the end of the year, many having gone to Mount Alexander, near Castlemaine, 65 kilometres north of Ballarat. Chris Peters, a hut-keeper on a sheep station at Mount Alexander, had broken off a piece of quartz from a reef in the pastures and seen gold. He and a companion resigned and worked at the rock, but were spied upon by a number of squatters. A Melbourne *Argus* journalist reported the location of the find wrongly. By the time corrections were made, the gold commissioner had arrived and taxed Peters and his offsider 10 per cent of the six pounds (2.7 kilos) of gold they had in their hut.

The diggings at Mount Alexander were spread across creeks, gullies and outcrops. The gold dug up was often hidden in concealed purses, in saddlebags and elsewhere, so an estimate of its wealth became impossible to make. But an eloquent symbol of how topography was variously prized was the placement of the Mount Alexander cemetery on Pennyweight Hill, a hill of little potential value, where, amongst the dead, the wives and children of miners were numerous, victims of childbirth in some cases, sudden fevers in others.

North of Castlemaine, in Bendigo Creek, gold was visible at a glance. One of the first to notice it for its value may have been Margaret Kennedy, wife of the overseer at Ravenswood Station, while she rode about delivering rations to the convict shepherds' huts. With the wife of a barrel-maker, she made a tent from a linen sheet. The women were the first diggers at Bendigo, soon joined by three male prospectors.

Lieutenant-Governor La Trobe was trying to manage the burgeoning fields with only forty-four soldiers. He also had fifty-five constables in Melbourne, but fifty of them wanted to resign and go digging. William Lonsdale, the Colonial Secretary in Victoria, told Doveton, the first Gold Commissioner, to be discreet in demanding fees and to take the money only from men who had it to pay from their earnings. Other diggers were to be given a card signed by the commissioner which would permit them to search till such time as they found gold. Doveton was also told to exact no fees for September, given that the month was so far advanced. But Doveton's behaviour does not seem to have been as lenient as instructed. Doveton and his notorious sergeant, the former blacksmith, Armstrong, behaved with that petty authoritarianism which was one of the sins of minor Britons, and corrupt ones at that. Armstrong would quickly penetrate every area of wealth and exchange on the goldfields. A Quaker visitor to Ballarat, William Howitt, described the appalling 'Hermstrong' as a monster who took money from diggers by illegal means, including blackmail. Armstrong was one of the initiators of the police practice by which men found without their licence, even if it were just metres away in their tent or spare shirt pocket, were chained overnight to trees. Liquor sales were banned on the goldfields, so sly grog shops abounded, and only the ones police were taking money from were permitted to survive. Police often confiscated liquor from the competitors of the Armstrong-sanctioned shops, and broke kegs, or mockingly poured out bottles in front of the men who had invested in them. When Armstrong retired to Melbourne after only two years, he boasted that he had cleared £15 000 by speculation and bribery and extorting miners. When the miners found that one of the streets in the new town of Ballarat, designed by the surveyor Frederic Charles Urquhart, was to be named in Armstrong's honour, they saw yet another sign that the authorities were making a mockery of them. The streets and cross streets were all named after commissioners, police functionaries or magistrates. A town where every laneway was named for a Peeler was to the diggers a questionable town.

As well, the diggers saw little civic improvement for the taxes they paid. The roads got worse, there was no hospital, the mails were unreliable, and the police, some of them ex-convicts from across Bass Strait who had learned corrupt habits as overseers, were grossly untrue to their charge.

But at least there could be no more transportation now. The escaped Irish political prisoner Thomas Francis Meagher, waiting on Waterhouse Island in Bass Strait for an American ship which was to leave Hobart to rendezvous with him and take him to the United States, one morning saw an eight-oared boat arriving from the direction of the Tasmanian mainland. It was full of escaped convicts from Hobart—they had stolen the cutter and were on their way to the gold rush in Port Phillip. They were well equipped with the contents of the cutter's chest, and with other gear including a tent. They stayed with Meagher for three days and when his American ship arrived, which would take him to Civil War glory and assassination in the United States, they rowed him out to it. Clearly, transportation had become an absurdity. Why would government bother sending prisoners for punishment to places that men were now willing to pay a high premium to reach?

CHAPTER 29

HOW GOLD MAKES ALL NEW

William Charles Wentworth, by now the consummate Tory, saw gold as an inconvenience to the pastoral princes, and was working as chairman of the New South Wales Select Committee to formulate a Goldfield Management Bill to limit the rights of miners and hold labourers in place on pastoral lands. In the proposed bill was a clause reserving any gold found on squatters' leaseholds to the squatter himself. Goldfield commissioners were to be empowered to tear down the homes of unlicensed residents. And while the miners' licence fee was to be reduced for locals to stop them going to Victoria, the fee was to be doubled for 'foreigners'.

Henry Parkes mocked the legislation. 'This is not the way for our legislature to vindicate itself in the eyes of the British nation . . . Men with brains, men with ambition, men with a ha'penny's worth of gumption and tuppence worth of nous were not going to sit in some shepherd's hut for the benefit of some big absentee shepherd king. No sir. And even an imbecile knew that to discourage the gold interest was a great public wrong.' Wentworth's bill was passed in modified form.

But busy with politics and his shop, Parkes himself did not go looking for gold. He was more interested in exalting Australia in the eyes of the imperial centre, a not uncommon Australian impulse.

Miners' associations existed on many goldfields, and the native-born and British were as one with newcomers in seeing the act as destructive (despite the token reduction in their own licence fees), and intended to make everyone return to being serfs of the pastoral interest. So passionately was this felt that at Sofala on the Turon, at Bathurst and elsewhere, mass meetings were held by the red-shirted miners, and there was talk of resisting the new Act by armed force and the old Irish Croppy weapon of the pike. On the day before the new licences were to be introduced, 7 February 1853, 1500 armed miners, aggrieved storekeepers and other traders who feared the goldfields being depopulated, marched on Sofala—there were speeches, and WC Wentworth, once the tribune of the populace, was burned in effigy.

Next day at Sofala the commissioner was nervously shifting in his saddle on the far side of the Turon waiting for troops of the 11th Regiment of Foot to arrive and restore order in the sprawling canvas town. Before they did, fourteen men crossed the river and defied him to arrest them, since they would not purchase a licence. They were arrested and charged. Waving pistols and shillelaghs, a furious crowd of miners then crossed in the face of the Gold Commissioner's troopers and the lately arrived redcoats. But a clergyman spoke up and managed for the moment to soothe the miners. The question was not finished with, however.

Gold, said the clever little Corkman Justice Therry, brought to the colony a state of society which combined the minimum of comfort with the maximum of expense. House rents rose 100 per cent when the diggers came back to town with their money. Hay quadrupled in price. Couples who had worked for an annual wage of £50 as domestics now demanded more than three times that. The salaries of all government officers had to be raised nearly 50 per cent to keep them from leaving for the Turon. At first, just before the discovery of gold and just after, Sydney looked tenantless, given that so many had gone to the diggings in California and others to the new ones near Bathurst. So the first fortunes of the gold rush derived, in the continuing spirit of Sydney, from a real estate killing made by men who remained in town and bought up rows of empty houses, banking on the inevitable coming demand. Within twelve months such men were selling the houses at twenty times their previous value. Similarly, those speculators who bought livestock from farmers and squatters when herdsmen and shepherds decamped for the diggings would soon make a fortune from them.

But the Victorian goldfields threw all former discoveries in any country and in New South Wales into the shade. The population of Victoria in 1851 was already 77 000. In the next three years it grew to 250 000. In spite of the difficulties of administration, La Trobe was comforted by the deposits made to the Government Savings Bank which implied the growth of settled life.

Roger Therry in New South Wales, where the phenomenon was not quite as intense as in Victoria, was nonetheless aware of the way fortunes were really made from gold. He met in Sydney an old friend, 'a lollipop maker', who was in steerage on the same ship on which Therry had returned to Australia in 1848. '"Then," I said, "You seem to have had good luck at the diggings?" His answer was, "I did not go near them."' The man had owned a pub on the high road to Ballarat from Geelong and had earned an enviable £6000 a year, and was going home again with £20 000, an improbable fortune for an ordinary immigrant.

Therry also entered a very elegantly fitted-out shop in Sydney and saw there that 'a red-shirted fellow, face hidden in hair, was smoking a large pipe that filled the room with smoke'. Therry mentioned the roughness of the man to the shopkeeper. '"Oh sir!" was his reply. "That gentleman has been just buying £70 worth of goods for the lady near him, so, you know, we must be civil to such a customer."'

Very early in the gold rush, radical opinion in the city and on the fields concentrated on the land issue—that the land was locked up by the squatters who sat in numbers on the Legislative Councils of both New South Wales and Victoria and who paid nominal rent, and denied any future prospect of land ownership to the miners who paid immensely per square metre for their minute claims. RL Milne, a conservative pamphleteer from Melbourne, witnessed a meeting on the issue in 1852. 'To my astonishment, [there] was a republican flag, the stars and stripes of North America, waving in prognosticating triumph, right over the British ensign, in full view of the city of Melbourne.'

He reported further that one of the speakers was in the habit of taking off his hat to salute the multitude of miners and workers at public meetings, stating that in doing so he paid them a compliment he did not pay to any queen—'thereby intimating the right of sovereignty in them, and not the Crown of England'.

The Melbourne *Age* set the tone for the new men—the city progressives and radicals, and those on the goldfields. It would say in 1857, 'The laissez-faire system will not answer in this country.' That is, there would need to be government intervention to ensure equity in land, employment and rights. These concepts caused undeniable grief to conservatives such as William a'Beckett, the first Chief Justice of Victoria, who was throughout the 1850s the champion of order, which to him meant not merely law and order but the accustomed order of classes without which, he believed, civilisation must end. Gold was dangerous because it had the power to turn class relations upside-down. He would write a pamphlet, *Does the Discovery of Gold in Victoria, viewed in relation to its Moral and Social Effects, as Hitherto Developed, Deserve to be Considered a National Blessing or a National Curse?*

It had certainly introduced into society a general contempt for polite dress and personal appearance, and an acceptance of squalid crowding-in. And of course smoking and drinking and swearing. Chief Justice a'Beckett saw this thrusting towards equality as 'the dream of a madman or the passion of a fiend'. It would be possible to call him a prig and a hypocrite, given that he married while in Melbourne his deceased wife's younger sister, a marriage which had been forbidden under British statute not yet enacted in Australia. But he would have argued, 'My act did not bring the very pillars of society down.'

For gold hunting, said William's brother, Thomas a'Beckett, also a lawyer, was 'not, *per se*, a desirable occupation. Its success is not dependent upon moral work, and it has a tendency to destroy rather than promote the observance of those rules of conduct which, while they contribute to wealth and welfare, elevate the individual who practises them and promote social happiness.'

It was believed that the goldfields could be unhinging too—that they increased the numbers of the insane. Gold, alcohol and harsh conditions were considered to bring on madness. Everyone dreamed of nuggets. James Thomas Harcourt, who ran for some years a private lunatic asylum in Victoria, stated in the course of a trial in the Victorian Supreme Court in 1852 that it was a 'common feature' with Victorian lunatics to place their excrement in their pockets and say it was gold.

A talented lawyer, the Irishman Redmond Barry, also chimed in on the side of the establishment. He had been spirited enough on his journey to Australia to have an affair with a married woman passenger and to be considered such a dasher as to be confined to his cabin by the captain. Now, in Melbourne, a man at the height of his talents, he was almost hyperactively beneficent in his civic activities and heavily involved in the founding of those bulwarks against barbarism, the University of Melbourne and the Victorian Institute. 'All this points to prove,' said Barry at the opening of the university in 1854, 'that the barren acquisition of money does not satisfy the cravings of the people who possess comprehension.'

Churchmen looked upon the gold craze as an enemy of piety. Anglican Bishop Perry declared gold could act 'to the increased prosperity of this colony, and for the happiness of its people; or for the destruction of social order, and the introduction of an age of barbarism amongst us'. Like the a'Beckett brothers, the bishop thought it a problem that gold threatened to make the poor rich, as the poor knew 'no other enjoyment than the gratification of their appetites'.

By contrast with some colonial gentlemen, Lord Robert Cecil, a promising 21-year-old Englishman and future prime minister of Britain, was cheered by the signs of good order in the great pitted and denuded landscapes of Ballarat and Bendigo. He was recovering from a nervous collapse in 1852 when he visited the goldfields. An Oxford and Eton man, he wore a jumper, since he had been warned that the diggers hooted 'gents', and he aspired to be called 'mate' according to the general tenor of the gold localities. Everyone was 'mate' except the Chinese diggers, and sometimes, in cases of personal relationships, even them. At the goldfields, found Cecil, 'there was less crime than in a large English town and more order and civility than I have myself witnessed in my native village of Hatfield'. That pillar of society Redmond Barry would come to agree with him and would give praise to the unwritten British Constitution and its moderating influence in saving Victoria from the worst excesses of Californian Yankeedom.

GOLDFIELD ARRIVALS

It is a truism that diggers emigrating to the Australian colonies in hope of a golden bonanza brought with them new attitudes, their backgrounds making them intolerant of police officiousness and sceptical of oligarchies.

Peter and Richard Lalor, for example, who arrived in Australia in 1853, might be taken as typical of the educated Irish. They had left a nation gutted by Famine and cowed by political repression, and they brought with them a family tradition of both civil resistance and physical force. Their father, a middling farmer, had been a supporter of Daniel O'Connell, and had been elected to the Westminster parliament as a member of the Irish Party in the House of Commons. Their brother, James Fintan, ideological force of the Young Ireland Movement and of the Irish uprising of 1848, was a friend to the famed Irish political prisoners transported to Van Diemen's Land—William Smith O'Brien, John Mitchel and Thomas Francis Meagher. He wrote that only those who worked the land should own it, a doctrine which anticipated Marx and Engels. In the midst of the Famine he urged farmers to go on a nationwide rent strike, and was arrested and then released from prison as his health declined. He agreed to take part in an uprising in the summer of 1849 to protest against the sending of the harvest out of starving Ireland, but nothing came of it and two days after its proposed date he died in Dublin. Peter and Richard Lalor therefore came from no vague tradition of nay-saying. Their father, Patrick, would state in the year of his sons' emigration to Australia, 'I have been struggling for upwards of forty years, struggling without ceasing in the cause of the people.'

Arrived in Melbourne, Richard and Peter entered a business partnership as spirit and provision merchants, which gave Peter finance sufficient to go to the Ovens goldfield late in 1853. In 1854 he moved to Ballarat where he tried several spots, finally sinking a shaft on Red Hill and living in a small hut made of logs on the Eureka goldfield.

John Basson Humffray arrived in Ballarat the same year Peter Lalor went to the Ovens. He had been born in north Wales in 1824, the son of a master weaver who made sure he was well educated. His home county, Montgomeryshire, and his hometown, Newtown, were centres of the Chartist movement, in which the young Humffray involved himself. In Ballarat, another young man of ideas, the Italian Raffaello Carboni, described Humffray as 'perplexed at the prosperity of the vicious and the disappointment of the virtuous in this mysterious world of ours'. He was, like Lalor's father, a believer in moral force and, despite the increasingly severe provocations offered by the Victorian police to the miners, rejected the concept of armed retaliation and resistance. Grubbing in the clay did not consistently attract him as a fit vocation for a man, so he opened a bookstore in Ballarat, but he was always a solid supporter of the diggers. He was appalled by the establishment and the attitudes emanating from 'the Camp', the cantonment occupied at the north end of Ballarat by the police and military. The British army, engaged so heavily in the war against Russia in the Crimea, did not have many troops to spare for the colony of Victoria, but the longer the miners' grievances went unaddressed, the more troops of the 12th and 40th Regiments marched up from Melbourne through the Eureka diggings and over Bakery Hill to take residence in the Camp.

Raffaello Carboni, an Italian nationalist in his early thirties, had been briefly imprisoned for his politics while a seminarian in Rome. Having left the Church to work in a bank, he became a member of the Young Italy movement which sought to unify Italy by driving the Austrians out of the north, taking the Papal

States from the Pope (who, said the rebels, should be content to be a spiritual prince), and the south from the heinously corrupt Bourbons who ruled the Kingdom of Naples and Sicily. When Giuseppe Garibaldi, the Young Italy general in exile, returned to Italy from Peru in 1848, he took Milan from the Austrians and marched on Rome. The Pope fled, and his restoration became an objective both of the French and the Austrians. Carboni was an officer in a Garibaldian battalion led by his friend Colonel Cattabeni, and was wounded three times in the leg during Garibaldi's defence of Rome. When the French assault finally drove out the Italian nationalists, Garibaldi went again into Peruvian exile, but Carboni settled in Cornhill in London, taught languages and read graphic accounts of the Australian goldfields in the *London Illustrated News*. He was in Melbourne by mid 1852 and was soon at Ballarat. 'I had joined a party; fixed our tent on the Canadian Flat; went up to the Camp to get our gold licence.' Then he walked to Golden Point and jumped into an abandoned hole. 'In less than five minutes I pounced on a little pouch [a seam]—the yellow boy [gold] was all there—my eyes were sparkling—I felt a sensation identical to a first declaration of love in bygone times—"*Great Works!*" at last was my bursting exclamation.' This was his favourite epithet, and the exuberant young man, one of whose wounds sometimes still reopened, was known and liked as Great Works Carboni.

In January 1853, Carboni saw a party working a claim at Canadian Gully in Ballarat find a golden rock weighing 93 pounds (42 kilos), and then shortly after another weighing 84 pounds (38 kilos). A few days later, at a depth of 15 metres, another monster weighing 136 pounds (62 kilos) was discovered, and named 'The Canadian'. Raffaello Carboni, with a claim on a hill above, declared 'Canadian Gully was as rich in lumps as other goldfields are in dirt.'

LETTERED MINERS

Not all diggers were as well educated or politically sophisticated as Peter Lalor, John Humffray and Raffaello Carboni, but many of them were. By the time of Carboni's arrival, there was a lending library established at Golden Point and it was passionately patronised by diggers. It proved that by 1854, the literacy rates in goldfield males were much higher than those prevailing in the British population. Eighty per cent of the goldfields Irish, for example, were literate.

This reality altered and even elevated the goldfields, though they did not look like salubrious locations. The Sabbath was well observed. Methodists were established by the end of 1853 with a resident preacher, and Father Matthew Downey, a Kerry man educated at Naples, was the first Catholic priest to take up residence on the Ballarat fields. His bishop described his habitation as 'the most miserable apology for a dwelling I have ever seen. A few wine casks serve as chairs . . .' Theatres were opened on the Gravel Pits field in late 1853 and on Eureka in 1854, while the Adelphi Theatre in Ballarat itself quickly followed. A racing club was formed and cricket was played in the summer.

The diggers seemed to be imposing their own version of order. Yet a new Victorian governor, Charles Hotham, wrongly believed he was dealing with anarchic and unlettered scum. Westminster, too, was thinking of putting an export duty on gold as well as the licence fee. The diggers pointed out that such a step would be 'class legislation, inasmuch as there is no export duty on wool or tallow'. They were not fools, but they felt they were counted as such. And they were the inheritors of the tradition of the year of revolutions, 1848, when that famous bloodless French coup had delivered a poet-president, Lamartine, when even the starving Irish rebelled abortively, when the Italians had risen against the French and the Austrians.

Indeed, as the Irish made their way to the ports to take ship to California or Australia, they were still likely to encounter cadavers, black with typhus, hollowed by hunger, in ditches. Homeless widows and children screamed their plaints of misery at them on their way. And they trod on, taking ship to a saner world. But in Victoria they found all they hated: the landlord, the bailiff, the equivalent of the tithe-gouger—anointed by authority—in their path. The old tyranny was encapsulated in the uniform of the Victorian police. And La Trobe, and Hotham after him, had not released even enough ground to allow the miners a vegetable garden.

Charles Hotham was a hardnosed naval captain of some diplomatic experience, but no appeaser. Victoria was for him a second choice—he had wanted a Crimean War command. New provisions for constitutional reform for Victoria and New South Wales were under consideration in Whitehall, as a result of pressure from colonists. In the meantime Victoria was to be wrung into shape like a warship might be. The policy, and Hotham's mindset, would be catastrophic. Feeling the gritty winds blowing off the goldfields in 1854, Hotham did not need a prefabricated hut—he lived in reasonable resplendence in a residence in Toorak, and received dispatch riders from the goldfields.

He was alarmed that the Americans on the goldfields had formed the Order of the Lone Star with the intention to extend to the citizens of Australia the benefits of liberty and republicanism. His predecessor La Trobe had written to London earlier to say that though 'some danger might be apprehended' from the Americans, he did not think republicanism was apparent on the goldfields. Indeed, La Trobe and Hotham, had the latter possessed the gift to see these things, would have noticed how regularly the diggers looked upon their situation as a violation of traditional British rights, not necessarily of republican ones. It was even so with Carboni.

In November 1853, he had gone to a meeting on Bakery Hill, just above Eureka, where four hundred diggers expressed sympathy with the plight of the police-plagued Bendigo diggers and a petition was raised for a reduction of fees. There was a 'great waste of yabber yabber', said Carboni, about the lack of digger representation in the Legislative Council, and much complaint about monopoly of the land. Before leaving the meeting, Carboni held a brief conversation with a medical man, Dr Carr, whom he would later meet under a more pernicious star. Carr complimented Carboni on his English, and then told him (as relayed in Carboni's shaky French) '*Nous allons bientot au revoir la Republique Australienne!* (We'll soon see an Australian republic).' Carboni, who believed in an independent but not necessarily republican Italy, remarked, '*Quel farce!* (What a joke!)'

'I understood very little of these matters at the time,' Carboni later admitted. 'The shoe had not pinched my toe yet.' But there was talk of a diggers' congress, and the storekeepers of Ballarat added to the diggers' petition their own protest declaring that the licence fee was 'unjust in principle, partial in collection'.

Soon afterwards, a new field was found on the Buckland River near Beechworth, towards the New South Wales border in the north-east, and five thousand men rushed there, forgetting their politics. On top of that nearly a thousand diggers, mainly Americans, sailed away to try the goldfields discovered at the headwaters of the Amazon, though they were replaced by 1500 supposedly apolitical Chinese.

Governor Hotham knew he must now visit turbulent Ballarat. Driving up the dusty main road from Melbourne with his wife, the grand-niece of the illustrious Lord Nelson, he arrived in the town on a Saturday evening and was pleased to find 'an orderly and well conducted people, particular in their observance of Sunday'. A digger carried his wife through the mud and a nugget of 75 pounds (34 kilos) was found and named in Lady Hotham's honour. The governor was pleased to note that shafts had to go deep to find gold, since that meant a digger had to stay fixed in one locality for the better part of six months before he bottomed out, either on a vein of gold or nothing. At nearby Bendigo Hotham was presented with a petition to do away with the licence fee, and met the diggers and spoke equably with them. Even so, his military eye had noticed that a soldier invading the surface of the goldfields would be poorly placed to deal with a digger firing upon him from within a shaft.

Hotham's brief, like that of any governor, was to cut debt. Revenue from the goldfields had declined in the last months of 1854. Hotham's advice, however, was that only half of the diggers paid their licence fee. He instructed his Gold Commissioners and the acting Commissioner of Police that an effective search be made on all the fields at least twice a week to raise revenue.

As far as the diggers were concerned, they would now be hounded even more by the corrupt police and officious soldiers of the Camp. A digger had described the Camp as 'a kind of legal store where justice was bought and sold, bribery being the governing element of success, and perjury the base instrument of baser minds to victimise honest and honourable men, thus defeating the ends of justice'. Yet His Excellency foolishly put his fondest hopes in it.

The soldiers and police lived well in the Camp, and the police were involved in the sly grog business not only as paid-off protectors but also as partners. Some had a business arrangement with James Bentley, a former Vandemonian convict, Melbourne confectioner and gold-buyer, who had built the first-class Eureka Hotel that could accommodate eighty people. Bentley's premises were always protected by the police. But Sergeant Major Milne, a notorious policeman, descended upon Frank Carey, an alleged American sly-grogger who would not pay him bribe money, and closed him down.

Many policemen also forced diggers to give them a share of their gold. By now, Carboni's contempt for colonial authority was complete. For a Gold Commissioner, Carboni's advice was, 'Get a tolerable young pig, make it stand on its hind-legs, put on its head the cap trimmed with gold lace, whitewash its mouth, and there you have the ass in the form of a pig. I mean to say a "man". With this privilege, that he possesses in his head the brain of both the abovementioned brutes.'

There were many Irish on the goldfields whom the police liked to rile. The new priest for the Irish was Father Patrick Smyth, who had a crippled Armenian servant, Yoannes Gregorius. Ministers of religion were exempt from having to purchase licences, but Gregorius was beaten by a policeman for not having one. The Acting Commissioner of Victorian Police, Evelyn Sturt, brother of the explorer Charles Sturt, arrived at the scene, and so did Father Smyth who had to pay £5 bail to get Gregorius released from a prison which, a few months later, would be crammed with digger prisoners. Gregorius was charged with assault upon a trooper. The Ballarat Catholics, whether Irish or otherwise, drew up a letter to the authorities.

When Governor Hotham saw the petition, he was impressed by its articulateness. 'The conduct of Mr Commissioner Johnston towards the Reverend Father Smyth,' the petition said, 'has been calculated to awaken the highest feelings of indignation in the breasts of his devoted flock; and they do call upon the Governor to institute an enquiry into the character and do desire to have him at once removed from Ballarat.' But the commissioner was not removed—in Hotham's mind he was keeping the lid on the pot—and the Irish and others remained aggrieved.

On 16 October 1854, four men in blue shirts, corduroy trousers and caps with black crepe veils held up the Ballarat branch of the Bank of Victoria and departed with £15 000. No one would ever find out, at least officially, who they were, but this robbery carried out within a stone's throw of the Camp might have given the miners the idea of the impotence of the Camp against, not a gang of men in crepe masks, but a mass of men who exposed their faces to the sun and spoke of greater freedom.

There had been an infuriating murder amongst the miners' ranks that helped fuel their resentment of the Camp. Earlier in October, two young Scots diggers had gone into town on the tear, and on the way back to camp tried to get a drink at Bentley's Eureka Hotel. Words were exchanged at the pub shutters, and the two were then pursued along the Melbourne Road by one of Bentley's servants who killed young James Scobie with a shovel.

Immediately the police network sprang into efficient action to save Bentley. But the miners called a meeting at the place where Scobie was killed. Because that was not far from the Eureka Hotel, there was a certain threat attached to the meeting. Bentley asked for police protection, and both the police and a number of soldiers turned up. Those who spoke at the protest meeting were Thomas Kennedy, a former Scots Chartist and a Baptist preacher; a man named Hugh

Meikle who had been a juror at the Coroner's inquest into Scobie's death; one Archibald Carmichael; and Peter Lalor, the Irish digger.

Next to the hotel was a bowling alley of canvas owned by John Emritson, a Bostonian, and he watched as mounted police advanced a short distance from the meeting place to the hotel. Cries broke out from the crowd demanding Bentley show himself. Some boys in the crowd began throwing stones, windows were broken, and then suddenly the crowd was pulling wooden boards from the walls. Lieutenant Broadhurst and some more men of the 40th Regiment arrived and lined up on the right of the building.

Robert Rede, the Gold Commissioner, also turned up, and mounted the windowsill to address the crowd, hopeful that his presence would remind men of their civic responsibilities. Eggs splattered him. All at once the bowling alley was alight. The winds were blowing as only the winds of the internal Australian desert, bearing down on central Victoria, can. The military refused to attempt to extinguish the flames, as their lieutenant thought it beyond the ambit of their duties. The police were left trying to beat the flames down while the military marched back to the Camp.

Later, Carboni would vividly recall the fire: 'The redcoats wheel about, and return to the Camp. Look out! The roof of the back part of the hotel falls in! "Hurrah! Boys, here's the porter and ale with the chill off." Bottles are handed out burning hot—the necks of two bottles are knocked together!—contents drunk in colonial style.—Look out, the roof, sides and all fall in! An enormous mass of flames and smoke arise to the roaring sound—the sparks are carried far, far into the air, and what was once the Eureka Hotel is now a mass of burning embers. As she burns the crowd calls, Hip Hip Hurrah!'

Later that afternoon hail and rain fell on Ballarat and the rumour in the Camp was that an attack would be made on them to capture Bentley. The women and children resident in the Camp were moved out and 1000 rounds of ball cartridge were issued. A small number of diggers were arrested that night but were quickly rescued from the police, who galloped back affrighted to the Camp. 'The people ask for justice, not bullets!' wrote Humffray. He declared that the Eureka Hotel had become 'a bundle of crayons with which to write the black history of crime and colonial misrule'.

A diggers' committee made an eight-page submission setting out the facts of Scobie's death and urging Governor Hotham to look into it. Down in his villa in Toorak, according to his wife an inadequate gubernatorial residence, he replied that he had offered a reward for the capture of Scobie's murderer, and that if he was to order an investigation into matters on the goldfields, an essential prelude to that would be the gold miners' obedience to the law of the land.

In the matter of the fire, Hotham soon found himself the victim of police stupidity, in that one of the accused, Andrew McIntyre, was a man who tried to restrain the crowd, while the other one, Thomas Fletcher, a printer, had not left his office that day. Many of those who had raised bail for McIntyre and Fletcher now wanted to storm the Camp instead and release them by force. Henry Holyoake, a London Chartist, addressed an impromptu meeting on Bakery Hill. He managed to contain the fury of those who were outraged by the indiscriminate arrests of the two men. The accused had been committed for trial at Geelong, since it was clear no goldfields jury would condemn them. A crowd of miners marched along the Melbourne Road, letting their pistols off.

Commissioner Rede was determined not to let things settle down quietly, since that would lessen the authority of the government. He looked forward to mass arrests and the imposition 'of a frightful lesson'. Rede, a former surgeon, was calling for blood. He was in unconscious unison with his governor who had been told by the Secretary of State for the Colonies in Britain, the Duke of Newcastle, to bring the issues of Victoria's goldfields to a head, if necessary. Before Rede followed up, though, he intended to wait upon the arrival of a detachment of the 12th Regiment from Melbourne 'in sufficient force to punish'. He sent out his troopers the next day to hunt for unlicensed diggers and to 'test the feelings of the people'.

CHAPTER 30

GOLDEN CELESTIALS

News of the gold discoveries in Australia reached southern China in 1852. The Chinese named the Australian goldfields Xian Jin Shan, New Gold Mountain. (California, its diggings in decline by the mid 1850s, was Jiu Jin Shan, Old Gold Mountain.) Their tickets funded on credit by Chinese merchants, about five hundred Chinese embarked as diggers for Australia in that year and the next, but then, in 1854, 10 000 arrived throughout the year. They came mainly from the Guangdong delta. Their villages were hard up, densely populated, frequently raided by warlords, and now paying English taxes as well. The countryside was involved in guerilla warfare against the Ching government, and rebels, outlaws and bandits sheltered in the mountains above the estuary.

Each of these miners who arrived in Australia was, as one modern Chinese scholar describes it, connected to his family back home the way a kite is by a string to the hands of its owner. As they walked to the goldfields from Geelong or Sydney, there were acts of petty spite by white miners, including the pulling of cues, called 'pigtails', by the Europeans, and the upsetting of Chinese diggers' gear carried, coolie-style, on both ends of a long bamboo pole. In that age, the Chinese miners' lack of Christianity, the essential marker of human worth, made them a butt of jokes or abhorrence. But it also made them subtly dangerous to the mind of colonial society. Nonetheless the major source of serious, as against flippant and oafish, opposition to Chinese immigration in the years 1856 to 1860 came not from the goldfields, but from politicians and newspapers.

Though a number of witnesses spoke of good order, sobriety and discipline amongst the Chinese, the Victorian Goldfields Commission of Enquiry would condemn them as practising 'degrading and absurd superstition', as being incurable gamblers and possessing other unspecified vicious habits. They were so undemanding of physical comfort that their overall effect was 'to demoralise colonial society', declared the Enquiry. These thunderings would have redoubled if the Enquiry had known that many households in China tolerated the idea that a married man who made good—or good enough—might marry also in Australia, and not necessarily to a Chinese woman. These Australian marriages were considered secondary marriages by the man, and a number of non-Chinese wives were shocked when they ultimately ventured to their husbands' villages and met the primary wives.

The one thing the Chinese were not accused of was political crime, but they were as political as the Irish. Many of the gold-rush Chinese in New South Wales and Victoria were refugees and had supported the Taiping (or Great Peace) rebellion, a revolt against Manchu rule led by a Christian-influenced seer, Hung-Hsui-Chuan, who attracted huge support and rallied an army from amongst the common people.

In June 1855, the Victorian Legislative Council passed an Act to make Provision for Certain Immigrants. It imposed a poll tax of £10, payable by the ship's captain, on every Chinese arrival. Furthermore, captains were permitted to land only one Chinese national per 10 tons of displacement. To avoid the tax, ships' masters began to disembark Chinese passengers in New South Wales, or at Robe on the coast of South Australia. From there the Celestials—the name commonly used and derived from China's self-description as the Celestial Kingdom—walked to the Victorian goldfields, a distance of 400 kilometres through hard country. On 8 April 1856, for example, a party of 150 Chinese left Adelaide for the Victorian diggings under the escort of an experienced bushman, Lionel Edwardson. Five two-horse drays carried food, utensils and general luggage. The leader of the Chinese group had already spent some years in South Australia, and had amassed a small fortune as a merchant, upon which he had returned to his native China and induced this large party to migrate with him to the goldfields. The average rate of travel was 19 kilometres a day. The overland route was boggy in winter but was much better than the Guichen Bay coastal route from Robe which suffered still more from heavy winter rains.

At Robe between 17 January and 3 May 1857, 10 000 Chinese immigrants were landed, from ships which had sailed from Hong Kong. Guichen Bay off Robe was not a very safe harbour, open to buffeting southerlies. So the ships landed their Chinamen and made a quick turnaround. The Sub-Collector of Customs at Robe remembered this Chinese invasion of the 1850s: 'The Government of the sister state [Victoria] never forgave South Australia for this loss to them of about £20 000. I had great difficulty securing the opium for Judy [his wife, who possibly took it for tuberculosis] and on one occasion Ormerod's store was broken open by the Chinamen to gain possession of the cases containing it. There were then about 3000 Celestials camping about the townships and Lieutenant Saunders and forty men of the 12th Regiment were sent to keep order.' He noticed how generally well-behaved the Chinese parties were, but 'their national vice, however, of gambling accompanies them while upon the road and it is singular, though painful, to observe how intensely the passions of play burn in this effeminate race'.

South Australia introduced its own poll tax in 1857, and a number of similar New South Wales bills were passed thereafter.

By 1861 there were more than 24 000 Chinese immigrants on the Victorian goldfields of Ballarat, Beechworth, Bendigo, Castlemaine and Maryborough. The *Argus* of 4 June 1856 said, 'The present Act for checking the introduction of the Chinese has proved at all events a partial failure. Like Southey's rats they seem to come in at the windows, and under the doors, and down through the ceilings and up through the floors.' At the same time there were 11 000 Chinese on the New South Wales goldfields in places like Armidale, Binalong, Bathurst, Braidwood, Lambing Flat (Young), Carcoar, Mudgee, Tamworth and Tumut. In 1857 there was an outbreak of violence against the Chinese at Buckland River in Victoria and the move to form anti-Chinese leagues spread to other Victorian goldfields and to New South Wales. In part response, Chinese Benevolent Societies, often based on clan or district ties, quickly developed across the goldfields of Australia to support the Chinese population.

OBJECTS IN A LANDSCAPE, OR ACTORS IN A FIELD

An observer of the Mount Alexander goldfields, north of Ballarat, near Castlemaine, wrote, 'The camp grew in regular lines of streets, narrow and primitive, but highly populous and busy, while the whole valley was alive with Chinamen as they swarmed in their paddocks and holds.' On that field, one in four adult males was Chinese. Contrary to accepted wisdom, Chinese and European miners often worked side by side, mutually dependent on adequate water to work their claims, and mutually subject to its ravages. The mineshafts at Mount Alexander's Moonlight and Pennyweight Flats, for example, were about 9 metres deep and all diggers of whatever stripe worked furiously to keep water out of them.

Yet, the full-throated entertainer, Charles Thatcher, very popular on the goldfields, depicted 'John the Chinaman' as a thief.

> 'Tis now the very witching time of night,
> Past twelve o'clock and not a star in sight.
> All nature sleeps until the coming morn
> And tired diggers steal a churchyard yawn.
> The thieving Chinaman sees night's black pall
> O'er hill and gully slowly mantling all.
> With bag in hand he threads his noiseless way
> A visit to the hen woods now to pay.

'John Chinaman', according to one of Thatcher's sketches, gradually adopted European habits, wearing a coat and trousers, making love to Irish girls and settling down to enjoy the privileges of an Englishman. 'John is gregarious, his religion is rather doubtful and consists of going into a joss house and burning fragrant sticks of sandalwood . . . strange to say there are no Chinese in Parliament at present, which is rather unfair, neither has any Chinaman been raised to the Bench.' Obviously all was not racial concord on the fields.

Despite social ostracism, there were women who married the Chinese and these were often Irish orphan girls. Marriages were more common than expected and a lot of them were stable and successful. But European women in relationships with Chinese men were described as lazy, degraded creatures, the victims of lewd Orientals and outcasts from European society. 'A lot of silly girls . . . too lazy to work.' 'Prostitutes of the lowest order . . . went to the Chinese to escape incessant beatings' by their clients.

It was also often presumed that the women who married Chinamen were opium addicts. Some may have been, and certainly some became opium abusers, but these cases were the notable ones, obvious to the authorities, who might then assume any woman with a Chinese husband or lover was an addict.

*

From 1854 onwards, there had been a number of anti-Chinese riots on Victorian and New South Wales goldfields. Those later in the decade occurred at a time when the colonial legislatures were framing legislation against Chinese immigration. In 1857 and 1858 at Adelong and Tambaroora respectively, and at the Buckland River field in Victoria in 1857, there were attacks on Chinese miners inspired by a complex of emotions on the part of white diggers. These included objections to the way the Chinese worked in gangs, their supposed exploitation of desirable sites, the existence of separate Chinese camps, which seemed sinister to other diggers, and the ethnic hysteria they evoked simply by being there. In 1860 a string of anti-Chinese riots began at Lambing Flat near Young, north-west of Goulburn in New South Wales, and would culminate a year later in a riot which destroyed Chinese camps and drove more than a thousand Chinese miners away.

The Lambing Flat riots are often taken to prove that digger society was endemically racist and that the Chinese were hapless and submissive victims of racial violence, and made their living off poor or abandoned ground. There was no denying the hysteria of the diggers or the savagery of the riots, but Chinese mining was not haphazard and confined to the margins. Chinese miners at Braidwood and Kiandra in southern New South Wales, for example, generally worked in large numbers under the control of a boss, who would have perhaps one hundred and fifty men under him organised into gangs of ten to thirty. The boss attended to the purchase of claims, the supply of provisions and payments, and charged the miners between 23 to 30 shillings a week for board.

The Chinese were willing to live rough, and that helped white miners sneer at them, but their solidarity also affronted some. Clan loyalty meant more than individual comfort for the men who signed on to come to the goldfields. Even on the goldfields, the Chinese gangs were connected by lineage and the boss came from a high clan family. The individual's passage from the Pearl River to the New Gold Mountain was probably advanced by Guangdong merchants—the basis for the many complaints that Chinese migrants remitted too much of their money back home and did not spend it in Australia.

The Chinese diggers indeed lived frugally and acquired whatever wealth they could for an eventual return to the Middle Kingdom. Once the alluvial gold played out many did return home. But from those who stayed came the population of Chinese labourers, market gardeners, cooks and urban businessmen who would beget Australian families and themselves grow old in Australia.

CHAPTER 31

THE REPUBLICAN PUSH

In 1847, Earl Grey, the Colonial Secretary, and James Stephen, his Undersecretary, had a plan for a new Constitution for New South Wales. Its benefits or disadvantages would wash along the Australian continent to the new and junior colonies of Victoria, South Australia, Western Australia and Queensland. It was a re-working of a constitution prepared that year for New Zealand. The plan envisaged a federation of the Australian colonies. District councils, instituted in 1842, were to remain, also the colonial legislatures, then a federal authority would be placed over all.

However, there were still very few federalists in Australia in the 1850s. Governor FitzRoy of New South Wales was one, though he kept quiet about it. JD Lang, who abominated the governor, was another. Throughout the early 1850s FitzRoy and his two sons—Captain Augustus FitzRoy, his aide-de-camp who would later be killed in the Crimean War, and George FitzRoy, his private secretary—acquired a reputation as notorious lechers. Dr Lang denounced 'the flagitious immorality' of the three of them, all the more shocking given that the sainted late Lady FitzRoy had been killed in a coach accident for which FitzRoy's ego and recklessness were to blame. Lang wrote: 'Sir Charles FitzRoy was engaged in one of his Vice-Regal progresses in New South Wales when he reached the inland town of Berrima . . . and took up his abode at the hostelry of an innkeeper of the name of See, formerly, I believe, the [boxing] champion of New South Wales.' See's daughter was 'by no means destitute of personal attractions'. Miss See became pregnant and paternity was laid at the door of Governor FitzRoy. Lang believed that by sending reports on 'the FitzRoy brothel' to the new Colonial Secretary the Duke of Newcastle, he had helped get rid of the FitzRoys. When Governor FitzRoy ultimately left New South Wales in 1855, an address of farewell was prepared in the Legislative Council, to which Lang tried to add his own clause: 'That the moral influence which has emanated from Government House during His Excellency's term of office has been deleterious and baneful in the highest degree to the best interests of the community.'

Lang's was the resonating voice of republican federalism. As early as 1843, in the New South Wales Legislative Council, he had stated, 'It is impossible for this House to regard His Excellency [at that time, Gipps] in any other light than as an agent of a despotic authority which has usurped the rights and trampled on the privileges of the people.' Lang's visit to America in 1840 had enlarged his republicanism and he had produced a book-length tract while at sea entitled *Freedom and Independence for the Golden Lands of Australia*, in which he divided the settled areas of the Australian continent into states named for heroes such as Cook and Flinders. Earl Grey's plan helped, said Lang, in as far as it paved the way for 'the President of the United States of Australia'. But it was a plan imposed from above, with the franchise rights of voters not yet defined, and Lang wanted to provoke a plan which flowed from the people. His Australian League was formed to establish 'one great Australian nation'. Federalism had its first domestic champion in this rambunctious Presbyterian minister.

Other republican sympathisers included notable Currency children grown to early manhood. Daniel Deniehy was a prodigiously gifted young man of fifteen by the time he travelled to Ireland and Europe with his former convict parents. His father, Henry, had been transported and had arrived in New South Wales in 1820 serving a seven-year sentence for vagrancy, a common enough way of off-loading some of the Irish poor. Mary McCarthy, his mother, had also served a seven-year sentence. The boy was born in 1828. The father began his free life as a labourer, moved into business as a produce merchant and then became a general merchant. Young Deniehy went to school at the Sydney Academy, which later became Sydney Grammar, and in later years remembered the sleepy schoolroom in Phillip Street 'with small old-fashioned windows encased with great vines and honeysuckles'. The Sydney he grew up in was still a wild town, characterised by garbage heaps and open sewage drains. Short of water, plenteous in grog, its population did not generally bathe, so that when the garrison corps paraded in the humid Sydney summer near Hyde Park, the passer-by could smell them.

Deniehy's visit to his parents' homeland, Ireland, a place of seasonal misery and close to perpetual unrest, sharpened his republican instincts, while the Continent rounded out his education as a colonial of sensibility. His sense of fashion was not impaired by his travels either. The Deniehys left Cork by the immigrant ship *Elizabeth* in January 1844 to return to Sydney. The town had trebled in size since Deniehy's youth to a population of 36 000, and the old struggle between the emancipists and the exclusives—the pure merinos as they thought of themselves—was in full play, as was the Currency–Sterling divide. In monetary terms, currency was of less value than sterling, and thus 'Currency' were implicitly themselves of questionable value. But young men like Deniehy accepted the term as a badge of honour.

The three big political issues of Deniehy's late adolescence were the question of self-government, the prevention of the renewal of transportation, and the making available to ordinary settlers of land from the vast estates held—some would say locked up—by the squatters. The Pastoral Association had been formed to protect the privilege of the squatters, and their ability to control numbers in the Legislative Council was helped by their votes being worth so much more than those of city merchants. The property qualification to vote was high as well. The Currency poet Charles Harpur wrote scathingly of the statesman of the pastoral interest, William Charles Wentworth,

> *Now behold him in his native hue,*
> *The bullying, bellowing champion of the few!*
> *Patriot!—he who has no sense nor heed*
> *Of public ends beyond his own mere need.*

Dan Deniehy of New South Wales, a mere articled clerk, also took up his pen to mock the squatters out of their claims, and to apply to their sons the nickname 'Geebungs', after a form of native shrub. Deniehy, who would soon be mounting platforms for the cause, considered the pastoralists a lumpen commercial crowd who would rather put a bullock driver into parliament, as long as he owned property, than 'an impoverished Fox or an O'Connell living on his rents'. The Geebungs did not want to mix with other Currency, at least as Deniehy depicted them, but could never become fully British.

Deniehy was characteristically hard upon a Geebung named James Martin from County Cork, who was emphatic that neither of his parents had been convicts. Yet despite his early opinions Martin would come to believe that the old world's customs had to give way to a new world of talent, and he would become ultimately premier of New South Wales and later its chief justice. Martin, because of his Catholic working-class Irish origins, could never quite belong to the true merinos. But his patriotism, like that of Wentworth, who despised him, and like that of another coming colonial politician, Bede Dalley, was a patriotism dedicated to Australia under the British Constitution rather than a specifically Australian one.

The man for whom Deniehy worked as an articled clerk was a literary patron of great generosity of spirit, Nichol Drysdale Stenhouse, a partner in the legal firm of Stenhouse and Hardy in Elizabeth Street, Sydney. Stenhouse was the perfect employer for Deniehy. As a young solicitor he had helped the famous— but cash-strapped—writer Thomas De Quincey, author of the notorious *Confessions of an English Opium Eater*. He had considered it a privilege to protect De Quincey during the years he was hiding from his creditors in Edinburgh.

In Deniehy, Stenhouse was about to acquire another literary cause, of the kind that he had lost when lack of legal opportunity in Edinburgh had forced him to become a steerage immigrant to Australia. Since arriving in his new homeland, Stenhouse had gathered a library of four thousand volumes, and a circle of literary friends, including Charles Harpur, to whom he sent books by post to soothe Harpur's solitude in Maitland. Now his clerk Deniehy began to publish fiction in the *Colonial Literary Journal*, and a critical piece, 'The Rise and Progress of the Drama in Australia'.

In his fiction Deniehy wrote of young love in an entirely Australian environment: a young couple meet on the Royal Mail coach running from Nash's Hotel in Parramatta to Sydney. 'We talked of Parramatta and its people—the banks of the river—steamers and stages—poetry—Lord Byron and peach pies— love and sorrow—cookery and curl papers—Governor Bourke and the last King Bungaree etc.' 'Sweet' St James swung into view as they passed the gothic portal which adorned the junction of Parramatta Road and South George Street. But as the hero of the story pursues Betsey, he becomes scared of matrimony, and this would characterise Deniehy's own attitudes.

In *The Legend of Newtown* the hero again reflects Deniehy's sentiments. He is 'the son of the soil, generous, ardent . . . his enthusiasm made him proud of the land of his birth, jealous and sensitive of the slights too often thrown on her, and the vapid sneers which expatriated witlings find so much gratification in showering on the land that supports them, and gives them their daily bread'. The heroine in this piece is Australian too. Her features 'were exquisitely fair and regular, and her figure possessed all that sylph-like grace and fragile delicacy of the Australian female form'.

And in his verse, Deniehy projected an Australian idyll for him and his kind:

A cottage shall be mine, with porch,
Enwreath'd with ivy green,
And bright some flowers with dew-fill'd bells
'Mid brown old wattles seen.

Stenhouse's residence and library at Balmain had become a regular meeting place for Sydney radicals, and through Stenhouse Deniehy, the literary patriot, was introduced to the explorer Ludwig Leichhardt, whose heroic if not always practical character made an impression on the young man's imagination. Here was a sort of rebel, a man who did not want to serve Prussian militarists by fulfilling his state duty of conscription, but instead sought the interior of a newer, freer, less constricted place.

The other great radical venue of the time was Henry Parkes's 'toyshop' back room. There Deniehy met David Blair, a journalist on Parkes's *Empire*, to which Deniehy also contributed. 'He was clad in the style of a finished man of fashion—in fact, a perfect little dandy,' Blair wrote of Deniehy. Blair thought that some of Deniehy's writing was so good that it took the breath away—it was like meeting an ancient Roman emperor walking in broad daylight in George Street.

Deniehy's friendship with the poet Charles Harpur also began in Parkes's parlour. Like Deniehy, Harpur was the son of convicts from County Cork. Harpur had just given up schoolteaching in the country and was in Sydney for a brief visit. Along with an Irish schoolteacher named John Armstrong from Tullamore, Harpur and Deniehy decided to take over the Mechanics School of Arts, the intellectual centre in Sydney prior to the foundation of the University of Sydney in 1852. Harpur dubbed it the 'school of charlatans', and the three put together a ticket to take over the committee. The new program, once that had been achieved, involved a series of lectures by Deniehy. In his lecture on modern English poetry, he praised his friend Harpur, calling him 'the earliest of those Sons of the Morning who shall yet enlighten and dignify our home, building up as with the hands of angels the national mind'.

Henry Kendall was another Currency visitor to Henry Parkes's back room. Born in Ulladulla on the New South Wales south coast in 1839, he had sailed on a whaler at the age of sixteen and returned to Australia in March 1857 to settle in Sydney's Newtown. Kendall, too, would pursue the Australian voice, and was encouraged by another literary solicitor, JL Michael, who made Kendall a clerk at Grafton, in the beautiful Clarence Valley of northern New South Wales. He agreed with the ultimatum which Harpur had laid down for himself:

> Be then the Bard of thy country . . .
> 'Tis the cradle of liberty!—Think and decide.

Australianisms appeared in Kendall's poetry—he called the dingo the warragul, a common coastal usage at the time. The kookaburra he called 'the settlers' clock'. He was particularly annoyed by the non-Currency belief that Australian birds had no song. The magpie certainly did, and the bellbird, and with colonial pride he pushed them in his writing. He possessed a sense of care for nature—he complained that the loss of many native species of birds was due to the extinction of Aboriginal hunters in many areas, which had led to a glut in the population of the huge lizard named the goanna, an eating delicacy which the Aboriginals had kept in check.

He yearned as only a colonial can for the power to combine the Australian landscape he devoted himself to with poetic sensibility. He wanted an Australian muse to possess him.

> A lyre-bird lit in a shimmering space,
> It dazzled my eyes and I turned from the place,
> And wept in the dark for a glorious face
> And a hand with the harp of Australia.

In 1851, young Dan Deniehy was admitted as an attorney to the Supreme Court of New South Wales. He took what work he could and kept writing, and within the year married Adelaide Elizabeth Hoalls, a young woman visiting Sydney as part of a world trip with her mother. She met Deniehy at the house of the Chief Justice, Sir Alfred Stephen. Miss Hoall's father held Deniehy in absolute detestation 'as having clandestinely won the affections of a young innocent girl [his daughter] in a strange land'.

At a public meeting in the School of Arts on 16 April 1850, Lang uttered a plaint which would echo and be repeated down generations. 'You have hitherto, even in the estimation of Great Britain herself, been the tail of the world, and every brainless creature of blighted prospects and broken fortunes from England ... has been systematically placed above you even in this the land of your birth. Why, it is the rule of the service under the present regime that no native of the colony, however able, talented and meritorious he may have proved himself, can be appointed by the governor to any office under government with a salary of above £100 a year.'

Lang was a strange creature in many ways—a papism-hating Presbyterian who found his friends amongst the papists like Deniehy. He never doubted that Australians would become a great and glorious people, even though he was not native-born, and even though he had personally intervened to recruit immigrants to prevent the population being excessively Irish or containing too great a proportion of ex-convicts.

To Deniehy as to everyone else, Lang was an enigmatic friend. Deniehy was so fond of Lang's republican and other political impulses, including the dream of a federal Australia, that the man's anti-Irish-ness seemed a small blemish in the patriot whole. Deniehy himself would, after all, speaking out against Archbishop John Polding's appointment of a particular man to a school board, incur temporary excommunication and abuse from some of his fellow-Irish. So he knew the limitations of his sect and his tribe both.

HOUSE OF COLONIAL LORDS

In 1853 a Select Committee of the New South Wales Legislative Assembly applied itself to the task, as first devised by Earl Grey, of drawing up a new Constitution with a bi-cameral system. The committee was chaired by William Charles Wentworth, who, along with James Macarthur, son of the great Perturbator, and Edward Deas Thomson, envisaged a Constitution which would ensure the control of parliament by the pastoral faction.

James Macarthur saw himself as a fine aristocrat. By 1832 his famous father

John Macarthur had been consumed by his demons and declared a lunatic, living under his wife Elizabeth's care. She and his household had been his chief supporters and comforts, but now amidst other rantings he accused her of sexual and commercial infidelities. He had died in unrelieved torment at Camden Park in 1834. His son's original ambitions were similar to those of his famous father—he hoped to continue to establish the Macarthurs' freehold lands within the Limits of Location in the manner of the great British, land-accumulating noble families. At first he thought squatting unworthy of a great family, but his brother William and his older, English-born cousin Hannibal drew him into the practice from the late 1830s onwards. He was a four-square conservative, and his caution helped the family survive the depression of the early 1840s, in which Hannibal lost a great deal. But he so despaired of the potential impact of the gold discovery in Australia that he thought of giving up the land of his childhood and living in England. Over time he became the friend or at least ally of that more opportunistic conservative William Charles Wentworth, and between them they knew they must produce a Constitution which best served the pastoral ascendancy.

The committee's report provided for a lower house elected by votes of unequal value and without secret ballot, favouring rural interests, and a nominated upper house based on the House of Lords. The idea of a lower house controlled by the men of the great pastures outraged the leading merchants, and the concept of a 'lordly' upper house appalled democrats. A People's Constitution Committee was formed to protest against the proposed upper house and Deniehy was its youngest member. It held a mass meeting at the Royal Victoria Theatre, filled to overflowing, where many speakers, including Deniehy, made their protests. Deniehy rose, small and stooped, and was at first called on to speak up. He certainly did speak up, to make one of the most famous speeches in colonial history. He said that Mr Wentworth's having repented of the 'democratic escapades' of his youth had led now to high Tory sins sufficient to cancel out a century of former service. Loud cheers began, and mounted. Deniehy denounced 'those harlequin aristocrats—these Botany Bay magnificos—these Australian mandarins'. He imagined that James Macarthur would style himself the Earl of Camden and his coat of arms would be a green field with the rum keg of the New South Wales order of chivalry. 'They cannot aspire to the miserable and effete dignity of the worn-out grandees of continental Europe.' As the common water mole is in Australia transformed to the duck-billed platypus, 'in some distant emulation of this degeneracy, I suppose we are to be favoured with a bunyip aristocracy'.

'If we are to be blessed with an Australian aristocracy,' Deniehy continued, 'I would prefer it to resemble, not that of William [Wentworth] the Bastard, but of Jack the Strapper.' He concluded, 'The domineering clique which makes up the Wentworth party are not representative of the manliness, the spirit and the intelligence of the free men of New South Wales.'

The next morning, with the air still ringing from Deniehy's insults, Wentworth spoke in Macquarie Street on the second reading of his Constitution Bill. This was an older, more successful Wentworth, but still rancorous, still haunted by society's earlier and, in some cases, still existing prejudices against him and his wife Sarah, who was the daughter of a former convict blacksmith and had borne him three children out of wedlock. He admitted that purely on a population basis, Sydney should have seventeen members in the Legislative Assembly instead of the six proposed. But he insisted that as the pastoral industry produced most of the colony's wealth, it should have more representatives in parliament. He defended the hereditary element of the proposed upper house. He said such a house would be a good and stable bulwark, while lack of titles was a great blemish in the American Constitution, declaring, 'We want a British, not a Yankee Constitution.'

A few weeks later there was another constitutional protest meeting on some vacant land near Circular Quay, where Deniehy took up the challenge strongly again. He attacked Wentworth's 'claptrap' about those who opposed Wentworth's system wanting to introduce American institutions into New South Wales. The Constitution Committee did not want to transplant American institutions holus bolus, he said, but to look at them as models, 'because the United States bore more resemblance to a new colony, such as Australia, than did the old countries of Europe'. And while the small constituencies of England elected youthful aristocrats, zealous about pointers and spaniels and aspects of the game laws, so 'we in the legislature of New South Wales saw a goodly sprinkling, nay, a majority of the representatives of bullocks, bunyips, sheep and gumtrees'. Deniehy, applauded again and again, was still talking when the sun went down, preventing journalists from making further notes. The potency of his voice was enhanced by a parody he wrote on the departure of Edward Deas Thomson for two years leave in England, declaring him as being treated to the sycophancy of the pastoral crowd:

. . . a knot of hirelings, moneyed knaves and those thy hand
Hath helped to heights that better men should hold . . .

Despite his gift for oratory, Deniehy was not prospering in business—he had, wrote his friend Miss EA Martin, 'careless and reckless generosity, and the utter want of business capacity which distinguishes men of genius'. He regretted the hardships to which his wife was thus subjected, believing that if she had not married him she would have had a comfortable position in English society. But if adoration of the public and his peers could have achieved a financial dimension, he would have been rich indeed.

Charles Harpur was teaching in the Hunter Valley when he read the report of Deniehy's speech in a newspaper sent him by Stenhouse. He ecstatically devoted a poem to his friend.

Little Dan Deniehy!
Brilliant Dan Deniehy!
Dear is the light of thy spirit to me!
Dear as a streaming ray
Out from a gleaming bay
Is to some weather-worn barque from the sea.

Harpur's wife, Mary, had married him in 1850 and their first son was named Washington. He farmed in the Hunter Valley until 1859, when he was appointed a gold commissioner at Araluen in southern coastal New South Wales. There he selected a residence on the Tuross River at Eurobodalla, and established a farm and lived a stable life with Mary and their children.

Thus his future prospects proved much happier than Deniehy's, who became gradually and increasingly a victim of alcohol and short finances.

THE ROOSIANS

On 8 March 1854, Britain and France declared war on Russia—already at war with Turkey. Nominally the Crimean War was about the guardianship of Christian shrines in Jerusalem, or at least that was what the War Department told the British public. In fact it was a war to prevent Russia expanding as Turkish power declined in eastern Europe. Australia had no pressing reason to be involved, although Russia was a Pacific power. But many Australian Britons were filled with a patriotic desire to fight for the Empire. Harpur, Lang and Deniehy lambasted the war. Harpur asked, as many would ask in later wars in which Australia saw itself involved, 'What is the eastern war to thee, it's craft and folly, blame and blunder?' The cry was that this was a war undertaken to uphold one despotism against another. The Australian supporters of the war projected a Russian invasion of Australia. A Russian naval vessel was said to be at loose in the Pacific. A patriotic meeting was held at John Malcolm's Sydney Circus, a popular venue even for meetings, in May 1854. Sir William Denison, the lieutenant-governor of Van Diemen's Land, declared that 'England is not fond of engaging in wanton wars, but when once embarked on a just war, there are no consequences which the country is not prepared to meet.' Henry Parkes spoke on behalf of a cause he believed to be so national and so great as to require Australian participation. Dean McEncroe said on behalf of the Catholic community that he hoped no invidious distinctions would be made with regard to the widows and orphans of Roman Catholic soldiers. He was sure that their blood would not be the least copious on the fields of Alma and Inkerman. Daniel Cooper, a former convict and rich merchant, subscribed £1000 to the war fund. With three cheers for Lord Raglan, the British commander-in-chief, and three groans for Tsar Nicholas, the meeting ended.

This was a question on which Deniehy and Parkes parted ways. 'He is rather too fond of "his Queen and his country",' Deniehy was suddenly writing, 'and a good deal too much in the habit of acquainting the public with this fondness.' He declared that 'Mr Parkes has too much, not of the English man in him, but of "Englishmanism" about him . . . the distinction is subtle. I fear his career as a senator will be a very curious one.' Such is the spirit of 'number one' [self-interest], said Deniehy, which ran through even 'the best of your imported men'. Dr Lang, though, was a solitary adherent to principle, who towered over the neighbouring attitudes like a cathedral spire. Whatever Englishmanisms was— and Deniehy saw it and disapproved of it as the inclusion of British imperial identity within the Australian one—it was the more common of the brands of Australian sense of nationality prevailing at the time.

The government announced its intention to send an officer to Goulburn to drill the Goulburn Yeomanry Cavalry Corps, and Deniehy wrote a letter to the *Goulburn Herald*, signing it 'Harold Flupsy Buffles', the name of the supposed officer involved, which declared, 'I can only say that if that Roosian "Ketchikoff" does land, I only hope he may try travelling upon the Goulburn Road. I have a notion that he would undoubtedly regret such a step.'

A number of plans were put in place to defend Sydney Harbour, Robert Towns suggesting a barrier composed of the hulls of vessels connected by chains, which could be sunk in a few minutes on a gun signal. The Attorney-General unsuccessfully suggested taxing the people of New South Wales £100 000 a year towards the expenses of war, and Deniehy denounced that idea as 'the most iniquitous . . . to be found in the whole history of colonial policy, teeming as it is with injustice, wickedness, and crime'.

CHAPTER 32

POLICE STATE?

The conservative fear that the more men sought gold, the more the goldfields would be scenes of blood and brawls and riots initially had proved unfounded. Even James Macarthur had begun to understand this by the end of 1851. Instead, gold was raising prices, property values, rents and incomes so high that the £10 voting franchise threshold would soon be easily reached by ordinary men. Samuel Sydney, an English publicist of immigration, wrote an 1852 manual for potential immigrants, entitled *Three Colonies of Australia*. Gold, he told his readers, had transformed Australia from a mere 'sheep walk tended by nomadic burglars' into the 'wealthiest offset of the British Crown—a land of promise for the adventurous—a home of peace and independence for the industrious—an El Dorado and an Arcadia combined'.

Riches and independence may well have been within the grasp of some lucky diggers, and the merchants who benefited from their largesse. But those left at home were not so enamoured with gold. Janet Kincaid wrote from Greenock in Scotland to her husband in the Victorian gold town of Maryborough complaining that he had embraced the independence of the gold-seeking life to the neglect of his family. 'You left the ship to better *yourself* and to get your *own money* to your *self*. You never cared much for your family, far less for your wife. You sent £5 two years and a half ago. Would £5 keep you since you left the ship?' He was, she said, a hard-hearted father who could sit down and eat up his children's meat. 'Let me know what you intend to do for the boys. We are still in the same house, 15 West Stuart Street, *where you left us*.'

An American digger received a letter from a female friend in California. 'Oh Chandler, did we not pass many happy hours together? I thought what a pleasant home you had and kind parents. With everything else that one could wish to make you happy and yet you left them all for *gold!* Oh Chandler, I hope you may be blessed with good health and get enough to pay you for the sacrifice you made in going.'

Indefatigable Caroline Chisholm, the Catholic promoter of female and then family immigration, also ran a personal family reunion program for the goldfields: 'I have promised parents to go in search of their children—I have promised wives to make enquiries of their husbands—I have promised sisters to seek their brothers, and friends to look for friends.' Chisholm was aware of how hostile gold rushes could be to the interests of women, not only those in foreign parts. Destitution and desertion were the lot of many colonial women too.

Frances Perry, wife of the Anglican bishop of Melbourne, was attracted to camp life when she and her husband visited the government compound on the goldfields. 'Life in the Camp is most amusing, and was quite a novelty to me. There is a large mess I can attend, where the commissioners, military officers, superintendent of police, etc. etc. take their meals, the Chief Commissioner presiding.' She was in no doubt that waves of resentment from the encircling miners broke against the ramparts of the Camp, in country another woman described as resembling 'one vast cemetery with fresh made graves'.

Jane Prendergast, a woman stuck on the fields with her husband, wrote to her father-in-law in 1853. 'On one point certain which I will never agree, he likes this country and I do not; I can understand the gentlemen liking it, their lives are so very free and independent, so much the reverse of the strength that society imposes upon them in England, but no ladies like it: the fortunes of their families and a wish to get some gold out of the land of gold have brought them here, and necessity obliges them to remain.'

Gavan Duffy, a much-tried Irish seditionist but by the 1850s a coming statesman who would ultimately be premier of Victoria, observed that the income of the gold seeker was not so great in the long run when compared with that of ordinary pursuits. 'But the employment had the unmistakeable charm of not being a servile one.' After all, said Duffy, 'It is a blessed land, seamed with gold, fanned with healthy breezes, and bathed in a transparent atmosphere like the landscapes of Guido.' This was a generation which had not been raised, as later Australians were, to see the threat of the landscape, the threadbare nature of the agricultural possibilities, or the deserts at the centre of the continent.

Nor was Raffaello Carboni, one of the many to raise the issue of land on the goldfields, deterred by Australia's shortcomings. From a tree-stump rostrum, Carboni told a meeting of miners at Ballarat in November 1854, 'I have a dream, a happy dream. I dream that we had met here together to render to Our Father in heaven for a plentiful harvest, such that for the first time in this, our adopted land, we have our own food for the year; and so each of us holding in our hands a tumbler of Victorian wine, you called on me for a song. My harp was tuned and in good order: I cheerfully struck up, "O Let Us Be Happy Together". Not so, Britons, not so! We must meet as in old Europe . . . for the redress of grievances inflicted on us, not by Crown heads, but by blockheads, aristocratical incapables, who never did a day's work in their lives.'

A sense of freedom and male independence characterised even the diggers' entertainments when they went into Melbourne.

The audiences for the concerts at Melbourne's Salle de Valentino and Black's Concert Room were almost exclusively male, though prostitutes, of course, broke the male solitude. Even the gaoler at Melbourne Gaol, John Castieau, described his own largely male social life as being to 'lounge about, drink, look at the whores, fool away my money at their homes, by paying for drink'.

But land would give them families, said city progressives, and turn them into citizens.

Nonetheless, Governor Charles Hotham was still edgy about law and order. He had a tendency of courting the miners while remaining clearly authoritarian. And in spite of broad popular opinion against mining licences, he would not abandon them. He regarded some of the speeches reported from the goldfields as akin to the Chartist assemblies, and the speeches and marches made in England in 1848, that year of revolution across Europe. RL Milne, a former soldier, wrote that nothing but moral supervision would 'save Australia from the gambling, stilettoing, vile abominations and desecrated Sabbaths of an assassinating Italy, infidel France, and republican America'.

In fact, 1848, the year of European revolutions, was coming their way, just a little delayed.

*

The police took on a function more akin to that of the Royal Irish Constabulary, attending and reporting on goldfields meetings, infiltrating diggers' groups and keeping a firm authoritarian grip on mining society. The goldfields essentially became a police state. By mid 1854, with 1639 men in the police force, Victoria was more strongly policed than California. Castlemaine had one police officer for every 46 residents. By comparison, San Francisco, a city with a population of 34 000 in 1852, had a police force that never exceeded eighty men, and was often only around thirty (though 'vigilance committees' with plentiful rope took up the slack).

The pay of police was increased, military pensioners were brought from Van Diemen's Land, and fifty London Metropolitan policemen were recruited. There was a special mounted cadet corps for gentlemen recruits. A number of respectable young men who were stranded in Melbourne by the gold rush joined up.

As the Miners' Reform League called 'Monster Meetings' to protest at police tyranny and to appeal to Governor Hotham, diggers were subjected to little daily dramas of arrest, corrupted evidence and a sequence of protection for police favourites and beatings and chainings for honest men.

By late 1854, meetings were being called on the goldfields every few days, which panicked the Gold Commissioner, Rede, and the Commissioner of Police—in a short period of October Catholic miners held a meeting; the next day a protest was held over the imprisonment of the two diggers arrested for the burning of Bentley's hotel; and two days later there was to be a meeting of the 'Tipperary Mob', that is, men from that Irish county. The police and soldiers at the Camp hoped that a promised detachment of the 12th Regiment would arrive before that meeting, and Rede was beginning to feel that the place could be defended only by cannon. Rede was determined to bring it all to a fight, however, if he could get the personnel in the Camp reinforced, and so it seemed, while ever the miners presumed to strike attitudes, did Hotham. In Ballarat there was an attempt by the authorities to sign up special constables amongst 'all loyal and respectable inhabitants of the goldfields'. Only three citizens presented themselves. On 19 October, more foot police arrived and then, within a few days, Captain White arrived with a detachment of the 40th Regiment. A number of diggers and other people, especially those with families, pulled out and left for Cressley's Creek, where the diggers were said to be bottoming out at 5.5 metres, 3.7 metres less than at Ballarat, with 8 ounces (226 grams) of gold. Two thousand people vanished from Ballarat.

Rede was planning further arrests and was organising the Camp to take action. Tents which obstructed its line of fire were simply pulled down, houses inside the walls were protected by piled-up bags of grain, loopholes cut in the walls, and barrels full of water placed to extinguish fires. All these preparations were to be made in silence, said Rede. He seemed confident of his power and arrested Henry Westbury, nicknamed Yorkey, a man who had been observed to have struck Bentley's hotel with his fists.

On 30 October, Hotham decided to dampen unrest by setting up a Board of Enquiry. The Board tried to get the *Ballarat Times* to give widespread publicity to its arrival on the goldfields, but the editor, Henry Seekamp, refused to do so. Carboni called him 'a short, thick, rare sort of man' with a hatred of humbug and 'yabber-yabber'. He had bought out the *Ballarat Times* and married a Dublin widow, Clara du Val, the leading actress in the Camden Theatre on the Gravel Pits, in December 1854. He had served on the Committee of the National Schools and had recently called a meeting to found a hospital for sick and destitute diggers. In early October, before Scobie was murdered, he had said that the Camp would have to behave with more courtesy, but even so he told Hotham in a letter, 'The corruption of every Department connected with the Government in Ballarat is become so notorious and so bare-faced that public indignation is thoroughly aroused; and though the expression of public feeling be for a time in abeyance, on account of the numerous armed mercenaries lately sent up from town, the fire of indignation is not extinguished; it still smoulders, only to burst forth again with unabashed and unabateable vigour . . . It is not fines, imprisonment, taxation and bayonets that is required to keep people tranquil and content. It is an attention to their wants and their just rights alone that will make the miners content, and that they must have, sooner or later, either given to them soon with a good will, or taken by them later with no will but their own.' Seekamp's advice was dismissed by the governor.

The honest Chartist bookseller, John Humffray, argued that those who did not now complain to the Committee of Enquiry had only themselves to blame, but the miners had no confidence in the committee. So the board left Ballarat satisfied that, with two exceptions—those of Magistrate D'Ewes and Sergeant Major Milne—the conduct of all in the Camp had been excellent. There had been a chorus of contempt and complaint against D'Ewes and Milne from publicans to storekeepers. The committee went back to Melbourne sure that the removal of the two men would be enough to pacify the goldfields. They also recommended a more equitable manner of deciding disputed claims and a decentralisation of the police, so that they could hunt for licences on their own initiative, and thus be more flexible. They also reported that the system was 'a great source of irritation', and that its abolition would bring only good. They advised Hotham both to listen to the diggers but also to overpower by stern means 'every attempt on the part of the populace to take the law into their own hands'.

The evidence the committee considered had come from only sixteen diggers, sixteen publicans and storekeepers, fifteen Camp officials and eight professional men. One of the non-British diggers who gave evidence, the German Frederick Vern, said that others would have come forward if they had had any confidence in the government.

The home of the 'Tipperary Mob', Eureka was removed physically from the Camp and had its own generally respected policemen, its priests and its pubs. After the burning of the Eureka Hotel, there were still other hotels, notably the Free Trade, to help assuage the thirst of diggers, together with sly grog tents and shanties. Those with independent capital, like Peter Lalor, were secure in their endeavours, but diggers who had not yet made it rich were at the mercy of storekeepers or small entrepreneurs who backed them. Carboni depicted Ballarat as a 'nuggetty El Dorado for a few, a ruinous field of hard labour for many, a profound ditch of sedition for body and soul to all'. And yet the gold finds were increasing. And the population was increasing despite those who left to escape the attentions of the Camp, including the continual licence hunts.

Meanwhile a jury in Melbourne had found three diggers guilty of burning down the Eureka Hotel. But the jury also made a statement: 'The jury feels, in returning a verdict against the prisoners at the bar, that in all probability they would never have had that fateful duty to perform if those trusted with government at Ballarat had done theirs properly.' The judge also took the chance to address the diggers at Ballarat, telling them that 'the eyes of the law are upon them, and, if necessary, they will be brought to justice'.

On 11 November 1854, the Ballarat Reform League was officially launched on Bakery Hill above Eureka in the presence of 10 000 miners and their wives and children. Anastasia Hayes, for example, Irishwoman, future creator of a miners' flag, was there, babe in arms. It was a Saturday afternoon. The meeting had begun in a large tent, where Dr Carr made a speech on equal representation in parliament and the unlocking of the land. The meeting then moved outside onto the hill where John Humffray, the fiery Scot Thomas Kennedy, and Frederick Vern, the German, addressed the crowd. Humffray was elected president of the league, and a number of motions were passed, the meeting noting that the people of the goldfields had been provoked 'beyond the bounds of human endurance'.

The assembly called on the governor 'to introduce the inalienable right of every citizen to have a voice in making the laws [they were] called upon to obey', declaring that 'taxation without representation is tyranny'. The meeting further determined 'That, being as the people have been hitherto, unrepresented in the Legislative Council of the Colony of Victoria, they have been tyrannised over, and it had become their duty as well as interest to resist, and if necessary to remove the irresponsible power which so tyrannises over them.' According to the meeting, 'this colony has hitherto been governed by paid officials, under the false assumption that law is greater than justice because, forsooth, it was made by them and their friends, and admirably suits their selfish ends and narrow-minded views.' It was not, however, 'the wish of the League to effect an immediate separation of this Colony from the parent country, if the equal laws and equal rights are dealt out to the whole free community. But . . . if Queen Victoria continues to act upon the ill-advice of dishonest ministers and wage obnoxious wars with the colony under the assumed authority of the Royal Prerogative, the Reform League will endeavour to supersede such Royal Prerogative by asserting that of the people which is the most royal of all prerogatives, as the people are the only legitimate source of all political power.'

The folk at the meeting then made a number of Chartist demands concerning universal suffrage, regular parliament, payment of members and so on. The immediate object of the Reform League was stated to be a change in the management of the goldfields by disbanding the commissioners and totally abolishing the diggers and storekeepers' licence tax.

Henry Seekamp was at the meeting, and wrote in the *Ballarat Times* that the formation of the League was 'not more or less than the germ of Australian independence'. The League, said Seekamp, would eventually become an 'Australian Congress'. Karl Marx would read of these matters in 28 Dean Street, Soho, in his two-roomed apartment. Engels had once told him Australia was the United States of 'murderers, burglars, ravagers and pickpockets'. But Marx looked at Ballarat as a symptom of a 'general revolutionary movement in the colony of Victoria'. He was sure it would be quickly suppressed.

In Melbourne on 27 November, George Black, editor of the *Diggers' Advocate*, and Thomas Kennedy presented themselves to a rather harassed Governor Hotham in Toorak with the resolutions. Hotham was an assiduous, incorruptible and rather stiff man, but not lacking in warmth. He had already ordered that the hated magistrate D'Ewes be sacked and his name erased from the Commission of Police. (As a lost soul of Empire he would ultimately suicide in Paris.) The much complained of Sergeant Major Milne's career was ended as well. Hotham was preoccupied with cutting the public service, and bravely trying to deal with corruption which had arisen under La Trobe. But his overriding concern was revenue, and for that he looked, not to the squatters with their vast land holdings, but to the miners and their licence fees. What did the miners expect? he must have privately asked himself. His deficit for 1854, so his auditors told him, was £2 226 616.

Black and Kennedy, on behalf of the League, also demanded the release of Fletcher, McIntyre and Yorkey, the men sentenced over the Eureka Hotel fire. His Excellency went into a fit of rage at the word 'demand'. The decision of the jury had to stand, said Hotham. He would not upset a verdict, though he could pardon the men if that was appropriate. But, 'I must make my stand on the word "demand". I'm sorry for it, but that is the position you place me in.' Kennedy thought the word 'demand' could be rescinded, and solemnly implored Hotham to consider the matter, if for no other reason than to keep back 'the spilling of blood which must be the case with infuriated men—let us have peace even if inconsistent with the dignity of the British Crown'.

Hotham listened to them but then, after they had gone, wrote the notation 'Put away' on the documents they had left him. This may well have been a synonym for 'File', but the phrase had a symbolic eloquence. Hotham would have loved to put it all away.

CHAPTER 33

THE BATTLE

Major General Sir Robert Nickle, Commander in Chief of troops in Australia, based since August 1854 in Melbourne, was a man approaching seventy. He had fought in his youth against Croppies in the Irish uprising of 1798 and Americans in 1815. He sympathised with the miners' cause, but was told by Governor Hotham to reinforce the Camp and to put his protégé Captain Thomas of the 40th Regiment in charge. The Camp was swollen to overflowing with almost five hundred armed men enclosed in its cramped spaces. At the Camp on the evening of 28 November, the day after the meeting with Hotham, the promised detachment of the 12th Regiment arrived carrying a wounded drummer boy, winged by a miner on Eureka as the detachment marched towards Ballarat on the Melbourne Road. After the young murdered Scobie, the drummer was the second victim of Eureka.

On Thursday, 30 November, Raffaello Carboni, who had been working from an early hour, went to his tent at 10 a.m. for a rest. He wanted to sign off on his letter to his friend, a WH Archer, in Melbourne, whom he begged to use his influence with the governor. (This a pious rather than realistic hope.) 'Just on my preparing to go and post this letter, we are worried by the usual Irish cry, to run to Gravel-pits. The traps [police] are out for licences, and playing hell with the diggers. If that be the case, I am not inclined to give half-a-crown for the whole fixtures at the Camp.' The time of resistance had come. At Bakery Hill, Carboni found Peter Lalor up on the stump, his rifle in his hand, calling on volunteers to fall into ranks. According to Carboni, Lalor took him by the hand and said, 'I want you, Signore: help these gentlemen (pointing to old acquaintances of ours, foreigners), that if they cannot provide themselves with fire-arms, let each of them procure a piece of steel, five or six inches long, attached to a pole, and that will pierce the tyrants' hearts.'

All the diggers fell in file two abreast and marched from Bakery Hill to Eureka. 'Captain Ross of Toronto was our standard-bearer. He hoisted down the Southern Cross from the flag-staff, and headed the march.' The Southern Cross flag had been run up by Anastasia Hayes and other women out of sheets. Its design was a white cross with the stars of the Southern Cross constellation at the end of the arms of the cross and one at the intersection in the middle, all on a field of blue. The Irishman Patrick Curtain, the chosen captain of the pike men, swapped his iron pike for Carboni's sword. 'We reached the hill where was my tent. How little did we know that some of the best among us had reached the place of their grave! Lalor gave the proper orders to defend ourselves among the holes in case the hunt should be attempted in our quarters.'

It seems that having marched to Eureka many of the miners then dispersed to their tents throughout the area. At the Gravel Pits close to Eureka, men held small, impromptu meetings and many still carried any arms, pikes or rifles, they possessed. Commissioner Rede advanced out of the Camp, supported by a skirmishing line of infantry and cavalry, to attempt to disperse them.

He had great trouble reading the Riot Act, partly because his horse kept rearing. A few shots were fired by both sides. Eight diggers were captured and taken to the Camp. Rede met Humffray in his role of pacifist but engaged observer, and admonished him: 'See now the consequences of your agitation?' Humffray responded, 'No, but see the consequences of impolitic coercion.'

That afternoon, a meeting of captains and interested parties occurred in a store run by Martin and Ann Diamond, and Carboni described black bottles and glasses being put on the tables to make it look like a social occasion. Amongst the others there was the young Prussian Edward Thonen, a little sliver of a man with intense eyes who sold lemonade to the diggers and was a brilliant chess player. The Irish were led by Timothy Hayes, Anastasia's husband, the tall well-built Irishman of liberal mind 'and, above all, of a kind heart, and that covers a multitude of sins'. John Manning, a bald-headed Irishman, about forty years of age, who had come young to the colony and had passed hard days, a self-educated man given somewhat to drinking, was there. Then long-legged Frederick Vern—from Hanover, and well-meaning Peter Lalor, the Irishman with a history, a man of some thirty-five years. There were two other 'John Bullish fellows', who took up the cause of the miners mainly because their sly grog was flagging, so Carboni believed.

Lalor, despite disclaiming any knowledge of military matters and recording his disappointment that Humffray was no longer their leader, declared: 'If you appoint me your Commander in Chief, I shall not shrink; I mean to do my duty as a man. I tell you, gentlemen, if once I pledge my hand to the diggers, I will neither defile it with treachery, nor render it contemptible by cowardice.'

Vern pointed out that he could provide a German rifle brigade of 500 men and felt that he could be an appropriate chieftain. But Carboni felt that a Briton, even an Irishman, should be in charge. Peter Lalor was elected by show of hands or as Carboni says, unanimous acclamation. All hands now fell to to make some improvised fortifications of slabs of timber, reinforced with rough earth work. There were a few stores laid by, and diggers camped in huts within the newly constructed stockade. The ruins of Bentley's hotel lay a few hundred metres away. Drilling went on throughout the rest of the evening while Henry Goodenough, police constable and agent provocateur, went around urging the miners to make an immediate attack on the Camp.

The stockade was the scene of another meeting at sunset. The Southern Cross was raised with Captain Ross, sword in hand, and his division standing beneath it—the matter of an instant but a moment which would never fail to inspire Australia. Lalor, rifle in his left hand, mounted the stump again and asked all to leave who were not prepared to swear an oath. The men fell in in their divisions around the flagstaff, led by their captains, who saluted Lalor. Yet of the thousand who had marched to Eureka, only half that number took the oath. Lalor knelt, bare-headed, and with his right hand pointed upwards. The oath of the Southern Cross flag was sworn on that late afternoon of Thursday 30 November by men who in large numbers still felt fealty to Britain. 'We swear by the Southern Cross,' went the oath as enunciated by Lalor, 'to stand truly by each other, and fight to defend our right to liberties.'

The five hundred oath-takers shouted 'Amen'. The Camp was on alert all night for an attack. It did not understand that the diggers' actions were intended to be defensive. Parties of miners and sympathisers had left the stockade to collect arms and provisions for which receipts were to be issued. Everyone was under orders to respect property. Sentries were posted between Eureka and the Camp. But there was a cost to the diggers' resistance in that their mineshafts were gradually filling with water. A deputation was sent to Rede. As long as the commissioner would give an assurance not to reinstate licence hunts, and to release the eight prisoners he held, the diggers would lay down their arms and return to work. Carboni, George Black of the *Diggers' Advocate* and Father Smyth were elected to take this message.

It had been raining that night and men would be glad to get back to their pits to bale them out if possible. When the delegation reached the bridge over the Yarrowee, the police intervened, but an inspector eventually took them to Rede, who came out from the Camp to meet them as he thought it prudent not to permit them to enter and see his fortifications.

'The deputation,' wrote Carboni, was at last 'before King Rede, whose shadow by moonlight, as he held his arm *à la Napoleon*, actually inspired me with reverence; but behold! Only a marionette is before us. Each of his words, each of his movements was the vibration of the telegraphic wires directed from Toorak [where Governor Hotham resided]. He had not a wicked heart; some knew him for his benevolence, and he helped many an honest digger out of trouble . . . I would willingly turn burglar to get hold of the whole of the correspondence between him and Toorak.'

They turned back on the road to Eureka and found miners anxious to hear from them. Carboni's opinion was that Rede would be out riding and hunting licence defaulters by the next day. Father Smyth made a further appeal to Rede later in the night, but found him more recalcitrant than he had been a few hours earlier. The priest said he would return to Eureka and have all the diggers back at work in the morning if the commissioner would tell him when he intended to go licence-hunting again. Rede refused to do this.

The next day, Friday, drilling of rebels continued at the stockade. Men who had gone back to their own tents to sleep turned up again for that. In solidarity, ten thousand diggers did not return to their work that day even though it was chiefly the five hundred oath-takers who were drilling in Eureka. On that Friday afternoon a 300- to 400-strong contingent of miners arrived from the goldfields at Creswick, some twenty kilometres away, but they were unarmed, unprovisioned and exhausted.

The same day, Major General Sir Robert Nickle started out from Melbourne with considerable reinforcements for the Camp, including marines from HMS

Electra, 600 further men of the 12th and 14th Regiments, and four pieces of field artillery. This was practically all that was left of the armed forces in Victoria.

To the shame of Lalor and Carboni, many gangs of Vandemonians went out seizing goods on behalf of the diggers. At the Star Hotel on the main road, another, more radical, committee had its headquarters, and called now, under a document drawn up by Alfred Black, for a 'Declaration of Independence'. Lalor and Carboni thought this talk suicidal—'hallucinated yabber-yabber'. Vern was initially party to it, but was brought back to the Eureka fold by Lalor's need for military advice. At the stockade, a German blacksmith was producing pikes 'as fast as his big strong arms allowed him; praising the while his past valour in the wars with Mexico, and swearing that his pikes would fix redcoats and blue pissants especially'.

The morning of Saturday 2 December saw a repeat of Friday with the men returning from their own quarters to the stockade. Lalor gave Father Smyth permission to speak to the Catholics, and he expressed to them his grave concern, knowing that a well-armed force he estimated at seven to eight hundred men occupied the Camp and that more were on their way. He asked them to attend mass the following morning, but when they were unable to guarantee that, the priest went away, saddened.

When by Saturday afternoon no licence hunt had occurred, the defenders of the stockade were so unfitted for military reality that they decided they would not be troubled again until Monday. The diggers went off to eat at noon and the stockade was almost deserted. They had already planned a meeting of the Reform League, to be held at two o'clock on Sunday at the Adelphi Theatre.

'I took notice of this very circumstance [the bareness of the population of the stockade] from my tent,' wrote Carboni, who had military experience, 'the second from the stockade, on the hill, west, whilst frying a bit of steak on the fire of my tent chimney, facing said stockade: Manning was peeling an onion.'

About four o'clock that afternoon, however, there were 1500 men in and around the stockade and James McGill, the captain of the Independent Californian Rangers, whom Carboni had earlier dismissed as a poseur, arrived with his men. The Americans had stayed fairly aloof till now. A few Americans had joined the oath-takers as individuals, but this was the first American company to join Lalor's men. McGill was appointed second-in-command to Lalor. The password into the stockade for Saturday evening was the name of both the old Irish and newer colonial battlefield—'Vinegar Hill'.

McGill rode out that night to set up a series of outposts to prevent the surprise arrival of reinforcements for the Camp from Melbourne. Lalor retired at midnight without appointing any second-in-command in McGill's absence. By then only about 120 diggers remained in the stockade.

In fact the Camp was ready for an attack. Fireballs had been prepared to throw on the houses to rob the diggers of vantage points. Rede had a notice put up ordering all lights in tents near the Camp to be doused by 8 p.m. and no firearms to be discharged. Offenders would be shot by the sentries. His information was that there were six companies formed at Eureka—one French, one composed of Swedish and Germans, one American and the others made up of Irishmen and Vandemonians. He had no overall sense of their number, but he believed they were 'determined men and the greatest guns in the Colony'.

Sometime during the night he heard from a spy that the stockade was almost deserted and that the Americans had wandered off on a mission of McGill's devising. The commissioner held a night council with Captain Thomas and others. Since Nickle was on his way from Melbourne, it was up to Thomas and his troops if they wished to make a pre-emptive move before the meeting of the Reform League at the Adelphi that afternoon. An approach to the stockade was planned that would not alert the men sleeping in it.

At about 2.30 a.m., 182 mounted and foot soldiers and 94 police were quietly and suddenly ordered to fall in. Thomas gave them their instructions and issued them with rum. The stockade was to be attacked, and the ambiguous order was that only those who 'ceased to resist' would be spared. The important thing was to get close to the stockade and thus confine the battle within it, rather than the holed ground the miners knew well. The Camp party set out at 3.30 a.m. past the Free Trade Hotel, the first glimmer of dawn showing beyond the hills named Buninyong and Warrenheip.

The attacking force quietly approached the stockade from the north, at its rear attended by three magistrates, to read the Riot Act if necessary. Henry de Longville, a digger, saw them approaching and fired a signal. Frederick Vern called, 'Here they are coming, boys: now I will lead you to death or victory!' There was some panic amongst the diggers. Few of them knew what to do in a real fight, and of course the soldiers and police did. Carboni was stuck nearby in his tent. But Lalor reacted quickly and prepared a knot of men around him to make a defensive stand. He kept cool, and told his men not to fire until the police and soldiers were close. The slaughter of miners had already begun on the edges of the stockade, and it was obvious that surrender was not a choice. The first returning fire of the diggers caused the troops to pause. Captain Wise fell wounded, but soldiers and police poured in upon the diggers. Under the leadership of Patrick Curtain, the pike men fought wildly. Only a handful in Curtain's group would survive.

Shots sang past Carboni's tent and penetrated his chimney. 'The shepherds' holes inside the lower part of the stockade had been turned into rifle pits and were now occupied by Californians of the IC Rangers' Brigade, some twenty or thirty in all . . . Ross and his division northward, Thonen and his division southward, and both in front of the valley, under the cover of the slabs, answered with such a smart fire, that the military who were now fully within range did unmistakeably appear to be swerved from their ground . . .'

Inevitably, the troops soon breached the flimsy rampart, and the cavalry started striking down those who tried to escape. Thonen, the lemonade seller, was killed when he was shot in the mouth. Captain Ross, the Canadian, had taken up a position at the foot of the Southern Cross flagpole but was lying mortally wounded in the groin when a constable hauled it down.

There was a spate of hand-to-hand fighting, and then the engagement ended. Three privates were dead, and Captain Wise was dying. The police had contributed little to the battle but now were guilty of atrocities against the wounded. The police also attacked the homes and tents of diggers, and harried any wives and children stuck inside the stockade. A digger, shot through the thighs, was fallen upon by three soldiers, one of whom knelt upon him while another tried to choke him and a third went through his pockets for money. A miner from Creswick, Henry Powell, appeared outside his tent well away from the stockade and mounted police struck him with a sword to the head, fired at him and rode over him several times. Another incongruous victim was the correspondent of the *Melbourne Morning Herald*. He was stopped by a mounted policeman three hundred metres from the stockade and shot through the chest. AW Crowe, an advocate of moral force, witnessed the killing of two Italians, neither of whom had taken any part in the uprising. One of these Italians had his tent on Specimen Hill, also three hundred metres from the stockade. The other had a tent in the stockade but had not joined in the battle. He was shot, and as he lay wounded, his gold was taken and then he was bayoneted to death. Of the wounded, Carboni wrote, 'What a horrible sight! Old acquaintances crippled with shots, the gore protruding from bayonet wounds, their clothes and flesh burning all the while. Poor Thonen had his mouth literally choked with bullets; my mate Eddie More, stretched on the ground, both his sides shot, asking for a drop of water. Peter Lalor, who had been concealed under a heap of slabs, was in the agony of death, a stream of blood from under the slabs heavily forcing its way downhill.'

Carboni went to fetch water. 'On my reaching the stockade with a pannikin of water for Teddy, I was amazed at the apathy showed by the diggers, who now crowded from all directions round the dead and wounded. None would stir a finger . . . The valorous who had now given such a proof of their ardour in smothering with stones, batons, and broken bottles the 12th Regiment on their orderly way from Melbourne on Tuesday, November 28, at the same identical spot on the Eureka, now allowed themselves to be chained by dozens, by a handful of hated traps.'

The dragoons, swords in hand, rifles cocked, brought them in chains to the lock-up in the Camp. Comissioner Rede wrote a notice: 'Her Majesty's forces were this morning fired upon by a large body of evil-disposed persons of various nations, who had entrenched themselves in the stockade on the Eureka, and some officers and men killed. Several of the rioters have paid the penalty of their crime, and a large number are in custody. All well-disposed persons are requested to return to their ordinary occupations.'

Lalor estimated there were 34 digger casualties, of whom 22 died, and said that the unusual proportion of the killed to the wounded was 'owing to the butchery of the military and troopers after the surrender'. Carboni, with his red hair and previous prominence in the movement, was not in the stockade during the engagement, but he was arrested by Sub-Inspector Carter soon after. Ironically, he was safe until he was released by Captain Thomas. As he walked away from his arrest that morning, a trooper fired his carbine at him. The shot struck the brim of his cabbage-tree hat.

Carboni was then called on by the physician Dr Carr to give assistance with the wounded at the nearby London Hotel. He was sent to procure some stretchers and to fetch Carr's box of surgical instruments from the hospital on Pennyweight Hill, six kilometres away. He returned with the instruments and another surgeon, Dr Glendinning. Re-entering the stockade, a friend of his from Canadian Gully took Carboni warmly by the hand and said, 'Old fella, I'm glad to see you alive, everyone thinks (pointing to a dead digger among the heap) that's poor Great Works!'

At about 8.30 a.m. Carboni was attending an American digger who had six gunshot wounds to his body when Henry Goodenough, a trooper and spy who knew the Italian well, burst in the door of the London Hotel. Goodenough arrested Carboni at pistol point. He was taken outside and chained to a dozen more prisoners and found himself marched into the Camp where he was stripped of his clothing, kicked, knocked down and thrown naked and senseless into the suffocating lock-up. He passed into a state of delirium. In the small hours of Monday, Rede had the prisoners removed to the storehouse, which was more commodious and better ventilated.

On Monday morning, Governor Hotham met with the Executive Council, and they jointly decided to proclaim martial law in and around Ballarat, though they were cautious enough to order that no death sentences be carried out without Hotham's express consent.

CHAPTER 34

THE AFTERMATH

The afternoon of Sunday 3 December, after the battle, Peter Lalor spent hiding at Warrenheip, but that evening or next morning, he walked into Ballarat, suffering greatly from his wounds. He sheltered for a while in the tent of a friend, Stephen Cummins, until it became clear that he was going to die without medical help. A desperate Cummins approached Father Smyth, who told him to get Lalor to the presbytery. Once darkness had fallen, Cummins managed to move Lalor across the gully to the priest's house where medical assistance was waiting. The two doctors fetched by Smyth, Doyle and Stewart, decided that amputation of Lalor's arm was an immediate necessity. They performed their task in the presbytery with the priest, Anastasia Hayes and Mrs Cummins present to assist. It is part of Lalor's legend that as he came to his senses during his period under ether, he cried, 'Courage! Courage! Take it off!'

Some days later Lalor was moved from the presbytery to the home of Michael Hayes, Timothy's brother, from where, after a few weeks, he was taken by dray to Geelong, to the house of his fiancée, Elysia Dunn. A reward of £200 had been offered for his apprehension.

There was a hunt on not only for Lalor but for George Black and Frederick Vern as well. But none of the rewards were paid. No one came forward. Vern was sheltered by various diggers and wrote blustering letters to the newspaper. Black was similarly saved from those searching for him.

On Monday morning, 4 December, Henry Seekamp, the editor of the *Ballarat Times* was arrested and joined the rebels in the Camp storeroom, where Timothy Hayes, John Manning and Carboni, among others, were still prisoners. Only about one-third of the 114 captives were Irish and only eleven were 'foreigners', that is, German, Spanish or Italian, which made it hard to pass off the uprising as an Irish–foreign plot. Yet, 'The insurgents are principally Foreigners,' Hotham told William Denison, lieutentant–governor of Van Diemen's Land, in a letter written the day after the battle. Nickle's view, in commemorating the death of Captain Wise, was that the Eureka Stockade was a place 'which a numerous band of foreign anarchists . . . had converted into a stronghold'.

When the prisoners were paraded that morning in the Camp, an Irish prisoner asked the others, 'Where do you read in history that the British lion was ever merciful to a fallen foe?' The prisoners believed that a mass grave was being dug, and even feared they might be buried alive.

John Dunmore Lang summed up a lot of public opinion in a letter to Henry Parkes's *Empire*. He was a former member of the Legislative Council at Port Phillip (even though he lived in New South Wales) and had travelled widely throughout Victoria. His was the normal democratic cry that government officials and government nominees and squatters had blotted out the voice of the people. 'There had not been a more incapable, a more extravagant, a more unprincipled or a more unjust and oppressive government in Christendom.' An *Age* editorial chimed in: 'Let the Government be undeceived. There are not a dozen respectable citizens in Melbourne who do not entertain an indignant feeling against its weakness, its folly and its last crowning error . . . they do not sympathise with injustice and coercion.'

A crowd of people was assembled in Swanston Street in Melbourne by the mayor and asked to show fealty to the Union Jack over the Southern Cross, but refused to do so. On Wednesday, 6 December, 6000 people who gathered outside St Paul's refused to support the government because to do so would betray 'the interests of liberty'. The countryside was full of similar meetings demanding redress, representation and land, the freeing of the prisoners, and a larger measure of justice. Independence from Britain was claimed as both a right and a necessity, and republican ideas were asserted. The days of arbitrary or despotic rule in Victoria were finished, but Hotham wanted the leaders of Eureka to face charges of high treason.

Carboni found himself hobbled to John Joseph, a black American alleged to have been one of those who shot Captain Wise, during preliminary hearings in front of the authorities at Ballarat, and listened while various government witnesses perjured themselves by claiming he had attacked them with a pike and that he had been captured inside the stockade. Carboni called his own witnesses, including Dr Carr, but as they did not present themselves, fearing retaliation from the Camp, he—like Joseph—was committed to stand trial for high treason.

Carboni spent the night of Tuesday, 5 December, shackled to another American, Charles Ferguson, who was kind enough to leave him his blue blankets upon his release from prison after claiming that he had been forcibly seized and detained by the stockaders and that his participation was involuntary. His countryman, Dr Kenworthy, had supported him in that. Similarly Captain McGill was let go, but not John Joseph, probably because he was black.

As Carboni waited for trial with Joseph, whom he called Joe, Hotham would not contemplate amnesty, even though William Westgarth, chairman of a new government-appointed Commission on the Goldfields, expressed the opinion that an amnesty was essential. Some weeks after the events at the stockade, the thirteen remaining state prisoners, including Carboni and Joseph, were moved under escort to Melbourne Gaol, taking two days to get there. Melbourne juries would be less prejudiced in their favour, it was believed: at Ballarat, Arthur Purcell Akehurst, a Clerk of the Peace, had been found guilty by a coroner's jury of wilfully and feloniously slaying the visiting Creswick digger, Henry Powell, but a Melbourne jury had later acquitted him.

In Melbourne Gaol, the prisoners were locked in their cells, four or five together, for thirteen hours at a time, with no tobacco, writing materials or newspapers. Their food was vile. They were stripped naked and searched. But that was nothing beside the consequences if they were found guilty of high treason. The thirteen men stood on trial for their lives.

The February and March trials of the Eureka accused would be crucial to the future of justice in the colonies. If they were found guilty, the old authoritarian and corrupt system would be validated. If not guilty, then political representation for diggers, good administration, the unlocking of the land and the abolition of a property basis for the electorate would be the unavoidable outfall.

Carboni was pleased to welcome in prison James Macpherson Grant, a canny Scottish solicitor. 'God bless you, Mr Grant!' he wrote. 'For the sake of you and Mr Aspinall, the barrister, I smother down my bitterness, and pass over all that I have suffered . . .' Richard Davis Ireland, an Irish barrister in the style of Daniel O'Connell, also defended the prisoners.

The first to stand trial was John Joseph—some thought this was because the jury would find it easier to bring down a guilty verdict against a black man, and then would be bound by precedent to find others guilty. Chief Justice a'Beckett, the arch conservative, was on the bench and the prosecutor was the Attorney-General, William Stawell. The Crown challenged all Irish potential jurors, and anyone who was a publican, while Joseph amusingly objected to gentlemen and merchants. Ultimately there were no men of 'doubtful exterior' or of Irish extraction in the empanelled jury and the trial began.

Two government spies swore to seeing Joseph in the stockade, and two privates of the 40th Regiment claimed he had fired a double-barrel gun at the military, perhaps wounding Captain Wise. The problem for the Crown, however, was to convince the jury that it had been Joseph's intention to make war 'against our Lady the Queen'. His defence barrister, Aspinall, made some fun out of the idea that Joseph, as 'a riotous nigger' or 'a political Uncle Tom' sought 'to depose our Lady the Queen from the kingly name and Her Imperial Crown'.

The jury came back quickly with a verdict of Not Guilty, and the cheering was so loud that a'Beckett singled out two members of the public in the gallery for a week in gaol.

John Manning, a former schoolteacher and possibly the author of an article deemed seditious in the *Ballarat Times*, was next. The same arguments were made and the jury again brought in a verdict of Not Guilty, which so enraged Mr Stawell that he sought a month's leave of proceedings so he could compile a new list of jurymen. All the Melbourne papers thought this a gross misuse of the jury system. The *Sydney Morning Herald*, however, anxious that the behaviour of the Melbourne juries and of the diggers would delay passage of the Constitution Bill for New South Wales, wrote, 'If the Melbourne jurors choose to perjure themselves under the intoxication of popular passion, that is their concern.'

Governor Hotham was now so unpopular that people cat-called him as he passed in the streets. But he did not have the flexibility to back away from pursuing the other prisoners, and by mid March the Attorney-General had a new list of 178 jurors. The first to be tried this time would be Timothy Hayes, a definite ringleader in the eyes of the Crown. Richard Ireland was his defence counsel.

All Irish and publicans were again kept out of the jury and Redmond Barry, a good Orangeman, was to be the judge. He and Ireland had been admitted to the Irish Bar together in 1839 after they had both graduated from Trinity College. Once more, police spies came forward and reported on Hayes's doings. In Hayes's defence, John O'Brien, a digger, testified that he was in Hayes's tent near the Catholic chapel while the firing was going on at the stockade and that Hayes had been in bed but got up to go to the priest's house. Father Smyth swore that Hayes had indeed come to him and told him that his services were needed at the stockade. Grey, an *Argus* journalist, testified that he heard no seditious words from Hayes, except perhaps the question that Hayes had asked at a meeting on Bakery Hill, 'Are you prepared to risk your lives in defence of your liberties?' And when Hayes had been arrested 300 metres from the stockade, a current licence had been found on his person.

The jury took only half an hour to bring down a verdict of Not Guilty. It was a great relief to Hayes's wife, Anastasia, who was worried publicly about why Tim had shown so little manhood as to get arrested in the first place. She had also complained to the police that the stockade had been attacked on Sunday rather than Saturday, 'when the men were ready for you'. Thousands assembled outside the courthouse talked of storming it to release Hayes were he found guilty. Now, freed, he was carried through the streets shoulder high by a cheering crowd.

Carboni had been under arrest four months by now, and his turn came on 21 March 1855. Attorney-General Stawell brought forth eight witnesses—four of the 40th Regiment and four constables, and it was not too late at all, if he could get this Italian, for honour and authority to be restored.

In prison until then, said Carboni, his daily routine had begun with a dish of hominy 'now and then fattened with grubs', then a lunch of scalding water with half a dozen grains of rice, a morsel of dried bullock flesh, and a bit of bread eternally sour. That was 'the cause of my suffering so much of dysentery'. A couple of 'black murphies'—potatoes—completed the daily diet with a similar dish of hominy as in the morning, 'with the privilege of having now and then a bushranger or a horse-stealer for my mess-mate, and often I enjoyed the company of the famous robbers of the Victoria Bank'.

John Manning and Michael Tuohy, both Irishmen, while awaiting trial would ask Carboni to entertain them with a favourite piece of Italian opera. Occasionally a kindly guard would drop a stick of tobacco through the wall. 'We decreed and proclaimed that even in Hell there must be some good devils.'

At the beginning of 1855 Carboni had received a copy of the indictment against him, and declared it 'the coarsest fustian ever spun by Toorak Spiders'.

In court, however, he rather liked Judge Barry, whom he said could manage his temper even among the vexations of the law.

A crown witness named George Webster declared that Carboni had made a speech on Bakery Hill to the effect that he'd come 16 000 miles to escape tyranny and that the diggers should put down the tyrants of the Camp. The prisoner tore up his licence and threw it towards a fire, added Webster. Mr Ireland for the defence, however, was able to hand the witness an intact gold licence covering the period when the licence was allegedly burned. One soldier declared that Carboni was armed with a pike in the stockade. Another stated that he saw Carboni and two other men chasing the first private. A third soldier said he was at the stockade and saw Carboni, and so did a number of troopers and a non-commissioned officer.

Mr Ireland warned the jury of the horrid reality of the punishment for high treason—hanging, drawing and quartering. 'Never mind the stench,' wrote Carboni later, recalling Ireland's words, 'each piece of the treacherous flesh must remain stuck up at the top of each gate of the town, there to dry in spite of occasional pecking from crows and vultures.'

The jury retired at nine o'clock at night to consider the evidence. 'To remain in the felon's dock while your jury consult on your fate is a sensation very peculiar in its kind.' At twenty minutes past nine, the jury came back. The verdict was Not Guilty. 'The people inside telegraphed the good news to the crowd outside and "Hurrah!" rent the air in the old British style. I was soon at the portal of the Supreme Court, a free man. I thought the people would have smothered me in their demonstrations of joy.'

Asked to speak, he used some notes he had scribbled in pencil in his cell, number 33: 'Lord God of Israel, Our Father in Heaven! We acknowledge our transgressions since we came into this our adopted land. Intemperance, greediness and the pampering of many bad passions have provoked Thee against us; yet, oh Lord our God, if in Thy justice, Thou are called upon to chastise us, in Thy mercy save this land of Victoria from the curse of the "spy system".'

To this, Tim Hayes shouted, 'Amen!'

The trials had become a farce now, but Hotham continued with them. The last prisoners were tried in a group of six, and acquitted. The governor was shaken in health and confidence. The Secretary for the Colonies, John Russell, wrote to him and told him that even if he had acted upon good advice to the best of his judgment, it had been inexpedient to charge the diggers with high treason. One of the acquitted, John Manning, spoke of the deliberately non-Irish juries that sat at the trials: 'The future history of Australia will remember them with honour, and posterity will exalt with a laudable pride that, in even the darkest and gloomiest moments of their history, their ancestors had been found to the very last moment, true to their post.'

When the report of the Commission on the Goldfields, authorised by Hotham in December, was tabled, it condemned 'the resort to arms'. Peter Lalor, still technically at large, wrote to the *Age* asking why nothing had been done to fix affairs 'before this bloody tragedy took place'. 'Is it to prove to us that a British government can never bring forth a measure of reform without having first prepared a font of human blood in which to baptise that offspring of their generous love? ... Or is it to convince the world that where a large standing army exists, the Demon of Despotism will have frequently offered at his shrine the mangled bodies of murdered men.'

The *Age* wrote of Hotham that he had 'brought the good faith in the government into disrepute by systematic breach of contract ... and a disgraceful system of espionage'.

Lalor, having survived his amputation, found that his friends had raised enough money for him to buy a portion of land near Ballarat. Even while the reward still existed for his apprehension he was moving around freely and had even bid publicly for his land.

It was an exhilarating time for Australian patriots. On 15 June 1855 the Gold Fields Act had been passed. It provided that local courts would undertake the majority of the work formerly done by the gold commissioners. The Act gave the diggers the right to elect members of the court, and its powers were wide, covering the regulation of conditions on the fields. On 14 July 1855, Raffaello Carboni was elected to the Ballarat Local Court and took his place with eight others. He was embittered by the loss of his money and personal belongings during his imprisonment, but he was delighted with his new position. In November 1855 he stood unopposed to represent Ballarat in the Legislative Council, and was again elected when a new Constitution came into force in 1856. By 1857 he denied he had ever been a Chartist, a republican or a Communist, but 'if democracy means opposition to a tyrannical people or a tyrannical government, then I have ever been, I still am, and will ever remain a Democrat'. He stayed in Australia until his book, detailing the Eureka battle and events leading up to it, was launched at the end of 1855, and then returned to Italy and to a place in Garibaldi's unification struggle.

John Basson Humffray was the other representative elected under the new Constitution from Ballarat. He founded a new group, the Victorian Reform League, but it did little since most of what it sought was achieved when Hotham despairingly implemented the recommendations of the Gold Fields Commission of Enquiry.

In November 1855, Hotham was induced to forward his resignation to the Colonial Office. When it was later moved in the Legislative Council that a sum of £1000 be expended on a monument to his memory, Lalor, elected that very month to the Assembly, rose and said he did not want to cast a slur on the dead (for Sir Charles by then had died), but that Sir Charles had a sufficient monument in the graves of those slain at Ballarat. Less than a year later Peter Lalor said he was 'free to confess that it was a rash act' he had taken part in at Eureka.

For Australia now seemed to the vast majority of its people—other than indigenes—a forum where crises could be resolved by constitutional and moral means. What would become an endemic cynicism about politics and the venality and jobbery of individual politicians had not yet possessed the souls of citizens. Peter Lalor would in 1856 be elected to serve in the Victorian Legislative Assembly, all property qualifications for being a voter having been removed in 1857 in that state. Backed by wealthier Irish and other well-off progressives in the Goulburn area, Daniel Deniehy, an oratorical catherine-wheel fuelled and hollowed by alcohol, would serve in the more limited Legislative Assembly in New South Wales before 1858, when the franchise was still restricted to payers of £10 rent or owners of property worth £100, and after, when property qualifications was abolished and the old Chartist option of the secret ballot was instituted. (It had after all been a year earlier in Victoria.) Following the arrival of the last convict ship in 1853, the former Van Diemen's Land, now naming itself Tasmania in an attempt to turn a new page or more accurately to rip out an old one, the political prisoner and Irish nobleman, William Smith O'Brien, wrote that had the bicameral institutions introduced there been in operation in Ireland they would have made peace and quashed rebellion.

As soon as the enormous colony based on Moreton Bay and containing a population of 25000 received its independence in 1859 under the name Queensland, elective government came into being, though the electoral districts were drawn in such a way as to give a pastoral vote much more value than a city one. South Australia, influenced constitutionally by its neighbour Victoria, held its first elections in 1857, whereas Western Australia, with its small population and commercial tenuousness, would be governed by viceroy and Legislative Council until the first elections for an assembly in 1890.

To keep a lid on radicalism, there existed in the new states Legislative Councils full of government appointees in the case of New South Wales, and in the more advanced politics of Victoria, elected on the basis that candidates owned property worth £50. The Legislative Councils were meant to thwart radical legislation.

Henry Parkes, never a brilliant businessman, had temporarily left the Legislative Assembly in New South Wales in an attempt to save his newspaper the *Empire*. He had earlier abandoned his attempts to make a living through his shops. But to him the new Legislative Assembly, which he soon re-entered and in which he was a robust liberal, provided a career, though one in which he was always hard-up. As for others, on one hand was the Reverend JD Lang, still turbulent, fighting off a libel charge brought by the South Coast landowner Alexander Berry, and regretting that his republican, federal vision had not emerged in the new constitutional arrangements. And on the other the aging and unappeasable William Charles Wentworth.

He and his family were in a self-imposed exile in Britain, where Wentworth mourned the waning of hope and the death of his teenage daughter Belle. Despite his role in creating the New South Wales constitution, he saw the finished item as 'a scandal to the British race and character'. Not only did he believe that the non-hereditary Legislative Councils would permit 'the folly of Democracy' to destroy the sylvan glories of the New South Wales he had written about in his youth, but his own proposal for a General Association of the Australian Colonies, a harbinger of an ultimate federal assembly, had been ignored. The universal franchise and a lack of an hereditary upper house seemed drastically radical to him and certainly likely to reduce the power of pastoralists. They would not do so to the extent he feared, given the influence of that group in the Legislative Councils of the various colonies and the squatters' capacity to adapt.

So that was Australia now, at the end of the 1850s, a country where most demands seemed to many people, including outside commentators, the Lalors of the earth, the Smith O'Briens, and the city progressives—to have been met; and where the penal past had been transmuted into a diverse future, in which Australians would bravely attempt to live down the origins of their society.

TIMELINE TO 1860

45 million BP	*circa* The landmass (Sahul) that was to form Australia began to break from Gondwana, the great southern super-continent.
60 000 BP	*circa* First *Homo sapiens* arrived on the continent.
35 000–30 000 BP	*circa* Oldest known Aboriginal tools found. Jinmium stone tools from the Northern Territory were dated at 130 000 BP, although this finding is yet to be widely accepted.
1600s–1800s	*circa* Makassan trepang (sea cucumber) divers reached the northern coastline and encountered Australian Aborigines.
1606	*March* Willem Jansz and crew of the Dutch ship *Duyfken* explored the western coast of what is now Cape York Peninsula and possibly encountered Australian Aborigines.
1606	*July–October* Luis de Torres sailed the southern coast of New Guinea, through the strait that now bears his name.
1616	*October* Dutch commander Dirk Hartog landed on an island on the western coast (now Shark Bay) and left behind a commemorative plate.
1629	*June* The Dutch East Indiaman *Batavia* was wrecked on a reef off the western coast. The commander, Francois Pelsaert, made Batavia in a ship's boat and returned to retrieve survivors. Two were left on the western coast.

1642	*August* Governor-General of the Dutch East Indies, Anthony van Diemen, sent Abel Tasman to explore south of the known land.
1642	*November–December* Tasman annexed part of a southerly island (now Tasmania) for Holland, calling it Van Diemen's Land.
1688	*January* English privateer William Dampier of the *Cygnet* anchored on the north-west coast. He undertook further exploration in the region in 1699.
1718	A system for the transportation of convicts from Britain to another country was established with the Transportation Act.
1760s	A series of Enclosure Acts transformed the British landscape, driving small farmers and agricultural workers into the cities. Widespread unemployment and social dislocation resulted.
1768	*August* Lieutenant James Cook of the *Endeavour* embarked from Plymouth to observe and record in Tahiti the transit of Venus across the face of the sun.
1768	During his around the world voyage, French explorer Louis Antoine de Bougainville sighted the Great Barrier Reef.
1769	*June* The observation of Venus completed, Cook then opened sealed orders that instructed him to search for the Great South Land.
1770	*April* Lieutenant Zachary Hicks sighted land, near the south-eastern tip of the Australian mainland. Later that month, Cook and others landed at Botany Bay.
1770	*August* Cook hoisted English colours and in the name of His Majesty King George III took possession of the whole eastern coast, giving it the name New South Wales.
1782	Britain was defeated in the American War of Independence. The transportation of British convicts to America soon ceased.
1783	Hulks were introduced on the Thames as a means of alleviating overcrowding in British gaols. They remained in use until 1853.
1786	*August* Minister for the Home Office, Lord Sydney, proposed the establishment of a convict settlement at Botany Bay. *The Heads of a Plan* was adopted later in 1786.

1788–92	Captain Arthur Phillip, Governor-in-Chief, New South Wales.
1788	*January* The First Fleet reached Botany Bay. Captain Arthur Phillip welcomed Count de la Perouse and two French vessels on their coincidental arrival in Botany Bay. In March the French ships departed to pursue Pacific explorations and were never seen again.
1788	*February* The formal proclamation of the colony took place in Sydney Cove. Phillip was appointed Governor. Lieutenant Philip Gidley King sailed in the *Supply* for Norfolk Island, where a penal station was to be established under his command.
1789	*April* An outbreak of smallpox was identified and soon constituted an epidemic among local indigenous communities.
1789	*November* Governor Phillip gave land at Rose Hill (near Parramatta) to James Ruse, an industrious former convict. In 1791, he drew his final rations from the government store. He is regarded as Australia's first independent farmer and settler.
1789	*November* Two Aborigines, Bennelong and Colby, were captured. Colby soon escaped but Bennelong remained at Government House for several months. In 1792 Bennelong accompanied Phillip to England, where he met George III. Bennelong returned to Australia in 1795.
1790	*June* The Second Fleet arrived, bringing more convicts and desperately needed supplies.
1790	*September* Governor Phillip was seriously wounded by a spear in an encounter with Aborigines at Manly Cove.
1791	*March* William and Mary Bryant, with their children and fellow convicts, escaped from Port Jackson and sailed to Timor in an open boat.
1791	*July–October* The Third Fleet arrived in Sydney.
1791	*October* Whaling from Sydney commenced using returning convict transports. By the late 1790s English, American and French whalers were also hunting in the region.
1791	*November* Twenty-one Irish convicts escaped and attempted to travel overland to China. A number soon died and the remainder were later recaptured.
1792–94	Major Francis Grose, administered the colony.

1793	*January* The first free immigrants arrived from England and took up land, in a district they named Liberty Plains (now Homebush), in February.
1793	*June* Reverend Richard Johnson commenced construction of the colony's first church. The first service was held in August.
1794–95	Captain William Paterson, administered the colony.
1795–1800	Captain John Hunter, Governor, New South Wales and its dependencies.
1795	*May* Open warfare broke out between settlers and Aborigines on the Hawkesbury. Paterson retaliated by sending a party of the NSW Corps and Aboriginal lives were lost. Violent encounters between Aboriginal and convict settlers would continue throughout the early years of the colony.
1796	*January* Escaped convicts banded together to plunder settlers' farms. They were Australia's first bushrangers.
1797	*May–June* Captain John Macarthur, Reverend Samuel Marsden, William Cox and Alexander Riley bought merino sheep imported from the Cape of Good Hope.
1798	*January* Sydney's first public clock was installed in a tower on Church Hill.
1798	Vessels were permitted to hunt seals in Bass Strait.
1798–99	George Bass and Lieutenant Matthew Flinders circumnavigated Van Diemen's Land, having earlier confirmed the existence of a strait between the mainland and the island.
1800–06	Captain Philip Gidley King, Governor, New South Wales.
1801	*February* Commander Matthew Flinders was given command of the *Investigator* and instructed to examine the 'the unknown coast'. Between 1801 and 1803 Flinders circumnavigated Australia.
1801	Passes, later known as tickets-of-leave, were introduced by Governor King to allow for greater flexibility in the convict labour force.
1803	*March* Australia's first newspaper, the *Sydney Gazette and New South Wales Advertiser*, was instigated by Governor King for

	the publication of government orders, proclamations and general information. It was published until 1842.
1803	*September* First settlement in Van Diemen's Land founded on the Derwent River.
1804	*March* Irish convicts, transported following the Irish rebellion of 1798, rioted at Castle Hill and marched on Parramatta. The NSW Corps checked their advance.
1804	*May* Settlers were authorised by Lieutenant Moore to shoot Aborigines at Risdon Cove, Van Diemen's Land. Hostilities between Aboriginal communities and convict settlers intensified.
1805	Robert Campbell's *Lady Barlow* was the first ship to sail directly to England with an all-colonial cargo, breaking the East India Company's monopoly on trade. The monopoly finally ended in 1834.
1806–08	Captain William Bligh, Captain-General and Governor-in-Chief, New South Wales and its dependencies.
1807	*February* Governor Bligh issued a regulation against the use of rum as currency. This measure was intended to weaken the hold on the colony's economy exercised by the NSW Corps (the 'Rum Corps').
1807	*August* Robert Davidson advertised the first dry-cleaning service in Sydney.
1808–10	Major George Johnston, Major Joseph Foveaux and Colonel William Paterson administered the colony throughout this period.
1808	*January* Governor Bligh was unlawfully removed from office by the NSW Corps, in what is known as the Rum Rebellion. Major George Johnston declared martial law and assumed authority as Lieutenant-Governor.
1809–17	Following the overthrow of Bligh, Macarthur and Johnston left the colony for England. Macarthur's wife, Elizabeth, administered his property during his time away.
1810–21	Colonel Lachlan Macquarie (later Major-General), Governor, New South Wales.
1810	*June* Governor Macquarie approved the establishment of a post office and Isaac Nichols as Australia's first postmaster.

1810	*October* A week-long sports carnival was held in Sydney. Activities included the first recorded race meeting, footraces and a boxing match.
1810	*November* Alexander Riley, Garnham Blaxall and Darcy Wentworth signed a contract with the governor to build Sydney Hospital, known as the Rum Hospital, as the men were granted a near-monopoly on the import of spirits.
1811	*May* Johnston was found guilty of mutiny for his role in Bligh's overthrow and sentenced to be cashiered. The NSW Corps was returned to England.
1811	*December* Reverend Samuel Marsden shipped the first commercial consignment of wool to England.
1813	*May* George Blaxland, William Charles Wentworth and William Lawson crossed the Blue Mountains west of Sydney, thus opening a way to the promising grazing lands beyond.
1813	*November* Governor Macquarie issued the 'holey dollar' and 'dump'—a Spanish coin with the central disc (the dump) removed—to prevent the colony's supply of coin becoming depleted. The holey dollar was outlawed as legal tender in 1842.
1814	*February* The Norfolk Island settlement was abandoned. It was later re-opened in 1825 and contained the worst convicts from New South Wales and Van Diemen's Land. It was again closed in 1854.
1815	*January* Governor Macquarie chose the site for Bathurst, the first settlement west of the Great Dividing Range.
1815	The end of the Napoleonic Wars prompted social and economic upheaval in Britain. The demobilisation of military forces, combined with poor harvests, contributed to an increase in crime and, subsequently, transportation.
1817	*April* Governor Macquarie, with Sydney merchants and officials, established Australia's first trading bank, the Bank of New South Wales.
1817	*December* The stonework for Australia's first lighthouse, designed by the convict architect Francis Greenway, was completed at South Head. It was lit by a revolving lantern in 1818.

1818	*May–November* New South Wales Surveyor-General John Oxley discovered the Warrumbungle Ranges, the Liverpool Plains and crossed the Great Dividing Range to make Port Macquarie.
1819	*January* The British government appointed John Thomas Bigge to investigate all aspects of the colony's government and convict system. *The State of the Colony of New South Wales* was published in 1822. Bigge's subsequent reports were published in 1833 and recommended widespread reform.
1820	*November* Governor Macquarie issued 'Order 25' which officially sanctioned limited grazing outside the Cumberland Plains. This marked the beginning of the movement of graziers inland.
1820	The dairy industry was founded in the Illawarra district. Butter and cheese were the primary products.
1820	Macarthur planted Australia's first commercial vineyard, using cuttings acquired in France.
1821	*March* The penal settlement for inveterate convicts was established at Port Macquarie. Following severe criticism of its management, it was closed in 1830.
1821–25	Major-General Sir Thomas Makdougall Brisbane, Governor, New South Wales.
1823	*July* The New South Wales Judicature Act included provisions for a legislative council, for Supreme Courts in New South Wales and Van Diemen's Land, and for trial by jury. This act was replaced by the Australian Courts Act in 1828.
1823	*July* William Charles Wentworth's ode 'Australasia: A Poem, Written for the Chancellor's Medal at the Cambridge Commencement, July 1823' was published in London, and is the first book of verse by an Australian-born author.
1824	*June* The first sitting of the Supreme Court of New South Wales took place, with Francis Forbes as Chief Justice.
1824	*June–July* A British act established the Australian Agricultural Company. It was granted one million acres of grazing land near Port Stephens. In 1828 it accepted a thirty-year lease of land and coalmines at Newcastle, effectively obtaining a monopoly in coal production.

1824	*August* The formation of a Legislative Council was proclaimed in New South Wales and met later that month.
1824	*September* A penal settlement was established at Moreton Bay.
1824	*September–October* Fort Dundas on Melville Island (Northern Territory) was established to prevent French encroachment. It was abandoned in 1829.
1824	*October* The *Australian*, published by William Charles Wentworth and Dr Robert Wardell, was first issued without government authority and advocated for 'a free press'.
1824	*October* Hamilton Hume and William Hovell explored the country south to Bass Strait, discovered the Australian Alps and the Upper Murray, and reached Port Phillip in December.
1825–31	Lieutenant-General Ralph Darling, Governor, New South Wales
1825	*June* Van Diemen's Land became a separate colony.
1825	*October* A board of trustees, chaired by Macarthur, was formed to coordinate the establishment of the Sydney Public Free Grammar School. The trustees included the former convict Mary Reibey who became the first woman to hold public office in her own right.
1826	*April* Sydney's first streetlight, an oil lamp, was lit in Macquarie Place.
1826	*June* Earl Bathurst, Secretary of State for the Colonies, ruled that Eliza Walsh, a single woman, was entitled to receive a land grant, provided she fulfilled the stipulations imposed by government.
1826	*July* Britain legislated for the use of sterling as the official currency in Australia. A branch of the Royal Mint opened in Sydney in 1855, at the height of the gold rushes.
1826	*December* Major Edmund Lockyer founded a settlement on King George Sound (now Western Australia) in an attempt to prevent French encroachment. The settlement was moved to the Swan River in March 1831.
1827	*April–September* Allan Cunningham explored north of Sydney to the Moreton Bay district, observing the fertile Darling Downs.

1827	*December* The first library in Australia, the Australian Subscription Library and Reading Room, opened in Sydney. The Hobart Town Book Society was formed; there had been a reading and newspaper room in Hobart since 1822.
1828	*April* The Australian Racing and Jockey Club was founded.
1828	*July* The Masters and Servants Act was made law in New South Wales. Servants and labourers who neglected or disobeyed orders could be gaoled, just as employers who mistreated their employees could be forced to pay compensation.
1828	*November* The first census of New South Wales was held. Twenty-four per cent of the total population was born in the colony. Aborigines were not included.
1829	*May–June* Captain Charles Fremantle took formal possession of the western third of Australia. The free settlement of Fremantle quickly followed. Perth was founded in August.
1829	*October* Governor Darling proclaimed the nineteen counties of New South Wales. The 'Limits of Location' (proclaimed in 1826) allowed settlement within a defined radius of Sydney. The restrictions proved unsuccessful. Graziers settled beyond the boundaries within a year.
1830	*September* Port Arthur penal station was founded on the Tasman Peninsula, south-east of Hobart. It was designed as a place of secondary punishment for the worst of recidivist convicts.
1830	*October* Lieutenant-Governor Arthur attempted to force the Aborigines of eastern Van Diemen's Land into the Tasman Peninsula where they were to be confined.
1831	*February* The commencement of government-assisted free migration brought about the end of the land grants system. The British government instructed through the 'Ripon Regulations' that remaining land in New South Wales and Van Diemen's Land was to be auctioned to support migration schemes.
1831	*July* The first assisted immigrants arrived in Australia.
1831	The first novel printed in Australia was Henry Savery's *Quintus Servinton: A tale founded upon incidents of real occurrence*, published in Hobart.

1831–32   Select Committee on Secondary Punishments inquired into the effectiveness of transportation following public attacks on its desirability. Its findings encouraged greater harshness in the treatment of convicts to emphasise the deterrent effect of transportation.

1831–32   The Land and Emigration Commission was set up in Britain to assist migration to Australia. Appointed commissioners were to compile information about the colonies and regulate emigration controls.

1831–37   Colonel Patrick Lindesay, administered briefly in 1831, to be replaced by Major-General Sir Richard Bourke, Governor, New South Wales.

1834   *August* South Australian Colonisation Act was approved. All land was to be sold and revenue was to finance emigration.

1834   *October* Governor James Stirling and a party of armed men attacked Aborigines near Pinjarra (now Western Australia). Many Aborigines were killed during the battle.

1835   *October* George Augustus Robinson took control of a settlement for Aborigines on Flinders Island in Bass Strait. The protectorate was abandoned in 1849.

1835   The Australian Patriotic Association was formed in New South Wales to advocate the establishment of representative government for the colony. The association disbanded in 1842.

1836   *June* Major Thomas Mitchell, New South Wales Surveyor-General, led an expedition into western Victoria, an area so fertile he named it 'Australia Felix'. His discoveries encouraged settlement.

1836   *September* Governor Bourke declared the Port Phillip district open for settlement, though squatters had already entered the area, many from Van Diemen's Land.

1836   *December* A ceremony was held to announce the commencement of settlement in South Australia.

1837   *March* Governor Bourke landed in Port Phillip and later named the site of a proposed township after the British prime minister Viscount Melbourne.

1837   *December* The first overland mail left Sydney for Melbourne. A few months later a regular fortnightly service was introduced.

1837–38	Lieutenant-Colonel Kenneth Snodgrass administered the New South Wales colony.
1837–38	*December–January* Major James Nunn's campaign, taking the form of mounted police raids against hostile Aborigines on the central north New South Wales frontier, commenced. In June 1838 the Myall Creek Massacre was committed. Acts of frontier warfare occurred frequently until 1845.
1838–46	Sir George Gipps, Captain-General and Governor-in-Chief, New South Wales and Van Diemen's Land and their dependencies.
1838	*August* Select Committee of Parliament on Transportation released its final report, attacking the penal system of New South Wales.
1838	*November* Prepaid letter sheets were introduced in New South Wales.
1839	*March* Land outside the 'Limits of Location' was divided into nine districts, in recognition of the squatting movement.
1839	*July* Moreton Bay penal settlement was closed and the area was later offered for private sale.
1839	*September* Port Darwin was discovered and named during a survey of the northern waters by *HMS Beagle*.
1840s	All the colonies suffered depressed economic conditions.
1840	*March* Paul Edmund Strzelecki, scientist and explorer, climbed Australia's highest mountain, which he named Mount Kosciuszko.
1840	*May–August* The British government ended transportation to New South Wales. The last convicts arrived in November. Convicts were still to be sent to Van Diemen's Land, Norfolk Island and later, Port Phillip.
1840	*June* Edward John Eyre commenced his explorations north of Adelaide, but he failed in his attempts and instead decided on an east–west crossing. He reached King George Sound in July 1841.
1841	*July* The convict assignment system was abolished in New South Wales and Van Diemen's Land.
1841	*October* Caroline Chisholm, a Catholic philanthropist, established the Female Immigrants' Home to help those unemployed on arrival.

1842	*September* Discovery of copper at Kapunda, and later Burra Burra Creek in 1845, led to the establishment of towns north of Adelaide. By 1850, South Australia's exports of copper had surpassed wheat and wool.
1843	*June–July* A general election for the reconstituted Legislative Council was held in New South Wales. The Act allowed for twenty-four members elected on a restricted franchise and twelve Crown nominees. The governor retained executive power. It was the first election for an Australian legislature.
1844	*January* The first peal of bells rang out in Australia from St Mary's Catholic Cathedral in Sydney.
1844	*April–May* Governor Gipps introduced new regulations in an attempt to reconfigure the squatting system; squatters were to be permitted to occupy runs on payment of a fee per square mileage. Squatters won security of tenure in 1846–47.
1844	For the first time in New South Wales exports exceeded imports.
1844–45	*August–January* South Australia Surveyor-General Captain Charles Sturt's expedition failed to find an inland sea in central Australia.
1844–45	*October–December* Ludwig Leichhardt set out from Moreton Bay and finally reached Port Essington (now the Northern Territory) despite major setbacks.
1846–55	Sir Charles Augustus FitzRoy, Governor-General, all Her Majesty's Australian possessions, and Captain-General and Governor-in-Chief, New South Wales, Van Diemen's Land and South Australia and their dependencies.
1848	*January* Last convicts disembarked at Port Phillip.
1848	*October* First shipload of Chinese indentured labourers arrived in Sydney.
1849	*February* Earl Grey, Secretary of State, announced the resumption of transportation. Prisoners considered reformed in Britain were sent as 'exiles', living free under conditional pardons.
1850s	The anti-transportation movement gained momentum. Resolutions against transportation were passed by the Legislative Councils of both New South Wales and Victoria in 1851.

1850s	Gold rushes dominated Australian life throughout this period.
1850	*January* The Australian Agricultural Company's monopoly on coal mining in New South Wales ended. Newcastle soon became the principal town of the Hunter region following the opening of the railroad between Newcastle and Hexham in 1857.
1850	*June* Transportation to Western Australia commenced where there was a demand for convict labour.
1850	*August* The Port Phillip District was separated from New South Wales and became the new colony of Victoria in July 1851. The Australian Colonies Government Act also gave the colonies permission to build their own constitutions, with provision for bicameral legislatures comprising elected and nominated members.
1851	*February* Edward Hargraves and John Lister found specks of gold not far from Bathurst.
1851	*May* The New South Wales government proclaimed all gold found in the colony the property of the Crown. Licences were introduced to dig or search for gold. Similar requirements were soon imposed in Victoria.
1851	*July–August* Gold was discovered in Victoria, just south of Ballarat.
1852	*July* Britain ended transportation to eastern Australia, including Van Diemen's Land.
1852	*July–August* The first mail steamer arrived in Sydney from England, after calling in to Melbourne.
1853	Gold surpassed wool as Australia's chief export.
1854	*January* The Cobb and Co coaching firm offered passenger services between Castlemaine, Bendigo and Melbourne, daily except Sundays.
1854	*February* Australia's first telegraph line opened between Melbourne and Williamstown. The first inter-colonial line was opened between Melbourne and Adelaide in 1858. The Sydney–Melbourne line followed shortly afterward.
1854	*September* The first public steam railway in Australia was opened, running between Melbourne and Port Melbourne.

1854	*October* The Van Diemen's Land Constitution Act became the first colonial constitution act to be passed. It provided for a bicameral legislature.
1854	*December* Police and troops raided the Eureka stockade, constructed by gold miners at Ballarat to resist government attempts to enforce a licensing system.
1855–61	During 1855, Sir William Thomas Denison, Governor-General, Her Majesty's colonies of New South Wales, Tasmania, Victoria, South Australia and Western Australia. He continued as Captain-General, Governor-in-Chief and Vice-Admiral, New South Wales and its dependencies from 1855–61.
1855	*June* Riots on the goldfields prompted the Victorian Parliament to introduce an act to limit Chinese immigration. South Australia passed similar legislation in 1857, as did New South Wales in 1858.
1856	*January* The name 'Tasmania', in honour of the Dutch navigator Abel Tasman, was officially adopted to replace Van Diemen's Land.
1856	*March* The Victorian Electoral Act introduced the secret or 'Australian' ballot.
1856	*May* In Victoria, many unions achieved an eight-hour working day.
1856	*August* The first inter-colonial conference was held. It dealt with the maintenance of lighthouses across the colonies.
1856	The first parliaments of New South Wales, Victoria and Tasmania, consisting of a legislative council and a legislative assembly, were opened. South Australia followed in 1857.
1858	*June* The 'Welcome' nugget was found in Ballarat and drew the world's attention.
1858	*July–August* Rules were drawn up for the game later known as Victorian or Australian Rules and formal competition commenced.
1859	*April* John McDouall Stuart opened a permanent 800 km route north from South Australia. He had earlier explored as far north-west as the present-day Coober Pedy.
1859	*December* The colony of Queensland was proclaimed.

| 1860 | *August* Robert O'Hara Burke and William John Wills left Melbourne to find a route to the northern coast. They reached the Gulf of Carpentaria in February 1861. Burke and Wills died on the return journey. |
| 1860–61 | Anti-Chinese riots broke out at Lambing Flat goldfields, New South Wales. |

Key Sources

Macquarie Book of Events
Edited by Bryce Fraser
Macquarie Library, Sydney, 1983

Australians
Volume 8: Events and Places
Fairfax, Syme and Weldon, Sydney, 1987

NOTES

ABBREVIATIONS TO NOTES

ADB	Australian Dictionary of Biography
BPP	British Parliamentary Papers
HRA	Historical Records of Australia
HRNSW	Historical Records of New South Wales
HO	Home Office
JACH	Journal of Australian Constitutional History
JRAHS	Journal of the Royal Australian Historical Society
ML	Mitchell Library, State Library of New South Wales
NLA	National Library of Australia
NSWSA	New South Wales State Archives
PRO	Public Record Office

EXPLANATION OF NOTES

1. When a book or document relates exactly to the subject matter of the section title, no subject tag is given. For example, in the section entitled 'The young gentleman', sources which relate to the young gentleman Joseph Banks are given without any introductory tag. But when a source covers only part of the section title, the source is introduced. Thus:

> Social and penal history of Georgian England: JM Beattie, *Crime and the Courts in England, 1600–1800* (Princeton 1986).

2. In the case of journal articles, apart from the author, title and name of the journal, the volume number, issue number and year are given. So, in the case of Charles S Blackton, 'The dawn of Australian national feeling', *Pacific Historical Review*, 24 (2), 1955, 24 stands for Volume 24; (2) stands for the second issue of that year.
3. Similarly, *HRA*, Series I (II) stands for *Historical Records of Australia*, Series I, Volume II. *ADB*, 1, means *Australian Dictionary of Biography*, Volume 1.

CHAPTER 1

Dinner at Cuddie Springs
Emigration of people across the land bridge from Asia to Australia, Cuddie Springs, Lake Mungo and Lake Nitchie: John Mulvaney & Johan Kaminga, *The Prehistory of Australia* (Sydney 1999).
Aboriginal pre-European world view: AP Elkin, *Aboriginal Men of High Degree* (Brisbane 1977); RL Kirk & AG Thorne (eds), *The Origins of the Australians* (Canberra 1976); AA Abbie, *The Original Australians* (Sydney n.d.); Geoffrey Blainey, *Triumph of the Nomads* (Melbourne 1975); Norman B Tindale & HA Lindsay, *Aboriginal Australians* (Brisbane 1963); David Unaipon, *Legendary Tales of the Australian Aborigines,* eds Stephen Muecke & Adam Shoemaker (Melbourne 2000, originally published 1927); Patrick Corbally Stourton, *Song Lines and Dreamings* (1996 London); John Ramsland, *Custodians of the Soil* (Taree 2001).

CHAPTER 2

The Makassar welcome
Makassan visitors: Henry Reynolds, *North of Capricorn: The untold story of the people of Australia's north* (Sydney 2003); RM & CH Berndt, *Arnhem Land: Its history and people* (Melbourne 1964); CM McKnight, *The Voyage to Marege: Macassan Trepangers in Northern Australia* (Melbourne 1976).

The Coy Coasts
Account of exploration: Evan McHew, *1606* (Sydney 2006); journals of early discovery of Australia, available on the Project Gutenberg Australia website <www.gutenberg.net.au>. Australia: JE Heeres (ed), *Abel Janszoonn Tasman's Journal of His Discovery of Van Diemen's Land and New Zealand in 1642 with Documents Relating to His Exploration of Australia in 1644*; Sir Ernest Scott, *Australian Discovery* (London 1929); George Collinridge, *The First Discovery of Australia and New Guinea* (1906); TD Mutch, *The First Discovery of Australia* (Sydney 1942).
Portuguese: Kenneth Gordon McIntyre, *The Secret Discovery of Australia: Portuguese ventures 250 years before Captain Cook* (Sydney 1982).

Pirating words
William Dampier, *A Voyage to New Holland, etc, in the Year 1699,* and *Continuation of a Voyage to New Holland* and *A New Voyage Around the World,* both available on Project

Gutenberg Australia; Diana & Michael Preston, *A Pirate of Exquisite Mind* (London 2004).

The grand intrusion
JC Beaglehole (ed), *The Life of Captain James Cook* (London 1974), and *The Journals of Captain James Cook on his Voyages of Discovery,* 5 vols (Sydney 1999); Nicholas Thomas, *Discoveries: The voyages of Captain Cook* (London 2003); Andrew Kippis, *Life of Captain James Cook* (London 1788); John Robson, *Captain Cook's World: Maps of the life and voyages of James Cook R.N.* (Sydney 2000).

The young gentleman
John Gascoigne, *Joseph Banks and the English Enlightenment* (Cambridge 1994); WH Wharton (ed), *The Endeavour Log of Sir Joseph Banks*, available on Project Gutenberg Australia.

Venus
As well as the journals listed above, Beaglehole, *Cook*; Thomas, *Discoveries*; Gascoigne, *Joseph Banks and the English Enlightenment*; Dr Tony Phillips, *James Cook and the Transit of Venus, 1769* at <www.FirstScience.com/SITE/ARTICLES/transit-of-venus.asp>.

The transit of Mercury, *Turaga* landfall and To *Gangurru* regions
See notes previous two sections.

CHAPTER 3

The England Cook returned to
Social and penal history of Georgian England: JM Beattie, *Crime and the Courts in England, 1600–1800* (Princeton 1986); Douglas Hay et al., *Albion's Fatal Tree: Crime and society in eighteenth-century England* (London 1975).
Society in general: Roy Porter, *English Society in the Eighteenth Century* (London 1982); Peter Ackroyd, *London: The biography* (London 2001); Tom Griffiths (ed), *The Newgate Calendar* (London 1997); William Blake, *The Poetical Works of William Blake* (London 1949).
Boswell: Frank Brady, *James Boswell: The later years, 1769–1795* (New York 1984).
Daniel Defoe's description of Newgate: Daniel Defoe, *Moll Flanders* (New York 1961, originally published 1772).

Campbell's hulks
Hulks: AGL Shaw, *Convicts and the Colonies: A study of penal transportation from Great Britain and Ireland and other parts of the British Empire* (London 1966); Beattie, *Crime and the Courts in England*; Hay et al., *Albion's Fatal Tree*; Dan Byrnes, *The Blackheath Connection*, cyberbook at <www.danbyrnes.com.au/blackheath/index.html>.

Get rid of them—but where?
Banks before the Commons Committee: CMH Clark (ed), *Sources in Australian History* (Melbourne 1957).

General reaction to the Commons Committee: Shaw, *Convicts and the Colonies.*
Magra's proposal: HO 7/1 microfilm at the Mitchell Library (ML) and other Australian libraries.
Final selection of New South Wales: 'Lord Sydney to the Lords Commissioners of the Treasury' in Clark, *Sources in Australian History*; Glynys Ridley, *Losing America and Finding Australia: Continental shift in an enlightenment paradigm*, The College of William and Mary website 2002 <www.wm.edu>.
Lord Sydney: Douglas Pike (ed), *Australian Dictionary of Biography* (hereafter *ADB*), 2, (Melbourne 1967) [The *ADB* is also available online, greatly enlarged and improved.]; Alan Atkinson, *The Europeans in Australia*, 1 (Melbourne 1997).
The period and the decisions: CMH Clark, *A History of Australia Volume 1: From the earliest times to the age of Macquarie* (Melbourne 1962).

A discreet officer and **The mysteries of Phillip**
For Phillip's career: Alan Frost, *Arthur Phillip, 1738–1814: His voyaging* (Melbourne 1987); M Barnard Eldershaw, *Phillip of Australia: An account of the settlement at Sydney Cove, 1788–92* (Sydney 1938); George Mackaness, *Admiral Arthur Phillip: Founder of New South Wales, 1738–1814* (Sydney 1937).
Phillip's service in the Portuguese navy: Kenneth Gordon McIntyre, *The Rebello Transcripts: Governor Phillip's Portuguese prelude* (Adelaide 1984).
The Heads of a Plan: Clark, *Sources in Australian History*; *Historical Records of New South Wales* (hereafter *HRNSW*), I, Part II.
Choice of Phillip: Michael E Scorgie & Peter Hudgson, 'Arthur Phillip's familial and political networks', *Journal of the Royal Australian Historical Society* (hereafter *JRAHS*), 82 (1), 1996.
Phillip's instructions: *Historical Records of Australia* (hereafter *HRA*), Series I (I).

Who were the convicts?
Enclosure Acts: Hay et al., *Albion's Fatal Tree*; Beattie's *Crime and the Courts in England.*
Individual convict trials at the Old Bailey: *The Old Bailey Papers*, ML and the National Library of Australia (NLA); John Cobley (ed), *The Crimes of the First Fleet Convicts* (Sydney 1972).
The background of convicts: LL Robson, *The Convict Settlers of Australia: An enquiry into the origin and character of the convicts transported to New South Wales and Van Diemen's Land, 1787–1852* (Melbourne 1965); Wilfrid Oldham, *Britain's Convicts to the Colonies* (Sydney 1990).

Flash talk
Living conditions of the criminal classes: Robson, *The Convict Settlers of Australia*; Oldham, *Britain's Convicts to the Colonies*; Shaw, *Convicts and the Colonies.*
Flash or Cant language: Captain Watkin Tench of the Marines, *Sydney's First Four Years*, ed. LF Fitzhardinge (Sydney 1961); Captain Grose, *1811 Dictionary of the Vulgar Tongue* (London 1981); Amanda Lougesen, *Convict Words: Language in early colonial Australia* (Melbourne 2002).

Phillip taking pains
Preparations for the departure to New South Wales: Charles Bateson, *The Convict Ships 1787–1868* (Sydney 1983).
Phillip's preparations and expeditionary philosophy: *HRNSW*, I, Part II; Frost, *Arthur Phillip*; Eldershaw, *Phillip of Australia*; Mackaness, *Admiral Arthur Phillip*.
William Richards and other contractors: Bateson, *The Convict Ships*; Byrnes, *The Blackheath Connection*.
Individual convicts: Mollie Gillen, *The Founders of Australia: A biographical dictionary of the First Fleet* (Sydney 1989).
The nature of provisions: Tench, *Sydney's First Four Years*; David Collins, *An Account of the English Colony in New South Wales*, 1, ed. Brian H Fletcher (Sydney 1975).
Individual ships: Bateson, *The Convict Ships*.
Preparation of ships: Paul G Fidlon & RJ Ryan (eds), *The Journal of Phillip Gidley King, Lieutenant R.N. 1787–1790* (Sydney 1980).
Loading of ships and Phillip's concern for condition of clothing, etc: Frost, *Arthur Phillip*; Eldershaw, *Phillip of Australia*; Mackaness, *Admiral Arthur Phillip*; *HRNSW*, I, Part II.

At Station, Plymouth and Portsmouth
John White, *Journal of a Voyage to New South Wales*, ed. Alec Chisholm (Sydney 1962); Paul G Fidlon & RJ Ryan (eds), *The Journal of Arthur Bowes Smyth: Surgeon, Lady Penrhyn 1787–1798* (Sydney 1979); *The Journal and Letters of Lt. Ralph Clark 1787–1792* (Sydney 1981); James H Thomas, *Portsmouth and the First Fleet* (Portsmouth c. 1987); Frost, *Arthur Phillip*; Eldershaw, *Phillip of Australia*; Mackaness, *Admiral Arthur Phillip*.
Condition of convicts: *HRA*, Series I (I).
Size, tonnage, and other aspects of ships: Bateson, *The Convict Ships*.
Sarah Bellamy's trial: Public Record Office (PRO) Assizes 2/25, ML and other state libraries; Madge Gibson, *Belbroughton to Botany Bay*, (Belbroughton, booklet).
The rest of the preparations for the fleet's departure from the Thames: Frost, *Arthur Phillip*; Eldershaw, *Phillip of Australia*; Mackaness, *Admiral Arthur Phillip*; Shaw, *Convicts and the Colonies*; Oldham, *Britain's Convicts to the Colonies*; *HRNSW*, I, Part II.

CHAPTER 4

The Passage
Collins, *An Account of the English Colony in New South Wales*, 1; White, *Journal of a Voyage to New South Wales*; John Hunter, *An Historical Journal of Events at Sydney and at Sea, 1787–1792* (Sydney 1968); Arthur Phillip, *The Voyage of Governor Phillip to Botany Bay* (London 1789); Tench, *Sydney's First Four Years*; Sergeant James Scott, *Remarks on a Passage to Botany Bay, 1787–1792* (Sydney 1963); John Easty, *Memorandum of the Transactions of a Voyage from England to Botany Bay, 1787–1792* (Sydney 1965); Thomas Keneally, *The Commonwealth of Thieves* (Sydney 2005); CMH Clark, *A History of Australia*, 1.

AUSTRALIANS

Meeting Eora
Early contact and early days: all First Fleet journals, especially King, Collins and Tench; John Cobley, *Sydney Cove 1788* (London 1962); Keith Vincent Smith, *Bennelong: The Coming in of the Eora* (Sydney 2001).
Aboriginal sexual prohibitions: Tindale & Lindsay, *Aboriginal Australians*.
Aboriginal response to European arrival: Inga Clendinnen, *Dancing With Strangers* (Melbourne 2003).
Shift in meaning of 'Botany Bay': Paul Carter, *The Road to Botany Bay: An exploration of landscape and history* (New York 1988).
European popular attitudes: Geoffrey C Ingleton, *True Patriots All: Or, news from early Australia* (Sydney 1952).

Botany Bay Blues
Limits of Botany Bay and move to Port Jackson: All the First Fleet journals; Charles C Dann (ed), *The Nagle Journal: A diary of the life of Jacob Nagle, sailor, from the year 1775–1841* (New York 1988).
La Pérouse: *ADB*, 1; Colin Foster, *France and Botany Bay: The lure of a penal colony* (Melbourne 1966).

Warrane-bound
The First Fleet journals, and Dann, *The Nagle Journal*.
Phillip's reaction to Port Jackson: Cobley, *Sydney Cove 1788*; Phillip's dispatches to Lord Sydney, *HRA*, Series I (I).

CHAPTER 5

Enquiries Ashore
The First Fleet journals.
Daniel Southwell and Dennis Considen: Cobley, *Sydney Cove 1788*; White, *Journal of a Voyage to New South Wales*; *ADB*, 1 and 2.
Canvas house: Hunter, *An Historical Journal of Events at Sydney and at Sea*; *HRA*, Series I (II).
Major Ross: *ADB*, 2; Clark, *A History of Australia*, 1; Alan Atkinson, *The Europeans in Australia*, 1.

Adam Delves
First agriculture: the First Fleet journals and Cobley, *Sydney Cove 1788*.
Ruse, and other convicts named: Gillen, *The Founders of Australia*; Collins, *An Account of the English Colony in New South Wales*, 1; Tench, *Sydney's First Four Years*.
Aboriginal language: Smith, *Bennelong*.

Honouring Bacchus and George
The debauch: Fidlon & Ryan, *The Journal and Letters of Lt. Ralph Clark*; *The Journal of Arthur Bowes-Smyth*; Collins, *An Account of the English Colony in New South Wales*, 1; Tench, *Sydney's First Four Years*; Cobley, *Sydney Cove 1788*.

Individual convict women: Gillen, *The Founders of Australia*.
Reading Phillip's Commission and subsequent speech and celebration: Collins, *An Account of the English Colony in New South Wales*, 1.
Contraceptive practice: Siân Rees, *The Floating Brothel* (Sydney 2001).
The prospects of convict women: Portia Robinson, *The Women of Botany Bay* (Melbourne 1988); Miriam Dixson, *The Real Matilda* (Melbourne 1976); Kaye Daniels & Mary Murnane, *Uphill All the Way: A documentary history of women in Australia* (Brisbane 1980); Monica Perrott, *A Tolerable Good Success: Economic opportunities for women in New South Wales 1788–1838* (Sydney 1983).
Reverend Johnson's reaction: J Bonwick, *Australia's First Preacher* (London 1897).

Island of innocence
Plans for Norfolk Island: Fidlon & Ryan, *The Journal of Phillip Gidley King*; Phillip's dispatch to Lord Sydney, *HRA*, Series I (I).
Jamison and Colley: *ADB*, 1.
Individual convicts: Gillen, *The Founders of Australia*.

The food question
Phillip on food shortage: Phillip's dispatch to Lord Sydney, *HRA*, Series I (I).
Rations and Barrett's execution: Collins, *An Account of the English Colony in New South Wales*, 1; Tench, *Sydney's First Four Years*; Phillip, *The Voyage of Governor Phillip to Botany Bay*; Cobley, *Sydney Cove 1788*; Frost, *Arthur Phillip*; Eldershaw, *Phillip of Australia*; Mackaness, *Admiral Arthur Phillip*.

A soldier's trial, and marriages
Private Bramwell, etc: Fidlon & Ryan, *The Journal and Letters of Lt. Ralph Clark*.
Individual convicts: Gillen, *The Founders of Australia*.
Convict women's affairs with sailors: Fidlon & Ryan, *The Journal of Arthur Bowes-Smyth*; Robinson, *The Women of Botany Bay*.
Reverend Johnson's background: Bonwick, *Australia's First Preacher*.
Assizes trials of Will Bryant and Mary Bryant: Cobley, *The Crimes of the First Fleet Convicts*.
Attitudes to smuggling: Hay et al., *Albion's Fatal Tree*.
The Kables' marriage: Cobley, *Sydney Cove 1788*; *ADB*, 2.
Johnson's first sermon: Bonwick, *Australia's First Preacher*.

Au Revoir, Monsieur le Comte
The First Fleet journals listed previously.
Phillip's dispatch to Lord Sydney, *HRA*, Series I (I).
La Pérouse: *ADB*, 2.

Finding an ambassador
Search for a native: *HRA*, Series I (I); Tench, *Sydney's First Four Years*; Collins, *An Account of the English Colony in New South Wales*, 1; Smith, *Bennelong*.
Keith Willey, *When the Sky Fell Down: The destruction of the tribes of the Sydney region, 1788–1850s* (Sydney 1979).

AUSTRALIANS

Who gave the Eora the smallpox?
Death of Arabanoo and others: the First Fleet journals of Hunter, White, Collins and
Tench; Alan Frost, *Botany Bay Mirages* (Melbourne 1994); Smith, *Bennelong*; Willey, *When
the Sky Fell Down*.
Estimates of Eora deaths: Frost, *Botany Bay Mirages*; Smith, *Bennelong*.

Food and men's minds
Food theft: Hunter, *An Historical Journal of Events at Sydney and at Sea*; Collins, *An Account
of the English Colony in New South Wales*, 1; Tench, *Sydney's First Four Years*; Fidlon & Ryan,
The Journal and Letters of Lt. Ralph Clark; Easty, *Memorandum of the Transactions of a
Voyage from England to Botany Bay*.
The return of *Sirius*: Phillip, *The Voyage of Governor Phillip to Botany Bay*; Hunter, *An
Historical Journal of Events at Sydney and at Sea*.

CHAPTER 6

The weight of prisoners
Condition of convicts: White, *Journal of a Voyage to New South Wales*; other First Fleet
journals, particularly Collins and Tench; Arthur Phillip, *Journal*, in Hunter, *An Historical
Journal of Events at Sydney and at Sea*; Byrnes, *The Blackheath Connection*.
Lady Juliana, and Catherine Heyland case: Rees, *The Floating Brothel*; Bateson, *The Convict
Ships*.
The Second Fleet in general: Phillip in Hunter, *An Historical Journal of Events at Sydney and
at Sea*; Shaw, *Convicts and the Colonies*; Oldham, *Britain's Convicts to the Colonies*; Michael
Flynn, *The Second Fleet: Britain's grim convict armada of 1790* (Sydney 2001); John Nicol,
Life and Adventures, 1776–1801, ed. Tim Flannery (Melbourne 1997).

Expirees
Cullyhorn: Collins, *An Account of the English Colony in New South Wales*, 1; Gillen,
The Founders of Australia; John Cobley, *Sydney Cove 1789–1790* (Sydney 1963).
John Harris and night guard: Collins, *An Account of the English Colony in New South Wales*,
1; Hunter, *An Historical Journal of Events at Sydney and at Sea*.

A second fleet
Grenville: Flynn, *The Second Fleet*; Atkinson, *The Europeans in Australia*, 1.
Richards and Camden, Calvert and King: Bateson, *The Convict Ships*; Flynn, *The Second
Fleet*; Byrnes, *The Blackheath Connection*.
Recruiting of New South Wales Corps: *HRA*, Series II; Michael Duffy, *Man of Honour:
John Macarthur—dualist, rebel, founding father* (Sydney 2003); MH Ellis, *John Macarthur*
(Sydney 1955); Flynn, *The Second Fleet*.

Antipodean Adam
Ross's attitude: Ross to Nepean, 10 July 1788, Cobley, *Sydney Cove 1788*.
James Ruse: Gillen, *The Founders of Australia*; *ADB*, 2.

Also Collins, *An Account of the English Colony in New South Wales*, 1; Tench, *Sydney's First Four Years*; Phillip in Hunter, *An Historical Journal of Events at Sydney and at Sea*; Atkinson, *The Europeans in Australia*, 1.

A new Arabanoo
Bennelong's capture: William Bradley, *A Voyage to New South Wales: The journal of Lieutenant William Bradley, 1786–1792* (Sydney 1961); also on State Library of New South Wales website, and photostat copy Ac 145, ML.
Bennelong's reception and Colby: Collins, *An Account of the English Colony in New South Wales*, 1; Tench, *Sydney's First Four Years*.

Famine
Increasing problems with food: the First Fleet journals; Frost, *Arthur Phillip*; Eldershaw, *Phillip of Australia*; Mackaness, *Admiral Arthur Phillip*; *HRA*, Series I (I).
Mutton birds: Hunter, *An Historical Journal of Events at Sydney and at Sea*; Fidlon & Ryan, *The Journal of Phillip Gidley King*.
Ross: Atkinson, *The Europeans in Australia*, 1.
The *Guardian* transport: Bateson, *The Convict Ships*.
Conditions in Sydney: Collins, *An Account of the English Colony in New South Wales*, 1; White, *Journal of a Voyage to New South Wales*.

Juliana: The face of shame
Arrival of *Juliana*: John Nicol, *Life and Adventures*; Rees, *The Floating Brothel*; Tench, *Sydney's First Four Years*.
Assembly of bulk of Second Fleet and supply situation: Flynn, *The Second Fleet*; Bateson, *The Convict Ships*; Shaw, *Convicts and the Colonies*; Oldham, *Britain's Convicts to the Colonies*.
Troubles on board *Neptune*, and Hodgetts: Flynn and Bateson as above.

Neptune's men
Macarthur: Duffy, *Man of Honour*; Ellis, *John Macarthur*.
Duel with Gilbert and correspondence with Nepean: Flynn, *The Second Fleet*.
D'Arcy Wentworth: John Ritchie, *The Wentworths: Father and Son* (Melbourne 1997); John Ritchie, 'The crimes of D'Arcy Wentworth', *Tasmanian Historical Studies*, No. 6 (I), 1998.

Neptune: The second face of shame
Conditions aboard: Flynn, *The Second Fleet*; Shaw, *Convicts and the Colonies*; Hazel King, *Elizabeth Macarthur and Her World* (Sydney 1980); Joy N Hughes (ed), *The Journal and Letters of Elizabeth Macarthur, 1789–1790* (Sydney n.d.); Duffy, *Man of Honour*; Ellis, *John Macarthur*.
D'Arcy Wentworth and Crowley: Ritchie, *The Wentworths*.
Captain Hill's compassion: Letter, 26 June 1789, *HRNSW*, I, Part II, and MDD 6821, ML.

CHAPTER 7

Confirmation of existence

Arrival of fleet and conditions aboard: Tench, *Sydney's First Four Years*; Collins, *An Account of the English Colony in New South Wales*, 1; White, *Journal of a Voyage to New South Wales*; Phillip in Hunter, *An Historical Journal of Events at Sydney and at Sea*; Flynn, *The Second Fleet*.

Trail's behaviour: Flynn, *The Second Fleet*; Bateson, *The Convict Ships*.

Reverend Johnson: Bonwick, *Australia's First Preacher*.

Captain Hill: 26 June 1789, *HRNSW*, I, Part II and MDD 6821, ML.

Self-sufficient Adam

Ruse: Tench, *Sydney's First Four Years*; Collins, *An Account of the English Colony in New South Wales*, 1; Flynn, *The Second Fleet*; Janice Ruse Israel, *My Mother Reread Me Tenderley: The life of James Ruse* (Sydney 1988).

For Sarah Whitelam: John Nicol, *Life and Adventures*.

Her subsequent behaviour: Flynn, *The Second Fleet*.

The whale and the spear

The First Fleet journals especially Tench, *Sydney's First Four Years*; Bradley, *A Voyage to New South Wales*; Phillip in Hunter, *An Historical Journal of Events at Sydney and at Sea*.

Interpretation of spearing: Clendinnen, *Dancing with Strangers*; Smith, *Bennelong*; Willey, *When the Sky Fell Down*.

On Aboriginal pronunciation: Collins, *An Account of the English Colony in New South Wales*, 1, Appendix; Smith, *Bennelong*.

Bennelong's marriages

Smith, *Bennelong*; Tench, *Sydney's First Four Years*; Collins, *An Account of the English Colony in New South Wales*, 1.

McEntire's enchanted spear

The Phillip and Tench journals; Smith, *Bennelong*.

Carrahdy: Elkin, *Aboriginal Men of High Degree*.

Tench's expedition: Tench, *Sydney's First Four Years*.

Dawes and Patyegarang: Smith, *Bennelong*.

Bennelong's ritual importance: Tench, *Sydney's First Four Years*; Collins, *An Account of the English Colony in New South Wales*, 1, Appendices on Aboriginal culture.

Anonymous painter, Port Jackson painter: Natural History Museum, London; John McDonald, *Art of Australia Volume 1: Exploration to Federation* (Sydney 2008).

A subtle response

Dutch snow: Phillip in Hunter, *An Historical Journal of Events at Sydney and at Sea*; Tench, *Sydney's First Four Years*; Collins, *An Account of the English Colony in New South Wales*, 1.

Phillip's business at home: Frost, *Arthur Phillip*.

Dispatch, Phillip to Grenville: 25 March 1791, *HRA*, Series I (I).

Letter to Banks: Cobley, *Sydney Cove 1791–1792*.

Blumenbach: Smith, *Bennelong*; Gasgoine, *Joseph Banks and the English Enlightenment*.

CHAPTER 8

Into the blue

Expedition to cross Hawkesbury River: Phillip in Hunter, *An Historical Journal of Events at Sydney and at Sea*; Tench, *Sydney's First Four Years*.

Phillip to Banks: Cobley, *Sydney Cove 1791–1792*.

Escape: CH Currey, *The Transportation, Escape and Pardoning of Mary Bryant* (Sydney 1983); Collins, *An Account of the English Colony in New South Wales*, 1; Tench, *Sydney's First Four Years*.

Recapture, etc: Ingleton, *True Patriots All*, segment named *The Memorandums*.

Phillip on Will Bryant and marriage: Collins, *An Account of the English Colony in New South Wales*, 1.

Bligh in Koepang: George Mackaness, *The Life of Vice-Admiral William Bligh, R.N., F.R.S.* (Sydney 1931).

A third fleet

Bateson, *The Convict Ships*; Byrnes, *The Blackheath Connection*; Oldham, *Britain's Convicts to the Colonies*; Shaw, *Convicts and the Colonies*.

Legal pursuit of Trail: Flynn, *The Second Fleet*.

The Irish on *Queen*: Kate Johnson & Michael Flynn, 'The Convicts of the *Queen*' in Bob Reece (ed), *Exiles from Erin: Convict lives in Ireland and Australia* (Dublin 1991); Bob Reece, 'Irish anticipations of Botany Bay', *Hibernian Chronicle*, 12, 1997.

Defenders: Samuel Clark & James S Donnelly Jr., *Irish Peasants: Violence and political unrest, 1780–1914* (Dublin 1983); Atkinson, *The Europeans in Australia*, 1; Thomas Keneally, *The Great Shame* (Sydney 1999).

Simeon Lord: *ADB*, 2.

Dispatch on *Gorgon*: Grenville to Phillip, 19 February 1791, *HRA*, Series I (I).

National Children: John Molony, *The Native-Born: The first white Australians* (Melbourne 2000); Portia Robinson, *The Hatch and Brood of Time: A study of the first generation of native-born white Australians, 1788–1828* (Melbourne 1985); Ken Macnab and Russel Ward, 'The nature and nurture of the first generation of native-born Australians', *Australian Historical Studies*, 339, 1962.

King's marriage: Jonathan King, *Philip Gidley King: A biography of the third governor of New South Wales* (Sydney 1981).

Gorgon and arrival in Sydney: Mary Ann Parker, *Voyage Round the World in the Gorgon Man of War*, annotated Gavin Fry (Sydney 1991).

Arrival of Great Seal: Collins, *An Account of the English Colony in New South Wales*, 1.

A brand name of crime

Barrington's history: Suzanne Rickard (ed), *George Barrington's Voyage to Botany Bay* (London 2001); *ADB*, 1.

Barrington's arrival: Phillip in Hunter, *An Historical Journal of Events at Sydney and at Sea*; Collins, *An Account of the English Colony in New South Wales*, 1; Tench, *Sydney's First Four Years*.

Gentleman go, gentleman stay
Reluctance to let Phillip go home: Grenville to Phillip, 21 February 1791, *HRA*, Series I (I).
Departures: Collins, *An Account of the English Colony in New South Wales*, 1.
Ann Yeates: Gillen, *The Founders of Australia*.
Phillip's desire to return: Phillip in Hunter, *An Historical Journal of Events at Sydney and at Sea*; Collins, *An Account of the English Colony in New South Wales*, 1.

Finding China
Collins, *An Account of the English Colony in New South Wales*, 1; Tench, *Sydney's First Four Years*.
Catherine Devereaux and James Kelly: *ADB*, 2; *HRA*, III.

Mercantile Dreams
Richards: Byrnes, *The Blackheath Connection*.
Tench's reconnaissance, and conversation with 'Chinese travellers': Tench, *Sydney's First Four Years*.
Land grants: Collins, *An Account of the English Colony in New South Wales*, 1.
Individual convicts visited: Tench, *Sydney's First Four Years*; Gillen, *The Founders of Australia*; Flynn, *The Second Fleet*.
Philip Schaeffer: *ADB*, 2; Tench, *Sydney's First Four Years*.
Ross's duel and embarkation: Cobley, *Sydney Cove 1791–1792*.

Barangaroo gives birth
Smith, *Bennelong*; Collins, *An Account of the English Colony in New South Wales*, 1; Tench, *Sydney's First Four Years*; Phillip in Hunter, *An Historical Journal of Events at Sydney and at Sea*.
Kinship vengeance and Pemulwuy: Collins, *An Account of the English Colony in New South Wales*, 2 and Appendices; Paul W Newbury (ed), *Aboriginal Heroes of the Resistance: From Pemulwuy to Mabo* (Sydney 1999).

An end to fleets
Individual ships: Bateson, *The Convict Ships*.
Arrivals: Collins, *An Account of the English Colony in New South Wales*, 1.
Grose: *ADB*, 1; Clark, *A History of Australia*, 1; Ellis, *John Macarthur*; Duffy, *Man of Honour*.
Dispatch, Phillip to Lord Grenville: *HRA*, Series I (II).
Johnson: Bonwick, *Australia's First Preacher*.

The devil with the children
Captain Edwards: Mackaness, *The Life of Vice-Admiral William Bligh*.
Mary Bryant and the *Gorgon*: Currey, *The Transportation, Escape and Pardoning of Mary Bryant*.

Tench and Bryant in Cape Town: Tench, *Sydney's First Four Years*.

Death of children: Tench, *Sydney's First Four Years*; Fidlon & Ryan, *The Journal and Letters of Lt. Ralph Clark*; Scott, *Remarks on a Passage to Botany Bay*.

Bryant in London: Frank Brady, *James Boswell* (New York 1984); Frederick A Pottle, *Boswell and the Girl from Botany Bay* (London 1938).

Oh! Shame, shame!

Harry Brewer: *ADB*, 1.

Richard Atkins: *ADB*, 1; *HRNSW*, I; *Journal of Richard Atkins During His Residence in New South Wales, 1791–1810*, NLA, manuscript.

Funerals and fishery: Collins, *An Account of the English Colony in New South Wales*, 1; Phillip in Hunter, *An Historical Journal of Events at Sydney and at Sea*.

David Burton: John Hunter, *Extracts of Letters from Arthur Phillip, Esq., Governor of New South Wales, to Lord Sydney* (London 1791).

Augustus Alt: *ADB*, 1.

Further deaths, and arrival of *Atlantic*: Collins, *An Account of the English Colony in New South Wales*, 1; Phillip in Hunter, *An Historical Journal of Events at Sydney and at Sea*.

Harvest and Atkins: Collins, *An Account of the English Colony in New South Wales*, 1; *HRNSW*, I.

Drought: Collins, *An Account of the English Colony in New South Wales*, 1.

Women and clothing manufacture: Phillip to Nepean in Cobley, *Sydney Cove 1791–1792*.

Discounting of notes, etc: Cobley, *Sydney Cove 1791–1792*.

Atlantic arrival and inadequacy of rations: Bateson, *The Convict Ships*; Collins, *An Account of the English Colony in New South Wales*, 1; *Journal of Richard Atkins During His Residence in New South Wales*, NLA.

Phillip to Dundas: 2 October 1792, *HRA*, Series I (I).

Chapman (visitor) on Phillip: *HRNSW*, I, Part I.

A governor longs for home

Royal Admiral: Bateson, *The Convict Ships*; Collins, *An Account of the English Colony in New South Wales*, 1.

Thomas Watling: *ADB*, 2; HS Gladstone, *Thomas Watling, Limner of Dumfries* (Dumfries 1938); Bernard Smith, *Place, Taste and Tradition* (Sydney 1945); John McDonald, *Art of Australia*, 1.

Mary Haydock (Reibey): *ADB*, 2, under 'R'; Kay Daniels, *Convict Women* (Sydney 1998); Robinson, *Women of Botany Bay*, and *The Hatch and Brood of Time*.

Officers take up *Britannia*: Collins, *An Account of the English Colony in New South Wales*, 1; Ellis, *John Macarthur*; Duffy, *Man of Honour*.

Officers expect land grants: Phillip to Dundas, 4 October 1792, *HRA*, Series I (I).

Phillip's decision to go: Collins, *An Account of the English Colony in New South Wales*, 1.

His report on state of colony: Phillip to Dundas, as above.

Phillip's departure: Collins, *An Account of the English Colony in New South Wales*, 1.

AUSTRALIANS

Spiriting away
Departure of Bennelong and other Aborigines: Smith, *Bennelong*; Isadore Brodsky, *Bennelong Profile* (Sydney 1973).
Phillip's journey home and later life: Frost, *Arthur Phillip*; Eldershaw, *Phillip of Australia*; Mackaness, *Admiral Arthur Phillip*.

CHAPTER 9

After Phillip
Grose's methods and the liquor business: *HRNSW*, I, Part II; Ellis, *John Macarthur*; Duffy, *Man of Honour*; Clark, *A History of Australia*, 1.
Liquor and gambling amongst convicts: Collins, *An Account of the English Colony in New South Wales*, 1; Atkinson, *The Europeans in Australia*, 1.
Individual convicts: Gillen, *The Founders of Australia*; Flynn, *The Second Fleet*.
Crowe, *Bellona*, marines attempted escape: Collins, *An Account of the English Colony in New South Wales*, 1.
Thomas Rose: *ADB*, 2; Collins, *An Account of the English Colony in New South Wales*, 1; JF Campbell, 'The dawn of rural settlement in New South Wales', *JRAHS*, 11, 1925.

Bennelong returns
Hunter, *An Historical Journal of Events at Sydney and at Sea*; Collins, *An Account of the English Colony in New South Wales*, 1; Miriam Estensen, *The Life of Matthew Flinders* (Sydney 2002); KM Bowden, *George Bass, 1771–1803* (Melbourne 1952).
Pemulwuy: Collins, *An Account of the English Colony in New South Wales*, 1; Willey, *When the Sky Fell Down*.
Earlier trial for murder of Aborigines, culprit Rickerby: *HRA*, Series I (II).
Wilson's story and retrieval of Tarwood: Collins, *An Account of the English Colony in New South Wales*, 1.
Grimes: *ADB*, 1; BT Dowd, 'Charles Grimes', *JRAHS*, 22, 1936.
Wilson's further expeditions: Collins, *An Account of the English Colony in New South Wales*, 1.
Wilson and others: William Joy, *The Other Side of the Hill: Two hundred years of Australian exploration* (Sydney 1984).

Politicals
The Scottish Martyrs: Margarot to Grose, 29 October 1794, *HRA*, II; M Roe, 'Maurice Margarot: a radical in two hemispheres, 1792–1815', *Bulletin of the Institute of Historical Research*, 31, 1958.
Argument between Maurice Margarot and Lieutenant Governor King: Margorot to King, 13 May 1800, *HRNSW*, IV; the same for Margarot to Undersecretary King.

Unhingeing a governor
On Hunter: Hunter, *ADB*, 1; Collins, *An Account of the English Colony in New South Wales*, 1; GA Wood, 'Governor Hunter', *JRAHS*, 14, 1928; Ellis, *John Macarthur*; Duffy, *Man of Honour*.

The heartsore Irish
Wentworth: Ritchie, *The Wentworths*.
Irish passions: Collins, *An Account of the English Colony in New South Wales*, 1; Thomas Pakenham, *The Year of Liberty* (London 1969); Anne-Maree Whitaker, *Unfinished Revolution: United Irishmen in New South Wales, 1800–1810* (Sydney 1994); Clark and Donnelly, *Irish Peasants*; TJ Kiernan, *The Irish Exiles in Australia* (Melbourne 1954); Atkinson, *The Europeans in Australia*, 1; Keneally, *The Great Shame*.
King's reaction: King, *Phillip Gidley King*; Whitaker, *Unfinished Revolution*; TC Croker (ed), *The Memoirs of Joseph Holt, General of the Irish Rebels in 1798* (London 1838).
King's concern: King to Portland, Whitaker, *Unfinished Revolution*.
Holt: Ruan O'Donnell, 'General Joseph Holt' in Reece (ed), *Exiles from Erin* (Dublin 1991); Croker, *The Memoirs of Joseph Holt*.
Fathers Dixon and Harold, floggings: Croker, *The Memoirs of Joseph Holt*; Patrick O'Farrell, *The Irish in Australia* (Sydney 1986); Whitaker, *Unfinished Revolution*; Kiernan, *The Irish Exiles in Australia*.
Foveaux: Foveaux, *ADB*, 1; Mackaness, *The Life of Vice-Admiral William Bligh*; Ellis, *John Macarthur*; Clark, *A History of Australia*, I.
Plans of rebellion on Norfolk Island: Fidlon & Ryan, *The Journal and Letters of Lt. Ralph Clark*; Foveaux papers, ML.
King's further unease about the Irish: Whitaker, *Unfinished Revolution*.
Sir Henry Browne Hayes: *ADB*, 1; CH Bertie, 'The story of Vaucluse House', *JRAHS*, 15, 1930.
The *Atlas* and *Hercules*: Bateson, *The Convict Ships*.
King's further suspicions: King to Duke of Portland, *HRA*, III; Whitaker, *Unfinished Revolution*.
Fathers O'Neil and Dixon: *HRNSW*, IV and V; *HRA*, I; JG Murtagh, *Australia: The Catholic chapter* (Sydney 1959); Whitaker, *Unfinished Revolution*; Patrick O'Farrell, *The Irish in Australia*; Collins, *An Account of the English Colony in New South Wales*, 1.
Loyal Associations: Whitaker, *Unfinished Revolution*; Collins, *An Account of the English Colony in New South Wales*, 1; King, *Phillip Gidley King*.

Trade and the Irish
Macarthur and King: Duffy, *Man of Honour*; Ellis, *John Macarthur*; Mackaness, *The Life of Vice-Admiral William Bligh*; Clark, *A History of Australia*, 1.
Sundry correspondence on issues involving King and Macarthur: *HRNSW*, II; Hazel King, *Elizabeth Macarthur and her World* (Sydney 1980).

CHAPTER 10

A new Vinegar Hill
Whitaker, *Unfinished Revolution*; King, *Phillip Gidley King*; Kiernan, *The Irish Exiles in Australia*; Lynette Ramsay Silver, *The Battle of Vinegar Hill: Australia's Irish rebellion, 1804* (Sydney 1989).

AUSTRALIANS

Marsden's experience: Piper Papers, ML. (Mrs Marsden and Mrs Macarthur gave an account to Captain Piper.)

A state of slaves
O'Farrell, *The Irish in Australia*; Whitaker, *Unfinished Revolution*; Croker, *The Memoirs of Joseph Holt.*
James Tuckey to Dundas: Tuckey manuscript, ML.

CHAPTER 11

The perturbator
Further Macarthur and King: Ellis, *John Macarthur*; Duffy, *Man of Honour*; King, *Phillip Gidley King*; Governor King to Lord Hobart and Undersecretary King, *HRNSW*, V; King to Lord Hobart, *HRA*, Series I and IV; King to Undersecretary King, *HRA*, Series I and V.
Staving Harris's casks: *HRNSW*, V.
Earl Camden: Pakenham, *The Year of Liberty*; Dr Marjory Bloy, *The Web of English History*, <www.historyhome.co.uk>.
King and the officers: Macarthur biographies as above.

A crisis in law
King's warning on need for lawyer, and his other problems: King, *Phillip Gidley King*; Duffy, *Man of Honour*; Ellis, *John Macarthur*.
Crossley: *ADB*, 1.
Robinson: *ADB*, 2.
Atkins: *ADB*, 1.
General conditions for coming mayhem: Duffy, *Man of Honour*; Mackaness, *The Life of Vice-Admiral William Bligh.*

Bligh the sinner
Bligh title cancellations: *HRA*, Series I and VI.
Complaint from Deputy Commissary Fitz to Undersecretary Chapman: 15 October 1807, *HRNSW*, VI.
Gore and Crossley: *ADB*, 1.
Bligh verbally attacks Macarthur: Duffy, *Man of Honour*; Ellis, *John Macarthur*; Mackaness, *The Life of Vice-Admiral William Bligh*; Stephen Dando-Collins, *Captain Bligh's Other Mutiny* (Sydney 2007); HV Evatt, *Rum Rebellion: A study of the overthrow of Governor Bligh by John Macarthur and the New South Wales Corps* (Sydney 1938); Ross Fitzgerald & Mark Hearn, *Bligh, Macarthur and the Rum Rebellion* (Kenthurst 1988).
Elizabeth Macarthur to Miss Kingdon: Sibella Onslow Macarthur (ed), *Some Early Records of the Macarthurs of Camden* (Sydney 1914).
Robert Campbell: *ADB*,1; M Stephen, *Merchant Campbell 1769–1846* (Melbourne 1965).
Andrew Thompson: *ADB*, 1.
His reports about Bligh's farm from the Hawkesbury: *HRNSW*, VI.

Blaxlands on Bligh: *HRNSW*, VI.

John Blaxland's discontented letter: *HRNSW*, VI.

D'Arcy Wentworth to Lord Castlereagh, 17 October 1807; Macarthur to Bligh, 1, 8 and 12 January 1808, both *HRNSW*, VI.

The grand impasse

Ellis, *John Macarthur*; Duffy, *Man of Honour*; Mackaness, *The Life of Vice-Admiral William Bligh*.

Mary Putland: *ADB*, 2; Penelope Nelson, *Bligh's Daughter* (Victoria, British Columbia, 2007).

Garnham Blaxcell and Anthony Fenn Kemp: *ADB*, 1.

Bligh's support base: *Settlers' Address to Governor Bligh*, 1 January 1808, *HRNSW*, VI.

Bringing a governor down

William Bligh, *Account of the Rebellion of the New South Wales Corps: Communicated to the Rt. Hon. Lord Castlereagh and Sir Joseph Banks, Bart* (Melbourne 2003).

Ellis, *John Macarthur*; Duffy, *Man of Honour* and Bligh as above; Evatt, *Rum Rebellion*; Dando-Collins, *Captain Bligh's Other Mutiny*; Nelson, *Bligh's Daughter*.

Johnston's motives in taking control: *HRNSW*, VI; *HRA*, Series I, VI, including Johnston to Castlereagh and evidence of Robert Campbell.

George Johnston: *A Charge of Mutiny: The court martial of Lieutenant Colonel George Johnston for deposing William Bligh in the rebellion of 26 January 1808* (Canberra 1988).

Maurice O'Connell: *ADB*, 2; Nelson, *Bligh's Daughter*.

Other aspects of the overthrow: Brian Fletcher, 'The Hawkesbury settlers and the Rum Corps', *JRAHS*, 59, 1969; Alan Atkinson, 'Jeremy Bentham and the Rum Rebellion', *JRAHS*, 64, 1987; Alan Atkinson, 'The British Whigs and the Rum Rebellion', *JRAHS*, 66, 1980.

CHAPTER 12

Comes the avenger

Ritchie, *The Wentworths*; Clark, *A History of Australia*, 1; MH Ellis, *Lachlan Macquarie: His life, adventures and times* (Sydney 1965); John Ritchie, *Lachlan Macquarie: A life* (Melbourne 1986); Russel Ward, *Finding Australia: The history of Australia to 1821* (Melbourne 1987).

Wentworths rising

Ritchie, *The Wentworths*; Wentworth Family Papers, A751–756, ML.

Pipes against King: *HRNSW*, V.

D'Arcy Wentworth as surgeon: Gillian Hull, 'From convicts to founding fathers: three notable surgeons', *Journal of the Royal Society of Medicine*, 94 (7), 2001.

The convict's child goes home

Ritchie, *The Wentworths*; Wentworth Family Papers, A751–756, ML.

In the heart of Empire

WC Wentworth in England and on the Continent: Wentworth Papers, A758, ML; Clark, *A History of Australia*, 1, and *A History of Australia Volume 2: New South Wales* and Van Diemen's Land, 1822–1838 (Melbourne 1968); DE Fifer, 'Man of two worlds: the early career of William Charles Wentworth', JRAHS, 90(3), 1984; CA Liston, 'William Charles Wentworth: the formative years, 1810–1824', JRAHS, 62 (1), 1973.

The arguments with Bennet: Wentworth Papers, ML.

Bennet's tract: HG Bennet, Letter to Viscount Sidmouth (London 1819).

Redfern: ADB, 2.

Eagar: ADB, 1.

The Commissioner visits

Bigge's three reports: The State of the Colony of New South Wales (London 1822); The Judicial Establishment of New South Wales (London 1823); and The State of Agriculture and Trade in New South Wales (London 1823).

Bigge: Ritchie and Ellis, Macquarie; Fifer, Man of Two Worlds; JB Hirst, Convict Society and its Enemies: A history of early New South Wales (Sydney 1984).

Macarthur and younger Wentworth: Ritchie, Wentworths, and Macquarie; Wentworth Papers, A757, ML.

A hothead's prose

WC Wentworth, A Statistical, Historical and Political Description of New South Wales and its Dependent Settlements in Van Diemen's Land (London 1819).

The poem 'Australasia': Ritchie, Wentworths; PR Stephenson, The Foundations of Culture in Australia (Sydney 1986); WC Wentworth, Austalasia, intro GA Wilkes (Sydney 1982). Wardell: ADB, 2.

The highwayman passes

Cookney to D'Arcy Wentworth: Wentworth Papers, A754, ML.

Death of D'Arcy: Ritchie, The Wentworths.

Who is Castlereagh, who is Sidmouth, and who in God's name is Bathurst?

JC Beaglehole, 'The colonial office 1782–1854', Historical Studies: Australia and New Zealand, 1 (3), 1941; Helen Taft Manning, 'Who ran the British Empire 1830–1850?', Journal of British Studies, 5 (1), 1965.

Castlereagh, Sidmouth and Bathurst: Pakenham, The Year of Liberty; P Ziegler, Addington (Sidmouth's common name) (London 1963); Hay et al., Albion's Fatal Tree; Dr Marjory Bloy, The Web of English History and The Victorian Web, <www.thevictorianweb.org>. Bathurst: ADB, 1.

CHAPTER 13

Radical transportees

Thomas Spence and his movement: Malcolm Chase, The People's Farm: British radical agrarianism, 1775–1840 (Oxford 1988); Ian McCalman, Radical Underworld: Prophets, revolutionaries, and pornographers in London, 1795–1840 (Cambridge, Mass., 1988).

Discontent: Gertrude Himmelfarb, *The Idea of Poverty: England in the early industrial age* (New York 1983); Hay et al., *Albion's Fatal Tree*; Bloy, *The Web of English History; The Victorian Web*.

Currency, not sterling
Currency: Robinson, *The Hatch and Brood of Time*; Molony, *The Native-Born*; Ken Macnab & Russel Ward, 'The nature and nurture of the first generation of native-born Australians', *Historical Studies*, 39, 1962; Charles S Blackton, 'The dawn of Australian national feeling', *The Pacific Historical Review*, 24 (2), 1955.

Lt. Bell evidence: Bigge Appendix, *The State of the Colony of New South Wales*; Alexander Harris, *Settlers and Convicts* (Melbourne 1953).

Charles Tompson and Harpur: *ADB*, 2; Molony, *The Native-Born*.

Native feeling: Anne Coote, 'Imagining a colonial nation', *JACH*, 1999 (1).

The poaching wars
Hay et al., *Albion's Fatal Tree*; PB Munsche, *Gentlemen and Poachers: The English game laws, 1671–1830* (Cambridge, Mass., 1981); Geneology UK and Ireland, *The Berkeley Castle Poaching Affray* <www.genuki.org.uk>.

The sealers' life and governance
Flinders in Bass Strait: Miriam Estensen, *The Life of Matthew Flinders*.

Sealers: John West, *The History of Tasmania*, 2 vols (Launceston 1852); James Boyce, *Van Diemen's Land* (Melbourne 2008); WA Townsley, *Tasmania from Colony to Statehood 1803–1945* (Hobart 1991); Brian Plompley & Kristen Anne Henley, 'The sealers of Bass Strait and the Cape Barren Island community', *Tasmanian Historical Research Association, Papers and Proceedings*, 37 (2 and 3), 1990; Iain Stuart, 'Sea rats, bandits and roistering buccaneers: what were the Bass Strait sealers really like?', *JRAHS*, 83 (1), 1997.

Relationship of sealers with Aboriginals: Rebe Taylor, 'Savages or saviours? The Australian sealers and Aboriginal Tasmanian survival', *Journal of Australian Studies: Vision splendid*, 66, 2000.

Some notes on Matthew Flinders
Estensen, *The life of Matthew Flinders*; Matthew Flinders, *A Voyage to Terra Australis*, 2 vols, (London 1814), available on Project Gutenberg Australia.

The tattoo and the lash
Punishment in general: Alan Atkinson, 'Four patterns of convict protest', *Labour History*, 37, 1979, and 'The government of time and space in 1838', *The Push from the Bush*, 9, 1981; Michael Ignatieff, *A Just Measure of Pain: The penitentiary in the Industrial Revolution, 1750–1850* (London 1989); David Neal, *The Rule of Law in a Penal Colony* (Cambridge 1991), and 'Free society, penal colony, slave society, prison?', *Historical Studies*, 22, (89), 1987.

Discipline at Port Macquarie: Bench Book, NSWSA, 4/5638, and Port Macquarie, NSWSA 4/5639; *Trial of Twelve Men*, 24 August 1833, for killing a constable, Port Macquarie, NSWSA, 4/5637; *Trial of Benjamin Ray*, 2 April 1832, Port Macquarie NSWSA, 4/5638; *A Convict Bullock Drivers' Strike*, 12 April 1834.

Moreton Bay: Jack Bushman, 'Passages from the life of a "lifer"', *Moreton Bay Courier*, Brisbane, Australia, 2, 9, 16, 23 and 30 April 1859; Raymond Evans, *A History of Queensland* (Melbourne 2007).
Female convicts: Jennifer Harrison, '"The very worst class": Irish women convicts at Moreton Bay' in Bob Reece (ed), *Irish Convict Lives* (Sydney 1993); Babette Smith, *A Cargo of Women: Susannah Watson and the convicts of the Princess Royal* (Sydney 1988).
Frank the Poet: Bob Reece, 'Frank the Poet' in Reece, *Exiles from Erin*.
Foster Fyans: James Backhouse, *A Narrative of a Visit to the Australian Colonies* (London 1843).
Punishment: JC Byrne, *Twelve Years Wanderings in the British Colonies from 1835 to 1847* (London 1848); Harris, *Settlers and Convicts*; Ian Duffield and James Bradley (eds), *Representing Convicts: New perspectives in convict forced labour migration* (London 1997); Backhouse, *A Narrative of a Visit to the Australian Colonies*.

Gangs
Grace Karskens, *Four Essays About the Great North Road* (Kulnura 1998), and 'The grandest improvement in the country: an historical and archeological study of the Great North Road, NSW, 1825–1836', MA thesis (University of Sydney 1985).
Solomon Wiseman: *ADB*, 2; R Therry, *Reminiscences of Thirty Years' Residence in New South Wales & Victoria* (London 1863).

Convict novelists
Savery and Tucker: *ADB*, 2; Henry Savery, *Quintus Servinton*, ed. and with biographical introduction by Cecil H. Hadgraft (Brisbane 1962); James Tucker, *Ralph Rashleigh*, ed. and with biographical introduction by Colin Roderick (Sydney 1952); State Library of Tasmania, Savery Papers; Henry Savery, *The Hermit of Van Diemen's Land*, ed. and with biographical introduction by Cecil Hadgraft (Brisbane 1964).

CHAPTER 14

Arriving at the end of things
Arrival of *Parmelia*: *Sydney Gazette*, 6 March 1834.
Convicts aboard *Parmelia*: Indent, 4/7076, AONSW; Keneally, *The Great Shame*.
Varieties of convicts and appearance of Sydney: Harris, *Convicts and Settlers*; James Mudie, *The Felonry of New South Wales* (Melbourne 1964).
Governor Bourke: *ADB*, 1; Hazel King, 'The early life of Sir Richard Bourke', *JRAHS*, 55, 1969, and 'Richard Bourke and his two colonial administrations', *JRAHS*, 9, 1964; Max Waugh, *Forgotten Hero: Richard Bourke* (Melbourne 2005); Bourke Family Papers, 1809–1855, Part 3 and Family Correspondence of the Bourke Family, 1822–1855, M 1863, ML.
Eliza Burns incident: *Sydney Herald*, 3 March 1834.
Slade: *ADB*, 2; 'Return of corporal punishment', *British Parliamentary Papers* (BPP), VI; EA Slade, *Evidence to Select Committee on Transportation*, BPP, XIX.

Secret societies: Clark & Donnelly, *Irish Peasants*; Donal McCartney, *The Dawning of Democracy: Ireland 1800–1878* (Dublin 1987); Keneally, *The Great Shame.*

Beyond the limits
Limits of Location: Stephen H Roberts, *The Squatting Age in Australia, 1835–1847* (Melbourne 1935); WK Hancock, *Discovering Monaro: A study of man's impact on his environment* (London 1972); Clark, *A History of Australia*, 2; Russel Ward, *The Australian Legend* (Melbourne 1958).
Assignments of *Parmelia* men: Memoranda Book, 1829–37, 2/2808, AONSW; and 1837 Muster, HO 10/30, AONSW.
Critics of assignment: JD Lang, *Evidence before the Select Committee on Transportation*, 30 May 1837, *BPP*, XIX; *Report from the Select Committee on Transportation* (House of Commons 1838); Mudie, *The Felonry of New South Wales*; Hirst, *Convict Society and its Enemies.*
Life of convict shepherds: Ward, *The Australian Legend.*
Bradley and Brodribb: *ADB*, 3; WA Brodribb, *Reminiscences of an Australian Squatter*, ed. AGL Shaw (Sydney 1883).
Land Commissioners and wool sales: Roberts, *The Squatting Age in Australia.*
Pastoral hope: John Perkins & Jack Thompson, 'Cattle theft: primitive cattle accumulation and pastoral expansion in early New South Wales, 1800–1850', *Australian Historical Studies*, III, 1998.
Ned Ryan: M Barnett, *King of Galong Castle* (Sydney 1978); Niamh Brennan, 'The Ballagh Barracks Rioters' in Reece, *Exiles from Erin.*

Meeting the seasonal people
Contact: Hancock, *Discovering Monaro*; Roberts, *The Squatting Age in Australia*; Australian Institute of Aboriginal and Torres Strait Islander Studies, Aboriginal Map of Australia, <www.aiats.gov.au>; Michael Young, *The Aboriginal People of the Monaro: A new documentary history* (Sydney 2005).
'The Convict and His Loubra': Ingleton, *True Patriots All.*
Sir George Gipps: *ADB*, 2; Roberts, *The Squatting Age in Australia.*
Protectors of Aborigines: Roberts, *The Squatting Age in Australia*; Henry Reynolds, *The Law of the Land* (Melbourne 1987); *The Australian Aborigines' Protection Society, Rules and Regulations* (Sydney 1838); *Report of the Parliamentary Select Committee on Aboriginal Tribes* (London 1837).

CHAPTER 15

The heady business of exploring
William Joy, *The Other Side of the Hill: Two hundred years of Australian exploration* (Sydney 1984); Kathleen Fitzpatrick, *Australian Explorers* (London 1959); Scott, *Australian Discovery*, available on Project Gutenberg Australia.
Oxley and Cunningham: *ADB*, 1 and 2; Joy, *The Other Side of the Hill*; John Oxley, *Journal of Two Expeditions into the Interior of New South Wales*, available on Project Gutenberg Australia.
Other explorers: Gregory Blaxland, *The Journal of Gregory Blaxland*; Hamilton Hume

and William Hovell, *Journey of Discovery to Port Phillip*; Thomas Mitchell, *Journal of an Expedition into the Interior of Tropical Australia*; *Three Expeditions into the Interior of Eastern Australia*; Charles Sturt, *Two Expeditions into the Interior of Southern Australia*, and *Narrative of an Expedition into Central Australia*. All available on Project Gutenberg Australia.
Hume and Hovell and Major Mitchell: Joy, *The Other Side of the Hill*; Fitzpatrick, *Australian Explorers*.
Sturt: *ADB*, 2; Sturt, *Two Expeditions into the Interior of Southern Australia*.

Dust and endurance
Mitchell, *Journal of an Expedition into the Interior of Tropical Australia*; Sturt, *Two Expeditions into the Interior of Southern Australia*.
Eyre: Edward John Eyre, *Journals of Expeditions of Discovery into Central Australia*, 2 vols, available on Project Gutenberg Australia.
Toas: Phillip Jones & Peter Sutton, *Art and Land* (Adelaide 1986).
Leichhardt: Alec H Chisholm, *Strange New World: The adventures of John Gilbert and Ludwig Leichhardt* (Sydney 1941); Ludwig Leichhardt, *Journal of an Overland Expedition in Australia, 1844–1845*, available on Project Gutenberg Australia.
Stuart and Burke and Wills: John Bailey, *Mr Stuart's Track: The forgotten life of Australia's greatest explorer* (Sydney 2007); Sarah Murgatroyd, *The Dig Tree: The extraordinary story of the ill-fated Burke and Wills expedition* (London 2000); Alan Moorehead, *Cooper's Creek* (London 1963).

CHAPTER 16

Merrie England
Conflict in Britain: Black Dwarf, history website <www.spartacus.schoolnet.co.uk>; William Cobbett, *Rural Rides* (London 1953).
John Anderson: *ADB*, 1.
Margaret and Alastair McFarlane: *The Scottish Radicals: Tried and transported in 1820* (Stevenage 1981).
Struggle for Reform Bill: Paul Scherer, *Lord John Russell: A biography* (London 1999).
Swing Riots: EP Thompson, 'The crime of anonymity' in Hay et al., *Albion's Fatal Tree*; George Rudé, *Protest and Punishment: The story of the social and political protesters transported to Australia 1788–1868* (Oxford 1978); Norma Townsend, 'Reconstructed lives: the Swing transportees in New South Wales', *Australian Studies*, 16 (2), 2001.

A steerage passenger
Bounty emigration: Robin Haines, *Life and Death in the Age of Sail: The passage to Australia* (Sydney 2003); Don Charlworth, *The Long Farewell* (Melbourne 1981); Don Watson, *Caledonia Australis: Scottish Highlanders on the frontier of Australia* (Sydney 1997); David Fitzpatrick, *Oceans of Consolation: Personal accounts of Irish migration to Australia* (Cork 1994); Chistopher O'Mahony & Valerie Thompson, *Poverty to Promise: The Monteagle emigrants, 1838–1858* (Sydney 1994).

Parkes's emigration: Henry Parkes, *An Immigrant's Home Letters*, ed. Annie T Parkes (Sydney 1896).
The Emigrant's Farewell: Thomas Campbell, *The Complete Poetical Works of Thomas Campbell* (London 1907).

The alma mater of immigrants
Steerage: Parkes, *An Immigrant's Home Letters*.
Manlius and other ships and passengers: Haines, *Life and Death in the Age of Sail*; Charlworth, *The Long Farewell*.
Sarah Davenport: Lucy Frost, *No Place for a Nervous Lady* (Sydney 1984).
The Immigrant's Vision: Charles Harpur, *The Poetical Works of Charles Harpur*, intro. Elizabeth Perkins (Sydney 1984).

The Scottish wave
Watson, *Caledonia Australis*; JD Lang, *Reminiscence of My Life and Times*, ed. DWA Baker (Melbourne 1972).

Reinventing Scotland
Triggers of Scots immigration, and Scots in the bush: William Cobbitt, *Ten Letters Addressed to the Tax-Payers of England* (London 1829).
MacDonnell: Watson, *Caledonia Australis*; George Dunderdale, *The Book of the Bush* (London 1870).
Other transplanted lairds: R Ian Jack, 'Andrew Brown, Laird of Cooerwull', *JRAHS*, 73, 1987–88.

Charles Darwin's New South Wales
FW & JM Nicholas, *Charles Darwin in Australia* (Melbourne 2008).

CHAPTER 17

'All freedom and sentiment'
JJ Spiegelman, 'Foundations of freedom of the press in Australia', *Quadrant*, 47 (3) 2003; RB Walker, *The Newspaper Press in New South Wales* (Sydney 1976); Sandra J Blair, 'The convict press: William Watt and the *Sydney Gazette* in the 1830s', *The Push from the Bush*, 5, 1979, and 'Patronage and prejudice: educated convicts in the New South Wales press', *The Push from the Bush*, 8, 1980.
Wardell: *ADB*, 2.
Barron Field: *ADB*, 1.
Massey Robinson: *ADB*, 2.
Freedom of press issues: *The Australian*, 22 September, 6 October, and 20 October 1825.
The anniversary dinner: Molony, *The Native-Born*.
The departure of Sir Thomas Brisbane: Wentworth in *The Australian*, 27 October 1825.
Ralph Darling: *ADB*, 1; Ritchie, *The Wentworths*.
Darling, Wentworth and others: Michael Roe, *Quest for Authority in Eastern Australia, 1813–1851* (Melbourne 1965).

Sudds and Thompson: Therry, *Reminiscences of Thirty Years' Residence in New South Wales & Victoria*; Roe, *Quest for Authority in Eastern Australia*; Walker, *The Newspaper Press in New South Wales*.

Arthur: *ADB*, 1.

Forbes: *ADB*, 1; Therry, *Reminiscences of Thirty Years' Residence in New South Wales & Victoria*.

Pedder: *ADB*, 2; Roe, *Quest for Authority in Eastern Australia*.

Hall: *ADB*, 1; Roe, *Quest for Authority in Eastern Australia*; Peter Cochrane, *Colonial Ambition* (Melbourne 2006).

Departure of Darling: *Monitor* and *The Australian*, 26 October 1831; Ritchie, *The Wentworths*; Cochrane, *Colonial Ambition*.

Sir Richard Bourke: *ADB*, 1; Max Waugh, *Forgotten Hero*.

The press of the 1830s

RB Walker, *The Newspaper Press in New South Wales*.

O'Shaughnessy and Watt: *ADB*, 2.

Watt in trouble: William Watt, *Party Politics Exposed* (signed *Humanitas*) (Sydney 1834); 'A report on the proceedings of the case of William Angus Watt', *HRA*, Series I, XVIII.

The Australian: Ritchie, *The Wentworths*; Walker, *The Newspaper Press in New South Wales*.

CHAPTER 18

New Holland

Australian Agricultural Company: Roberts, *The Squatting Age in Australia*.

James Stirling: *ADB*, 2; JS Battye, *Western Australia: A history from its discovery to the inauguration of the Commonwealth* (Nedlands, W.A., 1978); Clark, *A History of Australia*, 2.

Thomas Peel: *ADB*, 2; Battye, *Western Australia*.

Solomon Levey: *ADB*, 2; GFJ Bergman, 'Solomon Levey', *JRAHS*, 29, 1963–4.

Talking to the sulky one

Fremantle: Battye, *Western Australia*.

The Sulky One: George Fletcher Moore, *Extracts from the Letters and Journals of George Fletcher Moore* (London 1834), and *Diary of Ten Years Eventful Life as an Early Settler in Western Australia* (London 1884).

Molloy, Bussell: Alexandra Hasluck, *Portrait with Background: A life of Georgiana Molloy* (Melbourne 1955).

The founding years: EW Landor, *The Bushman, or Life in a New Country* (London 1847).

Oh Mr Wakefield

Wakefield's plans: Edward Gibbon Wakefield, *Sketch of a Proposal for Colonizing Australasia* (London 1829), and *A Letter from Sydney, the Principal Town of Australasia*, ed. R Gouger (London 1929).

South Australia in concept and reality: DH Pike, *Paradise of Dissent: South Australia*

1829–1857 (London 1957); Derek Whitelock, *Adelaide 1836–1976: A history of difference* (Brisbane 1977); Clark, *A History of Australia*, 2.
Angas, Gouger and Hindmarsh: *ADB*, 1 and 2.

Re-establishing Port Phillip
The Hentys: Margaret Kiddle, *Men of Yesterday: A social history of the western districts of Victoria, 1834–1890* (Melbourne 1961); Clark, *A History of Australia*, 2.
Gellibrand, Batman, Wedge, Lonsdale: all *ADB*, 1 and 2; Kiddle, *Men of Yesterday*; Joyce, *Van Diemen's Land*; L Bonwick, *John Batman* (Melbourne 1867); John Pascoe Fawkner, *Melbourne's Missing Chronicle: Being the journal of preparations for departure to and proceedings at Port Phillip*, ed. CP Billot (Melbourne 1982).
Neil Black: *ADB*, 1; Kiddle, *Men of Yesterday*.
La Trobe and his wife: *ADB*, 2; G Serle, *The Golden Age* (Melbourne 1967).

The colony of the saints
General conditions and problems: Pike, *Paradise of Dissent*; Whitlock, *Adelaide*.
Hindmarsh: *ADB*, 1.
Light: *ADB*, 2; G Dutton, *Founder of a City* (Melbourne 1960).

The maiden of Australind
Lucy Frost, *No Place for a Nervous Lady*.
Australind and other settlers: Hasluck, *Portrait with Background*; Battye, *Western Australia*; Jane Dodds, *A Swan River Colony Pioneer*, ed. Lilian Heel (Sydney 1988).

CHAPTER 19

Myall Creek … and beyond
Windradyne: *ADB* online <www.adbonline.anv.edu.au>; Bruce Elder, *Blood on the Wattle: Massacres and maltreatment of Aboriginal Australians since 1788* (Sydney 1988); T Salisbury & PJ Gresser, *Windradyne and the Wiradjuri: Martial law at Bathurst in 1824* (Sydney 1971); Bill Gammage, 'The Wiradjuri War, 1838–40', *The Push from the Bush*, 16, 1983.
Philanthropus: Reynolds, *Dispossession*.
Continued resistance: Michael Pearson, 'Bathurst Plains and beyond: European colonisation and Aboriginal resistance', *Aboriginal History*, 8 (1), 1984.
Snodgrass: *ADB*, 2.
Major Nunn: *HRA*, I; Clark, *A History of Australia*, 2; Reynolds, *Dispossession*.
Dangar: *ADB*, 1; Roberts, *The Squatting Age in Australia*; R Millis, *Waterloo Creek: The Australia Day massacre of 1838* (Melbourne 1992).
Individual account of the Myall Creek Massacre: *Sydney Herald*, 26 November 1838; *Sydney Monitor* and *Commercial Advertiser*, 19 November 1838; Elizabeth Webby, 'Reactions to the Myall Creek Massacre', *The Push from the Bush*, 8, December, 1980; Alan Atkinson (ed), '1838', *The Push from the Bush*, 1, May 1978; David Denholm, 'The Myall Creek Massacre', *The Push from the Bush*, 9, 1981.

Myall Creek and other conflicts: Clark, *A History of Australia*, 2; Bruce Elder, *Blood on the Wattle*; Don Watson, *Caledonia Australis*; Henry Reynolds, *Fate of a Free People* (Melbourne 1995), and *Dispossession* (Sydney 1989); Norma Townsend, 'Masters and men and the Myall Creek Massacre', *The Push from the Bush*, 20, 1985; Lyndall Ryan, 'Aboriginal policy in Australia: 1838—A watershed?', *The Push from the Bush*, 8, 1980.
For contrary view on massacres: Keith Windschuttle, *The Myth of Frontier Massacres in Australian History, Part I, II and III: The invention of massacre stories* (Quadrant 2000).

Contesting the land
Bennelong and Goat Island: Collins, *An Account of the English Colony in New South Wales*, 2.
European attitudes: Reynolds, *Dispossession*; Richard Windeyer, *ADB*, 2;
EE Landor, *The Bushman: Report from the Select Committee on Aborigines (British Settlements) together with the minutes of evidence, House of Commons Parliamentary Papers*, 1836; Saxe Bannister, *Evidence Before Select Committee on Aborigines*.
Relationships and depredations: Michael Cannon, *Who Killed the Koories?* (Melbourne 1990); Moore, *Diary of Ten Years*; Watson, *Caledonia Australis*; Dunderdale, *The Book of the Bush*.
Curr: Roberts, *The Squatting Age in Australia*; Cannon, *Who Killed the Koories?*

CHAPTER 20

Lost women, lost tribes
Lost woman in Gippsland: McMillan, *ADB*, 2; Watson, *Caledonia Australis*; Dunderdale, *The Book of the Bush*.
Eliza Fraser: DJ Mulvaney, 'John Graham: The convict as Aboriginal' in Reece, *Irish Convict Lives*; M Alexander, *Mrs Fraser on the Fatal Shore* (London 1971).

Rescuing Eliza
Graham's career and Eliza Fraser rescue: Mulvaney, 'John Graham'; Graham and Otter's Report, COD 183, AONSW; Ingleton, *True Patriots All*.

CHAPTER 21

Molesworth's committee
Molesworth and Grey: HCG Matthew & Brian Harrison (eds), *The Oxford Dictionary of National Biography* (London 2004).
Opposition to the system, and calls for greater harshness: Hirst, *Convict Society and its Enemies*; *Summary of the Report of the Select Committee on Transportation, together with Minutes of Evidence* (Westminster 1837); William Ullathorne, *Evidence before the Select Committee on Transportation, 1837*, BPP, XIX, 1; JD Lang, *Evidence before the Select Committee on Transportation*; James Macarthur, *Evidence before the Select Committee on Transportation*; Mudie, *Evidence before the Select Committee on Transportation*.

CHAPTER 22

The girl from the Female Factory

Female Factory: Annette Salt, *These Outcast Women: The Parramatta Female Factory, 1821–1848* (Sydney 1984); Kaye Daniels, *Convict Women* (Sydney 1998); Tony Rayner, *Female Factory Convicts* (Hobart 2004).

Mary Shields and other condemned: *Limerick Chronicle*, 9 January 1839.

Spring Crimes: Cormac O'Grada, *Ireland Before and After the Famine: Explorations in economic history, 1800–1825* (Dublin 1989); Margaret Crawford (ed), *Famine: The Irish experience 900 to 1900—subsistence crises and famines in Ireland* (Edinburgh 1989).

Irish Poor Law and workhouses: John O'Connor, *The Workhouses of Ireland* (Dublin 1995).

Convicts or Whitby and accompanying children: 2/8282, AONSW; Surgeons Log, Whitby, PRO 3212.

Irish women convicts in general: Peter Cunningham, *ADB*, 1; Peter Cunningham, *Two Years in New South Wales* (London 1827).

Further information on Van Diemen's Land female convicts: Sir John Franklin, *Confidential Dispatch from Sir John Franklin, 1843, addressed to the Secretary of State Lord Stanley*, Sullivan's Cove, 1996.

Neva: Bateson, *Convict Ships.*

Sir George Gipps to Glenelg: *HRA*, XIX.

Whitby arrives: *Sydney Gazette*, 26 June 1939.

Sisters of Charity: Richard Reid & Cheryl Mongan, *A Decent Set of Girls* (Yass 1996).

Female convicts: Mudie, *The Felonry of New South Wales*, and *Evidence Before the Select Committee on Transportation.*

Inside Female Factory: Salt, *These Outcast Women.*

Song, 'The Girl from the Female Factory': Douglas Stewart & Nancy Keesing (eds), *Old Bush Songs and Rhymes of Colonial Times* (Sydney 1957).

Assignment: Colonial Secretary's Correspondence, Female Factory 4/3691, AONSW.

Description of Shields and others: Tickets-of-leave, 4/4178, AONSW.

Nature of travel, NSW: Alexander Harris, *Emigrant Mechanic* (London 1850); Russel Ward, *The Australian Legend.*

Samuel Terry: *ADB*, 2.

Tallow: Roberts, *The Squatting Age in Australia.*

CHAPTER 23

The poor emigrant ashore

Arrival: Parkes, *An Immigrant's Home Letters.*

Depression, 1840s: Roberts, *The Squatting Age in Australia*; Sinclair, *Monaro*; Clark, *A History of Australia Volume 3: The beginning of an Australian civilisation, 1824–1851* (Melbourne 1986).

Mrs Meredith: see George Meredith, *ADB*, 2; Mrs Charles Meredith, *Notes and Sketches of New South Wales During a Residence in the Colony from 1839 to 1844* (Sydney 1973).

Henry Parkes's verse: Sir Henry Parkes, *Stolen Moments* (Sydney 1842).

Pastoral Might

All aspects: Roe, *Quest for Authority in Eastern Australia*; Roberts, *The Squatting Age in Australia*; Cochrane, *Colonial Ambition*; Kiddle, *Men of Yesterday*; Clark, *A History of Australia*, 3; Brian H Fletcher, 'Governor Bourke and squatting in New South Wales', *JRAHS*, 74 (4), 1989.

Governor Gipps: *ADB*, 1; Sydney Kendall Barker, 'The Governorship of Sir George Gipps', *JRAHS*, 16, (3 and 4).

CHAPTER 24

Fetching Spouses

Hugh's application and those of others: Returns of Applications, 1837–1843, 4/4992, AONSW.

The squatter's situation: Brodribb, *Reminiscences of an Australian Squatter.*

Laurencetown, etc: CG Otway, *A Tour in Connaght* (Dublin 1839).

William Forster: *ADB*, 4.

Squatters' reluctance: Roberts, *The Squatting Age in Australia*; Cochrane, *Colonial Ambition.*

A birth in the bush

Brodribb's marriage: Brodribb, *Reminiscences of an Australian Squatter.*

Shield's child: Baptismal Records, St Peter and Paul's Church, Goulburn, 22 August 1844; Mary, Baptismal Records, December 1947.

Convict marriage: Therry, *Reminiscences of Thirty Years' Residence in New South Wales & Victoria.*

Society's contest with the governor: Fitzroy, *ADB*, 1; Cochrane, *Colonial Ambition*; Roe, *Quest for Authority in Eastern Australia.*

Conditional pardon: 4/4459, 1 June 1848, AONSW.

Purchase of land: Land Deeds 48/11967, 25 October 1848, AONSW.

Brodribb loss: Brodribb, *Reminiscences of an Australian Squatter.*

Famine orphans: Reid & Mongan, *A Decent Set of Girls*; Trevor McClaughlin, *Barefoot and Pregnant? Irish famine orphans in Australia* (Melbourne 1991).

Mary and the Thunguddi

Mary McMaugh: Mary McMaugh, *Pioneering on the Upper Macleay* (Wingham, NSW, n.d.); Augustus Rudder, 'The Macleay River', *The Town and Country Journal*, LXIV, 1902; John Weingarth, 'The discovery and settlement of the Macleay River', *JRAHS*, 10, 1924.

Thunguddi: Clement Hodgkinson, *Australia from Port Macquarie to Moreton Bay* (London 1845); Geoffrey Blomfield, *Baal Belbora: The end of the dancing* (Sydney 1981).

CHAPTER 25

Canada Bay

Patriotes and other Canadian and American rebels: Beverley Boissery, *A Deep Sense of Wrong: The treason, trials and transportation to New South Wales of lower Canadian rebels after the 1938 rebellion* (Toronto 1995).

Buffalo: Bateson, *The Convict Ships.*

Experiences in Sydney: Léon Ducharme, *Journal of a Political Exile in Australia*, ed. George Mackaness (Dubbo 1976).

Reaction of residents: Therry, *Reminiscences of Thirty Years' Residence in New South Wales & Victoria.*

Clergy: Polding, *ADB*, 2.

Situation of *Patriotes* and other politicals: Rudé, *Protest and Punishment*; AGL Shaw, *Convicts and the Colonies.*

Governor Franklin: *ADB*, 1.

Tasmanian rebels: Linus Miller, *Notes of an Exile to Van Diemen's Land* (East Ardley, UK, 1968); Samuel Snow, *The Exile's Return* (Cleveland 1846).

The religious divide

Divide and internal conflict: Polding, *ADB*, 2; Nixon, *ADB*, 2.

Polding and Nixon: Roe, *Quest for Authority in Eastern Australia*; O'Farrell, *The Irish in Australia.*

O'Donahue: Kiernan, *The Irish Exiles in Australia*; Keneally, *The Great Shame.*

John McSweeney, *A Meddling Priest: John Joseph Therry* (Strathfield, NSW, 2000).

O'Donahue's espousing of Therry: *The Irish Exile*, July–November, 1850.

CHAPTER 26

Democracy

The ferment: Cochrane, *Colonial Ambition*; Roe, *Quest for Authority in Eastern Australia*; Clark, *A History of Australia*, 3; Beverley Kingston, *A History of New South Wales* (Melbourne 2006).

Lowe: *ADB*, 2.

Boyd: *ADB*, 1.

Moreton Bay separation: Evans, *A History of Queensland.*

Charles Harpur's poetry: Molony, *The Native-Born.*

The toyshop mob

Parkes's coterie: Cochrane, *Colonial Ambition*; Roe, *Quest for Authority in Eastern Australia*; John Hirst, *The Strange Birth of Australian Democracy: New South Wales 1848–1888* (Sydney 1988); Paul A Pickering, '"The oak of English liberty": popular constitutionalism in New South Wales, 1848 to 1856', *JACH*, 3 (1), 2001; Sir Henry Parkes, Letters, CY 2823 (A19), folios 114–243, ML.

General progressive and Chartist ideas at play: Clark, *A History of Australia*, 3; Andrew

Messner, 'Contesting chartism from afar: Edward Hawksley and the people's advocate, *JACH*, 1, (1999).

CHAPTER 27

East Indiamen
Alan Dwight, 'The use of Indian labourers in New South Wales', *JRAHS*, 62 (2), 1976; John Roe, *Quest for Authority in Eastern Australia.*
Robert Towns: *ADB*, 6; Robert Campbell, *ADB*, 3.

Trading in tea
Attempts at northern settlement: Alan Powell, *Far Country: A short history of the Northern Territory* (Melbourne 1982); Reynolds, *North of Capricorn.*
Tea trade: Marian Diamond, 'Tea and sympathy: foundations of the Australia/China trading networks', *Queensland Review*, 6 (2), 1999; James Broadbent, Suzanne Rickard & Margaret Steven, *India, China, Australia: Trade and society, 1788–1850* (Sydney 2003); Alan Lester, 'Imperial circuits and networks: geographies of the British Empire, *History Compass*, 4 (1), 2006.
Fort Dundas: *HRA*, Series III, V.

What about Chinese?
Recruitment, journey, and Australian existence: Maxine Darnell, 'Master and servant, squatter and shepherd: the regulation of indentured Chinese labourers, New South Wales, 1847–1853', in Henry Chan, Ann Curthays & Nora Ching (eds) *The Overseas Chinese in Australia: Settlement and interactions—proceedings* (Canberra 2001); Shirley Fitzgerald, *Red Tape, Gold Scissors* (Sydney 2008); Ian Jack, 'Some less familiar aspects of the Chinese in nineteenth century Australia' in Chan, Curthoys & Ching, *The Overseas Chinese in Australia*; Jan Ryan, *Ancestors: Chinese in Colonial Australia* (Fremantle 1995); Sing Wu Wang, *The Organisation of Chinese Emigration 1848–1888* (San Francisco 1978); Maxine Darnell, 'Life and labour for indentured Chinese shepherds in New South Wales, 1847–1855', *JACH*, 6, 2004; C.Y. Choi, *Chinese Migration and Settlement in Australia* (Sydney 1975); Alan Dwight, 'The Chinese in New South Wales law courts 1848–1854', *JRAHS*, 73 (2), 1987; *Indentured Chinese Labourers and Employers Identified, New South Wales, 1828–1856*, developed by Maxine Darnell at <www.chaf.lib.latrobe.edu.au/indentured.htm>.
Women who married Chinese: Kate Bagnall, 'Golden shadows on a white land: an exploration of the lives of white women who partnered Chinese men and their children in Southern Australia, 1855–1915', PhD Thesis, University of Sydney, 2008, and '"I was nearly broken hearted about him": stories of Australian mothers' separation from their "Chinese" children', *History Australia*, 1 (I), 2003.

CHAPTER 28

Golden Epiphany

Discovery of gold: Geoffrey Blainey, *The Rush That Never Ended: A history of Australian mining* (Melbourne 1969); David Goodman, *Gold Seeking: Victoria and California in the 1850s* (Sydney 1994); Charles Barrett (ed), *Gold: The romance of its discovery* (Melbourne 1970); Clark, *A History of Australia*, 3.

Hargraves: *ADB*, 4.

Deas Thomson: *ADB*, 2.

Impact of gold on Australian politics: Cochrane, *Colonial Ambition*; Roe, *Quest for Authority in Eastern Australia*.

Other claims of discovery: Blainey, *The Rush That Never Ended*; HME Heney, *In a Dark Glass: The story of Paul Edmund Strzelecki* (Sydney 1961).

Golden Victoria

Diggings: Clark, *A History of Australia*, 3, and *A History of Australia Volume 4: The earth abideth forever* (Melbourne 1978); Blainey, *The Rush That Never Ended*; Goodman, *Gold Seeking*; Barrett, *Gold*; John Molony, *Eureka* (Melbourne 2001); Ian D Clark, 'Another side of Eureka: the Aboriginal presence on the Ballarat goldfields in 1854', Working Paper (University of Ballarat 2005/07).

Meagher: Keneally, *The Great Shame*.

CHAPTER 29

How gold makes all new

Further developments: Clark, *A History of Australia*, 3 and 4; Blainey, *The Rush That Never Ended*; Goodman, *Gold Seeking*; Molony, *Eureka*.

Wentworth, Parkes and others: Cochrane, *Colonial Ambition*.

Impact of gold on society: Therry, *Reminiscences of Thirty Years' Residence in New South Wales & Victoria*.

a'Becketts and Redmond Barry: *ADB*, 3.

Goldfield arrivals

The Lalors and Humffray: Keneally, *The Great Shame*; Molony, *Eureka*.

Lalor: *ADB*, 5; Humffray, *ADB*, 4.

Carboni: *ADB*, 3; Molony, *Eureka*; Raffaello Carboni, *The Eureka Stockade*, intro. T. Keneally (Melbourne 2004); Desmond O'Grady, *Raffaello! Raffaello! A biography of Raffaello Carboni* (Sydney 1985).

Lettered miners

Standard gold-rush works as for previous two sections; Keneally, *The Great Shame*; Carboni, *The Eureka Stockade*; O'Grady, *Raffaello! Raffaello!*

Rede: *ADB*, 6.

AUSTRALIANS

CHAPTER 30

Golden Celestials
Jean Gittins, *The Diggers from China: The story of Chinese on the goldfields* (Melbourne 1981); Jan Ryan, *Ancestors: Chinese in colonial Australia* (Fremantle 1995); Wang, *Organisation of Chinese Emigration*; Kathryn Cronin, *Colonial Casualties: Chinese in early Victoria* (Melbourne 1982); Henry Chan, *The Overseas Chinese in Australasia* (Taipei 2001); Barry McGowan, 'Reconsidering race: the Chinese experience on the goldfields of southern New South Wales', *Australian Historical Studies*, 124, 2004.

Objects in a landscape, or actors in a field
Keir Reeves, 'A songster, a sketcher and the Chinese on central Victoria's Mount Alexander diggings: case studies in cultural complexity during the second half of the nineteenth century', *JACH*, 6, 2004; Barry McGowan, 'The Chinese on the Braidwood goldfields: historical and archaeological opportunities', *JACH*, 6, 2004; Barry McGowan, 'The economics and organisation of Chinese mining in colonial Australia', *Australian Economic History Review*, 45 (2), 2004; Dinah Hales, 'Lost histories: Chinese–European families of central western New South Wales, 1850–1880', *JACH*, (6), 2004.
Protests and race riots: Andrew Messner, 'Popular constitutionalism and Chinese protest on the Victorian goldfields', *JACH*, 2, 2000.

CHAPTER 31

The republican push
Cochrane, *Colonial Ambition*; Roe, *Quest for Authority in Eastern Australia*; Pickering, '"The oak of English liberty"'.
Fitzroy: *ADB*, 4.
Lang's judgments: Alan Martin, *Henry Parkes: A biography* (Melbourne 1980); JD Lang, *Freedom and Independence for the Golden Lands of Australia* (London 1852).
Deniehy: Cyril Pearl, *Brilliant Dan Deniehy* (Brisbane 1972); EA Martin, *The Life and Speeches of Daniel Henry Deniehy* (Sydney 1884); Deniehy's Letters, 869, ML. In MLMSS 868, Daniel Deniehy's letters from 1833–1860, there is a prospectus of his newspaper, *The Southern Cross*.
Betsey Bandicoot Letter: *Sydney Gazette*, 30 October 1823.
Stenhouse and others: Cochrane, *Colonial Ambition*; Pearl, *Brilliant Dan Deniehy*.
Henry Kendall: *ADB*, 5; Henry Kendall, *Poems and Songs* (Sydney 1862).

House of Colonial Lords and **The Roosians**
James Macarthur: *ADB*, 5.
The constitutional debate: Cochrane, *Colonial Ambition*; Roe, *Quest for Authority in Eastern Australia*; Pearl, *Brilliant Dan Deniehy*.

CHAPTER 32

Police state?

Police oppression: Goodman, *Gold Seeking*; Molony, *Eureka*; *Report of the Gold Fields' Commission of Enquiry* (Victorian Parliament 1855); Carboni, *The Eureka Stockade*; Blainey, *The Rush That Never Ended*; Clark, *A History of Australia*, 4.
Peter Lalor: *ADB*, 5.
Lalor family: Keneally, *The Great Shame*; Kiernan, *The Irish Exiles in Australia*.
Governor Hotham: *ADB*, 4; Molony, *Eureka*.

CHAPTER 33

The battle

Molony, *Eureka*; Carboni, *The Eureka Stockade*; Clark, *A History of Australia*, 4; *Age*, 6, 7 December; *Argus*, 6, 7, 8, 15 December 1854.

CHAPTER 34

The aftermath

Official reaction, escapes and trials: Raffaello Carboni, *Memoirs*; Molony, *Eureka*; Paul A Pickering, 'Ripe for a republic: British radical responses to the Eureka Stockade', *Australian Historical Studies*, 34 (121), April 2003.
Smith O'Brien: Keneally, *The Great Shame*.
Australian patriots and political developments: Kingston, *A History of New South Wales*; Anne Coote, 'Imagining the colonial nation: the development of popular concepts of sovereignty and nation in New South Wales between 1856 and 1860', *JACH*, 1 (1), 1999.
Wentworth: Cochrane, *Colonial Ambition*.

INDEX

AUSTRALIANS

attempts to educate British, 129
attempts to kill Pemulwuy, 160
capture of, 127
contrasted with Pemulwuy, 195
cremates wife, 193
death, 219
encounter with Phillip at Manly,
  154–7
at exchange of stolen property,
  158
given house in Sydney Cove, 161
gives whale meat to Phillip, 154
life at Government House, 129,
  130
love of women, 130, 131
marriages of, 161–3
meets Phillip, 128
meets Phillip on North Shore,
  159
names of, 87, 127
as peacemaker, 161
real property of, 405
returns from England, 216–17
returns to Sydney Cove, 159,
  169–70
son adopted by minister, 219
spears Willemerring, 193
treated for scabies, 183
trip to England, 210–11
wounds soldier, 218
Bennet, Henry, 269, 270–2, 276
Bent, Ellis, 260
Bentham, Jeremy, 269, 382
Bentley, James, 511
Bentley, Joshua, 98
Bentley, Joshua Jr, 98
Berkeley, Colonel, 293
Berry, Alexander, 557
Bertelson, PJ, 490
Betsey (ship), 241
Betts, Luckyn, 232
Bibbulmun people, 377, 380
Bidawal people, 331
Bidjigal people, 174, 194
Bigge, John Thomas, 272–4, 276–7,
  280, 286, 290–1, 305
bills of exchange, 204
Billy (guide), 456
Binalong, 517
Bird, Samuel, 176
Birmingham, England, 347
Bishop, Charles, 295–6
Bishop, Commandant, 419
Bishop, Joseph, 191
Black, Alfred, 544

Black, George, 539, 543, 549
Black, Neil, 390
Black Huts, 329
Blackall Range, 419
Black's Concert Room, 534
Blackstone, William, 36
Blair, David, 524
Blake, William, 34
Bland, William, 353, 428
Blatherhorn, William, 66
Blaxcell, Garnham, 253, 279
Blaxland, Gregory, 252, 267, 333,
  482
Blaxland, John, 252, 477, 482
Bligh, William
  becomes governor of NSW, 249
  on children born in NSW, 183
  criticised by William
    Wentworth, 274
  Crossley as advisor to, 249
  Donald Trail as master to, 141
  hears of Bryant's escape, 178
  officers conspire against, 250
  orders demolition of houses,
    250
  petitioned by Hawkesbury
    settlers, 252
  relationship with John
    Macarthur, 250–1, 253–8
  uprising against, 253–8
  voyage to Tahiti, 15
Bloodworth, James, 113, 154, 234
Blosset, Harriet, 17, 32
Blow, Lieutenant, 180–1
Blue Books, 282
Blue Mountains, 174, 175, 267,
  333, 340
Blue Shirt (Thunguddi leader), 458
Blumenbach, Johann Frederich,
  173
Bogan River, 337
bogong moths, 331
Bonaparte, Napoleon, 282, 302
Bond, Captain, 206, 207
Boonerah, 490
Boorong, 112
Booroo Berongal people, 174
Bossawa, Claude, 335
Boswell, James, 32, 38, 52, 59, 69,
  118, 200
Botany Bay, New South Wales, 23,
  27, 40, 71–2
Botany Bay Rangers, 125
bounty immigrants, 346–7, 356–7,
  390

Bounty mutineers, 198, 252
Bourbonnais, Désiré, 465
Bourdon, Louis, 461, 462, 464,
  465–6
Bourke, Anne, 496
Bourke, Catherine, 432
Bourke, Sir Richard
  appoints Lonsdale as police
    magistrate, 388
  asks for report on Port Phillip,
    387
  concerned about southern
    settlements, 386–7
  considered soft on convicts,
    322, 429
  considers coolie labour, 476, 477
  favours a free press, 370
  frames legislation for schools,
    402
  Gazette rails against, 372
  hears of John Graham's noble
    conduct, 423
  passes Church Act, 468
  on punishment, 308–9
  receives petition from free
    mechanics, 427
  removes superintendent of
    barracks, 323
  sends Watt to Port Macquarie,
    372
Bow, Huey, 489
Bowes Smyth, Arthur
  on arrival of women in the
    colony, 87–9
  on childbirth by lower class
    women, 69
  consulted by King, 92
  contact with Aborigines, 103
  on the death of John Fisher, 101
  on Phillip's speech to convicts,
    91–2
  as surgeon on Lady Penrhyn,
    62, 67
Bowman, James, 279
Boyd, Benjamin, 429, 447, 471, 486
Boyd, Thomas, 335
Boyne Day, 469
Bracefield, David, 421, 423, 424
Bradley, Emily, 455
Bradley, William, 76–7, 86–7,
  126–7, 326–8, 440–2, 455
Brady, Father, 462, 463
Braidwood, 340, 517, 519
Bramwell, Private, 97–8
Brataualung people, 416

608

arrives at Botany Bay, 74, 75
on Bennelong, 131, 216
claims Colby is Cadigal chief,
    128
as commander of *Sirius*, 114–15
departs from Botany Bay, 80
exonerated in court martial, 173
explores north of Botany Bay, 77
falls out with Macarthur, 225
hunts mutton birds, 133–4
inquires into Irish uprising, 229
on Irish convicts, 188
leaves for England, 172
lobbies on behalf of Macarthur,
    248
loses control of *Sirius*, 133
recalled to England, 225
relationship with D'Arcy
    Wentworth, 264, 265
relationship with Dr Margarot,
    224
returns to England, 231
returns to NSW as governor, 216
sceptical of Ross' farming plans,
    134
sends Irish convicts out on
    expeditions, 221–2
suffers disrespect of the military,
    225
on transportation from Ireland,
    180
Huon Mundy, 421, 422, 424
Hustler, William, 480
Hutt, John, 381
Hyde Park Barracks, 323, 465

The Immigrant's Vision (Harpur),
    355
*An Impartial...Narrative of the
    Present State of Botany Bay*
    (Barrington), 185
Impeta, 402
indentured labour, 476–81, 484–90
Indian labourers, 476–81
inflation, 204
Ingram, Mr (gamekeeper), 293
Innett, Ann, 92, 93, 133, 184
Investigator (ship), 301–3
Ireland, 225–8
Ireland, John, 464
Ireland, Richard Davis, 552, 554
Irish Catholics, 467–70
Irish convicts
    on the *Atlas* and the *Hercules*,
        231–2

escapes by, 221, 253
from the *Hercules*, 248
leaders of the 1798 uprising,
    227–9
Michael Dwyer sent to Norfolk
    Island, 256
perception of, 322
planned uprisings, 228–31
punishment of, 229–31, 240, 241
sent to Newcastle, 241
set out to find China, 187–8
in Sydney, 186, 188–9
in the Third Fleet, 179–82
women convicts, 430–4
see also Irish Rebellion (1804)
Irish diggers, 506–9, 511–12, 535,
    541–2
Irish Exile, 467
Irish Famine, 201, 447, 454, 455,
    506–7
Irish Party, 506
Irish Rebellion (1804), 237–41, 280
Irving, John, 151–2
Irving, Washington, 391
Isim, 490
Islanders (Scotland), 355, 356

Jacobites, 37
James, John Angell, 348
James, Mr (Cookney's brother-in-
    law), 279
Jamison, Sir John, 231, 428, 443
Jamison, Thomas, 93, 151
Jansz, Willem, 9
Jay, John, 93
Jemmy Green in Australia (Tucker),
    319
Jenkinson, Mr (Third Mate), 62
Jenner, Edward, 294
Jeoly (Mindanaoan), 13
Jew's Harp Inn, 464
Jinmium, 3
Johnson, John, 230
Johnson, Reverend Richard
    appalled by plan for retribution,
        166
    baptisms by, 67, 98, 176
    brings kittens to Australia, 69
    cares for orphans, 198
    on the cultivation of the glebe,
        198
    as member of Low Church, 99
    performs first marriages, 99–100
    prays with condemned man, 96
    shocked by condition of

convicts, 150
    volunteers to be hostage for
        Bennelong, 159–60
Johnson, Samuel, 32, 36, 52, 72–3,
    200
Johnson, William, 238, 240, 242
Johnston, George, 88, 105, 239–40,
    254–5, 256–8, 261, 281
Johnston, George Jnr, 267, 268
Johnston, James, 512
Johnston, John, 403, 404
Jones, Richard, 372
Jones, William, 348
Joseph, John, 551, 552
*Journal of a Voyage from Port
    Jackson...* (Gilbert), 136
Journals of Expeditions of Discovery
    (Eyre), 409
Journals of Two Expeditions...
    (Grey), 413
Justinian (ship), 142–3, 148, 149,
    151
Justitia (prison hulk), 38, 137, 294,
    314
Justitia II (prison hulk), 38

Kable, Henry
    affluence of, 287
    death sentence commuted, 61
    has child with Susannah
        Holmes, 70
    marries Susannah Holmes, 100
    sealskin business, 295–6, 298
    shipping business, 183
    superintendent of women
        prisoners, 86
    takes on apprentices, 289
    as a trader, 483
    tutors James Kelly, 189
Kable, Henry Jr, 61
Kamilaroi people, 401, 402, 477
Kang, 488–9
Kangaroo Island, 296, 297, 298,
    300, 301, 393
Kangaroo Valley, 334
Karubarabulu, 160, 161–2, 163,
    217, 219
Kaurna people, 393
Ke Tiam, 490
Kellow, Robert, 101
Kelly, James, 189, 289, 297, 483
kelpers, 357
Kemp, Anthony Fenn, 137, 255
Kempsey, 459
Kendall, Henry, 525

circumnavigation of, 295
naming of, 11
settlement of by Collins, 258
settlers move to Port Phillip
    from, 385, 387–8, 390–1
sighting of by First Fleet, 69–70
Vanuatu, 91, 102
Varney, R, 348, 445
Vatican, 468
Vaughan, Jack, 455–9
Vaughan, Mary (née McMaugh),
    455–9
Veal, Elizabeth, *see* Macarthur,
    Elizabeth
Venus, transit of, 14–15, 18–21
Vern, Frederick, 537, 538, 542, 544,
    545, 549
Victoria, Port Essington, 481–2
Victoria, Queen of England, 480
Victoria, settlement of, 385–92
Victorian Goldfields Commission
    of Enquiry, 516
Victorian Institute, 505
Victorian Reform League, 556
Village Magazine, 351
Vinegar Hill, 544

Waaksamheyd (ship), 172–3, 176
Waka-kabic language, 421, 424
Wakefield, Edward Gibbon, 382–4,
    392, 395
Wakefield, Priscilla, 382
Wakefield, William, 382
Walcheren, 281
Walgalu people, 330
Walker, George Washington, 307
Walker, Martha, 430
Walker, William, 219
Wallacea, 2
Wallumettagal people, 130
Walpiri people, 4
Walsh, John, 153
Walshe, Sergeant, 417
Wangal people, 130
Wanjon, Timotheus, 178
Warangu people, 341
Wardell, Robert, 278, 363, 365,
    367, 370
Warman, James, 416–17
Warner, Jonathon, 309–11
Warrane, 79
Warrior (ship), 377–8
Waterhouse, Lieutenant, 154–7
Waterloo, Battle of, 282
Waterloo Creek massacre, 402, 458

Waters, Mary Ann, 436
Waters, William, 145
Watling, Thomas, 207
Watt, William, 370, 371–2
Waugh, David, 409
Waugh, Mr (author), 390
Waverley (novel by Scott), 357
Waverley (ship), 434
Weaver, Esther, 288
Webster, George, 554
Wedge, JH, 386
Weekly Register, 469
Wellbank, Thomas, 432
Wellesley, Arthur, *see* Wellington,
    Duke of
Wellesley, Richard, Lord, 247
Wellington, Duke of, 282, 346
Wellington Valley, 367, 368
Wentworth, D'Arcy
    as assistant surgeon, 262, 263
    background, 139–40
    brought to task for son's satire,
        268
    death, 280
    defends himself against Bigge,
        276
    falls in love en route to Australia,
        143
    as farmer, 262
    as a highwayman, 140–1, 184
    loses money on Rum Hospital,
        279
    on Norfolk Island, 152, 261–2
    obliged to witness floggings, 152
    as police commissioner and
        principal surgeon, 267, 279
    politics of, 262
    as president of Bank of NSW,
        279
    receives annual pension, 276
    receives land grants, 262, 264,
        276
    removes mistress from home,
        270
    returns from Norfolk Island, 264
    seeks to recover debts, 264
    sent to Norfolk Island, 151
    suffers attacks on his character,
        264–5
    uneasy at Macquarie's arrival,
        261
Wentworth, D'Arcy Jnr, 266, 280
Wentworth, John, 266, 268, 270,
    279
Wentworth, Sarah, 528

Wentworth, Sophia, 480
Wentworth, Thomasin (Timmy),
    364
Wentworth, William Charles
    as acting provost-marshal, 266
    argues against Indian labour,
        477
    arrives in Port Jackson, 264
    attends Cambridge University,
        277–8
    attends school in England, 266
    becomes aware of father's past,
        270–2
    birth, 151
    bitterness over political
        developments, 557
    celebrates Darling's departure,
        370
    chairs Constitution Committee,
        526–7, 528
    challenges Bigge to duel, 276–7
    criticises Governor Darling, 369
    devotion to his father, 261–2,
        265
    discourages gold-mining, 502
    effigy of burnt by miners, 503
    employs coolie labour, 481
    employs Lepailleur, 464
    enters NSW society, 266–7
    explores Blue Mountains, 333
    fights new land policy, 447, 448
    founds *Australian*, 363
    Gazette rails against, 372
    gets chambers at the Temple,
        269–70
    greets the Macquaries in
        London, 273
    Harpur writes scathingly of,
        522
    has child with Sarah Cox, 364
    hosts anniversary dinner, 363
    lampoons Macarthurs, 266
    mentioned by Select Committee,
        428
    mourns death of daughter, 557
    opposes petition against
        Macquarie, 269
    receives land grant, 267
    returns from schooling in
        England, 266
    returns to England to study law,
        267–8
    returns to self-exile in England,
        557
    snobbery of, 266